THIRD EDITION

Fundamentals of Special Education

What Every Teacher Needs to Know

Margaret G. Werts
Appalachian State University

Richard A. Culatta
Appalachian State University

James R. Tompkins
Appalachian State University

PEARSON
Merrill
Prentice Hall

Upper Saddle River, New Jersey
Columbus, Ohio

Library of Congress Cataloging-in-Publication Data
Werts, Margaret G.
  Fundamentals of special education : what every teacher needs to know
  / Margaret G. Werts, Richard A. Culatta, James R. Tompkins. — 3rd ed.
    p. cm.
  Includes bibliographical references and index.
  1. Special education—United States. 2. Exceptional children—United
    States. 3. Exceptional children—Services for—United States.
I. Culatta, Richard. II. Tompkins, James R. III. Title.
LC3981.C85 2007
371.9073—dc22   2006002705

Vice President and Executive Publisher: Jeffery W. Johnston
Executive Editor: Ann Castel Davis
Editorial Assistant: Penny Burleson
Production Editor: Sheryl Glicker Langner
Production Coordination: Carlisle Publishing Services
Design Coordinator: Diane C. Lorenzo
Photo Coordinator: Monica Merkel
Cover Designer: Aaron Dixon
Cover Photo: Fotosearch
Production Manager: Laura Messerly
Director of Marketing: David Gesell
Marketing Manager: Autumn Purdy
Marketing Coordinator: Brian Mounts

This book was set in Helvetica by Carlisle Publishing Services
and was printed and bound by Von Hoffmann Printing. The cover was printed by Phoenix Color Corp.

Photo Credits: Anne Vega/Merrill, pp. 2, 30, 69, 106; Scott Cunningham/Merrill, pp. 9, 86, 126, 131, 161, 215, 226, 271, 306, 327, 378, 391; Dan Floss/Merrill, p. 20; George Dodson/PH College, p. 38; Barbara Schwartz/Merrill, pp. 47, 92, 172, 296, 358; Jason Lauré, p. 49 (left and right); UN/DPI/Marta Pinter (NJ) Copyright by Interfoto MTI Hungary, p. 75; Ken Karp/PH College, pp. 98, 141; John Paul Endress/Silver Burdett Ginn, pp. 110, 393; Anthony Magnacca/Merrill, pp. 118, 188, 197, 250, 255, 314, 351; Laima Druskis/PH College, pp. 148, 166, 204, 384; Teri Stratford/PH College, p. 153; PH College, p. 156; Todd Yarrington/Merrill, pp. 177, 182; Michal Heron/PH College, p. 220; Laura Bolesta/Merrill, pp. 240, 248; Patrick White/Merrill, p. 264; courtesy Gallaudet University, p. 276; Valerie Schultz/Merrill, p. 292; Michael Newman/PhotoEdit Inc., p. 318; Rhoda Sidney/PH College, p. 331; Doug Pensinger/Allsport Photography, p. 344; Tom Watson/Merrill, p. 364; Linda Kauffman/Merrill, p. 370.

Pearson Education Ltd.
Pearson Education Singapore, Pte. Ltd.
Pearson Education Canada, Ltd.
Pearson Education—Japan

Pearson Education Australia PTY, Limited
Pearson Education North Asia Ltd.
Pearson Educacíon de Mexico, S.A. de C.V.
Pearson Education Malaysia, Pte. Ltd.

10 9 8 7 6 5 4 3 2 1
ISBN: 0-13-171491-0

This book is dedicated to the children who fill our days:

Travis, Jarrod, Richard, Elizabeth, Katherine, Tim, Mark, and Moira.

We respect and admire each of you more each day.

And to the many other persons who are special who have contributed
to our understanding of their lives.

PREFACE

From the moment of the conceptualization through the final editing of the first, second, and third editions of this text, the authors have kept a guiding principle. We have dedicated ourselves to presenting the fundamental information that is necessary for beginning students, allied professionals, and concerned family members who are beginning to study the field of special education. We have presented the principles and foundations of special education that all teachers need to know and the practices that have evolved from those principles. By arranging the chapters on disabilities according to a uniform outline that describes each exceptionality category in a consistent manner, we hope that you will better understand the complexities of the categories of the disabilities and the sometimes subtle differences among them.

The authors share a combined total of well over a century of experience with exceptional students: children, youth, and adults. Our thinking and the wisdom of our mentors and teachers have been filtered through our experience as classroom teachers, administrators, psychologists, Washington Bureau of Handicapped staff, university faculty, speech-language pathologists, siblings of persons with disabilities, and persons with disabilities. We hope that our presentation of the basic parameters of each disability area and our definition of the current issues and interventions help you understand historical foundations, legal and practice foundations, and current practices.

ABOUT THIS BOOK

The purpose of this text is to gather into one source the critical information needed to understand students with disabilities. We have tried to present the information as concisely and yet completely as possible. In this third edition we have made several changes. We have updated the information, added information changed because of passage of new legislation, and added a chapter on autism. We have added to each chapter a section with a situation and questions about what you might do as a teacher or other concerned individual ("What Would You Do?"). The questions have a multitude of "correct" responses, and it is our hope that these vignettes will serve as a springboard for discussion rather than as an exercise to derive the "right" answer.

Throughout the text we have attempted to confront problematic and difficult issues head-on. Even at the introductory level we believe that knowledge of concerns and currently unanswered issues and questions can be as informative as explanations of the knowledge and hypotheses shown in the research of our colleagues.

Chapter 1 introduces the many basic concepts in special education. This chapter contains explanations of the laws that most affect the schools and their practices. It also defines the student in need of specially designed instruction, shares relevant demographics, and presents a brief history of special education. We highlight the professional preparation standards that special educators must meet in order to provide the best educational experience possible. Once armed with this basic understanding, you may proceed to any of the eleven separate chapters that deal with different categories of exceptionality. We do understand the complexities of identifying students by category. However, we have chosen to retain the format of "disability chapters" for the simple reason that the newly reauthorized IDEA retains categories for funding purposes. The chapters are as follows:

Chapter 2: Students with Communication Disorders

Chapter 3: Students with Mental Retardation or Intellectual Disabilities

Chapter 4: Students with Learning Disabilities

Chapter 5: Students with Attention Deficit/Hyperactivity Disorder

Chapter 6: Students with Emotional and Behavioral Disorders

Chapter 7: Students with Physical and Health Impairments

Chapter 8: Students with Autism Spectrum Disorders

Chapter 9: Students with Hearing Impairments

Chapter 10: Students with Visual Impairments

Chapter 11: Students with Severe or Multiple Disabilities

Chapter 12: Students Who Are Gifted and Talented

To make Chapters 2 through 12 consistent and easy to follow, we used the same structure for each chapter. Each chapter begins with a definition of the category of a fundable disability area to be discussed. As you will learn, defining each area of disability is not as simple as it may seem. Federal definitions, individual state definitions, and conceptualizations of scholars in each area are sometimes in conflict. We have attempted to highlight conflicting definitions and present the most commonly accepted information.

Each chapter presents prevalence figures that will help you understand how students are labeled. Unfortunately, differing definitions often lead to different counts. We present the conflicting data and explain how the different figures might occur.

The next section of each chapter deals with the most salient characteristics that identify a student as a member of a category in special education. These descriptions of observable behaviors and physical anomalies may help to identify students who may need special assistance. We strongly believe that students with special needs are more like their peers without labels than they are different from them. However, an understanding of the characteristic differences should provide the beginning teacher with critical information in understanding a disability.

The etiology or cause of each disability, as experts understand it to be, is also discussed in each disability chapter. A condition may be caused by a variety of factors, or by several factors acting together, or the cause may be unknown. In some cases we discuss experts' best guesses regarding the cause of the disability.

In the next section of each chapter we discuss in detail the identification process that is appropriate for each student referred and thought to be "at risk." Here you will learn the steps necessary for fulfilling the legal, professional, and ethical requirements for placing a label on a student. The label gives the student access to the services provided by the school, thus allowing him or her to receive the most appropriate educational experience.

We next highlight programs that are effective and widely used interventions for different groups of students with disabilities. Some of the interventions described are not etiology specific or specific to special education at all. They are simply good strategies to use. It is important to remember that teaching strategies for students with a label of disability should be planned with the individual student in mind, not a category of students.

Each categorical chapter has an "Issues of Importance" section to highlight some of the concerns of students, teachers, parents, and other professionals who deal with students with special needs on a daily basis. The goal of these sections is to sensitize you to the most compelling issues facing those who are providing services to students with special needs and their families. Throughout the text we make an effort to separate cultural differences from exceptionalities. A goal of special education is not to make everyone the same, or to teach some artificially determined level, but to provide access to a free and appropriate education for students who need special services. Students' cultural and ethnic heritages do not make them students with a disability. On the other hand, culturally and linguistically diverse students are not immune from having educational difficulties. In a section called "Diversity," we attempt to help you understand the differences and how to recognize them.

Because a variety of persons work with students with special needs, we have included a section in each chapter entitled "Professionals." In this section we describe roles of service providers. Students with disabilities will spend time with a variety of personnel each day, week, and month. Other professionals will be involved in a consultative fashion. We have attempted to describe the roles of these persons.

Each chapter contains a list of terms. These are included in the text of the chapter in bold, and they are defined in the chapter. These lists are by no means exhaustive. Rather, they are intended to give you a basic knowledge of vocabulary and to start your own brainstorming process.

The final section of each chapter provides resources and places to go for more information. In each chapter we include a listing of groups dedicated to improving all aspects of the lives of persons with disabilities. We also list professional publications, journals, and newsletters with information about the area of disability. The reference section that appears at the end of each chapter identifies the sources we used in pulling together the information we felt was critical. The inclusion of separate reference sections at the end of each chapter simplifies the search for references and readings in each area.

Our goal throughout the text was to translate material that is often complex and contradictory into a format that a novice reader could easily understand. We are well aware of the dangers of oversimplification. We tried as best we could not to lose the essence of an issue or concern in an effort to make the material palatable. The supplementary readings will help you examine information in greater depth. The source material we used in writing this book included the most accepted and accessible sources available to scholars and practitioners who work in special education and related fields. Although we bring many years of experience to the writing of this text, we have made an effort to keep our personal opinions and feelings separate from the material in the chapters. In this way we tried to present the most accepted theories and the most commonly accepted information available at the time. To accomplish this, we immersed ourselves in the writings of our expert and respected colleagues and the results of their research and conclusions that are found in the literature. From this roundtable of experts we have teased out a consensus of the beliefs and practices for each topic. At times we present divergent views. Research and work with students continually generate new ideas and theories. Divergent views may be brought to a consensus in time, and recommended practices will evolve from studying these views and the research accompanying them.

ACKNOWLEDGMENTS

While writing this text, we have not worked in a vacuum. Our mentors, colleagues, students, and the students we have worked with have taught us. Our mentors helped us with understanding special education. Our colleagues have argued with us, shaped our thinking, and judged our contributions. Our university students have taken us to task and forced us to clarify our thinking. The students with whom we have worked have validated the practices we have presented as well as our professional lives. They are a constant reminder that we must strive to learn more, refine the practices that are effective, and provide a better database for the next generation than we have for this one. We feel fortunate to have the opportunity to synthesize our reflections on these experiences and to present them in this text. We have, of course, been as meticulous as possible in attributing thoughts and ideas to the authors and originators. If we have slighted anyone, it was not only unintentional but also a direct function of the synthesis of their truths into our lives. Julius E. Heuscher, quoted in *Newsweek* (1991), explained that borrowing often occurs in texts because "[s]ome ideas become so true that they become our own." We like to believe that we are learners first and teachers second.

This text would not exist without the guidance and assistance of our current and former editors Ann Davis and Allyson Sharp, who allowed us to write a text that could present the information and protect the dignity of the knowledge base without resorting to "dumbing down" the material in a misguided attempt to sugarcoat it for the readers. We are grateful to our very competent and refreshingly human production coordinator, Mary Tindle, and her staff at Carlisle Publishing Services, who guided us flawlessly through production. We are also indebted to our colleagues at Appalachian State University for their continuing work through this project. Without these friends and colleagues this work would not have been completed. Their insights and suggestions saved us from oversights, unrecognized errors, and unfortunate assumptions. Finally, we thank the reviewers who guided us with ideas for this edition: Joyce Bergin, Armstrong Atlantic State University; James O. Burton, II, Marshall University; Gregory Conderman, Northern Illinois University; Ellen Contopidis, Nazareth College; Michael R. Dillon, Dowling College; Lloyd Kinnison, Texas Woman's University; and Ellen Marshall, San Antonio College.

Discover the Merrill Resources for Special Education Website

Technology is a constantly growing and changing aspect of our field that is creating a need for new content and resources. To address this emerging need, Merrill Education has developed an online learning environment for students, teachers, and professors alike to complement our products—the *Merrill Resources for Special Education* Website. This content-rich website provides additional resources specific to this book's topic and will help you—professors, classroom teachers, and students—augment your teaching, learning, and professional development.

Our goal with this initiative is to build on and enhance what our products already offer. For this reason, the content for our user-friendly website is organized by topic and provides teachers, professors, and students with a variety of meaningful resources all in one location. With this website, we bring together the best of what Merrill has to offer: text resources, video clips, web links, tutorials, and a wide variety of information on topics of interest to general and special educators alike. Rich content, applications, and competencies further enhance the learning process.

The *Merrill Resources for Special Education* Website includes:

- Video clips specific to each topic, with questions to help you evaluate the content and make crucial theory-to-practice connections.

- Thought-provoking critical analysis questions that students can answer and turn in for evaluation or that can serve as basis for class discussions and lectures.

- Access to a wide variety of resources related to classroom strategies and methods, including lesson planning and classroom management.

- Information on all the most current relevant topics related to special and general education, including CEC and Praxis™ standards, IEPs, portfolios, and professional development.

- Extensive web resources and overviews on each topic addressed on the website.

- A search feature to help access specific information quickly.

To take advantage of these and other resources, please visit the *Merrill Resources for Special Education* Website at

http://www.prenhall.com/werts

Teacher Preparation Classroom

YOUR CLASS. THEIR CAREERS. OUR FUTURE. WILL YOUR STUDENTS BE PREPARED?

We invite you to explore our new, innovative and engaging website and all that it has to offer you, your course, and tomorrow's educators! Organized around the major courses pre-service teachers take, the Teacher Preparation site provides media, student/teacher artifacts, strategies, research articles, and other resources to equip your students with the quality tools needed to excel in their courses and prepare them for their first classroom.

This ultimate on-line education resource is available at no cost, when packaged with a Merrill text, and will provide you and your students access to:

Online Video Library. More than 150 video clips—each tied to a course topic and framed by learning goals and Praxis-type questions—capture real teachers and students working in real classrooms, as well as in-depth interviews with both students and educators.

Student and Teacher Artifacts. More than 200 student and teacher classroom artifacts—each tied to a course topic and framed by learning goals and application questions—provide a wealth of materials and experiences to help make your study to become a professional teacher more concrete and hands-on.

Research Articles. Over 500 articles from ASCD's renowned journal *Educational Leadership*. The site also includes Research Navigator, a searchable database of additional educational journals.

Teaching Strategies. Over 500 strategies and lesson plans for you to use when you become a practicing professional.

Licensure and Career Tools. Resources devoted to helping you pass your licensure exam; learn standards, law, and public policies; plan a teaching portfolio; and succeed in your first year of teaching.

Brief Contents

CONTENTS

7 STUDENTS WITH PHYSICAL AND HEALTH IMPAIRMENTS   204

9 STUDENTS WITH HEARING IMPAIRMENTS   264

8 STUDENTS WITH AUTISM SPECTRUM DISORDERS   240

10 STUDENTS WITH VISUAL IMPAIRMENTS   306

Note: Every effort has been made to provide accurate and current Internet information in this book. However, the Internet and information posted on it are constantly changing, so it is inevitable that some of the Internet addresses listed in this textbook will change.

1

Introduction to Special Education

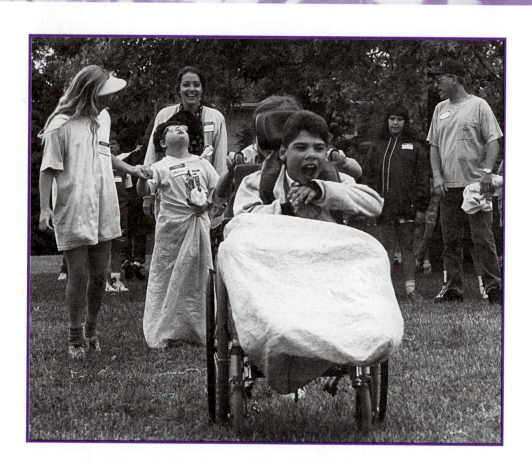

KEY TERMS

cascade of services   8

disability   5

due process   6

FAPE   6

impairments   4

inclusion   8

labeling   7

least restrictive environment   5

paraeducators   22

zero reject   6

WHAT WOULD YOU DO?

Eugene had been working very hard. He had to learn that alphabetic symbols had meaning. He had to learn that spoken language had a connection to written language. We had reinforced these notions for several months of his first-grade year. One afternoon in early November, he had read the first three pages of a preprimer with minimal prompting. He was excited and I was ecstatic. I raced down the hall after school. I ran into the first-grade room and shouted to his teacher, "Eugene read three pages. That's four whole words! Four different words!" She looked at me and shook her head. "He is so far behind the rest of my class," she said sadly.

Mary was working intently with her tutor. She was slowly sounding out words using short vowel sounds. Her teachers had worked out a new plan for her in math. The tutor was reading stories that included calculations in a meaningful context. Mary used pennies or other counting objects to "act out" the story.

Manuel used his joystick to guide his wheelchair down the wide hall to the library. He smiled as his friends called out to him "Hey, Manny!"

"Great wheels."

"Wanna race?"

Manuel continued down the hall giving a laugh and a high five to each friend he saw. He had outgrown his other wheelchair a few months ago. Last weekend, his friend Lamont had come over and painted flames on the arm rests and foot rests of his new one. It was getting rave reviews.

1. How is each of the students in need of special education?

2. How can one system of special education meet disparate needs?

Special education is specially designed instruction that is individualized to meet the unique educational and related needs of students with disabilities. It provides learning opportunities that are not provided in standard or general school curricula or by general school services. Special education programs are designed to be appropriate for the individual student; they must be provided and paid for by the school district and community, not individual students and their families. Individualized programming that is the core of special education must be provided in settings that best meet each special student's needs. Typical settings for special education programs are public schools, special classes in public schools, special schools, homes, rehabilitation hospitals, and residential schools and institutions. Special education includes related instructional services such as speech, physical, and occupational therapy, and transportation services. In addition, the special education movement supports the proposition that children and youth with disabilities need to be integrated or included in normal or general educational services or programs to the extent that it is reasonable.

Kirk (1972) defined the exceptional child (including gifted and talented children as well as children with disabilities) as follows:

> [the] child who deviates from the average or normal child (1) in mental characteristics, (2) in sensory abilities, (3) in neuromuscular or physical characteristics, (4) in social or emotional behavior, (5) in communication abilities, or (6) in multiple handicaps to such an extent that he requires a modification of school practices, or special education services, in order to develop to his maximum capacity. (p. 4)

Special education evolved when our society recognized and respected human differences and assumed the responsibility for the provision of individualized educational services for students with disabilities.

INDIVIDUAL DIFFERENCES

All people exhibit differences from one another. Often the differences are quite apparent; in other instances, the differences may be subtle. In addition, all students present different skill levels in academic subjects and different interest levels in educational activities. The degree of these differences determines whether a student is eligible for special educational services.

The definition of "normal" or "acceptable" or "typical" in our culture is elusive. One meaning is that a person is prepared to participate, in an independent fashion, in the cultural mainstream or milieu. People within a group may be characterized as normal when they conform to the group's rules or values. When individuals meet the social and educational expectations of the group, they are considered normal or typical.

People display a wide variety of physical, emotional, and learning differences. When a student differs from the norm (what is considered normal by virtue of what everyone else is doing) to such an extent that specialized and individualized educational programming is required to meet unique needs, the student is considered eligible for special education. Students who are eligible are those who are below average intellectually, display learning or behavioral differences, or have physical or sensory **impairments,** or limitation in skills or ability to perform a task in the same manner as most persons. Each student may show multiple impairments that are combinations of conditions. The student may also be gifted intellectually or show a remarkable talent. Categories of special education are the following:

- Specific learning disabled
- Speech or language impaired
- Mentally retarded
- Emotionally or behaviorally disturbed
- Physically impaired
- Other health impaired
- Hearing impaired
- Orthopedically impaired
- Visually impaired
- Autistic

- Deaf-blind
- Traumatic brain disordered
- Severely and multiply handicapped

and under the Jacob Javits Education Act:

- Gifted and talented

STUDENTS AT RISK

In addition to students who are identified as exceptional, some are referred to as students at risk. They are not identified as having a **disability,** or loss of function, although they may be at a later time. They are considered to have a high probability of developing a disability. The term at risk is also used with some very young children who, because of negative conditions surrounding their birth, nurturing, or environment, may be expected to experience developmental problems. At-risk students include students who may experience learning, socialization, and maturational difficulties in the general classroom; are failing academic subjects; or are at risk of overall school failure and thus may become identified as candidates for special education services (Heward, 2006; Mastropieri & Scruggs, 2000).

HISTORY OF SPECIAL EDUCATION

Public education for students with special needs in the United States can be traced back to the establishment of free public education in the early 1800s. However, by the early 1900s, although institutional programs for students with sensory impairments and mental retardation were widespread in the United States, only a few public schools served students with disabilities who did not fit the available curriculum (Kauffman, 2005).

From the early 1900s to the 1970s, attempts to serve students with special needs within public schools frequently took the form of special day schools that educated students with physical impairments, mental retardation, and serious emotional disturbance. The independent self-contained special education classroom within a regular public school also emerged at this time (Kauffman, 2005; Smith, 2001). The movement of students with special needs into the public schools was a large step. In the mid-1970s, Public Law 94-192, the Education for All Handicapped Children Act, allowed all students access to a free and appropriate education, and the regulation for the act required that the placement be in the **least restrictive environment** for that individual. The least restrictive environment is the placement that is as close as educationally appropriate to the school and classroom that the student would be in if there were not a disability or reason for specially designed instruction.

Special education has historically been supported by the U.S. Office of Education, which was a part of the former Department of Health, Education, and Welfare (HEW). It then evolved into the Bureau of Education for the Handicapped (BEH) in the Department of Health, Education, and Welfare. Currently, special education is under the authority of the Department of Education, Office of Special Education and Rehabilitative Services (OSERS), and has three components.

1. Office of Special Education Programs

The Office of Special Education Programs (OSEP) is primarily responsible for administering programs and projects relating to the free, appropriate public education of all infants, toddlers, children, youth, and adults with disabilities, from birth through age 21. OSEP is therefore responsible for ensuring that the principles of the Individuals with Disabilities Education Improvement Act (IDEA) are administered and adhered to in the projects that are funded through their programs. OSEP's Monitoring and State Improvement Programs division administers most of the special education funds. This program provides grants to states and territories to assist them in providing a free, appropriate public education to all students with disabilities. Early intervention and preschool programs provide grants to each state for students with disabilities, from birth through age 5.

2. Rehabilitation Services Administration

The Rehabilitation Services Administration (RSA) oversees programs that help individuals with physical or mental disabilities to obtain employment. They provide counseling, medical services, psychological services, job training, and other services based on individual needs. RSA's major program provides funds to state vocational rehabilitation agencies to provide employment-related services for individuals with disabilities, giving priority to individuals who are severely disabled.

3. National Institute on Disability and Rehabilitation Research

The third component of OSERS, the National Institute on Disability and Rehabilitation Research (NIDRR), provides leadership and support for a comprehensive program of research related to the rehabilitation of individuals with disabilities. Efforts are aimed at improving the lives of individuals with disabilities from birth through adulthood.

Beginning in 1975 and continuing to the present, the special education movement has been experiencing critical turning points. This is primarily due to the enactment of the federal laws and the subsequent reauthorizations. They include the Elementary and Secondary Education Act of 1965 (and its reauthorizations, including No Child Left Behind in 2002); the Rehabilitation Act of 1972; Public Law 94-142, the Education for All Handicapped Children Act and its amendments; PL 101-476, IDEA, and subsequent reauthorizations, including the Individuals with Disabilities Education Improvement Act of December, 2004. These laws and others with related amendments mandate a free, appropriate public education to all students with disabilities. The major points described in the special education laws, specifically in IDEA, have become the language of special education.

1. *Zero reject*—No child shall be refused an appropriate education by public schools. A free and appropriate education **(FAPE)** will be provided for every child regardless of extent of need.

2. *Nondiscriminatory evaluation*—Evaluations must be conducted in the child's native language, with an evaluator proficient in the child's language, and with assessment instruments validated in that language, if available.

3. *Least restrictive environment*—Every child with a disability must be educated in the most appropriate environment closest to what they would be in if there were no disability impacting their learning.

4. *Due process*—Fourteenth Amendment rights of the Constitution, which guarantee privacy, confidentiality of information, and protection of personal rights, are extended to those identified as disabled. No state may deny rights to one citizen or group of citizens that it extends to other groups of citizens.

5. *Individualized education program (IEP)*—Educators must plan individually tailored education programs for each exceptional child who qualifies for special education

services. An IEP determines the benchmarks, goals, and objectives; the placement; and the evaluation procedures for school-age students whose disabilities impede their educational progress.

6. *Individualized transition program (ITP)*—Educators must plan individually tailored transition programs from school to employment and adult life. These programs must be age appropriate, functional, and developmentally appropriate for the individual person.

7. *Preschool programs*—Early intervention programs for children from birth through age 3 must be developed and operational. These programs must be age appropriate, functional, and developmentally appropriate for the individual child. An individualized family service plan (IFSP) must be written for young children, and the documents may include objectives for their family members. An IFSP may be in effect for young children from birth to age 3.

8. *Parents' rights*—Parents or guardians have the right to be included in decision making and to be partners with the schools and related service personnel who are involved with their child. They are to be given notice of meetings and must have a majority representation on the state's advisory board. They also must have access to their child's records and assurance that the records are to be protected from those persons who are not teaching or involved in educating their child.

9. *Highly qualified teachers*—Every student deserves a highly qualified teacher. In the 2004 reauthorization, the term "highly qualified" was added and defined to align with the terms in No Child Left Behind (ESREA, 2002) When used with respect to any public elementary school or secondary school special education teacher teaching in a state, such term means that:

> The teacher has obtained full state certification as a special education teacher (including certification obtained through alternative routes to certification), or passed the state special education teacher licensing examination, and holds a license to teach in the state as a special education teacher, except that when used with respect to any teacher teaching in a public charter school, the term means that the teacher meets the requirements set forth in the state's public charter school law. (Mandlawitz, 2006; National Information Center for Children and Youth with Disabilities [NICHCY], 2005)

These terms and the concepts they represent have become the backbone of the special education movement. We will refer to them repeatedly throughout this text and further define them as we proceed.

LABELING STUDENTS

Labeling, or using a name or classifications to describe individuals with special needs, implies more than simply identifying students who need special educational services. Special educators have historically been concerned about the negative effects of labeling and categorizing exceptional students. Labeling has been viewed as demeaning, stigmatizing, and discriminatory (Turnbull, Turnbull, Shank, & Smith, 2004), especially with regard to the potential to label students based on low ability due to poverty or membership in specific ethnic or cultural groups. These concerns have been balanced by recognizing that the labeling process facilitates the passage of legislation; governmental program administration; and eligibility for resources in treatment, education, research, and personnel preparation (Vallecorsa, DeBettencourt, & Zigmond, 2000).

CONTINUUM OF SERVICES

The various special educational placements are often referred to as the **cascade of services.** The continuum of environments ranges from the least restrictive environment of the general classroom placement (full **inclusion** with aids and services necessary to ensure success) to the most restrictive placement (institutionalization). Figure 1.1 is a graphic representation of the model proposed by Evelyn Deno in 1979 for a student of school age. It has remained the basis for the continuum of services. The philosophy holds that, to the maximum extent appropriate, students with special education needs should be educated in the setting that closest approximates a general education setting. Students with special needs will participate with students who are typically developing; engaging in activities to meet their needs in academic, nonacademic, and extracurricular areas such as meals, recess, counseling services, recreational activities; and special interest groups and clubs sponsored by the local school. In this context, the least restrictive environment (LRE) means students with special needs will be educated with students who are not disabled. Among all of the alternatives for placement within an educational system, students with special needs will be placed where they can obtain the most appropriate educational services. The settings are defined as follows:

*   *General education class*—Students receive the majority of their education program in a general education classroom with appropriate aids and services but

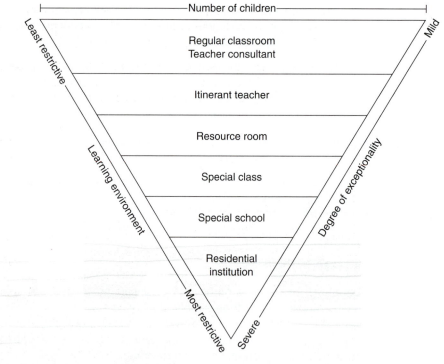

FIGURE 1.1
Cascade of Services: Special learning environments for exceptional children.

Note: Hospital and homebound services provided for children with disabilities who may be confined for long periods of time fall within the realm of the residential-institution setting on the scale of special education learning environments.

Source: From "Special Education as Developmental Capital" by E. Deno, 1979, *Exceptional Children, 37,* pp. 229–237. Copyright 1970 by The Council for Exceptional Children. Reprinted with permission.

may receive special education and related services outside general classrooms for less than 21 percent of the school day. Students may be placed in general classes and receive special education within the general classes, or they may be placed in general classes and receive special education outside the general class.

- *Resource rooms*—Students receive special education and related services outside general classrooms for at least 21 percent but not more than 60 percent of the school day. Students placed in resource rooms receive part-time instruction and assistance in general classes.

- *Separate class*—Students receive special education and related services outside general classes for more than 60 percent of the school day. Students may be placed in special classrooms, with part-time instruction in general classes, or in separate classes full time on the school campus or in the same building as students who are not labeled.

- *Separate schools*—Students receive special education and related services, free to the families, for more than 50 percent of the school day. These schools may be public or private institutions.

- *Residential facilities*—Students receive education in a public or private residential facility, at no expense to families, for more than 50 percent of the school day.

- *Homebound or hospital environments*—Students receive specially designed instruction in hospital or homebound programs. Hospital programs funded under IDEA can be for students classified as other health impaired or emotionally disturbed or for students who are labeled with another disability. Homebound instruction can be decreed by the IEP team as the most appropriate setting for the student to receive services (U.S. Department of Education, 2005).

Because for preschoolers, toddlers, and infants, the philosophical least restrictive environment may be the home setting, this cascade, or range of services, may not be the same. Similarly, for students age 18 to 21, a different hierarchy of services may be necessary.

EDUCATIONAL PLACEMENTS

Each year since 1978, the Office of Special Education has reported on the number of students with disabilities age 6 through 21 served in each different educational environment: general class, resource room, separate class (self-contained class), separate public or private school, public or private residential facility, and homebound or hospital placement (U.S. Department of Education, 2005). The present report to Congress lists the percentages of time students are in general education classes (less than 21 percent, between 21 and 60 percent, and over 60 percent) rather than regular classes, resource rooms, and separate classes. Table 1.1 lists the number of students in each educational placement for the school year 2000–2001. Table 1.2 lists the number and percentage change of students age 6 through 21 served under IDEA for the school year 2000–2001. The passage of time is reflected in the increase in the percentages of students served in each special education category. Regardless of placement, teachers should act on behalf of all students with labels. Suggestions are listed in Box 1.1, What Every Teacher Should Do.

BOX 1.1
WHAT EVERY TEACHER SHOULD DO
With IEPs

- Tell families their rights under the laws and assist them in advocating for their child.
- Become familiar with the other educators and professionals in the school and community who are involved with the student and coordinate services and activities. Coordinated services are likely to be more effective and less confusing to the students and their families.
- Stay up to date and familiar with the laws that affect students with disabilities. Amendments and litigation add to the complexities and the nuances of rights available to students with disabilities and their families.
- Read and reread the IEP of each student. The goals and the objectives that have been declared as important for this person are listed in the IEP along with information from the assessment process, which can help general and special education teachers choose effective and efficient teaching methods.
- Keep progress information in a portfolio for each student. Decisions on program changes are easily made when there is information to work from.
- Revise IEPs as students reach their goals and objectives. Use the paperwork as a tool to assist you in being a good teacher.
- Use interesting and motivating teaching strategies. Change methods often enough to retain interest but not so often that it is confusing. Check often to determine if the material you are teaching has been learned. Assist the student in building a solid foundation of mastered academic and nonacademic skills.
- Get to know the family of each student. The family can be the best source of ongoing knowledge as well as information about new events in students' lives.
- Teach all of your students.

TABLE 1.1

Number of students age 6 through 21 with disabilities served in different educational environments by disability, School year 2000–2001.

Disability	Outside <21%	Regular 21–60%	Class >60%	Separate School	Residential Facility	Homebound/ Hospital
Specific learning disabilities	1,277,162	1,162,977	414,728	19,606	4,630	5,013
Speech or language impairments	939,112	92,351	56,199	8,791	390	546
Mental retardation	80,958	178,159	316,812	31,178	3,359	2,690
Serious emotional disturbance	127,503	111,497	151,280	62,475	17,444	6,170
Other health impairments	133,256	100,092	49,271	4,855	1,109	7,044
Hearing impairments	29,998	14,186	15,962	4,442	6,264	148
Orthopedic impairments	33,889	17,093	17,726	3,039	201	1,165
Visual impairments	13,176	5,238	4,162	1,541	1,787	170
Autism	19,525	12,312	37,256	9,908	1,011	314
Deaf-blindness	240	132	454	252	225	25
Traumatic brain injury	4,826	4,171	4,396	1,050	172	328
Multiple disabilities	14,848	19,649	55,910	26,385	3,171	2,879
All disabilities	2,674,493	1,717,857	1,124,156	173,522	39,763	26,492

Source: U.S. Department of Education, 2005.

TABLE 1.2

Number and percentage change of students ages 6 through 21 served under IDEA: School years 1998–1999 and 2000–2001.

Disability	Number of Students		Change	
	1998–1999	2000–2001	Number	Percent
Specific learning disabilities	2,062,076	2,884,116	822,040	39.9
Speech or language impairments	974,256	1,097,389	123,133	12.6
Mental retardation	563,902	613,156	49,254	8.7
Serious emotional disturbance	381,639	476,369	94,730	24.8
Other health impairments	52,733	295,627	242,894	460.6
Hearing impairments	57,906	71,000	13,094	22.6
Orthopedic impairments	48,050	73,113	25,063	52.2
Visual impairments	22,866	26,074	3,208	14.0
Autism	53,576	80,326	26,750	49.9
Deaf-blindness	1,633	1,328	−305	−18.7
Traumatic brain injury	−	14,943	14,943	−
Multiple disabilities	87,957	122,842	34,885	39.7
Developmental delay	−	28,917	28,917	−
All disabilities	4,306,594	5,785,200	1,478,606	34.3

Source: U.S. Department of Education, 2005.

INCLUSION

As the rights of students with disabilities to obtain a free, publicly supported education in appropriate educational environments evolved, special education began to take on the form of separate education, with pull-out resource programs and increasingly one-to-one, tutoring type of instruction. Inclusion has several key components.

1. All students receive education in their "neighborhood school," that is, the school they would attend if they had no disability.
2. Placements are age and grade appropriate.
3. Special education supports exist within the general education class (Ruef, 2003; Sailor, 1991). Being a part of the general education classroom, a concept supportive of inclusion, refers to ". . . being a member of a real class, where and with whom you start the school day . . . You may not spend all of your time with your class, but it is still your group and everyone knows it." (Brown et al., 1991, p. 41).

One collaborative goal was for general education teachers and special education teachers to work cooperatively within the general education classroom to provide instruction for all students. In this model, the special education teacher and other support specialists provide instruction to students with special needs in the general education classroom rather than in separated classrooms (Salisbury, Strieker, Roach, & McGregor, 2001; Turnbull et al., 2004).

This is not as simple as it seems. The term LRE must be understood in the context of legal requirements established by precedents created through litigation. Schools still must provide or have the ability to provide a full continuum of alternative placements such as resource rooms or self-contained special education classrooms. The school also must consider whether harmful effects may result from such a placement on the student, others in the environment, or the quality of services. These considerations must be reevaluated when determining the IEP and the placement decision. (Grove & Fisher, 1999).

Part B of IDEA states a strong preference for educating students with disabilities in regular classes with appropriate aids and supports. This means that when implementing IDEA's LRE provisions, the general classroom in the school the student would attend if the student were not disabled is the first placement option that must be considered for a student with a disability before a more restrictive placement is considered. However, if the student's IEP cannot be implemented satisfactorily in that general education classroom, another placement is considered (Salend, 2001).

It is important to understand that even though general classroom placement is the placement that is least restrictive overall, IDEA does not require or mandate every student with a disability be placed in the general classroom for full or partial inclusion. Students should be placed according to their individual abilities and needs. This recognition that general class placement may not be appropriate for every student with a disability is reflected in the requirement that school districts make available a range of placement options. These placement options must be available to the extent necessary to implement the IEP of each student (Dybvik, 2004; Heward, 2003; Salend, 2001; Zigmond, 2001). General classroom teachers, who by necessity must become more involved with exceptional students with special needs as a result of inclusion, report they do not have the skills to adapt instruction and content to meet the needs of exceptional students (Magiera & Zigmond, 2005; Salend, 2001; Werts, Wolery, Caldwell, Snyder, & Lisowski, 1995; Werts, Wolery, Snyder, Caldwell, & Salisbury, 1996). Parents and educators of students with more severe disabilities are conflicted about the nature of the benefits that their students may receive from inclusion in general educational classrooms. Some are supportive of the social benefits and the opportunities to learn more if placed in the general education setting. Those who oppose inclusion feel the severity of their students' disabilities precludes any benefit and that the inclusive program is inappropriate (Palmer, Fuller, Arora, & Nelson, 2001). Clearly, placement is not a simple issue.

Full inclusion may not be the most appropriate environment for the student, and general education programs in many public schools are not organized or prepared to serve students with special needs. Classroom teachers have not been adequately trained to provide instruction to students with a variety of disabilities, and teacher preparation programs are only beginning to require courses in inclusion and collaboration. Dual certification programs are becoming more common, and training in special education is being provided in more programs for general education teachers. Educators seem to agree that there are considerable difficulties in (1) establishing good working relationships or collaboration with general teachers on the aims, goals, and sequences of teaching and (2) understanding the role of the special education teacher and agreeing on the level of support the special education teacher should provide in the general classroom (Friend & Cook, 1996; McLeskey & Waldron, 2002; Slater, 2004; Villa & Thousand, 2003; Voltz, Sims, & Nelson, 2005; Werts et al., 1995; Werts et al., 1996).

Even though the concept of full inclusion for students with special needs is currently a popular model with some educators, many questions need to be answered about its efficacy. Training in the components and implementation of inclusion must be provided for both general and special educators, students, and parents. Researchers, schools, teachers, and parents must remember the overriding goal of special education: that each student with a disability must be served and educated in the most appropriate individualized placement. Placement decisions and decisions about curriculum and objectives to master are determined by a team of persons and documented in an IEP.

THE LAW AND SPECIAL EDUCATION

Many commonplace occurrences, such as writing an IEP or including parents as part of the team that decides the best course of study, objectives and goals, and placement, did not occur until legislation was passed that mandated these and other activities.

The funding generated from a federal law is passed through the state administration, which retains a percentage for costs that cover all programs in the state. The state money, along with the remaining federal dollars, is given to the districts to supplement the costs of educating students with special needs. The money may be used in a variety of ways: salaries for extra teachers, paraeducators, related service personnel, equipment, therapy in or away from school, transportation, or any other manner specified as educationally relevant by the IEP team.

There is a rich history of legislative efforts by Congress for persons with disabilities. Table 1.3 highlights some of this legislation. This chronological summary of enabling legislation will help you understand the roots of special education and the directions in which it is currently growing. However, the path has not always been a straight or narrow one.

Prior to World War II, few federal laws authorized special benefits for people with disabilities. Students with disabilities were often excluded from schools in our nation's early history (Smith, 2001). Since the 1960s, however, there has been a great emergence of federal legislation in support of services and education for students with

TABLE 1.3

Federal legislation for people with disabilities.

Year	Legislation
1879	Funds to produce braille materials for the American Printing House for the Blind (PL 45-186)
1920	Vocational rehabilitation services authorized for World War I veterans are extended to civilians (PL 66-236)
1961	Provisions for production and distribution of captioned films for the deaf (PL 87-715)
1963	Funds to train teachers for all disabilities; research and demonstration projects are established to study education of exceptional children (PL 88-164)
1965	Provisions for extension of basic authorities allowing the development of research and demonstration centers (PL 89-105)
1965	Support to aid children with disabilities in state institutions (PL 89-313); National Technical Institute for the Deaf is established (PL 89-136)
1966	Authorization for establishing the Bureau of Education for the Handicapped and a National Advisory Committee on the Handicapped (PL 89-750)
1968	Experimental demonstration centers for preschoolers are established (PL 90-538); provisions are made for deaf-blind centers, resource centers, and expansion of media services for those with disabilities (PL 90-247); PL 90-480 eliminates architectural barriers to people with disabilities
1970	Facilities are required to be accessible to those with physical disabilities (PL 91-205)
1970	Consolidation into one act of all previously separate federal grant programs for children with disabilities; known as Part B of the Education of the Handicapped Act (PL 91-230)
1973	Rights of individuals with disabilities in employment and educational institutions receiving federal funds are guaranteed through Section 504 of the Rehabilitation Act Amendments (PL 93-112)
1974	Authorization of the Family Educational Rights and Privacy Act giving parents the right to examine records kept in the student's files (PL 93-380)
1975	Free, appropriate public education and other procedural guarantees are mandated for all children with disabilities (PL 94-142)
1978	Gifted and Talented Children's Act (PL 95-561) authorizes minimum appropriations to state agencies for programs for gifted and talented children
1983	PL 94-142 amended to provide added emphasis on parent education and preschool, secondary, and postsecondary programs for children and youth with disabilities (PL 98-199); amended in 1986 to extend its provisions to infants and toddlers from birth through age 2 (PL 99-457)
1984	The Vocational Education Act (PL 98-524) supports vocational programs and the provision of such programs to students with disabilities
1985	The need for specialized temporary care is recognized by the Temporary Childcare for Handicapped Children and Crisis Nurseries Act (PL 99-401)
1986	Rehabilitation Act Amendments of 1986 provide programs in supported employment services for individuals with disabilities (PL 99-504)
1987	Developmental Disabilities and Bill of Rights Act establishes Developmental Disabilities Councils as a part of advocacy systems for people with developmental disabilities (PL 100-146)
1988	Authorization for the establishment of statewide assistive-technology services (PL 100-407)
1990	Americans with Disabilities Act bans discrimination against people with disabilities in employment; public buildings, transportation, and communication systems must be made accessible (PL 101-335); PL 94-142 is reauthorized and renamed Individuals with Disabilities Education Act (PL 101-476)
1991	The Carl D. Perkins Vocational and Applied Technology Education Act focuses on improving programs leading to providing the skills needed to work in a technological society (PL 102-103)
1994	Reauthorization of PL 100-407 to develop a national classification system for easier access to assistive-technology devices and services (PL 103-218)

14

TABLE 1.3
Continued.

Year	Legislation
1994	Developmental Disabilities Assistance and Bill of Rights Act supports councils within states to help people with developmental disabilities achieve independence, productivity, and integration and inclusion into their communities (PL 103-230)
1996	Health Insurance Portability and Accountability Act (HIPAA) ensures that clients and medical patients have an assurance of privacy for their medical records (Public Law 104-191)
1997	Individuals with Disabilities Education Act reauthorization (IDEA, 1997) provides for strengthened parental rights, nonbiased testing, and disciplinary procedures for students whose misbehavior is a manifestation of their disability
2001	No Child Left Behind: Elementary and Secondary Education Act provides for highly qualified teachers, use of research-validated teaching methods in all classrooms, and accountability through yearly high-stakes testing
2004	Individuals with Disabilities Education Improvement Act adds provisions for aligning the law with NCLB (ESEA), highly qualified teachers, and research-based interventions

Sources: From NICHCY, 2005; Turnbull & Turnbull, 2000; Wehman, 1997; Yell, 2006.

disabilities. The many court decisions rendered and the state and federal laws passed since the 1960s now protect the rights of students with disabilities and guarantee that they receive a free, appropriate, publicly supported education (NICHCY, 2005).

Early Federal Education Laws and Court Cases

Although the Tenth Amendment to the Constitution implies that provision of education is the business of the states (Yell, 1998), federal law guarantees the educational rights of individuals with disabilities. Throughout the 1800s, special education programs emerged for people with mental retardation, deafness, blindness, behavioral disorders, and physical disabilities. Not until 1879, however, by way of Public Law 45-186, did Congress provide funds for the American Printing House for the Blind to develop materials in braille. Decades passed until Congress again acted on behalf of people with disabilities (PL 66-236) by providing vocational rehabilitation services for World War I veterans and extending these services to civilians (Hardman, Drew, & Egan, 2005; Heward, 2006). During the late 1950s Congress made limited and sporadic attempts to assist individuals with mental retardation and deafness. There were also some early attempts at preparing personnel to assist people with exceptionalities. The 1960s initiated a productive era for the early emergence of legislation for individuals with disabilities. In 1961, PL 87-715 provided for funds to develop, produce, and distribute captioned films. In 1963, PL 88-164 expanded federal interest in training personnel to assist individuals in all the disability categories recognized at the time. Monies for grants to research service delivery and instruction, as well as to demonstrate projects for model service-delivery systems, were provided (Horne, 1996; Smith, 2001).

Direct federal support for the education of students with disabilities has its modern roots in the Elementary and Secondary Education Act of 1965 (ESEA), which addresses the bulk of federal aid for K–12 education. At the heart of ESEA funding is Title I, Aid to Disadvantaged Children, which consumes the majority of the money spent on ESEA programs each year. The most recent reauthorization of ESEA was in 2001 when President George W. Bush signed into law the No Child Left Behind legislation.

The Elementary and Secondary Education Act Amendments of 1966, PL 89-750, established the first federal grant program for the education of students with disabilities at the local school level. This law also established BEH to administer all Office of Education programs for students with disabilities. Its function was to help the states implement and monitor programs, support demonstration programs, conduct research, and evaluate federally funded programs. The services included funding for regional resource centers, centers and services for students with deaf-blindness, expansion of instructional remedial programs, continued research in special education, and recruitment of education personnel. In addition, funds were provided to disseminate information concerning educational opportunities for students with disabilities. This law also provided financial support for training special educators, other teachers, support personnel, and parents and assisted in the production and distribution of educational media (Turnbull & Turnbull, 2000).

Legal Reform

In the mid-1970s, two precedent-setting cases took place in Pennsylvania and the District of Columbia. The Pennsylvania Association for Retarded Citizens (PARC) and parents of 13 school-age students with mental retardation brought a class-action suit against the Commonwealth of Pennsylvania for its alleged failure to provide all of its school-age students with mental retardation with a publicly supported education (Pennsylvania Association for Retarded Citizens (PARC) v. Commonwealth of Pennsylvania, 1972). The PARC suit was resolved by a consent agreement that specified that the state could not apply any law that would postpone, end, or deny students with mental retardation access to a publicly supported education. The agreement required the state to identify all school-age students with mental retardation who were excluded from the public schools and to place them in a free public program at no cost to the student or the student's family. The program was to consist of education and training appropriate for these students based on their capacity. The agreement claimed that it was highly desirable to educate these students in programs most like those available to students without disabilities.

Also in 1972, parents and guardians of seven District of Columbia students brought a class-action suit against the District of Columbia Board of Education on behalf of all out-of-school students with disabilities (*Mills v. District of Columbia Board-of-Education,* 1972). Unlike the settlement in the PARC case, Mills was resolved by a judgment against the district school board. The result was a court order that the District of Columbia must provide an appropriate education for all students with a disability, regardless of the severity of the disability, and it must be publicly supported, that is, paid for by the same monies that pay for education for all other students.

The courts had become an ally in the quest for the best education possible for all students. Many similar cases followed. Table 1.4 is a brief summary of some major court cases that have influenced the development of special education. The history of litigation, judgments for and against the students with disabilities, sustains the proposition that individuals with disabilities are entitled to equal protection and rights for education and other services without discrimination.

The Rehabilitation Act of 1973, Section 504 (PL 93-112), provides basic civil rights protection for qualified individuals with disabilities in programs and activities that receive federal financial assistance. No individual in the United States shall, solely by

TABLE 1.4
Selected history of litigation of special education.

Year	Court Case
1954	*Brown v. Board of Education of Topeka* (Kansas) Established the right of all children to an equal opportunity to education and ruled that separate was not equal.
1967	*Hobson v. Hansen* (Washington, DC) Declared the track system, which used standardized tests as a basis for special education placement, unconstitutional because it discriminated against African American and poor children.
1970	*Diana v. State Board of Education* (California) Declared that children cannot be placed in special education on the basis of culturally biased tests or tests given in a language other than the child's native language.
1972	*Mills v. Board of Education of the District of Columbia* Established the right of every child to an equal opportunity for education, declared that lack of funds was not an acceptable excuse for lack of educational opportunity.
1972	*Pennsylvania Association for Retarded Citizens v. the Commonwealth of Pennsylvania* Class-action suit that established the right to free public education for all children with mental retardation.
1972	*Wyatt v. Stickney* (Alabama) Declared that individuals in state institutions have the right to appropriate treatment within those institutions.
1979	*Larry P. v. Riles* (California) First brought to court in 1972; ruled that IQ tests cannot be used as the sole basis for placing children in special classes.
1982	*Board of Education of the Hendrik Hudson Central School District v. Rowley* (New York) Upheld for each child with a disability the right to a personalized program of instruction and necessary supportive services; services that might be useful but are not necessary for the student to function satisfactorily do not have to be supplied.
1983	*Abrahamson v. Hershman* (Massachusetts) Ruled that residential placement in a private school was necessary for a child with multiple disabilities who needed around-the-clock training; required the school district to pay for the private placement.
1984	*Department of Education v. Katherine D.* (Hawaii) Ruled that a homebound instructional program for a child with multiple health impairments did not meet the least restrictive environment standard; called for the child to be placed in a class with children without disabilities and provided with related medical services.
1988	*Honig v. Doe* (California) Ruled that children with disabilities could not be excluded from school for any misbehavior that is "disability related."
1989	*Timothy W. v. Rochester School District* (New Hampshire) Required that all children with disabilities be provided with a free, appropriate public education. The three-judge appeals court overturned the decision of a district court judge, who had ruled that the local school district was not obligated to educate a 13-year-old boy with multiple and severe disabilities because he could not "benefit" from special education.
1990	*W.G. v. Target Range School District No. 23 Board of Trustees* (Montana) Established that a parent is entitled to private-school cost reimbursement when a school district is in violation of EHA.

(continued)

TABLE 1.4
Continued.

Year	Court Case
1991	*Community Consolidated School District No. 21 v. Illinois State Board of Education* (Illinois) Established that the hostility of parents is of "obvious and direct relevance" in determining the benefits of an educational placement.
1991	*Theado v. Strongsville City School District* (Ohio) Established that compensatory education may be awarded to an individual with a disability after age 21 if an appropriate education was denied during the tenure in public education.
1991	*Corores v. Portsmouth School District* (New Hampshire) Established the right to compensatory education when a district is found not to have provided a free and appropriate education to a student with a disability.
1992	*Oberti v. Board of Education of the Borough of Clementon School District* (New Jersey) Established inclusion as a right, not a privilege, and found that to learn to function effectively, all children with disabilities need integration experiences.
1992	*Holland v. Sacramento City Unified School District* (California) Established that the school district was required to accept an 11-year-old girl with an IQ of 44 in a general class. In assessing the inclusion placement, the court considered benefits derived from full-time placement in general classrooms, nonacademic benefits, the impact of the exceptional student's presence on other students, and the costs of placement.
1996	*Mary P. v. Illinois State Board of Education* (Illinois) Established that academic achievement may be a component of an eligibility decision but might not form the sole basis for the determination.
1998	*Frank S. v. School Committee of Dennis-Yarmouth Regional School District* (Massachusetts) Ruled that, after graduation, the student was no longer eligible for FAPE because the school had discharged its duties in fulfilling the IEP.
1998	*Walczak v. Florida Union Free School District* (Florida) Established that, although IDEA does not establish any level of academic achievement for an IEP, the courts may look at passing grades and test scores to determine appropriateness.
1999	*Cedar Rapids Community School District v. Garret F.* (Iowa) Related services may include nursing services such as catheterization of bladder, suctioning, ventilator setting checks, and other specialized procedures if such procedures are necessary to keep the student in school where the student is progressing on IEP goals.
2001	*Chapman v. California Department of Education, the Superintendent of Public Instruction, and the State Board of Education.* Challenged high school exit exams as discriminatory against students with disabilities.
2005	*Porter v. Board of Trustees of Manhattan Beach Unified School District* (California) Awarded 6.7 million because the school district did not provide FAPE.
2005	*Shaeffer v. Weast* (Montgomery County Schools, Maryland) Required the complaintant to have the burden of proof for providing an appropriate educational program.

Sources: Heward, 2006; Meyen, 1996; Oakstone Legal and Business Publishing, 1999; Turnbull & Turnbull, 2000.

reason of a disability, be excluded from participation in, be denied benefits of, or be subjected to discrimination under any program or activity receiving money from the federal government. The U.S. Department of Education's implementation of Section 504 applies to preschool, elementary, secondary, postsecondary, vocational, and other programs and activities that receive or benefit from federal financial assistance. In essence, Section 504 prohibits discrimination against any student in educational institutions receiving federal funds. This includes most public schools.

Individuals with Disabilities Education Act

Following on the heels of the Elementary and Secondary Education Act, Congress passed the Elementary and Secondary Education Act Amendments of 1970, PL 91-230. This law consolidated into one act a number of previously separate federal grant programs related to the education of students with disabilities. By 1974 Congress had been confronted with two special education court cases (*Pennsylvania Association for Retarded Citizens v. Pennsylvania,* 1972; and *Mills v. District of Columbia Board of Education,* 1972). These cases each included a ruling on "child find" provisions that required the states to take the initiative to locate the students with disabilities and not wait for parents to bring the students to the attention of the school. These two cases, along with a growing number of parent groups calling for reform of special education, led to the passage of a more encompassing act, the Education for All Handicapped Children Act (PL 94-142), perhaps the single most far-reaching legislative act ever passed for students with exceptionalities. Congress passed this law in 1975 and has since reauthorized and retitled it the Individuals with Disabilities Education Act (IDEA). It was signed in November 1975 by Gerald Ford and first went into effect in October 1977 when the regulations were finalized. This act, as amended several times over the past few decades, governs eligibility for special education services, parental rights, IEPs, LREs, and the need to provide related services. The major purposes of this legislation, as amended over the years, are listed here:

- To guarantee that a "free, appropriate education," including special education and related service programming, is available to all students with disabilities who require it.
- To ensure that the rights of students and youth with disabilities and their parents or guardians are protected (for example, fairness, appropriateness, and due process in decision making about providing special education and related services to students with disabilities).
- To ensure and assess the effectiveness of special education.
- To assist financially the efforts of state and local governments in providing full educational opportunities to all students with disabilities through the use of federal funds.
- To inform parents or eligible students of their rights under this law, including the right to file a complaint with the U.S. Department of Education.

This legislation protects all families, in particular the families of students with special needs, from being subjected to arbitrary decisions that would affect the educational experience of students.

In 1983, through the Education of the Handicapped Act Amendments of 1983 (PL 98-199), Congress changed the law to expand incentives for preschool special education programs, early intervention, and transition programs for older students. All

programs under the Education of the Handicapped Act (EHA) became the responsibility of OSEP, which by this time had replaced BEH.

EHA was amended again through PL 99-457, the Education of the Handicapped Act Amendments of 1986, which lowered the age of eligibility for special education and related services for all students with disabilities to age 3. The law also established the Handicapped Infants and Toddlers Program. This program is directed to the needs of students from birth to age 3 who need early intervention services. Under this program, the infant or toddler's family may receive services to help them assist in the development of their child. PL 99-504, the Rehabilitation Act Amendment, was also passed in 1986. It provided programs for planned transition to work or other postsecondary activity.

In 1990 Congress passed the Education of the Handicapped Act Amendments (PL 101-476) and changed EHA to IDEA. Some new discretionary programs, including special transition programs, a new program to improve services for students with serious emotional disturbance, and a research and information dissemination program on attention deficit disorder, were created. In addition, the law added transition services and assistive-technology services as new definitions of special education services that must be included in a student's IEP. Rehabilitation, counseling, and social work services were included as related services under the law. Finally, the services and rights under this law were expanded to include students with labels of autism and traumatic brain injury.

In 1997 both houses of Congress overwhelmingly reauthorized IDEA, and President Clinton signed it into law. The most noteworthy features of that reauthorization dealt with discipline, IEP modifications, mediation, funding, and professional development. Schools now had the authority to place students with exceptionalities in alternative placements if they determined that the child's behavior was not a manifestation of the child's disability. This provision enabled educators to more easily remove violent or dangerous students with disabilities from their current educational placements. IEPs were to be more complex, requiring, among other mandates, statements of the student's current level of functioning, measurable short-term objectives, and annual goals. Transitional service needs must be specified, and the IEP must detail how parents and families are to be regularly informed of progress. When mediation is needed to resolve differences about placement, individual states are required to establish a mediation system in which parents and schools may voluntarily participate. However, mediation may not be used to deprive parents and families of their rights to due process.

IDEA makes it possible for states and localities to receive federal funds to assist in the education of infants, toddlers, preschoolers, children, and youth with disabilities. Basically, to remain eligible for federal funds under the law, states must ensure the following:

- *Zero reject*—All students with disabilities, regardless of the severity of their disability, can be served in the public schools.

- *Free, appropriate public education (FAPE)*—Education for students with disabilities will be provided at no cost to the families and students with disabilities, and it will be appropriate to their needs.

- *Least restrictive environment (LRE)*—Educators must justify any placement of a student outside the general education setting. IEP or an IFSP will be drawn up for each child or youth found eligible for special education or early intervention services, stating precisely the type of special education intervention related services needed. To the maximum extent *appropriate*, all students with disabilities will have access to a general education delivered in the LRE for that individual.

- *Evaluation and assessment*—Education of students with disabilities will be based on a complete, unbiased, and individual evaluation and assessment of the specific, unique needs of each student.

- *Parent rights to confidentiality*—Any information about a student with disabilities, including program decisions and placements, assessment data, and reports of progress, are confidential and must not be shared with anyone not working directly with the student.

- *Procedural safeguards*—Any decisions made about educational matters are made with parental and family input. In the event of a disagreement about procedures and placement, parents and families have the right to an impartial hearing or due process.

Students receiving special education have the right to receive the related services necessary to benefit from special education instruction. Related services include transportation and such developmental, corrective, and other supportive services as are required to assist a child with a disability to benefit from special education. This includes speech pathology and audiology, psychological services, physical and occupational therapy, recreation, early identification and assessment of disabilities in students, counseling services, including rehabilitation counseling, and medical services for diagnostic or evaluation purposes. The term also includes school health services, social work services in schools, and parent counseling and training (NICHCY, 1996, p. 6).

Families and parents have the right to participate in every decision related to the identification, evaluation, and placement of their student with a disability. They must give consent for any initial evaluation, assessment, or placement; must be notified of any change in placement that may occur; must be included, along with teachers, in conferences and meetings held to draw up individualized programs; and must approve these plans before they go into effect for the first time. The right of families to challenge and appeal any decision related to identification, evaluation, and placement, or any issue concerning the provision of FAPE, is fully protected by clearly spelled-out due process procedures. Parents also have the right to confidentiality of information. No one, except those with a legitimate educational need, may see a student's records without written permission from parents and families.

Funding formulas for special education have been modified. Most significantly, the expense of special education for local school districts can now be shared among state education departments and public agencies. For example, a public agency other than the school district may be assigned the responsibility to pay for assistive-technology devices or transitional services.

The 1997 reauthorization of IDEA ensured that states will provide more mechanisms for general and special educators to avail themselves of professional development opportunities, enabling them to be current in the knowledge and skills necessary to meet the needs of students with special needs. Examples of professional development programs might include those that provide general and special educators with content knowledge; collaborative skills; information about the latest research; or information about promising practices, materials, or technology (Oakstone Legal and Business Publishing, 1999).

The reauthorization in 2004 made several other significant changes in the laws. If a student is involved in conduct resulting in a disciplinary action, the school and the IEP team are to determine if the conduct is caused by the presence of a disability or is a result of the school's failure to implement the program or IEP correctly. If the team determines the behavior is a manifestation of the disability, then a functional behavioral analysis must be completed and all data used to write a behavioral intervention plan. If the behavior is not a manifestation of the disability, the student is subject to the discipline code of the school.

A teacher must be "highly qualified" under the statute. This means a special education teacher must have at least a bachelor's degree, hold a state license to teach special education, and be qualified to teach in the content area (e.g., elementary education, high school algebra, art, etc.). This legislation aligns IDEA with No Child Left Behind, which is the reauthorization of ESEA.

No Child Left Behind

No Child Left Behind (NCLB) was a reauthorization of ESEA. It applies to all schools and districts receiving Title I federal grants that provide funding for remedial education programs for poor and disadvantaged students. It is not a special education law, but many of the tenets affect special education programs and educators. The emphases of the provisions are on accountability and teaching methods that have been researched and shown to be effective. Many areas are legislated, and we will list a few of the most relevant. First, all teachers must be highly qualified, that is, they must hold a bachelor's degree and pass a state test or have course work in the areas in which they teach. For elementary teachers, this means having knowledge of how to teach math and reading. Second, all students must be proficient on state tests given at the end of the year. The scores from each school will be published each year, and schools whose students do not make adequate yearly progress are subject to sanctions. Tutoring and other services will be given to students in failing schools. Third, schools are encouraged to use research-validated teaching methods and materials. Fourth, **paraeducators** must have either 2 years of college or, for those employed before the act took effect, pass a test showing rigorous preparation in academic content. If a school, and subgroups of students within that school, fails to make adequate progress, students may elect to transfer out of the school or to have tutoring services. For continued failure, staff and administrators responsible for the failures will be replaced. The state may take over some schools and provide training for a new curriculum to address weaknesses.

Other Legislation

PL 93-380, the Family Educational Rights and Privacy Act (FERPA) passed in 1974, is often called the Buckley Amendment. It gives parents of students under the age of 18, and students age 18 and older, the right to examine records kept in the student's personal file. FERPA was designed to cover all students, including those in postsecondary education and those with and without disabilities. The major provisions of this early act are as follows:

- Family members and eligible students have the right to inspect and review the student's educational records.

- Schools must have written permission from family members or eligible students before releasing any information from a student's records. Although a school may disclose education records to some others without consent—such as other school officials, schools to which a student is transferring, certain government officials, and state and local authorities—the school must keep track, within the student's files, of the requests for these records. The family members or eligible student may inspect this information.

- Family members and eligible students have the right to have the records explained and interpreted by school officials.

- School officials may not destroy any education records if there is an outstanding request to inspect and review them.

- Family members and eligible students who believe that information in the education records is inaccurate or misleading may request that the records be amended. They must be advised if the school decides that the records should not be amended, and they have rights to a hearing (Turnbull & Turnbull, 2000).

The need for federal legislation for gifted and talented students was recognized in 1978 by PL 95-561, the Gifted and Talented Children's Act, which authorized an appropriation of $50,000 for each state education agency (SEA) to assist their planning, development, operation, and improvement of programs for the education of gifted and talented students. This legislation was followed in August 1988 by Senate Bill 373, entitled the Jacob K. Javits Gifted and Talented Student Education Bill, which provided $8 million for the identification of and service for gifted and talented students, training and professional development for teachers of the gifted, and the creation of the National Center for the Education of the Gifted.

The year 1984 saw the passage of PL 98-524, the Vocational Education Act, which is often referred to as the Carl D. Perkins Act or the Perkins Act. It authorized federal funds to support vocational education programs and to improve the access of those who either have been underserved in the past or who have greater-than-average education needs for these programs. This law is particularly important because it requires that vocational education be provided for students with disabilities. The law states that individuals who are members of special populations (including individuals with disabilities) must be provided with equal access to recruitment, enrollment, and placement activities in vocational education. In addition, these individuals must be provided with equal access to the full range of vocational education programs available to others, including occupationally specific courses of study, cooperative education, apprenticeship programs and, to the extent practical, comprehensive guidance and counseling services. Under the law, vocational education planning should be coordinated among public agencies, including vocational education, special education, and state vocational rehabilitation agencies.

The Temporary Childcare for Handicapped Children and Crisis Nurseries Act, PL 99-401, was first introduced in 1985 as part of an omnibus child-care bill and enacted by the 99th Congress in 1986. The act was later incorporated into the Children's Justice and Assistance Act of 1986 (PL 99-401). The act was most recently reauthorized and otherwise amended by the Child Abuse, Domestic Violence, Adoption and Family Services Act of 1992 (PL 102-295). This law provides funding through competitive grants to states and U.S. territories to develop nonmedical respite services (specialized temporary care) for students with disabilities or chronic or terminal illnesses and to develop crisis nursery services for those at risk of abuse and neglect. In addition to temporary child care, these programs also offer an array of family support services or referrals to such services.

Along with health and educational services, the legal and civil rights of individuals with exceptionalities were targeted by legislation. The Mental Retardation Facilities and Community Mental Health Centers Construction Act of 1963 (PL 88-164) and the Developmental Disabilities and Bill of Rights Act Amendments of 1987 (PL 100-146) provided a Bill of Rights section included in the 1987 amendments. People covered under these amendments included those with mental retardation, autism, cerebral palsy, and epilepsy. Grants were provided to states to establish Developmental Disabilities Councils to support the planning, coordination, and delivery of specialized services to people with developmental disabilities. The law also authorized formula awards to support the establishment and operation of state protection and advocacy systems. Discretionary grants were awarded to (1) university-affiliated programs that provide interdisciplinary training in the fields of developmental disabilities and (2) projects of national significance aimed at increasing the independence, productivity, and community integration of people with developmental disabilities. The 1987 amendments also established a federal interagency committee to plan for and coordinate activities related to people with developmental disabilities. The act was amended in 1990 (PL 101-496) and 1994 (PL 103-230) by the Developmental Disabilities Assistance and Bill of Rights Acts. The grants to support councils in the states are for promoting—through systematic change, capacity building, and advocacy activities—the development of a comprehensive consumer- and family-centered system and a coordinated array of culturally competent services, supports, and other assistance designed to help those with developmental disabilities achieve independence, productivity, and integration and inclusion into the community. Another key provision of these amendments was the definition of developmental disability:

> a severe, chronic disability of an individual 5 years of age or older that: (a) is attributable to a mental or physical impairment or combination of mental and physical impairments; (b) is manifested before the person attains age 22; (c) is likely to continue indefinitely; (d) results in substantial functional limitation in three or more of the following areas of major life activity: (i) self-care; (ii) receptive and expressive language; (iii) learning; (iv) mobility; (v) self-direction; (vi) capacity for independent living; and (vii) economic sufficiency; and (e) reflects the individual's need for a combination and sequence of special interdisciplinary, or generic services, supports, or other assistance that is of lifelong or extended duration and is individually planned and coordinated. (NICHCY, 1996, pp. 5–6)

The 1994 amendments make a specific exception to the age limitation for developmental disabilities to include individuals from birth through age 5 who have substantial developmental delays or specific congenital or acquired conditions with a high probability of resulting in developmental disabilities if services are not provided.

Programs, projects, and activities receiving assistance under PL 103-230 must be carried out in a manner consistent with a number of principles, including: (1) that individuals with developmental disabilities, including those with the most severe developmental disabilities, are capable of achieving independence, productivity, and integration and inclusion into the community, given appropriate support; (2) that these individuals and their families are the primary decision makers regarding the services and supports to be received; and (3) that services, supports, and other assistance should be provided in a manner that demonstrates respect for individual dignity, personal preference, and cultural differences.

The Americans with Disabilities Act (ADA), PL 101-336, was signed into law on July 26, 1990. The central purpose of the act is to extend to individuals with disabilities civil rights protections similar to those provided to individuals on the basis of race, sex, national origin, and religion. Based on the concepts of the Rehabilitation Act of 1973, ADA guarantees equal opportunity for individuals with disabilities in employment, public accommodation, transportation, state and local government services, and telecommunications. ADA is the most significant federal law to date ensuring the full civil rights of all individuals with disabilities.

Title II of ADA prohibits discrimination on the basis of disability by state and local government entities. The Office of Civil Rights is responsible for enforcing Title II with respect to all programs, services, and regulatory activities related to the operation of public elementary and secondary education systems and institutions and public institutions of higher education and vocational education.

The federal government has also attempted to provide assistance for individuals and their families who are dependent on technology but may be confused about obtaining appropriate services or equipment by the ever-growing array of devices and services available. The primary purpose of the Technology-Related Assistance for Individuals with Disabilities Act of 1988 (PL 100-407) was to assist states in developing comprehensive, consumer-oriented programs of technology-related assistance and to increase the availability of assistive technology to individuals with disabilities and their families. In 1990 and 1991 Congress amended this law by passing PL 101-392 and PL 102-103, respectively, changing the name of the law to the Carl D. Perkins Vocational and Applied Technology Education Act. This legislation concentrates resources on improving educational programs leading to the academic and occupational skill competencies needed to work in a technologically advanced society. It expands the term special population to include individuals who are economically and educationally disadvantaged (including foster children), individuals with limited English proficiency, individuals who participate in programs to eliminate sex bias, and those in correctional institutions. The act was reauthorized in 1994 and required the development of a national classification system for assistive-technology devices and services.

An assistive-technology device is defined as any item, piece of equipment, or product that is used to increase and help with the functional capabilities of an individual. It may be bought off the shelf, modified, or customized. It may have been designed as an assistive device or it may be modified to meet the purposes. It may be technologically oriented, such as a computer with voice capabilities, or it may be as simple as a rubber mat to keep objects from slipping. Assistive-technology services are any services that directly assist an individual with a disability to select, acquire, or use an assistive-technology device. This includes evaluating the needs of the individual, including a functional evaluation in the customary environment. Box 1.2 contains law text of the (IDEA) relating to technology and related device.

In summary, the federal laws require that all students with disabilities be educated and that students with disabilities receive a full, individualized evaluation before being placed in special education. This evaluation must be nondiscriminatory and fair for every student, including, but not limited to, nonverbal and nonreading students and those with different cultural, ethnic, linguistic, and other diverse backgrounds. Each

BOX 1.2
WHAT EVERY TEACHER NEEDS TO KNOW ABOUT TECHNOLOGY

Text of the Individuals with Disabilities Improvement Act (2004) dealing with assistive technology devices

§300.5 Assistive Technology Device. As used in this part, **assistive technology device** means any item, piece of equipment, or product system, whether acquired commercially off the shelf, modified, or customized, that is used to increase, maintain, or improve the functional capabilities of a child with a disability.

§300.6 Assistive Technology Service. As used in this part, **assistive technology service** means any service that directly assists a child with a disability in the selection, acquisition, or use of an assistive technology device.

The term includes:

- The evaluation of the needs of a child with a disability, including a functional evaluation of the child in the child's customary environment;
- Purchasing, leasing, or otherwise providing for the acquisition of assistive technology devices by children with disabilities;
- Selecting, designing, fitting, customizing, adapting, applying, maintaining, repairing, or replacing assistive technology devices;
- Coordinating and using other therapies, interventions, or services with assistive technology devices, such as those associated with existing education and rehabilitation plans and programs;
- Training or technical assistance for a child with a disability or, if appropriate, that child's family; and (f) training or technical assistance for professionals (including individuals providing education or rehabilitation services), employers, or other individuals who provide services to, employ, or are otherwise substantially involved in the major life functions of that child. (authority 20 U.S.C. 1041(2))

student must be provided with an IEP devoted to the student's needs and, to the extent appropriate, should be educated with peers who are not disabled. Parents, legal guardians, and other family members must be notified and give consent regarding the evaluation process and placement procedures. They have the right to a due process hearing when an agreement cannot be reached between them and the school. Special education decisions are made by teams composed of families, students, and school personnel. Parental input is mandated and is a very essential part of the laws (NICHCY, 1996; Turnbull & Turnbull, 2000; Westling & Fox, 2006; Yell, 2006).

Rights and Responsibilities Resulting from Legislation

We have outlined the step-by-step legal attainment of rights and responsibilities of students with disabilities and their parents. What follows is an explanation of how the legislation has been transformed into day-to-day procedures in providing services to students with special needs. Each of the following processes that form the structure of special education services can be traced back to the enabling legislation that made it a part of the education system for students with special needs.

DUE PROCESS

Students with disabilities, their parents or guardians and other family members, and the schools are guaranteed procedural due process safeguards in the determination of needs for services, identification, and placement of students with disabilities. This means that, at each of the various stages on the path to determining whether a child is eligible for special services, families must be advised of their rights under the law and must give written consent to proceed with each step. Due process provides protection from arbitrary decision making and requires families to take appropriate responsibility in the determination of an education program for their children. Box 1.3 summarizes due process rights in an outline format that will help you understand the usual process for determining and providing for a child's educational needs. These rights are determined by the legislation governing the educational rights to FAPE and by several amendments to the Constitution. These include, but are not limited to, the Fourteenth Amendment and the Fifth Amendment.

BOX 1.3
WHAT EVERY TEACHER SHOULD KNOW

Due Process Rights in a Nutshell

Right to Know. Parents must be informed before any action regarding:

- Identification
- Evaluation
- Programming
- Placement

Guaranteed Active Participation in the IEP Process. Parents must give permission for:

- Release of health and educational records
- Preplacement evaluation
- Initial placement

Appropriate Evaluation. Testing and evaluation materials must be selected and administered so as not to be racially or culturally discriminatory, must be provided and administered in the child's native language, and must be valid for the purposes for which they are to be used:

- Tests selected must accurately reflect the child's aptitude or achievement level and other factors they purport to measure.
- No single test may be used to determine educational programs.
- All areas that might have an impact on the disability must also be assessed.

Independent Evaluation. If parents are concerned about team decisions, they may obtain an independent evaluation:

- Usually at their own expense
- At the school system's expense in some cases

Placement Hearing Resolution. If parents disagree with the school's plans for the child and cannot resolve the disagreement informally, they are entitled to a hearing with an impartial hearing officer at no personal expense to help resolve differences.

(continued)

BOX 1.3   *Continued*

Input in the IEP. The IEP lays out the goals for the child and the services to be provided, including the extent of participation in general educational programs. The following criteria must be met:

- Parents must have the opportunity to attend each meeting of the IEP team.
- Parents must be given advance notification of each meeting.
- Parents must be allowed to participate in planning.
- Meetings must be scheduled at a mutually agreeable time.
- An interpreter must be provided if needed.

Communication of Team Decisions. All decisions must be clearly and simply communicated in the parents' native language and by a method of communication that can be understood by all members of the team. The school is responsible for providing all explanations required by team members.

Right to Information. Parents have the right to:

- Review all educational records
- Request copies of these records (there may be a charge)
- Request removal of information they think is false or misleading

Stay-Put Provision. Once a placement has begun, it may be changed only by the IEP team. If consensus including parent agreement cannot be reached, the child must "stay put" until the hearing process is concluded. In extreme circumstances, the courts can change a placement.

Right to Confidentiality. All information on any child with a disability must be kept confidential.

Right of Action in Federal Court. Any party aggrieved by the decision of a hearing officer has the right to bring civil suit in federal court.

Source: From NICHCY (1996) 34 C.F.R., pt. 300.

NONDISCRIMINATORY ASSESSMENT

Nondiscriminatory assessment is at the core of due process and of FAPE. Students with suspected disabilities must be assessed by public schools or a designated professional to determine whether they are eligible for special education services. The majority of students are initially referred by the classroom teacher or a parent or guardian for evaluation. During evaluation and assessment procedures, educators must use, as best they can, tests and testing protocols that are culturally and racially fair or unbiased. The tests must be in the native language of the child if such adequately standardized instruments exist. Use of multiple assessment tools and techniques safeguards against making judgments based on the results of one instrument, reducing but perhaps not eliminating bias. Observations of the student in classrooms, playground situations, home situations, and other natural environs are necessary. Nondiscriminatory assessment procedures counteract the possibility of a student being placed in special education based on cultural, linguistic, or ideological differences rather than identifiable disabilities.

INDIVIDUALIZED EDUCATION PLAN

All students who might be identified as eligible for special educational programming must have an evaluation that encompasses the areas of suspected need and areas of strength. If the student is found to qualify for specialized services through IDEA, the team will meet to write an IEP. This document must be developed by a team whose members meet to review the assessment information available about the student and design an educational program to meet the student's unique educational needs. This meeting, called an IEP meeting, must be held within 30 calendar days after the school district determines, through a multidisciplinary evaluation, that a student has a specified physical or mental impairment and needs special education and related services (North Carolina Department of Public Instruction Exceptional Children Suport Team, 1996; U.S. Department of Education, 2005). A student's IEP review must occur at least annually thereafter, unless the student lives in a state involved in a program for a 3-year reevaluation cycle. Even if the student is in the pilot program, if the family member responsible for approving the IEP does not agree, the IEP must be revisited every year or more often. Families and teachers can request an IEP meeting to review and revise the student's IEP more often than once a year. IDEA 2004 provides that the IEP team shall revise the IEP to address:

- Any lack of expected progress toward the IEP goals or in the general education curriculum
- The results of any reevaluation
- Information provided to or by the family members
- The student's anticipated needs
- Other matters (IDEA, 2004; Section 1414 [d] [4])

The following people comprise the IEP team and must be invited to attend the IEP meeting:

- One or both of the student's parents, foster parents, or other family members
- The student's general education teacher(s). If the child has more than one teacher, state policy or law may specify which teacher(s) should participate.
- The student's special education teacher
- A representative of the school other than the child's teacher. This person must be qualified to provide special education or supervise its provision and able to make fiscal decisions.
- Other individuals, at the discretion of the school or the parents. These could include advocates, attorneys, persons to take notes, neighbors, siblings, and others.
- The student, when appropriate. Appropriate, in this case, is determined by the family.

Depending on the purpose of the meeting, other participants may be involved. For example, when a student is being evaluated for the first time, the school must ensure that a member of the evaluation team participates in the IEP meeting so that someone knowledgeable about the evaluation procedures and results is present. A psychologist or a nurse may be needed to explain test results. If one of the purposes of the meeting is to consider transition services outside of the school setting for the student, then the school must also include the student and a representative of any other agency that will be responsible for providing or paying for the transition

services. For all students age 16 or older, one of the purposes of the annual meeting will always be the planning of transition services, which are a required component of the IEP for these students. The transition plan is generally referred to as an ITP.

The IEP and the ITP developed by the team are formulated from the assessment procedures during evaluation and from observation during and prior to the formal evaluation. Parents and others who know the student are generally asked to provide input as well.

Attending to the questions presented in Box 1.4 ensures that the IEP team will follow the procedures necessary to safeguard due process and to gather the information needed to write an IEP. Following are the 11 steps in developing the IEP document:

- Formulate a statement of the student's present level of educational performance.
- Formulate a statement of measurable annual goals.
- Formulate short-term instructional objectives written in measurable terms.
- Formulate a statement of the specific special education services to be provided.
- Determine the date when those services will begin and the length of time the services will be given.
- Describe the extent to which the student will be able to participate in general educational programs.
- Provide a justification for the type of educational placement the student will receive.
- Provide a list of the individuals responsible for implementing the IEP.
- Provide an outline of objective criteria, procedures, and time lines for evaluating whether the short-term objectives are being achieved.
- Compile all information on the appropriate form(s).
- Obtain the necessary signatures.

BOX 1.4
WHAT EVERY TEACHER SHOULD KNOW

Questions for IEP Participants

I. EVALUATION

Questions to Be Addressed

1. Has parental consent been obtained?
2. What areas of concern are identified in the referral?
3. What data sources will be used?
4. Who should administer and gather the evaluation information?
5. Does the student qualify for special education services?

Individuals Involved

1. Classroom teacher
2. Special education teacher
3. Local Education Teacher (LEA) representative
4. Psychologist
5. Related service providers
6. Parents
7. Others, when appropriate

II. IEP DEVELOPMENT AND PLACEMENT

Questions to Be Addressed

1 How do the evaluation results translate into the student's present level of performance?
2. What are the final student program outcomes?
3 What goals can the student reasonably achieve within 1 year's time?
4. What objectives will help the student accomplish the goals?
5. How will the goals and objectives be monitored?
6. Is the student placed in the least restrictive environment?

Individuals Involved

1. Parent[*]
2. Local Education Teacher (LEA) representative[*]
3. Special education teacher[†]
4. Student[†]
5. Psychologist
6. Classroom teacher

[*] mandated
[†] mandated for transition

III. IEP IMPLEMENTATION AND MONITERING

Questions to Be Addressed

1. Are the goals and objectives appropriate? Relevant? Functional?
2. Is the student making progress?
3. Does the IEP need to be amended?

Individuals Involved

1. Special education teacher
2. Other service providers as indicated on the IEP
3. IEP team members and appropriate consultants

IV. ANNUAL REVIEW

Questions to Be Addressed

1. Have the goals been achieved?
2. Does the student still require special education services?
3. What new goals and objectives need to be written?

Individuals Involved

1. Special education teacher
2. Local Education Teacher (LEA) representative
3. Parent
4. Student, when appropriate

Contents of the IEP

The IEP for each student must contain the following:

1. Demographic information
2. The following dates:
   a. The date the IEP document is completed
   b. The entry date to the program (date for initiation of services)
   c. The projected ending date of the IEP (may be no more than 1 year from the date of the completion of the IEP)
3. A statement of the student's present levels of educational performance, based on formal or informal measures
4. A statement of measurable annual goals
5. Measurable short-term objectives to be used in implementing annual goals (optional)
6. Appropriate objective criteria, evaluation procedures, and schedules for determining whether the short-term instructional objectives are being achieved
7. A plan for reporting to the family members the progress on the goals
8. A statement of the specific educational and related services to be provided to the student and the extent (amount of time) to which the student will be able to participate in general educational programs
9. The signatures and titles of all participants at the meeting and the date each one signed
10. Other information as needed

Figure 1.2 is a sample of an IEP.

Confidentiality and Record Keeping

IDEA and other federal laws, notably FERPA (PL 93-380), guarantee the protection of confidentiality of a student's education records. These provisions address the issues of (1) the use of identifiable information, (2) who may have access to the student's records, and (3) parents' right to request that their child's records be amended. Public Law 104-191 (1996), the Health Insurance Portability and Accountability Act (HIPAA), ensures that clients and medical patients have an assurance of privacy for their medical records. Records cannot be shared with persons, agencies, or others without the written consent of the patient. A medical agency must notify the patients about their privacy rights and how the information can be used.

LEAST RESTRICTIVE ENVIRONMENT

The final concern is that the services be provided in the least restrictive or least isolated setting in which the student can be successful. Students with disabilities are required, to the maximum extent appropriate, to be educated with students who are not disabled. Special classes, separate schooling, or other removal of students with disabilities from the general educational environment should occur only when the nature and severity of the disability is such that education in general classes with the use

Reading sample (middle school)
INDIVIDUALIZED EDUCATION PROGRAM (IEP)

DEC SHCA
(Part I)

Student Chris T.

Grade 7   School   Oak Middle

B. Date of Beginning and Duration of Special Education and Related Services

From September 3, 1991 To June 7, 1992
        (mo)   (day) (yr)   (mo) (day) (yr)

A. Present Level(s) of Performance
(Summarize evaluation results including strengths and needs or behavioral weaknesses)
- Accurately identifies initial and final consonants and short-long vowels; identifies similarities in word lists; can complete incomplete stories.
- Unable to select main idea in silent reading, use context clues or use phonetic or structural analysis.

C. Annual Goal(s) By using an individualized and linguistic approach, Chris will use phonetic clues to decode unfamiliar words and use strategic routines to summarize main ideas and details.

D.

Short-Term Instructional Objectives in Measurable Terms	Evaluation Procedures (How)	Evaluation Schedule (When)	Date Attained (Must be completed for each objective)
• Chris will be able to use decoding techniques to "chunk" unknown words with 99% accuracy.	• Informal probes using controlled level materials at the student's instructional level with progress charting.	by December 1	
• Chris will be able to use decoding techniques to attack and identify unknown words with 99% accuracy.	• Informal probes using controlled level materials equal to reading materials used in Chris's mainstreamed classes with progress charting.	by February 28	
• Chris will be able to use comprehension routines to improve recall of main ideas and details with 70% comprehension level.	• Informal comprehension probes using graded controlled reading level materials equal to reading materials used in mainstreamed placement.	by June 7	

FIGURE 1.2
Sample IEP.

Source: Courtesy of North Carolina Department of Public Instruction.

of supplementary aids and services cannot be achieved satisfactorily. A satisfactory level of success is determined by either trying the student in the LRE deemed appropriate for the age level or by reasonable, defensible professional judgment.

SPECIAL EDUCATORS: PROFESSIONAL PREPARATION STANDARDS

The final component of this chapter introduces the professionals most responsible for the provision of the services needed by students with exceptionalities: the special education teachers. These professionals may specialize in one or more of the categories of exceptionality listed in Table 1.1. They are certified as competent to provide services by the state in which they work. Speech-language pathologists are certified as clinically competent by the American Speech-Language-Hearing Association in addition to the state in which they provide services. In the past, there has been no national certification for special educators. With the advent of National Board Certification and other agency and organizational movement toward a national certification, this may change. Currently, each state determines the criteria a special educator must meet for each of the exceptionalities and awards the appropriate certification when a candidate meets its criteria. Information about specific guidelines and requirements for any given state can be obtained by contacting the state director of special education at the address listed in Appendix A. Although each state sets its own guidelines for special education teacher certification, this does not mean that each state operates in a vacuum, arbitrarily setting its own independent standards. The Council for Exceptional Children (CEC) has published suggested standards for the initial preparation and certification of teachers of students with exceptionalities (Council for Exceptional Children, 2003). Effective teacher training programs must attempt to meet these expectations when training college students who wish to teach students with special needs. The council mandates that graduates of university training programs have knowledge and skills in the following 10 areas as they relate to the various exceptionalities:

- Philosophy, history, and legal foundations
- Characteristics and development of learners
- Individual learning differences
- Instructional strategies and teaching methods
- Learning environments and social interactions
- Language development and atypical language development and use
- Instructional planning and decision making
- Assessment and evaluation
- Professional and ethical practice
- Collaboration

The full standards are found at the CEC Web site: *http://www.cec.sped.org/ps/ perf based stds/knowledge standards.html*

Special education teachers should be skillful in explaining the current trends in education, interpreting reports and diagnostic information from all professional sources, using and adapting assessment instruments, maintaining reports and records, developing individualized strategies, and choosing and using appropriate technologies for each student to accomplish objectives. Special educators need to be skillful in implementing generalization and maintenance plans and preparing and obtaining specially modified materials. It is their responsibility to lead in structuring an optimal learning environment for their students. When appropriate, they must be versed in teaching about human sexuality and recreational, social, and daily living skills. They are critical in helping with transition services, counseling families, and consulting with appropriate professionals.

The CEC standards follow the structure of the competencies of the National Council for Accreditation of Teacher Education (NCATE) to create national standards for training programs. In addition, the skills and knowledge specified in CEC's Standards for Professional Practice in Special Education were designed to serve as a reference for individual states in determining certification requirements for professionals. Each of the chapters on exceptionalities that follow will more specifically detail the contributions that the special education teacher makes as part of the IEP team.

CONCLUSION

This introductory chapter has explained the rationale behind the format of this text. We have introduced concepts of special education and students with exceptional needs in a general way and briefly traced the history of special education. A review of the law regarding special education has provided an understanding of how the current practices in providing service to students are based on legislative and judicial ruling. We have explained the process by which students are identified and the critical role that families play in the educational planning for students with exceptionalities.

The final section introduced the special education teacher and described the competencies needed to be an effective special educator. Armed with this initial knowledge of special education, special educators, students with special needs, legal standards, and mandated procedures for providing services, we can now turn our attention to discipline-wide and discipline-specific issues that are of importance to all who deal with students with special educational needs.

DISCUSSION QUESTIONS

1. List 13 areas of disability eligible for funding under IDEA.
2. What rights do parents and family members have regarding the education of their children with special needs?
3. What percentages of students with disabilities are classified within each category of disability?
4. Is full inclusion necessary for appropriate education of students with disabilities?
5. What court cases have had the most impact on education of students with disabilities? Why?
6. How do IDEA and NCLB address the education of students with disabilities?

REFERENCES

Brown, L., Schwarz, P., Udvari-Solner, A., Kampschroer, E. F., Johnson, F., Jorgansen, J., et al. (1991). How much time should students with severe intellectual disabilities spend in regular education classrooms and elsewhere? *Journal of the Association for Persons with Severe Handicaps, 16(1),* 39–47.

Council for Exceptional Children. (2003). *What every special education teacher should know: Ethics, standards, and guidelines for special educators* (5th ed.). Reston, VA: Author.

Dybvik, A. C. (2004). Autism and the inclusion mandate. *Education Next, 4(1),* 42–49.

Friend, M., & Cook, L. (1996). Interactions: *Collaboration skills for school professionals* (2nd ed.). White Plains, NY: Longman.

Grove, K. A., & Fisher, D. (1999). Entrepreneurs of meaning: Parents and the process of inclusive education. *Remedial and Special Education, 20,* 208–215.

Hardman, M. L., Drew, C. J., & Egan, M. W. (2005). Human exceptionality school, community, and family (8th ed). Boston: Allyn & Bacon.

Heward, W. L. (2003). Ten faulty notions about teaching and learning that hinder the effectiveness of special education. *The Journal of Special Education, 36,* 186–205.

Heward, W. L. (2006). *Exceptional children: An introduction to special education* (8th ed.). Upper Saddle River, NJ: Merrill/Prentice Hall.

Horne, R. L. (1996). The education of children and youth with special needs: What do the laws say? *National Information Center for Children and Youth with Disabilities (NICHCY).* Retrieved August 29, 2005, from www.nichcy.org/outprint.asp

Individuals with Disabilities Education Improvement Act. (2004). U.S.C. 20, 1400 et seq.

Kauffman, J. M. (2005). *Characteristics of emotional and behavioral disorders of children and youth* (8th ed.). Upper Saddle River, NJ: Merrill/Prentice Hall.

Kirk, S. A. (1972). *Educating exceptional children* (2nd ed.). Boston: Houghton Mifflin.

Magiera, K., & Zigmond, N. (2005). Co-teaching in middle school classrooms under routine conditions: Does the instructional experience differ for students with disabilities in co-taught and solo-taught classes? *Learning Disabilities Research & Practice, 20(2),* 79–85.

Mandlawitz, M. (2006). *What every teacher should know about IDEA 2004.* Boston: Allyn & Bacon.

Mastropieri, M. A., & Scruggs, T. E. (2000). *The inclusive classroom: Strategies for effective instruction.* Upper Saddle River, NJ: Merrill/Prentice Hall.

McLeskey, J., & Waldron, N. L. (2002). Inclusion and school change: Teacher perceptions regarding curricular and instructional adaptations. *Teacher Education and Special Education, 25(1),* 41–54.

Meyen, E. L. (1996). *Exceptional children in today's schools* (3rd ed.). Denver: Love.

Mills v. District of Columbia Board of Education , 348 F. Supp. 866 (D. D. C. 1972); contempt proceedings, EHLR 551:643 (D. D. C. 1980).

National Information Center for Children and Youth with Disabilities (NICHCY). (1996, October). Vol. 9, pp. 1–6.

National Information Center for Children and Youth with Disabilities (NICHCY). (2005). Retrieved August 8, 2005, from *http://nichcy.org/idealist.htm*

North Carolina Department of Public Instruction, Exceptional Children Support Team. (1996). *Individual education planning packet.* Raleigh, NC: Exceptional Children's Division (NCDPI).

Oakstone Legal and Business Publishing. (1999). *Students with disabilities and special education.* Burnsville, MN: Author.

Palmer, D. S., Fuller, K., Arora, T., & Nelson, M. (2001). Taking sides: Parent views on inclusion for their children with severe disabilities. *Exceptional Children, 67(4),* 467–484.

Pennsylvania Association for Retarded Citizens (PARC) v. Commonwealth of Pennsylvania , 334 F. Supp. 1257 (E. D. Pa 1971); 343 F. Supp 279 (E. D. Pa 1972).

Ruef, M. B. (2003). Including students with disabilities: Let's move forward together. *Action in Teacher Education, 25,* 1–4.

Sailor, W. (1991). Special education in the restructured school. *Remedial and Special Education, 12(6),* 8–22.

Salend, S. J. (2001). *Creating inclusive classrooms.* Upper Saddle River, NJ: Merrill/Prentice Hall.

Salisbury, C., Strieker, T., Roach, V., & McGregor, G. (2001). *Pathways to inclusive practices: Systems.* Pittsburgh, PA: Child and Family Studies.

Slater, L. (2004). Relationship-driven teaching cultivates collaboration and inclusion. *Kappa Delta Pi Record, 40(2),* 58–59.

Smith, D. D. (2001). *Introduction to special education: Teaching in an age of opportunity* (4th ed.). Boston: Allyn & Bacon.

Turnbull, H. R., & Turnbull, A. P. (2000). *Free appropriate public education: The law and children with disabilities* (6th ed.). Denver: Love.

Turnbull, R., Turnbull, A. P., Shank, M., & Smith, S. (2004). *Exceptional lives: Special education in today's schools.* Upper Saddle River, NJ: Merrill/Prentice Hall.

U.S. Department of Education. (2005). *Twenty-fifth annual report to Congress on the implementation of the Individuals with Disabilities Education Act.* Washington, DC: Author.

Vallecorsa, A. L., DeBettencourt, L. U., & Zigmond, N. (2000). *Students with mild disabilities: A guide for special educators.* Upper Saddle River, NJ: Merrill/Prentice Hall.

Villa, R. A., & Thousand, J. S. (2003). Making inclusive education work. *Educational Leadership, 61(2),* 19–23.

Voltz, D. L., Sims, M. J., & Nelson, B. (2005). M2ECCA: A framework for inclusion in the context of standards-based reform. *Teaching Exceptional Children, 37(5),* 14–19.

Wehman, P. (1997). *Exceptional individuals in school, community, and work.* Austin, TX: PRO-ED.

Werts, M. G., Wolery, M., Caldwell, N. K., Snyder, E. D., & Lisowski, L. (1995). Experienced teachers' perceptions of conditions and supports for inclusion. *Education and Training in Mental Retardation and Developmental Delay, 30,* 15–26.

Werts, M. G., Wolery, M., Snyder, E. D., Caldwell, N. K., & Salisbury, C. L. (1996). Supports and resources associated with inclusive schooling: Perceptions of elementary-school teachers about need and availability. *Journal of Special Education, 30,* 187–203.

Westling. D. L., & Fox, L. (2006). *Teaching students with severe disabilities.* Upper Saddle River, NJ: Merrill/Prentice Hall.

Yell, M. L. (2006). *The law and special education.* Upper Saddle River, NJ: Merrill/Prentice Hall.

Zigmond, N. (2001). Special education at a crossroads. *Preventing School Failure, 45,* 70–74.

2

Students with Communication Disorders

KEY TERMS

WHAT WOULD YOU DO?

Mateo, 7 years old, was learning English. He lived with his mother, father, two brothers, and three sisters in a suburb of a large metropolitan area. His father was in management in a manufacturing company. Mateo was the youngest child. The parents and all his siblings were bilingual. They spoke primarily Spanish in the home, English at school and in the community, and a mixture with each other and with friends. Mateo was in second grade. He had been receiving special education programming since his kindergarten year and had been fully included in the general education classroom this year. He received programming from his special education teacher, Ms. Ying, in Ms. Jones's classroom. Ms. Ying entered the classroom one morning as Ms. Jones was starting math class. Mateo was seated in the second row.

Ms. Jones begins, "O.K., everyone. Take out your math books and turn to the practice problems after the pages we worked on yesterday. Answer the first three problems and raise your hand when you are finished. Please use your regular pencils and we will correct them in red."

Mateo takes out his math book and turns to the page with the practice problems. He picks up his pencil and begins to tap it on the page. He looks around at the students seated beside him.

Ms. Jones observes and then says, "Mateo, I gave you your instructions. Would you please get to work?"

Mateo sits quietly and looks at the page of problems. He then looks at Ms. Jones and then again at the students around him.

"Are you having trouble with the math? Do you know how to work the problems? Ms. Ying will need to help you. Have your questions ready for her," says Ms. Jones to Mateo. Seeing Ms. Ying, she continues, "Oh, there you are! Mateo needs help. This happens all the time."

1. What evidence of deficits in auditory processing do you see in Mateo's behavior?

2. How could Ms. Ying assist Ms. Jones in scheduling the instruction and directions so that Mateo could focus on the math instruction?

Communication is more than just talking. It is understanding others' speech and gestures. It is reading and writing. An individual learns to understand the world by translating many experiences into language. As the individual matures, feelings, thoughts, and discoveries are shared with others by words joined together in ever increasing complexity. Language and speech make learning an efficient process. Our knowledge, history, culture, beliefs, myths, and fears are passed from generation to generation through some form of language, oral or written. It is this exchange of ideas, opinions, and facts between people interacting with each other that define communication (Bernstein & Tiegerman-Farber, 2002; Heward, 2006).

Communicative competence is an ability to use speech and language to uncover how the world works. It is how we obtain, store, analyze, and share information with others. Breakdowns or dysfunctions of this system make learning an enormously difficult task (Reichle, 1997; Stuart, 2002). Students with untreated communication problems suffer both social and educational isolation from their peers. Because much of speech and language is learned, early intervention can help all students with communication disorders to compensate and can enable some to completely overcome their disability.

DEFINITIONS

Communication disorders include both speech disorders and language disorders. However, before any logical discussion of disorders of communication can be attempted, it is important to discuss what is meant by speech and what is meant by language. Similarly, before we can explain what can go wrong with these processes, it is crucial to understand how the typical acquisition of these skills occurs.

TYPICAL DEVELOPMENT OF SPEECH AND LANGUAGE

As they are developing typical speech and language, children pass through a number of well-defined stages. Meaningful speech and language develop over time. The whole process begins with interactions between the typical neurological system and the student's environment (Owens, 2005).

Speech

Speech is the systematic use of sounds and sound combinations to produce meaningful words, phrases, and sentences. Specific parts of the body interact to produce and modify speech sounds. These include the lungs, larynx, soft palate (velum), nasal cavities, tongue, teeth, lower jaw (mandible), and lips. Air that is stored in the lungs passes over the vocal cords, which are located in the larynx. This passage of air causes the vocal cords to vibrate and produce a noise. This noise (voicing) travels up the throat (pharynx) and is changed by movements of the soft palate, lips, lower jaw, and tongue. It is also changed when it travels through the nasal cavities. Figure 2.1 illustrates the speech mechanism and the relationship of these components.

The production or generation of sound is called phonation. Modification of the sound by the mouth and nasal cavities is called resonation. The final movements of the mouth, lips, tongue, jaw, and soft palate are called articulation. This process shapes sounds into **phonemes,** which are the smallest meaningful units of sound we use in constructing speech. Each language has its own set of phonemes that are used to build words. Although several languages share many sounds, not all

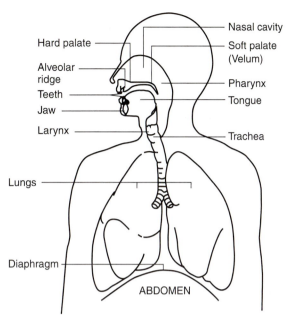

FIGURE 2.1
The speech mechanism and respiratory tract.

languages are made up of the same sound systems. Learning phonemes of a language requires motor behavior (physical movements) as well as intellectual understanding. Problems can arise when students cannot control the physical components of their bodies to produce sounds, cannot hear the differences between sounds, or do not possess the cognitive ability to learn the differences between phonemes.

Students master the consonant sounds of language over a considerable time period. Whereas all vowel sounds are usually mastered by age 3, some consonant sounds may not develop in students until age 8 (Menn & Stoel-Gammon, 1992; Olmstead, 1971; Polloway, Miller, & Smith, 2004). Many students are well into second grade before all consonant sounds are fully developed. However, sound development is not an exact science. Individual development varies greatly. We have selected the upper limits by which at least 90 percent of students have developed sounds and have included these figures in Table 2.1 (Hunt & Marshall, 2006; Menn & Stoel-Gammon, 1992).

Language

Language is much more complex than speech. Language puts meaning into speech and is used to express and receive meaning. Although most languages have speech as a component, not all do. Sign language is an example of a language system that fulfills all the requirements of language, yet does not use speech as the medium to transmit and receive messages. Languages enable communication to work by allowing composing and sending of messages (encoding) from one person to another, who receives them and understands them (decoding). Encoding and decoding skills develop over time and are dependent on intact neurological systems and experiences.

TABLE 2.1
Consonant sounds.

Phonetic Symbol	Orthographic Symbol	Illustrative Word	Age at which Sound is Produced Correctly by 90% of Children
/p/	p	*p*ig	3
/m/	m	*m*an	3
/n/	n	*n*ose	3
/w/	w	*w*ater	3
/h/	h	*h*at	3
/b/	b	*b*ounce	4
/d/	d	*d*og	4
/k/	k, c	*c*at	4
/g/	g	*g*o	4
/f/	f, ph	*f*un	4
/j/	y	*y*ear	4
/t/	t	*t*oes	6
/n/	ng	lon*g*	6
/r/	r	*r*ip	6
/l/	l	*l*ong	6
/θ/	th	*th*ink	7
/ʃ/	sh	*sh*oe	7
/tʃ/	ch	*ch*ew	7
/dʒ/	j	*j*oke	7
/z/	z	*z*ipper	7
/v/	v	*v*oice	8
/ð/	th	*th*is	8
/s/	s	*s*oup	8
/ʒ/	s, zh	trea*s*ure	8
/hw/	wh	*wh*ere	8

Language is innate to all human beings. It is common to all cultures and develops similarly in all people in every society. However, the process does not occur in a vacuum. It is social in nature and depends on interactions with the environment. An easy way to understand how humans develop language is to imagine that we each come equipped with a language acquisition device (LAD) in our brain that enables us to sift through all the speech, gestures, and vocal intonations that surround us as we grow. This device helps us attend to what is important and ignore unnecessary distractions. Over time, it helps us learn the systems that surround us, with increasing sophistication, so that we may join in and use them to communicate our own needs and experiences (Chomsky, 1957, 1981; Heward, 2006).

The major components of language are:

- Phonology
- Morphology
- Syntax
- Semantics
- Pragmatics

Each of these components develops as a child matures and allows humans of all cultures to express complicated concepts in a form that can be understood by other speakers and listeners of the same language. **Phonology** is the sound system of a language. The phonological rules of each language determine which combinations of sounds are permissible in that language to form meaningful words. **Morphology** deals with rules for transforming words and changing their basic meanings. For example, adding /s/ changes one horse to many horses, and adding /ed/ changes today's work to yesterday's worked. **Syntax** is the rule system governing the order and combination of words to form phrases and sentences. **Semantics** is the meaning of language. "I am hungry" is a sentence that is semantically appropriate to speakers of English. It has meaning. However, "Why is a mouse when it is spinning faster?" is a puzzling statement. It is phonologically appropriate because it contains sounds of English. It is morphologically sound because transformations of the words spin and fast are allowable. It breaks down on a semantic level, however, because it has no meaning. The final component is **pragmatics,** which involves the social aspects of language. It takes into account a knowledge and understanding of rules of turn taking, starting and ending conversations, choosing and maintaining appropriate topics, being sensitive to miscommunications, and being aware of what experiences are shared by listeners and which need supplemental information for understanding messages (American Speech-Language-Hearing Association, 1982). Languages have the following:

- Form (phonology, morphology, syntax)
- Content (semantics)
- Function (pragmatics) (American Speech-Language-Hearing Association, 1993a)

The first meaningful words of a typically developing child are usually spoken between 12 and 18 months. Table 2.2 is a schematic outline of the approximate ages and patterns of typical language development.

By age 6 most typically developing children have mastered the complexity of their native language well enough to use language to learn about concepts that have not been or cannot be directly experienced. Owens (2005) summarized language development into five age-related phases from birth to age 12. He suggested that the young child (ages 1 to 6 months) is an examiner who observes the environment with relatively little interaction. The child becomes an experimenter (at ages 7 to 12 months) when he or she begins to interact with others while beginning to cognitively understand the basics of language. Next comes the explorer stage (ages 12 to 24 months), wherein the child begins purposeful interaction with the environment and is learning language at a fast pace. By ages 3 to 5 years, the child has become the exhibitor, talking about experiences and feelings in a logical way that can be understood by strangers. From ages 6 to 12, the child is now an expert, with a huge vocabulary

TABLE 2.2
Language of a typically developing child.

Age	Attainment	Example
13 months	First words	here, mama, bye bye, kitty
17 months	50-word vocabulary	
18 months	First two-word combinations	more juice here ball more T.V. here kitty
22 months	Later two-word combinations	Andy shoe Mommy ring cup floor keys chair
24 months	Mean sentence length of 2.00 words First appearance of *-ing*	Andy sleeping
30 months	Mean sentence length 3.10 words First appearance of *is*	My car's gone!
37 months	Mean sentence length 4.10 words. First appearance of indirect requests	Can I have some cookies?
40 months	Mean sentence length of 4.50 words	

Source: From "Language Disorders in Preschool Children," by L. Leonard, 1994, in G. Shames, E. Wiig, and W. Secord (eds.), *Human Communication Disorders* (4th ed., p. 179), Boston, MA: Allyn & Bacon. Reprinted by permission.

and the ability to manipulate language to express many complicated and abstract ideas. Table 2.3 is a summary of Owens's (2005) conceptualizations of language development.

DISORDERS OF SPEECH AND LANGUAGE

Speech and language are vulnerable to disruptions that can lead to disorders. Because the entire communication system depends on neurological systems for cognitive processing of environmental experiences, disruptions in the neurological system, underdevelopment of cognitive skills, or a lack of appropriate language experiences can lead to speech disorders, language disorders, or both. Communication disorders include both speech disorders (producing language) and language disorders (understanding and formulating language).

We have divided communication disorders into speech disorders and language disorders and then further divided speech and language disorders into the discrete types of dysfunction that compose each category. Although many students may have a discrete communication disorder, it is possible to have multiple speech and language problems. Because speech and language are coexisting systems, a disruption in one system often has a negative effect on the other.

TABLE 2.3

Overview of language development: Birth to age 12.

Age	Characteristics
The examiner (1–6 mos.)	Responds to human voice; makes pleasure sounds (1 mo.) Produces strings of consonant-vowel or vowel-only syllables; vocally responds to speech of others (3 mo.) Smiles at person speaking to him/her (4 mo.) Responds to name; smiles and vocalizes to image in mirror (5 mo.) Prefers people games, e.g., peek-a-boo, I'm going to get you; explores face of person holding him/her (6 mo.)
The experimenter (7–12 mos.)	Recognizes some words; repeats emphasized syllables (8 mo.) "Performs" for family; imitates coughs, hisses, raspberries, etc. (9 mo.) Obeys some directives (10 mo.) Anticipates caregiver's goal and attempts to change it via persuasion/protest (11 mo.) Recognizes own name; engages in familiar routines having visual cues (e.g., bye-bye); uses one or more words (12 mo.)
The explorer (12–24 mos.)	Points to toys, persons, animals named; pushes toys; plays alone; begins some make-believe; has 4- to 6-word vocabulary (15 mo.) Begins to use 2-word utterances (combines); refers to self by name; has about 20-word vocabulary; pretends to feed doll, etc. (18 mo.) Enjoys rhyming games; tries to "tell" experiences; understands some personal pronouns; engages in parallel play (21 mo.) Has 200- to 300-word vocabulary; names most common everyday objects; uses some prepositions (*in, on*) and pronouns (*I, me*) but not always accurately (*in, on*); engages in object-specific pretend play and parallel play; can role-play in limited way; orders others around; communicates feelings, desires, interests (24 mo.)
The exhibitor (3–5 yrs.)	Has 900- to 1,000-word vocabulary; creates 3- to 4-word utterances; talks about the "here and now"; talks while playing and takes turns in play; "swears" (3 yrs.) Has 1,500- to 1,600-word vocabulary; asks many questions; uses increasingly complex sentence constructions; still relies on word order for interpretation; plays cooperatively with others; role-plays; recounts stories about recent experiences (narrative recounts); has some difficulty answering *how* and *why* (4 yrs.) Has vocabulary of 2,100–2,200 words; discusses feelings; understands *before* and *after* regardless of word order; play is purposeful and constructive; shows interest in group activities (5 yrs.)
The expert (6–12 yrs.)	Has expressive vocabulary of 2,600 words, understands 20,000–24,000 word meanings; defines by function; has many well-formed, complex sentences; enjoys active games and is competitive; identifies with same sex peers in groups (6 yrs.) Verbalizes ideas and problems readily; enjoys an audience; knows that others have different perspectives; has allegiance to group, but also needs adult support (8 yrs.) Talks a lot; has good comprehension; discovers may be the object of someone else's perspective; plans future actions; enjoys games, sports, hobbies (10 yrs.) Understands about 50,000 word meanings; constructs adultlike definitions; engages in higher-order thinking and communicating (12 yrs.)

Source: From *Language Development: An Introduction* (6th ed., pp. 74–95), by R. E. Owens, 2005. Copyright © 2005 by Allyn & Bacon, Needham Heights, MA. Adapted by permission.

Disorders of Speech

A speech disorder is characterized by any impairment of vocal production (voice), speech sound production (articulation), fluency (stuttering and related disorders), or any combination of these impairments (American Speech-Language-Hearing Association, 1993a). Speech disorders are present when a student's speech is so different from what is expected that it calls attention to itself, when it is so difficult to understand that it interferes with communication, or when it causes distress to the speaker or listener (Van Riper & Erickson, 1996).

Disorders of Language

A language disorder is abnormal development in understanding or using spoken, written, or other symbolic systems. The disorder may involve the rate of acquisition of language; the form of language (phonology, morphology, or syntax); the content of language (semantics); the function of language (pragmatics); or any combination of form, content, and function (American Speech-Language-Hearing Association, 1993a; Hunt & Marshall, 2006; Polloway et al., 2004).

Services provided under IDEA may be delivered both to students for whom a communication disorder is deemed to be the primary disability and to students whose speech and language problems are secondary to another condition requiring special education. Speech or language impairment is defined as a communication disorder such as stuttering, impaired articulation, a language impairment, or a voice impairment that adversely affects a student's educational performance (C.F.R., Part 300, Section 300.7, 1992). Although the definitions for communication disorders vary from state to state, most require that the student show some deficit in the components of language or in the areas of speech. This must usually be documented on a standardized test or by a sample of communication that was analyzed in the student's typical communication environment.

DIFFERENCES IN SPEECH AND LANGUAGE

The way students speak is a reflection of their culture (Heward, 2006). We learn speech and language by interacting with people in our environment when we are children. We imitate and learn to talk the way others talk. The United States is a linguistically and ethnically diverse country. This diversity is reflected in the language and speech of our children. Many factors contribute to linguistic diversity. The primary factors can be race, ethnicity, social and economic status, education, occupation, and geographic region. These factors can lead to the development of accents and dialects.

Accents are sound differences of spoken language and are usually attributed to geographic regions and the influences of foreign languages (Taylor & Payne, 1994). The pronunciation of the word Cuba as "Cuber" in certain areas of the Northeastern United States is an example of an accent.

Dialects are more complex and can be variations of the form, content, and use of a language. They are rule-governed differences that are consistently applied by individuals who are members of that geographical, regional, social, cultural, or ethnic group. Dialects are linguistically valid and legitimate ways of communicating. However, they are somewhat different from Standard English. The major dialects spoken in the United States are Black English, Southern English, Southern White Nonstandard English, and

Appalachian English. Most dialectal speakers can code-switch, which is the ability to move from one language or dialect to another as the situation demands (Gleason, 1973; McCormak & Wurm, 1976; Reid, 2000; Smith, 2001). We will give examples of dialectal differences in the "Characteristics and Etiology" section of this chapter.

PREVALENCE

Over 1 million of the 5.8 million students between ages 6 and 21 who were served during the 2000–2001 school year under IDEA were diagnosed as having speech or language impairments as their primary impairment (U.S. Department of Education, 2005). However, this 18.6 percent figure is deceptive because it fails to include students who have communication problems that coexist with another diagnosis. Students with cerebral palsy, mental retardation, severe and multiple disabilities, hearing impairments, and autism almost always have a disordered communication component to their disability that requires treatment. A study by the American Speech-Language-Hearing Association (Dublinski, 1981; Heward, 2006) revealed that 42 percent of all students with disabilities who are served by speech-language pathologists have other primary handicaps.

Other surveys suggest that speech disorders affect approximately 10 to 15 percent of all preschool students and 6 percent of all primary school students. Language disorders may be present in 3 percent of preschoolers and 1 percent of all school-age students (National Institute of Neurological and Communicative Disorders and Stroke, 1988). When the total population, including adults, is considered, communication problems affect approximately 10 percent of the population of the United States (American Speech-Language-Hearing Association, 1991; Hunt & Marshall, 2006; National Center for Health Statistics, 1988). The prevalence figures for the entire population include adults, many of whom acquire communication disorders later in life as the result of strokes, hearing loss, accidents, and degenerative diseases that negatively affect communication skills.

CHARACTERISTICS AND ETIOLOGY

The characteristics of many speech and language problems are directly related to the etiology of the problems. Physical, emotional, or faulty learning causes affect speech and language systems in unique ways and often produce different characteristics. This section will divide communication problems into speech disorders and language disorders and explain how different causes of speech and language impairment often manifest themselves with differing symptoms. These characteristics not only help in the identification of problems but also often point the way to the most effective programming.

Etiology and Characteristics of Speech Disorders

The most common speech disorders disrupt speech sound production (articulation), vocal sound production (voice), and the smooth flow of speech (fluency). Disorders of articulation, voice, and fluency are each divided into several major subtypes. Beginning with disorders of articulation, we will explore these subtypes, their etiology, and the characteristics common to each of them. The severity of each characteristic can range from being barely noticeable to the listener to being extremely conspicuous and detrimental to the student's educational progress.

Articulation Disorders

Articulation disorders are the most common problems among school students (Kirk, Gallagher, Anastasiow, & Coleman, 2005; Polloway et al., 2004). Students with articulation disorders have difficulty in producing the speech sounds of their language. Speakers with articulation disorders tend to make four types of errors in producing sounds. When speaking, they (1) substitute one sound for another (wabbit for rabbit or toup for soup); (2) omit sounds from words (nake for snake or oup for soup); (3) distort the typical production of sounds (the "Daffy Duck" kind of /s/ sound); or (4) add sounds that do not belong in words (balack for black).

Articulation disorders resulting from known anatomical or physiological problems are called organic articulation problems. Those resulting from unknown causes or faulty learning are called developmental phonological disorders (American Psychiatric Association, 1994; Shriberg, 1994). The most common causes of organic articulation disorders are clefts of the palate, cerebral palsy, traumatic brain injury, and hearing impairment. None of these conditions is in and of itself a speech disorder. The severity of each condition will determine whether an articulation disorder will result and how severe it will be.

Clefts of the Palate. A cleft is an opening that results from the failure of facial structures to fuse appropriately during prenatal development. Clefts of the lip and palate result when these structures do not join between the 6th and 12th weeks of the first trimester of pregnancy. The palate is composed of two structures. The anterior (closest to the face) portion is called the hard palate. It is an inflexible structure that forms the roof of the mouth and the floor of the nasal cavity. The posterior (closest to the pharynx) portion is called the soft palate and is made up of flexible tissues that bend to seal off the nasal cavities from the pharynx. The alveolar ridge, or gum ridge, is directly behind the lips and is the tissue that houses the teeth. Clefts may affect the lips, alveolar ridge, and hard and soft palates. No one single factor has been isolated

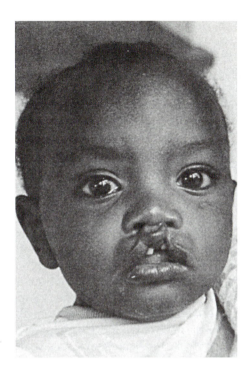 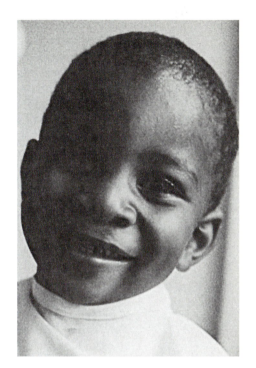

as the cause of clefts. A multifactor theory that combines genetic predispositions and prenatal environmental factors seems to be currently accepted (Hegde, 1995). The most commonly quoted incidence figure for the occurrence of clefts is 1 in every 750 births (McWilliams, Morris, & Shelton, 1990). However, the incidence appears to differ with different racial and ethnic groups. The highest rate in the United States was reported to be 1 in 220 births for Native American children in South Dakota, and the lowest incidence was 1 in 8,600 births for African American children (Hegde).

Clefts can affect the lip alone, the lip and gum ridge only, the hard palate, or the hard and soft palate, or there may be a total opening that extends from the lip all the way through to the soft palate. Clefts are first and foremost health problems. Depending on the severity of the cleft, the student may have significant feeding problems and be susceptible to ear infections because of an inability to suck on a bottle efficiently or to close off passages to the nose and ears while eating. Students with clefts may have a difficult time in producing sounds that require firm contact between the soft palate and the pharynx. This results in their inability to close off the nasal passages and means that their speech sounds are partially diverted from the normal pathway through the mouth and are overly influenced by passing through the nasal passages. This excess or hypernasality makes it very difficult for others to understand the student's speech.

Cerebral Palsy.   Cerebral palsy is brain damage resulting from infection, poisoning, oxygen deprivation, or trauma that occurs prior to, during, or immediately after birth. Students with cerebral palsy may have difficulty with coordination and controlling muscular activity. Cerebral palsy does not always cause articulation disorders. Only when the areas of the brain that control the speech mechanism are affected are articulation disorders present. If these areas of the brain are damaged, the student may not be able to coordinate the rapid and precise movements necessary for intelligible speech production. The student may be unable to efficiently use the breath stream in ways necessary to articulate sounds and produce running speech. As a result, individual sounds will be distorted, produced slowly, and slurred together in a manner that will make it difficult for the listener to understand the message. The term **dysarthria** is often used to describe the lack of coordination that is characteristic of the speech patterns of students with cerebral palsy. The brain damage that causes articulation disorders may also cause the student to experience language problems (Turnbull, Turnbull Shank, & Smith 2004).

Traumatic Brain Injury (TBI).   Traumatic brain injury, which is caused by any accident or injury to the brain (car accidents, gunshot wounds, child abuse), can also lead to many conditions, including articulation disorders. The observable characteristics may be very similar to those of cerebral palsy. A major difference is that TBI often occurs after sounds have developed normally, whereas in students with cerebral palsy, typical speech and sound development may never have occurred. Students with TBI may evidence dysarthric speech and in addition may show signs of apraxia. **Apraxia** of speech is a weakness and lack of coordination that manifests itself when voluntary movements are attempted. Speech is an activity that, unlike breathing or the circulation of the bloodstream, requires conscious volitional control. Students with apraxia might show little involvement in automatic uses of the speech mechanism, in swallowing and chewing food, but may have a difficult time purposefully making the sounds of speech and consciously coordinating the speech mechanism. As with cerebral palsy, the brain injury resulting from TBI can also lead to language disorders (Turnbull et al., 2004).

Hearing Loss.   The sound system of language is learned by hearing the sounds of language in our environment and learning to mimic them over time. A student with a hearing loss may not hear some sounds or may hear them in a distorted way due to hearing impairment. Students who are deaf may not hear speech or spoken language at any meaningful level. As a result, depending on the severity of the hearing impairment, students will omit sounds, distort sounds, or make inappropriate sounds that are a reflection of what they are hearing. If a student's hearing loss is severe enough, he or she will not spontaneously produce speech sounds at all. The implications of hearing loss and deafness on speech and language development will be discussed at length in Chapter 9, "Students with Hearing Impairments."

Developmental Phonological Disorders.   Students with developmental phonological disorders have difficulty making speech sounds without any identifiable structural, neurological, or physiological cause. As many as 80 percent of students identified as having articulation disorders may have developmental phonological disorders (Van Riper & Erickson, 1996). One explanation for the etiology of developmental phonological disorders suggests that they are based on the student's inability to understand the rules used to combine sounds, rather than difficulties in producing sounds. A student with an articulation problem may not be able to physically move his or her tongue to produce the /s/ sound. In contrast, a student with a developmental phonological disorder may not understand that /s/ sounds appear at the end of some words, or the student may not have learned the rules for making sounds. The idea that sound-production problems may be the result of phonological disorders links articulation and language together and suggests that sound-production disorders for students without organic problems may be closely related to language development. Research continues in this area. Some treatment approaches are based on helping students with possible phonological disorders learn rules for speaking instead of mastering individually defective sounds (Schwartz, 2006).

Another view is that developmental phonological disorders are the result of a student learning to say sounds incorrectly for some unknown reason. The implication is that, as a result of poor learning, the student has not mastered the ability to use the speech mechanism to produce sounds of language correctly, even though there is nothing deviant about his or her speech structures or neurological system.

Many conditions and syndromes have articulation problems as one of their components. However, regardless of the cause of the articulation disorder, penalties for the student can be the same. These students can become frustrated because their listeners cannot understand what they are attempting to say. They may become isolated from their peers because they sound different and are teased when they attempt to communicate. If they have multiple articulation problems (many sounds produced inappropriately), their teachers may not be able to accurately gauge their comprehension of curricular materials or even adequately meet their needs, share their discoveries, or answer their inquiries. In addition, they will have difficulty learning to read when reading is taught using phonically based instruction. Spelling and the comprehension of spoken instruction may also suffer. These negative characteristics will impair the learning process and adversely affect the entire educational process (McLoughlin & Lewis, 2005).

Voice Disorders

Voice disorders are characterized by abnormalities of pitch, loudness, and quality of vocal production. These vocal abnormalities may be transient in nature, lasting only a few days or weeks, or chronic, lasting until help is provided to correct them or the circumstances causing them. The transient nature of some disorders makes it difficult to estimate the incidence of voice problems in school-age children. In addition, many voice problems take time to develop and do not manifest themselves until late adolescence or early adulthood. The largest survey reported places the incidence of voice disorders in students at 6 percent of the population (Hunt & Marshall, 2006; Senturia & Wilson, 1968). Voice problems are the result of organic factors (structural anomalies and diseases) and functional factors (poor use of structures, serious emotional conflicts, and unknown causes). Voices often mirror inner conflicts and can be a warning sign of emotional distress. The sound of a student's voice can often indicate whether a problem exists. However, it cannot with any degree of accuracy identify whether the cause of the voice problem is organic or functional. Later in this chapter we will discuss the identification procedures necessary to pinpoint the possible causes of the abnormal voice characteristics listed here.

Pitch.   The pitch of the voice is produced when the vocal folds open and close as air expelled from the lungs rushes over them, causing vocal fold vibration. The more frequently the cords vibrate, the higher the perceived pitch of the voice. Stretching a rubber band and plucking it will mimic vocal fold vibration and pitch production. Each person has an optimal pitch level, which is the pitch that results when the most vocal fold vibrations are most efficiently used to make sound. Habitual pitch level is the pitch we use most often when making the laryngeal sounds used to form speech sounds. For most people, optimal pitch and habitual pitch are fairly similar most of the time. Most people laugh or clear their throats at their optimal pitch level. The optimal pitch level for a student changes as the student grows. By age 12 or 13, adolescent vocal structures have matured to where adult optimal vocal pitch should be established. Many persons, especially males, experience rather dramatic normal shifts (pitch breaks) in the pitch of their voices during puberty. For most, this is a transitory phase requiring no special attention. Disorders of pitch occur when the optimal pitch of the voice and the habitual pitch level do not match fairly closely. For the listener, a person with a voice disorder characterized by a pitch problem will have a voice that sounds too high or too low to be appropriate for the speaker's age or sex, or the voice will lack control as evidenced by recurring pitch breaks that draw attention away from the speaker's message.

Organic reasons for pitch problems can be failure of the vocal folds to grow properly, paralysis of the vocal cords, growths or diseases affecting the vocal cords, hormonal therapy, or the use of steroids or other muscle-enhancing substances. Functional pitch problems can result from using a pitch level too high or low for the person's age or sex for no known reason or for emotional reasons such as fear of maturity.

Loudness.   The amount of energy used to produce vocal sounds determines the loudness of the voice. Loudness is related to the volume of air that passes over the vocal cords and the tension of the vocal cords. Disorders of voice characterized by loudness manifest themselves in speakers with voices that are too loud or too soft for the situation in which communication occurs.

Organic reasons for loudness problems include hearing losses that make it difficult for the speaker to monitor loudness appropriately. Sometimes students with cerebral palsy or similar coordination disorders cannot control their vocal mechanism well enough to regulate the breath stream in a manner that will result in appropriate loudness levels. Functional loudness problems can result when a student uses an inappropriately loud voice as a result of being reared in an environment where he or she must habitually shout for attention. Other students may use inappropriately soft voices in an attempt to avoid drawing attention to themselves, for any number of reasons from potential child abuse to simple shyness. Our voices call attention to us. If for some reason attention has negative consequences for a student, that student may do all he or she can to avoid the spotlight, including speaking in a very soft voice. As with all other functional voice disorders, a student may use an inappropriately loud or soft voice for no discernible reason.

Quality.   The quality of the voice is its most complex feature. Pitch and loudness are a part of quality, but the quality feature of a person's voice is what gives it the unique characteristics that make it different from every other person's voice. The interaction of the vocal sound produced by the larynx with the cavities of the throat (pharynx), nasal cavities, and mouth provide characteristics that are unique to each voice. The range for acceptable voice quality is large. However, at least four parameters can be identified that will isolate deviant voice quality. The acceptable quality of the voice can be disrupted by any of the following:

- Excessive or insufficient nasal resonance
- Breathiness
- Harshness
- Hoarseness

Nasal resonance problems are caused when too much or too little air passes through the nose during speech production. Too much air flow (hypernasality) can distort speech sounds, as described in the section on articulation disorders. It can also negatively affect voice quality. The opposite of hypernasality is too little air flow into the nasal passages (hyponasality). Most speakers have experienced transitory hyponasality when they have colds or allergy reactions. Nasal swelling and blockages hamper typical nasal resonance and give the voice a flat and muffled quality. Chronic hypernasal resonance problems may be caused by clefts of the hard and soft palate or paralysis of the soft palate, which makes it unable to close the nasal passages. Hyponasality can be caused by chronic allergic reactions or by growths in the nasal cavities. Permanent structural damage to the nose can also lead to hyponasality. Either hypernasality or hyponasality can result after surgery to correct soft palate deformities.

Breathiness occurs when the vocal folds do not sufficiently hold back enough of the breath stream for vocal fold vibration to occur. As a result, breathy voices have a whisperlike quality. Breathy voicing can occur when the vocal folds are paralyzed and cannot come together to vibrate, when a growth or node appears on the cords and keeps them from vibrating, when a speaker uses the vocal system to affect a breathy voice, or sometimes for no known reason. It is also possible to have a breathy voice for a number of emotional reasons that are unique to each individual.

Harshness (stridency) is usually the result of excessive strain or tension. Some students who chronically abuse their voices with excessive loudness and tension over time will develop "screamer's nodes" on their vocal cords. These calluslike growths disrupt vocal fold vibration and will cause the voice to sound harsh or raspy. Some speakers have harsh-sounding voices because they do not use their voices efficiently to produce typical voicing.

Hoarseness is usually a transitory symptom that most speakers have experienced as the result of shouting too much or cheering too loudly. Another common cause of hoarseness is the swelling of the vocal apparatus that occurs with laryngeal infections (laryngitis). Cheerleaders or poorly trained singers who consistently abuse their voices for long periods of time can develop vocal fold growths that will result in harsh-sounding voices. Fortunately, most speakers will automatically desist those activities that lead to vocal damage and allow the tissues to heal before permanent damage can occur.

Pitch, loudness, and quality disorders of the voice do not necessarily occur in isolation from one another. Voice disorders can be characterized by any combination of these components. Each person has unique vocal system strengths and weaknesses. Some students can cheer or yell for hours with little or no consequences, whereas for others even the mildest allergic reaction or common cold will affect their voices. Any vocal difference that persists for an unusual amount of time should be suspect and lead to referral for possible services.

Fluency Disorders*

Fluency is the smooth flow of speech that most speakers experience when talking. Disfluencies take many forms and can result from different causes. Not all disfluencies are abnormal, and they cannot all be treated in the same manner. Stuttering is the most well-known type of disfluency, but it is not the only kind.

Normal Disfluencies of Speech. Normally fluent speech is not perfect speech. All speakers pause, hesitate, repeat, and misspeak in a variety of ways that are well within the limits of typical communication. In stressful situations that call for unfamiliar vocabulary use, most speakers may exhibit some disfluent speech. These disfluencies are not stuttering, nor are they abnormal. Speech is a complex activity that requires

*The concepts discussed in this section were originally discussed in the following works listed in the bibliography: Culatta & Leeper, 1987; Culatta & Leeper, 1989; and Culatta & Goldberg, 1995.

constant thought and rapid, precise movements of many structures. It is not surprising that a process this complex is never fully mastered. Even the most polished and proficient speaker will sometimes pause and hesitate when spontaneously composing and delivering a complicated or emotionally charged message.

Normal Developmental Disfluencies.   As students pass through the developmental stages of language learning, they will be more disfluent at certain times than others. These periods of developmental disfluency are typical occurrences. Typically communicating children are most disfluent between the ages of 2.5 and 4 years. These typical disfluencies are characterized by repetitions of whole words and phrases and with occasional interjections of "ers" and "uhs" and "ahs" (Heward, 2006; Perkins, 1971; Yairi & Lewis, 1984). This is a transitional stage that most children outgrow as they master speech and language.

Stuttering.   Stuttering is a disorder that begins in childhood. It becomes more complicated over time, and it follows a fairly predictable developmental path. At first, the behavior is episodic, with weeks passing during which the student's speech is normally fluent. Gradually these fluent intervals shrink until the student is consistently stuttering most of the time. Stuttering begins with simple whole-word and sound repetitions and, if the disorder is untreated, develops into more complicated patterns characterized by blocks, forcings, substitutions of nonfeared words for feared words, avoidances of speaking situations, eye closing, jaw tremors, and other facial and bodily contortions. The internal feelings of a person who stutters also progress through an evolutionary process. The student who is beginning to stutter shows very little reaction or concern about stuttering. This changes to self-identification as a stutterer and eventually strong emotional reactions, including fear of speaking, embarrassment when stuttering, and feelings of victimization (Bloodstein, 1960; Heward, 2006).

A diagnostic characteristic of stuttering is that the vowels used during repetition are different from those used when typical speakers are disfluent. When a person who stutters repeats a word, he or she tends to insert the schwa vowel /ə/ ("uh") in place of the vowel that would ordinarily occur. Thus "bae-bae-baseball" becomes "buh-buh-base-ball." Stuttering can also be manipulated in a number of ways that distinguish it from other types of disfluency. For example, reduction in stuttering often occurs with repeated readings of the same passage. This phenomenon is called adaptation. Stuttering can also be reduced when distracting noises are introduced while the person who stutters is speaking. Speaking in time to a metronome, singing, or group recitation can all alter or eliminate stuttering for brief periods of time. In fact, any temporary distraction may produce short-term fluent speech. In addition, people who stutter do not do so on every word they utter. Much of their speech is fluent, and during these fluent periods there is little or no sign of the characteristic behaviors that constitute stuttering.

Stuttering tends to run in families (Kidd, 1980). However, the presence of a "stuttering gene" has not been isolated. The cause of stuttering is unknown. The most widely held belief about the cause of stuttering is that it is the result of environmental experiences that interact with a genetic predisposition to bring about the disorder.

In summary, the following characteristics need to be present to differentiate stuttering from other types of disfluency:

1. The behavior must have a developmental history beginning in childhood.
2. There are no identifiable etiological or maintaining factors.
3. The repetition patterns differ from those of typical speakers.

4. The characteristics of stuttering can be modified in many ways.

5. The characteristics of stuttering are not present during fluent periods.

6. The person who stutters has internalized a belief system about the difficulty of communication in general and specific situations in particular.

Cluttering. This form of disfluency is characterized by speech that is so disorganized that it is difficult to understand. Words are spoken at an extremely fast rate, phrases are left uncompleted, and there are frequent repetitions and omissions of whole words and parts of phrases. Speech is slurred, articulation is disordered, the flow of words is jumbled, and speech is produced in spurts (Heward, 2006; Van Riper & Erickson, 1996). Students who clutter have little awareness of its effect on their speech or the listener. They do not develop speaking fears, nor do they avoid speaking situations. This lack of concern often results in resistance to help or lack of any real interest in modifying their speech patterns. Unlike students who stutter, students who clutter often have allied reading, language, and writing difficulties and a variety of motor coordination problems.

Mixed Disfluencies. Students who are disfluent are not excused from difficulties in any of the other areas. A student who already stutters may suffer neurological damage or emotional trauma, with resulting disfluent behaviors that are independent of the original stuttering. In practical terms this means that the teacher, parent, or speech-language pathologist who suspects multiple causality for disfluent behavior must share this information with all those concerned about the student and develop logical treatment protocols that account for all the relevant factors contributing to the disfluency pattern.

Etiology and Characteristics of Language Disorders

Approximately 2 to 3 percent of all preschool children and 1 percent of all school-age students have language disorders (National Institute of Neurological and Communicative Disorders and Stroke, 1988). Language disability is not a disease, but rather a failure to learn (Van Riper & Erickson, 1996). There are many reasons for this failure, some known and others unknown. Language disability may be the result of not having prerequisite conceptual knowledge or adequately developed cognitive processes. It may be developmental or acquired, expressive or receptive, and an isolated problem or a component of other disorders.

Conceptual knowledge of the environment is needed when attempting to communicate. It is impossible for a student to linguistically convey what he or she does not know. Students who have limited conceptual knowledge have difficulty symbolizing events (Owens, 2004). Students develop many concepts through play activities. The more sophisticated a student's play, the greater the student's knowledge of the world (Westby, 1988). Students deprived of experiences do not gain the concepts that those experiences teach. A youngster who has never visited a supermarket cannot understand how food gets to stores and from stores to homes. A 10-year-old whose knowledge of the world is at a 3-year-old's level cannot be expected to exhibit language beyond the 3-year-old level.

Several specific cognitive processes are prerequisites for language learning. Deficits in attention skills, memory, and auditory and visual perception will make language acquisition difficult. Attention is the ability to focus on one event while excluding all other competing distractions. Students who have difficulty attending will have problems attaching language symbols to their experiences and abstracting meaning from those experiences.

Long-term memory and short-term memory are the two types of memory needed to learn language. Long-term memory is needed to store the rules, meanings, and structures of language so that they can be accessed when needed. Short-term (working) memory is the brief holding of concepts while processing them. Short-term memory is needed to follow directions or store concepts while searching for meanings that are stored in long-term memory (Wagner & Torgesen, 1987). Students with deficits in long- and short-term processing of information will be unable to store and access the information they need to learn language.

Perception is the ability to recognize the commonalities in events. When learning language, students perceive the similarities in their visual and auditory experiences and associate them with the language they are hearing. This is how specific words, word forms, and syntax are learned. If students do not perceive the similarities in their experiences, they will not be able to convert these similarities into language symbols (Kemler, 1983).

Developmental language disorders are evidenced by students who have difficulty acquiring any or all of the components of language. Developmental language disability is considered congenital, and many believe that it stems from neurological damage that occurs before or during birth. However, it is not always possible to determine the specific nature of the suspected brain injury, which may be subtle and is often undetectable (Culatta & Culatta, 1993). In addition, students' environments that do not foster language development can play a major role in developmental language disorders.

Acquired or traumatic language disorders are the result of definable injuries that affect the language formulation or comprehension areas of the brain. These injuries often occur after typical language has been acquired or during childhood, interrupting or disturbing language as it is being learned.

Whereas speech deals with the production or modification of sounds, language is more complex in that it has both receptive (decoding) and expressive (encoding) components. Receptive language skills are evidenced by a student's ability to receive and translate messages into meaningful information. Receptive language abilities are critical for all language learning. Receptive language skills make it possible for the student to understand the rules of language, the meanings of words, the intent of instructions, and the relationship between experiences and their application to learning. A student's receptive skills must always precede and be more sophisticated than his or her expressive skills for language learning to advance. Expressive language skills are evidenced by the student's ability to formulate what he or she is thinking or feeling into meaningful words, phrases, and sentences. Language relies on speech in most cases, and gestures and signs in some cases, to transmit the messages that have been formulated. Disorders of a receptive nature can occur when a student is deaf or hearing impaired and does not receive messages or receives them in a distorted fashion. Receptive language disorders also occur when a student, for a variety of reasons, is unable to store and decode the messages received from others. Expressive language disorders are the result of a student being unable to encode and express thoughts, feelings, and experiences in logical, meaningful, and acceptable ways.

Language disabilities may occur in isolation without other coexisting conditions, or they may be causally linked to any of a number of other conditions. The conditions that are commonly linked with language disabilities are traumatic brain injury, cerebral palsy, hearing impairment, mental retardation, multiple handicaps, autism, severe illness, and environmental deprivations.

Brain damage that has destroyed tissues needed to comprehend and formulate language is a shared cause of traumatic brain injury and cerebral palsy. For both conditions, language disabilities are present only when the language formulation and comprehension areas of the brain are damaged. The damage that causes traumatic brain injury occurs after language has developed or while it is developing. The damage that causes cerebral palsy occurs prior to the student's development of language. Students affected by either condition may have difficulties in attending to messages, decoding them meaningfully, or using language effectively to respond to questions or follow instructions.

Students who are severely hearing impaired or deaf do not hear the language used in their environment. They may be taught language through signing and may learn to master the morphology, syntax, and semantics of language, but will have difficulty with the phonology and pragmatic aspects of spoken language. Because these students have to rely on visual and tactile language-learning experiences, they tend to have difficulty with abstractions and tend to be concrete in their linguistic performance (Van Riper & Erickson, 1996).

Students with mental retardation and multiple handicaps, depending on the severity of the conditions, may have all aspects of language impairment. For students who are mentally retarded, the degree of language involvement will depend on the severity of the retardation. As previously discussed, cognitive skills are necessary to learn the rules of language and the relationship of words to each other. Students with retardation may be slow in developing these needed skills and, as a result, may be slow in developing receptive and expressive language. Students with multiple handicaps may also have cognitive problems and, in addition, may be limited in their conceptual knowledge of the environment. Other prerequisite skills such as attention, memory, and perception may also be inadequate for typical language development.

Students with autism consistently display profound language dysfunctions. Many times a student with autism is suspected of being deaf because he or she fails to attend to voice or speech signals. The student does not learn language at expected rates and has little pragmatic function in communication. The student's lack of emotionality is mirrored in speech and language that can be devoid of expressions of feeling or totally lacking in attempts to reach out to others. Words that are learned are used in restricted contexts, and the student does not seem to generalize one experience to another. It is suspected that the perceptual problems of students with autism interfere with language learning (Bernstein & Tiegerman-Farber, 2002). If they speak at all, students with autism tend to use short, simple sentences, omitting grammatical features such as conjunctions and prepositions. Because the student tends to learn whole phrases as single units, morphological changes are rarely applied (Hegde, 1995).

Students who experience severe illnesses or environmental deprivation may fail to develop language for the same underlying reason as students with autism. Although for markedly different reasons, both groups may share cognitive deficiencies due to the lack of experiences needed to develop language. The severely ill student who is out of contact or marginally aware of his or her surroundings is not capable of abstracting the experiences needed to learn language. This student must often sacrifice even the most common enriching experiences while battling to survive. Manipulating objects, crawling, visiting a shopping center, doing a puzzle, or even playing with blocks may be activities unavailable to someone who is chronically ill. As a result, even if this student lives in the most stimulating environment, he or she might not be able to take advantage of the language-learning opportunities that the environment offers. The environmentally impoverished student may be capable of processing, abstracting, perceiving, and conceptualizing but may not be exposed to activities that lead to developing these prerequisite skills.

Students raised in barren environments devoid of toys, educational materials, and language-enriching experiences cannot develop language in a vacuum. Richness of experience does not equate with the expense of toys, but rather with the diversity of experiences to which a student is exposed. Frequent and meaningful conversations with family members or caretakers, travel outside of one's home or neighborhood, looking at pictures, and manipulating toys all add to the conceptual framework that the language-developing student is constructing. The fewer experiences the student has, the less information he or she will have for linguistic development, and the more restricted that developing framework will become.

Disorders of Form, Content, and Use of Language

Independent of their cause, the major aspects of language disability can be classified by discussing the components needed to learn language. Disorders of the morphologic, syntactic, semantic, and pragmatic components of language reveal characteristics of language disability that cross the boundaries of any given condition. The form of language may be defective when a student has difficulty acquiring the morphologic and syntactic aspects of language. This is evident in students who are mature enough to have developed a sense of the morphology of their language, yet use words and phrases without the appropriate endings. Students with morphologic problems may not express plurality or appropriate tenses or use articles, pronouns, and prepositions. Syntactic problems arise in faulty sentence construction. These students often speak in short sentences and use inappropriate word order. On a receptive level, students with morphologic problems may be confused by any sentences that are complex or unusual in form.

The content of language is represented by semantic acquisition. Students with language disorders are often slow in learning the meanings of words. Their vocabularies are smaller than those of their peers, and they have difficulty remembering the meaning of newly acquired words. Receptively, these students may not understand the meanings of abstract words or the concepts that they represent.

Pragmatics represents the meaningful use of language. Students with pragmatic problems may not know how to initiate or maintain conversations. They may be clumsy in taking turns, knowing how to interrupt, or giving a listener information needed to understand what they are trying to communicate. These students will have problems telling stories, asking questions, and relating the language they hear to personal experiences.

Characteristics of Speech and Language Differences

This section will highlight characteristic speech and language differences that are part of recognized dialects of Standard English. Most dialectal speakers can easily code-switch between their dialectal speech and Standard English; however, many students who have little contact with Standard English speakers may come to school competent only in their particular dialect. Teachers in these areas of the country must understand what the regional dialect is and be able to determine whether a given student is using language that is different from Standard English yet still valid and not disordered and in need of treatment. Table 2.4 highlights some of the differences between Standard English and the most prevalent dialects. This listing is illustrative of the differences but is by no means complete. Williams and Wolfram (1977) identified 29 linguistic rules of Black English that differ from Standard English. It is critical to emphasize the fact that dialects are rule-governed, valid differences in language use

TABLE 2.4
Selected phonological and grammatical characteristics of Black English (B), Southern English (S), Southern White Nonstandard English (SWNS), and Appalachian English (A). Presence of each feature in the dialect is denoted by (X).

Features	Descriptions	Examples	B	S	SWNS	A
Consonant cluster reduction (general)	Deletion of second of two consonants in word final position belonging to same base word	tes (test)	X		X	
	Deletion of past tense (-ed) morpheme from a base word, resulting in a consonant cluster that is subsequently reduced	rub (rubbed)	X		X	
	Plural formations of reduced consonant cluster assume phonetic representations of sibilants and affricatives	desses (desks)	X		X	
/θ/ phoneme	/f/ for /θ/ between vowels and in word final position	nofin (nothing) Ruf (Ruth)	X			
/δ/ phoneme	/d/ for /δ/ in word initial position /v/ for /δ/ between vowels and in word final positions	dis (this) bavin (bathing) bave (bathe)	X X			
Vowel nasalization	No contrast between vowels /I/ and /ɛ/ before nasals	pin (pin, pen)		X		X
The /r/ and /l/ phonemes	Deletion preceding a consonant	ba: game (ball game)	X	X		
Future tense forms	Use of gonna	She gonna go. (She is going to go.)	X		X	
	Gonna reduced to 'ngna, 'mana, 'mon and 'ma	I'ngna go. I'mana go. I'mon go. I'ma go. (I am going to go.)	X			
Double modals	Co-occurrence of selected modals such as might, could, should	I might coulda done it. (It is possible that I could have done it.)	X		X	X
Intensifying adverbs	Use of intensifiers, i.e., right, plumb, to refer to completeness	right large (very large)	X		X	X
Negation	Ain't for have/has, am/are, didn't	He ain't go home. (He didn't go home.)	X			
Relative clauses	Deletion of relative pronouns	That's the dog bit me. (That's the dog that bit me.)	X		X	X
Questions	Same interrogative form for direct and indirect questions	I wonder was she walking? (I wonder if she was walking.)	X		X	X

Source: From *Social Dialects: Differences vs. Disorders* (pp. 148–149), by R. Williams and W. Wolfram, 1977, Washington, DC: American Speech and Hearing Association. Adapted by permission of the American Speech-Language-Hearing Association.

and not errors or less correct language. Students who speak a dialect of a language are no less linguistically competent than their Standard English-speaking peers.

IDENTIFICATION PROCESS

Students with communication disorders are initially identified by referrals to the school speech-language pathologist, who then conducts screening examinations. Students who are referred and fail screening examinations then undergo more formal diagnostic procedures to identify the specific aspects of their communication disorder.

Referral Sources

The major referral source for students is the classroom teacher. The teacher observes the student attempting to communicate in day-to-day situations. The teacher observes when the student is expressing new information, telling well-known stories, explaining thoughts and feelings, and interacting with peers. In addition, most classroom teachers can compare the communication performance of students to their peers. Most school-based speech-language pathologists conduct periodic in-service sessions for teachers, during which they highlight the characteristics of students with communication disorders and explain treatment options that are available in the school setting. Teachers are encouraged to contact the speech-language pathologist if they suspect a student in their class has a communication disorder. Speech-language pathologists also routinely distribute checklists and charts outlining typical development to teachers to help them decide on referrals (Hunt & Marshall, 2006). Figure 2.2 is a typical checklist that can be used to help teachers identify students who might need special programming.

The next most productive source for referral is family members. Family members have the opportunity to observe their children in a variety of communication settings. Checklists of characteristics of speech disorders that are sent home and invitations to contact the school speech-language pathologist help to identify many students.

Professionals in areas that provide service to students also can identify and appropriately refer students for services. School nurses, pediatricians, dentists, preschool teachers, and coordinators and teachers affiliated with various early intervention programs can be sources for early identification. In some instances, students themselves can initiate a referral by sharing their concerns about how they talk with their parents, teachers, or allied health professionals.

Screening Procedures

Speech, language, and hearing screenings are procedures that briefly sample a student's communication skills and hearing acuity to determine whether a more formal diagnostic evaluation should be conducted. Public school speech-language pathologists usually screen students entering kindergarten and those in the primary grades. Receptive and expressive language skills, articulation, voice, and fluency are specifically isolated. Most school systems have guidelines that mandate when initial screening and follow-up screenings must be performed. Students who fail hearing screenings are referred to audiologists for in-depth diagnostic assessment (see Chapter 9). Students who fail screenings for the other parameters of communication are scheduled for more formal diagnostic testing.

The following behaviors may indicate that a child in your classroom has a language impairment that is in need of clinical intervention. Please check the appropriate items.

_____ Child mispronounces sounds and words.

_____ Child omits word endings, such as plural -s and past tense -ed.

_____ Child omits small unemphasized words, such as auxiliary verbs or prepositions.

_____ Child uses an immature vocabulary, overuses empty words such as *one* and *thing,* or seems to have difficulty recalling or finding the right word.

_____ Child has difficulty comprehending new words and concepts.

_____ Child's sentence structure seems immature or overreliant on forms, such as subject-verb-object. It's unoriginal, dull.

_____ Child's question and/or negative sentence style is immature.

_____ Child has difficulty with one of the following:

_____ Verb tensing	_____ Articles	_____ Auxiliary verbs
_____ Pronouns	_____ Irreg. verbs	_____ Prepositions
_____ Word order	_____ Irreg. plurals	_____ Conjunctions

_____ Child has difficulty relating sequential events.

_____ Child has difficulty following directions.

_____ Child's questions often inaccurate or vague.

_____ Child's questions often poorly formed.

_____ Child has difficulty answering questions.

_____ Child's comments often off topic or inappropriate for the conversation.

_____ There are long pauses between a remark and the child's reply or between successive remarks by the child. It's as if the child is searching for a response or is confused.

_____ Child appears to be attending to communication but remembers little of what is said.

_____ Child has difficulty using language socially for the following purposes:

_____ Request needs	_____ Pretend/imagine	_____ Protest
_____ Greet	_____ Request information	_____ Gain attention
_____ Respond/reply	_____ Share ideas, feelings	_____ Clarify
_____ Relate events	_____ Entertain	_____ Reason

_____ Child has difficulty interpreting the following:

_____ Figurative language	_____ Humor	_____ Gestures
	_____ Emotions	_____ Body language

_____ Child does not alter production for different audiences and locations.

_____ Child does not seem to consider the effect of language on the listener.

_____ Child often has verbal misunderstandings with others.

_____ Child has difficulty with reading and writing.

_____ Child's language skills seem to be much lower than other areas, such as mechanical, artistic, or social skills.

FIGURE 2.2

Behaviors resulting in teacher referral of students with possible language impairments.

Source: Language Disorders: A Functional Approach to Assessment and Intervention (4th ed., p. 355), by R. E. Owens, 2004. Needham Heights, MA: Allyn & Bacon. Reprinted by permission.

Diagnostic Procedures

The diagnosis of a communication disorder follows a fairly standard pattern that is modified to meet the needs of any given student. Figure 2.3 is an outline of a typical diagnostic protocol.

Obtaining of parental permission
Construction of case history
    Records
    Interviews
Observations of communication behavior
Evaluations
    Informal (nonstandardized)
    Formal (standardized)
Diagnostic findings
Prognosis
Intervention recommendation

FIGURE 2.3
Outline of a diagnostic protocol.

Parental Permission

Parents of students who fail screening tests are usually notified by letter that their student has not passed the speech, language, or hearing portion of the screening examination. The implications of failing the screening tests are usually outlined, and permission is requested to conduct a diagnostic evaluation. Parents have the options of granting permission for further testing, not granting permission, or having the diagnostic evaluation performed by a speech-language pathologist of their own choosing outside of the school setting, usually at their own expense. When possible, family members are asked to attend the diagnostic evaluation or at least provide pertinent historical data about their child on prediagnostic case history forms.

Case History

The speech-language pathologist, having obtained parental permission, proceeds to construct a case history of the student that focuses on communication. School and medical records may be requested to scan for possible organic, emotional, or environmental experiences the student may have had that could have an impact on present communication. Examples of significant medical events might be a history of seizures, periods of severe illness, specific illnesses such as rubella that have communication consequences, current medications being administered, and a history of diagnosed conditions that are often allied with communication disorders. Emotional episodes and diagnosed emotional conditions can also have an impact on communication. Environmental experiences of importance might include child abuse, family breakups, or frequent changes in living situations. The speech-language pathologist will also review the prediagnostic case history form filled out by the parents to see if any other possible etiological explanations might exist for a student's suspected communication disorder. Most prediagnostic forms also request family members to describe the student's communication patterns and to report whether the way the student communicates is of any concern to them. The case history is completed when the speech-language pathologist conducts interviews with family members during the diagnostic session prior to evaluating the student. Questions about school and medical records are discussed at this time, and family members are encouraged to share their view of the student's communication skills and describe in detail any concerns they may have about communication. The student may also be interviewed at this time to help in completing the case history.

Observations

It is becoming increasingly important to observe the student's communication prior to commencing evaluations. The concern is that relying only on the communication samples obtained and measured during the formal diagnostic setting might not be the most representative sample of the student's "real" communication. Observation can be accomplished in several ways. As a rule, the more natural the setting in which the student is observed communicating, the more valid will be the implications drawn from the sample. Naturalistic contexts for observation include observing students in group activities; in free-play situations; during task-oriented situations; and in social interactions with parents, adults, and peers. These observations can reveal how the student gains attention, initiates communication, takes turns speaking, and uses speech and language in general (Heward, 2006; McCormick, 1994). It is not always possible for the speech-language pathologist to observe in these naturalistic settings. A compromise might be to ask the parents to send prior to the diagnostic session, or bring to the diagnostic session, an audio- or videotape of the student communicating in natural settings. An advantage of the recordings is that the parents or the speech-language pathologist can point out instances of communication behavior about which there is concern.

Many of the suites used to conduct speech and language evaluations are constructed with one-way observation mirrors. Another common way of observing a student is to ask a parent, sibling, or peer to spend a few minutes in some activity with the student while the speech-language pathologist observes through the observation window. This technique is commonly used to enable observation on the scene during a diagnostic session.

Evaluation

After completing observations, the usual procedure is to begin informal and formal evaluations of the student. Informal evaluations include attempting to engage the student in conversation, listening to stories or descriptions of pictures, and playing games that elicit speech and language. The speech-language pathologist uses these samples to compare performance to expectations of age-appropriate behavior in communication. The speech-language pathologist will informally assess the student's use of the components of language. He or she will also listen for the correct articulation of sounds and appropriate use of voice and will assess the fluency displayed. The speech-language pathologist will also observe the ease with which the student is able to perform the movements of the articulators needed for speech.

Formal testing is usually accomplished by using standardized tests that enable the speech-language pathologist to compare any given student's performance on the parameters being tested to similar performance by peers. Many standardized tests are available to test specific aspects of communication. For example, Figure 2.4 is a reproduction of the Screening Test Checklist Form of the Dworkin-Culatta Oral Mechanism Examination and Treatment System (Dworkin & Culatta, 1996), a test routinely used to determine whether a student can manipulate his or her articulators to successfully perform the movements needed for speaking. An inability to perform any of

SCREENING TEST CHECKLIST FORM

Name: _____ ; Sex: _____

Age: _____ ; DOB: _____ ; File #: _____

Address: _____

_____ ; Phone # (___) _____

Referral Source: _____ ; Date of Exam: _____

Examiner: _____ ; Test Location: _____

SCREENING KEY

ABNORMAL = YES; NORMAL = NO; QUESTIONABLE = YES
[For "YES" response, place ✔ in Deep Test Box.]

	RESPONSE	DEEP TEST
I. FACIAL STATUS 1. Does the face look asymmetrical, or possess any abnormal signs at rest?	_____ →	▢
II. LIP FUNCTIONING 1. Are the movements of the lips asymmetrical, or are the repetitions too slow, dysrhythmic, or imprecise?	_____ →	▢
III. JAW FUNCTIONING 1. Are movements asymmetrical, limited in range, or accompanied by TMJ noises?	_____ →	▢
IV. HARD PALATE 1. Is the arch shape or tissue appearance unusual?	_____ →	▢
V. TONGUE FUNCTIONING 1. Do movements lack sufficient range and precision, or are the repetitions too slow, dysrhythmic, or imprecise?	_____ →	▢
VI. VELOPHARYNGEAL FUNCTIONING 1. Are there signs of hypernasal or hyponasal resonance?	_____ →	▢
VII. STATUS OF DENTITION 1. Are there gross abnormalities in the alignment and condition of upper/lower teeth or signs of gross gum disease?	_____ →	▢
VIII. MOTOR SPEECH PROGRAMMING ABILITIES 1. Are there signs of articulatory groping, or whole or part word transpositions of the sequence?	_____ →	▢
LIST EXAMINATIONS TO BE DEEP TESTED	_____ →	_____

COMMENTS:

FIGURE 2.4

Dworkin-Culatta oral mechanism examination and treatment system.

Source: The Dworkin-Culatta Oral Mechanism Examination and Treatment System, by J. Dworkin and R. Culatta, 1996, Farmington, MI

the screening test activities is a signal to administer more exhaustive activities in the weak areas.

Speech sound articulation is usually tested using pictures that contain key sounds. For example, the student might be asked to identify a picture of a cat or kitten to determine whether the student can produce the /k/ sound correctly. These tests are called articulation tests. They provide the examiner with a standardized set of pictures that require the student to articulate the speech sounds of language when identifying the pictures. A widely used test is the Goldman-Fristoe Test of Articulation–2 (Goldman & Fristoe, 2000).

Language testing is more complex; many different standardized tests can be used to determine the student's skills in each of the components of language. For example, the Peabody Picture Vocabulary Test–III (Dunn & Dunn, 1997) gives a standardized measure of a student's receptive vocabulary. The Test of Language Development (TOLD–III; McLoughlin & Lewis, 2005; Newcomber & Hammill, 1997) helps identify the student's level in the development of language skills. The Clinical Evaluation of Language Fundamentals–III (CELF–III; Semel, Wiig, & Secord, 1995) measures language comprehension and expression for 5th to 12th graders. The speech-language pathologist determines from the analysis of the samples collected during observations and from recordings just which language tests are appropriate for a given student.

Evaluations of possible voice problems, unlike those in other areas, begin with a medical evaluation. Because the symptoms (what a listener hears) of voice problems can be the same whether the problem is organic or functional in nature, it is imperative that diagnosis and treatment be a team effort between the otorhinolaryngologist and the speech-language pathologist. Otorhinolaryngologists—ear, nose, and throat (ENT) specialists—are physicians who specialize in diagnosing and treating disorders of the ear, nose, and throat. Many conditions that reveal themselves through voice problems (laryngeal cancers, vocal nodules, juvenile papilloma) can have serious and even life-threatening consequences. It is therefore imperative that a medical clearance be obtained for the safety of the patient prior to administering speech pathology services.

Fluency evaluations proceed in several stages depending on the type of disfluency the student is displaying. Much of the information discussed in the section on the characteristics of disfluency is diagnostic in nature. Instruments such as the Protocol for Differentiating the Incipient Stutterer (Pindzola & White, 1986) help the speech-language pathologist determine whether the disfluencies observed are typical developmental disfluencies or the beginning of stuttering. The Differential Screening Test for Stuttering Checklist (Culatta & Goldberg, 1995), reproduced in Table 2.5, helps the speech-language pathologist decide whether the disfluency in a student's speech is stuttering or another type of disfluency.

Diagnosis, Prognosis, and Recommendations

Once the case history information, observation information, and results of informal and formal testing are combined and analyzed, the speech-language pathologist is able to state a diagnosis of the communication disorder. For example, a student might be diagnosed as exhibiting a mild to moderate disorder of articulation, severe stuttering, or an expressive language disorder.

As a part of the diagnosis, the speech-language pathologist will usually make a prognostic statement and suggest recommendations for programming. A sample prognostic statement might be that a student exhibits a developmental phonological

TABLE 2.5
Differential screening test for stuttering checklist.

Number	Indicator	Associated with Stuttering	Associated with Other Forms of Disfluency
1	Onset	Before 7 years of age	After 7 years of age
2	Stages of development	Progressive	Abrupt
3	Family history	History of stuttering in family	No history of stuttering in family
4	Etiology	Unknown	Appears immediately following a specific event
5	Adaptation	Number of disfluencies reduces through fifth reading	Little or no reduction of disfluencies through fifth reading
6	Automatic speech–1 (days of the week)	Relatively fluent	Little or no change
7	Automatic speech–2 (months of the year)	Relatively fluent	Little or no change
8	Automatic speech–3 (count to 20)	Relatively fluent	Little or no change
9	Choral reading (reads for 1 minute, 30 seconds; disregard first 30 seconds)	Fluency level improves	No effect on fluency
10	Singing	Fluency level improves	No effect on fluency
	Total checks		

Instructions: Check the appropriate responses for each indicator. Although there is no specific number of indicators that unequivocally differentiates a stutterer from a person with another form of disfluency, a preponderance of checked items in one column can provide substantial evidence.
Source: From *Stuttering Therapy: An Integrated Approach to Theory and Practice* (p. 97), by R. Culatta and S. Goldberg, 1995, Needham, MA: Allyn & Bacon.

disorder that will probably improve with treatment, or that the student is severely dysarthric, resulting in the inability to use oral speech, and will need training in alternative forms of communication.

The diagnostic report, including case history information; results of observations; and evaluations, diagnosis, prognosis, and recommendations, is shared with the child's parents and also presented to the IEP team. Programming decisions are finalized based on the collaboration of the family members and the IEP team, of which the speech-language pathologist is a member.

PROGRAMS

Service Provision Settings

Speech therapy services are presented in all the traditional special educational settings. Speech-language pathologists provide service as consultants to the regular classroom teacher, in resource rooms, separate classes, residential facilities, and home and hospital settings. In addition, private practitioners work on a fee-for-service basis or by contract with families or schools. Requirements mandate that speech-language pathologists in training be directly supervised by the programs that train them. As a result, speech clinics that provide services while training student speech-language pathologists can be found at many colleges and universities. Students receiving speech therapy are the most highly integrated group of all those receiving special education services. Approximately 87 percent of students seen for speech or language therapy in the schools attend regular classrooms at least 60 percent of their time (U.S. Department of Education, 2005). However, that figure is deceptive because many of the students seen for speech therapy services—those who are less integrated and whose primary disability is not a communication disorder—are not counted in this tally.

Type of Service Delivery

Speech therapy services are delivered in several formats. Students with similar communication problems are often grouped together and receive direct service in small groups. Students with unique or more severe problems can be seen individually several times a week during the school year in resource room settings outside of the classroom. This format has been labeled the pull-out model; it is the most traditional service delivery model. It can be an appropriate service provision model for developing skills that take a long period to master. For some students, intensive services are provided daily for short periods of time. This is the block scheduling model; it can be effective in providing the intensive care some students need to master specific skills that can then be transferred into the classroom.

Consultation with regular and special education teachers is becoming an increasingly popular model of service provision. Prior to the implementation of IDEA, students with severe disabilities were more likely to receive all services, including speech therapy, in segregated facilities. Most of these students are now seen in the schools and in general education classrooms. Allied with this change in location is the currently popular belief that communication skills can be best mastered in naturalistic settings rather than in the traditional resource room (Ehren, 2000; Prelock, 2000). As a result, more speech therapy services are being delivered using the consultation model than ever before. Speech-language pathologists are increasingly viewing themselves as full participants in the education of the student.

Other trends that affect the type of service delivered to students with communication disorders include the increasing focus on families, literacy, and diversity. There is a growing recognition that students do not "have" communication disorders in a vacuum. The way a student communicates has an impact on his or her family. Successful treatment suggests that the family, as well as the student, be involved in many aspects of the therapy process, from the initial mastery of new skills to the eventual transferring of those skills to the naturalistic environment. Classroom teachers are often considered "family" in the sense that they are a significant part of the student's communication environment (Ehren, 2000).

Literacy is being seen as a more global concept that supercedes spoken language as the domain of the speech-language pathologist. Literacy is reading and writing, as well as speaking and understanding. All of these processes are essentially social procedures that are part of the student's culture. Thus, language and literacy become shared goals for teachers and speech-language pathologists (American

Speech-Language-Hearing Association, 2001a; American Speech-Language-Hearing Association, 2001b; McCormick, 1994).

A growing sensitivity to the linguistic and cultural diversity of students in the schools is also shaping service provision (Westby & Erickson, 1992). Speech-language pathologists are trained to teach students to speak not only in Standard English, but they are also learning about the dialectal differences discussed earlier in this chapter. Students who might have been treated as disordered a decade ago are now being serviced as competent speakers learning new forms of language.

Early Intervention Programs

Because much of speech and language development is completed by the time school begins, early intervention for most communication disorders is highly recommended. This is especially true for students who have severe language disabilities or who stutter.

Preschool programs for children with language problems are usually half-day programs that foster cooperative play, encourage spontaneous speech, and facilitate interaction among children. These activities contribute to the conceptual knowledge and cognitive processes needed to develop language. Most of these programs attempt to structure naturalistic settings where children are free to interact and explore. They are usually stocked with a variety of interesting materials and objects that encourage communication (Paul, 1985; Wilcox, 1984). The activities and techniques used are shared with family members so that they might use them at home to encourage communication and language learning.

Students who stutter and do not receive treatment develop more complicated patterns of stuttering and more negative views about the communication process as they mature. The earlier that treatments are initiated, the more successful will be their outcome. If treatment is delayed until adolescence or early adulthood, the disorder is more resistant to treatment and the likelihood of relapse is far greater (Culatta & Goldberg, 1995; Shames & Rubin, 1986). With many speech disorders, the longer the person practices speech errors, the more resistant those errors will be to modification.

Sample Therapy Techniques

This section will sketch a cross-section of the therapy techniques used to treat various speech and language disorders. Most therapy approaches, regardless of the disorder, attempt to make the student aware of acceptable communication behavior, explain how and why the student is not producing the target behavior, model methods for producing the desired speech or language, and structure opportunities to use the newly acquired correct behavior in situations outside of therapy.

Articulation Therapy

The treatment of articulation disorders caused by clefts of the palate, cerebral palsy, traumatic brain injury, or hearing loss requires that the student somehow compensate for a speech mechanism that is not functioning properly. Articulation problems that are developmental phonological disorders require no such compensation.

Prior to initiating articulation therapy for students with clefts, the cleft must somehow be repaired or at least temporarily sealed. For most students with clefts of the palate, this means surgery to seal the cleft. However, surgical repair of a cleft does

not guarantee typical functioning of the mechanism or typical speech articulation. Even after surgery, exercises and drills may be necessary to train the newly repaired system to function adequately. Students must be made aware of the sounds that they are misproducing, be taught how to make them correctly, and practice saying them until they become automatic. For some students with clefts of the palate, surgery is postponed for medical reasons. These students will be fitted with prosthetic devices, essentially "false palates," that will achieve the closure necessary to articulate sounds. These devices are usually temporary in nature and require modification as the student grows.

Students who have cerebral palsy and articulation problems must be taught to use their defective articulatory system as efficiently as possible. This may mean slowing speech so that they can articulate more clearly, or it may mean that they will have to learn to gain more control over their speech mechanisms through drills and exercise. For many of these students, speech production will improve the intelligibility of their speech, but they will never articulate speech sounds normally. Some students who have severe disabilities may never be able to use oral speech for communication. **Intelligibility** is a listener's rating of the ability to understand the speech and language of a speaker.

The section of this chapter on alternative and augmentative communication will describe the options for communication available with technology.

Students who have suffered traumatic brain damage may regain the articulation skills they once had through a well-planned program of speech exercises and drills that will rehabilitate damaged systems. They may have to relearn on a conscious level how to make sounds they originally learned automatically. The degree of improvement will depend on the severity of the dysarthria that followed the TBI and the degree of recovery made within the first 6 months after the trauma. These students are similar to students with cerebral palsy in that decisions have to be made about how successful any rehabilitation aimed at producing oral speech can be.

Students who are hearing impaired or deaf must learn to produce sounds that they either do not hear or that they hear only in a distorted form. Programs to teach sound production to these students rely on the use of tactile and visual stimuli to produce sounds and memorization of where those sounds belong so they can be used in oral communication. A student who cannot hear /s/ can learn to produce it by feeling the air stream on his or her hand or by blowing on a pinwheel. After learning to produce this sound, the student must then learn which words have the /s/ sound and remember to produce it. The more residual hearing a student possesses, the more possible this task is.

Students with functional articulation disorders can be taught to produce correct speech sounds in numerous ways. The success rate for these students is much higher than for those who have organically based articulation disorders. Many times these students need only to be made aware of the sounds that they are omitting or distorting, and they will use this information to correctly produce those sounds. This process is called auditory stimulation and is used to make students sensitive to speech sounds. Other students with functional articulation problems must not only be taught to recognize correct sound production but must also be taught how to physically produce the problem sound correctly. This method, called phonetic placement, requires a student to consciously learn how sounds are made and use this knowledge when producing speech. Drill and practice are needed to learn to automatically replace the incorrect sound and produce the newly corrected sound.

Voice Therapy

Treating students with voice problems is always a team effort. If the voice problem is organic in nature, initial treatment is usually medical. If the voice problem is the result of emotional distress, initial treatment will usually be counseling. Even when these preliminary treatments are successful, speech therapy may still be needed. After surgery, the student may need to learn how to use the vocal system as efficiently as possible. Many times, the structures used for voicing are damaged as a consequence of surgical procedures. The student will need instruction on how to prevent further damage to a weakened system. For some students, all that is required after surgery is vocal rest so that tissues can heal.

Students with functional voice problems often have the potential to learn to produce normal-sounding vocal tones. Learning to use an appropriate voice may be a step-by-step process wherein the speech-language pathologist models appropriate voicing and the student imitates the model, initially in sound production and finally in speech production. Computers and specially designed voice monitors can often be used to graphically represent appropriate voice use for the student as he or she is speaking. Using the appropriate voice must become automatic. Parents, teachers, peers, and siblings are often recruited to aid in this process.

Fluency Therapy

Different types of disfluency require different treatments. Parents and students who are overly concerned about the typical disfluencies of speech or developmental disfluencies may only need information about the routine nature of typical disfluencies and the transitory nature of developmental disfluency to alleviate their concerns.

More abnormal types of disfluency may need more rigorous treatments. Disfluent speech that results from neurogenic damage will in all probability be treated as a part of the motor planning exercises and language retrieval strategies that focus on the speech and language problems caused by the neurological damage. As these neurogenically involved speakers gain or regain control of their speech and language systems, the disfluencies that they are experiencing will decline. Psychogenic disfluency treatment is in the realm of the psychologist, psychiatrist, social worker, or guidance or family counselor. Because this disfluency is in reaction to emotional stress, it is only tangentially a communication problem and is best treated by professionals other than speech-language pathologists. The disfluencies that arise from language impairment are best treated by techniques that improve language skills. The limited research available seems to indicate that treatment that increases language skills, in spite of emerging disfluencies, will eventually alleviate what appears to be temporarily created fluency failure (Culatta & Goldberg, 1995).

The treatment of cluttering involves teaching the student to be aware of the problem so that he or she can learn to slow the rapid, jerky, jumbled speech that characterizes cluttering. Over time and with repeated practice, the student will need to build a tolerance for the normal speech being practiced and use it in daily communication.

Students who stutter can be treated by any one of more than 50 separate protocols that are available to speech-language pathologists (Culatta & Goldberg, 1995). However, many of the therapy techniques are similar; when Culatta and Goldberg analyzed these treatment protocols, they noticed that stuttering is actually treated in a limited number of ways. Speech-language pathologists teach students who stutter to make adjustments of the speech mechanism that will bring about more fluent speech. They teach students to slow their rate of speech to gain control. Speech-language pathologists also use operant conditioning techniques to reinforce fluency and fluency-generating behaviors and to punish stuttering. By manipulating the length and complexity of a student's utterance, starting from one-word utterances and carefully increasing their length, speech-language pathologists can bring about fluency for some students. In other cases, the negative attitudes that students have developed about communication must be changed before progress can be made. A commonality in all therapy protocols is that they require students to monitor their speech and be aware of whether they are being fluent or are stuttering. Providing treatment for students who stutter and the goals of that treatment have been issues of controversy. Speech-language pathologists have evolved from not being willing to directly treat students who stutter to advocating early intervention. The goals of therapy have vacillated between teaching students to control their stuttering as best they can, to expecting them to be typically fluent as the result of treatment.

Language Therapy

Developmental disorders of language that affect language acquisition and traumatically acquired disorders of language that result in the loss of linguistic competence are treated differently. When dealing with developmental disorders, the task is one of habilitation, or teaching a student to gain skills he or she has never mastered. Traumatically acquired language disorders call for rehabilitation, or helping the student regain the skills or potential to develop skills he or she had prior to the accident.

Therapy for Developmental Disorders of Language.   The overall goal of language therapy for students who have been identified as having developmental disorders of language is to engage in procedures that will facilitate the acquisition of language. Therapy activities will not be successful if they are administered without the full participation of parents, teachers, and family members. Early intervention objectives focus on preparing parents and caregivers to provide language stimulation in play and routine caregiving activities. Exploring, manipulating objects, and experiencing new situations will provide for later concept development (Westling & Fox, 2000). Preschool language therapy focuses on participating in verbal and nonverbal games and guiding parents in initiating communication activities. Speech-language pathologists, family

BOX 2.1
WHAT EVERY TEACHER SHOULD DO

Suggestions for Facilitating Language

1. *Be responsive to the child's spontaneous communicative attempts.* A child learns language by engaging in communicative interactions. If the communication partner is responsive to the child's communicative acts, the language learning process will continue. Being responsive to communicative attempts includes repeating the content, carrying out the child's requests, listening intently, and commenting on the message.

2. *Modify input.* The language trainer should slow speech, pause, repeat, and use gestures as well as intonation to convey meaning. Modified input makes the language signal of more interest to the child. It also permits the child to make associations between words and the aspects of the environment for which they stand.

3. *Provide opportunities for the child to communicate.* A child who communicates a great deal is actively practicing communication skills. There are several mechanisms for increasing the frequency with which the child communicates:
   - Do not anticipate needs.
   - Arrange for unusual or novel events to occur.
   - Arrange for the child to convey information to others.
   - Provide the child with choices.

4. *Model or expand the child's language.* Once the child's communicative attempts are accepted, the trainer or parent can expose the child to a slightly better or more complete way of saying the same thing. If the child says, "I want the big, big ball," the trainer can say, "Yes, you want the *very* big ball."

5. *Talk about things of interest to the child.* Provide language input that corresponds with the child's own intentions. Say the same thing that the child is saying, but in slightly different ways. A spilled drink at lunchtime can become a beneficial language learning experience.

members, and teachers model how to request objects, respond to the communication of others, and follow directions (McCormick, 1994).

Family members and caregivers are encouraged to engage in parallel-talk activities, which provide a running narration of what the student is doing. They are also coached in self-talk activities, which provide a running narration of their own activities, and are taught to expand the student's communication attempts. An example of parallel talk is a family member observing a student playing with blocks and saying, "Bobby has the red block in his hand. It is a big block." Self-talk would be exemplified by a caregiver making chocolate milk with the following commentary: "I'm putting milk in Bobby's blue cup. Now the powder goes in. Where is the spoon? Here it is. Stir, stir, stir." Expansions occur after a student says, "My book," and the family member replies, "Yes, it is your book, and I would like to read it to you."

Language therapy for school-age students focuses on strengthening the specific components of language that are disordered in the context of the classroom curriculum or ongoing social activities (McCormick, 1994). Box 2.1 lists some suggested procedures for facilitating language development.

BOX 2.1 *Continued*

6. *Provide many clear examples of language rules.* If children are learning the word *break,* they should be exposed to many repetitions of the word associated with many examples of things that break. For example, they might break cookies and crackers, encounter objects that keep falling apart, break spaghetti in order to glue the pieces on a picture, and break carrot sticks for lunch.

7. *Use words the child already knows to teach new words.* For a child who doesn't know the meaning of the word *blend,* the trainer can say, "When we blend, we make things go together smoothly." The trainer can then give examples such as, "When we blend *b* and *e* together, we get *beeee,* not *buh-eee.*" By hearing the meanings of new words explained in simple ways, children easily expand their vocabulary.

8. *Reduce complexity.* Language that is too complex is of little or no benefit to the child. To be optimally effective, the language signal must be only slightly more complex than the child's current level of functioning. Thus, if the child is at the single-word level of language development, communication partners should be speaking in simple two-word combinations.

9. *Tell and retell stories and experiences.* Practice in telling and retelling stories and experiences provides the child with the opportunity to relate events in an organized manner. At first, a child's retelling can be prompted with questions and pictures. Children may need several exposures to a simplified version of a story or event before trying to relate it entirely on their own.

10. *When the child has a profound hearing loss or a motor disability, communicate in the child's mode or form of communication.* Children with hearing losses often need to be exposed to several modes of communication; for example, words paired with gestures or signs. Likewise, a child who is using a picture board to communicate will need to have others acknowledge or incorporate that communication board in interactions that occur in all sorts of natural contexts.

Source: From "Students with Communication Problems," by B. Culatta and R. Culatta, 1993, in A. E. Blackhurst and W. H. Berdine (Eds.), *An Introduction to Special Education* (3rd ed., pp. 251–252). Copyright © 1993 by HarperCollins College Publishers. Reprinted by permission of Addison-Wesley Educational Publishers Inc.

Therapy for Acquired Disorders of Language. The overall goal of language therapy for students who have been identified as having acquired disorders of language is to engage in procedures that will facilitate the reacquisition of the specific language skills that are impaired as a result of the brain damage. Analyzing diagnostic test results and samples of the student's spontaneous language will often provide the speech-language pathologist with an outline of a student's strengths and weaknesses in receptive and expressive language skills. Therapy activities can then be targeted to use the student's strengths to compensate for weaknesses. For example, if a student is having difficulties processing complicated instructions, the speech-language pathologist may teach the student how to appropriately ask that instructions be repeated. Rather than say, "I don't know what to do," the student might ask, "What do I do on page 25?" Teachers and family members can also be instructed in efficient ways to help the student process information, such as simplifying instructions, writing them on the board, or presenting them slowly. If a student is having trouble retrieving words as the result of brain injury, the speech-language pathologist may help him or her develop strategies, such as thinking of what the word does or who uses the object. These attempts at association often result in successful word retrieval. Language exercises that systematically target the components of form, content, and use can help strengthen language weaknesses or enable students to relearn lost skills.

GENERALIZATION AND MAINTENANCE

None of the gains achieved in speech or language therapy will be of any consequence unless they are applied outside of the therapy setting (generalized) or become a permanent part of the student's communication (maintained). The current emphasis on naturalistic settings for speech therapy provision is, in part, an effort to foster more efficient generalization and maintenance of therapy gains. Classroom teachers, special educators, and family members must all be active participants in the therapy process so that they are aware of what the student is accomplishing and how the communication gains may be used in daily communication.

TECHNOLOGY

Technological advances have had an impact on service provision for students with communication disorders in two major areas. The first is in using technology to assist individuals who will not be able to use oral communication effectively. This use of technology is called alternative and augmentative communication (AAC). The second is providing equipment that facilitates learning appropriate speech and language.

Alternative and Augmentative Communication

AAC devices can be as low tech as communication boards with photographs pinned to them or as high tech as computers that can be programmed to synthesize speech. Once it is determined that a student requires an alternative to spoken language, it is the responsibility of the speech-language pathologist and IEP team to decide what might best meet the student's needs. Factors that enter into the decision are the cognitive ability of the student, the physical dexterity required to operate the selected device, and the sophistication of the language to be transmitted. It is not unusual for a student to progress from simple to complex devices as he or she becomes more linguistically competent. For example, a communication board with pictures of simple activities and written instructions beneath them might be appropriate in initially helping the student learn vocabulary and how to request basic needs. As the student progresses, a device with selected preprogrammed requests that are produced by the machine might better suit the student's needs. Eventually, the student might learn to use a computer that will generate appropriately complex language that the student composes on the device. Speaking devices can be activated by keyboards, touchpads, and a variety of switches that can be adapted to the manual dexterity the student possesses.

Alternative and augmentative communication systems can open new worlds to the student who is unable to use oral communication, but they cannot take the place of learning language. A student cannot use a device beyond his or her level of competence. A sophisticated speech synthesizer will not enable a student functioning linguistically at the level of a 2-year-old to compose intricate and complex sentences. However, it can help a student who is linguistically sophisticated but motor impaired express his or her needs in an increasingly acceptable manner.

AAC devices and systems are rarely the first choice for teaching a student to communicate. Oral speech or sign language are usually the primary goals in teaching speech or language. (Chapter 9, "Students with Hearing Impairments," discusses the technology available to students who are hearing impaired or deaf.) However, the limitations of any given student's ability to use typical communication must be recognized and accepted by the student and the student's family members, teachers, and speech-language pathologists in order to efficiently maximize the student's learning experience.

Facilitating Devices

Technology in the form of aids to help students master typical communication skills has changed speech therapy provisions. Tape recorders and video recorders are routinely used to demonstrate the correct and incorrect production of target behaviors. They help the student understand and practice concepts developed during therapy and provide a way to bring outside experiences with communication to the therapy session. Most speech-language pathologists would not consider conducting therapy sessions without tape-recording or video-recording them for later analysis. Personal computer programs are available to help students learn vocabulary items, develop conceptual knowledge, and practice specific speech and language skills. The materials available range from programs designed to meet special communication needs to programs available to the general public that can be used with little modification. As computers become increasingly sophisticated in speech and sound discrimination ability, they will increasingly be a part of therapy.

BOX 2.2
WHAT EVERY TEACHER SHOULD KNOW
ABOUT TECHNOLOGY

- Augmentative communication devices assist students in expressing needs, desires, and thoughts. These devices can be sophisticated with electronic and programmable messages spoken at the touch of a button. The process also can be as simple as pointing to a photo or other picture on a board.
- Computers with speech capabilities are used to assist students in speaking in class. The machines can be programmed to speak sentences when activated with a switch or a keystroke, or the student can type messages for others.
- Computer programs are capable of providing feedback to students as they are speaking. For instance, it can flag speech that is disfluent and provide a visual or auditory prompt to the student. The student can generate a record of events of disfluency, and progress can be maintained. The student may also use the software as a practice monitor.
- Functional magnetic resonance imaging (FMRI) is a technique that uses the blood flow in organs (e.g., the brain) to detect structure activity. Physicians can use this technology to find areas of structural damage.

Several devices have been designed to specifically help students master the skills needed for typical communication. The Computer-Aided Fluency Establishment Trainer (CAFET), designed by Martha Goebel, director of the Annandale Fluency Clinic in Virginia, uses hardware and software that enable the student to learn speech behaviors needed for fluent speech. Physical movements of the articulatory system are electronically monitored, and age-appropriate programs help students practice the required skills. The Visipitch is a complex device that analyzes many components of voice production and provides graphic feedback on a video screen when correct vocal production is produced. This direct and immediate feedback provides initial practice in correct vocal productions and facilitates generalization and maintenance. Many other devices and programs have been specifically designed to help speech-language pathologists obtain the behavior initially needed to correct speech and language disorders. The Society for Augmentative and Alternative Communication and the American Speech-Language-Hearing Association, listed at the end of this chapter, can provide information about AAC devices and commercially available devices and programs used in speech therapy. Focus tips for using computers and technology are included in Box 2.2.

ISSUES OF IMPORTANCE

Issues that have an impact on providing effective service to students with communication disorders will be discussed in this section. The issues selected are only a few of the issues of concern to speech-language pathologists. However, they are selected to provide some insight into the controversies affecting this area of serving students with special needs.

Appropriate Settings for Service Provision

Most speech therapy is provided in separate therapy rooms using the pull-out model. This model has been criticized because it isolates students from the classroom, stigmatizes them by focusing attention on their disabilities, and isolates the speech-language pathologist from the educational mission of the schools (Nelson, 1998). Generalization and maintenance are more difficult to maintain using a pull-out model. Even though the resource room may be highly structured and may encourage the establishment of skills, generalization tends to be minimal because the skills being learned have little relevance to the classroom activities and the play activities with students' peers. The pragmatic aspects of communication suffer from lack of peer interaction (McCormick, 1994). Advocates of providing speech therapy in more naturalistic settings suggest that more speech therapy services be provided on a consultation and collaboration basis and that in-service training be provided to give general classroom teachers increasing responsibility for speech and language services. In addition, they advocate for the presence of paraeducators and other support staff to monitor communication in the classroom. A more moderate view acknowledges that although much of what is happening in isolated resource rooms can be transferred to the classroom, there will always be a need for one-on-one therapy conducted in the privacy of the clinical suite or resource room.

Treatment of Developmental Phonological Disorders

A significant proportion of students seen for speech therapy are diagnosed as having developmental phonological disorders that might self-correct as they mature. The concern is whether treatment should be applied conservatively or withheld until there is no doubt that a problem exists. Withholding treatment would free the speech-language pathologist's time for other disorders and help alleviate the chronic shortages of speech-language pathologists in the schools. The downside to this approach is that many of the students who would be denied early service will not self-correct and thus will present more entrenched problems that are resistant to therapy when it is finally presented. Treating these older students would be more costly and time consuming in the long run. The decision of what would be best practice requires clinical judgment, prioritizing provision of services, and collaborating and consulting with classroom teachers and assistants. Clinical experiences with students who stutter and students with exceptionalities of all types tend to indicate that early intervention is both more effective and less costly in most situations.

Technology and Alternative and Augmentative Communication

Alternative and augmentative communication devices and systems have clearly had a liberating effect on students who cannot master oral communication. However, providing a student with an augmentative or alternative system is significantly more complex than simply ordering the most appropriate tool and handing it to the family involved. Issues to address include the costs of equipment, who pays for the equipment, who updates or replaces it, how it is serviced, and who provides training for the student and the family. The complexity of programming many of the devices may be beyond the skill level of the student, his or her family members, and in some cases the speech-language pathologist who recommended it. The portability and reliability of some devices is highly suspect. Some are usable only in restricted situations because of inherent auditory or visual transmission features. Even the most reliable and sturdy machines may be laborious to operate, due to either the speed of the equipment itself or the skills of the user (Beukelman, 1991; Nelson, 1992). Slowness results in frustration for the communicator and the listener. Students who use communication devices often have to rely on the programming and language selections of others who are attempting to guess what the students will wish to say in situations that have not yet been encountered. The cumbersome programming needed to make some devices functional can threaten to turn speech pathologists into computer technicians and remove them from service provision duties more in line with their training and interests. As anyone who has ever experienced even the most minor glitch in a personal computer can attest, technical service is not only difficult to obtain but also frustratingly complex to apply, especially to machines that are used at home and in community settings away from the computer specialist.

Psychologically, family members, students, teachers, and speech-language pathologists often expect more from devices than they are capable of delivering. It is tempting to hope that a "magic machine" will solve a student's communication problems and devastating when the reality of the limitations of the device become apparent.

The more positive side of the concern is that many of even the most basic devices are still in their infancy. In all fairness, they must still be considered experimental models rushed into service because they are so desperately needed. It is not unrealistic to expect that within the next decade, devices will become less expensive, more portable, less fragile, and easier to operate. Even in their crudest form, many of these devices do free students from the isolation imposed by not being able to communicate with their peers and enable them to be included, more than has ever been possible, in the typical activities of the classroom.

DIVERSITY

Three of the most pressing minority concerns are (1) acceptance of the validity of linguistic diversity, (2) appropriate provision of services to students with linguistic diversity, and (3) lack of minority professionals available to provide services.

Validity of Linguistic Diversity

Despite data that show that the dialects of Standard English are legitimate, rule-governed forms of English, political, social, and educational biases against these forms of English still exist (Taylor, 1986). Dialectal speakers run the risk of being considered disordered rather than different and can be judged cognitively inferior to their Standard English-speaking peers. They may be discriminated against in the workplace and penalized in the classroom. The fact that speech-language pathologists, rather then teachers of English as a second language, see many of these students is significant, because the American Speech-Language-Hearing Association (ASHA) has specifically stated that no dialect of English is a disorder or a pathological form of speech or language (American Speech-Language-Hearing Association, 1982). Attempts to recognize that Black English is the primary language of some students and to teach these students to code-switch have been derided as a "cruel joke" by NAACP president Kweisi Mfume and a "ridiculous theory" by the press secretary of California governor Pete Wilson (Leland & Joseph, 1997). Inflammatory rhetoric and uninformed public statements do little to help family members and teachers understand that dialects exist in many languages besides English, and confusion can occur when students and teachers speaking different forms of the same language interact during the educational process. Those who teach in Standard English in areas where dialects of English are commonly spoken must be aware of the differences in language and the confusions that could occur.

Service Provision to Dialectal Speakers

Being a dialectal speaker does not exempt a student from having communication problems. One unintended consequence of sensitivity to dialectal speech is that some speakers of other dialects with communication disorders are being denied service due to the mistaken belief that their speech disorders are merely speech differences and therefore need not be treated. An interesting and potentially harmful paradox exists when both the inclusion and exclusion of dialectal speakers in special service programs can be viewed as discriminatory (Nelson, 1998). One obvious answer is that the legal requirement that students must be evaluated by professionals fluent in the student's native language be applied to dialectal speakers as well as to speakers of foreign languages.

The format of service provision to dialectal speakers is also a concern. Because dialectal speakers do not automatically have speech and language disorders, it would appear that when the only differences in language or speech are dialectal, these students should be as capable as their Standard English-speaking peers in learning the parallel forms of expression that constitute Standard English. Understanding the dialectal form and helping the student translate it into Standard English appears to be the most effective teaching strategy rather than grouping these students with those that need remediation for speech or language disorders.

Minority Professionals

Although it is not necessary to be a minority group member to work with minority students, there is no denying that minority professionals can bring a sensitivity and interest to the problems of minority individuals that mainstream speech-language pathologists might not. In addition, minority professionals can serve as role models to minority and majority students alike. Despite active recruiting programs by colleges and university training programs and federally funded minority group grants, minority speech-language pathologists make up fewer than 7 percent of all the members of ASHA. Fewer than 2 percent are Hispanic. Fewer than 3 percent are African Americans, and fewer than 0.5 percent are Native Americans. Unfortunately, these figures have remained stable even as the number of speech-language pathologists in the United States grows (American Speech-Language-Hearing Association, 1993b).

PROFESSIONALS

Speech-Language Pathologists

Speech-language pathologists are the specialists on the educational team who are primarily responsible for the identification, diagnosis, design, and application of programs for students identified as having speech and language disabilities. They provide service directly to students and serve as consultants and collaborators with regular and special education teachers, family members, and allied health and medical practitioners. Speech-language pathologist is a professional title conferred by ASHA. This national professional association is the research and credentialing organization for approximately 90,000 speech-language pathologists and audiologists. Audiologists are professionals who deal with students who are hearing impaired and deaf. Their role is explained in Chapter 9 of this text. Approximately 45 percent of all speech-language pathologists work in school settings.

Speech-language pathologists are awarded a nationally recognized certification called the Certificate of Clinical Competence (CCC) once they have completed a course of study that leads to a master's or doctoral degree from an academic institution that has been accredited by the American Speech-Language-Hearing Association. In addition to academic courses, at least 500 hours of supervised clinical practice must be completed with a variety of clients with different speech and language disorders. Upon completing master's training, the speech-language pathologist must complete a Clinical Fellowship Year (CFY) of employment under the supervision of a certified speech-language pathologist and a national examination before the CCC is awarded.

In addition, approximately 45 states require licensing of speech-language pathologists. These licensing requirements are different from the teacher certification requirements that are also mandated in most states to practice in the schools. ASHA considers it unethical to provide services in any setting prior to completing or being in the process of completing the requirements for the CCC. However, a diminishing number of states require only a bachelor's degree in communication disorders to obtain teacher certification. Most of these states also require that bachelor's-level service providers be in the process of obtaining a master's degree in communication disorders in order to maintain a position in the public schools. The American Speech-Language-Hearing Association is committed along with most state professional organizations to have the master's degree as the entry-level credential for school speech-language pathologists (American Speech-Language-Hearing Association, 1993b).

Communication Aides or Assistants

Communication aides or communication assistants are support personnel who work under the direct guidance of a speech-language pathologist, who is directly responsible for their actions. The requirements to become a licensed communication assistant vary from state to state. Approximately 30 states have regulations and laws governing the use of communication aides (American Speech-Language-Hearing Association, 1988). For example, in North Carolina the communication assistant must have completed an associate's degree in speech-language pathology assisting from a community college or equivalent program, or a BA degree with specific courses outlined in the licensing requirements. The services the communication assistant may provide are limited to managing the behavior of clients and positioning and escorting patients.

They may also complete observation checklists, administer binary screening protocols, record behaviors, and provide prompts. Communication assistants are also empowered to set up appointments, obtain records, organize records, send reports, compile data, arrange the clinical setting, manage and maintain equipment, and program assistive devices (North Carolina Board of Examiners, 1997).

Educational Professionals

As we have repeatedly mentioned throughout this chapter, classroom teachers and special education teachers are a vital part of the services provided to students with communication disorders. They are vital as collaborators for the generalization and maintenance of gains made in therapy and are becoming increasingly important as members of the team providing direct remediation. As more services are delivered in classrooms, teachers and paraeducators will become more involved in teaching language skills in natural settings to facilitate generalization of language skills (Harn, Bradshaw, & Ogletree, 1999).

Educational professionals have always played a critical role in the identification of students who might need help with communication problems and in helping speech-language pathologists counsel the families of students with communication disorders.

Medical and Allied Health Professionals

Depending on the type of communication disorder, ear, nose, and throat specialists (otorhinolaryngologists); family counselors; psychologists; psychiatrists; and social workers could all be part of the team that determines what might be the best treatment protocol for the students with a communication disorder.

DISCUSSION QUESTIONS

1. How are disorders of speech and language different?
2. What does it mean to "code-switch" between Standard English and dialectic English?
3. Outline steps in screening and evaluation of speech or language disorders. What steps are seen as critical?
4. How can technology enhance the use of speech?
5. How can technology enhance the use of language?
6. Describe the students who might need the following therapies:
   a. fluency therapy
   b. voice therapy
   c. articulation therapy

   Which of these students would be more likely to be in general education classes with minimal support? Which would need more intensive support?
7. In what setting should language therapy be implemented? Why?
8. What aspects of dialects should be considered in therapies for speech and or language?

PROFESSIONAL ASSOCIATIONS AND PARENT OR SELF-HELP GROUPS

American Academy of Otolaryngology
1101 Vermont Avenue NW, Suite 302
Washington, DC 20005

American Cleft Palate–Craniofacial Association
1218 Grandview Avenue
Pittsburg, PA 15211

American Speech-Language-Hearing Association
10801 Rockville Pike
Rockville, MD 20852

Division of Children's Communication Development
Council for Exceptional Children
1110 North Glebe Road, Suite 300
Arlington, VA 22201-5704

International Fluency Association
457 Old Farm Road
Wyncote, PA 19095

National Center for Neurogenic Communication Disorders
University of Arizona
Tucson, AZ 85721

National Center for Voice and Speech
Wendell Johnson Speech and Hearing Center
University of Iowa
Iowa City, IA 52242

National Council on Stuttering
558 Russell Road
Dekalb, IL 60115

National Institute of Communication Disorders, Hearing and Deafness
National Institutes of Health
Bethesda, MD 20892

National Stuttering Project
2151 Irving Street, Suite 208
San Francisco, CA 94122

Stuttering Foundation of America
5139 Klingle Street NW
Washington, DC 20016

U.S. Society for Augmentative and Alternative Communication
202 Barkley Memorial Center
University of Nebraska
Lincoln, NE 68583

American Journal of Speech-Language Pathology
10801 Rockville Pike
Rockville, MD 20852

Augmentative and Alternative Communication
P.O. Box 1762
Station R
Toronto, Ontario M4G 4A3
Canada

Augmentative Communication News
Sunset Enterprises
One Surf Way, Suite 213
Monterey, CA 93940

Journal of Childhood Communication Disorders
1110 North Glebe Road, Suite 300
Arlington, VA 22201-5704

Journal of Communication Disorders and Journal of Fluency Disorders
Elsevier Science Publishing Co.
655 Avenue of the Americas
New York, NY 10010

Journal of Speech and Hearing Research and Language, Speech and Hearing Services in the Schools
10801 Rockville Pike
Rockville, MD 20852

Our Voice
365 West 25th Street, Suite 13E
New York, NY 10001

REFERENCES

American Psychiatric Association. (1994). *Diagnostic and statistical manual of mental disorders–IV*. (DSM–IV) Washington, DC: Author.

American Speech-Language-Hearing Association. (1982). Definitions: Communicative disorders and variations. *ASHA, 24,* 949–950.

American Speech-Language-Hearing Association. (1988). Utilization and employment of speech-language pathology support personnel with underserved populations. *ASHA, 30,* 55–56.

American Speech-Language-Hearing Association. (1991). *Fact sheet on communication disorders*. Rockville, MD: Author.

American Speech-Language-Hearing Association. (1993a). Definitions of communication disorders and variations. *ASHA, 35,* 40–41.

American Speech-Language-Hearing Association. (1993b). Implementation procedures for the standards for the certificates of clinical competence. *ASHA, 35,* 76–83.

American Speech-Language-Hearing Association. (2001a). Roles and responsibilities of speech-language pathologists with respect to reading and writing in children and adolescents. Position statement, executive summary of guidelines, technical report. *ASHA, supplement 21,* 17–27. Rockville, MD: Author.

American Speech-Language-Hearing Association. (2001b). *Scope of practice in speech-language pathology.* Rockville, MD: Author.

Bernstein, D. K., & Tiegerman-Farber, E. (Eds.). (2002). *Language and communication disorders in children* (5th ed.). Needham, MA: Allyn & Bacon.

Beukelman, D. R. (1991). Magic and cost of communicative competence. *Augmentative and Alternative Communication, 7,* 2–10.

Bloodstein, O. (1960). The development of stuttering: Part II developmental phases. *Journal of Speech and Hearing Disorders, 25,* 366–376.

Chomsky, N. (1957). *Syntactic structures.* The Hague, Netherlands: Mouton.

Chomsky, N. (1981). *Lectures on government and binding.* Dordrecht, Netherlands: Doris.

Council for Exceptional Children (2001, September). Where we are in special education? *Today, 8(3),* 1.

Culatta, B., & Culatta, R. (1993). Students with communication problems. In A. E. Blackhurst & W. H. Berdine (Eds.), *An introduction to special education* (3rd ed.). New York: HarperCollins.

Culatta, R., & Goldberg, S. (1995). *Stuttering therapy: An integrated approach to theory and practice.* Needham, MA: Allyn & Bacon.

Culatta, R., & Leeper, L. (1987). Disfluency in childhood: It's not always stuttering. *Journal of Childhood Communication Disorders, 10,* 96–106.

Culatta, R., & Leeper, L. (1989). The differential diagnosis of disfluency. *National Student Speech-Language-Hearing Association Journal, 17,* 50–59.

Dublinski, S. (1981). Action: School services. *Language, Speech and Hearing Services in Schools, 12,* 192–200.

Dunn, L. M., & Dunn, L. (1997). *Peabody Picture Vocabulary Test–III.* Circle Pines, MN: American Guidance.

Dworkin, J., & Culatta, R. (1996). *The Dworkin-Culatta Oral Mechanism Examination and Treatment System.* Farmington, MI: Edgewood.

Ehren, B. J. (2000). Maintaining a therapeutic focus and sharing responsibility for student success: Keep to in-classroom speech language services. *Language, Speech, and Hearing Services in Schools, 31,* 219–229.

Gleason, J. B. (1973). Code switching in children. In T. E. Moore (Ed.), *Cognitive development and the acquisition of language.* New York: Academic.

Goldman, R., & Fristoe, M. (2000). *Goldman-Fristoe Test of Articulation–2.* Circle Pines MN: AGS.

Harn, W. E., Bradshaw, M. L., & Ogletree, B. T. (1999). The speech-language pathologist in the schools: Changing roles. *Intervention in School and Clinic, 34,* 163–170.

Hegde, M. N. (1995). *Introduction to communicative disorders* (2nd ed.). Austin, TX: PRO-ED.

Heward, W. L. (2006). *Exceptional children* (8th ed.). Upper Saddle River, NJ: Merrill/Prentice Hall.

Hunt, N., & Marshall, K. (2006). *Exceptional children and youth: An introduction to special education* (4th ed.). Boston: Houghton Mifflin.

Kemler, D. (1983). Wholistic and analytic modes of perceptual and cognitive development. In T. J. Tighe & B. E. Shepp (Eds.), *Interactions: Perception, cognition and development.* Hillsdale, NJ: Erlbaum.

Kidd, R. D. (1980). Genetic model of stuttering. *Journal of Fluency Disorders, 5,* 187–201.

Kirk, S. A., Gallagher, J. J., Anastasiow, N. J., & Coleman, M. B. (2005). *Educating exceptional children* (11th ed.). Boston: Houghton Mifflin.

Leland, J., & Joseph, N. (1997, January 13). Hooked on ebonics. *Newsweek,* 78–79.

McCormak, W. C., & Wurm, S. A. (1976). *Language and man: Anthropological issues.* The Hague, Netherlands: Mouton.

McCormick, L. (1994). Communication disorders. In N. G. Haring, L. McCormick, and T. G. Haring (Eds.), *Exceptional children and youth* (6th ed.). Upper Saddle River, NJ: Merrill/Prentice Hall.

McLoughlin, I. A., & Lewis, R. B. (2005) *Assessing students with special needs* (6th ed.). Upper Saddle River, NJ: Merrill/Prentice Hall.

McWilliams, B. J., Morris, H. L., & Shelton, R. L. (1990). *Cleft palate speech* (2nd ed.). Philadelphia: Decker.

Menn, L., & Stoel-Gammon, C. (Eds.). (1992). *Normal and disordered phonology in children.* Austin, TX: Pro-Ed.

National Center for Health Statistics. (1988). Current estimates from the National Health Interview Survey, United States, 1988. *Vital Health Statistics,* Series 10, No. 173. DHHS Publication No. (PHS) 89-1501.

National Institute of Neurological and Communicative Disorders and Stroke. (1988). *Developmental speech and language disorders: Hope through research.* Bethesda, MD: National Institutes of Health.

Nelson, N. W. (1992). Performance is the prize: Language competence and performance among AAC users. *Augmentative and Alternative Communication, 8,* 3–18.

Nelson, N. W. (1998). *Childhood language disorders in context: Infancy through adolescence* (2nd ed.). Boston: Allyn & Bacon.

Newcomber, P. L., & Hammill, D. (1997). *Tests of language development* (3rd ed.). Austin, TX: PRO-ED.

North Carolina Board of Examiners. (1997, February). *Newsletter.* Greensboro, NC: Author.

Olmstead, D. (1971). *Out of the mouths of babes.* The Hague, Netherlands: Mouton.

Owens, R. (2004). *Language disorders: A functional approach to assessment and intervention* (4th ed.). Needham, MA: Allyn & Bacon.

Owens, R. (2005). *Language development: An introduction* (6th ed.). Boston, MA: Allyn & Bacon.

Paul, L. (1985). Programming peers' support for functional language. In S. F. Warren & A. K. Rogers-Warren (Eds.), *Teaching functional language.* Baltimore: University Park Press.

Perkins, W. (1971). *Speech pathology: An applied behavioral science.* St. Louis, MO: Mosby.

Pindzola, R., & White, D. T. (1986). A protocol for differentiating the incipient stutterer. *Speech and Hearing Services in the Schools, 17,* 2–15.

Polloway, E. A., Miller, L., & Smith, T. E. C. (2004). The development of language. In E. A. Polloway & T. E. C. Smith (Eds.), *Language instruction for students with disabilities* (3rd ed.). Denver: Love.

Prelock, P. A. (2000). Epilogue: An intervention focus for inclusionary practice. *Language, Speech, and Hearing Services in Schools, 31(3),* 296–298.

Reichle, J. (1997). Communication instruction with persons who have severe disabilities. *Journal of Special Education, 31,* 110–134.

Reid, D. K. (2000). Discussion in classrooms. In K. R. Fahey & D. K. Reid (Eds.), *Language development, differences, and disorders.* Austin, TX: PRO-ED.

Schwartz, R. G. (2006). Articulatory and phonological disorders. In N. Anderson & G. H. Shames (Eds.), *Human communication disorders* (9th ed.). Boston: Allyn & Bacon.

Semel, E., Wiig, E., & Secord, W. (1995). *Clinical evaluation of language fundamentals–3.* San Antonio, TX: Psychological Corporation.

Senturia, B. H., & Wilson, F. B. (1968). Otorhinolaryngic findings in children with voice deviations. *Annals of Otology, Rhinology and Laryngology, 77,* 1027–1042.

Shames, G., & Rubin, H. (1986). *Stuttering then and now.* Upper Saddle River, NJ: Merrill/Prentice Hall.

Shriberg, L. D. (1994). Developmental phonological disorders: Moving towards the 21st century—forewards, backwards, or endlessly sideways. *American Journal of Speech-Language Pathology, 3,* 26–28.

Smith, D. D. (2001). *Introduction to special education: Teaching in an age of opportunity* (4th ed.). Boston, MA: Allyn & Bacon.

Stuart, S. (2002). Communication: Speech and language. In M. L. Batshaw (Ed.), *Children with disabilities.* Baltimore: Paul H. Brookes.

Taylor, O. (1986). *Nature of communication disorders in culturally and linguistically diverse populations.* San Diego, CA: College-Hill.

Taylor, O. L., & Payne, K. (1994). Culturally valid testing: A proactive approach. *Topics in Language Disorders, 3(7),* 8–20.

Turnbull, A. P., Turnbull, H. R., Shank, M., & Smith, S. (2004). *Exceptional lives: Special education in today's schools* (4th ed.). Upper Saddle River, NJ: Merrill/Prentice Hall.

U.S. Department of Education. (2005). *Twenty-fifth annual report to Congress on the implementation of the Individuals with Disabilities Education Act.* Washington, DC: Author.

Van Riper, C., & Erickson, R. (1996). *Speech correction: An introduction to speech pathology and audiology* (9th ed.). Boston, MA: Allyn & Bacon.

Wagner, R., & Torgesen, J. (1987). The nature of phonological processing and its causal role in the acquisition of reading skills. *Psychological Bulletin, 101,* 192–212.

Westby, C. (1988). Children's play: Reflections of social competence. *Seminars in Speech and Language, 9,* 1–14.

Westby, C., & Erickson, J. (1992). Prologue. *Topics in Language Disorders, 12(3),* v–viii.

Westling, D. L., & Fox, L. (2000). *Teaching communication skills: Teaching students with severe disabilities.* Upper Saddle River, NJ: Merrill/Prentice Hall.

Wilcox, M. J. (1984). Developmental language disorders: Preschoolers. In A. Holland (Ed.), *Language disorders in children: Recent advances.* Austin, TX: PRO-ED.

Williams, R., & Wolfram, W. (1977). *Social dialects: Differences vs. disorders.* Washington, DC: American Speech and Hearing Association.

Yairi, E., & Lewis, E. (1984). Disfluencies at the onset of stuttering. *Journal of Speech and Hearing Research, 27,* 155–159.

3 Students with Mental Retardation or Developmental Disabilities

KEY TERMS

WHAT WOULD YOU DO?

Logan was a 12-year-old with dimpled cheeks, blonde hair, and blue eyes. He was slightly overweight and clumsy. His foster mother enrolled him in school. His school records were incomplete, but there were indications that he had been in special education classes in his former school. Telephone calls and e-mails had not yet been effective in securing more complete records. Logan was tested as soon as possible and was found to have a verbal IQ of 58, a performance IQ of 63, and a full-scale IQ of 60. He was below average in functional skills such as mobility in the community, dressing skills, and communications skills. His reading and math scores were both below first-grade level. He was placed in a class for students with mental retardation and developmental delays. He was older than most of the students in that class and initiated rough play with them. He broke the arm of one student. He shouted at the teacher and refused to complete worksheets. He would not participate in circle time.

In January, he was placed in a class for students with behavior disorders. The class had five students including Logan and a teacher and a paraeducator. The students in the new class ranged in age from 7 to 15. Logan was not a behavior problem in this very structured setting. He soon began to learn some sight words. After 4 months, he could count to 20 and could write numbers to 10. He could write his first and last name. An IEP meeting was held to determine whether another placement should be considered for Logan. His foster parents did not want him to be moved. The teacher of his current class felt that he was witness to too much inappropriate behavior and had made enough academic progress to attempt some general education classes and some time in the class for students with developmental delays. The foster parents expressed that he was making so much progress that they wanted him to stay with the teacher he had and in the smaller class setting. He had plenty of appropriate socializations with friends and cousins at home.

1. Which placement do you consider most appropriate for Logan?

2. If you were Logan's teacher, what would be the area you would consider most important in his IEP?

Historically, mental retardation (MR) or intellectual disability has been conceptualized, defined, and diagnosed in a variety of ways by a number of professionals. Educators, medical personnel, vocational-rehabilitation professionals, psychologists, and others are actively involved in the treatment of individuals with mental retardation. Individuals with mental retardation come from all levels of society, racial groups, ethnic groups, and both genders. Some types of mental retardation are predominantly found in families who are socioeconomically disadvantaged and in those who receive little or no prenatal medical care. Some types are specific to males or females; others are pervasive.

Persons with retardation are able to make adequate degrees of adjustments to many life circumstances but, because of limited intellectual and adaptive capacities (NICHCY, 2004; Spruill, Oakland, & Harrison, 2005; Wehman, 1997), they are unable to make progress in all areas at the same rates as persons who are typically developing.

The level of instruction and level of support needed characterizes persons with mental retardation. This instruction or support is provided in homes, preschool settings, playgroups, community sites, general education classrooms, resource rooms, separate classes, separate schools, home and hospital school-type settings, sheltered workshops, and other specialized settings. The cause or type of disorder, the availability of training or instructional technology, and the availability of early intervention combine to determine ability levels. Many individuals with mental retardation have or can develop capabilities in some areas. Other individuals have pervasive disorders in many life areas that remain underdeveloped. However, mental retardation is not considered a "curable" or time-limited disability. The condition, by definition, continues throughout the person's lifetime (Luckasson et al., 2002; Taylor, Richards, & Brady, 2005; Westling & Fox, 2000).

The condition of mental retardation does not exist in a vacuum. Taylor et al. (2005) pointed out that socioeconomically disadvantaged individuals are overrepresented among the mildly retarded. Some cases of mental retardation may be conceptualized as a sociological phenomenon within society observed through the limited performance of some of the individuals in that society (Gold, 1980; Heward, 2006; Smith, 1997). Beirne-Smith, Ittenbach, and Patton (2002) took the concept of sociopolitical forces on the definition of mental retardation a step further. During times in our history when physical skills were vital for survival, persons with cognitive difficulties were not at a disadvantage. In the past few decades, academic skills of reading, writing, and math are seen as important for daily living. Persons who have difficulties with these skills are at a disadvantage.

The label mental retardation is considered by some to be a pejorative term, and many organizations have moved to using intellectual disability (Friend, 2005). According to The Presidents Committee on Intellectual Disabilities (2004), attitudes about people with disabilities has changed substantially. The name of the committee was changed in 2003 to reflect the new language of intellectual disability rather than mental retardation.

DEFINITIONS

Individuals with mental retardation have, by definition, limited intellectual development with concurrent deficits in adaptive skill areas (communication, self-care, home living, social skills, community use, self-direction, health and safety, functional academics, leisure) with an onset before the age of 18 years. A diagnosis of MR indicates nothing about causality, an individual's past, or future potential. Luckasson et al. (2002) stated that, given appropriate supports over the lifetime, the functioning of the person with mental retardation generally improves. Therefore, the label tells us only that the individual has substantial limitations in intellectual and adaptive development and ability at the present time. Persons identified as mentally retarded are often not learning the same things at the same rate as persons who are typically developing. However, many people with mental retardation learn in the same way as those who are typically developing, and their motor development follows the same sequence and pattern. The rate and extent of development varies. They have the same desires, anxieties, aspirations, and frustrations as anyone else, but they may not express those desires or articulate what they need adequately.

Often the conceptualization of mental retardation depends on the specialist defining it. For example, physicians may find some types of mental retardation due to a chemical imbalance or the inability of the body to assimilate and digest certain foods. Sociologists and developmental psychologists may feel that mental retardation is a reflection of a lack of stimulation, such as intervention provided early enough to counteract the effects of poor prenatal care, genetic disorders, or familial and environmental conditions. Thus, they consider it a symptom of inadequate social concern and an inadequacy of social structure. Educators may see it as a lack of adequate instruction or adequate learning. Employers may define it as a lack of flexibility in job roles. Family members may see it as a difference in learning to adjust to family roles and social norms.

The definition of persons with mental retardation has been a changing concept. In fact, the definition of mental retardation has been changed 10 times in the past 100 years. The concept of supports was added to the definition in 2002. Adaptive skill areas were emphasized in the definition in American Association on Mental Retardation [AAMR], 1992 (Luckasson et al., 2002). Earlier, levels of mental retardation were part of the definition. In the current reauthorization of IDEA (2004), the term mental retardation is retained. A new definition was not included. According to the law, mental retardation is

> . . . significantly subaverage general intellectual functioning, existing concurrently with deficits in adaptive behavior and manifested during the developmental period that adversely affects a child's educational performance. (IDEA amendments of 1997, P.L. 105-17, 11 stat 37 [20 U.S.C. 1401 9260] 34 C.F.R. 300.7 [c] [6])

The definition of mental retardation did not change in the 2004 reauthorization of IDEA. The American Association on Mental Retardation (Luckasson et al., 2002) provided the following definition for mental retardation:

> Mental retardation is a disability characterized by significant limitations both in intellectual functioning and in adaptive behavior as expressed in conceptual, social, and practical adaptive skills. This disability originates before age 18.

> Five Assumptions Essential to the Application of the Definition

> 1. Limitations in present functioning must be considered within the context of community environments typical of the individual's age peers and culture.
> 2. Valid assessment considers cultural and linguistic diversity as well as differences in communication, sensory, motor, and behavioral factors.
> 3. Within an individual, limitations often coexist with strengths.
> 4. An important purpose of describing limitations is to develop a profile of needed supports.
> 5. With appropriate personalized supports over a sustained period, the life functioning of the person with mental retardation generally will improve (Luckasson et al., 2002).

Intelligence

The concept of intelligence is hypothetical. We define **intelligence** by tests of observed performance based on the assumption that it takes more intelligence to perform some tasks than it does to perform others (Gold, 1980; Salvia & Ysseldyke, 2001; Taylor et al., 2005). There are many component processes or operations underlying performance on IQ tests (Fletcher, Blair, Scott, & Bolger, 2004; Nyborg, 2003). IQ scores are a generally good predictor or indicator of current performance in school tasks or daily life. Technically, an intelligence score refers to outcome scores of verbal and performance tasks. Verbal tasks include defining and comparing words, repeating sequences, mathematical exercises, and responding to questions. Performance tasks include puzzle piece arranging, sequencing story cards, and completing mazes. Significantly, subaverage general intellectual functioning is defined by one or more standardized intelligence tests and a person scoring at two or more standard deviations from the average or mean IQ score on these tests. The mean standard score (100) represents the average score of same-age students who have taken the intelligence test. Therefore, the score at the second standard deviation from the mean (100) would fall around or beyond the score of 68 to 70. State laws and regulations determine cutoff points for applying a label of mental retardation.

Adaptive Behavior

Adaptive behavior refers to actions of a person to manage various environments; for instance, to take care of personal needs, communicate with peers, engage in social activities, and to adapt to changing conditions. For a fair diagnosis of mental retardation, deficits or areas of limitation must exist in some adaptive skill areas, even though the individual may exhibit relative strengths in other skill areas. Areas of adaptive skills (conceptual, social, and practical) are considered essential to socially successful individuals who function independently without substantial support in effectively adapting to environmental demands (Baumeister & Baumeister, 2000; Bijou, 1966; Kirk, Gallagher, & Anastasiow, 2000). Preschool children are expected to grow and mature appropriately within their families. Youngsters are expected to learn academic skills and interact socially with peers, forming stable, meaningful relationships. Adults are expected to be gainfully employed, pay taxes, get along in the community, and form long-lasting emotional bonds. Adaptive behavior refers to the individual's ability to respond to the demands of the total social environment. The 2002 definition from AAMR reflects the notion of context when considering the functioning of a person with mental retardation (Luckasson et al., 2002). A person may need supports in the context of an academic setting but have no need in social or community settings. In such cases, the label of mental retardation may not be appropriate in all situations.

Adaptive behavior is often difficult to assess directly (Cuskelly, 2004). Family members, teachers, friends, and others who are well acquainted with the person suspected of being mentally retarded usually fill out checklists of skill areas and individual skills, listing or identifying those that are completed easily and those that are difficult for the person. The lists are then compared with the performance of age or grade peers to determine the relative position of an individual within the general population (Beail, 2003; Harrison & Oakland, 2000; McLoughlin & Lewis, 2000).

Age of Onset

AAMR defines the age of onset for mental retardation as prior to age 18, because it is at this age that people in our society are legally expected to carry out the responsibilities of adult behavior. The condition or disability of mental retardation is manifested during the developmental period but usually (especially with mild mental retardation) is initially identified when the student shows academic deficits (Hallahan & Kauffman, 2006). It is generally identified in early elementary school unless there is a reason for the condition to be known at birth.

Some experts believe that the occurrence of mild mental retardation may not be a stable condition and that, given appropriate assistance, performance of individuals with mild mental retardation will improve (Hallahan & Kauffman, 2006; Smith, 1997). Mild mental retardation may be a description of present functioning rather than prediction of future capacity. Because any individual's functioning will vary depending on circumstance, age, or task, a person with intellectual limitations may (at least in theory) move in and out of the categorization of low functioning. When students who are **at risk,** or have a higher than usual chance of developing an impairment, disability, problem, or deficiency, receive enriching early education programs, they can often escape a diagnosis of mild mental retardation. Because we live in socially and otherwise demanding environments, limitations are often an outcome of environmental mismatches, meaning the demands of the environment exceed the current capabilities of the individual. Thus, competency of individuals may be determined by their experiences in certain environments and their abilities to meet environmental demands (Hardman, Drew, & Egan, 2006; McClimens, 2003; McLoughlin & Lewis, 2000).

PREVALENCE

The Twenty-Fifth Annual Report to Congress on the Implementation of IDEA (U.S. Department of Education, 2005) identified 607,291 school-age students as having mental retardation, with an additional 45,128 identified as having a developmental delay. However, the lack of professional agreement about the definition of mental retardation, data collection and reporting problems, sociocultural and socioeconomic issues, and state regulations all cause difficulties in estimating the number of school-age students who are mentally retarded. Historically, it has been estimated that 3 percent of the general population (approximately 7 million people) could be considered mentally retarded (NICHCY, 2004). State education officials report varying estimated figures closer to 4 percent of the population. In addition, mental retardation is a coexisting factor in approximately 13 percent of all students with disabilities. A large majority of persons classified as mentally retarded are mildly retarded. In the late 20th century, the trend tended toward decreasing numbers of students with mild mental retardation. This was linked with an increase in the number of school-age students identified as LD which was seen as a more socially acceptable diagnosis. Conversely, those from poor families, especially minority families, reveal a rising trend for becoming identified as mentally retarded.

Several problems influence prevalence figures, such as bias in testing, prejudice in placement, and litigation (Croen, Grether, & Hoogstrate, 2002; Smith, 2001; Smith, Dowdy, Polloway, Patton, & Blalock, 1997). Because most of the students fall in the mild range of mental retardation, identified primarily as a result of poor academic performance, there is a higher incidence of identified mental retardation during the school-age years and a lower identified incidence during the preschool years. For students ages 6 through 11, the third largest disability category is mental retardation, following learning disabilities and speech and language disorders. For students in the 12 through 17 and 18 through 21 year age groups, mental retardation was the second largest disability category. The category of specific learning disabilities is the largest.

CHARACTERISTICS
General Cognition

Aside from being labeled as cognitively different or mentally retarded, individuals with mental retardation have little more in common with each other than do people without retardation. Persons with mental retardation vary physically and emotionally, as well as by personality, disposition, and beliefs. However, despite the diversity of the groups who compose the population of persons with mental retardation, there are some common characteristics. Their apparent slowness in learning may be related to the delayed rate of intellectual development (Wehman, 1997). For instance, adults with mental retardation may not learn certain skills or concepts efficiently and as a result tend to perform more poorly than comparative normal groups. Yet when they attend to appropriate aspects of presented learning stimuli versus inappropriate aspects, their rate and amount of learning can be acceptable (Vakil, Shelef-Reshef, & Levy-Shiff, 1997; Wehman, 1997; Werts, Wolery, Gast, & Holcombe, 1996).

Learning is dependent on intellectual development (although not necessarily intellectual levels). Intellectual development, in turn, determines the complexity and level of learning that can take place at any specific time. In comparing the learning ability of two groups of students at the same intellectual developmental level, and assuming the same degree of readiness to learn in terms of background experiences, attitudes, desires, quality of instruction, and similar factors, one would expect that they would learn a skill or concept in the same period of time. If specific educational supports are implemented, some research indicates students with mental retardation may achieve at the same rates but overall remain behind their peers (Vakil et al., 1997; Wehman, 1997).

The score on an IQ test is less important in determining the general **cognition,** or ability and facility in obtaining information, of a person with mental retardation than the types and amount of support needed to function at specified tasks or levels (Hourcade, 2002). A person may need intermittent support with tasks of daily living. At this level, the need would be episodic.

Attention

To acquire information, students must attend to the learning task for the required length of time and control distractions. Students with mental retardation may have difficulty distinguishing and attending to relevant questions in both learning and social situations (Saunders, 2001). The problem is not that the student will not pay attention, but rather that the student does not understand or does not filter the information to get to the salient features (Hunt & Marshall, 2002; Meyen & Skrtic, 1988). A related problem is that some students with mental retardation may have difficulty shifting their attention to new material. Task analysis, a process in which a task is broken down into component steps and those components are taught separately and then joined into a sequence, can be successfully used to assist a person to perform tasks that involve more than one step (Lifshitz, 1999; Xin & Holmdal, 2003).

Memory

Students with mental retardation may have problems with either long- or short-term memory or rehearsal processes necessary for placing information in memory. The more severe the retardation, the greater the memory deficit may be. Students may not spontaneously use appropriate learning or memory retention strategies and may have difficulty in realizing the conditions or actions that aid learning and memory. However, these strategies can be taught (Fletcher, Huffman, & Bray, 2003; Hunt & Marshall, 2002; Werts, Wolery, Holcombe, & Gast, 1995; Wolery & Schuster, 1997). Students with mental retardation have trouble recognizing recurring patterns or repetitions and are slower to transfer information to short-term memory and from short-term memory to long-term memory.

Language

Individuals with mental retardation (depending on the degree of retardation) may have language comprehension and formulation difficulties. They experience delayed language development and often exhibit less fluent and less articulate speech than their peers. Individuals with mild mental retardation may exhibit few and minor difficulties, whereas some individuals with severe mental retardation may have severely limited language skills. Other language deficits may be seen in expressive and receptive language, conversational skills, giving or receiving directions, determining central or essential issues, and telling stories (Meyen & Skrtic 1988; Turnbull, Turnbull, Shank, & Smith, 2004). Individuals with mental retardation also may show delayed functioning on pragmatic aspects of language, such as turn taking, selecting acceptable topics for conversation, knowing when to speak, knowing when to be silent, and similar contextual skills (Haring, McCormick, & Haring, 1994; Yoder, Retish, & Wade, 1996). However, as noted with other tasks, specific instruction may improve the student's functioning (Facon, Facon-Bollengier, & Grubar, 2002; Levy, Tennenbaum, & Ornoy, 2003; Tekin-Iftar, Acar, & Kurt, 2003; Yoder & Warren, 2002).

Academic Achievement

The cognitive inefficiencies of students with mild to moderate mental retardation lead to persistent problems in academic achievement (Hughes et al., 2002; Macmillan, Siperstein, & Gresham, 1996; Quenemoen, Thompson, & Thurlow, 2003; Turnbull et al., 2004). Students with mild and moderate mental retardation may lag behind their typically developing age peers academically. Instructional strategies such as peer instruction (Greenwood et al., 1992; Greenwood, Delquadri, & Carta, 1997; Wolery, Werts, Snyder, & Caldwell, 1994), modeling, demonstrations, and active engagement (Heward, 2006) can enable the student to learn from instruction in the classroom and offer an opportunity to interact socially as well. The specific training of skills that most people acquire without training, along with supports and resources in classrooms, can be of significant assistance in the education of students with MR and in their successful transition to adulthood (Wehmeyer, Lance, & Bashinski, 2002)

Metacognition

Depending on the degree of retardation, some individuals with mental retardation have difficulties in metacognitive skills, including planning how to solve a problem, monitoring the solution strategy, proceeding with the strategy implementation, and evaluating the outcome. The lack or underdevelopment of these skills notably affects memory, rehearsal skills, organizational ability, and being in control of the process of learning (Erez & Peled, 2001; Hunt & Marshall, 2002)

Motivation

Individuals with mental retardation may approach the learning situation with significant anxiety. Past experiences of failure and the anxiety generated by those failures may make them appear to be less goal/task directed and lacking in motivation. They may have learned to avoid failure. This avoidance, teamed with limited metacognitive skills, results in helplessness in the engagement for learning. They or others may limit their goals and aspirations, and they may become dependent (Utley, Hoehn, Soraci, & Baumeister, 1993; Weisz, 1999). The history of failure is likely to lead to dependence on external sources of reinforcement or reward rather than on internal sources of reward. They are less likely to be self-starters motivated by self-approval (Beirne-Smith et al., 2002; Taylor et al., 2005).

Physical Characteristics

Some persons with mental retardation will appear to the public to have no differences at all. Others, with differing biological etiologies, may exhibit coexisting problems, such as physical, motor, orthopedic, visual and auditory impairments, and health problems (Hallahan & Kauffman, 2006). Individuals with mild mental retardation may be below their typically developing age peers in measures of height, weight, and skeletal maturity. Some students with mental retardation may also have cerebral palsy, convulsive disorders, and sensory impairments. As noted earlier in this chapter, many persons with other disabilities also have cognitive deficits. They may be more susceptible than their peers to disease, illness, and dental problems. However, some students with mental retardation can participate in sports and physical education activities and keep up with other students, and some may even excel in certain sports (Colacello, 2001; Daughtrey, Gillentine, & Hunt, 2002; Haring et al., 1994; Hallahan & Kauffman, 2006; Vanderslice, 2002; Weiss, Diamond, & Demark, 2003).

Labels

In the past, the terms mild retardation, moderate retardation, severe retardation, and profound retardation were used to characterize the extent of a person's intellectual capabilities and adaptive skills. Mild mental retardation referred to the highest level of performance or functioning, and profound mental retardation referred to the lowest level of performance. Corresponding numerical IQ scores were associated with each category, with all scores falling two standard deviations below the mean on a bell curve. School systems typically still use these categories: mild mental retardation (IQ of approximately 50 to 70), moderate mental retardation (IQ of approximately 35 to 50), severe mental retardation (IQ of approximately 20 to 35), and profound mental retardation (IQ scores below 20; Hallahan & Kauffman, 2006). These scores reflect the most commonly used measure of intellectual functioning as an IQ score of 70, two standard deviations below the mean of 100 used by the standard IQ tests. Allowing for measurement error, AAMR recommends a higher ceiling of about 75. The Social Security Administration defines mental retardation as lower intellectual functioning along with deficits in adaptive functioning, demonstrated before the age of 22, to qualify for disability benefits for intellectual impairment. If the student's full-scale IQ score is below 60, however, the individual qualifies for benefits regardless of scores on measures of adaptive functioning.

Another difficulty with reliance on IQ scores is a difficulty with IQ tests. Since IQ tests were introduced early last century, there has been a steady rise in IQ scores, necessitating a need to restandardize the tests. This occurs periodically. For instance, the Wechsler Intelligence Scales for Children (WISC) was first introduced in 1949 and restandardized in 1974, 1991, and 2003. The phenomenon of rising scores is called the Flynn Effect and is well documented for those who score in the average ranges of the test (within one standard deviation from the mean). Less is documented in the lower ranges (those that lead to a label of mental retardation); however, scoring in the range that would qualify for a diagnosis of mental retardation might depend heavily on the IQ test norms being used the year an individual is tested (Flynn, 2000). The implication of this effect on the policies of the nation, specifically for our purposes the policies in the schools, is staggering (Kanaya, Scullin, & Ceci, 2003).

Currently, levels of mental retardation are described by the levels of support needed. Supports are resources that are intended to promote the functions as well as the development and improvement of the person. Supports can be natural, given by those naturally in the environment (e.g., family, friends), or service based, given by professionals (e.g., teachers, job coaches). Four levels are described. Intermittent supports are those needed on a one-time or as-needed basis, such as assistance in job searches, that may be intense but are short lived. Limited supports are those needed consistently over time, such as employment training. Extensive supports include those needed regularly in at least some environments, such as support in home living. Pervasive supports are those needed constantly and across environments. These are usually needed for safety and well-being. The supports are usually needed from professionals and are intrusive on life activities.

ETIOLOGY

It is nearly an impossible task to identify each cause of each case of mental retardation. There may be more than 1,000 known causes of mental retardation. It is not always clear which causes apply to a particular individual. In addition, mental retardation is rarely the result of a single cause, but is more often the result of complex interactions among multiple causes (Taylor et al., 2005; Turnbull et al., 2004). AAMR (1992) classified the causes of mental retardation into three groups.

1. Prenatal causes include errors of maternal metabolism, chromosomal damage or defects, developmental brain disorders, maternal diet, and environmental influences.
2. Perinatal causes include neonatal disorders, birth injuries, and low birth weight.
3. Postnatal causes include child abuse, neglect, accidents, injection, and exposure to toxins.

Injuries may occur to the child at any time during pregnancy, during the birthing process, and during development and can result in cognitive difficulties.

Prenatal Causes

Infection and Intoxication

Infections contracted during pregnancy can cause mental retardation. Infections such as rubella, syphilis, meningitis, AIDS (HIV), and toxoplasmosis (blood poisoning) can all have negative effects on fetal development. Drug usage during pregnancy—including legal prescriptive and nonprescriptive drugs such as alcohol and tobacco; illegal substances such as LSD, heroin, morphine, cocaine; and metals such as lead—can cause mental retardation. Chronic maternal illnesses such as diabetes, kidney disease, thyroid deficiency, and hypertension may affect the nutritional environment of the fetus or cause premature delivery and accompanying mental retardation (Hallahan & Kauffman, 2006; Hunt & Marshall, 2002; Taylor, Richards, & Brady, 2005). Blood type Rh incompatibility between fetus and mother in pregnancies after the first birth may also cause maternal antibodies to damage the fetus. Gestational maternal illnesses such as high fevers, measles, and others may cause difficulties as well.

Fetal alcohol syndrome and fetal alcohol effects can also be a concern. These refer to damage to the fetus resulting from maternal or paternal alcohol consumption. The newborn may show facial anomalies, heart problems, low birth weight, and eventually mental retardation (Hardman et al., 2006). Inadequate maternal nutrition may also be a causal factor. The fetus may not be able to draw enough nutrients from the mother's poor diet.

Chromosomal Abnormalities

Chromosomal abnormalities are defective cell division such as missing parts, translocations (sections that have moved), or fragmentation of chromosomes. These differences in chromosomal material may result in differences in the individual. Death may be one result. Down's syndrome, a genetic disorder, occurs when there are 47 chromosomes instead of the normal 46. It routinely leads to mental retardation and a variety of other health problems. The presence of Down's syndrome may be related to maternal age, with the incidence increasing in children born to mothers aged 35 and older. It can also be caused by a chromosomal abnormality called translocation. The person may have 46 chromosomes, but one pair breaks, and the broken part fuses to another chromosome. Persons with Down's syndrome have facial features marked by distinctive epicanthic folds, prominent cheekbones, and a small, somewhat flattened nose (Kirk et al., 2000; Turnbull et al., 2004). They generally have a short stature and barrel chest and frequently have syndactyly of fingers or toes.

Fragile X syndrome is now considered the most frequent known inherited cause of mental retardation and developmental disability. It is a single-gene disorder on the X chromosome (Hagerman & Cronister, 1996). The syndrome affects development (including development of cognitive functions), patterns of behavior, and physical features (Abbeduto & Hagerman, 1997; Bailey, Aytch, Odom, Symons, & Wolery, 1999; Bailey, Hatton, & Skinner, 1998; Hatton, Wheeler, & Skinner, 2003). Males, if affected, have more severe symptoms than females.

Phenylketonuric disorder (PKU) is another example of a genetic defect that can produce severe retardation. In PKU, the absence of a specific enzyme in the liver leads to a buildup of the amino acid phenylalanine. The effects of PKU, when detected, can be controlled by modifying early infant nutritional intake, especially milk (Hardman et al., 2006).

Unknown Prenatal Influences

Unkown prenatal influences may cause mental retardation. For example, the causes of hydrocephalus and microcephaly are not fully understood. Yet, if untreated, both will result in multiple disorders, including mental retardation. Hydrocephalus is the presence of slow-draining cerebrospinal fluid in the skull, which increases the size of the skull and causes pressure on the brain. Microcephaly is a condition in which the skull is significantly smaller than normal, which will also destroy brain tissue (Taylor et al., 2005).

Perinatal Causes

Anoxia and asphyxia (deprivation of sufficient oxygen at birth), umbilical cord accidents, head trauma, mix of incompatible blood types, infections, radiation, and other unforeseen factors may happen during birth and cause mental retardation. Gestational disorders such as prematurity and low birth weight are risk factors for mental retardation. The more extreme these conditions, the higher the level of risk (Hunt & Marshall, 2002). Low-birth-weight babies are 25 percent more likely to have cerebral palsy and 50 percent more likely to be in special education classes (Ball, 1999). Currently, the advances in knowledge and abilities of medical personnel allow more infants with birth difficulties to survive. Although medical and other advances have made strides in preventing mental retardation some infants will have difficulties that result in mental retardation.

Postnatal Causes

Youngsters who have suffered abuse can show reduced response rates and may have lower IQs, although the reasons for the link are not clear. The result is not from brain damage but may be from frustration, a disruption of language development, or the association of failure with punishment (Smith, 2001). Many parents with mental retardation do not understand the needs of infants and toddlers and therefore are not able to deliver the care needed. Other parents, due to poverty or problems of their own, are not ensuring good medical care and nutrition. These situations often lead to delayed and retarded development (Feldman & Walton-Allen, 1997). Accidents may or may not be related to neglect, but if the onset of **brain injury,** or a physical injury or damage to the brain that impedes normal development, is before the age of 18, the condition may be termed either mental retardation or traumatic brain disorder.

Environmental or Psychosocial Disadvantage

Students with mild mental retardation make up a majority of all identified cases. Within this group, etiology is mostly unknown. There is a strong belief that psychosocial disadvantage, the combination of a poor social and cultural environment early in life, may contribute significantly to this population. Professionals must be careful to distinguish between social and cultural deprivation and social and cultural difference. There does not appear to be any intrinsic value that makes one rich cultural experience more valid than another. Instead, it is the absence of experiences rather than the type of experiences that appears to be critical. Findings from studies consistently reveal that a large percentage of cases of mild mental retardation are caused by environmental issues, most notably deprivation in the early years of life. Poverty and social disorganization in the home environment increase health risks and contribute to early and progressive language deficits and variety of cognitive problems. Families at the poverty level may also have lower expectations for academic or school achievement. They often are unable to prepare students for school, receive poor health care, and experience poor nutrition. Some reject dominant cultural values supporting school achievement (Greenwood, Hart, Walker, & Risley, 1994; McDermott, 1994; Ramey & Finkelstein, 1981).

Gross Brain Disease

Gross brain disease conditions include disorders such as neurofibromatosis (tumors in the skin, peripheral to nerve tissue and the brain). Tuberous sclerosis is characterized by the growth of tumors in the **central nervous system (CNS),** the brain or spinal cord, and the degeneration of cerebral white matter (Hardman et al., 2006). Mental retardation is often a concomitant condition with both of these disorders.

Psychiatric Disorders

The Diagnostic and Statistical Manual of Mental Disorders (American Psychiatric Association, 2000) characterizes mental disorders as behavioral or psychological syndromes that currently affect a person's functioning at many times (Brown, Aman, & Lecavalier, 2004). At any given time, mental illness can depress intellectual functioning. A diagnosis of mental retardation would be false if the cause is known to be from an identifiable psychiatric condition.

IDENTIFICATION PROCESS

Several types of assessment are needed for students to be labeled as mentally retarded. **Assessment** is a process for determining a student's strengths and weaknesses. It involves screening, diagnosis, classification, placement, and monitoring. By law, a student may not be labeled on the basis of one test, and the AAMR requires information about intellectual functioning, adaptive behavior, and levels of support needed. Therefore, assessment procedures should include, at a minimum, observations of behavior from teachers, family members, and others involved in the circles of support, the results of standardized achievement tests, and results from valid and reliable tests of cognitive functioning. Other assessment approaches are encouraged, such as curriculum-based assessments, interviewing, and sociometric ratings (Hessels-Schlatter, 2002; Hunt & Marshall, 2002; Kirk et al., 2000; Quenemoen et al., 2003; Taylor et al., 2005).

Intelligence Testing

Cognitive functioning is measured by standardized intelligence tests, which usually consist of a series of questions and problem-solving tasks assumed to require certain amounts of intelligence to answer or solve correctly. Because the test sample limited skills and abilities, the outcome score is only a representation of overall intelligence. The IQ is based on the relationship between the individual's chronological age (CA) and mental age (MA). These tests are standardized, which means that they use the same questions and tasks, always presented in the same way, and are scored using the same procedures each time the test is given. A concern is that many IQ tests are culturally biased, favoring white middle-class students by examining prior learning that only a white middle-class student is likely to experience.

Most of the time, IQ scores do not change significantly. However, the scores are neither static nor stable, and for students who are mildly retarded, IQ scores can be influenced by experience. Scores in the 70–85 range can change as much as 20 points after a period of significant instruction. Intelligence testing outcomes can be influenced by motivation, time, location of the test site, testing administrators, and testing procedures (Anastasi, 1988; Hallahan & Kauffman, 2006; Heward, 2006; McLoughlin & Lewis, 2000). Intelligence tests are imperfect instruments, imperfectly understood, that are used as a part of the process for classification purposes, assignment of labels, and placement in special programs. They are sometimes of questionable validity because generally no more than 50 percent of academic achievement is associated with intelligence. The remainder of individual difference is presumably determined by the student's motivation, work habits, experience in taking tests, and cultural and other experiences. Intelligence tests are heavily weighted toward

language skills, and the performance portions of the tests require a ready under-standing of verbal instructions. Students who speak nonstandard English or are not facile in standard English will probably do poorly on these tests.

Despite these limitations, intelligence tests, when used appropriately, can be highly useful when making special education eligibility and entitlement decisions. They are useful also for predicting future academic success.

The Stanford-Binet Intelligence Scale (SB5)

The fifth edition of the *Stanford-Binet Intelligence Scales (SB5)* covers five factors—Fluid Reasoning, Knowledge, Quantitative Reasoning, Visual-Spatial Processing, and Working Memory. Further, professionals are able to compare relative capabilities in verbal and nonverbal performance (Roid, 2003). A version for younger students (ages 2.0 to 7.3 years) is available. The early SB5 includes a Test Observation checklist and software-generated Parent Report with the subtests from the SB5.

The Revised Wechsler Intelligence Scale for Children (WISC–IV)

WISC–IV (Wechsler, 2003) has 16 subtests. Twelve subtests measure verbal compre-hension, perceptual reasoning, working memory, and processing speed. Supplemen-tal subtests are available for each category. Results from the subtests can be calculated as a Full-Scale IQ (FSIQ) score or as a General Ability Index (GAI), which is a sum-mary score that is less sensitive to the influence of working memory and processing speed. Because difficulties with working memory and processing speed may result in lower FSIQ scores (Wechsler, 2003), a rating with a GAI may be more informative and representative of abilities than an FSIQ (Raiford, Weiss, Rolfhus, & Coalson, 2005).

The Kaufman Assessment Battery for Children (K–ABC–II)

This alternative test measures intelligence as manifested by information-processing abilities (Kaufman & Kaufman, 2004): The resulting scores are stated as a global scale and as subscales of mental processing, fluid-crystallized knowledge, and a non-verbal index. It is now normalized for students aged 3 to 18.

Adaptive Functioning Assessment

A measurement of adaptive functioning is required for the identification of mental re-tardation. A student cannot be considered mentally retarded unless there are deficits in the effectiveness or degree to which the individual meets societal standards of per-sonal independence and social responsibility expected of his or her age and social group (Sandler & Hatt, 2004). Adaptive behavior refers to how a person meets or fails to meet the challenges and requirements of daily living and the extent to which that per-son can function and interact with others in the environment. Adaptive behavior mea-sures do not consider the quality of a person's home life, the level of poverty, or the experiences to which the student has been exposed. They do not consider whether the student can reason or perform certain tasks at school, at home, or in an assessment situation. The items on these measures involve tasks requiring students to feed them-selves, dress themselves, get on a bus, or go to the store and buy a hamburger.

Adaptive behavior measures are essential in identifying mild mental retardation and avoiding the misdiagnosis and misplacement of students with problems other than retardation. Adaptive behavior is also a measure of how well students adapt to school as well as to the environment outside of school. Macmillan et al. (1996) made the point that mild mental retardation can be understood only in terms of cognitive inefficiencies and the environmental demands for problem solving. Mild mental retardation is highly contextual and relative to the environment; people with retardation may not appear retarded in certain settings.

It is difficult to measure adaptive behavior directly. If a task is difficult or not in a student's repertoire, it will not be observable. Therefore, checklists of selected behaviors are used. Two scales have emerged as the dominant means of measuring adaptive behaviors, the American Association on Mental Deficiency Adaptive Behavior Scale (Nihira, Foster, Shellhaas, & Leland, 1974) and the Vineland Social Maturity Scale (Doll, 1947; Sparrow, Cucchetti, & Balla, 2005). The norms have been updated, but the checklists continue to reflect the same major domains of functioning: communication, daily living, socialization, and motor skills. These two scales have been developed to assist in better identifying specific skills that allow the person to cope with their environment (Matson, Dixon, Matson, & Logan, 2005).

The Vineland Adaptive Behavior Scale

This checklist relies on questions related to age-appropriate self-help, locomotion, communication, occupation, socialization, and self-direction skills. It also attempts to measure social competence (deBildt, Kraijer, Sytema, & Minderaa, 2005; Sparrow, Balla, & Cucchetti, 2005). There are three versions: a survey interview form, an expanded interview form, and a classroom edition. Information is gathered from the student, family members, teachers, related service personnel, siblings, and others involved with the student.

The Adaptive Behavior Scale–Public School Version (ABS–PS)

This highly regarded and widely used scale is an outgrowth of a project begun in 1965 by Parsons State Hospital and AAMR to develop a measure of adaptive behavior that could be used to help plan programs for patients with disabilities (Debell, 1980). Lambert revised this instrument in 1974 in order to use it with public school students, and it was further revised in 1993 (Lambert, Nihira, & Leland, 1993). Most of the 21 ABS domains have low-to-moderate correlations with IQ test performances, indicating the items are measuring different areas. They load onto five factors: personal self-sufficiency, community self-sufficiency, personal-social responsibility, social adjustment, and personal adjustment.

The adaptive behavior scales are important instruments used in the identification and placement of students with mental retardation. These measures indicate how the student functions outside the school environment. The examiner can determine whether low intelligence and achievement scores are indeed an indication of mild mental retardation or are just reflective of academic problems of origins other than intelligence.

PROGRAMS
Educational Services

The special education movement has emphasized the need for students with special needs to be fully or partially included in regular education classrooms and programs to the extent appropriate. These full and partial inclusion efforts encompass most students with mental retardation, especially the higher functioning students. Special educators collaborate and cooperate with general education teachers to integrate students with mental retardation into the general education classrooms and provide activities for both educational and social opportunities with normal peers while continuing individualized programs. Students with mental retardation participate in all classroom and extracurricular activities with their typically developing peers (Smith, 2001; Vallecorsa, DeBettencourt, & Zigmond, 2000).

Traditionally, services for students with mental retardation have been offered in regular classrooms, special education resource rooms, self-contained classes, special schools, and hospital or institutional settings. There have been great efforts in the past three or more decades to provide community-based services for all students with mental retardation and to reduce the institutionalized population. Deinstitutional programs have resulted in an increase in community-based programs and smaller locally based programs. Emphasis is placed on teaching the mentally retarded, to the extent to which they can learn, the functional and academic skills needed and used in everyday life. Emphasis is on the transition from school to community living skills programs for adulthood and especially on employment and socialization.

Services for students with mental retardation begin with early intervention programs that focus on providing guidance for families and a direct focus on the infant's acquisition of sensory-motor skills. Early intervention programs also provide family members with stimulation techniques that might facilitate intellectual development. Preschool programs, such as Head Start programs for students with mental retardation and economic disadvantages, focus on school readiness and socialization activities. General education classroom programs for students with mild and moderate retardation provide individualized academic and other functional programs and interaction with nondisabled peers. Resource room programs are provided for some students while they attend a special services program part of the day for remedial help. In self-contained classroom programs, students in need of more academic support are in a segregated classroom for most of the day. Their programs focus on age-appropriate but also developmentally appropriate skills.

In resource rooms and self-contained special education classrooms, which are generally placements for lower functioning students who function in the mild to moderate range, the curriculum is organized within the framework of persisting life problems, such as behaving in and managing the home and family, using leisure time, managing money, understanding health and safety issues, and traveling. These life situations are crucial at all age levels and directly involve the individual with their environment. The curriculum can be organized around the behaviors and information needed for adequate functioning within the context of life problems. The curriculum can also accommodate traditional academic subject matter areas, such as reading, math, science, health, and other school subjects, to facilitate functioning in society. In this setting the teacher must be responsive to the following concerns:

1. The teacher must have a good grasp of each student's abilities in each domain area so lessons can build on a student's background knowledge.
2. The teacher must structure the learning situation and reduce distractions.
3. The teacher must present material clearly, sequentially, and with positive reinforcement for correct responses.
4. When the student has an incorrect response, the teacher should encourage the student and reevaluate whether he or she has overestimated the student's ability, whether parts of the lesson were confusing, or whether the student is not ready to engage in that particular learning situation and needs more preparation.

Other teaching strategies are listed in Box 3.1.

BOX 3.1
WHAT EVERY TEACHER SHOULD DO
Effective Teaching Strategies

- Students with mental retardation respond to many of the same instructional strategies as students without labels. Frequently they may need more time or more trials than other students to achieve mastery.
- The focus of the curriculum for students with mental retardation should be on functional tasks. The IEP team must make decisions on what will be functional for each student. For instance, functional reading may include signs for one student and sections of a newspaper for another.
- Another focus of the curriculum should be developmentally appropriate tasks. The student should learn tasks and information that are important to his or her developmental level.
- Teachers should provide opportunities for students to practice and to achieve supervised success with tasks before they have independent practice.
- Teachers should provide supportive and corrective feedback as often as possible, especially in the early stages of acquisition of a behavior.
- Teachers should reinforce the processes of the desired tasks rather than just the products.
- Teaching the tasks and behaviors in the setting where they will be used as much as possible can be very helpful; for instance, teachers could teach menu reading in a restaurant, zipping while dressing to go outside, and how to make change in a store.
- Teachers should use task analysis when the task to be taught is complex. The component parts may be taught independently and then taught as a sequence.
- Proximity of an adult to the student has been shown to be an effective management tool to keep the student on task (Werts, Zigmond, & Leeper, 2001). Being close to the student can also allow the teacher to provide more opportunities to respond and more praise.
- Teachers should arrange the lesson and the prompts for responses so the student will respond correctly a majority of the time. More praise will lead to continued success.

In all this, the planning of individualized curriculum and instruction for students with mental retardation considers readiness, motivation, and performance evaluation (Goldstein, 1966; Hunt & Marshall, 2002; Wolery, Ault, & Doyle, 1992; Wolery & Wilbers, 1995). There are many assistive technology devices and methods available to teachers of students with intellectual disabilities. A few examples are listed in Box 3.2.

Inclusion Programs

Inclusion is the practice of educating students with disabilities in general education classrooms in which they would be placed if they did not have a disability. Advocates of full inclusion, defined as spending all time in school in the general education classroom with appropriate aids and services, hold that fragmentation of services for students with

BOX 3.2
WHAT EVERY TEACHER NEEDS TO KNOW ABOUT TECHNOLOGY.

- To facilitate zipping coats, attach a key ring or chain or small toy to the existing tab, using a ribbon or nylon string loop. Replace existing zippers with larger ones.
- Shoes that tie can be laced with corded elastic so that the shoe does not need to be untied each time it is taken off and put on. The elastic will stretch to accommodate the student's foot.
- Full featured keyboards with keys 4 times bigger than the traditional keyboard are manufactured with multi-colored or white keys. The multi-colored key layout lets users take advantage of computer learning programs and become visually acquainted with the letter arrangement on a standard keyboard.
- Bump and go toys can teach cause and effect. Flashing lights and sirens can reinforce that actions happen when a switch is activated.
- Communication aids are booklets or tablets organized by topic. The student can select a topic and then select people, or objects, or places to talk about. These aids can be used as conversation starters or as a total conversation if the student lacks intelligible speech.

special needs and segregated classrooms often cause students with disabilities to experience loss of self-esteem, feelings of stigmatization, and negative attitudes about school. The current educational thrust is for general educators to take more responsibility for the instruction of students with retardation and other disabilities, while receiving appropriate support systems (Cross, Traub, & Hutter-Pishgahi, L., & Shelton, G. 2004; Henley, Ramsey, & Algozzine, 2002). Special classes, separate schools, and other restrictive environments for students with special needs should be used only when the nature or severity of the disability is such that education in the general class cannot be achieved satisfactorily. The increased effort to include some students with mild and moderate retardation is the result of the realization that partial inclusion and resource or self-contained classroom programs do not meet the needs of some students, for instance, students with retardation who have socialization as a major goal. Special education teachers, general education teachers, service providers, and family members should collaborate on multidisciplinary teams to plan programs for the educational and socialization needs of these students. In fact, these teams met infrequently to review test results, placement options, and other administrative concerns but not programming issues. This created a breakdown in communication and reduced chances for effective programming for students (Nowacek, 1992).

A current belief, among some educators, is that students with mild mental retardation may best be served in inclusion programs that use a functional curriculum and academics, where they can develop the skills necessary to make a successful transition from school to adult responsibilities, including personal/social, daily living, and occupational adjustment skills. If students with mental retardation are to be successfully integrated into general educational settings, they will need to acquire classroom-related survival skills and behaviors, develop appropriate social skills, and participate in cooperative ventures with nondisabled peers. Then, they can be perceived as performing reasonably well (Patton, Beirne-Smith, & Payne, 1990). For example, while the class is working on addition of two-digit numbers, a student with mental retardation could use manipulatives to add single digits; while the class is taking a written spelling test, the student with mental retardation could match written words to pictures or arrange letters to match the written words. Similarly, while the class is working on Fahrenheit and centigrade temperatures, the student with mental retardation could work on the concepts of hot and cold. More drastic curriculum change may be necessary for students with differing needs. A student who needs continued help in self-care skills, such as dressing and traveling independently, will need time to develop and practice such basic behaviors under guidance. Other educators cite a lack of evidence that inclusive programs have had a positive effect on students with cognitive differences (Fuchs & Fuchs, 1994; Kavale & Mostert, 2003).

Davis (1994) reported that the Association for Retarded Citizens (The Arc) encourages efforts for the inclusion of youngsters with mental retardation. The Arc position is as follows:

1. All students have value and should be included in all aspects of school life.
2. Students can best develop life skills in educational settings designed to meet their individual needs with peers of various abilities and backgrounds.
3. Students should be educated with nondisabled peers in an age-appropriate setting.
4. Students have the right to an individualized education that addresses their strengths and needs and provides options and appropriate resources for support.

There is also a need to identify programs that successfully include students with retardation and to examine the components of these programs. Early studies indicated that peers who were typically developing did not accept socially students with cognitive differences, whether the students with retardation were in the regular classroom or the special education classroom (Kirk & Gallagher, 1986). Other studies (Kennedy & Itkonen, 1994) indicated that older students were well accepted if they were perceived as "nice" people. If they were not, they were not well accepted. This follows the social pattern that is prevalent for students who are typically developing.

Individualized Education Programs (IEPs)

All students who receive special education services, including students identified as mentally retarded, must have an IEP to detail the services they will receive, who is to deliver them, and how much time is to be spent in special programming and how much time in general education programming. This IEP is the result of the collaborative efforts of a team composed of family members, general and special education teachers, the student, and any specialists that will be involved in service provision. The IEP details the student's needs and specifically describes how the school system will meet them. According to IDEA (2004), the IEP team meets regularly and modifies the program as the needs of the student change. One member of the team, usually the special education teacher, is responsible for monitoring the implementation of the IEP and periodically ascertaining from all persons involved whether the program is effective.

Behavioral Therapy Programs

In public and other schools, behavior modification is used to decrease disruptive and inappropriate behavior, help the student attend to learning tasks, maintain attention, and shape new learning behaviors by reinforcing appropriate behavior. Training procedures incorporating the use of behavioral analytic techniques facilitate the cognitive process. This is especially effective when adults model the performance of a task for a student who repeats the task and is reinforced at each stage of performance (Alberto & Troutman, 2006; Wolery, Bailey, & Sugai, 1988). These programs provide readiness skills that are prerequisites for learning to attend, following directions, developing language, developing self-help skills, and acquiring socialization skills (Hallahan & Kauffman, 2006).

ISSUES OF IMPORTANCE

There are a wide variety of issues and problems in the education of students with mental retardation, ranging from what constitutes intelligence and mental retardation to what are appropriate placements. We have discussed some of these issues throughout this chapter. However, four major concerns bear emphasis:

1. What constitutes intelligence and how it is measured
2. The negative stereotyping of individuals with retardation
3. The absence of standardized educational placement criteria
4. The paucity of preventive and preschool services

Intelligence and Measurement

There is considerable disagreement as to what intelligence is and how to measure it. Because the theoretical concept of intelligence is not directly observable, we can only infer it from observing acts that are thought to require it. These acts are usually measured by intelligence tests that are often culturally biased and heavily weighted in favor of those with developed language skills. In addition, the scores derived from these tests are not stable, and with young students they are not particularly reliable. The tests also measure performance at only one point in time. The results are better used for predicting performance than for assisting in planning interventions. Yet despite these problems, deficits in intellectual functioning as measured by intelligence tests are often more heavily weighted than are deficits in the more revealing adaptive behavior of students suspected of being mentally retarded.

Negative Stereotyping

Individuals with mental retardation differ from one another in more ways than they are similar. The degree of retardation, the environment in which the person functions, and individual innate characteristics make each person identified as mentally retarded significantly different from every other person, labeled mentally retarded or not. Yet, stigmatizing and prejudicial labels and attitudes, such as "stupid," "moron," and "unqualified," are routinely applied by society in general. Dehumanizing myths, such as the inaccurate perceptions that individuals with mental retardation do not get bored while performing repetitive tasks or that persons so labeled have little pride and do not suffer humiliation when abused, continue to thrive. Perhaps the isolation imposed on those diagnosed as retarded by separate schools and special classrooms has reinforced these negative stereotypes. The inclusion movement and its resulting interaction between students who are identified as mentally retarded and their peers who are typically developing should lead to greater understanding and sensitivity. The key seems to be in how the educational system highlights students who are different and how teachers structure the interactions among students.

Placement Criteria

In spite of AAMR guidelines for identification and placement of students with mental retardation, intelligence levels and adaptive behavior criteria vary widely across school districts. Quite often, financial pressures placed on a school system or parental pressures for a more socially acceptable label influences identification and placement. For many, the diagnosis of LD is more acceptable than the diagnosis of mentally retarded. As a result, the misdiagnosis of many students with mental retardation is occurring. Not only does this tend to mask the occurrence of the real problem for many students, but it also leads to the potential provision of ineffective or misdirected services and educational experiences.

Preventive and Preschool Services

Because the identification as mentally retarded, especially mildly mentally retarded, often waits until initial testing at school, preventive programs cannot be introduced until relatively late in the cognitive developmental process. Early identification and early treatment could drastically lower the numbers of students who are identified as mentally retarded during their school years. Research indicates that more than 50 percent of all instances could have been prevented (Beirne-Smith et al., 2002; Hallahan & Kauffman, 2006; Taylor et al., 2005). A weakness in early identification is the underutilization of educational and treatment services for infants and preschool children with mental retardation. Once again, it is clear that early services for any developmental disability are usually more effective than services after the person has matured. Perhaps as the data about early identification and intervention are accepted by society, family members and professionals will be more willing to make earlier referral for infants and young children who are exhibiting developmental delays.

DIVERSITY

Over 12 million persons below the age of 18 live in poverty, live in single-parent families, or are linguistically diverse, speaking a language or dialect other than standard English. The two measures most frequently used to identify students with mental retardation—intelligence testing and adaptive behavior skills—may be influenced greatly by economic disadvantage and cultural and linguistic diversity. Medical issues related to high mortality rates of infants, poor nutrition, and poor health care, and which can lead to a higher incidence of mental retardation, occur at a higher level for those living in poverty. Social issues such as overcrowded homes, substandard living environments, lack of stimulation, and instability correlate with low intelligence test scores, regardless of a student's ethnicity (Greenwood et al., 1994). Families preoccupied with survival may appear to be unresponsive to intellectual development and, from their own experiences, have low academic expectations for their children. The disproportionate number of minority students identified as mentally retarded reflects these restrictions on opportunities to learn.

Since the 1970s, the norms for the most often used tests to estimate intelligence, WISC–IV and Stanford Binet–5, have been recalculated. The proportions of persons in the normalized samples more closely represent the proportions of persons in the nation. Some samples include persons with disabilities in the natural proportions to the population. As a result, they more closely represent the population, and comparisons of persons with and without disabilities are more accurate. However, some intelligence tests rely heavily on linguistic facility and information tied to cultural experiences. Individuals from culturally and linguistically diverse backgrounds may do poorly on these tests as a result of their different experiences and be misdiagnosed as mentally retarded.

A similar bias may occur with adaptive behavior measures. What is considered socially appropriate, adjusted, or competent behavior for one group may not be for another group (Hallahan & Kauffman, 2006; Heward, 2006). Often minority students identified as mentally retarded in part on the basis of their inappropriate adaptive behaviors are not considered retarded at home or in their neighborhoods.

PROFESSIONALS

Many career opportunities exist for those interested in helping individuals with mental retardation. Intervention programs are geared to infant stimulation, early education, elementary- and secondary-level education, postsecondary education, transition from school to work, case management, job coaching, and teaching leisure skills (O'Reilly, Lancioni, & Kierans, 2000). Administrative roles include directing special education programs and teaching positions that provide direct service. There are roles for social service caseworkers; paraeducators; vocational rehabilitation workers; speech-language pathologists; and physical education, physical therapy, and occupational therapy workers, as well as general and special education teachers.

As you have read in this chapter, general classroom teachers increasingly must accommodate students with mental retardation in their classrooms (Dore, Dion, & Wagner, 2002; Hallahan & Kauffman, 2006). They must be able to modify their lessons to include individualized attention and instruction, alternative learning materials and strategies, and appropriate practice sessions to facilitate acquisition of skills by students who may or may not be learning the same material as the majority of students in the class. Many techniques are possible to assist the student to learn easily beside typically developing peers: multilevel teaching (Werts, Wolery, Venn, Demblowski, & Doren, 1996), differentiated learning (Tomlinson, 2000), transition-based teaching (Werts, Wolery, & Holcombe-Ligon, 1992), among others.

Special education teachers work in a variety of settings, dependent primarily on severity of the disability and needs of individual students. Resource room teachers emphasize tutorial, one-to-one, remedial instruction combined with some programmed experiences. Academic skills are important for students served in a resource room. They receive some academic instruction in the pull-out classroom and some in the general education setting. They may also receive instruction in social skills, appropriate behavior in the community, and behavior supports.

Segregated self-contained classroom teachers provide services exclusively to students with mental retardation during the school day. These special education teachers teach classes with smaller enrollments than general education classes. The self-contained classroom may be a full-day placement, and its curriculum may include instruction in life skills as well as academic skills.

Teachers in special schools or institutions are specially trained to serve students with moderate to severe retardation. Their concentration of studies differs from that of the resource room special educator or self-contained classroom teacher. The primary concerns in these settings are instruction in practical daily living skills, social skills, and vocational skills. Vocational rehabilitation personnel provide vocational assessment, counseling, and placement assistance. The professionals in these settings include medical personnel, psychologists, occupational therapists, social workers, rehabilitation counselors, and prospective employers.

Sheltered workshops provide on-the-job training and employment for individuals with mental retardation. The professionals in this primarily adult setting are usually counselors, social workers, volunteers, and employers.

The CEC publishes standards for training special education teachers. These were detailed in Chapter 1. In addition, each professional role has specialized training and licensure requirements. Appendix A lists the addresses of each state special education director in the United States. Because each state has its own licensing or certification standards, interested readers are encouraged to contact the appropriate state director of special education for information about certification and training requirements to assist students with mental retardation.

Historically, family members have probably been the most neglected source of support and expertise. In the past, schools took it upon themselves to test, place, and educate students, rarely consulting family members to ascertain their needs and desires. Family members were seldom informed of decisions until after the special education program was initiated. However, families would not be denied their rights and, as a result, family members of students with disabilities have advocated successfully for an appropriate education. Families have organized support systems and political groups and continually engage in lobbying efforts to combat any lingering resistance to their full participation in school activities and educational decisions. The skills and knowledge that families possess to assist educators is fully recognized (Hardman et al., 2006).

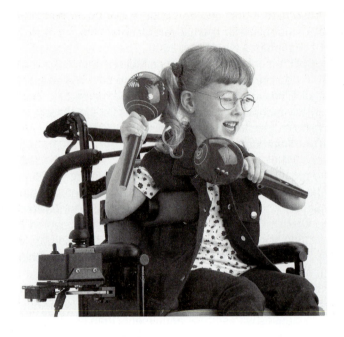

A school may disagree with families' decisions about a student's placement. When this occurs, the school may initiate a process hearing (due process guaranteed by the Fourteenth Amendment). The matter first goes to a mediator who hears both sides of the issue and tries to help the family members and the school reconcile differences and place the student in the most appropriate setting. If the issues cannot be resolved in mediation, the matter may be taken to a due process hearing and then to court, if necessary. Although this is not the preferred way to operate, it is certainly legal and is, in fact, within the scope of responsibilities written into school law.

Paraprofessional assistance provided by educational personnel who are hired in capacities other than as certified or licensed professionals is used in many early elementary classrooms (Ashbaker & Morgan, 2006; Causton-Theoharis & Malmgren, 2005). Elementary teachers list paraprofessionals as a desirable support for the inclusion of students with disabilities (Nowacek, Werts, Harris, & Tillery, 2005; Werts, Wolery, Snyder, Caldwell, & Salisbury, 1996; Wolery, Werts, Caldwell, Snyder, & Lisowski, 1995). The use of paraprofessionals has many potential benefits. They provide increased numbers of personnel to supervise and monitor activities, control problem behavior, provide clerical help, give help in case of emergencies, assist with instruction (both individual and with groups), and give the teacher another adult with whom to share ideas (Wolery et al., 1997). The most recent authorization of IDEA (2004) states that personnel standards for each state should "allow paraprofessionals and assistants who are appropriately trained and supervised . . . to be used to assist in the provision of special education and related services to children with disabilities . . ." (Sec. 612.15). Conversely, extra personnel in the classroom may also be perceived as a source of stress. Unless available resources are used effectively, they may produce little benefit and be perceived as a burden (Janney, Snell, Beers, & Raynes, 1995; Wolery et al., 1997). Teachers also have stated that "traffic" in the classroom can be distracting and that extra adults in the class are not necessarily supportive. Additionally, a paraprofessional can be a social barrier, inhibiting the interactions between students with disabilities and their peers (Giangreco, Edelman,

Luiselli, & MacFarland, 1997). Peer support might be as beneficial to students with mental retardation as paraeducators (Carter, Cushing, Clark, & Kennedy, in press; Giangreco, & Broer, 2005).

A paraprofessional's duties and responsibilities in elementary classrooms may vary from situation to situation. In some cases, reported activities include being a member of the collaborative team (Salisbury, Palombaro, & Hollowood, 1993), guiding students in drill and practice exercises (Zigmond, 1995), or teaching instructional groups (Vallecorsa et al., 2000). Frank, Keith, and Steil (1988) found that teachers reported that tasks for which they needed help varied with the type of program they were teaching. Werts, Wolery, Snyder, and Caldwell (1993) found that some teachers used paraprofessionals only for transition from one area of the building to another, whereas others used the extra assistance for teaching small groups and monitoring academic tasks. This variability may be desirable, just as variability in teaching styles is desirable. However, the lack of a clear job description has been cited as a barrier to the effective use of extra personnel in the classroom and to the implementation of effective practices (Hall, McClanahan, & Krantz, 1995; Nowacek et al., 2005; Werts, Tillery, Roark, & Harris, 2004).

DISCUSSION QUESTIONS

1. As you compare definitions of mental retardation or intellectual disabilities, do you prefer the older or the newer versions? Why?

2. It has been suggested that the term "mental retardation" be replaced by "intellectual disabilities." Do you support this change? Why or why not?

3. What should be taught to persons with mental retardation?

4. What is the teacher's responsibility for teaching economic sufficiency for persons with severe mental retardation?

5. A young woman, aged 16, wants to get a driver's license. She has a measured IQ of 41. She can read some sight words, and can read numbers of 1 and 2 digits. She has a slight palsy of the hands generally controlled by medication. What curricular goals would you write with her?

PROFESSIONAL ASSOCIATIONS AND PARENT OR SELF-HELP GROUPS

American Association on Mental Retardation
444 North Capitol Street NW
Suite 846
Washington, DC 20001-1512
202-387-1968 or 800-424-3688
Fax: 202-387-2193
Web: *www.aamr.org*

The Arc of the United States
1010 Wayne Avenue, Suite 650
Silver Spring, MD 20910
301-565-3842
E-mail: *info@thearc.org*
Web: *www.thearc.org*

Beach Center on Disability
The University of Kansas
Haworth Hall, Room 3136
200 Sunnyside Avenue
Lawrence, KS 66045-7534
785-864-7600 (V/TTY)
E-mail: *beach@ku.edu/*
Web: *www.beachcenter.org*

Center for Universal Design
North Carolina State University, College of Design
Campus Box 8613
Raleigh, NC 27695-8613
800-647-6777 or 919-515-3082 (V/TTY)
E-mail: *cud@ncsu.edu*
Web: *www.design.ncsu.edu/cud*

Council for Exceptional Children (CEC)
1110 North Glebe Road, Suite 300
Arlington, VA 22201-5704
703-620-3660 or 888-CEC-SPED toll free
TTY: 703-264-9446
Fax: 703-264-9494

National Down Syndrome Congress
1370 Center Drive, Suite 102
Atlanta, GA 30338
800-232-6372 or 770-604-9500
E-mail: *info@ndsccenter.org*
Web: *www.ndsccenter.org*
Parent packet available in Spanish

National Down Syndrome Society
666 Broadway, 8th Floor
New York, NY 10012-2317
800-221-4602 or 212-460-9330
E-mail: *infor@ndss.org*
Web: *www.ndss.org*
Materials available in Spanish; Spanish speaker on staff

National Fragile X Foundation
P.O. Box 190488
San Francisco, CA 94119-0488
800-688-8765 or 925-938-9315
E-mail: *NATLFX@Fragilex.org*
Web: *www.fragilex.org*
Materials available in Spanish

National Organization on Fetal Alcohol Syndrome (NOFAS)
900 17th St NW, Suite 910
Washington, DC 20006
800-666-6327 or 202-785-4585
E-mail: information@nofas.org
Web: *www.nofas.org*
Materials available in Spanish; Spanish speaker on staff

Prader-Willi Syndrome Association
5700 Midnight Pass Road, Suite 6
Sarasota, FL 34242
800-926-4797 or 941-312-0400
E-mail: *national@pwsausa.org*
Web: *www.pwsausa.org*
Materials available in Spanish

Williams Syndrome Association, Inc.
P.O. Box 297
Clawson, MI 48017-0297
800-806-1871 or 248-244-2229
E-mail: *infor@williams-syndrome.org*
Web: *www.williams-syndrome.org*
Materials available in Spanish

American Journal on Developmental Disabilities
1719 Kalorama Road, NW
Washington, DC 20009

Council for Exceptional Children
Division on Mental Retardation
1110 North Glebe Road, Suite 300
Arlington, VA 22201-5704

REFERENCES

Abbeduto, L., & Hagerman, R. J. (1997). Language and communication in fragile X syndrome. *Mental Retardation and Developmental Disabilities Research Reviews, 3,* 313–322.

Alberto, P., & Troutman, A. (2006). *Applied behavior analysis for teachers* (7th ed.). Columbus, OH: Prentice Hall/Merrill Publishing.

American Association on Mental Retardation (AAMR), (1992). Ad Hoc Committee on Terminology and Classification. *Classification in mental retardation* (9th ed.). Washington, DC: American Associates on Mental Deficiency.

American Psychiatric Association. (2000). *Diagnostic and statistical manual of mental disorders: Text revision (DSM–IV–TR)* (4th ed.). Washington, DC: Author.

Anastasi, A. (1988). *Psychological testing* (5th ed.). New York: Macmillan.

Ashbaker, B. Y., & Morgan J. (2006). *Paraprofessionals in the classroom* . Boston: Pearson/Allyn & Bacon.

Bailey, D. B., Aytch, L. S., Odom, S. L., Symons, F., & Wolery, M. (1999). Early intervention as we know it. *Mental Retardation and Developmental Disabilities Research Reviews, 5,* 11–20.

Bailey, D. B., Jr., Hatton, D. D., & Skinner, M. (1998). Early developmental trajectories of males with fragile X syndrome. *American Journal on Mental Retardation, 103,* 29–39.

Ball, W. (1999). Examining the link between tobacco use and low birth weight. *Early Childhood Reports, 10,* 3.

Baumeister, A. A., & Baumeister, A. A. (2000). Mental retardation: Causes and effects. In M. Hersen & R. T. Ammerman (Eds.), *Advanced abnormal child psychology* (2nd ed., pp. 327–355). Mahwah, NJ: Lawrence Erlbaum Associates.

Beail, N. (2003). Utility of the Vineland Adaptive Behavior Scales in diagnosis and research with adults who have mental retardation, *Mental Retardation, 41,* 286–289.

Beirne-Smith, M., Ittenbach, R. F., & Patton, J. R. (2002). *Mental retardation* (6th ed.). Upper Saddle River, NJ: Merrill.

Bijou, S. S. (1966). A functional analysis of retarded development. In N. R. Ellis (Ed.), *International review of research in mental retardation* (Vol. 1). New York: Academic.

Brown, E. C., Aman, M. G., & Lecavalier, L. (2004). Empirical classification of behavioral and psychiatric problems in children and adolescents with mental retardation. *American Journal on Mental Retardation, 109,* 445–455.

Carter, E. W., Cushing, L. S., Clark, N. M., & Kennedy, C. H. (in press). Effects of peer support interventions on students' access to the general curriculum and social interactions. *Research and Practice for Persons with Severe Disabilities.*

Causton-Theoharis, J. N., & Malmgren, K. W. (2005). Building bridges: Strategies to help paraprofessionals promote peer interactions. *Teaching Exceptional Children, 37(6),* 18–24.

Chandler, L., & Dahlquist, C. (2006). *Functional assessment: Strategies to prevent and remediate challenging behavior in school settings* (2nd ed.). Upper Saddle River, NJ: Merrill.

Colacello, S. C. (2001). Challenging healthcare and winning at Special Olympics' Wellness Park. *The Exceptional Parent, 31(10),* 63–65.

Costenbader, V., & Readney-Brown, M. (1995). Isolation time-out used with students with emotional disturbance. *Exceptional Children, 61,* 353–363.

Croen, L. A., Grether, J. K., & Hoogstrate, J. (2002). The changing prevalence of autism in California. *Journal of Autism and Developmental Disorders, 32,* 207–215.

Cross, A. F., Traub, E., Hutter-Pishgahi, L., & Shelton, G. (2004). Elements of successful inclusion for children with significant disabilities. *Topics in Early Childhood Special Education, 24,* 169–183.

Cuskelly, M. (2004). The evolving construct of intellectual disability: Is everything old new again? *International Journal of Disability, Development and Education, 51,* 117–122.

Daughtrey, C., Gillentine, A., & Hunt, B. (2002). Student collaboration in community sporting activities. *Strategies, 15(5),* 33–36.

Davis, S. (1994). *The 1994 update on inclusion in education of children with mental retardation.* Arlington, TX: The Arc.

deBildt, A., Kraijer, D., Sytema, S., & Minderaa, R. (2005). The psychometric properties of the Vineland Adaptive Behavior Scales in children and adolescents with mental retardation. *Journal of Autism and Developmental Disorders, 35(1),* 53–62.

Debell, S. (1980). Adaptive behavior and its measurement. *NASP Communique, 8,* 4–5.

Doll, E. A. (1947). *Vineland social maturity scale: Manual of directions.* Minneapolis, MN: Educational Test Bureau.

Dore, R., Dion, E., & Wagner, S. (2002). High school inclusion of adolescents with mental retardation: A multiple case study. *Education and Training in Mental Retardation and Developmental Disabilities, 37,* 253–261.

Erez, G., & Peled, I. (2001). Cognition and metacognition: Evidence of higher thinking in problem solving of adolescents with mental retardation. *Education and Training in Mental Retardation and Developmental Disabilities, 36,* 83–93.

Facon, B., Facon-Bollengier, T., & Grubar, J. C. (2002). Chronological age, receptive vocabulary, and syntax comprehension in children and adolescents with mental retardation. *American Journal on Mental Retardation, 107,* 91–98.

Feldman, M. A., & Walton-Allen, N. (1997). Effects of maternal mental retardation and poverty on intellectual, academic, and behavioral status of school-age children. *American Journal on Mental Retardation, 101,* 352–364.

Fletcher, K. L., Blair, C., Scott, M. S., & Bolger, K. E. (2004). Specific patterns of cognitive abilities in young children with mild mental retardation. *Education and Training in Developmental Disabilities, 39,* 270–278.

Fletcher, K. L., Huffman, L. F., & Bray, N. W. (2003). Effects of verbal and physical prompts on external strategy use in children with and without mild mental retardation. *American Journal on Mental Retardation, 108,* 245–256.

Flynn, J. R. (2000). The hidden history of IQ and special education: Can the problems be solved? *Psychology, Public Policy, and Law, 6,* 191–198.

Frank, A. R., Keith, T. Z., & Steil, D. A. (1988). Training needs of special education paraprofessionals. *Exceptional Children, 55(3),* 253–258.

Friend, M. (2005). *Special education: Contemporary perspectives for school professionals.* Upper Saddle River, NJ: Merrill.

Fuchs, D., & Fuchs, L. S. (1994). Inclusive schools movement and the radicalization of special education reform. *Exceptional Children, 60,* 294–309.

Giangreco, M. F., & Broer, S. M. (2005). Questionable utilization of paraprofessionals in inclusive schools: Are we addressing symptoms or causes? *Focus on Autism and Other Developmental Disabilities, 20(1),* 10–26.

Giangreco, M. F., Edelman, S. W., Luiselli, T. E., & MacFarland, S. Z. C. (1997). Helping or hovering? Effects of instructional assistant proximity on students with disabilities. *Exceptional Children, 64(1),* 7–18.

Gold, M. W. (1980). An alternative definition of mental retardation. In M. W. Gold (Ed.), *"Did I say that?" Articles and commentary on the Try Another Way System.* Champaign, IL: Research.

Goldstein, H. (1966). Fostering independent, creative thinking in educable mentally retarded children. In E. M. Kelly (Ed.), *The new and more open outlook for mentally retarded* (pp. 17–29). Washington, DC: Catholic University of America Press.

Greenwood, C. R., Carta, J. J., Hart, B., Kamps, D., Terry, D., Delquadri, J. C., et al. (1992). Out of the laboratory and into the community: Twenty-six years of applied behavior analysis at the Juniper Gardens Children's Center. *American Psychologist, 47,* 1464–1474.

Greenwood, C. R., Delquadri, J., & Carta, J. J. (1997). *Together we can: Classwide peer tutoring to improve basic academic skills.* Longmont, CO: Sopris West.

Greenwood, C. R., Hart, B., Walker, D., & Risley, T. (1994). The opportunity to respond and academic performance revisited: A behavioral theory of developmental retardation theory of developmental retardation and its prevention. In R. Gardner III, D. M. Sainato, J. O. Cooper, T. E. Heron, W. L. Heward, J. Eshleman, & T. A. Grossi (Eds.), *Behavior analysis in education: Focus on measurable superior instruction* (pp. 213–223). Pacific Grove, CA: Brooks/Cole.

Grossman, H. (1990). *Trouble-free teaching: Solutions to behavior problems in the classroom* (pp. 133–156). Mountain View, CA: Mayfield.

Hagerman, R. J., & Cronister, A. (Eds.). (1996). *Fragile X syndrome: Diagnosis, treatment, and research* (2nd ed.). Baltimore: Johns Hopkins University Press.

Hall, L. J., McClanahan, L. E., & Krantz, P. J. (1995). Promoting independence in integrated classrooms by teaching aides to use activity schedules and decreased prompts. *Education and Training in Mental Retardation and Developmental Disabilities,* September, 208–217.

Hallahan, D. P., & Kauffman, J. M. (2006). *Exceptional learners: Introduction to special education* (10th ed.). Boston: Allyn & Bacon.

Hardman, M. L., Drew, C. J., & Egan, M. W. (2006). *Human exceptionality: School, community, and family, IDEA 2004 update edition* (8th ed.). Needham, MA: Allyn & Bacon.

Haring, N. G., McCormick, L., & Haring, T. G. (1994). *Exceptional children and youth: An introduction to special education* (6th ed.). Upper Saddle River, NJ: Merrill/Prentice Hall.

Harrison, P. L., & Oakland, T. (2000). *Adaptive Behavior Assessment System.* San Antonio, TX: Psychological Corp.

Hatton, D. D., Wheeler, A. C., & Skinner, M. L. (2003). Adaptive behavior in children with fragile X syndrome. *American Journal on Mental Retardation, 108,* 373–390.

Henley, M., Ramsey, R. S., & Algozzine, R. F. (2002). *Characteristics of and strategies for teaching students with mild disabilities* (4th ed.). Boston: Allyn & Bacon.

Hessels-Schlatter, C. (2002). A dynamic test to assess learning capacity in people with severe impairments. *American Journal on Mental Retardation, 107,* 340–351.

Heward, W. L. (2006). *Exceptional children: An introduction to special education* (8th ed.). Upper Saddle River, NJ: Merrill/Prentice Hall.

Hourcade, J. (2002). *Mental retardation: Update 2002* . Arlington, VA: ERIC.

Hughes, C., Copeland, S. R., Agran, M., Wehmeyer, M. L., Rodi, M. S., & Presley, J. A. (2002). Using self-monitoring to improve performance in general education high school classes. *Education and Training in Mental Retardation and Developmental Disabilities, 37,* 262–272.

Hunt, N., & Marshall, K. (2002). *Exceptional children and youth: An introduction to special education.* Boston: Houghton Mifflin.

Individuals with Disabilities Education Act, 20- U. S. C., 1400 et seq. (1997).

Individuals with Disabilities Education Improvement Act (IDEA), (2004).

Janney, R. E., Snell, M. E., Beers, M. K., & Raynes, M. (1995). Integrating students with moderate and severe disabilities in general education classes. *Exceptional Children, 61,* 425–439.

Kanaya, T., Scullin, M. H., & Ceci, S. J. (2003). The Flynn effect and U.S. policies: The impact of rising IQ scores on American society via mental retardation diagnoses. *American Psychologist, 58,* 778–790.

Kaufman, A., & Kaufman, N. (2004). *Kaufman Assessment Battery for Children, Second edition* (KABC–II). Circle Pines, MN: American Guidance Service.

Kavale, K. A., & Mostert, M. P. (2003). River of ideology, islands of evidence. *Exceptionality, 11,* 191–208.

Kazdin, A. E. (1992). Overt and covert antisocial behavior: Child and family characteristics among psychiatric inpatient children. *Journal of Child and Family Studies, 1,* 3–20.

Kennedy, C. H., & Itkonen, T. (1994). Some effects of regular class participation on the social contacts and social network of high school students with disabilities. *Journal of the Association for Persons with Severe Handicaps, 19,* 1–10.

Kirk, S. A., & Gallagher, J. J. (1986). *Educating exceptional children* (5th ed.). Boston: Houghton Mifflin.

Kirk, S. A., Gallagher, J. J., & Anastasiow, N. J. (2000). *Educating exceptional children* (9th ed.). Boston: Houghton Mifflin.

Lakey, B. B., McNees, P. M., & McNees, M. C. (1973). Control of an obscene verbal tic through time out in an elementary school classroom. *Journal of Applied Behavioral Analysis, 6,* 104–106.

Lambert, N. K., Nihira, K., & Leland, H. (1993). *Adaptive Behavior Scale–School* (2nd ed.). Austin, TX: PRO-ED.

Levy, Y., Tennenbaum, A., & Ornoy, A. (2003). Repair behavior in children with intellectual impairments: Evidence for metalinguistic competence. *Journal of Speech, Language, and Hearing Research, 46,* 368–381.

Lifshitz, H. (1999). Comparison of two methods of teaching word-processing skills to persons with mental retardation. *Education and Training in Mental Retardation and Developmental Disabilities, 34,* 90–98.

Luckasson, R., Borthwick-Duffy, S., Buntinx, W. H. E., Coulter, D. I., Chaig, E. M., Reeve, A., et al. (2002). *Mental retardation: Definition, classification, and systems of supports* (10th ed.). Washington, DC: American Association on Mental Retardation.

Macmillan, D. L., Siperstein, G. N., & Gresham, F. M. (1996). A challenge to the viability of mild mental retardation as a diagnostic category. *Exceptional Children, 62(4),* 356–371.

Matson, J. L., Dixon, D. R., Matson, M. L., & Logan, J. R. (2005). Classifying mental retardation and specific strength and deficit areas in severe and profoundly mentally retarded persons with the MESSIER. *Research in Developmental Disabilities, 26(1),* 41–45.

McClimens, A. (2003). The organization of difference: People with intellectual disabilities and the social model of disability. *Mental Retardation, 41,* 35–46.

McDermott, S. (1994). Explanatory model to describe school district prevalence rates for mental retardation and learning disabilities. *American Journal on Mental Retardation, 99,* 175–185.

McLoughlin, J. A., & Lewis, R. B. (2000). *Assessing students with special needs* (5th ed.). Upper Saddle River, NJ: Merrill/Prentice Hall.

Meyen, E. L., & Skrtic, T. M. (1988). *Exceptional children and youth: An introduction* (3rd ed.). Denver: Love.

NICHCY (2004). *Mental Retardation FS8: A publication of the National Dissemination Center for Children with Disabilities* . Arlington, VA: Author.

Nihira, K., Foster, R., Shellhaas, N., & Leland, H. (1974). *AAMD adaptive behavior scale, manual.* Washington, DC: American Association on Mental Deficiency.

Nowacek, E. J. (1992). Professionals talk about teaching together: Interviews with five collaborating teachers. *Intervention in School and Clinic, 25(5),* 262–276.

Nowacek, E. J., Werts, M. G., Harris, S. D., & Tillery. C. Y. (2005). *Paraeducators' and teachers' perceptions of knowledge needed to collaborate in classrooms.* Unpublished manuscript.

Nyborg, H. (Ed.). (2003). *The scientific study of general intelligence: Tribute to Arthur R. Jensen.* Oxford, UK: Elsevier.

O'Reilly, M. F., Lancioni, G. E., & Kierans, I. (2000). Teaching leisure social skills to adults with moderate mental retardation: An analysis of acquisition, generalization, and maintenance. *Education and Training in Mental Retardation and Developmental Disabilities, 35,* 250–258.

Patton, J. R., Beirne-Smith, M., & Payne, J. S. (1990). *Mental retardation* (3rd ed.). Upper Saddle River, NJ: Merrill/Prentice Hall.

Quenemoen, R., Thompson, S., & Thurlow, M. (2003). *Measuring academic achievement of students with significant cognitive disabilities: Building understanding of alternate assessment scoring criteria. Synthesis report*. Minneapolis, MN: National Center on Educational Outcomes; Washington, DC: Council of Chief State School Officers; Alexandria, VA: National Association of State Directors of Special Education.

Raiford, S. E., Weiss, L. G., Eric Rolfhus, E., & Coalson, D. (2005). *WISC–IV: General ability index: Overview*. San Antonio, TX: PsychCorp.

Ramey, C. T., & Finkelstein, N. W. (1981). Psychosocial mental retardation: A biological and social coalescence. In M. J. Begab, H. C. Haywood, & H. L. Garber (Eds.), *Psychosocial influences in retarded performance: Issues and theories in development*. Baltimore: University Park Press.

Roid, G. (2003). *Stanford Binet–5*. Chicago, IL: Riverside.

Salisbury, C. L., Palombaro, M. M., & Hollowood, T. M. (1993). On the nature and change of an inclusive elementary school. *Journal of the Association for Persons with Severe Handicaps, 18(2)*, 75–84.

Salvia, J., & Ysseldyke, J. E. (2001). *Assessment* (8th ed.). Boston: Houghton Mifflin.

Sandler, A. G., & Hatt, C. V. (2004). Mental retardation. In M. Hersen (Ed.), *Psychological assessment in clinical practice: A pragmatic guide* (pp. 321–345). New York: Brunner-Routledge.

Saunders, M. D. (2001). Who's getting the message? *Teaching Exceptional Children, 33*, 70–74.

Schloss, P. L., & Smith, M. A. (1994). *Applied behavior analysis in the classroom* (pp. 178–196). Needham, MA: Allyn & Bacon.

Smith, D. D. (2001). *Introduction to special education: Teaching in an age of opportunity* (4th ed.). Needhan, MA: Allyn & Bacon.

Smith, J. D. (1997). Mental retardation as an educational construct: Time for a shared view? *Education and Training in Mental Retardation and Developmental Disabilities, 32*, 167–173.

Smith, T. E. C., Dowdy, C. A., Polloway, E. A., Patton, J., & Blalock, G. (1997). *Children and adults with learning disabilities*. Boston: Allyn & Bacon.

Sparrow, S. S., Balla, D. A., & Cucchetti, D. V. (2005). *Vineland adaptive behavior scales: Interview edition, survey form manual*. Circle Pines, MN: American Guidance Service.

Sparrow, S. S., Cucchetti, D. V., & Balla, D. A. (2005). *Vineland II: Adaptive behavior scales*. Circle Pines, MN: AGS Publishing.

Spruill, J., Oakland, T., & Harrison, P. (2005). Assessment of mental retardation. In D. H. Saklofske, L. G. Weiss, & A. Prifitera (Eds.), *WISC–IV clinical use and interpretation: Scientist practitioner perspectives* (pp. 299–331). San Diego, CA: Elsevier Academic Press.

Taylor, R. L., Richards, S. B., & Brady. M. P. (2005). *Mental retardation: Historical perspectives, current practices, and future directions*. Boston: Allyn & Bacon.

Tekin-Iftar, E., Acar, G., & Kurt, O. (2003). The effects of simultaneous prompting on teaching expressive identification of objects: An instructive feedback study. *International Journal of Disability, Development and Education, 50*, 149–167.

The President's Committee for People with Intellectual Disabilities (2004). *A charge we have to keep: A road map to personal and economic freedom for people with intellectual disabilities in the 21st century*. Washington, DC: Committee. Retrieved 2/13/2006 from http://www.acf.hhs.gov/programs/pcpid/index.html

Tomlinson, C. A. (2000). Reconcilable differences? Standards-based teaching and differentiation. *Educational Leadership, 58(1)*, 6–11.

Turnbull, A. P., Turnbull, H. R., Shank, M., & Smith, S. (2004). *Exceptional lives: Special education in today's schools* (4th ed.). Upper Saddle River, NJ: Merrill/Prentice Hall.

U.S. Department of Education (2005). *To assure the free appropriate public education of all children with disabilities: Individuals with disabilities education act*. Twenty-fifth Annual Report to Congress on the Implementation of the Individuals with Disabilities Education Act. Washington, DC: U. S. Department of Education.

Utley, C. A., Hoehn, T. P., Soraci, S. A., & Baumeister, A. A. (1993). Motivational orientation and span of apprehension in children with mental retardation. *Journal of Genetic Psychology, 154*, 289–295.

Vakil, E., Shelef-Reshef, E., & Levy-Shiff, R. (1997). Procedural and declarative memory processes: Individuals with and without mental retardation. *American Journal on Mental Retardation, 102*, 147–160.

Vallecorsa, A. L., DeBettencourt, L. U., & Zigmond, N. (2000). *Students with mild disabilities in general education settings: A guide for special educators*. Upper Saddle River, NJ: Prentice Hall.

Vanderslice, R. (2002). Special Olympics: Beneficial to all. *The Delta Kappa Gamma Bulletin, 68(2)*, 5–10.

Walker, J. E., & Shea, T. M. (1987). *Behavioral management: A practical approach for education* (5th ed.). Upper Saddle River, NJ: Merrill/Prentice Hall.

Wechsler, D. (2003). *WISC-IV technical and interpretive manual*. San Antonio, TX: Psychological Corporation.

Wehman, P. (1997). *Exceptional individuals in school, community, and work*. Austin, TX: PRO-ED.

Wehmeyer, M. L., Lance, G. D., & Bashinski, S. (2002). Promoting access to the general curriculum for students with mental retardation: A multi-level model. *Education and Training in Mental Retardation and Developmental Disabilities, 37*, 223–234.

Weiss, J., Diamond, T., & Demark, J. (2003). Involvement in Special Olympics and its relations to self-concept and actual competency in participants with developmental disabilities. *Research in Developmental Disabilities, 24*, 281–305.

Weiss, J. R. (1999). Cognitive performance and learned helplessness in mentally retarded persons. In D. Bennett-Gates & E. Zigler (Eds.), *Personality development in individuals with mental retardation* (pp. 17–46). New York: Cambridge University Press.

Werts, M. G., Tillery, C. Y., Roark, R. R., & Harris, S. (2004). What parents tell us about paraeducators. *Remedial and Special Education, 25,* 232–239.

Werts, M. G., Wolery, M., Gast, D. L., & Holcombe, A. (1996). Sneak in some extra learning by using instructive feedback. *Teaching Exceptional Children, 28(3),* 70–71.

Werts, M. G., Wolery, M., & Holcombe-Ligon, A. (1992). Efficacy of transition-based teaching with instructive feedback. *Education and Treatment of Children, 15,* 320–334.

Werts, M. G., Wolery, M., Holcombe, A., & Gast, D. L. (1995). Instructive feedback: Review of parameters and effects. *Journal of Behavioral Education, 5(1),* 55–75.

Werts, M. G., Wolery, M., Snyder, E. D., & Caldwell, N. K. (1993). *Report from the follow-through institute of best practices.* Unpublished manuscript. Pittsburgh, PA: Allegheny-Singer Research Institute.

Werts, M. G., Wolery, M., Snyder, E. D., Caldwell, N. K., & Salisbury, C. L. (1996). Supports and resources associated with inclusive schooling: Perceptions of elementary school teachers about need and availability. *Journal of Special Education, 30,* 187–203.

Werts, M. G., Wolery, M., Venn, M. L., Demblowski, D., & Doren, H. (1996). Effects of transition-based teaching with instructive feedback on the acquisition of skills by children with and without disabilities. *Journal of Educational Research, 90,* 75–86.

Werts, M. G., Zigmond, N., & Leeper, D. C. (2001). Effects of paraprofessional proximity on academic engagement of students with substantial disabilities in primary general education classrooms. *Education and Training in Mental Retardation and Developmental Disabilities, 36,* 407–420.

Westling, D. L., & Fox, L. (2000). *Teaching students with severe disabilities* (2nd ed.). Boston: Allyn & Bacon.

Wolery, M., Ault, M. J., & Doyle, P. M. (1992). *Teaching students with moderate to severe disabilities.* New York: Longman.

Wolery, M., Bailey, D. B., Jr., & Sugai, G. M. (1988). *Effective teaching: Principles and procedures of applied behavior analysis with exceptional students.* Needham, MA: Allyn & Bacon.

Wolery, M., & Holcombe, A. (1993). *Procedural fidelity.* Pittsburgh, PA: Allegheny-Singer Research Institute.

Wolery, M., & Schuster, J. W. (1997). Instructional methods with students who have significant disabilities. *Journal of Special Education, 31,* 61–79.

Wolery, M., Werts, M. G., Caldwell, N. K., Snyder, E. D., & Lisowski, L. (1995). Experienced teachers' perceptions of conditions and supports for inclusion. *Education and Training in Mental Retardation and Developmental Delay, 30,* 15–26.

Wolery, M., Werts, M. G., Dunst, C., Schuster, J., Hemmeter, M. L., Salisbury, C. L., et al. (1997). *Interim report from the follow-through institute of best practices.* Unpublished manuscript. Pittsburgh, PA: Allegheny-Singer Research Institute.

Wolery, M., Werts, M. G., Snyder, E. D., & Caldwell, N. K. (1994). Efficacy of constant time delay implemented by peer tutors in general education classrooms. *Journal of Behavioral Education, 4,* 415–436.

Wolery, M., & Wilbers, J. S. (1995). *Including children with special needs in early childhood programs.* Washington, DC: National Association for the Education of Young Children.

Xin, J. F., & Holmdal, P. (2003). Snacks and skills: Teaching children functional counting skills. *Teaching Exceptional Children, 35,* 46–51.

Yoder, D. I., Retish, E., & Wade, R. (1996). Service learning: Meeting student and community needs. *Teaching Exceptional Children, 28(4),* 14–18.

Yoder, P. J., & Warren, S. F. (2002). Effects of prelinguistic milieu teaching and parent responsivity education on dyads involving children with intellectual disabilities. *Journal of Speech, Language, and Hearing Research, 45,* 1158–1174.

Zigmond, N. (1995). Models for delivery of special education services to students with learning disabilities in public schools. *Journal of Child Neurology, 10(1),* S86–S92.

4

Students with Learning Disabilities

KEY TERMS

WHAT WOULD YOU DO?

Josh was at the center of the controversy whether he knew it or wanted to be. He had moved into my district that fall. I read through his records and slotted him into my resource program. He was 9 years old and soon to have a birthday. He was enrolled in third grade. He was learning letter sounds and having difficulty recognizing differences between letter forms. He had some of the same form difficulties with numbers. He did have good identity matching skills. He was great with word find puzzles and with hidden objects. He would involve himself with these activities for several hours, given the worksheets. In his third-grade classroom, the teacher had a wonderfully developed opening exercise of news exchange. The students, Josh's friends, were charged to bring in newspaper articles. They read them to the class and then the class would discuss the meaning of the news. Josh never brought articles because he could not read them. However, he loved the discussions. His quick mind gathered information and synthesized it. He loved the back-and-forth discussion of viewpoints. He listened avidly to these discussions between the teacher and the student who brought the article. Josh rarely got to be a part of the active discussion. The teacher had a rule about talking and being involved if you did not have an article to share. However, he did come to the resource room immediately after the sharing time each day, and I found myself to be the recipient of the wonderful "download" of information Josh gathered. This exercise accomplished several functions. Josh was able to talk and discuss the information. He was able to teach me about current events, and I was able to see the thought processes he was producing in these areas. In other words, he was able to impress me with his synthesis of information. It showed me a side of Josh that was not evident as we struggled together in instruction of phonemic awareness.

So, I was happy with Josh's placement. He came to me for 1 hour a day of individual instruction and an additional 1/2 hour of instruction in a small group with another student at the same reading level. His third-grade teacher was not happy, however. She did not perceive that Josh was learning anything in her class, and she wanted him pulled out for instruction for more time in the morning and for at least some afternoon time. Josh's IEP was written and signed by his mother, a general education teacher, a special education teacher, and the director of special education. I, as his current special education teacher, refused to rewrite the IEP. It called for Josh to spend the majority of his time in the general education classroom. His teacher was not happy with my stance and decided to use the teachers' union as a method of forcing me to change his placement. She filed a union grievance.

1. What are the legal ramifications of the stance of the special education teacher?

2. Did Josh belong in the general education class? Would you have changed his placement? ▨

Historically, the concept of a student having learning disabilities resulting from neurological impairment was derived from the pioneering work of William Cruickshank at Syracuse University in the late 1950s and early 1960s. At a parent meeting in the early 1960s, Samuel Kirk suggested the term specific learning disability for the wide variety of symptoms and characteristics of students who were having difficulty. A variety of professional and parent groups contribute to a diverse understanding of what it means to be learning disabled (LD). They all appear to agree (1) that LD is a chronic condition of probable neurological origin; (2) that it varies in its manifestations and severity; (3) that it influences how individuals value themselves; and (4) that it is defined primarily by exclusion of other disability categories (Hallahan & Kauffman, 2006; Individuals with Disabilities Education Improvement Act, 2004; Lerner, 2006). A learning disability that is untreated or treated poorly can have an adverse effect on educational, vocational, social, and activities of daily living.

There is general agreement that LD frequently occurs with some other handicapping or disabling conditions and that LD can be found in all socioeconomic, racial, and cultural categories. Learning disabilities in students are often complicated by problems with adjustment, frustration, and poor peer interactions. As these students are identified and interventions are planned for them, many disciplines may be involved, including special education, psychology, psychiatry, social work, and medicine. Students with learning disabilities may experience emotional adjustment and social skill deficits as secondary problems manifested by disruptive behavior, frustration shown through lack of work, or poorly attempted work. Their frustrations with academic deficits have been shown to contribute to poor school adjustment (Lerner, 2006). However, a label of Specific Learning Disabilities excludes reasons such as poor instruction, emotional disturbance, or intellectual disabilities.

There is considerable dissatisfaction with current definitions, and labels, for students with learning disabilities. Questions surrounding cause or etiology are speculative. Controversy over identification procedures continues. In this chapter, we will discuss these concerns and provide clarifications on conceptual and program approaches. We will also emphasize the issues of definition, identification procedures, and program intervention.

DEFINITIONS

The most influential definitions about learning disorders, derived from federal legislation and professional associations, although not exactly the same, share more similarities than differences. These similarities include recognition of a need for testing, an unexpected discrepancy of actual performance from predicted performance, a list of exclusions from other causes, and recognition of the possible neurological complications in defining learning disabilities (Kavale & Forness, 2005; Lerner, 2006).

Legal Definition

The most widely accepted definition of learning disabilities is the one endorsed by OSERS in the Department of Education:

> Specific learning disability means a disorder in one or more of the basic psychological processes involved in understanding or in using language, spoken or written, that may manifest itself in an imperfect ability to listen, think, speak, read, write, spell, or to do mathematical calculations, including conditions as perceptual handicaps, brain injury, minimal brain dysfunction, dyslexia, and developmental aphasia. The term does not include learning problems that are primarily the result of visual, hearing, motor handicaps, mental retardation, emotional disturbance, environmental, cultural, or economic disadvantage (U.S. Department of Education, 1999).

This definition has been retained, but with the reauthorization of IDEA in 2004, the methods of identification and determination of eligibility have been broadened.

National Joint Committee on Learning Disabilities Definition

Educators and other interested professionals and parents often refer to the 1997 definition of specific learning disabilities by the National Joint Committee on Learning Disabilities (NJCLD), which states that:

1. Learning disabilities are a heterogeneous group of disorders. Individuals with learning disabilities exhibit many kinds of behaviors and characteristics.
2. Learning disabilities result in significant difficulties in the acquisition and use of listening, speaking, reading, writing, reasoning, or mathematical skills.
3. The problem is intrinsic to the individual. Learning disabilities are due to factors within the person rather than to external factors, such as the environment or the educational system.
4. The problem is presumed to be related to a central nervous system dysfunction. There may be a biological basis to the problem.
5. Learning disabilities may occur along with other disabilities or conditions. Individuals can have several problems at the same time, such as learning disabilities and emotional disorders (NJCLD, 1997).

Labels

Numerous terms and labels are used in reference to students with specific learning disabilities. The more acceptable labels appear to be specific learning disability, language learning disability, or learning disability. From the historical and medical perspective, the following labels were used at some time (Bender & Larkin, 2003):

- Brain damage
- Minimal brain dysfunction
- Brain injury
- Psychoneurological learning disorder
- Strauss syndrome
- Perceptually handicapped (disabled)

- Educationally handicapped
- Language disordered
- Dyslexic

Confusion about appropriate labels can be circumvented when educators provide descriptions of assessment results and students' learning performance and profiles when referring to individual students. This approach facilitates comprehension and overall communication about the student and the learning problems. The value of the label learning disabilities for these students would seem to be that it makes a renewed plea for specially designed instruction based on an understanding of the child's individual educational needs and of the implied continued advocacy to promote educational and overall welfare.

Definition: Some Qualifications

Both of the definitions presented medically oriented variables as well as educational factors, suggesting that the underlying cause of LD may be a neurological condition. Research is ongoing in this area (Hallahan & Mercer, 2002; Joseph, Noble, & Eden, 2001; Sousa, 2001). Most state and local education agencies identify three factors as essential in defining learning disabilities: severe discrepancy between intellectual ability and achievement, specific achievement areas, and exclusion factors. The differences in interpretation vary considerably (Reschly & Hosp, 2004).

Aptitude-Achievement Discrepancy

A *discrepancy* generally refers to a notable or severe gap in a student's achievements compared to potential as measured by a standardized individual intelligence test. Although neither of the generally accepted definitions of **aptitude-achievement discrepancy** mentions a specific level of intelligence, an IQ test is generally used as a pivotal point for the identification using a discrepancy model (Stanovich, 2005). The IQ score is the point from which the other assessment scores must deviate. The definitions specify an unexpected deficit. These students might exhibit a severe discrepancy, as calculated by comparing achievements in their school performance in one or more academic areas, to their intellectual potential, as measured by standardized tests. CEC opposes the use of these formulas because there is no national, consistent, agreed-upon formula to reliably measure these discrepancies. In addition, the testing instruments used to measure aptitudes and achievements may be unreliable for these students. If the student performs in a manner that does not reflect accurate levels on a test of aptitude, usually the WISC–IV (Wechsler, 2003) or the Stanford Binet–5 (Roid, 2003) or on any of the tests of academic achievement, then the formula based on the scores will reveal a faulty conclusion.

Central Nervous System Dysfunction

Some scholars suggest that, by definition, students with learning disabilities have some neurological or brain dysfunction, whether it can be documented or not. It has been suggested that for students with learning disabilities, perceptual systems (expressive or receptive) are either not functioning or are functioning differently from those of other students. As a result, these students experience difficulty in acquiring, retaining, and processing information. Some students may show evidence of central nervous system dysfunction, whereas others exhibit no evidence (Pugh et al., 2000). However, this view is not held by all experts in special education (Mercer, 1997). Medical technology has allowed further exploration of the working areas of the brain. It does appear that those persons with learning disabilities may have differences in the manner in which the brain processes solving problems and using language. Recent research results with brain imaging appear to indicate differential working areas for persons with learning disabilities as compared to other students (Shaywitz et al., 1998; Sousa, 2001).

Psychological Processing Disorders

Historically, students with learning disabilities have been perceived as having deficits in their ability to perceive and interpret stimuli but not as having learning problems because of visual acuity, hearing acuity, or motor handicaps (Kavale & Forness, 2000). Learning disabilities may be the result of a perceptual impairment, affecting perceptual skills such as thinking and reasoning. Students with learning disabilities demonstrate language problems, especially with listening and speaking. Additional examples of problems in psychological processes are deficits in attention and memory. Auditory and visual skills are correlates of reading abilities and are useful in making predictions of reading difficulties.

Exclusions

Most definitions of learning disabilities exclude students who are not learning due to economic disadvantage, mental retardation, or emotional disturbance. Outside influences or extrinsic environmental determinants such as poor teaching, poor health, poor home environment, family instability, low motivation, or disadvantaging social, cultural, or ethnic influences are also excluded. Therefore, a learning disability is not "caused" by any of the mentioned circumstances. However, students with learning disabilities may have other disabilities that coexist with and may complicate the teaching of persons with learning disabilities. Many of the problems in determining appropriate strategies concern the teacher taking all the factors into consideration in planning for the student.

General Issues

Learning disabilities are a mixed group of disorders, with subgroups across the areas in which the disorder is primarily manifested. Problems caused by being LD transcend the school setting and persist into adulthood. Students with learning disabilities who are eligible or entitled for services must clearly demonstrate a need for special intervention.

Because these students are typical or average in intellectual functioning—that is, they are students who score in a range on intelligence tests that would indicate no difficulties in cognitive skills—the learning disability lies in their ways of learning, in their perceptual systems, and in how they interpret and integrate information to make sense of their environment. Students with learning disabilities are not labeled LD because they are lazy, undisciplined, or unmotivated. Some students may experience frustration because they recognize the gaps in their learning, and this frustration may lead to behavioral problems. This is not to indicate that students with learning disabilities do not have coexisting disabilities that could be labeled as emotional disturbance. The question of which came first is difficult to sort out and of little educational utility.

A difficulty in defining LD relates to the variety or heterogeneity of this population. In practice, many students labeled as LD do not demonstrate the presence of hard neurological signs, but rather soft signs, such as reversals of letters and numbers beyond the age this would be expected. Other difficulties lie in not being able to identify students earlier in their educational career, in retaining students because this frequently leads to students dropping out of school (Smith, 2005), in differentiating lack of motivation from inability, and a host of other conflicting factors. Although many special educators advocate for a more restrictive or tighter LD definition to define a distinct population, there is no agreement on what will constitute the definition's conceptual elements (NJCLD, 2001). Moreover, although the current definition indicates that psychological processes are associated with learning disabilities, we have no precise indication of how these processes are translated into differential teaching strategies. Finally, the difficulty of using a significant discrepancy between intelligence and achievement has many difficulties. There are different manners of calculating the discrepancies (Reschly & Hosp, 2004). Many states have arbitrary cut points that do not account for errors inherent in assessment scores, and the pivotal scores (the score calculated from performance on a test of aptitude or intelligence) are frequently depressed as a result of the academic difficulty that spurred the referral.

PREVALENCE

The category of students with learning disabilities has grown to be the largest category of students in special education. Over 5 million students with disabilities are served in U.S. public schools; and over half of these students are classified as learning disabled. This means that approximately 50 percent of students with disabilities who are being served are identified as being learning disabled. Estimates of learning disabilities in the U.S. school-age population vary from the modest estimate of 2 percent to extreme ranges of 20 to 40 percent. Moderate estimates and apparently more realistic estimates range from 5 to 10 percent of the school-age population. The forces that drive the confusion about estimates are the result of different definitions, conceptual models, assessment approaches, state education agency guidelines, and professional and parent advocacy group definitions (Reschly, 1996; Turnbull, Turnbull, Shank, & Smith, 2004). The report to Congress (U.S. Department of Education, 2005) lists 2,887,115 students between the ages of 6 and 21 receiving services under the label of LD. Perhaps the lack of serious social stigma associated with learning disability, as compared with the perceived stigma associated with other areas of classifications such as mental retardation or emotional disturbance, is a factor that encourages this classification to be used so frequently (MacMillian, Siperstein, & Gresham, 1996; U.S. Department of Education, 1999).

CHARACTERISTICS

Persons with learning disabilities belong to a very diverse group of people. They do not exhibit characteristic physical features, actions, symptoms, precise genetic patterns, or other markers. They do, however, share one characteristic: They do not learn in the same way or as efficiently as their classmates. However, they frequently do not learn in the same way as their peers who are also labeled LD. Although persons labeled LD have average to above average intelligence, their academic performance is unexpectedly lower than would be predicted. Learning disabilities span the lifetime of persons, but for very young children and for adults it is less noticeable. Persons of school age have fewer choices of activities, and their disability may be more markedly evident. As adults, those same persons may find careers or jobs that do not require them to perform tasks that are in the area in which their disability is manifested. Similarly, some students may avoid difficult tasks in preference to activities that are "more fun" and thus less frustrating.

Each characteristic observed in a given student can range from mild to severe. Often students appear unmotivated, passive, or inactive about involving themselves in the learning situation of the classroom, yet some appear to have a higher level of physical activity than do the other students in their classes. There are more males than females (a 3-to-1 ratio) identified as LD. Students with learning disabilities are more often retained in a grade than are their peers. One difficulty is in distinguishing students with learning disabilities from low-achieving students. As we previously mentioned, students with learning disabilities are not emotionally disturbed—that is, behavior problems or emotional problems are not the primary cause of their learning disability. These students may exhibit a learning problem in one area and not in another (Mercer, 1997). Many of these characteristics could also be listed as characteristic of students with attention deficit/hyperactivity disorder (ADHD). IDEA lists students with ADHD in the category of other health impaired (OHI).

The 10 most cited characteristics are:

1. Delay in developmental milestones
2. Impulsivity
3. Emotional lability
4. General coordination deficits
5. Disorders of attention
6. Perceptual-motor impairment
7. Disorders of memory and thinking
8. Specific academic problems (especially in linguistic and calculation skills)
9. Disorders of speech and learning
10. Some central nervous system signs or irregularities (Heward, 2006)

Intelligence

Generally, students with learning disabilities are of average or near average intelligence. Some students have above average intelligence and may even be gifted, whereas others have measured IQ scores in the lower ends of the average range. College students are the fastest growing group of adults being identified with learning disabilities and who are receiving services (Mercer, 1997; Rath & Royer, 2002).

Perception and Motor Skills

Perception is the ability to organize and integrate sensory stimuli. Students with learning disabilities often experience poor auditory/visual discrimination, which means that they are unable to adequately distinguish one stimulus from another or to correctly orient the stimuli in the space that they occupy. They may not be perceptually aware of their environment and may experience confusion in directional

orientation. They tend to be awkward, clumsy, and uncoordinated. They often have poor handwriting and may experience problems in figure-background difficulties or distinguishing an object or sound from its background. Students with learning disabilities often have problems in impulse control, sustaining attention (the ability to focus on information), short- or long-term memory (acquiring and recalling information), and metacognition (the ability to monitor and evaluate their own performance). Organizing, categorizing, arranging, and planning may not be strong skills. Some students tend to **perseverate,** repeating or continuing the same response repeatedly. Poor motor skills are sometimes associated with learning disabilities (Smith, 2005). Unfortunately, the knowledge of what perceptual difficulty a student may exhibit has not reliably translated into choosing effective teaching strategies for individual students.

Metacognition Skills

Metacognition consists of an awareness of the skills, strategies, and resources needed to perform a task effectively. It requires the ability to use self-regulatory mechanisms such as planning movements, evaluating the effectiveness of ongoing strategies, checking the outcomes of efforts, and remediating difficulties. Metacognitive skills ensure the successful completion of tasks. Students with learning disabilities may exhibit metacognitive deficits in some areas of self-monitoring (Mercer, 1997).

Behavior and Affective Characteristics

Students who are LD may be **hyperactive** (with excessive body activity) or **hypoactive** (lethargic). They can be easily distracted, have short attention spans, show memory deficits, act impulsively, and overreact with intense and sometimes surprising emotion. These students can also have serious difficulties in social adjustment because they may tend to act impulsively and may violate recognized social norms or values. They may be unable to predict the consequences of their behaviors and lack social comprehension skills, which results in their misjudging the feelings of others. They provoke negative reactions from others and become socially undesirable. This inability to interact effectively with others frequently results in low self-esteem. Most researchers have concluded that students with learning disabilities are at a greater risk for experiencing low social acceptance. Yet some students who are LD are not rejected and are in fact popular in the class/school milieu. The relationship between the student's misbehavior and academic difficulty is not known. Perhaps much of their misbehavior is a result of frustration, depression, or withdrawal reactions caused by their learning disability (Hallahan & Kauffman, 2006; Lerner, 2006).

Problems in Academic Learning

Students with learning disabilities are often several years behind their peers in some areas such as reading decoding, comprehension, fluency, and spelling. They tend to experience number, letter, word, and sound reversals. In general, these students have serious reading problems (often termed dyslexia), in which they have problems identifying words or understanding what they read. These difficulties are often compounded by serious oral and written language impairments. They also exhibit poor handwriting, spelling, sentence structure, and composition skills (Deshler et al., 2001; Schumaker & Deshler, 2003). Poor math performance is evident in recalling math facts, writing numbers legibly, learning arithmetic terms and concepts, and abstract math reasoning. Some high school level students reach a learning plateau and make little progress in academic skills, have deficiencies in study skills, and reflect ineffective problem-solving skills (Hunt & Marshall, 2002).

Communication Disorders

Students with learning disabilities may have a more difficult time learning to articulate the sounds of language. They may repeat sounds, stumble over words, and in general have halting speech delivery. They may have difficulty in grasping the pragmatic or social aspects of language, such as turn taking and sharing information needed for meaningful communication, which might result in rambling and continuous conversation. These students have problems in language comprehension, processing, and formulation (expression). They often have word-finding difficulties (Kuder, 2003).

Memory and Thinking Disorders

Many students with learning disabilities have difficulty memorizing words and remembering the sounds that constitute words. They may evidence both short-term and long-term memory deficits for tasks that require semantic processing. However, it is unclear whether learning disabilities result from problems in storing and retrieving information from the long-term memory, or whether they result from a deficit in the memory system itself (McNamara & Wong, 2003; Nelson, Benner, & Gonzalez, 2003; Swanson, 2003).

Specific Academic or Achievement-Related Characteristics

The following characterizations are school or achievement related and are oriented to specific areas. For example, students with reading problems can exhibit (1) insecurity with reading tasks, (2) tension manifested physically during the reading activity, (3) inability to keep place during reading, (4) omission of words, (5) insertion of words, (6) substitution of words, (7) reversal of words, and (8) comprehension errors and fluency problems. A student with learning disabilities in reading may exhibit any combination of these characteristics (Reschly, 1987).

According to Mercer (1997), math-related learning disabilities are generally characterized by some of the following: (1) motor problems reflected in illegible or slowly written numbers; (2) memory problems including mastery of facts, following steps in an algorithm, and multiple-step problem solving; (3) language problems, which includes processing words with multiple meanings, vocabulary processing, and oral mathematical problem solving; (4) abstract reasoning problems, which includes word problems, comparisons, and symbol meaning; and (5) metacognition problems, which includes the inability to select appropriate preliminary problem-solving strategies and a lack of ability for generalization of strategies across mathematical problems (Geary, 2004).

Written expression problems usually are characterized by the inability to produce written documents that reflect complete sentences, adequate spelling, proper grammar, and thematic writing. These problems are compounded by the inability of students with learning disabilities to remember the sentences they intended to construct. They may also display problems in spacing and paragraphing (Mercer, 1997).

In summary, not all students with learning disabilities share all the noted symptoms or characterizations detailed here. Many of the behaviors identified may also be discovered in students who do not qualify for a label of LD. Students with learning disabilities appear to have an immature view of life, impulsivity, and a lack of awareness of their potential for personal development and change for the better. They tend to have lower self-evaluations. They do not always perceive social situations correctly and consequently act inappropriately and exhibit a general lack of inhibition, causing them to sometimes appear silly or obnoxious to their peers (Lerner, 2006).

ETIOLOGY

Speculations about the causes of learning disabilities are numerous, and the cause of learning disabilities for an individual student may be unknown. The more accepted causes for LD fall into the following categories: environmental/ecological, brain damage, organic or biological, and genetic. Research in medicine, psychology, linguistics, and education is ongoing to discover the causes of learning disabilities. Currently, explanations about causes are speculative. Experts suggest that there are various levels of severity, multiple problems, influences, and at-risk vulnerabilities that vary from student to student. The cause of learning disabilities may be embedded in the student as well as in the environment and may be complicated by organic, genetic, or biological anomalies (Hallahan & Kauffman, 2006; Hallahan & Mercer, 2002).

Environmental/Ecological Model

Poor learning environments, unstable abusive families, disadvantaged environments, and inappropriate school instruction may contribute to the learning and socialization problems of students with learning disabilities. Emotional disturbances, lack of motivation, ingestion of lead, drug abuse, school suspension, or death in the family appear to contribute to adjustment problems. On the other hand, direct systematic instruction and removal of painful, unhealthy, or negative influences seem to correct some LD and socialization problems. Studies indicate that team teaching, direct instructional procedures, and the use of a teacher aide make significant influences in correcting, preventing, and ameliorating the difficulties of students with learning disabilities (Slaton & Morsink, 1993). However, it is important to remember that, by federal definition, none of these factors are included in those that cause learning disabilities.

Research also indicates that poor quality teaching negatively influences some students with learning disabilities. Advocates of this model suggest that the learning disabilities of the students so labeled are exacerbated by teachers who are frustrated and do not fully understand the modifications, adaptations, and differential teaching strategies that could be of assistance to these students and perhaps others in their classes. They view learning and socialization as a result of the relationship between the student, the learning environment, and the teacher. There may be a mismatch between the student's predisposition to learn and how the classroom program requires performance to demonstrate the learning. This mismatch can result in poor school performance outcomes. The greater the teacher's instructional ability and positive relationship to the child, the greater the positive match and subsequent child school success (Smith, 2005; Turnbull et al., 2004).

Finally, there is evidence that lack of uniform and consistent nurturing, lack of opportunity to learn, absence of personal challenges, and family-related difficulties are more likely to occur with students with learning disabilities than with other students. As these students fail in school, they are seen as "dumb" and "lazy" and often are scapegoated, frustrated, and suspended from school and become dropouts.

Brain Damage Model

The term *minimal brain dysfunction* was used in the past, in spite of the lack of evidence for brain or neurological impairment or knowledge of what caused the suspected damage. Currently, there is still little empirical evidence of brain trauma, but there is growing literature on neurological dysfunction documented by functional magnetic resonance imaging. Researchers are gathering evidence for a structural and functional difference of the brains of students with learning disabilities and those without a disability. Structural differences include size of various areas. Functioning refers to the activity levels of areas of the brain while performing different tasks (Hallahan & Kauffman, 2006; Kibby & Hynd, 2001; Richards, 2001).

Organic and Biological Model

Suspicion has been touted that chemical agents found in food colorings or specific food flavorings could cause learning disabilities. Similar speculation exists about the result of vitamin deficiencies, especially the B complex. These possibilities have no scientific support. Theories that there may be imbalances in the neurotransmitters (biochemical), which in turn interfere with neural impulse transmission, thus causing LD, are also inconclusive. Research does not confirm the links between LD and malnutrition; allergies to milk, sugar, and chocolate; salicylates (biochemicals found in certain fruits and vegetables); toothpaste; perfumes; or aspirin. There is an additional position that a developmental or maturational lag (i.e., a neurological developmental lag) may underlie some learning disabilities.

Genetic Model

There is evidence that some families have a history of learning disabilities. Studies of identical (monozygotic) twins indicate in some instances that if one twin is dyslexic, the other twin will likely experience a reading disability. Other evidence suggests that there is an inherited genetic influence on reading and language problems among students and other members of their families. More research is required to discover relationships between genetic determinants and specific learning disability outcomes.

In summary, the causes of learning disabilities are varied; despite technological advances, it is still difficult to ascertain causes for most learning disabilities. Although we have presented the models as separate entities, there is no reason to believe that the causes offered by one model are independent from the causes offered by another model. This interaction may lead to learning disabilities being understood as the result of multiple causes that transcend the limits of any given model (Lerner, 2006; Mercer, 1997). The causes of learning disabilities are not as important as finding the teaching methods that are both effective and efficient for the student. There is a large body of literature related to effective instruction. One of the challenges is to determine what works for each student.

IDENTIFICATION PROCESS

Early detection of learning disabilities is extremely difficult due to the definitional aspect that requires an unexpected substantial deficit between expected performance and actual performance. It is difficult to document a deficit as a student begins to learn academic subjects. The longer LD goes unnoticed, the more difficult it will be to remedy the problem and the more at risk the student will be to serious adjustment problems and possible juvenile delinquency. Early detection or screening is dependent on early observation of behavioral and learning characteristics. No person is more qualified in early detection or screening procedures than the classroom teacher. The teacher is with the student throughout the school day and in a key position to screen students with learning disabilities. The symptoms or characteristics of specific learning problems that have been identified and knowledge of them should sensitize the teacher to the possible existence of a learning disability.

Discrepancy Method

One method of identifying students with learning disabilities is that of determining an aptitude and expected achievement discrepancy. Federal and state legislation and other guidelines recommend detailed procedures for identifying and assessing students with suspected learning disabilities. The public school must use a multidisciplinary evaluation team including the student's general classroom teacher, the school psychologist, and other clinical personnel. The team must determine the degree of discrepancy between intellectual ability and age- or grade-level academic achievement or actual performances. By means of appropriate and competent testing, if a severe discrepancy between achievement and intellectual ability is discovered and documented in areas of oral expression, listening, comprehension, linguistic processing, written expression, basic reading skill, reading comprehension, mathematics calculation, or mathematics reasoning, the student may be considered LD. This student may not be identified LD if the discrepancy is due to other handicaps or impairments or environmental, cultural, or economic disadvantage (Turnbull et al., 2004).

Critical to identification procedures are continuous and direct teacher measurements of achievement, especially the use of inventories to assess reading and calculation skills. These are compared to and assessed in conjunction with tests of aptitude. Some of the tests and materials used in the identification and assessment of LD are the *Wechsler Intelligence Scale for Children–IV (WISC–IV),* which measures a student's cognitive abilities or intelligence (Wechsler, 2003); the *Woodcock-Johnson Psycho-Educational Battery–Revised (WJ–III),* which measures achievement in reading, writing, and mathematics by age and grade level (Woodcock & Mather, 1989); and the *Brigance Diagnostic Inventory of Basic Skills,* which measures a variety of skill sequences in readiness, reading, language arts, and math (Brigance, 1983), and other tests of academic achievement.

An identification sequence is as follows. A student suspected of being LD may become a concern to teachers when he or she does not meet educational or social-behavioral expectations in school. These concerns may initiate an assessment/diagnostic procedure, with parental approval. A multidisciplinary team evaluates all areas related to the possible learning disability, using appropriate testing instruments administered by highly trained personnel who attempt to control for racial or cultural bias. Both general and special education teachers must be on the team. They must document the student's present level of functioning, strengths and weaknesses, and unique learning needs. The gap or discrepancy between academic achievement and intellectual ability in one or more areas related to communication skills and math/arithmetic abilities must be clearly demonstrated. Members of the team must observe the student in the general classroom and confirm that the gap or discrepancy is not a result of sensory or motor impairment, mental retardation, serious emotional disturbance, or other exclusionary factors (Hunt & Marshall, 2002; Meyen, 1996).

Academic achievement levels can be determined by teacher-made tests, curriculum-based measurement, and standardized tests that provide standard scores. Intellectual ability can be determined by the administration of individual standardized intelligence tests. Criterion-referenced testing is used to examine a student's performance on a specific task—that is, comparing the performance of an individual to what has been taught and judging how well the task was mastered. Individual educational goals and objectives set the standards for instruction and guide the teacher and the team in measuring the student's performance. Once the results of tests and observations are compiled, the team meets and writes a remediation plan for the student that specifies the type and level of services needed.

Response to Intervention Method

Because there are many problems with the discrepancy model of identification of learning disabilities (Fletcher, Francis, Morris, & Lyon, 2005; Francis et al., 2005; Fuchs, 2003), it has been legislated that identification could be determined by the student's **response to intervention.** This is a process used during the prereferral stage to determine whether lack of good instruction may be the cause of the student's difficulties. The teacher uses scientifically validated methods to teach the student. The methods are documented and data is collected on the student's learning. If the methods appear to work, they are continued and the student is not thought to have a disability. The general education teacher continues to be responsible for the student's education. If the student does not progress or learn after several trials, then he or she can be referred for a full evaluation. The data from the teaching is considered when planning for remediation (Kavale, Holdnack, & Mostert, 2005; Lerner, 2006; Vaughn & Fuchs, 2003).

The process includes four components.

1. Students are described in terms of the academic area in which they have difficulty. The areas of exclusion are not considered at this point. The academic problem is described as accurately as possible.

2. The teacher strives to get an accurate definition of the deficits and the strengths that are relevant to the problem. **Criterion-referenced tests,** those that test the area under concern and are scored and analyzed in reference to what skills are present, are useful here. **Norm-referenced tests,** those that have a large standardization sample and can be used to compare the student to a peer group, can also yield data that is useful.

3. The teacher uses proven procedures to eliminate the possibility that poor instruction is causing the student to have academic difficulty.

4. Documentation is gathered on the methods attempted and the relative success of all attempts to teach over time. The methods that show success are continued, and the student is retained in the general education classroom. If there continues to be difficulty in learning, the student is referred for further evaluation and possible programming and specially designed individual instruction (Friend, 2006; Lyon et al., 2001).

Misidentification

Although the two procedures described here may, at first glance, appear relatively straightforward, there is the potential for students to be misidentified as LD due to:

- Confusion about the LD definition
- Lack of uniformity among the criteria for determining the discrepancy between ability and achievement

- Misplacement of non-LD students in LD programs to avoid the social stigma associated with the diagnosis of retardation or severe emotional disturbance
- Inappropriate teaching methods applied either before or after the prereferral stage
- Confusion between slow learners and students with LD
- Poorly implemented testing leading to questionable results
- Confusion in admission or exclusion procedures and guidelines

While waiting for the diagnostic workup, classroom teachers find the following techniques helpful in managing the at-risk student:

1. Discipline the student with kindness in a quiet and firm manner. Spell out, enforce, and reinforce consequences for definite limits on behavior.
2. Allow the student to select the area in the classroom in which to complete assigned tasks most effectively. Many students need an environment relatively free of distractions and interruptions.
3. Make instructions short and to the point.
4. Keep the student's routine highly structural; the student should always know what is expected in behavior and school assignments.
5. Keep the interpersonal relationship gratifying, warm, and fulfilling. The student should receive praise and encouragement for appropriate behaviors, and the manner of relating should be consistent (Vallecorsa, DeBettencourt, & Zigmond, 2000).

PROGRAMS

Teaching a student with a learning disability requires individualizing learning experiences to his or her unique needs. Using all the information obtained in the assessment procedures, a specific teaching program is designed. As the teacher works with the student, the teacher modifies teaching procedures and plans as new needs become apparent. The following commentary will illustrate some of the more widely used interventions.

Direct Instruction

Direct instruction approaches consist of data-based instruction, in which specific target learning tasks are identified, analysis of the behavior and learning is conducted, and progress to achieving targets is charted. This approach provides a highly structured and organized teaching strategy for students with specific learning disabilities and provides structured phases for lesson delivery. These phases are the provision of the lesson's focus or a review of the prior lesson; a clear, succinct statement of the lesson's objective; and the provision of structured, guided, and independent demonstration and practice of skill application with feedback, positive reinforcement, correction, examples, illustrations, and questions/answers directed to the student (Hallahan & Kauffman, 2006; Pullen, Lane, Lloyd, Nowak, & Ryals, 2005).

Direct instructional approaches appear to be successful for students as the teacher generates a high rate of student responses, proceeds at a brisk pace, and uses social praise and other reinforcements as well as modeling the skill or response. Feedback is essential and is provided intermittently as well as through the lessons and evaluations (Pullen et al., 2005).

Cognitive Instruction

In this approach, the teacher uses a highly structured lesson focusing on an identified learning problem. The learning or instructional activities emphasize attending, responding, rehearsal, recall, and transfer of information. The lesson reflects highly structured strategies for monitoring and controlling the thought process. The student with learning disabilities uses a limited number of learning strategies, monitors his or her responses, and progresses with self-correction. The teacher helps with motivation, reinforcement, and progress charting. Direct instructional procedures are used. The teacher provides the student with detailed data profiling strengths and weaknesses and emphasizing successes and achievements. Teachers and students set goals and emphasize self-monitoring, self-recording of progress, and self-reinforcement procedures. Teacher reinforcement for independent learning, coupled with expression of high expectations for the student, is essential. Teachers use lesson content enhancements, which provide visual or graphic aides to identify, organize, understand, and retain information. Content enhancement procedures employed by teachers include graphs, organizers, charts, and diagrams. The cognitive instructional approach demands the reduction of skills into discrete component elements, the use of sequential steps in task analysis, and the use of many strategies such as mnemonic devices and acronyms to facilitate recall, and self-direction (Jitendra, Edwards, & Sacks, 2004; Lerner, 2006; Turnbull et al., 2004).

Study Skills Training

Study skills training, or metacognitive skills training, assists students in learning how to take notes and tests; prepare compositions, projects, and reports; and remember to bring necessary materials (paper, pen, pencil, etc.) to class for assignments. It also helps students learn to use charts, organizers, outlines, recorders, and computers. This approach emphasizes assessing and planning how to approach learning tasks (Elliott, DiPerna, & Mroch, 2004). Even more specifically, skills in following oral and written instructions may be necessary. For example, learning how to skim to locate information in a text and remembering when assignments are due might be critical skills. Other skills considered essential are budgeting time, requesting help when it is needed, using library references effectively, and working independently (Knowlton, 1993). In fact, classroom teachers rank the ability to work independently, efficiently, and effectively as a critical study skill (Mercer, 1997; Olson & Platt, 2004). They expect students to be able to organize information and resources such as notes, textbooks, and worksheet information in productive ways that lead to the completion of assignments (Schumaker & Deshler, 1984).

Social Skills Training

Social skills training, using positive reinforcement and stressing understanding of feelings, helps the student in specific skill areas such as getting along with peers and adults in various settings and circumstances. The affective levels include helping the student achieve self-esteem, self-appreciation, worthwhileness, control, mastery over feelings and events, and a sense of adequateness and competency. Social skills training focuses the student on skills needed to resolve conflict, manage frustration and aggression, employ conversational skills, express feelings, and learn how to make and keep friends (Miller, Lane, & Wehby, 2005; Smith, 2005). Another form of social skills training is that of teacher-pleasing behavior. Students with learning disabilities frequently forget to bring homework, books, and pencils to class, or to be prepared for the activities that have been announced (tests, discussions, etc.) Several techniques are helpful in assisting students in helping teachers to have better opinions of them and their efforts. One is to teach students to ask questions in class. According to Naomi Zigmond (personal communication, 2000), one of the most useful early questions is: "Would you repeat that please?" Using this question requires the student to listen for a pause after an explanation or set of instructions that would make the question appropriate. This question would cue the teacher to the student's level of listening and participating in class.

Inclusion Strategies

Special education laws (IDEA) stipulate that students with disabilities should be educated with their nondisabled peers to the maximum extent appropriate. This is translated to mean that, when given the correct supports and resources, if students with learning disabilities can be accommodated in general education classrooms, then they should be included with age peers. If they cannot be successful there, then an alternative instructional model should be employed.

Regardless of the model employed, general classroom teachers are expected to teach students with learning disabilities in the general classroom when it is possible for the student to learn in that setting. Commentators indicate that one guideline for modifying instruction and material is to make use of whatever it takes to successfully teach students with learning disabilities. This may mean experimentation and creative presentations of curriculum to determine the appropriate instructional approach. Teachers can increase student success by ensuring that the approach and materials are presented at the students' instructional level and that the students are able to and do complete the assignments. Worksheets and exercises should be attractive and interesting and present information in a logical sequence. Teachers may need to repeat instructions more frequently for students with learning disabilities, write instructions on the board or on a card for the student to place on the desk, allow more time for task completion, task analyze and break down tasks into smaller units for instruction, and divide assignments into smaller-than-usual segments ranging from simple to complex. Peer teaching, special seating arrangements, specific and uncomplicated directions, and clarifications at the onset of a learning experience or lesson will increase successful performances.

Other general instructional modifications may include having a daily assignment sheet posted in view, using charts or graphic organizers, and using color-coded materials that highlight directions or changes in assignments. In addition, talking or rehearsing students through tasks, giving samples or illustrations of assignments, and supplying students with a calendar that lists important dates and assignment deadlines may prove to be helpful to students with learning disabilities (Jitendra, Edwards, Choutka, & Treadway, 2002).

General education teachers can prepare students with learning disabilities to read in content areas by using audiotapes, reading aloud to the student, pairing students to work with nondisabled peers in small cooperative groups and, when possible, using electronic media and computer programs in place of textbooks (Bender & Larkin, 2003). Teachers can help students with learning disabilities in math with numerous simple techniques (Espin, Busch, Shin, & Kruschwitz, 2001). For example, they might assign the student with a learning disability fewer problems; grade assignments on different scales;

allow the student more time; give the student graph paper to help keep the numbers in line; provide clear, neat examples of the work assignment; keep problems of the same type grouped together; highlight the signs that the student needs to notice (numbers, mathematical signs, etc.); and provide reinforcers for completing work (Greenbaum & Markel, 2001).

Teachers can modify their programs to help students improve writing by having students read aloud (privately or with the teacher) samples of their own writing, providing samples of finished writing assignments, providing two grades for writing (one for idea and one for technical skills), providing practice with story starters and open-ended questions, setting realistic and mutually agreed-upon expectations for neatness, and providing students with a copy of the teacher's notes (Baker, Gersten, & Graham, 2003; Graham & Harris, 1994).

A wide variety of teaching behaviors can positively influence educational and achievement outcomes for students with learning disabilities and can be integrated in general classes. Suggested interventions, listed in Box 4.1, can help to meet the instructional needs of these students. Finally, the general educator, by collaborating with the special educator, can make modifications of instruction and overall programming more appropriate to the level of functioning of students with learning disabilities, which will allow students to be more successful and will in turn create a positive learning environment that keeps students on task.

Peer Mediated Instruction

Peer mediated instruction is a time-tested technique that uses an alternative teaching arrangement in which students serve as instructional agents for their classmates or other students. Successful programs are logically structured and consistent with principles of effective instructional practice. To be successful, peer teachers, just like their adult mentors, must present information systematically, draw out peer responses, monitor the accuracy of these responses, and provide immediate feedback (Burkes, 2004; Mastropieri, Scruggs, & Graetz, 2003; Werts, Caldwell, & Wolery, 1996; Werts, Wolery, Anthony, Snyder, Caldwell, & Heckathorn; 1995; Wolery, Werts, Snyder, & Caldwell, 1994).

Peer mediated approaches can be used as alternative practice activities after information has been introduced, discussed, and reviewed by the classroom teacher, and it can be used to teach new material in groups and with students working in dyads as tutors for one another. Two peer programs that have been promoted are Classwide Peer Tutoring (CWPT) and Classwide Student Tutoring Teams (CSTT) (Greenwood, Arreaga, Utley, Gavin, & Terry, 2001; Mortweet et al., 1999; Utley et al., 2001). CWPT, developed at the Juniper Gardens Children's Project in Kansas City, Kansas, was designed to improve the basic skills performance of low-achieving students from minority groups and disadvantaged families and those with mild disabilities. CWPT consists of four major parts: (1) weekly competing teams, (2) highly structured teaching procedures, (3) daily point earning and public display of student performance, and (4) direct practice of functional academic skills. Each week the class is randomly divided into two teams. The teacher assigns students within each team to tutoring pairs. While in pairs, students must follow prescribed instructional procedures. When the tutee gives correct answers, the tutor awards points. If the tutee gives incorrect answers, the tutor provides the correct response, requires the tutee to write the answer three times, or gives one point if the tutee corrects the mistake. If the mistake is not corrected, no points are given. Students are encouraged to complete as many items as

---

BOX 4.1

WHAT EVERY TEACHER SHOULD DO

Effective Teaching Strategies

- Use explicit instruction when the material is needed by the student. Direct instruction can save time and quickly teach information for students to use in discussions.
- Listen to the student. Some methods and strategies will become apparent as the student works.
- Use games and puzzles for repetitive work and practice.
- Provide structure and routine for the student. Energy can be spent on academic learning rather than on adjusting to changing routines.
- Use strategies that have a research base with students with learning disabilities. Students with learning disabilities learn differently, and techniques and strategies that work with students without LD may or may not work with students with learning disabilities.
- Use guided notes and teach note-taking strategies.
- Use mnemonic instructional strategies. Many facts must be learned or memorized. It is easy to remember HOMES for the Great Lakes (Huron, Ontario, Michigan, Erie, and Superior) or "My Very Educated Mother Just Served Us Nine Pizzas" for the planets in sequence (Mars, Venus, Earth, Mercury, Jupiter, Saturn, Uranus, Neptune, Pluto).
- Collect data to track progress. The student, teachers, and family members need to know about the progress being made. Lack of progress can signal a need for a different method of teaching or a different level of instruction.
- Provide feedback as quickly as possible. Immediate feedback on performance is more helpful than delayed feedback.
- Use strategies to assist students in participation in active learning. For example, SLANT stands for Sit up, Lean forward, Activate your thinking, Nod or take Notes, and Track the speaker.

---

possible so that they earn more points for themselves and their team. At the end of the week, all points are totaled and the winning team of the week is announced (Buzhardt, Abbott, & Greenwood, 2005).

Use of peer mediated instructional approaches is justified for a number of reasons. These procedures are effective and implementation is feasible. Social relationships and academic performance have the potential to be improved. The existing teacher force is expanded. Finally, peer mediated approaches are advocated because students seem to like them (Werts et al., 1995).

Computer Assisted Instruction (CAI)

Computer assisted instruction (CAI) is the use of computers and software that is organized to provide a broad range of instruction including drill and practice, tutorial sessions, educational games, simulations, problem-solving experiences, word processing programs, and spelling and grammar checking programs (Hall, Hughes, & Filbert, 2000). The use of CAI for students with learning disabilities has become an effectively used teaching tool and a highly rewarding learning activity for students (Patra & Rath, 2000). CAI is an attractive and motivating learning approach that appears to engage students with learning disabilities in successful learning experiences. It also allows the students to receive immediate feedback, reduces errors by presenting material in a sequenced manner, and allows teachers to track and graph student learning curves. This is important so that a student does not spend too much or too little time on a concept. The teacher must be alert to the data that the computer is capable of generating so that the student is allowed to progress at the most efficient rate for his or her own style, generalization, and maintenance needs. It also helps reduce emphasis on student handwriting requirements. Computerized speech synthesizers can be useful for students with reading problems. When the students want the text to be read aloud, they can access a speech device and read along with the computerized narrator or use a read-along pen device (Okolo, 2000). The CAI approach facilitates group discussion and cooperative learning and provides a powerful reinforcement for nonjudgmental learning. The important aspect of computer assisted instruction is the quality of the software and its appropriateness for the individual student. It is very important for the teacher to use the computer as an assistive tool, not as a babysitter. In other cases, the computer can be used as a reinforcer as well as educational tool.

It appears that student achievement usually is greater when CAI supplements teacher direct instructional practices. It is a promising attractive instructional intervention for students with learning disabilities, whether presented to group settings or individually. Several procedures are recommended to help teachers establish effective CAI learning environments. Teachers should start their CAI programs at the beginning of the year to establish ground rules and routines. Computer instruction should be made available for students at the same time each day and in the same room. The software that is selected should be attractive and age- and ability-level appropriate. Of course, the equipment should be functional, well maintained, and up to date (Montague & Fonseca, 1993). Further suggestions for using technology in the classroom are included in Box 4.2.

Other Classroom Accommodations

Bradley, King-Sears, and Tessier-Switlick (1997) provided some suggestions for classroom accommodations for students with learning disabilities that have been recommended by teachers to support full integration in general classrooms.

When using written materials, provide copies that are clear and uncluttered so that the student is not distracted and "stuck" in an aspect of the presentation that has little to do with the targeted behavior. It is also useful for some students to sit close to the chalkboard or whiteboard to have an uncluttered and clear view of the material written there. Many teachers find that it is also useful to provide both written and verbal instructions. Some students will need to have the book on tape to use alone or to use in conjunction with the printed text.

When lecturing to a class that includes some students with learning disabilities, it is helpful to provide an overview of the content that was covered at the previous session so the students can have a "running start" on the current material. It is useful to check the notes that are being taken to ensure key points are recorded. Some

> **BOX 4.2**
> **WHAT EVERY TEACHER NEEDS TO KNOW ABOUT TECHNOLOGY**
>
> - Software that responds to speech can assist a student in producing typed works. The student will need to "train" the software to recognize his or her own voice and language patterns.
> - Electronic spellers (either stand alone spellers or checkers provided with word processing programs) allow students to choose from a list of correctly spelled words. The student will need instruction in choosing the correct word from an array.
> - Paper that makes carbonless copies (NCR paper) is useful if a student needs to have notes taken by another. The notetaker can write the notes once, and pass the copy on to the student who needs assistance.
> - Small digital recorders or tape recorders can record the lectures and provide a means of having the student re-listen to a class and check to see if the notes are correct and complete.
> - Text to speech capabilities of computer can be used by students with learning disabilities. Free services such as "ReadPlease" are available as web based applications. Others have a nominal cost. The student uses cut and paste features for text from a document or web site and places the text in the appropriate box. The computer will "read" the text and highlight the words so the student can follow along.

teachers will use an alternate note taker who will use carbon paper or photocopy the notes for another student. It is important to pause periodically, review an important concept, and to allow time for questions and for notes to be completed. Some teachers use note outlines and have found some students will do well with the key points pointed out for them so they can listen to lectures more fully. In reading class, new vocabulary should be introduced systematically, and any reasons for doing an assignment or for learning new vocabulary should be clearly articulated. Many students find it easier to follow notes when they are color coded and when they are allowed to work with a peer.

With many assignments, students will do better if they are allowed to verbalize the steps or the concepts as they are learning them. Separate areas of the room can allow this to occur without disturbing students who need an environment that is quieter. Individual notebooks for troublesome words or concepts, study sheets, and lists of things to be used frequently (multiplication facts, history dates, etc.) can be helpful.

ISSUES OF IMPORTANCE

The issues we will highlight in this section are the implications of students being routinely misdiagnosed as LD and the controversy about the appropriate educational setting for students with learning disabilities.

Misdiagnosing Students as Learning Disabled

We have reported in this chapter that the criteria for identification of students as LD are inconsistent throughout the United States. There is extensive confusion regarding definitions, prevalence estimates, characterizations, labels used, determination of degrees or levels of severity, diagnostic procedures, etiology, and appropriate program intervention. There appear to be no absolute criteria for diagnosis, and some criteria vary from state to state. Assessment and testing procedures, especially the use of IQ tests and determination of the discrepancy formula, are questioned regarding validity, relevance, and measurement of error. Some experts even suspect that some students with learning disabilities score in the mild retardation levels because assessment instruments are not appropriate for the population being tested. Many tests do not include students with disabilities in the sample population for validation and reliability. Yet large numbers of students are identified as being LD, and the numbers are growing each year.

The circumstances suggest that learning disabilities are complex conditions with a wide variety of possible influencing causes, ranging from neurological impairments of various types that cannot be readily diagnosed to difficulties in adapting to inflexible styles of teaching. We know that these students perform below expected academic achievement levels and that they might exhibit social or adjustment difficulties as a result. We know that they sometimes act out their frustrations and are rejected by peers. In a few cases they can be socially alienated and at risk for juvenile delinquency and causing disturbances at school and in the community. One of the characteristics of students with learning disabilities is that they do not have good impulse control. Given the number of uncontrolled variables surrounding the diagnosis of learning disabilities, it is not unreasonable to suspect that some students having problems in learning and behavior at school are being misidentified and misdiagnosed as LD. It is possible that some students who are mentally retarded, emotionally disturbed, and otherwise sensory impaired are also being labeled as LD. Some of these students have concomitant disabilities and LD may be listed under the alternative diagnosis. On the other hand, many students have learning disabilities as well as other diagnoses (e.g., hearing impairments, visual impairments, cerebral palsy, and others) and they are counted in the schools' reports as LD. Differential rates of development and motivational differences with some students without disabilities also place them at risk for misidentification as LD. Because of the low stigmatizing influences that accompany the diagnosis of learning disability, there has been an extraordinary increase in the number of students identified as LD. Parents who might not accept a diagnosis of serious emotional disturbance, mental retardation, or organic language processing difficulties will often readily accept a label of LD.

This issue is worthy of discussion because misdiagnosed students, with their divergent needs, tend to further confuse the perception of learning disability. In addition, programs and treatments designed for the student with a learning disability may not be successful when applied to students with different needs dictated by their true disabilities. Perhaps most important, misdiagnosis may prevent students from receiving the appropriate special education services.

Use of the discrepancy formula has been a controversial issue since its inception. Students who show a discrepancy or a difference in what is expected and in how they perform are termed "disabled." In reality, though, determining "what is expected" is almost impossible (Stanovich, 2005). Many districts have implemented a prereferral intervention stage in the process. Students are given "diagnostic-prescriptive" teaching to determine effective strategies or methods of teaching. This concept has been extended by IDEA–2004: The notion of response to instruction (RTI) was proposed as

a possible replacement for the discrepancy formula. In the reauthorization, SEAs (states) or LEAs (districts) may choose to use RTI. It is not mandated.

Appropriate Educational Settings

Despite the current focus on inclusion, there is continued debate about where students with learning disabilities should be educated. One reason for the debate is that the decision is not one that may be made in the abstract. IDEA–2004 and each of its predecessors have called for a continuum of services to be offered so that students with individual needs may have them met in the most appropriate setting. It is easy to forget that special education is a process and a set of instructional procedures designed to provide the most appropriate educational opportunities to each student. A wide variety of curricular and organizational options and instructional strategies are effective for these students. Full inclusion in the general classroom has become a more popular setting than resource rooms or special education self-contained classrooms; however, full inclusion without the appropriate services and supports is not special education. The demands on general classroom teachers require assistance for students with learning disabilities to receive appropriate and effective instructional programs. If this is not the case, the IEP team needs to reconvene and initiate alternative services and strategies to deliver specially designed and individualized instruction.

A parallel issue is that program intervention and support for preschool students who will be diagnosed as LD when they reach school age are, on a national scale, modest or nonexistent. At-risk preschool students can be helped remarkably through early preschool programs. Yet, although early intervention programs continue to grow and show their value in other special education areas, they cannot have the same emphasis in the specific area of learning disability because learning disabilities cannot be diagnosed in early childhood. By their very nature, they relate to language-based academic learning (reading, writing, mathematical calculations) to which the young student has not yet been exposed. One cannot diagnose an academic deficiency before academic learning has formally begun.

DIVERSITY

The label or term learning disabilities is a loose, appealing, cosmetic, and popular label because it carries diminished social stigma and little parental or student responsibility for its occurrence. It appears to carry reduced blame of families and students when compared with mental retardation, serious emotional disturbance, or other disabilities categories. There is no implication of neglect or abuse. There is no implication of lack of motivation on the part of the student. Initially (in the 1970s), students at a low socioeconomic level who were in trouble with learning and behavior at school were more likely than their middle-class peers to be regarded as mentally retarded or emotionally and behaviorally disturbed. However, Sattler (1988), Meyen (1996), and Coutinho, Oswald, and Best (2002) indicated that a growing number of students from ethnic minorities are being classified as LD. There is even a growing concern that students from ethnic minorities are overrepresented in LD programs. The limited commentary about this issue suggests that careful or competent consideration and evaluation of test results, adaptive behavior inventories, classroom performance, and cultural influences on learning and behavior may be lacking. Another question is that of testing practices and the misuse or misunderstanding of discrepancy formulas to document the required deficits. However, it is also possible that these students who speak different languages also have learning disabilities. The problems of decoding, copying, and understanding language occur in students who learn alphabet-based languages (such as English) and logographic or pictorial systems of written language (such as Chinese or Japanese). It also occurs in languages in which the grammatical rules are regular (Spanish) and in those that do not always follow rules (English) (Lerner, 2006).

PROFESSIONALS

The professionals most likely to work with students with learning disabilities and their families are general classroom teachers, special educators, physicians, and psychological counselors. Because most students with learning disabilities are included, as much as educationally appropriate, with their peers without labels, many remedial services are provided in the general education classroom. The general education teacher provides some of this instruction with assistance from the special education teacher or other types of supports. A special education teacher, often acting as a consultant or a coteacher, provides the general education teacher with support in remediation in certain skill areas for the student and adapting activities when it is necessary. In this collaborative role with the general education teacher, the special educator assists in assessment, selecting curriculum materials, modeling strategies, and using them in direct instructional activities. In addition, some special education teachers provide full- or part-time service to students with learning disabilities in self-contained classrooms, resource rooms, or general education classrooms. For a while, medical personnel were the largest contributors of referrals to a school for students with learning disabilities. Medical and paramedical professionals, including family physicians and psychotherapists, depending on their familiarity with the behavioral and other accompanying symptoms often coexisting with learning disability, may provide medication, behavioral therapy, counseling, and other related services. They often assist the general and special educator and ask for information about daily functioning of the student in natural environments. Physicians no longer primarily diagnose learning disabilities. Generally, a general education teacher or a parent is the first to notice some differences in learning and some evidence of discrepancy. The referral process then is initiated and a team assesses and makes decisions about entitlements and services needed in the school and community settings.

CEC provides standards for the preparation and certification of teachers for students with learning disabilities. The program of studies they require of college and university training programs typically includes courses in education philosophy and history; characteristics of students with learning disabilities; assessment, diagnosis, and evaluation knowledge and experience; instructional intervention knowledge; classroom and student behavioral-management knowledge and practice; and knowledge of advocacy and training in collaboration with allied professionals and parents. Coursework in ethical and professional practice is also mandated. Although CEC sets the guidelines for training programs, each individual state has its own criteria for certification of teachers specializing in working with students with learning disabilities. Appendix A is a listing of the directors of special education for each state. Interested readers may contact their offices to obtain the specific requirements for any state.

DISCUSSION QUESTIONS

1. How has the definition of learning disability changed over the decades since 1975?
2. List some of the labels used for learning disabilities and explain why they were not deemed adequate.
3. What is thought to cause learning disabilities?
4. Of the 13 categories of disabilities served under IDEA, the largest is learning disability. Discuss reasons for this.
5. What characteristics of students with learning disabilities might make it difficult to get along socially in school groups? Why?
6. What characteristics of students with learning disabilities might make it difficult to get along academically in school groups? Why?
7. Is inclusion a preferred setting for educating students with learning disabilities?
8. What problems are inherent in the discrepancy formula approach to identification of students with learning disabilities?

PROFESSIONAL ASSOCIATIONS AND PARENT OR SELF-HELP GROUPS

Association for Children with Learning Disabilities
Learning Disabilities Association of America
4165 Library Road
Pittsburgh, PA 15234

Council for Exceptional Children
Division for Learning Disabilities
1920 Association Drive
Reston, VA 20191-1589

Council for Learning Disabilities
P.O. Box 40303
Overland Park, KS 66204

ERIC Clearinghouse on Disabilities and Gifted Education
Council for Exceptional Children
1920 Association Drive, Reston, VA 20191-1589

National Center for Learning Disabilities
99 Park Avenue, New York, NY 10016
(212) 687-7211

National Center to Improve Practice in Special Education through Technology, Media, and Materials (NCIP)
Education Development Center, Inc.
55 Chapel Street
Newton, MA 02160

Orton Dyslexia Society
Chester Building, Suite 382
8600 LaSalle Road
Baltimore, MD 21286

U.S. Department of Education
National Library of Education
555 New Jersey Avenue NW
Washington, DC 20208-5121
Library Administration

Journal of Learning Disabilities
PRO-ED
8700 Shoal Creek Boulevard, Austin, TX 78757

LD Forum
Council for Learning Disabilities
P.O. Box 40303
Overland Park, KS 66204

Learning Disability Quarterly
Council for Learning Disabilities
P.O. Box 40303
Overland Park, KS 66204

Learning Disabilities Research and Practice
Lawrence Erlbaum Associates
365 Broadway
Hillsdale, NJ 07642-1487

REFERENCES

Baker, S., Gersten, R., & Graham, S. (2003). Teaching expressive writing to students with learning disabilities: Research-based applications and examples. *Journal of Learning Disabilities, 36,* 109–123.

Bender, W. N., & Larkin, M. J. (2003). *Reading strategies for elementary students with learning difficulties.* Thousand Oaks, CA: Corwin Press, Inc.

Bradley, D. F., King-Sears, M. E., & Tessier-Switlick, D. (1997). *Teaching students in inclusive settings: From theory to practice.* Boston: Allyn & Bacon.

Brigance, A. (1983). *Brigance diagnostic inventory of basic skills.* North Billerica, MA: Curriculum Associates.

Burkes, M. (2004). Effects of classwide peer tutoring on the number of words spelled correctly by students with LD. *Intervention in School and Clinic, 39,* 301–304.

Buzhardt, J., Abbott, M., & Greenwood, C. (2005). Usability testing of the classwide peer tutoring–learning management system. *Journal of Special Education Technology, 20,* 19–29.

Coutinho, M. J., Oswald, D. P., & Best, A. M. (2002). The influence of sociodemographics and gender on the disproportionate identification of minority students as having learning disabilities. *Remedial and Special Education, 23,* 49–59.

Deshler, D. D., Schumaker, J. L., Lenz, B. K., Bulgren, J. A., Hock, M. F., Knight, J., et al. (2001). Ensuring content-area learning by secondary students with learning disabilities. *Learning Disabilities Research and Practice, 16,* 96–108.

Elliott, S. N., DiPerna, J. C., & Mroch, A. A. (2004). Prevalence and patterns of academic enabling behaviors: An analysis of teachers' and students' ratings for a national sample of students. *School Psychology Review, 33,* 302–309.

Espin, C. A., Busch, T. W., Shin, J., & Kruschwitz, R. (2001). Curriculum-based measurement in the content areas: Validity of vocabulary matching as an indicator of performance in social studies. *Learning Disabilities: Research & Practice, 16,* 142–151.

Fletcher, J. M., Francis, D. J., Morris, R. D., & Lyon, G. R. (2005). Evidence-based assessment of learning disabilities in children and adolescents. *Journal of Clinical and Adolescent Psychology, 34,* 506–522.

Francis, D. J., Fletcher, J. M., Steubing, K. K., Lyon, G. R., Shaywitz, B. A., & Shaywitz, S. E. (2005). Psychometric approaches to the identification of LD: IQ and achievement scores are not sufficient. *Journal of Learning Disabilities, 38,* 98–116.

Friend, M. (2006) *Special education: Contemporary perspectives for school professionals, IDEA 2004 update edition.* Boston: Allyn & Bacon.

Fuchs, L. S. (2003). Assessing intervention responsiveness: Conceptual and technical issues. *Learning Disabilities: Research & Practice, 18,* 172–186.

Geary, D. C. (2004). Mathematics and learning disabilities. *Journal of Learning Disabilities, 37,* 4–16.

Graham, S., & Harris, K. (1994). Implications of constructivism for teaching writing to students with special needs. *Journal of Special Education, 28,* 275–289.

Greenbaum, J., & Markel, G. (2001). *Helping adolescents with ADHD and learning disabilities: Ready-to-use tips, techniques, and checklists for school success.* Upper Saddle River, NJ: Merrill/Prentice Hall.

Greenwood. C. R., Arreaga, M. A., Utley, C. A., Gavin, M. K., & Terry, B. J. (2001). Classwide peer tutoring learning management system: Applications with elementary-level English language learners. *Remedial and Special Education, 22*(1), 34–47.

Hall, T. E., Hughes, C. A., & Filbert, M. (2000). Computer assisted instruction in reading for students with learning disabilities: A research synthesis. *Education and Treatment of Children, 23,* 173–193.

Hallahan, D. P., & Kauffman, J. M. (2006). *Exceptional children: Introduction to special education* (10th ed.). Boston: Allyn and Bacon.

Hallahan, D. P., & Mercer, C. D. (2002). Learning disabilities: Historical perspectives. In R. Bradley, L. Danielson, & D. P. Hallahan (Eds.), *Identification of learning disabilities: Research to practice* (pp. 1–67). Mahwah, NJ: Lawrence Erlbaum.

Heward, W. L. (2006). *Exceptional children: An introduction to special education* (5th ed.). Upper Saddle River, NJ: Merrill/Prentice Hall.

Hunt, N., & Marshall, K. (2002). *Exceptional children and youth: An introduction to special education.* Boston: Houghton Mifflin.

Individuals with Disabilities Education Improvement Act (IDEA) (2004). Public law 108-446.

Jitendra, A. K., Edwards, L. L., & Sacks, G. (2004). What research says about vocabulary instruction for students with learning disabilities. *Exceptional Children, 70,* 299–322.

Jitendra, A. K., Edwards, L. L., Choutka, C. M., & Treadway, P. S. (2002). A collaborative approach to planning in the content areas for students with learning disabilities: Accessing the general curriculum. *Learning Disabilities: Research & Practice, 17,* 252–267.

Joseph, J., Noble, K., & Eden, G. (2001). The neurobiological basis of reading. *Journal of Learning Disabilities, 34,* 566–579.

Kavale, K. A., & Forness, S. R. (2000). Auditory and visual perception processes and reading ability: A quantitative re-analysis and historical interpretation. *Learning Disability Quarterly, 23,* 253–270.

Kavale, K. A., & Forness, S. R. (2005). What definitions of LD say and don't say. *Journal of Learning Disabilities, 33,* 239–256.

Kavale, K. A., Holdnack, J. A., & Mostert, M. P. (2005). Responsiveness to intervention and the identification of specific learning disability: A critique and alternative proposal. *Learning Disability Quarterly, 28,* 2–16.

Kibby, M. Y., & Hynd, G. W. (2001). Neurological basis of learning disabilities. In D. P. Hallahan & B. K. Keogh (Eds.), *Research and global perspectives in learning disabilities: Essays in honor of William M. Cruickshank* (pp. 25–42). Mahwah, NJ: Lawrence Erlbaum.

Knowlton, E. K. (1993). *Secondary regular classroom teachers' expectations of learning disabled students.* Research Report No. 75. Lawrence, KS: University of Kansas Center for Research and Learning.

Kuder, S. J. (2003). *Teaching students with language and communication disabilities.* Boston: Allyn & Bacon.

Lerner, J. (2006). *Learning disabilities and related disorders: Characteristics and teaching strategies* (10th ed.). Boston: Houghton Mifflin.

Lyon, G. R., Fletcher, J. M., Shaywitz, S. E., Shaywitz, B. A., Torgeson, J. K., Wood, F. B., et al. (2001). Rethinking learning disabilities. In C. E. Finn, A. J. Rotherham, & C. R. Hokanson, (Eds.), *Rethinking special education for a new century* (pp. 259–287). Washington, DC: Thomas B. Fordham Foundation and Progressive Policy Institute.

MacMillan, D. L., Siperstein, G. N., & Gresham, F. M. (1996). A challenge to the viability of mild mental retardation as a diagnostic category. *Exceptional Children, 62,* 356–371.

Mastropieri, M. A., Scruggs, T. E., & Graetz, J. E. (2003). Reading comprehension instruction for secondary students: Challenges for struggling students and teachers. *Learning Disability Quarterly, 26,* 103–116.

McNamara, J. K., & Wong, B. (2003). Memory for everyday information in students with learning disabilities. *Journal of Learning Disabilities, 36,* 394–406.

Mercer, C. D. (1997). *Students with learning disabilities* (5th ed.). Upper Saddle River, NJ: Merrill/Prentice Hall.

Meyen, E. L. (1996). *Exceptional children in today's schools* (3rd ed.). Denver, CO: Love.

Miller, M. J., Lane, K. L., & Wehby, J. (2005). Social skills instruction for students with high-incidence disabilities: A school-based intervention to address acquisition deficits. *Preventing School Failure, 49*(2), 27–39.

Montague, M., & Fonseca, F. (1993). Using computers to improve story writing. *Teaching Exceptional Children, 25*(4), 46–49.

Mortweet, S. L., Utley, C. A., Walker, D. D., Harriett. L., Delquadri, J. C., Reddy, S. S., et al. (1999). Classwide peer tutoring: Teaching students with mild mental retardation in inclusive classrooms. *Exceptional Children, 65,* 524–536.

National Joint Committee on Learning Disabilities (NJCLD). (1997). Operationalizing the NJCLD definition of learning disabilities for ongoing assessment in schools. *Perspectives: The International Dyslexia Association, 23*(4), 29–33.

National Joint Committee on Learning Disabilities (NJCLD). (2001). Learning disabilities: Issues on definition. Position paper of the National Joint Committee on Learning Disabilities. In *Collective perspective on issues affecting learning disabilities: Position papers and statements.* Austin, TX: PRO-ED.

Nelson, J. R., Benner, G. J., & Gonzalez, J. (2003). Learner characteristics that influence the treatment effectiveness of early literacy interventions: A meta-analytic review. *Learning Disabilities Research and Practice, 18,* 255–268.

Okolo, C. M. (2000). Technology for individuals with mild disabilities. In J. Lindsey (Ed.), *Technology and exceptional individuals* (3rd ed., pp. 243–301). Austin, TX: Pro-Ed.

Olson, J. L., & Platt, J. M. (2004). *Teaching children and adolescents with special needs.* Upper Saddle River, NJ: Merrill/Prentice Hall.

Patra, J., & Rath, P. K. (2000). Computer and pedagogy: Replacing telling with computer assisted instruction for teaching arithmetic skills to mentally retarded children. *Social-Science-International, 16*(1–2), 70–78.

Pugh, K. R., Mencl, W. E., Shaywitz, B. A., Shaywitz, S. E., Fulbright, R. K., Constable, R. T., et al. (2000). Task-specific differences in functional connections within the posterior cortex. *Psychological Science, 11,* 51–56.

Pullen, P. C., Lane, H. B., Lloyd, J. W., Nowak, R., & Ryals, J. (2005). Effects of explicit instruction on decoding of struggling first-grade students: A data-based case study. *Education and Treatment of Children,* 63–75.

Rath, K. A., & Royer, J. M. (2002). The nature and effectiveness of learning disability services for college students. *Educational Psychology Review, 14,* 353–381.

Reschly, D. (1987). Learning characteristics of mildly handicapped students: Implications for classification, placement, and programming. In M. Wang, M. Reynolds, & H. Walberg (Eds.), *Handbook of special education: Learner characteristics and adaptive behavior.* New York: Pergamon.

Reschly, D. (1996). *Disproportionate minority representation in general and special education programs: Patterns, issues, and alternatives.* Des Moines, IA: Iowa Department of Education.

Reschly, D. J., & Hosp, J. L. (2004). State SLD identification policies and practice. *Learning Disability Quarterly, 27,* 197–213.

Richards, T. L. (2001). Functional magnetic resonance imaging and spectroscopic imaging of the brain: Application of fMRI and fMRS to reading disabilities and education. *Learning Disability Quarterly, 24,* 189–203.

Roid, G. H. (2003). *Stanford Binet Intelligence Scales* (5th ed.). Itasca, IL: Riverside Publishing.

Sattler, J. (1988). *Assessment of children* (3rd ed.). San Diego, CA: Author.

Schumaker, J. B., & Deshler, D. D. (1984). Setting demand variables: A major factor in program planning for the LD adolescent. *Topics in Language Disorders, 4*(2), 22–40.

Schumaker, J. B., & Deshler, D. D. (2003). Can students with LD become competent writers? *Learning Disability Quarterly, 26,* 129–141.

Shaywitz, S. E., Shaywitz, B. A., Pugh, K. R., Fulbright, R. K., Constable, R. T., Mencl, W. E., et al. (1998). Functional disruption in the organization of the brain for reading in dyslexia. *Neurobiology, 5,* 2636–2641.

Slaton, D. B., & Morsink, C. V. (1993). Students with learning disabilities. In A. E. Blackhurst & W. H. Berdine (Eds.), *An introduction to special education* (3rd ed.). New York: HarperCollins.

Smith, D. D. (2005). *Introduction to special education: Teaching in an age of challenge.* Needham, MA: Allyn & Bacon.

Sousa, D. A. (2001). *How the brain learns* (2nd ed.). Thousand Oaks, CA: Corwin Press.

Stanovich, K. (2005). The future of a mistake: Will discrepancy measurement continue to make the learning disabilities field a pseudoscience? *Learning Disability Quarterly, 28,* 103.

Swanson, H. L. (2003). Age-related differences in learning disables' and skilled readers' working memory. *Journal of Experimental Child Psychology, 85,* 1–31.

Turnbull, A. P., Turnbull, H. R., Shank, M., & Smith, S. (2004). *Exceptional lives: Special education in today's schools.* Upper Saddle River, NJ: Merrill/Prentice Hall.

U.S. Department of Education. (1999). Assistance to states for education of children with disabilities and the early intervention program for infants and toddlers with disabilities: Final regulations. *Federal Register, 64*(48), CFR parts 300 and 303.

U.S. Department of Education. (2005). *Annual report to Congress,* Washington, DC: Author.

Utley, C. A., Reddy, S. S., Delquadri, J. C., Greenwood, C. R., Mortweet, S. L., & Bowman, V. (2001). Classwide peer tutoring: An effective teaching procedure for facilitating the acquisition of health education and safety facts with students with developmental disabilities. *Education and Treatment of Children, 24,* 1–27.

Vallecorsa, A. L., DeBettencourt, L. U., & Zigmond, N. (2000). *Students with mild disabilities in general education settings: A guide for special educators.* Upper Saddle River, NJ: Merrill/Prentice Hall.

Vaughn, S., & Fuchs, L. (2003). Redefining learning disabilities as an inadequate response to instruction: The promise and potential problems. *Learning Disabilities Research and Practice, 18,* 137–146.

Wechsler, D. (2003). *The Wechsler Intelligence Scale for Children–IV.* San Antonio, TX: Psychological Corporation.

Werts, M. G., Caldwell, N. K., & Wolery, M. (1996). Peer modeling of response chains: Observational learning by students with disabilities. *Journal of Applied Behavior Analysis, 29,* 53–66.

Werts, M. G., Wolery, M., Anthony, L., Snyder, E. D., Caldwell, N. K., & Heckathorn, J. K. (1995). *Peer tutoring using response prompting strategies.* Pittsburgh, PA: Allegheny Singer Research Institute.

Wolery, M., Werts, M. G., Snyder, E. D., & Caldwell, N. K. (1994). Efficacy of constant time delay implemented by peer tutors in general education classrooms. *Journal of Behavioral Education, 4,* 415–436.

Woodcock, R. W., & Mather, N. (1989). *The Woodcock-Johnson psycho-educational battery–revised.* Allen, TX: DLM Teaching Resources.

5

Students with Attention Deficit/Hyperactivity Disorder

KEY TERMS

WHAT WOULD YOU DO?

Raising a child with attention deficit disorder with hyperactivity (ADHD) is frustrating, agonizing, heartbreaking, and sometimes heartwarming. Shannon came into the world with a zeal for life exceeding all others. Her energy seemed at first just a bit more than others. She was exquisitely attuned to all that occurred. Little did I know at the beginning that it was an awareness that would grow to cause many unwanted disruptions and problems. Shannon rushed through life in a feverish pace, actively engaging in a myriad of tasks. Most of these activities involved play, and they were socially acceptable, but interestingly, sometimes Shannon was extremely focused on certain tasks, such as building cities from Legos. She soon added to the Legos boxes, blocks, newspaper clippings of ads, old holiday decorations, and countless other items that could become part of the structures she envisioned. Her creativity, coupled with her immeasurable observational skills and awareness of her surroundings, never indicated an attention problem. I was quite active and creative as a child, as was my wife, so we never considered the idea of a problem.

Around age 7 we began to notice a slight, or so it seemed then, focusing problem. Shannon was unable to block out movement, sounds, and other activities in her environment. A fly, car, or siren would send her leaping up from whatever she was doing to rush to see what was going on. The simple ruffling of a curtain, the sound of the heater coming on, or even the ticking of the clock attracted her. But she was only a child and her creativity far surpassed other children her age and, therefore, concern over her distractibility was not our primary concern.

When she was in the second grade, we became concerned. Shannon's school papers began to show signs of not staying on task. In conferences with her teacher, we were told she was up and down constantly, never finishing tasks or assignments before she was off playing, dancing about, singing, or making loud outbursts. The teacher was never sure what to expect. She had no bounds. In a discussion with Shannon, we discovered she was completely clueless to the disruptive nature of her actions, and she was clueless that she was so easily distracted. We began to tighten our reins at home and administered punishments for bad reports from school. Grades got worse, and the notes from the teacher continued. I read every article I could find on learning disabilities. One day I stumbled upon a new article and found I was reading about my daughter, my Shannon. Every paragraph defined her actions and her inability to focus. Was this possible? Could a chemical imbalance in the body and brain cause such disruption? About a week or so after I was deep into reading about the problem that plagued my daughter, her teachers, and us, I found a name—ADHD or attention deficit disorder with hyperactivity. Could this really be the answer? If so, now what do we do? Many doctors suggested behavioral modifications or the use of psychopharmaceutical drugs. Medication was not a cure or solution, just a help with symptoms. The drugs had side effects. The dangers and changes were too much. We opted to go with behavioral modifications. Combining information we read with what we knew about Shannon, we began to make playtime into learning time. We created treasure hunts that required Shannon to complete tasks and assignments to find and retrieve a desired reward. We rhymed things she had to memorize. We sang songs about history. The plan worked. She was not disabled or dumb; she was quite intelligent and capable of doing the work she was failing in school. But sitting for more than 15 minutes caused the ill-focused behaviors described in the reports from school.

Shannon was very well liked by her peers and had no problems fitting into a group. But this teacher was not aware of ADHD. I went into the classroom and observed Shannon and found myself observing the teacher more: a teacher who was very set in her ways and incapable of change from her ultimately planned routine. Meanwhile the little girl who was so excited about getting up to greet each day was solemn and moping. I reached my all-time frustration level. I marched into the teacher's room and let her know how illiterate she was and how unmannerly her conduct to my daughter was and that I planned to prove her wrong. After slamming the door, I fumed all the way home. It was not appropriate, but it felt good to me. (Adapted from a letter from a parent.)

1. What behaviors of Shannon would be indicative of a diagnosis of ADHD?

2. What interventions would have been effective with teachers who did not comply with the family's requests for modifications?

Students with ADHD are easily distracted, frequently find their thoughts wandering to a subject only superficially related, if at all, to the one being taught, and are likely to speak out impulsively. They are full of energy and prone to act without sufficient planning for others to understand the steps they intend to take. Teachers may have noted on progress reports that these students "fail to listen to directions," "are underachieving," "are bright enough, but will not listen to directions," or "are lazy." Sometimes, there is an attention inconsistency. These students may spend inordinate amounts of time on projects, but are unable to sit still for meals.

Since the 1997 reauthorization of IDEA and the implementation of regulations in March 1999, ADHD has been a fundable condition, not on its own, but under the area of Other Health Impaired, Learning Disabilities, or Emotional Disturbance, depending on the manifestation of the symptoms (Yell, 2006). The federal law governing the rights to a free, appropriate education for all children and students with disabilities does not mention ADHD as its own category of disability. ADHD is considered a medical condition and, therefore, the appropriate category for students diagnosed with this disorder is Other Health Impaired. However, we have included it here in a separate chapter because so many students with ADHD are enrolled in public schools. It occurs across all cultural, racial, and socioeconomic groups. It can cause problems for adults as well as children and affects persons at all levels of intelligence (Fowler, 1992).

Although ADHD is listed as a health impairment, the manifestation of the condition as it affects student learning determines entitlement for special education services or services under ADA. In other words, a person may be diagnosed as having ADHD but be functioning adequately in school; that is, having no specific difficulties in academic areas. Such a student would not qualify for special education. If, however, the condition of ADHD is determined to have an adverse effect on the student's ability to learn from the general education curriculum, or in a general education classroom without supports, then the student would need to have an IEP written that would specify the assistance needed in the areas in which there are difficulties. Similarly, a person may be diagnosed with ADHD and need accommodations in the community or the workplace, or medications and therapy. Learning to deal with personal differences may mean persons are able to make their own accommodations and not need special considerations from others. Modifications or accommodations outside of school and for adults would be covered, with a different set of specifics, under ADA (ADA, 1990).

As stated, students with ADHD receive services under the category of Other Health Impaired. We discuss ADHD in this separate chapter for two reasons. First, in the past decade there has been an enormous growth in the number of students being referred for services as ADHD. Second, educators and others involved with these students are dealing with a growing but as yet incomplete body of research literature describing recommended practices, both education and medical, for these students.

DEFINITIONS

ADHD is a neurological syndrome generally characterized by impulsivity, distractibility, and hyperactivity that is inconsistent with the age of the person (American Psychiatric Association, 2000). Some research shows persons with ADHD exhibit deficits in several areas such as in selective attention, executive attention, sustained attention, and orienting of attention (Tsal, Shalev, & Mevorach, 2005). The condition is present in persons of all ages, genders, ethnic groups, socioeconomic statuses, educational levels, and intelligence levels. Students are diagnosed with ADHD according to the criteria listed in the Diagnostic and Statistical Manual of Mental Disorders–Fourth Edition–Text Revision (DSM–IV–TR) (American Psychiatric Association, 2000). The three types of ADHD listed include (1) the predominantly inattentive type; (2) the predominantly hyperactive-impulsive type; and (3) the combined type. Males are identified three to four times more often than females, and males are generally identified as either the combination type or the predominantly hyperactive and impulsive type (Weyandt, 2001).

Students with ADHD often have symptoms that are inappropriately diagnosed as other disabilities, such as learning disabilities or conduct disorders. Approximately 30 percent of all students with ADHD have a learning disability as well (Dykman & Akerman, 1991). Some students will perform poorly in academic settings, but the performance can be affected by the symptoms and does not necessarily reflect a cognitive deficit (Morrison, 1995). The DSM–IV–TR notes that approximately 50 percent of clinic-referred persons with ADHD also have oppositional defiant disorder, which is characterized by patterns of negativistic, hostile, and defiant behavior toward authority figures.

PREVALENCE

One of the fastest growing categories of students within special education is that of ADHD. It is the most common childhood psychiatric disorder (Daley, 2004; Nolan, Volpe, Gadow, & Sprafkin, 1999). In schools, the percentage of students with ADHD probably varies from 3 to 5 percent of the population (Barkley, 1995; Faraone, Sergeant, Gillberg, & Biederman, 2003), although the demands of a particular school and the structure imposed may make the symptoms more or less noticeable and disturbing to teachers. Actual prevalence is difficult to determine. Students with ADHD are served in the category of Other Health Impaired, and no distinction is made to isolate any one category of health impairment. Also, students may be treated for ADHD but not have a need for educational interventions and not be included in the head counts that are sent to Congress. They are "invisible" as special education students. According to the Twenty-Second Report to Congress, the number of students ages 6 to 21 being served under the category Other Health Impaired has increased over 318 percent in 10 years from 52,733 in 1989 to 220,831 in 1999 and then to 338,672 in 2002 (U. S. Department of Education, 2005).

Prior to the reauthorization of IDEA in 1997 (IDEA, 1997), students with ADHD were served in a variety of ways or not at all. Many of them were served as students with learning disabilities or as students with emotional disturbances. Some states had regulations that provided services through state money; others offered no monetary support. Many states used the regulations from the Rehabilitation Act of 1973, Section 504, to write plans for students needing modifications who did not qualify for entitlements through IDEA. Some states had chapters written into state educational regulations. The difficulty with this range of plans was that few monetary resources existed, and some students with ADHD, depending on where they lived, were not served.

IDEA (IDEA, 2004) is a federal law that governs all special education for individuals, but **Section 504** of the Rehabilitation Act of 1973 is a civil rights law. This statute prohibits institutions that receive federal funds, including public and private schools, from discriminating against students with disabilities. There are no fiscal resources associated with Section 504; however, plans for modifications must be in place and implemented if the student is designated as having a mental or physical impairment that affects a major life function.

CHARACTERISTICS

Students with ADHD differ from their peers because they are unable to concentrate or control their impulses. ADHD has been labeled an invisible disorder because no discernable psychological or physiological tests are useful in differentiating these students from others. The symptoms cited in this section are indicative of ADHD only when they are persistent and extreme. DSM–IV–TR states that symptoms must be present before the age of 7; they must be present in two or more settings; and there must be evidence of clinical impairment in social, academic, or occupational functioning (Smith, Polloway, Patton, & Dowdy, 2001). Although the symptoms must be present before the age of 7, the disorder can be identified later. Because there is no definitive test, the behaviors may be noticeable but not troublesome to the family or to the teachers in some grade levels; therefore the identification of the disorder, and treatment or accommodations, may be delayed.

Three types of ADHD are generally referenced. One type is predominantly inattentive, with the student displaying characteristics for at least 6 months and to a degree that is maladaptive and does not match maturational expectations when observed. Of the nine symptoms listed for inattention, the student must display at least six of them to be categorized as an inattentive type. The symptoms are as follows:

1. Failing to give close attention to details, leading to careless mistakes
2. Having difficulty sustaining attention to tasks and to play activities
3. Having difficulty listening to what is being said
4. Having difficulty following through and completing homework assignments, classroom assignments, chores, or occupational duties

5. Having difficulty organizing tasks

6. Avoiding tasks that require strenuous mental activity

7. Losing materials that are necessary to complete tasks

8. Being easily distracted by extraneous activity

9. Forgetting schedules of daily activities

Most students forget assignments on occasion; fail to bring pencils to class; or fail to complete tasks, such as making their beds in the morning. The distinguishing overriding characteristic for students labeled ADHD is that these behaviors are persistent—present for at least 6 months—and maladaptive—preventing the student from accomplishing tasks that lead to adequate educational progress.

Another type of ADHD is predominantly hyperactive-impulsive. Hyperactivity is a condition of displaying excessive energy and is characterized by restlessness and agitation. Persons displaying impulsivity appear to act before they think. These symptoms, leading to a diagnosis of hyperactive-impulsive ADHD, are markedly different from those that lead to a diagnosis of inattentiveness. Multiple symptoms are listed in the DSM–IV–TR. For a diagnosis to be made, at least six of these characteristics must be present and ongoing for at least 6 months. The student with this form of ADHD displays the following behaviors:

1. Fidgets and squirms in seat

2. Leaves desk or seat in the classroom at inappropriate times

3. Runs and climbs in situations when it is inappropriate

4. Avoids engaging in quiet leisure activities

5. Acts as if driven and is always "on the go"

6. Talks excessively

7. Blurts out answers impulsively, often before the question has been completed

8. Displays difficulty waiting in lines and taking turns

9. Butts into conversations or other people's games, interrupting and intruding on others

We must remember that for services to be provided, the symptoms must be persistent and extreme to the extent that the student cannot function adequately in the environment. For educational services to be provided by the school, the student must be performing poorly in school activities and be in need of interventions in school.

The third type of ADHD is a combined type, with the student showing both types of behavior, hyperactive-impulsive as well as inattentive. In addition, to be diagnosed with ADHD, the individual must not have these symptoms as a part of another disorder, such as pervasive developmental disorder, autism, schizophrenia, or other psychiatric disorders. The American Psychiatric Association (APA, 2000) also stated that the symptoms should not be more easily explained by a mood disorder, anxiety disorder, or personality disorder. The population of students diagnosed as ADHD is diverse; few display all of the symptoms listed in the DSM–IV–TR. In addition to these major symptoms, there are other characteristics. Students may demonstrate low self-esteem, moodiness, temper outbursts, manifestations of frustration, obsessive-compulsive behaviors, and aggressiveness. Males are more likely to exhibit aggressive behaviors than females (Arnold, Ickowicz, Chen, & Schachar, 2005; Gaub & Carlson, 1997).

In the last decade or so, professionals have begun to understand the lasting nature of the problems individuals have with ADHD. The problems in school do not go away as the individual grows to adulthood. Only about one third of people with ADHD outgrow the symptoms. Ninety percent of students with ADHD fail at least one grade, approximately 1.3 percent drop out of high school, and very few finish a 4-year college program (Reeve, 1996).

ETIOLOGY

Several theories exist about the causes of ADHD, but no conclusive evidence has been shown. Traditionally, it was seen as a disorder of attention only: a result of the brain being unable to filter salient features from a large amount of stimuli. ADHD is now viewed as the result of a neurological, medical disorder rather than as a purely behavioral problem (Smith et al., 2001). Many professionals agree that it is neurologically based, and although no specific cause has been determined, neurological imaging and scanning may offer some hope for etiological information. The causes may be related to the structure of the brain, chemical imbalances such as an excess level of seratonin in the bloodstream, some function of the brain, or a combination of these or other factors.

To date, no specific gene or genes have been identified that may be a factor in causing the behaviors. Swanson et al. (1998) found a strong correlation between a dopamine receptor gene and ADHD. However, they concluded that, though this may be a factor in some cases, there might be other prenatal influences as well.

Several researchers have examined the possibility that the disorder is inherited. Levy (1999) found correlations in the behaviors of twins in a study conducted in Australia. Barkley (1998) reported on studies indicating a student with ADHD was likely to have a sibling with ADHD, and parents of students with ADHD are likely to exhibit the disorder. Given the complex nature of the disorder and the subtypes, however, most researchers believe that there are a number of influences and that the causes may be just as complex (Weyandt, 2001). Anecdotal evidence from teachers indicates that hyperactivity or inattentiveness may be prevalent in siblings or in parents of students referred for ADHD. However, research has not isolated a gene or other factor that indicates that ADHD runs in families (Hallowell & Ratey, 1994).

Other theorists have stated that students with ADHD have anatomically unique brain structures (Stevenson, Pennington, Gilger, DeFries, & Gillis, 1993) or an imbalance or deficiency in brain receptors (Hechtman, 1994). These are manifested in a series of neurologically based tasks that represent analytic and executive functioning (Barkley, Grodzinsky, & duPaul, 1992). Some researchers have theorized that ADHD is correlated with a dysfunction of the frontal lobes and the tasks associated with those lobes (e.g., attention, self-regulation, impulsivity, planning). Karatekin and Asarnow (1999) found that students with ADHD had fewer **fixations,** spent less time, and were less systematic with eye movements when scanning a picture, than students without the disorder. Other researchers have found that total brain volume was 5 percent less in a sample of boys with ADHD than in a sample of boys without the symptoms (Castellanos et al., 1994), and Berquin et al. (1998) found that cerebellum size was smaller in boys with ADHD compared to boys without ADHD. These correlations are indicative of some differences in brain anatomy, but the reasons for the differences are not clear. Weyandt (2001) cautioned that these differences are correlated but do not necessarily cause or have any relation to the condition. With advances in medical technology, we may discover more about the causes and treatment of ADHD.

Teratogens are toxins in the environment that can block the normal development of a fetus, such as smoke or pollution. These have been postulated as a cause of ADHD. Lead in the paint in the surroundings, cigarette smoke in the environment, and alcohol consumption before and after birth may affect the behavior of the child. Research does not support these theories as causes, although there may be correlations between these factors and the appearance of ADHD in students (Barkley, 1998).

Many myths exist about the causes of ADHD. One of the most widely accepted is that poor diet could be a cause. No rigorous research is available to back up this claim. Most of the diets prescribed for alleviating the symptoms stem from the work of Benjamin Feingold (1975), who claimed that preservatives and food additives were responsible for hyperactive behaviors. Once considered to be a promising area of controlling behavior, research has found diet to be an ineffective, although relatively harmless, treatment (Barkley, 1998; Connors, 1990; Kavale & Forness, 1983). More recent research indicates that some people may be allergic to some foods and will be calmer and more comfortable without these substances in their diets. This, however, may be a function of an allergic reaction and should not be labeled ADHD. Several factors such as fluorescent lighting, sugar, food additives, poor parenting, classroom organization, and poor teaching do not, according to the research, cause ADHD. Modifying any or all of these factors may cause a difference in the behaviors of a student, but the difference may not be due to "curing" ADHD. The confusion occurs when changing one of the factors results in an improvement in the student's behavior. Because other factors are often not controlled, the change may have been influenced by a combination of factors.

IDENTIFICATION PROCESS

Students with ADHD are as likely as any other population to have a **dual diagnosis,** or more than one diagnosable disability concurrently. Determining whether impulsive behavior is indicative of a learning disability or a hyperactivity problem is very difficult. Only after a battery of assessments; observations across times and places; analysis

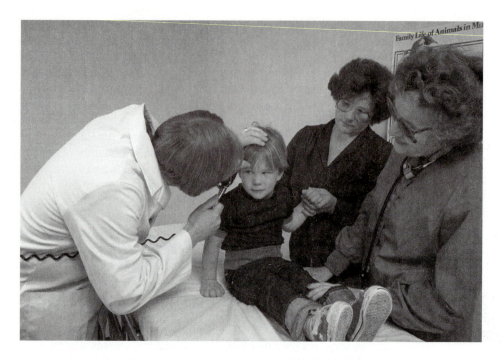

of student work; and analysis of interview data from parents, other family members, teachers, and the student can an appropriate diagnosis be made. Those with dual diagnoses are likely to have more severe problems and are more difficult to diagnose (Paternite, Loney, Salisbury, & Whaley, 1999).

A sequence of steps is important for identifying a student with ADHD. Although they differ in ordering, the processes are approximately the same. All include a variety of assessment methods, both norm and criterion referenced, as well as the subjective opinions of teachers, family members, and sometimes physicians, students, and other significant people in the student's life. Following is one sequence for assessment and identification following a referral:

1. Administering and collecting rating scales from relevant persons
2. Orienting the family and the student to the evaluation
3. Interviewing the student
4. Administering normed tests such as IQ, achievement, and continuous performance tests
5. Conducting direct observations in several settings, including school, community, and home if possible
6. Interviewing the parent(s) and other family members
7. Conducting a medical evaluation
8. Integrating all the data
9. Giving feedback and recommendations to the team

In most cases, many of the tests and assessments will be conducted by a variety of experts, with one person needed to oversee the process. Sometimes parents or other family members see that the pieces are in place. More often the school guidance

The Council for Exceptional Children recommends the following six-step procedure when attempting to identify a child with ADHD:

Step 1. Document behavior observed by both parents and teachers that is indicative of ADHD.

Step 2. Re-evaluate tests such as group intelligence tests, group achievement tests, and vision and hearing tests to determine whether they are accurate measures of potential or whether poor performance may be the result of attention problems. A physician may be consulted to see whether an identifiable physical condition is causing inattention or hyperactivity.

Step 3. Attempt classroom management to correct or control behaviors leading to poor academic performance. If such attempts are unsuccessful, request a referral for ADHD placement.

Step 4. Conduct psychological evaluations to see whether the student meets criteria for ADHD placement. Administer individual tests and behavioral rating scales. Review medication recommendations.

Step 5. Have the team, including the child's parents, plan for the special educational needs of the child.

Step 6. Implement the Individual Education Plan.

FIGURE 5.1
Identification guidelines (ADHD).
Source: Council for Exceptional Children's Task Force on Children with ADHD, 1992.

counselor or the school psychologist is responsible for following through and gathering the data from various sources (Demaray, Schaefer, & Delong, 2003). The special education teacher is sometimes the person responsible for collecting the data, but because the disorder is medical, the teacher is not always in the position of case manager. Another sequence, suggested by CEC, is found in Figure 5.1.

Rating Scales for Behavior

Many checklists are available, depending on the needs of the student and the problems that are presented. Checklists are useful because they are relatively inexpensive, easily understood, and quick to administer (Salvia & Ysseldyke, 2001). However, rating scales or checklists provide a means for gathering only subjective information or perceptions about students from those who deal with them. Teachers, parents, the student, and others are given a set of statements on which to rate the behaviors or questions to answer. These lists provide a picture of each rater's perceptions of the behaviors observed. For instance, teachers in different classes may see the targeted behaviors as extremely disruptive to the student's leaning process or to the learning of other students in the class. Family members may see frustration and signs of depression. Physicians may see the same behaviors as neurological signs of stress, and some teachers may not be bothered by the behaviors at all. In comparing the different subjective ratings, the teams can see where the student is doing well and where he or she is doing poorly and use the information to help establish an atmosphere in the classroom that will promote success. Checklists by themselves are nothing but a collection of opinions about students. They resemble the data in the old joke about the men who are visually impaired describing parts of an elephant—none of them gives the entire picture of the student. However, combined with other sources of data, they are valuable in building a picture of the type of intervention needed by a particular student (Salvia & Ysseldyke, 2001; Sattler, 2002).

The most frequently used checklists are those in the Child Behavior Checklist series by Achenbach and Rescorla (2001) and McConaughy (1993). The items in the six scales are designed to provide behavior descriptions rather than to document diagnostic inferences. In other words, the results of several ratings on one student will result in a list of strengths and weaknesses. This information can then be used along with other test results and information from observations and classwork to determine a need for special education services for the student.

The Connors' Rating Scale (Connors 1997) is a paper-and-pencil or computer-administered test evaluating problematic behaviors in students as reported by the students, teacher, parent, guardian, or caregiver. It is designed for use with students from 3 to 17 years of age and consists of two teacher-rating scales (ages 3–17 and ages 4–12) and two parent-rating scales (ages 3–17 and ages 6–14). The information asked in the questions are the same as the symptoms listed for ADHD in the DSM–IV–TR.

The Attention Deficit Disorders Evaluation Scale–Revised (ADDES) (McCarney, 1989) has the greatest number of persons in the normative sample of any of the rating scales. Scoring is quick and efficient with the computer edition. There are two versions, one each for teachers and parents or guardians to complete. They are appropriate for students who are 4 to 18 years of age. The instrument is intended to measure the three components of ADHD as listed in the DSM–IV–TR. The informant (teacher or parent) rates each item on a 5-point scale with 0 meaning the student does not engage in the behavior and 5 meaning that the student engages in the behavior one to several times per hour.

Many instruments and rating forms may be used to determine areas of strengths and weaknesses or areas of problem behaviors. They produce subjective information but allow comparisons of different persons' perceptions of the behaviors of one student. Rating scales are available for different aged students, for direct observation, and for recall of information about specific episodes of behavior. Some have been normed with large samples and provide standardized scores. A comprehensive description of the many scales is beyond the scope of this text. Salvia and Ysseldyke (2001) provided descriptions including information on reliability, validity, and norming procedures.

Observations

A systematic observation is conducted most often in a naturalistic setting for the student (e.g., home, school, work) and is designed to determine the presence or absence of certain targeted behaviors. Observations can be used to obtain global impressions, record a variety of behaviors, or record the occurrence or nonoccurrence of specific troublesome or desirable behaviors. It is frequently useful to observe students with their peer group to compare how often a behavior occurs in typically developing peers. After observing global behaviors, the observer analyzes the field notes and determines whether the targeted behavior occurs at a significant rate. The observer may also look for other behaviors the teacher or family members did not mention as problematic.

After determining the troublesome or acceptable behaviors to be documented, the observer can focus successive observations on these targeted behaviors. These behaviors will probably include the ones in the referral list from teachers, family members, or students themselves. However, it may also include behaviors that are noted during the global impressions and in the field notes, which include a running account of behavior that can be examined for patterns that trouble or please professionals.

Another important aspect of observations is the timing of the behaviors under scrutiny, including what happens before and after the events, how long the behavior lasts, and the amount of time that passes between the suspected trigger event and the start of the behavior.

A final caution about looking for specific behavior is to be aware of the **ecology of the classroom,** including the physical and social environment and any unexpected events that occur during the observations. If unusual events happen that may be a cause of the trouble, the observer could make incorrect assumptions. It is important to conduct more than one observation to have a complete and more truthful picture of the student's typical behavior.

The definition of ADHD states that the symptoms must be evident before age 7. It is often difficult to determine hyperactivity in toddlers because what may be considered lack of behavioral inhibition, time management, and goal directedness may be age appropriate. However, recent research (Fewell & Deutcher, 2001) indicates that a correlation may exist between behaviors of children 2.5 to 3 years of age and a physician diagnosis or special education placement for ADHD at the age of 8 years. The investigators isolated behaviors such as clumsiness and slowness in the acquisition of communication skills in young children. Later, when the students were age 8, many were in special education classes with a diagnosis of ADHD. This early identification may or may not be helpful in treatment options. As research continues in this area, we hope to determine more effective interventions for a range of ages.

Ecological assessments are often conducted to find the settings or classrooms that will be the best placement for the student. They focus on the physical environment and the social interactions in the settings in which the student is required to function. The variables may include the physical arrangement of furniture, the temperature of the room, lighting, extraneous noises, teacher tone and loudness, and relationships with the teacher and peers.

Standardized Tests

Intelligence and academic assessments are not necessary for a medical diagnosis of ADHD, but they are a part of the educational identification process. It is necessary to rule out other disabilities or to determine whether the student may qualify in another category of disability. Gathering information on aptitude (intelligence) and achievement can help in developing the best possible plan for educational interventions and devising a plan that will allow the student to receive an appropriate education. Standardized tests are those with scores based on norms derived from a large number of participants at all levels of ability. Aptitude tests are not infallible; however, the results can be used to predict a student's performance in school.

Many teachers have expressed confusion over the degree to which deficits in social skills for a student with ADHD are a function of the disorder or an aftereffect (Marchant & Siperstein, 1997). Assessment instruments with social aspects in the subtests can be helpful in determining students' social skills. The level of the student's social skills knowledge can be compared with the student's use of appropriate skills in school and other settings. Checklists that are useful in these comparisons include the Connors' Parent and Teacher Rating Scales–Revised, the Vineland Adaptive Behavior Scale (Sparrow, Balla, & Cicchetti, 1984), and the AAMR Adaptive Behavior Scale–School (Lambert, Nihira, & Leland, 1993).

Interviews

Parents, family members, and teachers have information about students with ADHD that can be critical in planning educational interventions. The main purposes of interviews with members of the student's family are to gain the rapport of the parents and others and to gather information about the student's behavior in settings other than school (home and community). Family members can tell educators their perceptions of behaviors outside school, background information about the student and the family, family moves, the medical history of the student and others in the family, the student's academic history in other schools or at tutoring, the social and emotional history of the family, and the results of previous examinations.

Interviews with teachers can provide the team with information on the background of the student, behavior in class, the student's academic history from this and other years in the school, and the duration of difficulties. The teacher may also note, through systematic observation (see "Functional Behavioral Analysis" under "Diagnosis" in Chapter 6), what triggers certain behaviors and what is being reinforced by the reactions of teachers and peers. Constructing an accurate, comprehensive picture that all parties agree is valid is not an easy task when the behaviors of the student with ADHD vary from setting to setting.

Medical Exams

Medical reasons for conditions other than ADHD must be ruled out. As with other aspects and symptoms of ADHD, this is not an exact science. Many of the symptoms can point to more than one problem. Medical exams can also assist physicians in prescribing appropriate medications.

PROGRAMS

Many of the programmatic changes in schools aimed at helping students with ADHD are similar to those needed for students with learning disabilities. Interventions are designed to assist with time management, controlling outbursts, memory, and attention to salient features of a situation.

A multifaceted treatment approach is usually most effective for students with ADHD. Most treatment plans contain some of the following features. Not all students will need assistance in all areas, but some may. For others, the comorbidity of other disabilities will be the deciding factor.

- Medical management
- Psychological counseling
- Structure
- Educational planning
- Environmental reorganization
- Behavior modification

Medical management refers to the involvement of a physician who determines whether or not medication may be effective. Continued monitoring of the medication and the dosage is necessary to see if the side effects are less troublesome than the behaviors the medication is lessening. The medications most often prescribed are stimulants such as Ritalin and its counterparts. Because **stimulants** have an arousal effect, for many years doctors and educators referred to the paradoxical effect of the medication. The most current theories suggest that the arousal effects of the medications are providing stimulation to the brain and lessening the student's need to seek stimulation through hyperactivity. Side effects that sometimes occur with stimulant medications are loss of appetite and depression. Stimulants such as Ritalin, Alderol, or Cylert have been 70 to 80 percent effective in reducing hyperactivity/impulsivity behaviors (Fowler, 1992; Spencer et al., 1996; Spencer et al., 2005).

Medication will often increase the student's ability to attend and will help control interfering behaviors. This makes the student more available to instruction. Although teachers do not generally understand medications, they tend to have a positive view of the process for students with ADHD (Snider, Busch, & Arrowood, 2003). However, medications alone do not improve learning and achievement. Expectations for improved learning based solely on the effects of medication are unreasonable. It must be combined with effective academic intervention and frequently with cognitive behavior therapy. Both the medications and the academic intervention should be continuously monitored for improvements and difficulties. Changes should be made based on the student's progress. All should be alert for possible side effects, including sleeping and eating problems, the appearance of tics, and emotional changes in the student (Swanson et al., 1993).

Psychological counseling helps the student understand and cope with ADHD and the negative effects that often result before the problem is recognized. It is most effective when the student's entire family is involved (Blum & Mercugliano, 1997). The family members, parents and siblings, need to understand the effects of the condition, the side effects of the medications, if used, and the dynamics and struggles of the school situations for the student. The student must understand the amount of control that he or she has over behaviors, the consequences of the behaviors, and how to handle the consequences. The student also needs to understand the changes in personality that will accompany any medications used to assist in controlling behaviors and the reactions others may have to those changes (Hall & Gushee, 2002). Family members also need to understand what the medications will and will not do.

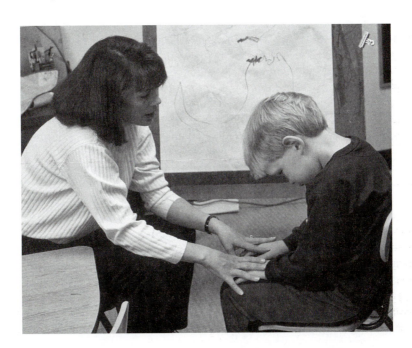

Structure, the arrangement of the environment (classroom or school) in a manner that enhances the student's success, is important in serving students with ADHD. Ironically, another important factor for teachers to remember is the need to be flexible and permit students to move when necessary and work where they can most effectively achieve and complete assignments. The purpose of educational interventions is to establish the impetus for appropriate behavior from the student, not from authority figures.

Structure and how it molds the relationship between the teacher and student permeates the entire teaching concept. For students with ADHD whose lives have been characterized by a lack of structure, the externally imposed rules and regulations of school may be either a relief or a nightmare. Some students with ADHD react well to knowing what is expected of them and what the consequences will be. Others are constrained by the rules. They have difficulty remembering them until after they have taken action. Their impulsivity makes it difficult for them to move into a classroom situation without disrupting the teacher and the class. There are some ways to help students with ADHD manage the structure. The teacher can arrange desks so the student is sitting near peers who are not bothered by movement. The student may need to work standing at his or her desk or at the chalkboard (or whiteboard) to be effective in completing assignments. Some students may even want to lie on the floor. The goal is to modify the learning environment in educational programming so that it facilitates rather than frustrates the student. Individual modifications range from establishing quiet zones for study to simplifying and repeating instructions and planning with the student to establish the best ways he or she can learn. Other suggestions are listed in Box 5.1. In some cases, assistive technology can be of help to the teacher. Some examples are listed in Box 5.2.

BOX 5.1
WHAT EVERY TEACHER SHOULD DO

Effective Teaching Strategies

- Make sure you know who made the diagnosis and what treatment was prescribed for each student.
- Many students are reluctant to take medications at school. Allow students to have a schedule that makes them comfortable and makes it easy to remember when to take medication. If students do not wish their peers to know they are on medications, arrange times during the day, such as during transitions to lunch or other classes, and respect the student's wish for privacy.
- Create a supportive and organized classroom environment. Students with ADHD need specific places to find materials and texts.
- Ensure that materials are of an appropriate difficulty level. Some students need to reduce the level of work they need to complete. Others need to be challenged to keep their minds stimulated.
- The tasks assigned in class and for homework should be meaningful. Busywork is not helpful and can cause anger and frustration.
- Use praise that is specific. It should specify the criterion met and the relationship between student effort and achievement, and it should promote student satisfaction with the completed task.
- Encourage students to monitor their own behaviors. They can chart their grades, their behaviors that disturb teachers or peers, and their behaviors that are on task and appropriate.

BOX 5.1 *Continued*

- Teach students to study in small blocks of time and to schedule the study time along with assignments. A calendar with assignments due and notes on when parts should be started is helpful.
- Monitor the student's progress on IEP goals. If the goals are written to reduce problematic behavior, collect data regularly and systematically. Graphs can be used to determine if the intervention, either psychotropic or behavioral, is effective. If the interventions are not reducing the targeted behaviors, a change is needed. **Psychotropic therapy** includes medication that alters perceptions, feelings, and behaviors. These may include Ritalin, Cylert, Alderol, and others.
- Make academic goals extremely clear to the student. Ensure that the student understands the directions for each task. It is helpful to have the directions in a written form as well as a verbal form.
- Be patient if the student needs to have the directions repeated. Repeat them in a calm manner.
- Converse with the parents and other family members frequently. Report positive aspects of their student's school day. Then, if a problem must be resolved, you will know the family well and they will know you.
- Slip in an IEP-related question or two during a routine activity in the classroom, such as lining up to leave the room, getting out books for the next activity, or between pages of a reading assignment. This method of systematically asking the questions 4 to 10 times per day addresses IEP objectives that are different from the material that is being taught to the remainder of the class.
- Teach from the general curriculum when it is working and, when necessary, modify with the individual student in mind.
- Involve the student in learning appropriate, effective, and efficient learning strategies. The student will need strategies to use in all classes.
- Teach behaviors to get along in school and in other settings. Social skills need to be practiced to appear natural.

BOX 5.2
WHAT EVERY TEACHER SHOULD KNOW ABOUT TECHNOLOGY

- Allow for podcasting of lectures or information given in class. The teacher can digitally record the class sessions and allow students to download them and listen to them multiple times. The student can also listen to a lecture in stages.
- Paper that has raised lines can assist a beginning writer in knowing when to stop a pencil stroke.
- Use e-mail with your students to enforce and encourage both reading and writing skills. Questions, comments, and feedback can all be delivered using e-mail. You can insist on journaling through blogs, in e-mails, or on class listservs.
- Provide audio tapes of classic literature for listening while engaged in other tasks.
- Masking a page can reduce distractions. A page-sized card with a window in it can be used to isolate a line of text.

Educational planning is accomplished most effectively through the use of a multidisciplinary team consisting of all the persons in the school setting who are involved with the student: medical personnel, the family members, and the student. This process, outlined in IDEA, is designed to produce an IEP for the student that will address the needs present in this setting. The problems in other settings may be addressed in an IFSP if the child is under the age of 8. These plans include counseling for the family, respite care, leisure activities, and other services. IFSPs are generally written for students in preschool settings. Each service agreed on by the team and written into the plan must be provided by the local education agency—in most cases, this is the public school.

In the case of a student with ADHD whose problems manifest in more than one setting, writing an IEP for school problems alone can be frustrating to the family members and others outside that setting. However, many of the interventions that are implemented at school may work at home and in community settings.

Behavior management instruction helps the student recognize behaviors that interfere with normal functioning. Once the student can recognize the behaviors, he or she can develop strategies for monitoring their occurrence and controlling or eliminating their negative effects on learning. Behavior modification involves more than passing out rewards. Students with ADHD need to have consistent consequences applied to their behaviors. Students need to learn when it is appropriate to move around the room and when it is not. Teachers should attempt to reinforce successive approximations. When a student is to be in his or her seat, the teacher reinforces being by the seat, then reinforces again when the student sits. When the student has mastered the skill (sitting, getting a pencil from the box, settling down by the time the bell rings, etc.), the teacher systematically fades the reinforcers so the student is getting external rewards only some of the time. Praise can be a powerful reinforcer, and although it needs to be faded to some degree, a praise-rich environment is good for most students. Reinforcers applied to desired behaviors, and negative reinforcers or withholding of reinforcing agents applied to undesirable behaviors, can control inappropriate behaviors. A more complete description of behavior analysis and how it may be used in classrooms is outlined in Chapter 4, "Students with Learning Disabilities," and Chapter 6, "Students with Emotional and Behavioral Disorders." Resources are also listed at the end of this chapter.

ISSUES OF IMPORTANCE

Accurate Diagnoses

Ensuring that diagnoses are based on a student's attention deficit, hyperactivity, or inattentiveness and not simply teacher disapproval of the student's classroom behavior is a major concern. Because there are no specific tests for identifying ADHD at this time, diagnosis is more subjective than for other disabilities. Legally, behaviors that cause a student to be labeled with ADHD must occur in two or more settings. If the school is one setting, then an IEP can be written. If the student is doing poorly in some academic areas, then the school becomes the primary site for intervention. If the student is not failing but rather doing as well as many of the students in his or her grade level, then there may be symptoms enough to write a Section 504 plan, a plan to assist students who are at risk. General education teachers then become extremely important in modifying activities in the classroom to ensure adequate performance. Because Section 504 of the Rehabilitation Act of 1973 is part of a civil rights law, the plans may be written to assist the student in school, community settings, or wherever the student needs accommodations.

Ruling Out Underachievement

Underachievement is a concern with students who are labeled ADHD. Students with ADHD may have a depressed IQ score, although most do not (Schuck & Crinella, 2005). Students may have a condition of learned helplessness, knowing that if they wait or are distracted too long, the teacher or another student will complete the task. Students may try to have others do their work for them. It is difficult to sort out whether students have become dependent on help because they needed it at one point or whether they have used the help to avoid doing the work that is required of them. In this respect, the problem is much like that of students labeled with other disabilities. Teachers should not allow students with ADHD to draw them off tasks with tangential or off-the-subject chatter.

Early Identification

DSM–IV–TR requires that the conditions associated with ADHD be present before age 7. Family members and teachers frequently have no difficulty noticing that their children and students are different in some way from other students after they enter school. Noticing an exceptionally high activity level in a preschool-aged child is difficult, even for children in structured settings. However, some children are so active that the family members and others recognize difficulties before school age. Many times a team is called together to decide on interventions for preschool-aged children or toddlers who need modifications to learn to play and grow socially and to gain information from their environment. In some cases, an IFSP can be written and implemented. The plan can include treatment plans for the child and for the needs of family members.

Many believe that students with ADHD will grow out of the condition. The research does not support this. The difficulties with inattentiveness or hyperactivity persist into adulthood. Usually, the individual finds a place to work or a career in which the symptoms do not impede success. Some are not so fortunate.

Transition Services

Transition services are required for each student with a disability who is served under IDEA. These services assist the student into school, work, or other placements after the age of 21 or graduation from high school. If a student with ADHD has an IEP under IDEA, this planning is mandated to begin at the age of 16. If the student has a Section 504 plan, or is not served in the school setting, transition services are not a legal mandate. In such cases, the family, student, physician, or any agency involved must begin the planning process. Transition services include conducting interest inventories and placing the student into internships or volunteer situations. Other needed services include managing the follow-through so that the student has several opportunities to explore options, fill out applications, and set life goals.

DIVERSITY

Some important cultural issues may need to be considered when determining whether a student from a nondominant culture should be considered for ADHD classification. Some students may exhibit activity levels that are culturally appropriate but different from the majority culture of their peers. The Council for Exceptional Children's Task

Force on Children with ADHD (1992) recommended that at least one member of the evaluation team be either a member of the same minority group as the student (ethnic, cultural, or linguistic) or be familiar with evaluating students from that minority group. Evaluation instruments such as the Child Behavior Checklist–Direct Observation Form (Achenbach & Rescorla, 2001) allow an evaluator to compare any given student to control peers from the same minority group in the same setting. Another concern is that males dominate every category of ADHD. Males are identified as ADHD far more often than females (Lumley, McNeil, & Hershell, 2002; Vail, 2002).

Female students may not be identified and therefore may not be receiving the services needed to have successful educational experiences. In fact, students of the inattentive type who are not aggressive may not be identified as ADHD. These students are still at risk of being ignored and considered lazy, disinterested, or not intelligent.

Students may be misidentified in many disability categories because of issues associated with having English as their second language. Students may appear to be unfocused and not paying attention when they do not understand what is being said to them. Some students, those from several cultures, consider it impolite to ask for help and will sit quietly and miss the conversation or the directions.

PROFESSIONALS

Educational Personnel

Both general and special education teachers may be involved in the programming provided for students with ADHD. The student may spend a large part of the school day in the general education classroom, especially if medications are effective. Special education teachers can be of assistance in teaching and helping the student to organize materials, take required items to class, write homework assignments correctly, and understand the assignments.

General education teachers can help by ensuring that the student is actively engaged in meaningful tasks for as large a percentage of the day as possible. By being close by, the teacher or paraprofessional encourages active engagement (Werts, Zigmond, & Leeper, 2001). The student also has the opportunity to ask questions. Getting bogged down on a task is less likely if a student's questions are handled immediately and the teacher encourages active engagement in an interesting task.

Frequently, students with ADHD will have a paraeducator or teacher's assistant assigned to them for help for all or part of a day. Sometimes an assistant is assigned to help the classroom teacher because of the presence of the student with ADHD in the class. The paraeducator can aid successful inclusion and help the student with ADHD to stay on task by immediately reinforcing desired behaviors, following a systematic reinforcement schedule, and helping other students. The paraeducator can help the student with ADHD participate in groups by curbing the impulsivity of the student by asking for other students to answer questions, equalizing the opportunities for each student in the group to participate, and reinforcing collaboration. Persons in the community such as scout leaders, club sponsors, community sports coaches, and others must have an understanding of the conditions and the symptoms exhibited by the student with ADHD. These adults need clear instructions on how to handle behaviors, when to ask about medications, when to allow the student to run off excess energy, and when it is appropriate to calm the student. Most of all, the adults or youths in charge of community activities must understand that the behaviors are symptomatic of a disorder and not just the outbursts of an unruly student.

Counselors can be helpful in school settings (Hall & Gushee, 2002). They may or may not be instrumental in identification of students with ADHD, but they can assist the students in dealing with impulsive behavior outbursts, coordinating interventions with teachers, and talking with parents about students' inappropriate behaviors. For instance, when students begin to change classes, the counselor can help implement organization systems. When homework assignments are varied across classes or subject areas, the counselor can assist the students with modifications for remembering assignments, getting completed assignments to the teachers, and managing time at home and at school (Schwiebert, Sealander, & Dennison, 2002).

Medical Personnel

Medical and paramedical professionals, including family physicians and psychotherapists, may provide medication, behavioral therapy, counseling, and other related services. They often assist the regular and special educator in monitoring the effects of medications. They work in collaboration with general and special education teachers to document typical behaviors in several settings to determine whether medications and prescribed dosages are effective. Although teachers and other educators are not qualified to suggest or prescribe medications for ADHD, they are in a position to provide medical personnel with information that will render their decisions more effective. Often medical personnel will ask parents and teachers to complete questionnaires on the frequency or intensity of behaviors, and depending on the age of the student, they may have the student complete a questionnaire as well.

DISCUSSION QUESTIONS

1. Should ADHD be funded as its own category or remain in the category of OHI? Why or why not?
2. What characteristics define a person with ADHD?
3. How can ADHD be underidentified or overidentified?
4. What interventions are effective for students with ADHD?
5. Should medications be used for students with ADHD?
6. Do students with ADHD outgrow the condition?

PROFESSIONAL ASSOCIATIONS AND PARENT OR SELF-HELP GROUPS

Children with Attention Deficit Disorder (CHADD)
8181 Professional Place, Suite 201
Landover, MD 20785
301-306-7070 or 800-233-4050
Fax: 301-306-7090
E-mail: national@chadd.org

ADD Warehouse
300 Northwest 70th Avenue, Suite 102
Plantation, FL 33317

Attention Deficit Disorder Association (ADDA)
8901 South Ireland Way
Aurora, CO 80016

National Attention Deficit Disorder Association (ADDA)
1788 Second Street, Suite 200
Highland Park, IL 60035
847-432-ADDA
Fax: 847-432-5874
E-mail: mail@add.org

Attention Deficit Disorder Ontario Foundation (ADDO)
Station R
Box 223

Toronto, Ontario
CANADA
M4G 3Z9
416-813-6858
E-mail: ADDO@addofoundation.org

Jumping Johnny Get Back to Work—A Child's Guide to ADHD/Hyperactivity
Michael Jordan, Ph.D., Connecticut Association for Children with LD
18 Marshall Street
South Norwalk, CT 06854
203-838-5010

Brakes: The Interactive Newsletter for Kids with ADHD
Magination
19 Union Square West
New York, NY 10003
800-825-3089

Teaching Exceptional Children
Council for Exceptional Children (CEC)
1110 North Glebe Road, Suite 300
Arlington, VA 22201-5704

REFERENCES

Achenbach, T. M., & Rescorla, L. (2001). *Manual for the ASEBA school-age forms and profiles.* Burlington, VT: Research Center for Children, Youth, & Families/Achenbach System of Empirically Based Assessment (ASEBA).

American Psychiatric Association. (2000). *Diagnostic and statistical manual of mental disorders: Text revision (DSM–IV–TR)* (4th ed.). Washington, DC: Author.

Americans with Disabilities Act of 1990 (ADA), 42U.S.C.A.: 12101 et seq.

Arnold, P. D., Ickowicz, A., Chen, S., & Schachar, R. (2005). Attention-deficit hyperactivity disorder with and without obsessive-compulsive behaviours: Clinical characteristics, cognitive assessment, and risk factors. *Canadian Journal of Psychiatry, 50,* 59–67.

Barkley, R. A. (1995). *Taking charge of ADHD: The complete, authoritative guide for parents.* New York: Guilford.

Barkley, R. A. (1998). *Attention deficit hyperactivity disorder: A handbook for diagnosis and treatment* (2nd ed.). New York: Guilford.

Barkley, R. A., Grodzinsky, G., & duPaul, G. J. (1992). Frontal lobe functions in attention deficit disorder with and without hyperactivity: A review and research report. *Journal of Abnormal Child Psychology, 20,* 163–188.

Berquin, P. C., Giedd, J. N., Jacobsen, L. K., Hamburger, S. D., Krain, A. L., Rapoport, J. L., et al. (1998). The cerebellum in attention deficit hyperactivity disorder: A morphometric study. *Neurology, 50,* 1087–1093.

Blum, N. J., & Mercugliano, M. (1997). Attention-deficit/hyperactivity disorder. In M. L. Batshaw (Ed.), *Children with disabilities* (4th ed.). Baltimore: Paul H. Brookes.

Castellanos, F. X., Giedd, J. N., Eckburg, P., Marsh, W. L., Vaituzis, C., Kaysen, D., et al. (1994). Quantitative morphology of the caudate nucleus in attention deficit hyperactivity disorder. *American Journal of Psychiatry, 151,* 1791–1796.

Connors, C. K. (1990). *Food additives and hyperactive children.* New York: Plenum.

Connors, C. K. (1997). *Connors' parent and teacher rating scales–Revised* (CSR–R). North Tonawanda, NY: Multi Health Systems.

Council for Exceptional Children's Task Force on Children with ADHD. (1992). *Children with ADHD: A shared responsibility.* Reston, VA: Author.

Daley, K. C. (2004). Update on attention-deficit/hyperactivity disorder. *Curricular Opinion Pediatrics, 16,* 217–226.

Demaray, M. K., Schaefer, K., & Delong, L. K. (2003). Attention-deficit/hyperactivity disorder (ADHD): A national survey of training and current assessment practices in the schools. *Psychology in the Schools, 40,* 583–597.

Dykman, R. A., & Ackerman, P. T. (1991). Attention deficit disorder and specific reading disability: Separate but often overlapping disorders. *Journal of Learning Disabilities, 24,* 96–103.

Faraone, S. V., Sergeant, J., Gillberg, S., & Biederman, J. (2003). The worldwide prevalence of ADHD: Is it an American condition? *World Psychiatry, 2,* 104–113.

Feingold, B. (1975). *Why your child is hyperactive.* New York: Random House.

Fewell, R. R., & Deutcher, B. (2001, December). *Early predictors of ADHD in children under the age of three years.* Paper presented at the Division for Early Childhood International Conference, Boston, MA.

Forbes, G. B. (1998). Clinical utility of the test of variables of attention (TOVA) in the diagnosis of attention-deficit/hyperactivity disorder. *Journal of Clinical Psychology,* Vol. 54 (4), 461–476.

Fowler, M. (1992). *C.H.A.D.D. educators' manual: An in-depth look at attention deficit disorder for an educational perspective.* Fairfax, VA: CASET Associates.

Gaub, M., & Carlson, C. L. (1997). Meta-analysis of gender differences in ADHD. *Attention, 2,* 25–30.

Hall, A. S., & Gushee, A. G. (2002). Medication interventions for ADHD youth: A primer for school and mental health counselors. *Journal of Mental Health Counseling, 24,* 140–153.

Hallowell, E. M., & Ratey, J. J. (1994). *Driven to distraction: Recognizing and coping with attention deficit disorder from childhood to adulthood.* New York: Touchstone.

Hechtman, L. (1994) Genetic and neurobiological aspects of attention deficit hyperactivity disorder: A review. *Journal of Psychiatry and Neuroscience, 19,* 193–201.

Individuals with Disabilities Education Act Amendments of 1997 (IDEA), Pub. L. 105-17, 105th Congress, 1st Session.

Individuals with Disabilities Education Improvement Act of 2004 (IDEA), Pub. L. 108-14, 108th Congress, 2nd Session.

Karatekin, C., & Asarnow, R. F. (1999). Exploratory eye movement to pictures in childhood onset schizophrenia and attention deficit hyperactivity disorder (ADHD). *Journal of Abnormal Child Psychology, 27,* 324–330.

Kavale, K. A., & Forness, S. R. (1983). Hyperactivity and diet treatment: A meta-analysis of the Feingold hypothesis. *Journal of Learning Disabilities, 16,* 324–330.

Lambert, N., Nihira, K., & Leland, H. (1993). *AAMR adaptive behavior scale–School* (2nd ed.). Austin, TX: PRO-ED.

Levy, F. (1999). DSM–IV subtypes: A genetic perspective. *The ADHD Report, 7*(1), 8–9.

Lumley, V. A., McNeil, C. B., & Hershell, A. D. (2002). An examination of gender differences among young children with disruptive behavior disorders. *Child Study Journal, 32,* 89–100.

Marchant, C., & Siperstein, G. N. (1997) Meeting the needs of students with AD/HD by addressing the professional development needs of their teachers. *Teacher Education and Special Education, 20,* 92–102.

McCarney, S. B. (1989). *Attention deficit disorders evaluation scale–Revised.* Columbia: MO: Hawthorne Educational Services.

McConaughy, S. H. (1993). Advancement in the empirically based assessment of children's behavioral and emotional problems. *School Psychology Review, 22,* 285–307.

Morrison, J. (1995). *DSM–IV made easy.* New York: Guilford Press.

Nolan, E. E., Volpe, R. J., Gadow, K. D., & Sprafkin, J. (1999). Developmental, gender, and co-morbidity differences in clinically referred children with ADHD. *Journal of Emotional and Behavioral Disorders, 7*(1), 11–21.

Paternite, C. E., Loney, J., Salisbury. H., & Whaley, M. A. (1999). Childhood inattention-overactivity, aggression, and stimulant medication history as predictors of young adult outcomes. *Journal of Child and Adolescent Psychopharmacology, 9,* 169–184.

Reeve, R. E. (1996). *Module I—Characteristics and identification. In A continuing education program on attention deficit disorder.* Reston, VA: Council for Exceptional Children.

Salvia, J., & Ysseldyke, J. E. (2001). *Assessment* (8th ed.). Boston: Houghton Mifflin.

Sattler, J. M. (2002). Assessment of children: Behavioral and clinical applications (4th ed.). San Diego: Sattler.

Schuck, S. E. B., & Crinella, F. M. (2005). Why children with ADHD do not have low IQs. *Journal of Learning Disabilities, 38,* 262–280.

Schwiebert, V. L., Sealander, K. A., & Dennison, J. L. (2002). Strategies for counselors working with high school students with attention-deficit/hyperactivity disorder. *Journal of Counseling & Development, 80,* 3–10.

Smith, T. E. C., Polloway, E. A., Patton, J. R., & Dowdy, C. A. (2001). *Teaching students with special needs in inclusive settings* (3rd ed.). Boston: Allyn & Bacon.

Snider, V. E., Busch, T., & Arrowood, L. (2003). Teacher knowledge of stimulant medication and ADHD. *Remedial and Special Education, 24,* 46–56.

Sparrow, S. S., Balla, D. A., & Cicchetti, D. V. (1984). *Vineland adaptive behavior scale (VABS).* Circle Pines, MN: American Guidance Service.

Spencer, T., Biederman, J., Wilens, T., Doyle, R., Surman, C., Prince, J., et al. (2005). A large, double-blind, randomized clinical trial of methylphenidate in the treatment of adults with attention-deficit/hyperactivity disorder. *Biological Psychiatry, 57,* 456–463.

Spencer, T., Beiderman, J., Wilens, T., Harding, M., O'Donnell, D., & Griffin, S. (1996). Pharmacotherapy of attention deficit hyperactivity disorder across the life cycle. *Journal of the American Academy of Child and Adolescent Psychiatry, 35,* 409–432.

Stevenson, J., Pennington, B. F., Gilger, J. W., DeFries, J. C., & Gillis, J. J. (1993). Hyperactivity and spelling disability: Testing for shared genetic aetiology. *Journal of Child Psychology and Psychiatry, 34,* 1137–1152.

Swanson, J. M., McBurnett, K., Wigal, T., Pfiffner, L. J., Lerner, M. A., Williams, L., et. al. (1993). Effect of stimulant medication on children with attention deficit disorder: A "review of reviews." *Exceptional Children, 60,* 154–161.

Swanson, J. M., Sunohara, G. A., Kennedy, J. L., Regino, R., Finear, E., Wigal, T., et al. (1998). Association of the dopamine receptor D4 (DRD4) gene with a refined phenotype of attention-deficit/hyperactivity disorder (ADHD): AQ family-based approach. *Molecular Psychiatry, 3,* 38–41.

Tsal, Y., Shalev, L., & Mevorach, C. (2005). The diversity of attention deficits in ADHD: The prevalence of four cognitive factors in ADHD versus controls. *Journal of Learning Disabilities, 38,* 142–157.

U.S. Department of Education. (2005). *Twenty-fifth annual report to Congress on the implementation of the Individuals with Disabilities Education Act.* Washington, DC: Author.

Vail, K. (2002). ADHD in girls is under-diagnosed. *The American School Board Journal, 189*(12), 12.

Werts, M. G., Zigmond, N., & Leeper, D. C. (2001). Paraprofessional proximity and academic engagement: Primary-aged students with disabilities in general education classrooms. *Education and Training in Mental Retardation and Developmental Disabilities, 36,* 424–440.

Weyandt, L. L. (2001). *An ADHD primer.* Boston: Allyn & Bacon.

Yell, M. L. (2006). *The law and special education.* Upper Saddle River, NJ: Merrill/Prentice Hall.

6

Students with Emotional and Behavioral Disorders

KEY TERMS

WHAT WOULD YOU DO?

Ashlynn was a 16-year-old junior in a public school. She had a 1.8 grade point average. Since seventh grade she had been active in drama, having the lead in the annual school play as a freshman and parts in the plays each year. She also played in a school band and was instrumental in coordinating a group interested in writing songs, especially those that spoofed the government, the administration of the school, and other current events. She played an electric guitar and she played regularly in one of the restaurants in town.

Her teachers found she had interesting and insightful comments to make in class discussions although she rarely prepared for class. She didn't turn in homework in spite of several systems of homework notebooks signed by teachers and parents. Ashlynn merely wrote the assignments in pencil and changed them after each adult had signed them. She had a few friends and had little trouble getting people to follow her. Her parents were worried her leadership abilities were "too good" and that she would get into serious trouble without realizing it.

In her junior year, she had a supporting part in the annual play. She was faithful in attendance of rehearsals and compliant in assisting with producing a quality performance. The play was performed for three nights (Thursday, Friday, and Saturday) and the performances were notable for no outlandish events or jokes. It was tradition that the cast have a party following the Saturday night performance. This year, Ashlynn's grandmother offered her home for the gathering. The house was about 10 miles out of town and the site included six acres of land. The cast planned the party for outdoors. The party started about 11:00 p.m. after the last curtain and when the cast members could get to the grandmother's home. Most of the students drove and carpooled to the home. Some parents dropped off their children. Ashlynn provided some snacks and soft drinks and cast members also brought food. A couple of Ashlynn's friends brought some kegs of beer. Grandma brought out some large disposable cups to use with the kegs of beer. The high school students, including Ashlynn, began to drink and get louder and louder. Because the home was out in the "country," the noise did not bother anyone for a while. Eventually, some neighbors called and complained to the grandmother. Some parents arrived about 2:00 a.m. to pick up their teens. One parent, a friend of Ashlynn's parents, aware of the underage drinking and the potential liability of having teenagers driving home after drinking, called Ashlynn's parents. Ashlynn's father took a van and drove to his mother's home and parked it across the entrance to the property. Ashlynn's mother drove out, went to the house and started taking keys away from students who had cars. Together, with the phone at the house and cell phones, they began calling parents, telling them the situation, and asking them to come and get the young men and women. Some

173

people had left the party before Ashlynn's parents arrived. Some parents came to retrieve their children. Others asked that the students be sent home.

The principal of the school was called early on Sunday morning and told of the party and the drinking. On Monday, he informed Ashlynn there would be consequences to her behavior.

1. Does Ashlynn have symptoms that would lead to a referral for behavioral disorders? Why or why not?

2. Does the incident of the cast party warrant intervention? What interventions would be appropriate?

Teachers are confronted with students whose behavior is out of control, and who are so depressed and **withdrawn,** pulled away from social interactions, that they resist learning or interacting with others. School may become irrelevant to students who experience the absence of a parent, a pregnancy, a friend's runway or suicide, drug addiction, or any of the other multiple problems current in our society. All teachers observe and confront behaviors that reflect home influences, situational and social stresses, and fears and anxieties about new learning tasks. Students experience abuse, neglect, divorce, broken families, poverty, homelessness, drug and alcohol abuse, and a decreased supportive social program. Students with emotional and behavioral disorders exhibit an ongoing and pervasive pattern of antisocial, noncompliant behaviors that inhibit learning in a school environment.

The special education area of emotional and behavioral disorders (EBD) or socially and emotionally disturbed (SED) or severely emotionally disturbed (SED) or emotionally disturbed is not easily named, described, or defined. Definitions, prevalence estimates, characteristics, and etiology are often divergent and sometimes the result of a consensus of expert opinion. There is also debate and little agreement about whether a specific philosophy, curriculum, or approach is preferred in the education of students with EBD (Grosenick, George, & George, 1990). Furthermore, students with EBD may have additional impairments that complicate their already difficult circumstances. Students with emotional and behavioral disorders come from all socioeconomic levels, age levels, and ethnic and racial groups. Even the term emotional and behavioral disorder is in flux, although it is the term used by the Council for Children with Behavioral Disorders (Heward, 2006; Theodore, Akin-Little, & Little, 2004).

DEFINITIONS

The definitions of emotional and behavioral disorders vary. Some are subjective and others are educationally irrelevant. Some emphasize medical or psychological terms. The fundamental issue that complicates defining students with EBD is the uncertainty about what constitutes human **deviance,** or a difference from typical development. The more widely accepted definitions propose that the problem behaviors have the following characteristics:

1. They exist to a marked extent and are notably serious.
2. They are chronic or exist over a long period of time (3 to 6 months or more).
3. There is a high rate or frequency of exhibited behavior.
4. There is an intense, dramatic, or overwhelming behavioral response.

5. Unacceptable behavioral episodes last far beyond expected.

6. Unacceptable behavior occurs consistently in at least two settings, one of which is school related.

7. Personal difficulties adversely affect school performances.

8. The behavior is age inappropriate and regarded as deviant from cultural or sociological standards of the child's background (American Psychiatric Association, 2000; Hardman, Drew & Egan, 2005; Heward, 2006).

The definitions highlight several common areas. Students with emotional and behavioral disturbances exhibit some or all of the following characteristics:

1. Serious learning problems; they are often failing all their subjects and are often two or more years behind their peers academically.

2. Serious problems with making or sustaining happy, gratifying relationships with others

3. **Social alienation** problems; they are frequently ostracized, having few social contacts; some are withdrawn.

4. Behaviors that are often obnoxious and surprisingly inappropriate; the behaviors puzzle, frighten, and disgust observers.

5. Inappropriate anxiety and sadness

6. Complaints about psychosomatic illnesses, especially stomach pains, nausea, and headaches

Students with EBD can be notably anxious and depressed; some act out and others are withdrawn. **Anxiety** refers to feelings of apprehension, fearfulness, or dread, whereas depression refers to feelings of sadness, self-depreciation, or worthlessness. Students who act out appear hostile, angry, and sometimes aggressive or assaultive. Students who are experiencing a temporary situational crisis or developmental lags or problems or those whose behavior is a reflection of economic disadvantage or specific social, cultural, or ethnic-determined behavioral reactions are not included in the definitions of EBD (Bauer, Keefe, & Shea, 2001; Lane, Wehby, & Barton-Arwood, 2005; Turnbull, Turnbull, Shank, & Smith, 2004).

Legal Definition

IDEA details the following definition originally written in 1978:

> The term means a condition exhibiting one or more of the following characteristics over a long period of time and to a marked degree that adversely affects a child's educational performance:
>
> - An inability to learn that cannot be explained by intellectual, sensory or health factors.
> - An inability to build or maintain satisfactory interpersonal relationships with peers and teachers.
> - Inappropriate types of behavior or feelings under normal circumstances.
> - A general pervasive mood of unhappiness or depression.
> - A tendency to develop physical symptoms or fears associated with personal or school problems.
> - The term includes children who are schizophrenic or autistic. The term does not include children who are socially maladjusted, unless it is determined that they have an emotional disturbance (U.S. Department of Education, 1999, p. 12422).

In 1990, the federal government moved autism to a separate category under IDEA.

This legal definition has the potential to be misleading in several ways because students can have emotional and behavioral disturbance and yet still not meet the criteria stated in the definition. There are issues with vague terms such as inability to learn and inability to build or maintain satisfactory interpersonal relationships (Forness & Kavale, 2000). It is an exclusionary definition and contains language that is subjective. Further, the definition does not allow for discrimination among students who are EBD, students who are socially maladjusted, and students who have behaviors that are simply disturbing (Merrell & Walker, 2004). For example:

1. Some students who have emotional difficulties can and do learn as a result of specialized remedial programs. Gifted students who are disturbed may be functioning below their potential but still be at grade level. **Intelligence quotient (IQ)** scores that indicate students with EBD to be slow learners or even educable mentally retarded may be predictive of school failure only if special services are not available. Although there is a greater likelihood of adjustment problems or EBD for students who are mentally retarded, LD, and sensory or health impaired, these disabilities are neither synonymous nor interchangeable with EBD. However, students with EBD may have concurrent disabilities that further confuse the identification difficulties.

2. Although troubled students are resistant and suspicious about entering into relationships, with adult persistence, care, and loving affection, these students can experience satisfying interpersonal relationships.

3. Behaviors are often deemed inappropriate based on the subjective personal judgments and opinions of adult observers. Phrases such as "tendency" and "long period of time" make objective decisions difficult.

Any written definition should be clearly understood, as positive as possible, and appropriate to present school conditions. It should address important skills, such as impulse control and attention, and the teacher's role with EBD students. The previous definition reflects the current professional preference because it is inclusive of both emotional and behavioral disorders, is school centered, reflects cultural and ethnic diversity concerns, excludes minor problems in students' lives, and includes the full range of concerns shared by mental health and education professionals (Kauffman, 2005). Any attempt to interpret the definition of EBD for general educators, special educators, and the lay public must highlight that these students are consistently and seriously troubled at home, in school, and in the community (Kauffman; Kerr & Nelson, 2006).

Descriptions of the unacceptable behavior patterns often illustrate the difficulties these students experience with greater clarity than do clinical diagnostic categories or classification terms. For example, instead of simply labeling a student obsessive-compulsive neurotic, one could instead describe the behaviors, such as repeated hand washing or an inability to suppress thoughts about injuring another person. These typical complaints are more easily understood using behavioral descriptions than a classification term. Clear descriptions of the unacceptable behaviors often lead to intervention strategies that evolve from the detailed behavioral analysis. Descriptions can also lead to better hypotheses of the functions of the behaviors rather than merely labeling them.

A final danger is that the EBD concept may be applied to any deviant behavior in the classroom for which there is no other available concept. Students may be so labeled because they violate classroom rules (Heward, 2006). The risk in this practice is that the label may not only misdiagnose students but it may also not be stable from year to year. However, it may be a lasting label. Some teachers are more tolerant of certain types of behaviors than others. Professionals making judgments about labeling must cautiously discriminate between behaviors that indicate disturbance and behaviors that are simply disturbing to a teacher.

Students with Conduct Disorders

Students with conduct disorders are excluded from the IDEA definition of EBD (Hughes & Bray, 2004; Merrill & Walker, 2004; Stinnett, Bull, Koonce, & Aldridge, 1999; Theodore et al., 2004). The Diagnostic and Statistical Manual of Mental Disorders (American Psychiatric Association, 2000) characterizes conduct disorders or social maladjustment as occurring when there is a repetitive and persistent pattern of behavior that violates the rights of others or violates societal rules or norms that are age appropriate. Conduct disorders take the following forms:

- Aggression toward people or animals
- Destruction of property
- Deceitfulness or theft
- Serious rule violation

Students with conduct disorders are further classified as either undersocialized or so-cialized. Undersocialized students are characterized by impulsivity, irritability, and ar-gumentativeness. They are social isolates, and disobedient, and can be threatening or assaultive. The socialized conduct disorder is displayed by more covert antisocial behavior typified by lying, stealing, arson, destructiveness, gang membership, tru-ancy, and running away (Kauffman, 2005; Rhode, Jensen, & Reavis, 1998). These students often get into trouble with the law, go before a juvenile court judge, and become labeled delinquent by the courts. The terms delinquency, social maladjust-ment, and conduct disorder are used interchangeably. The term EBD is not the same as these terms, and it is not interchangeable with them according to the federal defi-nition. Forness and Kavale (2000) and Turnbull et al. (2004) have stated that it is more important to describe the problem than to engage in discussions of meaningless distinctions when a problem clearly exists.

PREVALENCE

There are notable problems with estimating the number of students with EBD; as a result, estimated figures vary considerably (Heward, 2006; Kauffman, 2005). The National Institute of Mental Health in the U.S. Department of Health and Human Services has consistently estimated 10 percent of the school-age population as expe-riencing mental disorders (Haring, McCormick, & Haring, 1994). Some surveys even extend the estimates of students and youth with EBD to more than 20 percent (Meyen, Vergason, & Whelan, 1996). OSERS has estimated that between 1.2 and 2 percent of the school-age population has EBD. The number being served represents about half of the estimated 2 percent (Bullis & Cheney, 1999). Therefore, many students who may qualify are not being served. Of all the estimate ranges, which potentially identify between 1 and 10 million students disabled by EBD, only 477,627 students with EBD receive special education public school services (U.S. Department of Education, 2005). This number represents almost a 25 percent change over those receiving ser-vices in the 1989–1990 school year, ranking students with EBD as the fourth largest category of students receiving special education services. However, the category rep-resents only 8.2 percent of these students.

Estimating the number of students with severe emotional disturbance who qual-ify for special education services is difficult for a variety of reasons. The most obvious is the lack of an objective definition (Heward, 2006; Kauffman, 2005) and the exclu-sion of students with social maladjustment. Another factor is that the number of stu-dents identified with EBD rises as students' ages rise. However, many high schools do not have classes for students with EBD, and the labels may be changed to reflect only a co-occurring disability (Bauer et al., 2001). Other reasons for the difficulty in es-timating the numbers of students with EBD include subjectivity of judgments regard-ing screening, identification, diagnosis, and placement; governmental reluctance to include conduct disorders in the operational definition, in spite of evidence that stu-dents with emotional disturbance exhibit similar patterns of behavior; and public school personnel rejection of and reluctance to respond to these students, and the re-sulting tendency to force them out of school or to ignore their needs (Tompkins, 1996).

Students may have a disability in any category and still not qualify for special ed-ucation services. IDEA clearly states that students must need specially designed in-struction (i.e., they must be in need of an individually tailored curriculum or program) to qualify for special education services. Therefore, a student who could profit from general education programs may not need to be served under IDEA. Students who are emotionally disturbed but whose objectives and education can be delivered in the general education classroom without the benefit of aids and supports also would not qualify for special education services under this law. The student may need a behavior intervention plan that is required by IDEA when necessary and Section 504 of the Rehabilitation Act of 1973 when that is a better fit. Other students, not counted in the special education roles, may receive community-based support, private counseling, family counseling, medical interventions, or other interventions and combinations of interventions. Family members may be reluctant to sign IEPs that use a label of EBD when students can get help under a 504 plan. This is an individual plan written under the auspices of the Rehabilitation Act of 1973 and is designed to help students who do not have a special education label but may have some reason for needing extra consideration in some areas.

Schools may be reluctant to label students if they have no resources with which to treat the problems. It may be that these students are being ignored. These variables tend to confound one another. We do know that male students are more likely to be referred and labeled than females (a ratio of 4:1) and that males will more likely have externalized behaviors than internalized ones (Gilmour, Hill, & Place, 2004). In spite of all the difficulties, the number of students actually served in special education for the emotionally disturbed is 477,627 (U.S Department of Education, 2005) or 8.1 percent of all special education students.

CHARACTERISTICS

Intelligence and Achievement

Despite the limited research on intelligence of students with EBD compared with students who are typically developing, the philosophical problems associated with what is intelligence and the procedural flaws in intelligence testing create many difficulties in accurate measurement of the intellectual potential of students labeled as EBD. Studies over several decades have indicated that students with disturbances tend to have average to marginally lower-than-average measured IQs compared with students who are typically developing (Bortner & Birch, 1969; Bower, 1981; Duncan, Forness, & Hartsough, 1995; Graubard, 1964; Kauffman, 2005; Lyons & Powers, 1963; Motto & Wilkins, 1968; Nelson, Benner, & Rogers-Adkinson, 2003; Rubin & Balow, 1978). However, true scores may be much higher if the emotional difficulties caused depressed scores of the students' abilities. The scores on an IQ test generally serve as a predictor of school success, and lower scores are accurate in reflecting the academic and school failure that is a dominant characteristic of students with emotional and behavioral disorders. Many of these students are two or more academic years behind their peers, fail more courses, evidence higher absenteeism rates, have a higher dropout rate, and experience more disciplinary actions than students in other disability categories (Anderson, Kutash, & Duchniwski, 2001; Bradley, Henderson, & Monfore, 2004; Lane et al., 2005; Wagner et al., 2003). The more severe the disturbance, the lower the performances appear to be. The traditional position has been that these students tend to be regarded at the average or above-average intellectual functioning level, and their scores are complicated by inattention to school subjects during instruction as well as inattention to the tasks of the tests (Hardman et al., 2005; Heward, 2006).

Some common school-related behaviors include the following:

- A high rate of absenteeism and tardiness
- Failing most subjects
- Being two or more years behind academically
- Not completing assignments
- Returning assignments late, soiled, messy, sometimes with written profanity directed toward the teacher
- Experiencing difficulty in following directions
- Experiencing difficulty in maintaining attention to school tasks

Social and Interpersonal Characteristics

Several educators have suggested that students with EBD have the potential to succeed in school but lack secondary skills such as attending, following directions, and using tools appropriately, which leads to school failure (Rhode et al., 1998; Smith, 2001). Some students experience social isolation and have difficulty in developing meaningful interpersonal relationships. They may have a tendency to misinterpret cues as hostile (Gresham, 2002). They appear at the fringe of school extracurricular and social activities, exhibiting antisocial behavior. About two thirds of students with serious disturbances who are placed in special education programs exhibit **externalizing behaviors** such as failure to remain seated, fighting, stealing, using profanity, interference with others and the educational program, destroying property, noncompliance, being argumentative, lying, exhibiting temper tantrums, being verbally abusive, and physically and aggressively attacking others, disrupting the school environment and impeding instruction for all students (Lane, Gresham, & O'Shaughnessy, 2002; Walker, 1997). Yet other students labeled EBD exhibit **internalizing behaviors** such as withdrawal, apprehensiveness, reduced or little social interactions, sad or depressive feelings, daydreaming, and guilt feelings (internalizing behavior disorders). They can be shy, disinterested, or immature. Some frequently exhibit hyperactivity, overactivity, and impulsivity. Most troubled students are characterized as anxious and subject to depression (Hallahan & Kauffman, 1996; Kirk, Gallagher, Anastasiow, & Coleman, 2006). As a result, these students frequently join gangs, become substance abusers, are truant, become delinquent, or are adjudicated.

Labels

Many labels or terms are used in reference to students in trouble. Frequently used labels are emotionally disturbed, behaviorally disordered, emotional-behavioral disordered, and mentally disordered or mentally ill. Other labels used in the professional educational literature are behavioral disabilities, emotionally handicapped, behaviorally handicapped, behaviorally-emotionally handicapped, and socioemotionally impaired. Some professionals prefer to use nonclinical terms, such as students in conflict, to reduce social stigma and confusion in making reference to these students (Hunt & Marshall, 2006; Stinnett et al., 1999). Many educators prefer to use behavioral descriptors rather than labels, believing that in doing so they avoid misleading others by a negatively stereotyping label, allowing them to draw their own conclusions about the student (Dyck et al., 2004).

ETIOLOGY

The specific causes of EBD in any individual student are usually difficult to ascertain (Kauffman, 2005). Although no causal relationships have been conclusively identified, several predisposing and precipitating factors are considered important. These include everything from watching too much television to environmental pollutants to genetic abnormalities. However, to assume that any behavior is caused by one factor would be unwise. As a result, assigning blame to any one factor is usually untenable. There are several ways to understand the causes of EBD. However, a conceptual framework is only beneficial if it is believable, defensible, and useful in explaining the causes of human behavior and how to devise interventions for the students.

Some theorists believe that interventions based on social learning principles are preferable because they have practicality for teachers. Still others believe that an integrated model applied to the spectrum of events in the educational life of a student with EBD will result in a better outcome. The independent description of influences or causes presented here does not deny the proposition that influences across the models presented may be at play and that their interaction can contribute to a given student's adjustment problems.

Organic Factors

Although there is little question of a possible genetic cause for some disorders, such as schizophrenia, a psychotic disorder characterized by delusions or hallucination and depression, available data does not suggest conclusive proof for many other manifestations of students' behaviors (Eaves, Silberg & Erkanli, 2003; Eley et al., 2003). Similarly, depression most likely has a genetic determinant, and it certainly has biochemical **comorbidity,** or a concurrence of two or more conditions simultaneously, with emotional and behavioral difficulties. However, most experts suggest that the biological, genetic, or organic influences often interact with environmental experiences (e.g., in utero exposure to drugs or alcohol) to produce socially unacceptable behaviors (Fergusson & Woodward, 2002; Youngblade & Nackashi, 2003). Central nervous system dysfunction and brain disorders also can play a role in the development of behavior disorders. However, EBD cannot be tied to a single gene or chromosomal anomaly. Within the context of this model, EBD emerges as an outcome of a genetic aberration or a physiological or biochemical determinant (Heward, 2006).

Psychodynamic and Psychoeducational Models

Psychodynamic or **psychoeducational** models, sometimes referred to as psychoanalytic models, suggest that behavior disorders may result when the student has been traumatized very early in life. These traumas generate conflicts, from which anxiety emerges. The anxiety in turn causes feelings of apprehension to develop, forming the basis of subsequent reactions. Unconscious processes and other unobservable actions, such as intrapsychic events (relative to the psychosexual stages of development and personality structures such as the id, ego, and superego), play a role in the development behaviors. The models suggest that the interactions of mental process are out of balance. Conflicts, anxieties, and distortions make it hard to function rationally. In this model, EBD is regarded as a disease, with symptoms that are the result of past unsatisfactorily resolved childhood conflicts,

especially those influenced by parents. This model does not lead to practical applications for educators. It relies on psychiatric or family therapy (Coleman & Webber, 2002; Hardman et al., 2005).

Behavioral Model

According to this model, unacceptable behaviors are learned; therefore, the student's environment must be closely examined. Factors in the environment not only initiate unacceptable behaviors but also reinforce them. Students often learn undesirable behaviors because important people in their lives, including friends, reinforce such behaviors. Students may fail to develop necessary age-appropriate behaviors because such behaviors have not been elicited or reinforced, and they may become confused and erratic in their behavior because they are treated inconsistently (Alberto & Troutman, 2006; Kauffman, 2005).

Social Learning Model

Adherents to the social learning model do not deny the existence of private events or setting events that occur some time other than immediately before the maladaptive behavior. They emphasize stimuli (events that bring about or elicit behavior), responses (reactions to stimuli), and the use of reactions (consequences) to change behaviors. They admit that there may be underlying conflicts relative to the emergent unacceptable behavior, but they do not try to diagnose underlying unconscious problems (Alberto & Troutman, 2006; Kirk et al., 2006).

Ecological Model

The ecological model advocates that deviance (disturbance) is the result of a misfit between the behavior of individuals and the setting in which the student is placed. Discrete social or cultural forces outside the student create emotional disturbance. Behavior is regarded in the context of the environment or living circumstances. Therefore, disturbance is a result of a mismatch between individuals and their context. These environments (settings) contain inductive forces, which may be supportive for desired behavior, or seductive forces for unwanted behavior. Change the individual, change the context, or change both and the "disturbance" may be reduced or eliminated (Turnbull et al., 2004).

Ecology theories implies one of two things: (1) All students have a reactive aspect to their behavior even when they have already practiced considerable unacceptable behavior; or (2) if we adequately reduce the external stress or restore balance, students will often recover on their own. The student needs a positive nurturing milieu that minimizes undesired behavior and fosters normal growth. This model emphasizes the self-fulfilling prophecy: When stigmatizing labeling communicates negative feeling and expectations to a student, he or she will then exhibit unacceptable behavioral responses.

Integrated Model

Few teachers and other practitioners stay with one conceptual model in dealing with students in their classes; in fact, to do so would be in violation of IDEA's tenet of an education that is appropriate for each individual student. Teachers and other educators generally look at an integration of what is known about a student and how best to plan an intervention. It is a multiple interaction among the student, personal variables involved, the environment, and the behavior in question. Regardless of the conceptual model chosen, it is important not to oversimplify the magnitude of the problem and expect that any theory-based approach will provide a quick fix (Forness, Kavale, Sweeney, & Crenshaw, 1999).

IDENTIFICATION PROCESS

Students suspected of having emotional and behavioral disorders generally are referred for screening only after teachers become concerned about their notable misbehaviors. The unacceptable behavior is usually observed for some time, discussed in more than one conference with family members and other school personnel, and should be well documented. After the referral, a school assessment team or school-based committee composed of teachers and others involved with the student will observe the student and implement assessment procedures (Hardman et al., 2005; McLoughlin & Lewis, 2001).

Typically, behavior rating or inventory scales are used to provide a profile for behavior analysis. This screening procedure should eliminate students who are not truly disturbed and those who are exhibiting mild adjustment problems. Many screening checklists are in use; some are appropriate for different situations and ages of students, and some have multiple forms for teachers, family members, and students to complete (Demaray, Elting, & Schaefer, 2003). The following list is not exhaustive but representative: The Achenbach Child Behavior Checklist series (Achenbach & Rescorla, 2001), the Conners' Rating Scales–Revised (Conners, 1997), the Behavioral Assessment for Children, Second Edition (BASC–2; Reynolds & Kamphaus, 1992), the Behavior Rating Profile, Second Edition (BRP–2; Brown & Hammill, 1990), and the Scale for Assessing Emotional Disturbance (SAED), a standardized, norm-referenced instrument based on the federal definition of emotional disturbance (ED). The main purpose of the SAED is to assist in identifying children with ED by operationally defining ED as stated in IDEA (Epstein, Nordness, Cullinan, & Hertzog, 2002). These inventories or rating scales are organized for teacher, parent, and student use, with some allowing for peers to rate the student. They specific behaviors of notable maladjustment that appear serious and chronic, are in high frequency, and are intense. Some scales ask the respondent to simply note whether the behavior occurs, whereas others ask the respondent to indicate the behavior on a scale from "true" to "not true." One scale provides a classification system over six clinical dimensions, whereas another classifies students as having difficulties in separate items. Another scale rank orders students of profiles of two dimensions: externalizing problems (antisocial behavior, acting out, **aggression** or hurtful actions directed toward another) and internalizing problems (withdrawal, anxiety, social isolation).

Teachers' ratings may be very accurate, but they are not sufficient for a complete assessment (Hardman et al., 2005; Heward, 2006). Rating scales are easy to administer, but they have varying validity and reliability. They should not be used for diagnostic purposes; they are useful devices to distinguish students who are vulnerable or potentially EBD from other students, but they must be used with other assessment instruments, observations, analyses of work samples, and interviews (Carr, Langdon & Yarbrough, 1999; Kauffman, 2005). In addition to checklists, other identification procedures are routinely used to validate the information gathered from the rating scales.

Interviews.   A representative of the school or the evaluation team may interview the student and other important people in the student's life to attempt to find a focus for the overriding problem. Interview data can be as biased as ratings and comprise only a part of the process of screening or of evaluation.

Ecological Assessments.   Observations are conducted at home, in the classroom, and other places the student generally habituates. The observer attempts to find patterns in the behaviors before and after the problem behaviors, isolating dynamics that appear to either ameliorate or exacerbate the student's reaction to life circumstances. Very often, social workers, case workers, home-based teachers, or others who are regularly involved with the families perform these evaluations.

Self-Reports/Self-Concept Measures.   These instruments may inform educators about students' level of anxiety, impulsivity or aggression, self-esteem, or how worthwhile they see themselves (Kauffman, 2005; Salvia & Ysseldyke, 2001). Some self-report measures are given as written exercises and their usefulness depends on the student's ability and willingness to read.

The most effective approach in conducting identification and diagnostic procedures is a systematic, comprehensive, and multidisciplinary approach. The student should be evaluated by general and special education teachers and appropriate clinicians across the cognitive, affective, social, academic, medical, and functional domains. Additional information regarding adaptive behavior, motor skills, neurological functioning, and perceptual abilities may be needed. When students with EBD are compared with peers who have no labels, they usually tend to score lower on measures of intelligence and academic achievement. This characteristic is considered to be an underestimate in at least some cases. In any test, the score is made up of a true estimate of the person's ability and error. For students who habitually do not pay attention to school tasks and for whom school is not a preferred activity, it is reasonable to assume some variability.

DIAGNOSIS

Achievement and Aptitude Assessment Instruments

Students with emotional and behavioral disorders should be tested on an individual basis using validated and reliable measures of intelligence and achievement. Achievement tests measure the level of mastery that the student must have to progress to a new skill. Curriculum-based achievement tests use actual items from the classroom curriculum for testing purposes to determine classroom progress. Standardized tests measure and compare the student to others in the same peer group (age or grade level) and provide standardized scores that can be examined in reference to other tests. Teacher-made achievement tests or performance assessments determine what the student has learned over a period of time without necessarily using a paper-and-pencil test (Hardman et al., 2005).

Functional Behavioral Analysis

Functional behavioral analysis (FBA) is a method of discovering what is reinforcing the student for the exhibited behavior (O'Neill et al., 1997; Watson & Steege, 2004). It is a system built on several assumptions: (1) Behaviors, both challenging and appropriate, are supported by the current environment; (2) the behavior serves one of two functions (either to avoid something or to get something); (3) inappropriate behaviors can be changed using positive interventions when the function of the behavior is known; and (4) the process is best conducted by a team (Chandler & Dahlquist, 2002). The process is one of observing the student and determining the extent of the problem. If the problem is short lived or is not persistent, an intervention may not be necessary. However, if the problem is troublesome, the observers determine where the behavior occurs and antecedent and consequent events for the behavior. With this information, the teacher can plan a behavioral improvement plan that will substitute another, more appropriate behavior for the unacceptable one (Scott, Nelson, & Zabala, 2003).

An FBA consists of several steps. It generally begins with indirect analyses, including records reviews, interviews, and behavior rating scales. These are classified as indirect analyses because they are generally subjective. Opinions are the basis of the data. Behavioral ratings by teachers, parents, and the student may be a part of school records or they may be part of the data gathering. In addition to the paper-and-pencil ratings of adaptive and maladaptive behaviors, there may be a series of interviews with family members, teachers, and the student about typical behaviors. School records contain report cards, teacher comments, and earlier test data.

After a careful description of the targeted behavior is developed, the teacher, psychologist, or other educator can observe the frequency and duration of the behavior. Direct observation of the targeted behavior can identify other variables, such as environmental events, that could trigger or reinforce the behavior. Anecdotal record keeping involves observing the student within the natural setting. The narrative can contain descriptions of the disturbing or desired behavior and the events that occur immediately prior to and immediately following the behaviors. In addition, these notes may contain cues about the settings in which the behaviors occur. Direct observation of the number of times a behavior occurs (frequency) and the length of time (duration) it occurs will assist in making recommendations for interventions.

The point of an FBA is to plan interventions based on, among other relevant variables, when, where, how often, and how long the behaviors occur. A positive behavior support plan helps the student reduce undesirable behaviors and develop adaptive and socially acceptable habits. The plan would identify triggers and suggest routes to avoid or reduce interfering behaviors. Teaching and reinforcing adaptive replacement actions should follow.

Projective Tests

Projective tests are often used in the diagnosis of students with emotional and behavioral disorders (Heward, 2006). These tests present vague, ambiguous stimuli such as inkblots, cartoonlike characters, and sentence or word completion tests. The responses are open-ended, "whatever comes to your mind" responses with no right or wrong answers. Projective tests are developed and used to help individuals reveal inner wishes, conflicts, feelings, or fantasies. The Rorschach Psychodiagnostic Plates (Rorschach, 1942), The Children's Apperception Test (Wicks-Nelson & Israel, 1991), and the Draw a Person: Screening Procedure for Emotional Disturbance (Nagheri, McMeish, & Bardos, 1991) are administered and analyzed by psychologically trained professionals who attempt to determine whether themes indicative of emotional disturbance appear during the responses. Some students may also undergo psychiatric diagnostic interviews conducted by medical or clinical personnel such as psychiatrists, psychiatric social workers, nurses, and clinical psychologists. Teachers do not give these projective tests but may see results of such tests in reports or folders.

The entire assessment and diagnostic evaluation procedure should cover all of the previously mentioned domains and areas, including screening test results and information from educators, clinicians, and other appropriate personnel. The placement or IEP committee will then convene to review the gathered information to determine eligibility for a particular entitlement and for needed services relative to the judged degree of emotional disturbance needs of the student.

Misdiagnosis Possibilities

Students are vulnerable to misdiagnosis and misplacement as a result of any of a myriad of factors. The following are examples:

- Self-fulfilling prophecy, in which negative attitudes, feelings, and expectations of significant people can markedly influence the student to act in a manner they perceive as expected
- Social/cultural/racial issues, in which significant adults in students' lives are consciously or unconsciously prejudiced against them, negatively influencing behavior
- Counteraggressive school personnel, or adults who act out physically, sexually, verbally, or emotionally and abuse students to retaliate or relieve their own frustrations or psychological difficulties

PROGRAMS

Educational programs for students with emotional disturbance need to include several factors: mastering academics, developing social skills (Dong & Juhu, 2003), and increasing self-awareness, self-esteem, and self-control. Programming can be based on any of several models and, in many cases, models must be combined to find the best plan for a student, the teacher, and the situation involved. Two types of interventions are needed: (a) those that reduce the problematic behaviors or the likelihood of those behaviors, and (b) those that increase the likelihood of academic engagement and acquisition of skills. Additional suggestions for teaching are listed in Box 6.1.

Students with emotional disorders may qualify for psychological services under IDEA. These related services would be provided by a qualified social worker, psychologist, guidance counselor, or medical personnel. Teachers, although not a part of the ongoing intervention, may be called on to supply information and support.

There is a need for the family as well as the student to have supports and services. Working with a student and the family in several situations through the day and week give support and continuity of care and services. This system has been termed wraparound services. It is generally staffed at several levels (Epstein et al., 2003). A behavior specialist consultant is responsible for leading the treatment team, writing treatment and behavior plans, observing the student's behavior across various settings, leading meetings of the professionals from multiple disciplines, and working with all other agencies that may be involved (e.g., juvenile justice system, public schools, etc.). This person also supervisies the work of any therapeutic support staff who work with the student, family, school personnel, and agency personnel. The support staff

---

BOX 6.1
WHAT EVERY TEACHER SHOULD DO

Effective Teaching Strategies

- Document the baseline levels of behavior and graph learning curves and behavioral data for each student.
- When a student has mastered a task or activity, move to the next step. Boredom creates problems.
- Work on building and maintaining a solid relationship with your students. Respect is the best behavior manager.
- Use empirically validated teaching strategies. Students who are behind their peers have no time to waste with ineffective teaching.
- Remember to allow students to act their age. Adolescents without labels and with labels have many of the same characteristics. Work on the inappropriate behaviors only.
- Determine whether the behavior is problematic. Is it a behavior that will cause difficulties for the student in other settings, or is it just bothering you as the teacher?
- Be alert to internalizing behaviors as well as externalizing ones.
- Be consistent with rules, reinforcer schedules, expectations, and consequences.
- Provide a high level of supervision in all school settings.
- Strive for a high level of parent involvement.

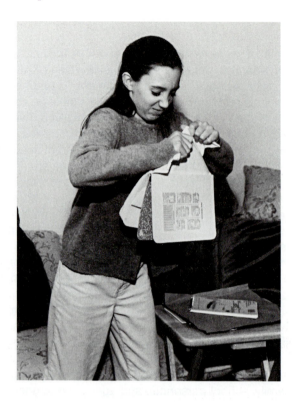

persons are responsible for providing behavioral interventions to the student across multiple settings (home, school, community) as directed by the behavioral consultant. These programs rely less on controlling the behavior of the student and more on providing instruction in adaptive behaviors and support for using acceptable modes of interacting. These programs generally share the following characteristics designed to provide support to the students and their families.

1. Use of clinicians and other personnel to work with students, families, and school programs
2. Use of school-based case management to coordinate and facilitate services and to manage changes in programming when needed
3. Provision of schoolwide prevention programs
4. Use of family liaisons to strengthen and empower the family members (Hardman, Drew, & Egan, 2005)

Increasing Appropriate Behaviors

Positive reinforcement increases the likelihood of appropriate behaviors, thereby reducing the opportunity for negatively viewed behaviors to occur. It is effective regardless of age, gender, culture, or disability of the student (Wielkiewiez, 1995). It is a natural occurrence in every classroom, but to be maximally effective, it must be used systematically and in a planned manner (Watkins & Slocum, 2003; Wolery, Ault, & Doyle, 1992). The intervention is focused on the belief that behavior is a function of its consequences. Typically, a pleasant or rewarding stimulus is applied immediately following an appropriate behavior. The teacher or instructor provides some type of external reward, usually paired with praise, when the student performs the targeted behavior. The external reinforcer is initially given for each occurrence of the preferred behavior in the beginning stages of acquisition. Once appropriate behavior is occurring regularly, the reinforcement is then faded on a systematic schedule as the student gains the ability to perform the tasks or sequence of tasks. The goal is to fade the external reinforcer and to substitute the internal satisfaction of doing well or having the tasks completed.

Negative reinforcement is similar to positive reinforcement in that it results in an increase of appropriate behaviors. The procedure involves removing a negative stimulus contingent on the desired behavior. The instructor places a restriction on the student until the behavior is completed or attempted. For instance, a student may need to finish a spelling test before being allowed to use the computer. The restriction on going to the computer is removed when the spelling test is finished.

Extinction may be used to reduce the number, intensity, or duration of undesirable behaviors. This is simply the discontinuation or withholding of a reinforcer for a behavior that has previously been reinforced. Many teachers unintentionally reinforce problematic behaviors, such as moving from an assigned place or talking inappropriately, by calling attention to the behavior. The student then has the attention of the teacher and the class and may enjoy it. If the teacher then consistently ignores the inappropriate talking, the student may at first talk louder or more often to get the attention but, eventually, if the behavior is consistently ignored, the student will cease talking because it does not produce the attention from the teacher or the class. Extinction calls for consistent and persistent implementation. If the student can get the teacher's attention occasionally, the behavior will persist for some time.

Rule setting is sometimes an easy and effective way to manage behaviors in the classroom. The rules should be simple enough for the students to understand them, few in number, and realistic. The teacher should set consequences for rule breaking, remembering that positive reinforcement is, in the long run, more effective overall. Sometimes a signal from the teacher can let the student know that the rule has been broken. These signals can be as simple as eye contact, a pause in the lesson or activity, or other subtle cues.

Pacing a lesson so that the students are not bored and changing activities when interest wanes is an effective way to manage behavior. Other techniques include humor, learning games, proximity control, and praising one student and letting others follow the example. Teachers can also model desired behavior. Sometimes they may model the behaviors without verbal cues. Other behaviors may need explanation. Clear statements of expectations can assist students in adopting appropriate behaviors.

Reducing Problematic Behaviors

Punishment is a tool on which people have relied extensively to suppress inappropriate behavior displayed by students with MR. Punishment may be considered the presentation of an adverse stimulus contingent on a specific behavior. Punishment serves to reduce the possibility of future inappropriate responses and reduces the rate of emission of the behavior (Alberto & Troutman, 2006).

Verbal statements in the form of reprimands, warnings, or disapprovals can be punishing. The effectiveness of these statements depends a great deal on the manner in which they are delivered. Reprimands delivered quietly and privately to the student have been shown to suppress disruptive behavior better than loud reprimands delivered either alone or followed by disapproving looks. Loud reprimands shouted across a classroom often draw attention to a student and may reinforce the disruptive behavior (Alberto & Troutman, 2006; Wolery et al., 1992).

Time-out is not a punishment but a procedure for reducing unwanted or undesirable behaviors. It is a procedure in which the student is removed from the possibility of receiving positive reinforcement for a certain (and generally predetermined) period of time. The crucial ingredient of time-out is delineating a time period in which reinforcement is unavailable because all sources of reinforcement are withdrawn. A variety of different time-out procedures have been used effectively. Schloss and Smith (1994) and Lakey, McNees, and McNees (1973) recommended using a time-out room to suppress obscene verbalizations or noncompliance with classroom rules. When the unwanted behaviors occur, the student can be placed in another room for a specified time period. In another variation of time-out, the student is not removed from the situation. When a disruptive behavior occurs, the student is told that the behavior is inappropriate and removed from the activity. The student is allowed to observe the activities and the other students. After a brief period, the student is allowed to return. This partial removal from an activity can markedly decrease disruptive behavior. Time-out should be limited to approximately 2 minutes after the student has regained composure. Longer times in time-out situations are not instructive and may lead to more disruptive behavior rather than compliance (Costenbader & Readney-Brown, 1995; Walker & Shea, 1987).

Response cost refers to loss of a positive reinforcer or to a penalty involving some work or effort (Alberto & Troutman, 2006; Chandler & Dalhquist, 2002). There is no necessary time period in which positive events are unavailable, as in the case of time-out. In using response cost, a penalty of some sort, usually in the form of fines, is required. The following is an example of an effective response cost procedure that was implemented by family members to control a student's behavior during shopping trips. The student was told that he could spend 50 cents at the end of shopping in the store. However, for each instance of inappropriate behavior, such as inappropriately touching merchandise, roughhousing, or being beyond a certain distance from the caretakers, a penalty of 5 cents would be subtracted from the original 50 cents. The results indicated that by placing a fine on inappropriate behavior, that behavior rapidly decreased. To be effective, response cost should not be used too frequently. If used too much, the student will become discouraged. In addition, the magnitude of the fines should be within reasonable limits. Discouragement and frustration behaviors are likely to result if the fine is excessive. The student should also be provided an opportunity to regain reinforcers or engage in reinforcing events following appropriate behavior. This strategy combines a positive reinforcement procedure with the response cost. The combined approach results in the strengthening of appropriate behaviors that will compete with the undesired ones. Understanding the rules of behavior that will govern the removal of the reinforcing events is also vital. In addition, the student should have alternative appropriate behaviors in his or her repertoire and be aware of the rules for using these behaviors to avoid a response cost.

In summary, each of the procedures described has been shown to suppress unwanted behaviors. Kazdin (1992) stated that the procedure selected should be determined by the severity of the behavior, the danger of the behavior to the student or to others, the ease of implementing the technique, the training required of the persons who will administer the program, and the acceptance or social validity (Wolery & Holcombe, 1993) of the specific treatment in the setting where it will be applied. Schloss and Smith (1994), Grossman (1990), and Gardner (1974) presented the guidelines in Box 6.2 for the use of punishment procedures that will produce the most desirable behavioral effects and the smallest number of negative side effects.

BOX 6.2
WHAT EVERY TEACHER SHOULD KNOW
Guidelines for Using Punishment Procedures

- Punishment should be used infrequently.
- The inappropriate behavior, the conditions under which it occurs, and its strength must be precisely defined.
- The punishment procedure to be used should be well articulated.
- The circumstances in which punishment will be used must be explicit.
- Alternative behaviors that will replace the punished one, and the reinforcement procedures to be used to strengthen them, should be readily identifiable.
- Time-out or response cost should be used whenever possible, rather than a procedure involving the presentation of aversive events.
- The student should be informed in a clear and precise manner about behaviors that will result in positive consequences and those that will result in negative consequences.
- Rules regarding punishment should be implemented consistently and immediately.
- The teacher should always provide alternative behavioral possibilities.
- Maximum intensity of the aversive event must be present from the beginning.
- When using a punishment procedure, the teacher must be careful to ensure that the consequences are in fact unpleasant to the student.
- The unpleasantness of the aversive consequences must be stronger than the positive consequences associated with the undesired behavior.
- After the punishment rule has been presented to the student, the teacher should avoid the routine use of threats or warnings that the behavior will produce unpleasant consequences if the student does not stop (or following the next time the inappropriate behavior occurs).

Positive Behavior Support

Positive behavior support (PBS) is an approach based on understanding the purpose of the challenging behavior and has been proposed as a viable alternative to punishment. The students are taught new skills that exclude the occurrence of challenging behavior. The support plan is written by a team of persons and includes strategies for adapting curriculum, environments, and activities to prevent occurrences of the challenging behavior. Skills are taught to replace the challenging behavior (Fox, 2003). In many cases, schools can implement a schoolwide system of behavior supports (Hawken & Horner, 2003; Lewis, Powers, Kely, & Newcomer, 2002). The approach emphasizes presenting a strong achievement orientation for academics, clear behavioral expectations, and consistent consequences. Consequences that are applied to students (both positive and negative) should be applied similarly across both the classroom and schoolwide settings. Staff should be trained to listen to students, to implement age-appropriate and culturally sensitive interventions, and to help students to make connections between their behaviors and the consequences. Students should understand that their efforts to engage in positive behavior contribute directly to the successes of other students, their classroom, and the entire school. Family support is important in this system of supports because if families and schools agree and work collaboratively on the behaviors, the students can make more rapid transitions into appropriate choices. Finally, it is imperative that school personnel collect and monitor data on the behavioral progress of students to determine the effectiveness of the interventions and to support teachers in their efforts.

Increasing Academic Engagement

Because many students with emotional and behavioral problems are already lagging behind their peers academically, focusing only on problematic behaviors allows them to fall further behind. Academic strategies should be planned as effectively and efficiently as possible. Schedules and routines are generally helpful to students who are experiencing anxiety. Routines provide stability. Direct instruction is a method that is effective and has the advantage of being efficient as well. Direct instruction is a teacher-directed, clear-cut manner of teaching a specific behavior. The initial task involves assessing the particular behavioral needs of the student. Baseline data (measures taken before any intervention is attempted) must be collected to determine the frequency of those behaviors one wishes to change (targeted behaviors), as well as the context in which those behaviors occur. Although standardized assessment instruments can provide information regarding the particular skills a student has compared to others, baseline data provide information about a specific student's level of performance. These data also provide a basis from which to measure the effectiveness of direct instruction, because frequency, or duration, of the occurrence of the target behavior can be measured and compared to baseline data as the intervention program proceeds. Once baselines have been established, one must identify the undesirable behaviors and those desirable alternative behaviors that one wishes to substitute and foster. A teacher needs to be cautious when selecting behaviors for modification. The type, frequency, duration, and intensity of the target behavior must be analyzed. The behaviors most often selected are those that interfere most with classroom processes or the student's overall functioning. The behaviors, or material that is taught, must be discrete, observable, and measurable (Watkins & Slocum, 2003)

The teacher provides instruction on a part of the material until it is mastered. Several direct instruction strategies are useful. Response-prompting strategies allow the student to practice skills with near errorless sessions (Wolery et al., 1992). The key element is to provide a prompt that the student can imitate so that no errors are practiced. These fast-paced strategies are effective with students with EBD, as well as students with other diagnoses, because they allow for few errors and therefore more positive reinforcement, positive teacher attention, and rapid learning.

Cognitive strategy approaches include self-monitoring, self-instruction, and self-control strategies. These approaches are organized to help students develop their self-awareness and self-direction while they are being reinforced to be more socialized and better learners. These are relatively simple procedures in which students record their own behaviors or academic scores. Sometimes the teacher scores the behaviors and then the student and the teacher compare the ratings. The charts and recording sheets frequently become reinforcing, reducing the need for other external reinforcers. Self-management also allows the student to generalize the intervention from one setting to another. The special education teacher may be able to monitor behavior in one room, but one teacher cannot monitor all students who are included into their appropriate classrooms. However, the students can bring the self-monitoring sheets to the teacher for approval, praise, and reinforcers as necessary. These self-evaluation sheets can assist students in understanding when and where the undesirable behaviors occur and what triggers them. Thus they can be the focus of discussions about behavior and self-determined behavior plans. Finally, they can serve as communication tools between home and school. The student or the teacher can explain the self-monitoring to the family member who will then attend to the information on the chart (Heward, 2006).

Many students with EBD lack confidence in their abilities. Using strategies that foster independence and the ability to do well can often lessen outbursts in school settings that are due to frustration. One set of strategies, called the cognitive model or information-processing model, emphasizes strategies for memory, storage and retrieval, and metacognition. One example of teaching using a cognitive strategy is that of using mnemonics (Mastropieri & Scruggs, 1991). The students use one image or word to remind them of the list or concept that is being taught. For instance, HOMES contains the first letters of the Great Lakes (Huron, Ontario, Michigan, Erie, and Superior). To remember the planets, some student use the sentence, "My very educated mother just ordered us nine pizzas." (Mars, Venus, Earth, Mercury, Jupiter, Uranus, Neptune, and Pluto). Another cognitive strategy is learning prefixes and suffixes to assist in knowing the meanings of words. If a student knows that ante means before and anti means against, then the words antebellum and anti-inflammatory will cause no problems on a vocabulary test (Lovitt, 1995).

Strategies have been devised that assist students in remembering how to control their behaviors. A strategy is generally conceptualized as a plan or a tool, such as a series of steps to assist in remembering how to behave or how to act. It has been shown that confident and effective learners generally use verbalizations, visualizations, mnemonics, tracking, self-questioning, and other cues to solve problems, attack work, and complete tasks. Given appropriate strategies, such as the SLANT strategy, students can be taught to be successful in the classroom. The SLANT strategy is based on a mnemonic of the first letters: Sit up, Lean forward, Activate thinking, Name key information, and Track the talker. Each of the action verbs alerts the student to perform an activity that will enhance appearance in the class and will likely lead to greater retention of the material being taught.

Other Interventions

Drug treatment provides appropriate medications to ameliorate students' depressions, hyperactivity, and other coexisting severe symptoms. Antidepressants are frequently prescribed for students who are feeling depressed, anxious, or panicky. Neuroleptics are prescribed for psychoses, extreme destructive behavior, and neurological tics or spasms. Tranquilizers can be used for distorted perceptions, and lithium can be used for bipolar disorders (Hardman et al., 2005).

Instructional methods and curriculum content are often manipulated when attempting to respond to each student's interests and ability level. Curricular emphasis ranges from teaching life, academic, and social skills to helping students cope with their current problems and prepare for future independent functioning. Direct instruction procedures in concert with direct teaching methods are regarded as effective approaches. Social skills training uses behavioral modification, whereas effective strategies are typically employed using volunteers, family members, and student peers in the academic and socialization programming (Clarke et al., 1995; Lewis, Hudson, Richter, & Johnson, 2004). Some experts have suggested that the content of the curriculum may not need to be different from that used with students who are not disabled, except that the curriculum may be modified for reading levels or entry skill levels. Following are some therapeutic elements common to all of the major remedial interventions:

1. Programs are structured; the arrangement of the learning environment is carefully designed with established routines, rules, and limits. Curricular and other activities are carefully planned and implemented. Clear directions, expectations that the student will do as directed, and consistent follow-through in applying consequences for behavior characterize a good classroom environment.

2. Programs are established so that the adults using them communicate acceptance.

3. Programs of effective remedial education are initiated.

4. Programs are developed to increase appropriate socialization and social skills.

5. Family members collaborate with teachers to support the student (Tompkins & Tompkins-McGill, 1993).

ISSUES OF IMPORTANCE
Manifestation

Manifestation of disability is a process that was placed into the law (IDEA) in 1997. It requires the IEP team to determine whether the behavior or misbehavior is a result of the disability or whether it is unrelated. The determination of whether or not the behavior is a result of a student's disability is called a **manifestation decision.** For instance, an act of vandalism by a student with ED who has difficulty recognizing or judging right from wrong might be considered a manifestation of the disability. If another student who can tell right from wrong and does not have anger control issues, but may have depression, committed the same act of vandalism, it might not be considered a result of the disability. Of course, all decisions are based on a full review of the student's disabilities and how the disability impacts behavior.

In determining whether a disability "caused" the behavior, several issues must be considered:

1. The student's placement must have been appropriate for the disability. If the student was placed inappropriately, the school may be at fault for not addressing the needs of the student.

2. The disability must not have impaired the student's ability to understand his or her actions and the consequences of the actions.

3. The disability condition must not impair the ability to control actions. In the case of an infraction involving weapons, drugs, or bodily injury, the determination of the part played by the disability may be waived before removing the student (Mandlawitz, 2006). Safety of all students is an important consideration. Students who are removed from the general education setting are still eligible for specially designed instruction, enabling progress toward IEP goals or general educational standards. Programming must continue regardless of the placement of the student. Any change in placement must be considered and agreed to by the IEP team.

Psychopharmacology

Coverage in the media often suggests that large numbers of students are being prescribed medication for only minor problems. Studies suggest that only a small fraction of students with serious psychiatric disorders are actually receiving such medication

(Jensen, 2005; Jensen et al., 1999; Zito et al., 1998). In the hands of a competent pediatrician or child psychiatrist, moreover, these medications are not only effective but an essential component of an overall treatment program for many, if not most, students with psychiatric disorders.

Transitions from School to Postsecondary Activities

When special education is judged by its "product," that is, the students who graduate from our public schools, it is the student's accomplishments in work, postsecondary training, or other activity that is the measure of success. Transition from school to work, community life, and adulthood is as critical a period for students with disabilities as it is for students who are typically developing. It is essential to develop and implement effective program plans to help exceptional students develop as independent, productive adults. The purpose of transition planning is to maximize the success of students with disabilities to the greatest extent possible, with cooperative linkages with a variety of postschool opportunities in education, vocational training, employment, recreation, and residential living. The support services during the transition period focus on the need to bridge school and adult life.

IDEA mandates that every student with disabilities over age 16 receiving special education services must have an ITP in addition to an IEP. Transition services are defined by IDEA as a coordinated set of activities for a student, designed within an outcome-oriented process that promotes movement from school to postschool activities, including postsecondary education, vocational training, integrated employment (including supported employment), continuing and adult education, adult services, independent living, and community participation (IDEA 300.18 [a]). The transition component is designed to provide instruction and community experiences that lead to successful postschool outcomes in a variety of life experiences (Brody-Hasazi, Furney, & DeStefano, 1999; Hunt & Marshall, 2006).

Dropouts

The term school dropout refers to students who leave high school before completion without reenrolling in another school or enrolling in a related educational program. Mandatory attendance laws limit the dropout label to students who are 16 and older. However, significant numbers of students leave school before age 16 or before reaching the 10th-grade level (Kortering, Hess, & Braziel, 1998; Lewis, 2005).

Research and professional commentary agree that there is a high rate of school dropout among special education students. The evidence suggests that students with learning disabilities, MR, and behavioral disorders (BD), otherwise noted as SED, drop out of school at significantly higher rates than their general education peers. Unlike their regular education peers who drop out, these students are rejecting programs that have been specially designed to meet their individual needs (Blackorby, Edgar, & Kortering, 1991; Landrum, Katsiyannis, & Archwamety, 2004). Black (2003) reported that special education students dropped out of school because they were not doing well in school, high-stakes tests were difficult and frustrating, they preferred to get out of school to get a job, they were not getting along with their teachers or other students, or their friends or peers dropped out of school. Some surveys and evidence (Kortering, 1993) suggest that students with disabilities are also dropping out of school because of enduring patterns of frustration, school failure, and social alienation from peers and teachers.

The need for positive rapport with teachers is the single most recurring issue in the education of EBD students (Devereaux, 1956; Edgar & Kinney, 1995; Kortering, Braziel, & Tompkins, 2002; Morse, 1985).

Mislabeled Students

When students are viewed as disturbed simply on the basis of rule breaking, serious misdiagnosis can occur. It is incumbent upon the teacher and others in the school environment to differentiate between students' short-term disturbing behaviors and emotional disturbance. Viewing rule-breaking students in the same light as students with behavioral and emotional disorders will often lead to inappropriate placement and exposing the student to inappropriate teaching and behavior modification strategies. Such mislabeling and misplacement may lead to a student modeling the behaviors of those in the same environment. This can lead to behaviors that mimic disturbance by the mislabeled student. Mislabeling can have effects that reach beyond school and the school years as well.

Needs of Institutionalized Students

When students are appropriately institutionalized, they are probably affected by the most profound mental disturbances. They may be psychotic, perpetrate aggravated aggression, or experience heightened anxiety reactions. The primary need of these students is often the stabilization that can be brought about by medical and pharmacological interventions. In these cases, educational programming is appropriate only when the student can tolerate it. Many institutions have short-term and long-term educational programs. Educational laws require students be given appropriate educational interventions.

DIVERSITY

Students from diverse racial and ethnic minorities are especially vulnerable to the effects of negative stereotyped expectations. They are frequently stigmatized and discriminated against on the basis of their race, ethnicity, or economic status. These students are often misdiagnosed and misplaced in the most overly restrictive and inappropriate settings on the proposition of perceived divergent social, behavioral, or academic standards. They are often seen in a deprecating point of view and are expected to misbehave and fail in schoolwork. Caught in a cycle of self-fulfilling prophecy, they are often mislabeled and misclassified (Council for Children with Behavioral Disorders, 1996; Cullinan, Evans, & Epstein, 2003; Yeh, Forness, & Ho, 2004).

For decades, social class and socioeconomic status have influenced educators and clinicians in schools toward misdiagnosis and misclassification. Antisocial or neighborhood-determined behavior from students in a ghetto or lower-class neighborhood may lead them into the correctional system, while white middle- to upper-class students enter psychotherapy (Church, Lewis, & Batshaw, 1997; Hobbs, 1975). Culturally and racially diverse students continue to be overrepresented in special education classes for troubled students. They tend to be in more restrictive settings and have a higher dropout rate and earlier arrest rate after leaving school than white middle-class students (Heward, 2006).

PROFESSIONALS

A wide variety of clinical and educational professionals are involved in the treatment and education of students with behavioral and emotional disorders. Professionals include regular and special education teachers, school psychologists, school nurses, case or psychiatric social workers, paraeducators, psychiatric aides, LPNs, psychiatric nurses, clinical psychologists, and psychiatrists. These professionals work in a variety of settings, such as public schools, residential programs and schools, group homes, and hospital or daycare centers; they provide service to students of all age levels. Some collaborate extensively with others, and some work with limited contact outside their professional interests. However, all of these service providers collaborate with students' families.

Medical Professionals

Psychiatrists are medical doctors trained in the understanding and treatment of mental illness and disorders via medication, psychotherapy, and other medical practices. Psychiatric nurses and social workers are trained in the clinical aspects of mental illness associated with the particular needs of nursing, casework, or therapy in treatment settings and in their own private practices. These medical professionals are trained to determine the causes of mental illness and classifications, prescribe or administer medications, and provide counseling or psychotherapy.

Educators

The CEC publishes standards for the preparation and certification of special teachers for the SED (or EBD) special education category. The program of studies typically recommended includes academic work in (1) a foundation course in educational philosophy and history; (2) characteristics of SED students; (3) assessment, diagnosis, and evaluation; (4) instructional intervention; (5) classroom and student behavioral management; (6) advocacy and consultation-collaboration with professional partnerships; and (7) professional and ethical practices (Council for Exceptional Children, 2003). We have described these competencies in more detail in Chapter 1. Technology is frequently used in the classroom. Some suggestions are listed in Box 6.3.

Paraeducators are frequently assigned to students who act out in classrooms to assist in including such students in general education classrooms. Paraeducators are persons who are not necessarily licensed or trained in special education but who work under the direct supervision of the special education teacher or other licensed personnel. According to NCLB, any paraeducator who works in a Title I school or in a Title I program must be rigorously prepared. They must earn an associate's degree or pass a state-approved test in basic skills (CEC, 2004; Wall, Davis, Winkler Crowley, & White, 2005). The duties of the paraeducator vary but include monitoring the activities of the student, assisting with transitions from one place to another in the building, assisting with bus riding, assisting with academic tasks, and keeping the student on task in class. The paraeducator, under the supervision of a licensed teacher, is frequently in charge of data collection for the behavior improvement plan, reporting to the teachers, communicating with family members if the school or teachers choose, and observing social and interpersonal interactions. Frequently, the paraeducator is assigned to a student labeled EBD for crisis management. There are many controversies surrounding the training that the assistant needs. Much research is needed to isolate the variables that would be effective in using a second adult in the classroom (Ashbaker & Morgan 2006; Nowacek, Werts, Harris, & Tillery, 2005; Werts, Tillery, Roark, & Harris 2004).

BOX 6.3
WHAT EVERY TEACHER SHOULD KNOW ABOUT TECHNOLOGY

- Students can use personal digital assistants (PDAs) to monitor their use of appropriate strategies. PDAs can also be used to structure the student's day and week.
- Teachers and parents can text message or send phone messages (nonringing) to students to provide feedback and to reinforce behavior.
- Teachers and parents may want to access several advisory Web sites. These sites can provide an opportunity to post problems with students, read about solutions and strategies, and perhaps to give advice. Examples of these sites include that of Torey Hayden, author of books about students with emotional difficulties, a site by Thomas McIntyre from Hunter College called Behavioradvisor.com, and Psychoed.net.
- Sticky notes can be used for quiet praise and attention getting. Teachers can place notes on a student's desk as they circulate. The student can be reminded which page to be on or be reinforced for attending or getting a problem worked. The advantage of the notes is that the student is guided privately.
- Simulations in science and other subjects can be experienced and practiced with instructional computer software. The "hands-on" experience can be reinforcing for students with attention difficulties.

DISCUSSION QUESTIONS

1. What factors are included in definitions of ED?
2. Should "conduct disorders" and "social maladjustment" continue to be excluded as part of the defined group? Why or why not?
3. Is psychopharmacology appropriate for school-aged students?
4. What part do family members play in the programming for students with ED?
5. What factors should be included in planning programming for students with labels of ED or BD?
6. What information would be available from screening instruments?
7. What information would be available from an FBA?

PROFESSIONAL ASSOCIATIONS AND PARENT OR SELF-HELP GROUPS

American Association for the Advancement of
Behavior Therapy
15 West 36th Street
New York, NY 10018

Beyond Behavior: A Magazine for Exploring Behavior in Our Schools and Council for Children with Behavioral Disorders, Council for Exceptional Children
1110 North Glebe Road, Suite 300
Arlington, VA 22201-5704

Federation of Families for Children's Mental Health and
National Mental Health Association
1021 Prince Street
Alexandria, VA 22314-2071

Journal of Emotional and Behavioral Problems
National Educational Service
1610 West Third Street, P.O. Box 8
Bloomington, IN 47402

Institute of Mental Health
5600 Fishers Lane
Rockville, MD 20852

Office of Special Education Programs and Rehabilitation Services Administration (OSERS) and National Institute on Disabilities and Rehabilitation Research
400 Maryland Avenue, SW
Washington, DC 20202

REFERENCES

Achenbach, T. M., & Rescorla, L. (2001). *Manual for the ASEBA school-age forms and profiles.* Burlington, VT: Research Center for Children, Youth, & Families/Achenbach System of Empirically Based Assessment (ASEBA).

Agran, M. (1997). *Student-directed learning: Teaching self-direction skills.* Pacific Grove, CA: Brooks/Cole.

Alberto, P., & Troutman, A. (2006). *Applied behavior analysis for teachers* (7th ed.). Upper Saddle River, NJ: Merrill/Prentice Hall.

American Psychiatric Association. (2000). *Diagnostic and statistical manual of mental disorders* (DSM–IV–TR) (4th ed.). Washington, DC: Author.

Anderson, J. A., Kutash, K., & Duchniwski, A. J. (2001). A comparison of the academic progress of students with EBD and students with LD. *Journal of Behavioral Disorders, 9,* 106–115.

Ashbaker, B. Y., & Morgan J. (2006). *Paraprofessionals in the classroom.* Boston: Pearson/Allyn & Bacon.

Bauer, A. M., Keefe, C. H., & Shea, T. M. (2001). *Students with learning disabilities or emotional/behavioral disorders.* Upper Saddle River, NJ: Merrill/Prentice Hall.

Black, S. (2003). Angry at the world. *American School Board Journal, 190*(6), 43–45.

Blackorby, J., Edgar, E. B., & Kortering, L. J. (1991). A shred of our youth? The problem of school dropout among youth with mild handicaps. *Journal of Special Education, 25,* 102–113.

Bortner, M., & Birch, H. G. (1969). Patterns of intellectual ability in emotionally disturbed and brain-damaged children. *Journal of Special Education, 3,* 351–369.

Bower, E. M. (1981). *Early identification of emotionally handicapped children in school* (3rd ed.). Springfield, IL: Thomas.

Bradley, R., Henderson, K., & Monfore, D. A. (2004). A national perspective on children with emotional disorders. *Behavior Disorders, 29,* 211–223.

Brody-Hasazi, S., Furney, K. S., & DeStefano, L. (1999). Implementing the IDEA transition mandates. *Exceptional Children, 65*(4), 555–566.

Brown, L. L., & Hammill, D. D. (1990). *Behavior rating profile: An ecological approach to behavior assessment* (2nd ed.). Austin, TX: PRO-ED.

Bullis, M., & Cheney, D. (1999). Vocational and transition interventions for adolescents and young adults with emotional or behavioral disorders. *Focus on Exceptional Children, 31,* 1–24.

Carr, E. G., Langdon, N. A., & Yarbrough, S. C. (1999). Hypothesis-based intervention for severe problem behavior. In A. C. Repp & R. H. Horner (Eds.), *Functional analysis of problem behavior: From effective assessment to effective support.* Bellmont: CA: Wadsworth.

Chandler, L. K., & Dahlquist, C. M. (2002). *Functional assessment: Strategies to prevent and remediate challenging behavior in school settings.* Upper Saddle River, NJ: Merrill/Prentice Hall.

Church, R. P., Lewis, M. E. B., & Batshaw, M. L. (1997). Learning disabilities. In M. L. Batshaw (Ed.), *Children with disabilities* (4th ed.). Baltimore: Paul H. Brookes.

Clarke, S., Dunlap, G., Foster-Johnson, L., Childs, K. E., Wilson, D., White, R., et al. (1995). Improving the conduct of students with behavioral disorders by incorporating student interests into curricular activities. *Behavioral Disorders, 20,* 221–237.

Coleman, M., & Webber, J. (2002). *Emotional and behavioral disorders: Theory and practice.* Boston: Allyn & Bacon.

Conners, C. K. (1997). *Conners' rating scales–revised.* Tonawanda, NY: Multi-Health Systems.

Costenbader, V., & Readney-Brown, M. (1995). Isolation time-out used with students with emotional disturbance. *Exceptional Children, 61,* 353–363.

Council for Children with Behavioral Disorders (CCBD). (1996). Guidelines for providing appropriate services to culturally diverse youngsters with emotional and/or behavioral disorders: Report of the task force of the CCBD ad hoc committee on ethnic and multicultural concerns. *Behavioral Disorders, 21*(2), 137–144.

Council for Exceptional Children (CEC). (2003). *What every special educator must know: Ethics, standards, and guidelines for special educators* (5th ed.). Alexandria, VA: Author.

Council for Exceptional Children (CEC). (2004). *The CEC paraeducator standards workbook.* Alexandria, VA: Author.

Cullinan, D., Evans, C., & Epstein, M. H. (2003). Characteristics of emotional disturbance of elementary school students. *Behavioral Disorders, 28,* 94–110.

Demaray, M. K., Elting, J., & Schaefer, K. (2003). Assessment of attention-deficit/hyperactivity disorder (ADHD): A comparative evaluation of five, commonly used, published rating scales. *Psychology in the Schools, 40,* 341–361.

Devereaux, G. (1956). *Therapeutic education.* New York: Harper & Row.

Dong, H. C., & Juhu, K. (2003). Practicing social skills training for young children with low peer acceptance: A cognitive-social learning model. *Early Childhood Education Journal, 31,* 41–46.

Duncan, B. B., Forness, S. R., & Hartsough, C. (1995). Students identified as seriously emotionally disturbed in day treatment: Cognitive, psychiatric and special education characteristics. *Behavioral Disorders, 20,* 238–252.

Dyck, M. J., Hay, D., Anderson, M., Smith, L. M., Piek, J., & Hallmayer, J. (2004). Is the discrepancy criterion for defining developmental disorders valid? *Journal of Child Psychology and Psychiatry 45,* 979–995.

Eaves, L., Silberg, J., & Erkanli, A. (2003). Resolving multiple epigenetic pathways to adolescent depression. *The Journal of Child Psychology and Psychiatry and Allied Disciplines 44,* 1006–1014.

Edgar, D., & Kinney, D. (1995). The effect of middle school extracurricular activities on adolescents' popularity and peer status. *Student and Society, 26,* 298–324.

Eley, T. C., Bolton, D., O'Connor, T. G., Perrin, S., Smith, P., & Plomin, R. (2003). A twin study of anxiety-related behaviours in pre-school children. *Journal of Child Psychology and Psychiatry and Allied Disciplines, 44,* 945–960.

Epstein, M. H., Nordness, P. D., Cullinan, D., & Hertzog, M. (2002). Scale for assessing emotional disturbance: Long-term test-retest reliability and convergent validity with kindergarten and first-grade students remedial and special education, *Remedial and Special Education, 23,* 141–148.

Epstein, M. H., Nordness, P. D., Kutash, K., Duchnowski, A., Benner, G. J., & Nelson, J. R. (2003). Assessing the wraparound process during family planning meetings. *Journal of Behavioral Health Services and Research, 30,* 352–362.

Fergusson, D. M., & Woodward, L. J. (2002). Mental health, educational and social role outcomes of depressed adolescents. *Archives of General Psychiatry, 59,* 225–231.

Forness, S. R., & Kavale, K. A. (2000). Emotional or behavioral disorders: Background and current status of the EBD terminology and definition. *Behavior Disorders, 25,* 264–269.

Forness, S. R., Kavale, K. A., Sweeney, D. P., & Crenshaw, T. M. (1999). The future of research and practice in behavioral disorders: Psychopharmacology and its school implications. *Behavioral Disorders, 24*(4), 18–43.

Fox, L. (2003). Positive behavior support: An individualized approach for addressing challenging behavior. *What Works Briefs.* Arlington, VA: Council for Exceptional Children.

Gardner, W. (1974). *Children with learning and behavior problems.* Needham, MA: Allyn & Bacon.

Gilmour, J., Hill, B., & Place, M. (2004). Social communication deficits in conduct disorder: A clinical and community survey. *Journal of Child Psychology and Psychiatry and Allied Disciplines, 45,* 967–978.

Graubard, P. S. (1964). The extent of academic retardation in a residential treatment center. *Journal of Educational Research, 58,* 78–80.

Gresham, F. M. (2002). Social skills assessment and instruction for students with emotional and behavioral disorders. In K. L. Lane, F. M. Gresham, & T. E. O'Shaughnessy (Eds.), *Interventions for children with or at risk for emotional and behavioral disorders* (pp. 242–258). Boston: Allyn & Bacon.

Grosenick, J. K., George, M. P., & George, N. L. (1990). A conceptual scheme for describing and evaluating programs in behavioral disorders. *Behavioral Disorders, 16*(1), 70–73.

Grossman, H. (1990). Trouble-free teaching: Solutions to behavior problems in the classroom (pp. 133–156). Mountain View, CA: Mayfield.

Hallahan, D. P., & Kauffman, J. M. (1996). *Exceptional children: Introduction to special education* (8th ed.). Boston: Allyn & Bacon.

Hardman, M. L., Drew, C. J., & Egan, M. W. (2005). *Human exceptionality: Society, school, and family* (8th ed.). Needham, MA: Allyn & Bacon.

Haring, N. G., McCormick, L., & Haring, T. G. (1994). *Exceptional children and youth: An introduction to special education* (6th ed.). Upper Saddle River, NJ: Merrill/Prentice Hall.

Hawken, L. S., & Horner, R. H. (2003). Evaluation of a targeted intervention within a schoolwide system of behavior support. *Journal of Behavioral Education, 12,* 225–240.

Heward, W. L. (2006). *Exceptional children: An introduction to special education* (8th ed.). Upper Saddle River, NJ: Merrill/Prentice Hall.

Hobbs, N. (1975). *The future of children.* San Francisco: Jossey-Bass.

Hughes, T. L., & Bray, M. A. (2004). Differentiation of emotional disturbance and social maladjustment: Introduction to the special issue. *Psychology in the Schools, 41,* 819–821.

Hunt, N., & Marshall, K. (2006). *Exceptional children and youth: An introduction to special education* (5th ed.). Boston: Houghton Mifflin.

Jay, D., & Padilla, C. (1987). *Special education dropouts: The incidence of and reasons for dropping out of special education in California.* Menlo Park, CA: SRI International.

Jensen, P. S. (2004) *Making the system work for your child with (ADHD).* New York: Guilford Press.

Jensen, P. S., Kettle, L., Roper, M. T., Sloan, M. T., Dulcan, M. K., Hoven, C., et al. (1999). Are stimulants overprescribed? Treatment of ADHD in four U.S. communities. *Journal of the American Academy of Child and Adolescent Psychiatry, 38,* 797–804.

Kauffman, J. M. (2005). *Characteristics of emotional and behavioral disorders of children and youth* (8th ed.). Upper Saddle River, NJ: Merrill/Prentice Hall.

Kazdin, A. E. (1992). Overt and covert antisocial behavior: Child and family characteristics among psychiatric inpatient children. Journal of Child and Family Studies, *1,* 3–20.

Kerr, M. M., & Nelson, C. M. (2006). *Strategies for addressing problem behaviors in the classroom* (5th ed.). Upper Saddle River, NJ: Merrill/Prentice Hall.

Kirk, S. A., Gallagher, J. J., Anastasiow, N. J., & Coleman, M. R. (2006). *Exceptional children and youth* (11th ed.). Boston: Houghton Mifflin.

Kortering, L. (1993). *School dropout among youth with learning disabilities or behavior disorders: A look at potential factors and outcomes.* Boone, NC: Appalachian State University.

Kortering, L., Braziel, P., & Tompkins, J. (2002). The challenge of school completion among youths with behavioral disorders: Another side of the story. *Behavioral Disorders, 27,* 142–154.

Kortering, L., Hess, B., & Braziel, P. (1998). School dropout. In G. Bear, K. Munke, & A. Thomas (Eds.), *Children's needs II: Development, problems, and alternatives* (pp. 511–521). Bethesda, MD: American Association of School Psychologists.

Lakey, B. B., McNess, P. M., & McNess, M. C. (1973). Control of an obscene verbal tic through time out in an elementary school classroom. *Journal of Applied Behavioral Analysis, 6,* 104–106.

Landrum, T., Katsiyannis, A., & Archwamety, T. (2004). An analysis of placement and exit patterns of students with emotional or behavioral disorders. *Behavioral Disorders, 29,* 140–153.

Lane, K. L., Gresham, F. M., & O'Shaughnessy, T. E. (2002). Identifying, assessing, and intervening with children with or at risk for behavior disorders: A look to the future. In K. L. Lane, F. M. Gresham, & T. E. O'Shaughnessy (Eds.), *Interventions for children with or at risk for emotional and behavioral disorders* (pp. 317–326). Boston: Allyn & Bacon.

Lane, K. L., Wehby, J., & Barton-Arwood, S. M (2005). Students with and at risk for emotional and behavioral disorders: Meeting their social and academic needs. *Preventing School Failure, 49*(2), 6–9.

Lewis, A. C. (2005). Who graduates? *The Education Digest, 70*(6), 68–70.

Lewis, T. J., Hudson, S., Richter, M., & Johnson, N. (2004). Scientifically supported practices in the emotional and behavioral disorders: A proposed approach and brief review of current practices. *Behavior Disorders, 29,* 247–255.

Lewis, T. J., Powers, L. J., Kely, M. J., & Newcomer, L. L. (2002). Reducing problem behaviors on the playground: An investigation of the application of schoolwide positive behavior supports. *Psychology in the Schools, 39,* 181–190.

Lovitt, T. C. (1995). *Tactics for teaching.* Upper Saddle River, NJ: Merrill/Prentice Hall.

Lyons, D. F., & Powers, V. (1963). Follow-up study of elementary school children exempted from Los Angeles city schools during 1960–1961. *Exceptional Children, 30,* 155–162.

Mandlawitz, M. (2006). *What every teacher should know about IDEA 2004.* Boston: Allyn & Bacon.

Mastropieri, M. A., & Scruggs, T. E. (1991). *Teaching students ways to remember: Stategies for learning mnemonically.* Cambridge, MA: Brookline Books.

McLoughlin, J. A., & Lewis, R. B. (2001) *Assessing students with special needs* (5th ed.). Upper Saddle River, NJ: Merrill/Prentice Hall.

Merrell, K. W., & Walker, H. M. (2004). Deconstructing a definition: Social maladjustment versus emotional disturbance and moving the EBD field forward. *Psychology in the Schools, 41,* 899–910.

Meyen, E. L., Vergason, G. A., & Whelan, R. J. (1996). *Strategies for teaching exceptional children in inclusive settings.* Denver, CO: Love.

Morse, W. (1985). *The education and treatment of socio-emotionally impaired children and youth.* Syracuse, NY: Syracuse University Press.

Motto, J. J., & Wilkins, G. S. (1968). Educational achievement of institutionalized emotionally disturbed children. *Journal of Educational Research, 61,* 218–221.

Nagheri, J. A., McMeish, T. J., & Bardos, A. N. (1991). *Draw a person: Screening procedure for emotional disturbance.* Austin, TX: PRO-ED.

Nelson, J. R., Benner, G. J., & Rogers-Adkinson, D. L. (2003). An investigation of the characteristics of K–12 students with comorbid emotional disturbance and significant language deficits served in public school settings. *Behavioral Disorders, 29,* 25–33.

Nowacek, E. J., Werts, M. G., Harris, S. D., & Tillery. C. Y. (2005). *Paraeducators' and teachers' perceptions of knowledge needed to collaborate in classrooms.* Unpublished manuscript.

O'Neill, R. E., Horner, R. H., Albin, R. W., Sprague, J., Storey, K., & Newton, J. S. (1997). *Functional assessment and* program development for problem behavior: A practical handbook. Pacific Grove, CA: Brookes/Cole.

Reynolds, C. R., & Kamphaus, R. W. (1992). BASC, behavior assessment system for children: Manual. Circle Pines, MN: American Guidance Service.

Rhode, G., Jensen, W. R., & Reavis, H. K. (1998). The tough kid book: Practical classroom management strategies. Longmont, CO: Sopris West.

Rorschach, H. (1942). Rorschach psychodiagnostic plates. New York: Psychological Corporation.

Rubin, R. A., & Balow, B. (1978). Prevalence to teacher identified behavior problems: A longitudinal study. Exceptional Children, 45, 102–111.

Salvia, J., & Ysseldyke, J. E. (2001). Assessment (8th ed.). Boston: Houghton Mifflin.

Schloss, P. L., & Smith, M. A. (1994). Applied behavior analysis in the classroom (pp. 178–196). Needham, MA: Allyn & Bacon.

Scott, T. M., Nelson, C. M., & Zabala, J. (2003). Functional behavior assessment training in public schools: Facilitating systemic change. Journal of Positive Behavior Interventions, 5, 216–224.

Smith, D. D. (2001). Introduction to special education: Teaching in an age of challenge (4th ed.). Needham, MA: Allyn & Bacon.

Stinnett, T. A., Bull, K. A., Koonce, D. A., & Aldridge, J. O. (1999). Effects of diagnostic label, race, gender, educational placement, and definitional information on prognostic outlook for children with behavior problems. Psychology in the Schools, 36, 51–59.

Theodore, L. A., Akin-Little, A., & Little, S. G. (2004). Evaluating the differential treatment of emotional disturbance and social maladjustment. Psychology in the Schools, 41, 879–886.

Tompkins, J. R. (1996). Special education movements in the education of students who are seriously emotionally disturbed: Motto—Move as slowly as you can. In B. L. Brooks & D. A. Sabatino (Eds.), Personal perspective on emotional disturbance/behavioral disorders. Austin, TX: PRO-ED.

Tompkins, J. R., & Tompkins-McGill, P. L. (1993). Surviving in schools in the 1990s: Strategic management of school environments. Lanhan, MD: University Press of America.

Turnbull, A. P., Turnbull, H. R., Shank, M., & Smith, D. (2004). Exceptional lives: Special education in today's schools (2nd ed.). Upper Saddle River, NJ: Merrill/Prentice Hall.

U.S. Department of Education. (1999). Assistance to state for the education of children with disabilities and the early intervention program for infants and toddlers with disabilities, final regulations. Federal Register, 64(48), CFR Parts 300 and 303.

U.S. Department of Education. (2005). Twenty-fifth annual report to Congress on the implementation of the Individuals with Disabilities Education Act. Washington, DC: Author.

Wagner, M., Marder, C., Blackorby, J., Cameto, R., Newman, L., Levine, P., et al. (2003). The achievements of youth with disabilities during secondary school. Menlo Park, CA: SRI International.

Walker, H. M. (1997). The acting-out child: Coping with classroom disruption (2nd ed.). Longmont, CO: Sopris West.

Walker, J. E., & Shea, T. M. (1987). Behavioral management: A practical approach for education (5th ed.). New York: Macmillan.

Wall, S., Davis, K. L., Winkler Crowley, A. L., & White, L. L. (2005). The urban paraprofessional goes to college. Remedial and Special Education, 26(3), 183–190.

Watkins, C., & Slocum, T. (2003). Components of direct instruction. Journal of Direct Instruction, 3, 75–110.

Watson, T. S., & Steege, M. W. (2004). Conducting school-based functional behavioral assessments: A practitioner's guide. New York: Guilford Publications.

Werts, M. G., Tillery, C. Y., Roark, R. R., & Harris, S. (2004). What parents tell us about paraeducators. Remedial and Special Education, 25, 232–239.

Wicks-Nelson, R., & Israel, A. C. (1991). Behavior disorders of children (2nd ed., pp. 99–100). Upper Saddle River, NJ: Prentice Hall.

Wielkiewiez, R. M. (1995). Behavior management in the schools: Principals and procedures. Boston: Allyn & Bacon.

Wolery, M., Ault, M. J., & Doyle, P. M. (1992). Teaching students with moderate to severe disabilities. New York: Longman.

Wolery, M., & Holcombe, A. (1993). Procedural fidelity. Pittsburgh, PA: Allegheny-Singer Research Institute.

Yeh, M., Forness, S. R., & Ho, J. (2004). Parental etiological explanations and disproportionate racial/ethnic representation in special education services for youths with emotional disturbance. Behavioral Disorders 29, 348–358.

Youngblade, L. M., & Nackashi, J. (2003). Evaluation of children's spontaneous reports of social difficulties: 'I don't have any friends'. Pediatric Case Reviews, 3(3), 157–167.

Zito, J. M., Safer, D. J., Riddle, M. A., Johnson, R. E., Speedie, S. M., & Fox, M. (1998). Prevalence variations in psychotropic treatment of children. Journal of Child and Adolescent Psychopharmacology, 8, 99–105.

7

Students with Physical and Health Impairments

KEY TERMS

WHAT WOULD YOU DO?

Barbara is a beautiful 15-year-old girl. She attends the public high school in her suburban area. She is enrolled in her sophomore year and takes the classes that the majority of her classmates are taking. She is in English, geometry, French, biology, and world history. She is doing well but has turned in some assignments late. Her teachers are tolerant. Barbara had cancer and had surgery resulting in an ostomy, an unnatural, surgically created hole in her abdomen that admits a small part of her large intestine. She had surgery last year following treatments with radiation and chemotherapy for an advanced case of colorectal cancer. Chemotherapy and radiation left her bowel in a state of reduced functioning. The lower third of her large intestine was removed in the surgery. Her rectum was removed and a permanent colostomy was formed. This meant she had to wear an adhesive patch around the opening and waste matter (feces) would be collected in a disposable plastic pouch. The pouch must be changed or cleaned frequently. At school, Barbara wears a small pouch. Because she cannot regulate the flow of waste matter, it is sometimes continuously accumulating in the pouch. She must empty the pouch at regular intervals to avoid leakage or odors. She takes a pill that functions as an "internal deodorant" to assist in controlling odors when she changes or empties the bag in the restrooms. She needs a restroom with a toilet and a sink in the same cubical so she can change and then clean up without leaving the cubical.

Barbara has a restricted diet, not necessarily because of the colostomy, but because of the radiation to the remainder of her bowel. The walls of the organ are damaged, and the process of digestion is not as efficient as it once was. Barbara is limited to bland and low-fiber foods and as a result has regular checkups to evaluate her overall health, as well as to check for recurrent and metastatic cancer. This diet makes it hard for her to maintain a healthy weight. She is able to participate in physical activities as her stamina allows and is enrolled in a general gym class.

1. What modifications to school routines may be necessary for Barbara?

2. What information about Barbara's condition should be given to teachers and students?

The concept of physical and health impairment as an issue for schools is multidimensional. It consists of two related areas: physical conditions that affect a student's education and health conditions that affect a student's education. These two large categories are further divided into many possible diseases and disorders. The specific

205

disorders may be as unrelated to each other as muscular dystrophy and TBI and as different as asthma and hemophilia. Yet students with these uniquely different conditions rely on the same legislation to guarantee them the right to the most appropriate educational experience as delineated by their IEP teams. Students with these conditions are served under the same law in different categories. Those with physical impairments are served as students with orthopedic impairments, and those with health impairments are served as students with OHI. The purpose of this chapter is to identify and explain some of the issues affecting their education. How often these conditions occur, causes of conditions, major characteristics, and characteristics of appropriate educational programs for students with disabilities will be discussed. The lengthy list of professional and parent or self-help organizations and the wide variety of references for further information presented at the end of the chapter underscore the diversity of the physical and health impairment needs of these students.

Hundreds of physical and health impairments can affect students' educational performance (Hallahan & Kauffman, 2006); however, only about 350,000 students ages 6 to 21 in public schools are served under the categories covered in this chapter. The 30-plus conditions we will highlight are those that are, in general, the most commonly occurring or most illustrative of types of impairment for students.

DEFINITIONS

Differentiating Physical and Health Impairments

A physical disability affects skeletal, muscular, or neurological systems. In general, federal legislation uses the term orthopedic impairments, whereas special educators and local service agencies use the term physical disabilities. Examples of physical or orthopedic impairments are cerebral palsy, epilepsy, and juvenile rheumatoid arthritis. Physical disabilities imply that students have problems with the structure or functions of their bodies. Health impairments put limitations on the body's physical well-being and require medical attention. Health impairments are diseases, infections, or conditions that affect the life-maintaining systems of the body. They can impair the student's ability to perform well at school because of their life-threatening or sometimes physically debilitating nature. Examples of health impairments are asthma, HIV, cancer, diabetes, and sickle cell anemia.

Federal Definitions of Physical and Health Impairments

IDEA defines both the categories of physical and health impairment. An orthopedic (physical) impairment is defined as one that "adversely affects a child's educational performance. The term includes impairments caused by **congenital** anomaly (one that is present at birth but is not inherited, such as a clubfoot, absence of some part of the body, etc.), impairments caused by disease (poliomyelitis, bone tuberculosis, etc.), and impairments from other causes (e.g., cerebral palsy, amputations, and fractures or burns that cause contractures)" (C.F.R. Sec. 300.7 [b] [7]).

Individuals with Disabilities Education Improvement Act (2004) and subsequent reauthorizations define students with health impairments as "having limited strength, vitality, or alertness due to chronic or acute health problems such as a heart condition, tuberculosis, rheumatic fever, nephritis, asthma, sickle cell anemia, hemophilia, epilepsy, lead poisoning, leukemia or diabetes, that adversely affects a child's educational performance" (20 U.S.C.,\\1400 et seq.).

As a result of their impairments, these students may require special school services, including special instruction schedules, counseling, various therapies, special equipment, medication, and technological aids. They are likely to be absent from school with a higher frequency than their peers and may in some cases have to accept and confront their own limited life span or impending death (Turnbull, Turnbull, Shank, & Smith, 2004). The conditions can be acute or chronic. **Acute** conditions develop or hit quickly and the symptoms are intense but will abate. **Chronic** conditions may develop quickly but are more likely to be progressive. The symptoms will either remain or get progressively worse.

PREVALENCE, CHARACTERISTICS, ETIOLOGY, AND TREATMENT OF SELECTED PHYSICAL AND HEALTH IMPAIRMENTS

This discussion of the frequency of occurrence, signs and symptoms, and causes of physical and health impairments differs from the discussions presented in most of the other chapters in this text because the umbrella term physical and health impairment comprises so many discrete disorders. As a result, it is more efficient to deal with each of the disorders and highlight its important features in one place in the text rather than in three separate sections. The brief explanations of treatments that follow the descriptions are usually descriptions of the medical interventions available. Educational intervention will be discussed later in this chapter in the section devoted to instructional programming. The following paragraphs are not meant to be an exhaustive listing of all the physical and health impairment possibilities, nor are they meant to be all-encompassing descriptions of the selected conditions described. Instead, their function is to serve as introductory outlines on the journey to a deeper understanding of how impairment can affect the social, emotional, and educational life of a student. Table 7.1 is a listing of how conditions affecting students might be classified.

Orthopedic Impairments

Cerebral Palsy

Cerebral palsy (CP) is a disorder that affects movement and posture. It is a result of brain damage. The brain injury, sometimes caused by oxygen deprivation, can occur prior to birth, typically as the result of placental separation; during the birth process, due to birth cord strangulation or by the direct brain damage caused by forceps delivery; or soon after birth as the result of contracting brain-damaging viral diseases. Accidental poisoning and direct trauma to the brain early in life while the brain tissues are still developing can also cause CP. **Palsy** refers to the lack of muscle control. As a result, students with CP, depending on the severity of the condition, may not be able to adequately control their movements. CP is not a disease. It does not become progressively worse, nor is it infectious in any form. It is not hereditary. The three major types of CP are **spastic** (hypertonic form, characterized by stiff, tense, poorly coordinated movements), **athetoid** (low tone form, characterized by purposeless uncontrolled involuntary movements and contorted purposeful movements), and **ataxic** (characterized by balance problems, poor depth perception, and poor fine and gross motor skills). Depending on which areas of the brain are affected, a person with CP may exhibit any of the types just described, and it is possible to have a mixture of types (Best, Heller, & Bigge, 2005).

TABLE 7.1
Classification of orthopedic (physical) and health impairments.

Orthopedic Impairments	Health Impairments
Amputations	Attention deficit/hyperactivity disorder
Cerebral palsy	Acquired immunodeficiency syndrome (AIDS)
Epilepsy (seizure disorder)	Asthma
Juvenile rheumatoid arthritis	Burns
Marfan syndrome	Cancer
Multiple sclerosis	Child abuse
Muscular dystrophy	Congenital heart disease
Osteogenesis imperfecta	Cytomegalovirus
Poliomyelitis	Cystic fibrosis
Spina bifida	Fetal alcohol syndrome
Spinal cord injuries	Fragile X syndrome
Traumatic brain injury	Medically fragile/technology dependent
	Hemophilia
	Human immunodeficiency virus (HIV)
	Hypoglycemia
	Juvenile diabetes
	Leukemia
	Nephritis
	Ostomies
	Prenatal substance abuse
	Sickle cell anemia
	Tuberculosis

Estimates of occurrence range from 4 to 5 children in every 2,000 live births (Miller & Bachrach, 1995). Other children may be diagnosed with CP later. Approximately 500,000 to 700,000 people currently living in the United States have some degree of CP (National Information Center for Children and Youth with Disabilities, 1997, 2002), and about 8,000 babies are identified each year (United Cerebral Palsy, 2001).

The problems associated with poor movement and balance skills may complicate educational activities. Sometimes associated conditions further complicate students' educational experiences. Each student with CP does not automatically exhibit the following associated conditions, but many do have associated communication, sensory, intellectual, and seizure disorders. The majority of people with CP have problems with motor coordination, which makes it difficult for them to make the fine movements needed for writing, turning pages, manipulating small items, and producing intelligible speech. Language comprehension and formulation difficulties as a result of the brain damage are also not unusual. Hearing and vision problems of all types are also quite common. Jones (1983) estimated that as many as 30 percent of all people with CP have hearing losses. Although it is difficult to accurately measure, and not all people with CP are automatically intellectually impaired, estimates identify 50 to 60 percent of this population as having cognitive deficits (Hallahan & Kauffman, 2006). Seizure disorders and their upsetting effect on the educational experience will be discussed later in this chapter. Students with CP exhibit concurrent seizure disorders as an associated condition somewhere between 25 and 50 percent of the time (Best et al., 2005; Brown, 1997).

Damage to the brain associated with CP cannot be reversed, but proper management of the student can curtail physical damage due to poor posture, increase strength, and compensate for functional skill deficiencies. Braces, canes, crutches, and wheelchairs can facilitate movement and independence. Specially designed tools and augmentative devices can help in self-care and communication. An augmentative device can be any aid or device that replaces natural speech and helps the student communicate. Devices range from simple picture boards that contain pictures of the student's basic requests to sophisticated computers programmed with head pointers that a student can program to produce complicated language (Heward, 2006; Turnbull et al., 2004).

Each student with CP presents a unique pattern of symptoms and resulting needs. For some, the disorder may be a minor inconvenience requiring minimal adjustment to regular classroom education. For others, CP may make regular classroom experiences nearly impossible. Those falling between these two extremes require sensitive team-constructed plans that will allow them to function as well as possible within the restrictions of the disorder.

Seizure Disorders (Epilepsy)

Seizures are the result of spontaneous abnormal discharges of electrical impulses in the brain. Epilepsy is a disorder characterized by recurring seizures. Epilepsy is considered to be the most common neurological impairment in school-age students (Lerner, 2002; McDermott et al., 2005; Smith 2001). Approximately 0.5 percent to 0.7 percent of the population has epilepsy (Hardman, Drew, & Egan, 2006). Seizures may be of unknown origin or may appear after accidents or high fevers that injure brain tissue (Bowe, 2000; Cross, 1993). As brain imaging improves, we are coming closer to understanding seizure disorders. Each type of seizure results in different behaviors by the person with the seizure disorder.

Generalized absence or petit mal seizures often last only a few seconds. The student may not even be aware of them as they occur. The student may appear to be daydreaming or staring into space. A slight eyelid tremor may be the only noticeable physical sign. Students may appear not to be following directions or may seem inattentive.

Generalized absence seizures can develop into more severe forms of seizure behavior, such as generalized tonic-clonic (grand mal) seizures. Grand mal seizures are considered the most serious type of convulsion and are characterized by prolonged loss of consciousness and a stiff or tonic phase, during which muscles become extremely rigid. The tonic phase is followed by a clonic phase characterized by the limbs thrashing about in a purposeless way. During the seizure, teeth grinding and loss of bladder control are common occurrences. Physical injury as a result of the uncontrollable movements is a real possibility. After the seizure is finished, the student may be disoriented and sleepy. The emotional and educational effects of grand mal seizures are both obvious and potentially devastating to the student experiencing them (Hunt & Marshall, 2002).

Complex partial or psychomotor seizures result from focal or localized brain electrical discharge. Behaviors may vary, but often the student can appear to be in a stupor or might experience a period of inappropriate and purposeless movement or behavior before returning to preseizure behavior. The following sequence is typical:

The student ceases an activity and replaces it with automatic purposeless movements accompanied by incoherent and irrelevant speech (sometimes called automatisms). These behaviors are sometimes followed by rage attacks of which the student is unaware after the seizure is terminated and normal behavior is resumed (Cross, 1993). It is not difficult to understand why those exhibiting psychomotor seizures often perform poorly academically and are routinely mislabeled as mentally ill or emotionally disturbed.

Myoclonic seizures are brief muscular contractions that are involuntary and may involve only one part of the body, such as a hand or the whole body in a whole-body spasm. They are more common in younger students than in older ones and typically occur during periods of drowsiness or arousal from sleep (Batshaw, 1997; Epilepsy. com, 2005).

Seizures may occur as isolated one-time events or may take place many times each day. Bright lights, certain sound combinations, or even odors can initiate seizures. An **aura,** or warning, can sometimes signal that a seizure will be occurring. Auras can take the form of an increase in sensory perception in taste, smell, visual perception, or hearing sensitivity. Occasionally, an aura can be used as a signal to engage specific behaviors that prevent seizures from occurring (Brown, 1997).

Treatment often focuses on controlling seizures through medication. Curative surgery that removes brain tissue can be successful with some syndromes that include seizure activity (such as Sturge-Weber disease). Surgery is most successful with infants and toddlers, who are still neurologically plastic and able to more readily compensate for the tissue loss than are adolescents (Blakeslee, 1992). The primary medical assistive role of the classroom teacher is to monitor the effects of the medication administered to the student. Side effects such as drowsiness, dullness, lethargy, and behavioral change need to be brought to the attention of family members and health care specialists. Often the classroom teacher, with or without the assistance of the parent, explains what seizures are to the other students in class or even to the student with the disorder. Seizure disorders alone are not enough of a disability to require special class placement unless they result in a need for specially designed instruction. However, they often occur in conjunction with other disorders, resulting in difficulties acquiring educational concepts and keeping up with classmates.

Multiple Sclerosis

Multiple sclerosis (MS) is a degenerative neuromuscular disease. This means that as the disease progresses, more and more damage will be done to the nerves that are affected, causing them to fail to transmit messages from the brain or to transmit them inaccurately. MS destroys the myelin sheathing that surrounds and protects the nervous system. Neither the cause of MS nor a cure for it is known. A currently accepted theory is that somehow MS is the result of a virus that causes the body to attack and destroy healthy myelin tissue as if it were an invading disease. MS is not infectious and cannot be transmitted from one person to another by close contact. The disease does not always progress in a systematic way. Some people experience mild attacks and then recover completely. Others have a series of attacks interspersed with periods of remission, during which the myelin-damaging process is suspended. However, with each attack more damage is done to the nervous system. Initial symptoms include muscle weakness, poor coordination, and fatigue. If the degenerative process continues, tremors, **spasticity** (uncontrolled tightening of muscles), blindness, or severe visual impairment and speech slurring are possibilities. The person may eventually lose bowel or bladder control and become partially or totally paralyzed. Because a person with MS has a good chance of living a normal life span, school years are preparation years that allow the person to knowledgeably anticipate future needs. Between 250,000 and 500,000 people in the United States are affected with MS (Smith, 2001).

Muscular Dystrophy

Muscular dystrophy (MD) is also a neuromuscular disease presenting as a weakening of the muscles. It tends to run in families and is usually transmitted to male children from their mothers (Cross, 1993). The cause of MD is not known. The term is used to cover any one of nine hereditary muscle-destroying disorders. The Duchenne type, which usually occurs between the ages of 3 and 6, is most common. During the course of the disease, muscles become progressively weaker as muscle tissue is replaced by fat and fibrous cells (Best et al., 2005; Turnbull et al., 2004).

MD progresses slowly. Initial signs may include difficulty in walking and climbing stairs and an awkward swaying walking pattern (Hill, 1999). Rising from a sitting position can be a problem. Students may grasp at table legs or desktops to pull themselves upright. As the disease progresses, students find it difficult to rise after falling and show back deformities and protruding abdomens. Often by age 10, the student loses the ability to walk and will need a wheelchair to move about (Heward, 2006). During the final stage, students become bedridden and totally dependent on others. They are particularly fragile; even the gentle tension that occurs during lifting can cause dislocations. There is no known cure, and death is usually attributed to heart failure or lung failure as a result of muscle weakness. MD affects between 1.4 and 2 people per 10,000 births (Batshaw, 1997). Genetic counseling is the only form of prevention. Active treatment includes exercises that will help maintain range of motion and promote efficient breathing.

Spina Bifida

Spina bifida is a neural tube defect caused by the failure of the spinal column to properly seal around the spinal cord. The **spinal cord** is a chain of nerves that extends from the base of the brain to the end of the spinal column. Three major neural tube defects (NTDs) are spina bifida, encephalocele, and anencephaly. The most common is spinal bifida, and the most common form is spina bifida occulta. This is a relatively benign condition in which the separation of the section of vertebral arches is hidden. In more severe cases, the infant does not generally survive. The spinal cord does not close properly during early fetal development, perhaps as early as the first month of prenatal development. The reason this genetically linked disorder occurs is unknown. However, the result is that the spinal cord and the **meninges** that cover it are unprotected. The resulting damage prevents the nerves of the spinal cord from transmitting messages from the brain to other parts of the body. Depending on just where on the cord the damage occurs (the closer to the neck, the more severe the symptoms) and the number of nerve fibers affected, this condition could cause infections, brain damage, and paralysis (Liptak, 1997; Smith, 2001).

Spina bifida occurs in approximately 1 of every 1,000 live births (Hardman et al., 2006). This affects a total of approximately 2,000 babies per year in the United States (March of Dimes, 1992). Females are three to seven times more likely to be born with spina bifida than males. It rarely occurs in African Americans or Asian Americans (Turnbull et al., 2004). The odds of a second child having the disorder increase if the first child is affected. The incidence of spina bifida is declining due to prenatal detection and parental decisions to terminate pregnancies (Lorber, 1990; Stone, 1987). The prevalence of NTDs varies among countries, but worldwide the incidence is falling.

There are several reasons. One is the use of maternal serum to determine the prenatal existence of NTDs. In addition, the use of folic acid in the mother's diet during pregnancy may have an effect on the reduction of the number of cases of NTDs.

Infants with spina bifida usually are candidates for surgical closure of the spinal cord exposure. Surgery helps avoid infection and facilitates normal development by preserving motor, sensory, and intellectual functions; however, the neural blockages are not repaired by surgery. Cosmetically, the back and spine are improved with surgery and are easier to care for. Without surgical repair, the prognosis is much more guarded, with the possibility of recurring infections that might bring about severe deficits in intellectual functioning. Successful treatment leads to expectations of higher intellectual functioning. Intellectual development is normal in 73 percent of students, and most do not need wheelchairs. Forty-eight percent of those who require **shunts** to drain fluids from the brain do not require repeated surgery. On the downside, some combination of crutches and wheelchairs is required for mobility, and 87 percent of students have urinary incontinence (Best, 2005; Liptak, 1997). Most students require medical monitoring and need clean intermittent catheterization (CIC) to allow their bladders to empty. The CIC procedure is typically performed every 3 to 4 hours. The procedure became controversial when students with spina bifida in the public schools met with resistance from teachers who refused to perform the procedure. The Supreme Court ruled that the schools are required to perform CIC either with a school nurse or some other person trained in the procedure (Palfrey, 1995; Taylor, 1990; Turnbull & Turnbull, 2000).

Traumatic Brain Injury

Traumatic brain injury (TBI) is caused by severe trauma to the head that results in lasting physical and cognitive impairments. Head injuries are linked to alcohol and drug abuse, which cause automobile accidents (the most common cause), and falls, especially from bicycles, motorbikes, and skateboards. Motor vehicle accidents are the second leading cause of TBI (Centers for Disease Control, 2004). Head injuries are also linked to gunshot wounds and other blows to the head that might cause brain damage. They are the most common cause of death for those under the age of 34 (Smith, 2001) and the most common cause of acquired disability in childhood (Best, 2005; Michaud, Duhaime, & Lazar, 1997). Congress added TBI as a category of disability in IDEA. IDEA defines TBI as follows:

> An acquired injury to the brain caused by external physical force, resulting in total or partial functional disability or psychosocial impairment, or both, that adversely affects a child's educational performance. The term applies to open or closed head injuries resulting in impairments in one or more areas, such as cognition; language; memory; attention; reasoning; abstract thinking; judgment; problem solving; sensory; perceptual and motor abilities; psychosocial behavior; physical functions; information processing and speech. The term does not apply to brain injuries that are congenital or degenerative, or brain injuries produced by birth trauma. (34 C.F.R. § 300.7 [b][12])

TBIs are classified as closed head injuries, when the damage is the result of the brain bouncing against the skull due to rapid acceleration and deceleration in accidents, or open head injuries, when there is direct external trauma to the brain. The specific problems caused by the impairments listed in IDEA might include chronic fatigue, pain, epilepsy, memory impairments, poor judgment, and poor organization skills. Motor problems such as paralysis, poor balance, and poor coordination are common (Smith, 2001). The person affected may be impulsive, aggressive, or destructive; have temper tantrums; be irritable; be unable to self-monitor; and display high levels of anxiety. After the accident, the student may have vision, hearing, and speech problems that were not evident prior to the trauma. The ability to understand and produce language may be severely impaired, depending on which areas of the brain were injured. Some or all of the problems that result from the accident may be transitory or last for the remainder of the person's life. With closed head injuries, a period of spontaneous recovery can occur in the first 6 months. During this period, many functions, skills, and abilities can return. After this time passes, recovery is less likely to occur without intensive therapy.

The statistics on TBI are readily available because in most cases the accidents causing the brain damage are severe enough to require the assistance of law enforcement and medical personnel, either at the scene of the accident or shortly after it occurs. Smith (2001) reported that, according to the National Head Injury Foundation, 100,000 of the 500,000 cases of TBI that occur each year are fatal. Another 100,000 people become debilitated for life. TBI occurs at the rate of 23 instances per 10,000 people a year (Best et al., 2005). One in 500 school students is expected to be hospitalized with TBI each year (Kraus, Fife, & Conroy, 1987). As many as 3 percent of the adolescent population of the United States have sustained head injuries serious enough to affect school performance (Forness & Kavale, 1993). Child abuse causes more than 60 percent of head injuries among infants. Shaken infant syndrome, in which a caregiver shakes a young child violently enough to cause brain and spinal cord injury, results in 10 to 25 percent fatality and TBI in many of those who survive (Mitiguy, 1991; Schroeder, 1993).

Hardman et al. (2006) listed the treatment sequence for TBI as including the following stages:

1. Applying whatever medical procedure is needed to maintain life
2. Minimizing complications that occur with the traumatic event
3. Restoring consciousness
4. Reorienting the patient after a coma
5. Initiating therapies that will help restore lost skills
6. Preparing for the return home
7. Providing counseling for the family and child

Depending on the severity of the damage, students and adolescents with TBI will often need a variety of special education services in addition to medical and rehabilitation therapies. Although restoration of skills to a preaccident level is always a goal, in many cases the best result possible is to help the student compensate for the traumatically induced weakness. Some students and adolescents will never again return to their level of functioning prior to the accident. Thinking, language, and attending skills, as well as emotional control and judgment and reasoning skills, may all require long-term retraining efforts from a variety of professionals, including speech-language pathologists, psychologists, and special education teachers.

Low-Incidence Physical and Health Impairments

The following briefly outlined orthopedic disabilities occur less frequently than those disabilities just described. The sources quoted will provide a deeper understanding of the conditions.

Marfan Syndrome

Marfan syndrome is a genetic disorder that affects approximately 20,000 people each year (Kirk, Gallagher, Anastasiow, & Coleman, 2006). Students tend to have long, thin arms and legs, prominent shoulder blades, long fingers, and spinal curvature. Most critical is the typical accompanying heart weakness that can lead to heart failure and death. Limited physical exercise is usually prescribed.

Juvenile Rheumatoid Arthritis

Juvenile rheumatoid arthritis is relatively rare, with an estimated occurrence of 3 new cases per 100,000 in the population. It affects female students twice as often as male students. There is complete remission in 75 to 80 percent of all cases (Hallahan & Kauffman, 2006). The disease itself affects muscles and joints, causing inflammation and swelling. As a result, movement becomes painful or impossible due to the resulting stiffness. Teachers can manage students' activities to lessen pain during ongoing routines (Hallahan & Kauffman, 2006; Heller, Alberto, & Meagher, 1996).

Osteogenesis Imperfecta

Osteogenesis imperfecta is also known as brittle bone disease. The bones of the students affected are easily fractured. As a result of the repeated fractures, limbs tend to be underdeveloped and bowed. These students are extremely fragile and require frequent hospitalizations. They may have hearing problems because the bones in the middle ear responsible for transmitting sounds to the brain can be defective (Cross, 1993). As the students mature, their bones become less brittle and the students are less fragile. Osteogenesis imperfecta affects approximately 1 in 20,000 students (Heward, 2006).

Treatment of osteogenesis imperfecta relies on bracing the student and surgery when needed. Students may use wheelchairs for ambulation. Their physical activity must be severely restricted. Bones may break even when they are shifting positions in a wheelchair. The students show a normal range of intelligence and, aside from specialized physical accommodations, do not usually require special education classroom placements.

Poliomyelitis

Polio, a viral infection that attacks the nerve cells of the spinal cord that control muscle function, can cause paralysis. It was once a major disease affecting school-age children, but preventive medical treatment (vaccines) has reduced the incidence.

Spinal Cord Injuries

Spinal cord injuries usually are caused by auto accidents or falls. Injury to the spinal cord often results in loss of sensation or paralysis. The higher on the cord the injury, the greater the loss of function. Depending on the injury, a wheelchair may be needed for ambulation. In severe cases, total paralysis may result in the person needing a respirator to assist in breathing (Heward, 2006). Spinal cord injuries affect approximately 3 of every 100,000 people in the United States (Hardman et al., 2006). Physical therapy and the use of adaptive devices for mobility and independent living, combined with counseling to adjust to the sudden trauma that caused the injury, constitute the core of the rehabilitative treatment procedures.

Many orthopedic conditions can occur and affect the educational progress of students. Table 7.2 is a summary of the incidence and prevalence of orthopedic impairments that affect students.

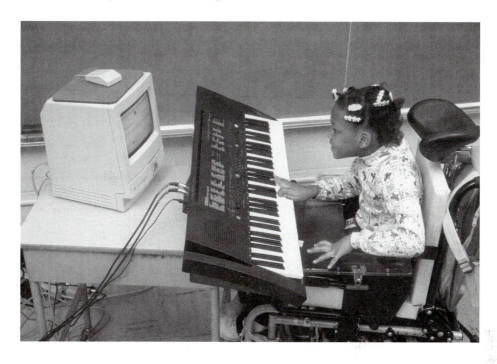

TABLE 7.2
Incidence and prevalence of orthopedic impairment.

Orthopedic Impairment	Statistics	Source
Cerebral palsy	28 per 10,000 births	Murphy, Yeargin-Allsopp, Decoufle, & Drews, 1993
Seizure disorders	1% of the population of the United States	Epilepsy Foundation of America, 2001
Multiple sclerosis	250,000–500,000 active cases	Smith, 2001
Muscular dystrophy	1.4–2 per 10,000 births 200,000 active cases	Batshaw, 1997 Hardman, Drew, & Egan, 2006
Spina bifida	20.13 per 100,000 live births	Mathews, 2004
Traumatic brain injury	1.4 million people per year 475,000 per year for students ages 0 to 14 years	CDC, 2005b

Health Impairments

Human Immunodeficiency Virus (HIV) and Acquired Immunodeficiency Syndrome (AIDS)

HIV and AIDS are related conditions. HIV, which is responsible for AIDS, is contracted from the exchange of diseased bodily fluids such as during unprotected sex or from using contaminated hypodermic needles. It can also be transmitted to a fetus from an infected mother. HIV gradually infects and eventually destroys the body's immune system, which normally protects the body from diseases. HIV progresses through distinct stages. During the earliest stage, the virus is in the bloodstream but there are no outward signs of illness. During the middle stage, minor symptoms appear as the immune system begins to lose its effectiveness. People who have been infected experience unusual fatigue, fevers, night sweats, chronic diarrhea, vaginal yeast infections, swollen glands, and frequent illnesses of all types. During its final stage, HIV becomes AIDS or AIDS-related complex. All of the following symptoms are possible: seizures, memory lapses, impaired vision, blindness, weight loss, cancerous lesions, and respiratory infections. Students may lose cognitive skills. Bouts of severe pain and death usually follow. The Centers for Disease Control reported 1 million cases of AIDS in 1993 (Turnbull et al., 2004). Approximately 2 percent of those infected are students. However, the number of infants and children with HIV is on the rise (Smith, 2001).

Treatment for students with HIV infection includes medical care and educational services to families. Although good hygienic practices are critical, there is no evidence that HIV has ever been transmitted from one student to another in a school, daycare, or foster care setting (HIV/AIDS, 1990). Cohen et al. (1991) reported that children who became HIV positive as a result of neonatal blood transfusions show an ability to maintain intellectual functioning for years. However, they may show some slowness in motor tasks and have impaired attention abilities and resultant academic problems.

Asthma

Asthma is a chronic condition of breathing difficulty, wheezing, coughing, and shortness of breath. The cause is unknown. Current speculation is that asthma is an allergic response that occurs in those who are predisposed to develop the disorder. It is the leading cause of school absences among all chronic diseases (Altman, 1993; Heller, Forney, Alberto, Schwartzman, & Goeckel, 2000). Although emotions and stress can influence the conditions that bring about asthma attacks, they are not the only causes of asthma (Best et al., 2005). No amount of stress can bring about asthma unless the student already has defective airways. Relaxation, although it is useful in avoiding more lung constriction after an attack begins, by itself cannot prevent asthma (Turnbull et al., 2004). However, a clear relationship does exist between emotional stress and asthma attacks in that stress increases the likelihood of episodes, and attacks produce stress (Heward, 2006). Approximately 4.5 percent of all children have asthma (Raj, Mishra, Feinsilver, & Fein, 2000). Twice as many males as females develop severe asthma. However, boys tend to improve as they age, whereas girls tend to develop more complications as they enter adolescence (Paul & Fafoglia, 1988). Of an estimated total of 18 million cases, 4 million are under age 18 (Turnbull et al., 2004).

Treatment for asthma revolves around eliminating allergens. This might entail special air filtrating, extra classroom cleaning, and vacuuming and wiping of surface. Outdoor play might be restricted during certain seasons, class pets may need to be moved, playing materials might need to be screened for content before use, and field trips may need to be more closely monitored (Smith, 2001). Specific medications might be prescribed to help the student resist allergens in general, or they may be used only during asthma attacks to help open closed lung passages. Periodic breathing exercises and mechanical lung drainage activities might be necessary. Often no special educational programming is needed aside from the allergen-removing environmental activities described. By consulting with family members and appropriate health care professionals, classroom teachers can be prepared to deal with asthma attacks if they occur at school.

Cancer

Cancer is a condition that causes uncontrollable growth of cells (tumors) in body organs and tissues. Students who develop tumors or undergo radiation therapy or chemotherapy often develop learning difficulties. Approximately 1,500 students and adolescents per year die from cancerous conditions. One third of the cancer deaths reported in 1993 were due to leukemia, a cancerous blood condition. There are approximately 8,000 cases of childhood cancer each year (Turnbull et al., 2004).

Improved medical treatment has dramatically improved the survival rates of students with cancers. For example, in the 1960s the survival rates for students with leukemia was 4 percent. It is currently at 72 percent. Similarly, the survival rate for Hodgkin's disease, another form of cancer, is between 68 and 88 percent (Turnbull et al., 2004). However, both the chemotherapy and radiation used to control or eliminate cancerous conditions can have side effects that range from physically unpleasant (hair loss) to educationally debilitating (acquired learning disabilities). The American Cancer Society (1988) recommended that all students treated for cancerous conditions have an IEP completed before they reenter school. For some students, the plan provides for the eventuality of home schooling. The current practice is to inform even young persons about the disease so that they can actively participate in their treatment programs.

Child Abuse

Each state has its own definition of child abuse. Public Law 93-247, passed in 1974, defines child abuse and neglect as "physical or mental injury, sexual abuse, negligent treatment or maltreatment of a person under 18 by someone who is responsible for the student's welfare under circumstances which indicate that the student's health or welfare is harmed or threatened" (Hallahan & Kauffman, 2006). Battered students often display suspicious burns, bruises, abrasions, and broken limbs. Long-lasting damage as a result of abuse can affect the central nervous system and the physical and psychosocial development of the student. Students who come to school with repeated swellings and bruises and show sudden onset of behavioral problems, such as sudden acting-out episodes or violent aggressive behaviors toward other students, are often in abusive situations. Attempts to disguise injuries and cover bruises should also alert teachers (Hallahan & Kauffman, 2006). Shaken infant syndrome, previously mentioned as a cause of TBI in infants and young children, is a form of child abuse that is a significant cause of death and brain injury.

Child abuse occurs at all socioeconomic levels and all cultural subgroups. It is estimated that 60 to 90 percent of all adults who abuse were abused themselves. Child abuse is most likely to occur when there are high levels of stress in a family, when expectations are too high, and when parents or caregivers are emotionally or socially isolated from support services of any type (Hunt & Marshall, 2002). All citizens have the legal responsibility to report suspicions of child abuse to social service and law enforcement agencies. Failure to do so is punishable by laws that vary in each state, with punishments ranging from loss of employment to imprisonment. Approximately 1.5 percent of all persons under age 18 have experienced abuse (Hardman et al., 2006).

Cytomegalovirus (CMV)

CMV, a virus of the herpes group, is usually harmless; it is estimated that 40 percent of the students and adults in the United States have contracted CMV with no apparent long-term disability (Taylor & Taylor, 1989). However, when it affects a fetus, it is classified as cytomegalic inclusion disease and can result in brain damage, blindness, and hearing loss. Although approximately 1 percent of all unborn children may be exposed to CMV, only about 10 to 15 percent of those exposed develop any disabilities (Smith, 2001). The virus is suspected of transmitting through bodily fluids and can remain active on surfaces for several hours. The most effective method of fighting this virus is by using proper infection control measures such as disinfecting surfaces and hand washing (Best et al., 2005). Pregnant women working in daycare settings appear to be at greater risk than others of infecting their unborn children. Although there is no cure, the disease can be identified with prenatal testing. The occurrence of the disease and its resulting disabilities appear to be reduced with frequent hand washing, sanitary diaper disposal, and keeping shared toys and play areas clean.

Cystic Fibrosis

Cystic fibrosis (CF) is a chronic genetic disorder that can affect the pancreas, the lungs, or both. When the lungs are affected, mucus matter does not drain properly, causing blockages, difficulty in breathing, and susceptibility to lung infection (Hunt & Marshall, 2002). Digestive problems that result in malnutrition and poor growth due to failure to absorb nutrients from food result when the pancreas is involved. Although the responsible gene has been identified and prenatal screening tests are available to determine whether a potential parent carries the disease, no cure is presently available (Cross, 1993). The life expectancy for people with CF is approximately 20 years (Hunt & Marshall, 2002).

Although the long-range outlook is improving for this disease, which was once fatal, no reliable cure exists. Proper treatment can retard the progression of the disease. Treatment includes medications that facilitate digestion and solutions that thin and loosen the mucus buildup in the lungs (Heward, 2006). Medications are combined with treatment designed to dislodge the mucus. The student is placed in a position that will make drainage easier and then the chest is clapped vigorously or vibrated. This procedure might be repeated several times a day (Best et al., 2005). As a rule, students with CF are of normal intelligence. Educational compensations are usually necessary only for restricting physical activity and for the class time lost during percussions.

Juvenile Diabetes and Hypoglycemia

Juvenile diabetes can be an inherited metabolic disorder, or it can develop after a viral infection. In either event, the pancreas does not produce enough insulin to metabolize or absorb the sugar in the bloodstream. Hypoglycemia occurs when too much insulin is produced (Turnbull et al., 2004). As unabsorbed sugar builds up in the bloodstream of students with diabetes, it can produce diabetic comas (unconsciousness), nerve damage, and eventually a weakened circulatory system (Little, 1991). Students show increased thirst, frequent urination, weight loss, headaches, and slow healing of incidental cuts and scrapes. Visual and kidney problems are common co-occurrences. Without proper medical intervention, students with diabetes lack energy and vitality. Type I diabetes is most common in 10- to 16-year-olds, whereas Type II is more common in adults and is related to obesity and genetic factors (Heward, 2006). Diabetes affects approximately 5 percent of the population (Hardman et al., 2006) and 1 in 600 school-age students (Martz, 2003).

Appropriate medical intervention for diabetes includes dietary control and doses of insulin administered on a prescribed schedule. Hypoglycemia is more dependent on dietary modifications. Both disorders require that the student eat appropriate snacks to regulate insulin levels. Teacher observation is critical to spot behaviors that indicate unbalanced insulin levels. Family members and health care professionals can inform the classroom teacher which behaviors are indicative of potential insulin shock, resulting when too much insulin is present, or diabetic coma, resulting when too little insulin is in the student's system.

Sickle Cell Anemia

Sickle cell anemia is an inherited blood disease that occurs most commonly among African Americans and Hispanics of Caribbean ancestry. The disease results in oxygen-carrying red blood cells losing their round shape and becoming crescent or sickle shaped. These distorted cells do not circulate as efficiently and cause oxygen transmission to be inefficient. Students experience severe pain in the abdomen, legs, and arms. They are unusually fatigued and vulnerable to infections. The poor blood circulation may lead to degeneration of joints throughout the body. As a result of pain and fevers brought about by infections, school attendance usually suffers (Sirvis, 1996). Sickle cell anemia affects approximately 1 of every 600 African American infants (Hardman et al., 2006). Medical treatment consists of administering massive doses of penicillin until the immune system is capable of warding off infections (Kirk et al., 2006).

Prenatal Substance Abuse

A pregnant woman's use of drugs and alcohol can affect her unborn child. Affected children have a greater risk of developing learning and behavioral problems, in addition to the physical damage they are at greater risk of sustaining. Some prescription drugs, illegal drugs, and nicotine can affect the unborn child depending on the drug, the dosage, and when during the pregnancy the child was exposed. For example, prenatal exposure to cocaine can lead to elevated heart and respiratory rates, hyperirritability, poor eating, diarrhea, gastrointestinal problems, and neurological damage of various types (Hardman et al., 2006). However, 20 to 40 percent of the babies born to mothers who have used illicit drugs do not show any symptoms (Carta et al., 2001; Treaster, 1993).

Fetal Alcohol Syndrome and Fetal Alcohol Effects

Fetal alcohol syndrome (FAS) and fetal alcohol effects (FAE) are the most common results of prenatal alcohol abuse. Alcohol abuse and the resultant FAS have been blamed for causing 5 percent of all congenital anomalies and from 10 to 20 percent of all cases of mild MR. Yet it is also estimated that even among chronic abusers, 50 to 70 percent of babies born are symptom free (Conlon, 1992). However, even moderate use of alcohol can lead to FAS (Hallahan & Kauffman, 2006). Overall, 1 of every 1,000 children born show signs of FAS (Hardman et al., 2006). It is most evident in families of low socioeconomic status and among Native American populations, but it is by no means confined to these populations. Students with FAS tend to evidence a variety of symptoms including learning impairments. They show a higher incidence of facial deformities, microcephaly, congenital heart defects, low birth weight, and small size (Turnbull et al., 2004). During infancy, children with FAS may be more irritable and difficult to handle, feed, and diaper. They may have a high-pitched cry and be unresponsive to parental attempts to comfort them. The majority of students with FAS will experience normal development. However, 20 to 30 percent will have language-learning problems and attention deficits (Griffith, 1991). Vincent, Paulsen, Cole, Woodruff, and Griffith (1991) divided growing students born with FAS into three groups. The first group experienced developmental disabilities of all types, including seizure disorders, CP, MR, and various physical abnormalities. The second group developed normally.

The final group was at high risk for developing learning and behavioral problems. Some could not process information as quickly or as readily as their peers. They did not use good judgment, often behaved impulsively, and had difficulty developing a strong moral system. These students tended to test the limits of caregivers because they often were socially insensitive, were easily overstimulated, and developed poor peer relationships.

Although some students are easily identified as having FAS, many others have been affected by their birth mothers' alcohol use and have not been identified. Shortly after birth, the child may exhibit signs of alcohol withdrawal. FAS and FAE are syndromes that are completely preventable with prenatal advice about alcohol before conception and during pregnancy (Batshaw & Conlon, 1997).

Fragile X Syndrome

This syndrome is thought to be a hereditary cause of MR. It is associated with the 23rd pair of chromosomes and involves a pinched X chromosome. There are pronounced physical characteristics for the syndrome, including a larger than average head size, large flattened ears, and nontapering fingers. The syndrome is more common in boys than girls, because girls have two X chromosomes. Despite reports suggesting numerous academic and social behavior deficits in boys with fragile X syndrome (FXS), little information is available concerning their actual classroom academic and social behavior. Symons, Clark, Roberts, and Bailey (2001) collected observational data on the behavior of 26 boys (5 to 12 years old) with FXS during academic activities in self-contained special education classrooms. Results indicated moderate levels of engagement during periods of academic instruction. Classroom engagement was not related to intrasubject variables such as severity of delay, autism status, or medication usage. A general measure of classroom quality and instruction was

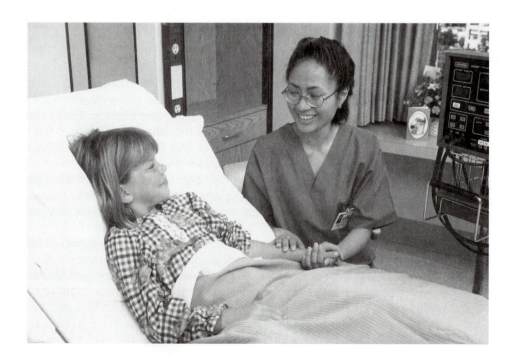

significantly correlated with engagement. Relatively low levels of stereotypic or self-injurious behavior were observed.

Technology Dependent or Medically Fragile

Students who are medically fragile or technology dependent require constant attention for survival. These students may require ongoing medical care and rely on a technological device to replace some vital nonfunctioning body part. Affected students fall into four subgroups—those who are sustained by (1) mechanical ventilators (breathing assistance machines); (2) nutrition or medication delivered intravenously; (3) periodic (daily) ventilator or nutritional help; and (4) long-term use of mechanical devices or processes such as kidney dialysis machines, urinary catheters, or any of a variety of life support monitors. The Task Force on Technology-Dependent Children uses the term technology dependent, whereas the Council for Exceptional Children uses the term medically fragile to identify the population of students who require special health care and life support during the school day.

Depending on the severity of the condition, these students may simply require periodic monitoring at school, or they may be able to function only in the most restricted level of special education service, the hospital or home setting. Students who are hospitalized or homebound are visited by itinerant teachers and, when possible, can interact with peers over closed-circuit television and speakerphone systems. Improvements in miniaturization, durability, and efficiency of medical devices have enabled an increasing number of technology-dependent students to attend school on a regular basis.

Other health impairments that might affect a student's strength, vitality, or alertness and thus adjustment problems are burns, congenital heart diseases, hemophilia, leukemia, nephritis, and tuberculosis. Table 7.3 is a listing of the incidence and prevalence of health impairments that might affect students.

TABLE 7.3
Incidence and prevalence of health impairments.

Health Impairment	Statistic	Source
HIV/AIDS	1–3 cases per 1,000 live births 1 million active cases	Hardman, Drew, & Egan, 2006
Asthma	9 million under age 18	Dey & Bloom, 2005
Cancer	11,900 children per year	U.S. Cancer Statistics Working Group, 2004
Child abuse	906,000 children in the United States	DHHS, 2005
Cytomegalovirus	1% of all fetuses	NCID, 2002
Cystic fibrosis	1 in 2,500 live European American births	Heward, 2006
	1 in 17,000 live African American births	Hardman et al., 2006
Juvenile diabetes	More than 1.3 million Americans have type 1 diabetes	JDRF, 2004
Sickle cell anemia	1 in 600 African American infants	Hardman et al., 2006
Prenatal substance abuse	1 in 10 live births exposed to illegal drugs	Chasnof, 1988
Fetal alcohol syndrome	2–15 cases per 10,000 live births	CDC, 2005a

IDENTIFICATION PROCESS

A physician usually performs the initial evaluation that determines whether a student has a particular health or physical impairment. After a medical diagnosis and identification are completed, school personnel must decide whether the student needs and qualifies for any of the special educational services supported by IDEA.

Determining which special services may be needed is a complex process that requires evaluations and judgments from several medical, educational, and related service personnel. Students with health and physical impairments require collaboration among professionals, perhaps more than students in other areas identified by IDEA. Dealing with health impairments that affect cognitive functioning or behavior requires persons qualified in each area to evaluate and interpret the results of tests. The team members, including the parents, guardians, other family members, and students, will then discuss, review, and combine the results to ensure a program of education that is appropriate, not so redundant that it leaves no time for other important areas, and covers all of the areas deemed important by the team. IDEA ensures that each student has access to the general or standard curriculum as appropriate, but the student's needs and the goals based on those needs take precedence over the standard or state curriculum. Not all students will require all of the services about to be discussed. A comprehensive identification would assess all of the following areas to see whether services are necessary in any or all of them.

Activities of Daily Living

Assessment in this area would evaluate the student's ability to engage in tasks that allow independence. Eating, drinking, dressing, toileting, and personal hygiene self-help skills are analyzed to determine current and possible future independent functioning. Older students' daily living skills expand to cooking, housekeeping, managing money, purchasing needed items, transportation, and other tasks. Assistive technology can be useful to the student and the teacher. Examples of technological ideas are listed in Box 7.1.

Mobility Assessment

A large component of independence is the ability to move about independently. Assessment might consist of evaluating current mobility skills and anticipating any future mobility needs that could be more easily attained with appropriate therapy or education. Some mobility involves assistive technology and the appropriate education to use it. Students may need to be able to use a lift to get into a van, call a taxi, or access a bus.

Physical Abilities Assessment

Physical potential needs to be assessed in order to write the IEP or IFSP. What physical actions a student can currently perform and what limitations the condition affecting the student might impose in the future must be anticipated. Based on the assessment, appropriate professionals can become part of the habilitation or rehabilitation team. Teachers will also need to know what procedures are appropriate in the classroom, what emergency procedures are necessary, and how to teach with maximum effectiveness.

BOX 7.1
WHAT EVERY TEACHER SHOULD KNOW ABOUT TECHNOLOGY

- In planning for a student with a wheelchair, remember that the hallways and aisles must be wide enough for comfortable cruising—usually 36″—and there must be areas for turnaround.
- Students can use a short plastic or wooden stick attached to the palm of their hand to type or point to a communication device. When using a pointing device, a visual keyboard can be displayed on a computer screen. The on-screen board can be accessed through the accessibility options for a Windows system.
- Book holders can be purchased that allow the student to read in bed. The book is suspended above his or her head. Other book holders can be fashioned from music stands, recipe book holders, or typing holders.
- Building up a spoon handle or a pencil with tape or other modeling material can make it easier to grip the item. Handle grips can be made from insulating foam wrap. Slip the appropriately sized wrap down the side and slid it over the handle of the spoon, hairbrush, or other object. Wrap or tape the insulation securely to prevent the object handle from turning inside the jacket.
- A remote for an environmental control system consists of a handheld infrared transmitter that enables the user to operate any electrical device or function within an area using either direct selection or scanning. It can activate or deactivate security-coded devices, lighting, and appliances. It can be used by any single-function control, such as a sip or puff switch, head-actuated switch, or hand or foot switch.

Psychosocial Abilities Assessment

A student's self-image and the ability to initiate and maintain social relationships are only two of many psychosocial processes that may need to be assessed. How well the student adapts emotionally to a disability may be the most facilitative or impeding component to successful education and living. Adjustment depends on many factors. These include the support of the student's family, the medical community, access to supports, and general ability levels. Sometimes psychological help is needed.

Communication Assessment

The ability to understand and use language is critical for much of the learning that takes place in the classroom. The skills necessary to formulate thoughts into language and the ability to program the appropriate organs needed to speak are critical for meaningful interaction within the learning environment. A communication assessment can determine a student's language and speech skills and potentials and help educators develop a plan for attainment of deficient skills or suggest compensations for skills that might never be attained.

Academic Potential and Achievement Assessment

Aptitude testing, reading comprehension skills testing, achievement tests, classroom work samples, observations of authentic tasks, and many other measures may be needed to help forecast a student's academic potential before recommending an IEP. Before services can be requested, the IEP team must decide what academic and other goals might be appropriate for any student with health or physical impairments.

Setting Assessment

The setting in which learning and living will take place must also be evaluated to determine whether modifications will be necessary. Doorway width, lighting, bathroom accessibility, air filtration, extra space for equipment, rest areas, and any other accommodations students with physical impairments may need will have to be integrated into the setting. Modifications of the learning setting may require the teacher to modify or change teaching techniques or use classroom modifications and supports to assist with instruction. A careful review of the curriculum and how it will be presented to the class will pinpoint the modifications necessary to effectively instruct students with physical or health impairments.

Assistive-Technology Assessment

Integrated into the assessments already listed is assistive-technology assessment. A determination of the value of available assistive technology and how using it might combine with other areas of assessment must be made. For example, for a student with cerebral palsy that affects the ability to effectively move the speech organs (dysarthria), using an augmentative speech device might be more effective than remediation attempts focused on using natural speech. The potential of the student to function with or without a device, the ability of the student to master the use of a device, the willingness of the family to accept the use of an augmentative system, and the cost and availability of the technology must all be factored into decisions to recommend assistive technology.

The following example illustrates how identification and assessment processes might be applied to one student with TBI.

After a student has sustained a head injury that caused either a closed or an open head injury, the medical procedures previously described—ranging from life-maintaining procedures to initial reorientation—are administered. After a period, when it is felt that spontaneous recovery of previous skills may no longer be a factor, neurologists might perform some brain imaging tests (e.g., CAT scan, MRI, fMRI, PET scan, EEG) to uncover the possibility of permanent brain damage. A psychologist or psychometrist might administer tests that measure information-processing skills or problem-solving abilities and compare the results to any pre-trauma measures that might exist. Family members will inform the team about how the student is functioning at home. The speech-language pathologist will test for receptive and expressive language abilities as well as evaluating motor speech skills. Physical and occupational therapists might evaluate mobility and the motor skills needed for daily living. The school counselor or a psychologist will contribute information on the student's emotional adjustments. From all of this information and other sources that might be needed, an appropriate IEP including educational setting recommendations will evolve. This plan may deal with short-term needs as well as long-term concerns.

PROGRAMS

Educational programming and medical treatment for students who have health or physical impairments are related but different processes and sometimes have different goals. Medical treatments stabilize, reverse, or control the conditions. Educational programming has as its general goals helping the person gain independence of all types. This includes physical independence and the mastery of daily living skills; self-awareness; social maturation (including acceptance and coping adjustments and academic growth beyond content mastery and into application of knowledge); and success with life skills such as employment, independent living, community involvement, and leisure activities. Most students with physical- or health-related disabilities are included in educational programs on the basis of their learning needs, not their handicaps (American School Health Association, 2003; Heward, 2006). Many are never identified as impaired for special educational purposes. These students do not need curriculum modifications or special related services. Some, however, do require modification of curricula, teaching methods adapted to their needs, and classroom or setting modifications.

Of the students identified as physically or health impaired, approximately 40 percent can be educated in regular classrooms, with resource room help in some cases. Often, simple adjustments, such as additional space for a student's necessary support equipment or a resource teacher to help the student catch up on missed classwork, can make a regular classroom less restrictive. Depending on the extent of the modifications needed, regular classroom placement can foster independence, improve social and communication skills development, and even sensitize nondisabled students to the potential of their peers with disabilities (Heward, 2006). Thirty percent of students with these disabilities require a separate classroom. Those remaining are best educated in separate schools, hospitals, or residential facilities (U.S. Department of Education, 2002).

Program Options

Public Law 99-457 mandates that students under age 3 who need special education have an IFSP (Hallahan & Kauffman, 2006). Similar to an IEP, this plan must specify family needs as well as student needs. Family needs can include, but are not limited to, respite care, psychological services, assistance for siblings, and transportation.

Early intervention and preschool programs begin as soon as needs are identified. Services often begin at the birth of the child. Initially, support for the family and information about available treatments and service options are provided along with assistance in learning how to care for the child at home. Regardless of the impairment, early programs tend to focus on motor development, self-help in daily living, and social skills. Family members play the most critical role in the early development of their child. Much of the preschool curriculum plan and instruction takes place in the home and is administered by family members. Members of the student's educational team provide support and structure for the interventions applied. Team members may include occupational therapists, speech-language pathologists, physical therapists, and nurses. Constant contact between the habilitation professionals and family members is vital.

A student usually moves beyond the home setting and into school if the medical conditions allow for attendance. Schools assume responsibility for educational and

physical management, including adapting spaces for wheelchairs, worktables, and other equipment. The school nurse or other informed persons may administer medicines. Bathroom stalls, sinks, mirrors, towels, and door handles need to be adapted to the student's needs. Younger students may require toileting assistance.

Academically, students with physical and health impairments often have high absence rates due to the demands of medical treatment and sometimes their own fragile health. Instruction may need to be modified to help these students keep up with their peers. Videotapes of missed experiences, telephone communication, and use of schoolmates as tutors are all critical adaptations that maintain academic and social connections within a classroom. Some students may require untimed exams or need to use specialized equipment to participate in classroom activities.

Family members and, most important, the students themselves, are critical members of the IEP team. Quite often, students are best able to describe their difficulties in the classroom and suggest sound solutions. Sometimes only minor environmental manipulations are needed. There are at least four types of simple environmental manipulations that can be helpful. The first is simply changing the location of materials and equipment so that the student with a handicap can reach them without disrupting classroom activities. The second is to modify work surfaces, as needed, so that they become more user friendly. The third is to modify commonly used objects that might be difficult to use in their usual form, and the fourth is to provide aids to help in manipulating objects or sources of frustration. It can be as easy as facilitating the use of a water fountain for a student who uses a wheelchair by placing a paper cup dispenser within easy reach (Heller, Bigge, & Allgood, 2005). Box 7.2 provides additional tips for teachers.

Many of the adaptations are carried through to middle school and high school instruction. By the middle school and high school years, many of the problems initially encountered in instructional modification and presentation have been solved. Students of middle school and high school age with physical and health-related disabili-

BOX 7.2
WHAT EVERY TEACHER SHOULD DO
Effective Teaching Strategies

- Students with physical disabilities respond to the same instructional strategies as students without labels. Frequently they may need more time or modifications to accomplish the same tasks or tasks that teach the same information.
- Familiarize yourself with the condition presented by the student. The student or the parent can generally be a great help in providing information about his or her own particular situation and for gathering and sharing pamphlets and information on the condition in general.
- Permit the use of computers, calculators, watches that speak and have databases, recorders, and other equipment that will facilitate learning.
- Organize the furniture and other objects in the rooms so that the student with extra equipment (wheelchair, standing board, computers, etc.) can get into the room and to his or her area.
- Arrange materials so that the student can access the materials without assistance as much as possible.
- Pace the lessons so that the student with a physical disability can have rest time between lessons. The IEP may require that a balance of work and rest be followed each day. The student may not have the stamina to attend to every aspect of the school day.
- Arrange to have tube feeding, ostomy cleaning, and other special procedures provided at a time that is comfortable for the student. The student may need to have a private time in the bathroom but may wish to eat lunch with his or her peers even if tube feeding.
- Ensure that the student understands directions. This can be accomplished by having the student repeat them, writing them on the board as well as giving them verbally, and having a peer buddy available for assistance when necessary.
- Have a reliable system for keeping track of assignments when the student must miss school for illnesses or doctor appointments. Have the student do assignments that are important for learning. Avoid extra drill and practice assignments if they are not necessary.
- Talk with the counselor or other mental health professional if you are having difficulty teaching a student with a severe or life-threatening illness. Remember that the student and the family are the ones that need support and that you must use other means of learning to cope rather than complaining to the student or family.

ties may be particularly sensitive to being different and be most concerned about their appearance. Both students with physical needs and their peers may need information about a given disability and its effects on physical and intellectual functioning. The student who is affected must be provided with the guidance and support necessary to realistically accept his or her condition.

Transition to adulthood continues this process. Employment and independent living are the goals. Legislation such as ADA has helped make adult living easier by mandating accessibility to public services and buildings and making illegal the discrimination against employment candidates on the basis of a physical handicap. Students with physical disabilities and health impairments have the lowest dropout rates of all special education students (U.S. Department of Education, 2002). Many go on to higher education. Colleges and universities are as responsible as all other institutions for providing appropriate accommodations, both physical and instructional, for these students. Adaptation and modification of public buildings, such as those on college campuses, are subject to regulations under Americans with Disabilities Act of 1990 (1990).

Technology

Advances in medical and adaptive technology have made it possible for students who would not have previously survived to live and attend school. Technology-dependent students may require ventilators that assist in breathing, pacemakers, kidney dialysis, sophisticated insulin delivery systems, urinary catheters, and even organ transplants to survive, remain with their families, attend school on a regular basis, and lead more normal lives. These life-sustaining medical advancements have their educational counterparts. Technology as sophisticated as computers and electronic communication aids and as simple as specially designed spoons can dramatically improve the lives of students with physical impairments and enable them to take advantage of the experiences available in their environment. Computers controlled by any number of inventive switches and head pointers are augmentative communication devices that make written and programmed spoken communication more possible. Less complex devices, such as communication boards with pictures of frequently used requests, can open up communication channels. Calculators can help in math drills, and calculators with speech synthesizers and watches that "speak" can help persons with limited mobility and those with visual impairments to write. Special switches can turn lights on and off as needed. Newly designed wheelchairs and motorized vehicles of all types provide freedom of movement, increased privacy, and the personal independence needed. Modern braces make it possible to be comfortable enough to read and study. Specially trained guide dogs can assist in many tasks. The cost and maintenance of equipment and resources are the only clouds on the horizon. The technological advances that make living easier for all people will substantially improve the quality of life for people with physical and health-related impairments.

ISSUES OF IMPORTANCE

There are many issues of concern for students and adolescents with physical and health-related impairments and their families. Some are not unique to this population and are shared by other disability groups discussed in other chapters of this text. The issues discussed in this section are neither all-inclusive nor sufficiently detailed to be comprehensive presentations. However, they highlight some real and pressing concerns with which families and the professionals who deal with physical and health-related impairments struggle daily.

Prevention

Many physical and health-related impairments are easily preventable. The use of seat belts, car seats, and helmets for bicycles and motor bikes could drastically reduce the incidence of TBI and spinal cord injuries. Education can help us all understand how safety equipment, responsible gun use and weapons training, vaccinations, abstinence from alcohol during conception and pregnancy, prenatal care, appropriate supervision of infants and young children, responsible use of medications, and safe sex can all lessen or prevent health and physical impairments. Most of these issues require an understanding of the consequences of the failure to routinely employ them. Obviously, the role of genetic counseling in the prevention of physical and health related disorders is a more complex issue. Decisions in these areas are often based on personal beliefs and religious and lifestyle principles. However, even in the most sensitive areas, information and the understanding of consequences can better prepare families for the outcomes of their decisions.

Family Concerns

We have highlighted the importance of the family in the total management of the child with a physical or health-related impairment. However, we have not highlighted the emotional and economic costs that can be placed on a family attempting to act responsibly. This section will highlight some of the pressing concerns families of students and adolescents with physical and health-related impairments must face daily.

Bernheimer & Keogh (1995) listed the demands that a student's chronic illness or disability can place on a family. Included in the discussion were fatigue, restricted social life, and a preoccupation with the numerous decisions that need to be made about the student. Decisions about accommodations to the student's needs, such as changes in diet and choices of activities, are sometimes seen as family changes (Gregory, 2005). In addition, the economic burdens can be staggering. Employment and career decisions are often made based on the availability of health insurance and maintaining it. Technology is both alluring and expensive. Often insurance carriers do not pay for the latest technological advances. Motorized wheelchairs, computers, electronic communication aids, and even special spoons can be very costly. Even when a student is eligible, government regulations are complex, and record keeping for reimbursements can put further strain on a family. Services are not provided equally in all areas of the country or even all areas of a state. Larger urban areas generally have more resources within a reasonable distance and can provide more support than can rural areas. Families have had to sever ties with communities and other family members to move to areas that can provide needed services for a student. Most homes are not designed with the spaces that might be needed for wheelchairs, ramps, or other large equipment. Costly remodeling or relocation might become a necessity (Livneh & Antonak, 2005).

Special planning and complicated arrangements are often necessary for the simplest tasks such as a weekend trip, an adult dinner, or a family vacation. The frequent absences from school that are a predictable characteristic of many health and physical impairments usually require at least one family member or other adult to be with the student, which causes conflicts and often unsatisfactory compromises.

Parent self-help groups and support groups of all types (see the listings provided at the end of this chapter) can help with creative ideas and solutions, joint baby-sitting arrangements, emotional support, and tips for dealing with professionals who may be less than sensitive to a family's conflicts.

Discrimination

Individuals with physical and health impairments are often noticeably different, have different needs for equipment, and may look different from those around them in schools, recreational facilities, and the workplace. In addition to their own possibly unresolved feelings, they must continually face potentially negative or stereotypical behaviors from people with whom they interact. Fear, rejection, or pity can cause a student to internalize these attitudes and become withdrawn, angry, and overly dependent.

Equally troublesome is architectural discrimination in the form of barriers that deny people with physical impairments access to facilities easily available to those without disabilities. ADA (PL 101-336, 1990) mandates that all new buildings, buildings undergoing renovations, and all public transportation and public facilities must be accessible to people with disabilities. The most commonly visible results of this legislation are the ramps, street corner pavement breaks, elevators, special parking spaces, special telephones, wheelchair accessible water fountains, and toilet modifications routinely available in many public places and businesses. These modifications have made and continue to make inroads into the prospect, for people with disabilities and their families, of traveling from a known environment to an unknown one.

Death and Grief in the Classroom

Sometimes students do not overcome their disability. Occasionally a disease runs its course prematurely, and students die. Although death is not a common occurrence in the classroom, it does occur with enough frequency that all involved need to be cared for. Obviously, the dying person and the family need support, but so do the student's teachers, other educational personnel, and classmates (Reid & Dixon, 1999).

Dying students need support during their illness and reassurance that they will not be forgotten. They may need to be absolved of the guilt they feel for the pain and suffering they are causing their friends and families (Turnbull et al., 2004). Families often feel abandoned while a child is dying and immediately after the death of a child. Surviving siblings need support as much as their parents do. Visits are usually welcomed and are times to show support and refrain from giving advice (Cassini & Rogers, 1990). Guilt is a complex emotion that often accompanies grief. Siblings are subject to feelings of why the other child died instead of themselves as well as relief and guilt over both feelings. Parents are not immune from the same thoughts.

Classmates need to be updated on the terminally ill student's condition. Honesty establishes credibility. Code words for death and dying, such as "going away," can confuse young students and can lead to misunderstanding of what is occurring. Reassurance that a young student dying is a rare event can be comforting to young classmates. This is not the time to lecture about safety or give warnings about good health practices. Different age groups will react differently. Preschoolers may not fully comprehend death or dying, but can certainly react to the sadness they perceive in the environment. Kindergarten and first grade students may believe that death is reversible or that it may be a consequence of common ailments such as head colds or stomachaches. Primary-level students need more information than younger children. They may feel responsible for the death or fear it will bring about other deaths. Middle school students are concerned about how the death affects them personally; they may feel the loss and express it emotionally and openly by acting out, by withdrawing, by deciding that school is not worth their time, or by attempts at suicide. High school students can react the same way as adults and their younger classmates, experiencing all the feelings of loss and grief without the maturity or experience to handle them (Schaefer, 1988).

Teachers must not be left out of the circle of those affected by a dying student (Munson & Hunt, 2005). They also need to grieve and feel anger and frustration and to be allowed to express these feelings. It is not unusual for a teacher who has spent time as a primary figure in a dying student's life to be irritable, depressed, or unwilling to confront feelings, or even to withdraw from the dying student. School administrators, counselors, and fellow teachers should be aware of these characteristic signs and provide support or, if necessary, recommend and assist in getting counseling for the teacher.

DIVERSITY

Disabilities and Farm Workers

The children of migrant agricultural workers, many of whom are culturally and linguistically diverse, are at highest risk for disabilities, including physical and health-related disabilities (Baca & Harris, 1988; National Commission on Migrant Education, 1992; Romo, 1996; Salend, Taylor, & Whittaker, 1998). The Education Commission of the States, Migrant Education Task Force (1979) reported that the life expectancy of migrant workers is 49 years, as compared to the national average of 79 years, and that infant mortality is 25 percent higher in this group than the national average. The commission noted that, among this group, lack of prenatal care and postnatal care resulted in birth injuries and disabilities. In addition, higher instances of poor nutrition and lack of access to health care lead to poor mental and physical development. Many of the health and physical disabilities prevalent in the children of migrant agricultural workers are preventable.

AIDS and Minorities

HIV infection is currently a growing cause of death in minority infants. The disease and its fatal consequences is growing especially fast among Hispanic and African American women and children (Indacochea & Scott, 1992). Although there is no indication that members of these two minority groups are any more susceptible to HIV or AIDS than any other groups, many members of these minorities are exposed to lifestyle risks that coexist with the transmission of the viruses. The transmission of HIV and its resultant AIDS could be drastically reduced by safe sex practices and the curtailment of intravenous drug use or even lessening the sharing of hypodermic needles.

PROFESSIONALS

Students with physical and health impairments and their families come into contact with many medical specialists, educational specialists, teachers, physicians, and therapists. These professionals are part of the interdisciplinary team that shares its expertise to provide the best habilitation and educational plan possible for a student (Able-Boone, Crais, & Downing, 2003). They are also responsible monitors who make certain that the plans are carried out and modified when changes occur in the needs and developmental levels of the student. Individual team members need to communicate with one another as well as with the student's parents to maintain health and, at the same time, develop whatever capabilities are possible in educational and independent living skills (Best et al., 2005; Heller et al., 2000; Verhaaren & Connor, 1981).

General and special education teachers who provide direct instruction to students with physical and health impairments may interact with dozens of specialists and service providers as they help the student achieve his or her maximum potential. Related services and service providers are not always the same for each student. However, related services might include members from the following long list: transportation co-ordinators, speech-language pathologists, physical therapists, occupational thera-pists, audiologists, psychological specialists, recreational therapists, school health service specialists, social workers, early identification and early assessment special-ists, music therapists, art therapists, media specialists, vocational education teachers, reading teachers, guidance counselors, assistive-technology specialists, mobility specialists, dietitians, and others who may have been inadvertently left off this list. It is not surprising that families often need the assistance of special educators to explain the function of some specialists and to help them become aware of what services are available and necessary for their student. Family members often grant special educa-tors or regular classroom teachers permission to work directly with paramedical and medical specialists. Students whose parents are directly involved with their education are more successful than students whose parents are less involved (Rainforth, York, & Macdonald, 1992). Obviously, no one student can be served by all these specialists at once, but it would not be unheard of for a student with serious impairments to have worked with a representative of every field listed here and others not mentioned as well. Any service that directly benefits a student being educated in a school program can be classified as a related service (Turnbull & Turnbull, 2000).

Paraeducators are often an important part of these students' school experiences. Paraeducators are hired to perform many complex tasks. Some school districts hire li-censed practical nurses for these jobs if they can find a person who is willing to work with a particular student.

A transdisciplinary team is necessary. Table 7.4 is a listing of some of the most commonly consulted professionals and the services that they provide.

TABLE 7.4
Frequently consulted professionals.

Professional	Service
Speech-language pathologist	Evaluates speech, language, and communication deficits and implements remedial services. Recommends and programs augmentative and adaptive equipment. Provides swallowing therapy.
Physical therapist	Directly provides exercises to maintain and enhance range of movement, modify positioning, and perform motor tasks.
Occupational therapist	Enhances self-care activities (feeding, dressing, toileting) and fine motor coordination (buttoning, dressing, eating). May also provide counseling related to social and psychological issues.
Assistive-technology specialist	Assesses needs for assistive and adaptive equipment. Aids in selection and modification of equipment.
School nurse	Responsible for health monitoring activities, classroom education, and performing unusual health-related procedures.
Special educator	Coordinates services and provision of direct instruction.
Homebound teacher	Provides direct instruction outside the school setting.
Social worker	Assists in family management issues.
Resource teacher	Provides direct and indirect services, such as mobility instruction, counseling, and consultation with other professionals.
Classroom teacher	Communicates and collaborates with other team members. Evaluates efficacy of programs. Provides direct instruction.

DISCUSSION QUESTIONS

1. What are health impairments?
2. What are physical impairments?
3. What do students in these two categories have in common?
4. What limitation should teachers expect when a student with a physical impairment or health impairment is enrolled in a general education classroom?
5. How much information should a general education teacher have about the students with physical or health impairments?
6. A student has a physical impairment and uses a wheelchair. He also has severe asthma. He wants to compete in Special Olympics. His father is afraid it would be too much for him. What advice would you give the student? What advice would you give the father?

PROFESSIONAL ASSOCIATIONS AND PARENT OR SELF-HELP GROUPS

Asthma and Allergy Foundation of America (AAFA)
1233 20th Street NW, Suite 402
Washington, DC 20036
202-466-7643
Fax: 202-466-8940
www.aafa.org

Allergy Foundation of America
801 Second Avenue
New York, NY 10017

American Academy of Allergy, Asthma and Immunology
Online Communications Department
611 East Wells Street
Milwaukee, WI 53202
E-mail: onlinemgr@aaaai.org

American Academy for Cerebral Palsy and Developmental Medicine (AACPDM)
6300 N. River Rd., Suite 727
Rosemont, IL 60018-4226
847-698-1635
Fax: 847-823-0536
E-mail: Woppenhe@ucla.edu

American Allergy Academy
P.O. Box 7273
Menlo Park, CA 94126

American Association for Protecting Children
9725 E. Hampden Avenue
Denver, CO 80231

American Cancer Society
1599 Clifton Road
Atlanta, GA 30329

American Cleft Palate Association/Cleft Palate Foundation (ACPA/CPF) National Office
104 South Estes Drive, Suite 204
Chapel Hill, NC 27514
919-933-9044
Fax: 919-933-9604
www.cleftline.org

American Diabetes Association
National Service Center
P.O. Box 25757
1660 Duke Street
Alexandria, VA 22313
703-549-1500 or 800-232-3472
www.diabetesnet.com/ada.html

American Heart Association
7320 Greenville Avenue
Dallas, TX 75231
800-AHA-USA1

American Leprosy Foundation
1600 Nebel Street, Suite 210
Rockville, MD 20852
301-984-1336
Fax: 301-770-0580
E-mail: lwm-alf@erols.com

American Lung Association
1740 Broadway
New York, NY 10019
212-315-8700
E-mail: webmaster@lungusa.org

American Occupational Therapy Association
4720 Montgomery Lane
P.O. Box 31220
Bethesda, MD 20824-1220
301-652-2682 or TDD: 800-377-8555
Fax: 301-652-7711

Association of Birth Defect Children
5400 Diplomat Circle, Suite 270
Orlando, FL 32812

Association for the Care of Children's Health
Member and Customer Service Representative
7910 Woodmont Avenue, Suite 300
Bethesda, MD 20814-3015
301-654-6549 or 800-808-2224
Fax: 301-986-4553

Brain Injury Association
105 North Alfred Street
Alexandria, VA 22314
703-236-6000
Fax: 703-236-6001

Center for Children with Chronic Illness and Disability
Box 721-UMHC
420 Delaware Street SE
Minneapolis, MN 55455-0374
612-626-0644

Cerebral Palsy Association of NY State
90 State Street, Suite 929
Albany, NY 12207-1709
528-436-0178

Childhelp USA National Headquarters
15757 North 78th Street
Scottsdale, Arizona 85260
480-922-8212
Fax: 480-922-7061

Childhelp USA National Child Abuse Hotline
800-4-A-CHILD or TDD: 800-2-A-CHILD

Children's Brain Diseases Foundation (CBDF)
350 Parnassus Avenue, Suite 900
San Francisco, CA 94117
415-566-5402
Fax: 415-863-3452
E-mail: Jr.der6022@aol.com

CDC National AIDS Clearinghouse
Information Specialist/Publications
Centers for Disease Control and Prevention
P.O. Box 6003
Rockville, MD 20849-6003

Children's Hospice International
901 North Pitt Street, Suite 230
Alexandria, VA 22314
703-684-0330 or 800-2-4-CHILD
Fax: 703-684-0226
E-mail: chiorg@aol.com

Cystic Fibrosis Foundation
6931 Arlington Road, Suite 200
Bethesda, MD 20814
301-951-4422 or 800-FIGHT-CF (344-4823)
Fax: 301-951-6378
E-mail: info@cff.org

Division for Physical and Health Disabilities
Council for Exceptional Children
1110 North Glebe Road, Suite 300
Arlington, VA 22201-5704

Epilepsy Foundation of America
4351 Garden City Drive, Suite 406
Landover, MD 20785
800-332-1000
E-mail: webmaster@efa.org

Foundation for Children with AIDS
55 Dimock
Roxbury, MA 02119

Pediatric AIDS Association
2950 31st Street, #125
Santa Monica, CA 90405
310-314-1459
Fax: 310-314-1469
E-mail: info@pedaids.org

or

41 Madison Avenue, 29th Floor
New York, NY 10010
212-448-6654
E-mail: Ny@pedaids.org

or

1730 Rhode Island Avenue NW, Suite 400
Washington, DC, 20036
202-296-9165
Fax: 202-296-9185
E-mail: Dc@pedaids.org

or

888-499-HOPE (4673)
E-mail: info@pedAIDS.org

Huntington's Disease Society of America
158 West 29th Street, 7th Floor
New York, NY 10001-5300
800-345-hdsa
Fax: 212-239-3430

International Center for the Disabled
340 East 24th Street
New York, NY 10010-4019
212-585-6000
Fax: 212-585-6161
E-mail: info@icdrehab.org

Juvenile Diabetes Research Foundation International
120 Wall Street
New York, NY 10005-4001
800-533-CURE (2873) or 212-785-9500
Fax: 212-785-9595
E-mail: info@jdrf.org

Little People of America
Box 745
Lubbock, TX 79408
888-LPA-2001 (English and Spanish)
E-mail: LPADataBase@juno.com

March of Dimes Birth Defects Foundation
1275 Mamaroneck Avenue
White Plains, NY 10605
888-MODIMES (663-4637)
www.modimes.org

Muscular Dystrophy Association
3561 E. Sunrise Drive
Tucson, AZ 85718
800-572-1717
E-mail: mda@mdausa.org

Muscular Dystrophy Association of America
810 Seventh Avenue
New York, NY 10019

Myasthenia Gravis Foundation
53 West Jackson Boulevard, Suite 909
Chicago, IL 60064

National AIDS Information Clearinghouse
P.O. Box 6003
Rockville, MD 20850

National Amputation Foundation
12–45 150th Street
Whitestone, NY 11357

National Association for the Craniofacially Handicapped
P.O. Box 11082
Chattanooga, TN 37401
615-266-1632 or 800-332-2373
Fax: 615-267-3124

National Association for the Physically Handicapped
Jim Truman, National President
754 Staeger Street
Akron, OH 44306-2940
330-724-1994
E-mail: jim@naph.net

National Resource Center on Child Abuse and Neglect
63 Inverness Drive East
Englewood, CO 80112-5117
303-792-9900
Fax: 303-792-5333

National Center for Youth with Disabilities
University of Minnesota
Box 721, UMHC
Minneapolis, MN 55455

National Committee for Prevention of Child Abuse
332 South Michigan Avenue, Suite 950
Chicago, IL 60604

National Council on the Handicapped
800 Independence Avenue SW, Suite 814
Washington, DC 20591

National Cystic Fibrosis Foundation
6931 Arlington Road
Bethesda, MD 20814

National Cystic Fibrosis Research Foundation
3379 Peachtree Road NE
Atlanta, GA 30320

National Easter Seals Society for Crippled Children and Adults
2023 Ogden Avenue
Chicago, IL 60612

National Foundation for Asthma
P.O. Box 30069
Tucson, AZ 85751

The National Foundation—March of Dimes
P.O. Box 2000
White Plains, NY 10602

National Head Injury Foundation
1140 Connecticut Avenue NW, Suite 812
Washington, DC 20036

National Huntington's Disease Association
128–A East 74th Street
New York, NY 10021

National Kidney Foundation
30 East 33rd Street, Suite 1100
New York, NY 10016
800-622-9010 or 212-889-2210
Fax: 212-689-9261

National Organization on Disability
910 Sixteenth Street NW, Suite 600
Washington, DC 20006
202-293-5960
E-mail: ability@nod.org

National Organization on Fetal Alcohol Syndrome
216 G Street NE
Washington, DC 20006
202-785-4585
Fax: 202-466-6456

National Organization for Rare Disorders
P.O. Box 8923
New Fairfield, CT 06812

National Rehabilitation Association
633 South Washington Street
Alexandria, VA 22314

National Rehabilitation Information Center
8455 Colesville Road, Suite 935
Silver Spring, MD 20910
703-836-0850 or TDD: 703-836-0849
Fax: 703-836-0848
E-mail: info@nationalrehab.org

National Society for Children and Adults with Autism
1234 Massachusetts Avenue NW, Suite 1017
Washington, DC 20005

National Spina Bifida Association of America
4590 MacArthur Boulevard NW, Suite 250
Washington, DC 20007-4226
800-621-3141 or 202-944-3285
Fax: 202-944-3295
E-mail: sbaa@sbaa.org

National Spinal Cord Injury Association
6701 Democracy Boulevard, Suite 300–9
Bethesda, MD 20817
301-588-6959
Fax: 301-588-9414

Osteogenesis Imperfecta Foundation
804 West Diamond Avenue, Suite 210
Gaithersburg, MD 20878
301-947-0083 or 800-981-2663
Fax: 301-947-0456

Spina Bifida Association of America
209 Shiloh Drive
Madison, WI 53705

Tourette Syndrome Association
42–40 Bell Boulevard
Bayside, NY 11361
718-224-2999

United Cerebral Palsy Association
1522 K Street NW, Suite 1112
Washington, DC 20005

Accent on Living
P.O. Box 700
Bloomington, IL 61701

Assistive Technology
RESNA
1101 Connecticut Avenue NW, Suite 700
Washington, DC 20036

Catalogue of Educational Materials
National Head Injury Foundation
1140 Connecticut Avenue NW, Suite 912
Washington, DC 20036

Closing the Gap
P.O. Box 68
Henderson, MN 56044

Disabilities Studies Quarterly
Department of Sociology
Brandeis University
Waltham, MA 02254

Disability Rag
P.O. Box 145
Louisville, KY 40201

Disabled USA
President's Commission on Employment of the Handicapped
1111 20th Street NW, Suite 600
Washington, DC 20036

Exceptional Parent: Annual Technology and Products-Services Issues
Psy-Ed Corporation
209 Harvard Street, Suite 303
Brookline, MA 02146

International Journal of Rehabilitation Research Quarterly
International Society of Rehabilitation of the Disabled
Rehabilitation International
432 Park Avenue South
New York, NY 10016

Journal of Head Trauma Rehabilitation
Aspen Publishers
200 Orchard Ridge Drive
Gaithersburg, MD 20878

NeuroRehabilitation: An Interdisciplinary Journal
Andover Medical Publishers
125 Main Street
Reading, MA 01867

New Mobility
Spinal Network
1911 Eleventh Street, Suite 301
Boulder, CO 80303

Rehabilitation Literature
National Easter Seal Society
2030 West Ogden Avenue
Chicago, Il 60612

Rehabilitation: Traumatic Brain Injury Update
University of Washington
Rehabilitation Medicine RJ-30 (Attention TBI Newsletter)
Seattle, WA 98195

Spinal Network EXTRA
P.O. Box 4162
Boulder, CO 80306

Straight Talk: A Magazine for Teens
The Learning Partnership
P.O. Box 199
Pleasantville, NY 10507

REFERENCES

Able-Boone, H., Crais, E. R., & Downing, K. (2003). Preparation of early intervention practitioners for working with young children with low incidence disabilities. *Teacher Education and Special Education, 26,* 79–82.

Altman, L. K. (1993, May 4). Rise in asthma deaths is tied to ignorance of many physicians. *New York Times,* p. B8.

American Cancer Society. (1988). *Back to school: A handbook for teachers of children with cancer.* Atlanta, GA: Author.

American School Health Association. (2003). Meeting the health needs of chronically ill students. *Journal of School Health, 73,* 131–132.

Americans with Disabilities Act of 1990, 42 U.S.C. [Section] 12101 et seq. (2003).

Baca, L., & Harris, K. C. (1988). Teaching migrant exceptional children. *Teaching Exceptional Children, 20,* 32–35.

Batshaw, M. L. (1997). *Children with handicaps: A medical primer* (4th ed.). Baltimore: Paul H. Brookes.

Batshaw, M. L., & Conlon, C. J. (1997). Substance abuse: A preventable threat to development. In M. L. Batshaw (Ed.), *Children with disabilities* (4th ed.). Baltimore: Paul H. Brookes.

Bernheimer, L. P., & Keogh, B. K. (1995). Weaving interventions into the fabric of everyday life: An approach to family assessment. *Topics in Early Childhood and Special Education, 15,* 415–433.

Best, S. J. (2005). Physical disabilities. In S. J. Best, K. W. Heller, & J. L. Bigge (Eds.), *Teaching individuals with physical or multiple disabilities* (5th ed.). Upper Saddle River, NJ: Merrill/Prentice Hall.

Best, S. J., Heller, K. W., & Bigge, J. L. (2005). *Teaching individuals with physical or multiple disabilities* (5th ed.). Upper Saddle River, NJ: Merrill/Prentice Hall.

Blakeslee, S. (1992, September 29). Radical brain surgery, the earlier the better, offers epileptics hope. *New York Times,* p. B6.

Bowe, F. (2000). *Physical, sensory, and health disabilities: An introduction.* Upper Saddle River, NJ: Merrill/Prentice Hall.

Brown, L. (1997). Seizure disorders. In M. L. Batshaw (Ed.), *Children with disabilities* (4th ed.). Baltimore: Paul H. Brookes.

Carta, J. J., Atwater, J. B., Greenwood, C. R., McConnell, S. R., McEvoy, M. A., & Williams, R. (2001). Effects of cumulative prenatal substance exposure and environmental risks on children's developmental trajectories. *Journal of Clinical Child Psychology, 30,* 327–337.

Cassini, K. K., & Rogers, J. L. (1990). *Death in the classroom.* Cincinnati, OH: Griefwork.

Chasnof, I. J. (1988, October). A first: National hospital incidence survey. *NAPARE Update,* 2.

Centers for Disease Control (2004). *Traumatic brain injury in the United States: Emergency department visits, hospital-izations, and deaths.* Retrieved June 27, 2005, from *www.cdc.gov/injury*

Centers for Disease Control (2005a). *Monitoring fetal alcohol syndrome.* Retrieved June 27, 2005, from *http://www.cdc.gov/ncbddd/factsheets/FAS monitoring.pdf*

Centers for Disease Control (2005b). *Traumatic brain injury in the United States: Emergency department visits, hospitaliza-tions, and deaths.* Retrieved June 27, 2005, from *http://www.cdc.gov/ncipc/pub-res/TBI in US 04/TBI ED.htm*

Cohen, C. B., Mundy, T., Karassik, B., Lieb, L., Ludwig, D. D., & Ward, J. (1991). Neuropsychological functioning in human immunodeficiency virus type 1 seropositive children affected through neonatal blood transfusion. *Pediatrics, 88,* 58–68.

Conlon, C. J. (1992). New threats to development: Alcohol, Cocaine, and AIDS. In M. L. Batshaw & Y. M. Perret, *Children with disabilities: A medical primer* (3rd ed., pp. 111–136). Baltimore: Paul H. Brookes.

Cross, D. (1993). Students with physical and health-related disabilities. In A. E. Blackhurst & W. H. Berdine (Eds.), *An introduction to special education* (3rd ed., pp. 351–397). New York: HarperCollins.

Department of Health and Human Services (DHHS) (US), Administration on Children, Youth, and Families (ACF). (2005). *Child maltreatment 2003* [online]. Washington, DC: Government Printing Office. Retrieved May 5, 2005, from *www.acf.hhs.gov/programs/cb/publications/cm03.pdf*

Dey, A. N., & Bloom, B. (2005). Summary health statistics for U.S. children: National health interview survey, 2003. *Vital Health Statistics, 10*(223). Retrieved June 23, 2005, from *http://www.cdc.gov/nchs/data/series/sr 10/sr10 223.pdf*

Education Commission of the States, Migrant Education Task Force. (1979). *Migrant health. Report no. 131.* Denver: Author.

Epilepsy Foundation of America. (2001). *Questions and answers about epilepsy.* Landover, MD: Author.

Epilepsy.com (2005). *Myoclonic seizures.* Retrieved June 15, 2005, from *www.epilepsy.com/epilepsy/seizure myoclonic.html*

Forness, S. R., & Kavale, K. A. (1993). The balkanization of special education: Proliferation of categories and subcategories for "new" disorders. *Oregon Conference Monograph, 5,* ix–xii.

Gregory, S. (2005). Living with chronic illness in the family setting. *Sociology of Health & Illness, 27,* 372–392.

Griffith, D. R. (1991). Intervention needs of children prenatally exposed to drugs. *DD Network News, 4*(1), 4–6.

Hallahan, D. P., & Kauffman, J. M. (2006). *Exceptional children* (8th ed.). Boston: Allyn & Bacon.

Hardman, M. L., Drew, C. J., & Egan, M. W. (2006). *Human exceptionality: School, community, and family, IDEA 2004* (Update Edition). Needham, MA: Allyn & Bacon.

Heller, K. W., Alberto, P. A., & Meagher, T. M. (1996). The impact of physical impairments on academic performance. *Journal of Developmental and Physical Disabilities, 8,* 243.

Heller, K. W., Bigge, J. L., & Allgood, P. (2005). Adaptations for personal independence. In S. J. Best, K. W. Heller, & J. L. Bigge (Eds.), *Teaching individuals with physical or multiple disabilities* (pp. 309–335). Upper Saddle River, NJ: Merrill/Prentice Hall.

Heller, K. W., Forney, P. E., Alberto, P. A., Schwartzman, M. A., & Goeckel, T. M. (2000). *Meeting physical and health needs of children with disabilities: Teaching student participation and management.* Belmont, CA: Wadsworth/Thompson Learning.

Heward, W. L. (2006). *Exceptional children: An introduction to special education* (8th ed.). Upper Saddle River, NJ: Merrill/Prentice Hall.

Hill, J. L. (1999). *Meeting the needs of students with special physical and health care needs.* Upper Saddle River, NJ: Merrill/Prentice Hall.

HIV/AIDS (1990). *HIV/AIDS education: Resources for special educators.* Joint publication of the Council for Exceptional Children and the Association for the Advancement of Health Education. Reston, VA: Council for Exceptional Children.

Hunt, N., & Marshall, K. (2002). *Exceptional children and youth* (3rd ed.). Boston: Houghton Mifflin.

Indacochea, J. J., & Scott, G. B. (1992). HIV-1 infection and the acquired immunodeficiency syndrome in children. *Current Problems in Pediatrics, 22,* 166–204.

Individuals with Disabilities Education Improvement Act (2004).

Jones, M. H. (1983). Cerebral palsy. In J. Umbriet (Ed.), *Physical disabilities and health impairment: An introduction* (pp. 41–58). Upper Saddle River, NJ: Merrill/Prentice Hall.

Juvenile Diabetes Research Foundation International (2004). *Type I diabetes: Fact sheet.* New York: Author.

Kirk, S. A., Gallagher, J. J., Anastasiow, N. J., & Coleman, M. R. (2006). *Exceptional children and youth* (11th ed.). Boston: Houghton Mifflin.

Kraus, J. E., Fife, D., & Conroy, D. (1987). Pediatric brain injuries: The nature, clinical course, and early outcomes in a defined United States population. *Pediatrics, 79,* 501–507.

Lerner, J. (2002). *Learning disabilities: Theories, diagnosis, and teaching strategies* (9th ed.). New York: Houghton Mifflin.

Liptak, G. S. (1997). Neural tube defects. In M. L. Batshaw (Ed.), *Children with disabilities* (4th ed.). Baltimore: Paul H. Brookes.

Little, M. (1991). *Diabetes.* New York: Chelsea House.

Livneh, H., & Antonak, R. F. (2005). Psychosocial adaptation to chronic illness and disability: A primer for counselors. *Journal of Counseling and Development, 83,* 12–20.

Lorber, J. (1990). Where have all the spina bifida gone? *Midwife Health Visitor & Community Nurse, 22,* 94–95.

March of Dimes. (1992). *Spina bifida: Public health education information sheet.* White Plains, NY: Author.

Martz, E. (2003). Living with insulin-dependent diabetes: Life can still be sweet. *Rehabilitation Counseling Bulletin, 47,* 51–57.

Mathews, T. J. (2004). *Trends in spina bifida and anencephalus in the United States, 1991–2002.* National Center for Health Statistics. Retrieved June 27, 2005, from *www.cdc.gov/nchs/products/pubs/pubd/hestats/spine an en.htm*

McDermott, S., Moran, R., Platt, T., Wood, T., Isaac, T., & Dasari, S. (2005). Prevalence of epilepsy in adults with mental retardation and related disabilities in primary care. *American Journal on Mental Retardation, 110,* 48–56.

Michaud, L., Duhaime, A., & Lazar, M. F. (1997). Traumatic brain injury. In M. L. Batshaw (Ed.), *Children with disabilities.* Baltimore: Paul H. Brookes.

Miller, F., & Bachrach, S. (1995). *Cerebral palsy: A complete guide for caring.* Baltimore, MD: The Johns Hopkins University Press.

Mitiguy, J. (1991). Cycles of abuse: Alcohol and head trauma. *Headlines, 2,* 2–11.

Munson, L. J., & Hunt, N. (2005). Teachers grieve! What can we do for our colleagues and ourselves when a student dies? *Teaching Exceptional Children, 37*(4), 48–51.

Murphy, C. C., Yeargin-Allsopp, M., Decoufle, P., & Drews, C. D. (1993). Prevalence of cerebral palsy among ten-year-old children in metropolitan Atlanta, 1985 through 1987. *Journal of Pediatrics, 123,* 13–20.

National Commission on Migrant Education. (1992). *Invisible children: A portrait of migrant education in the United States.* Washington, DC: U.S. Government Printing Office.

National Information Center for Children and Youth with Disabilities. (1997). *General information about spina bifida.* Available from *www.nichcy.org*

National Information Center for Children and Youth with Disabilities (2002). *Cerebral palsy.* Fact sheet = La paralysis cerebral. Hojas informativas sobre discapacidades. Washington, DC: Author.

Palfrey, J. S. (1995). Amber, Katie, and Ryan: Lessons from children with complex medical conditions. *The Journal of School Health, 65,* 265–267.

Paul, G. H., & Fafoglia, B. A. (1988). *All about asthma and how to live with it.* New York: Sterling.

Rainforth, B., York, J., & Macdonald, M. A. (1992). *Collaborative teams for students with severe disabilities: Integrating therapy and educational services.* Baltimore: Paul H. Brookes.

Raj, A., Mishra, A., Feinsilver, S. H., & Fein, A. M. (2000). An estimate of the prevalence and impact of asthma and relaed symptoms in a New York City middle school. *Chest, 118*(4) 84S.

Reid, J., & Dixon, W. (1999). Teacher attitudes on coping with grief in the public school classroom. *Psychology in the Schools, 36,* 219–228.

Romo, H. (1996). The newest "outsiders": Educating Mexican migrant and immigrant youth. In J. L. Flores (Ed.), *Children of la frontera: Binational efforts to serve Mexican migrant and immigrant students* (pp. 61–92). Charleston, WV: Clearinghouse on Rural Education and Small Schools.

Salend, S. J., Taylor, L. S., & Whittaker, C. R. (1998). Diversifying the special education training curriculum to address the needs of migrant students and families. *Teacher Education and Special Education, 21,* 174–186.

Schaefer, D. (1988). *How do we tell the children? Helping children understand and cope when someone dies.* New York: Newmarket.

Schroeder, H. (1993). Cerebral trauma: Accidental injury or shaken impact syndrome? *Headlines, 4*(5), 18–21.

Sirvis, B. (1996). Physical impairments. In E. L. Meyen & T. M. Skrtic (Eds.), *Exceptional children and youth: An introduction* (3rd ed.). Denver: Love.

Smith, D. D. (2001). *Introduction to special education: Teaching in an age of opportunity* (4th ed.). Needham, MA: Allyn & Bacon.

Stone, D. H. (1987). The declining prevalence of anencephalus and spina bifida: Its nature, causes and implications. *Developmental Medicine and Child Neurology, 29,* 541–549.

Symons, F. J., Clark, R. D., Roberts, J. P., & Bailey, D. B. (2001). Classroom behavior of elementary school-age boys with fragile X syndrome. *Journal of Special Education, 34,* 194–202.

Taylor, J. M., & Taylor, W. S. (1989). *Communicable disease and young children in group settings.* Boston: College-Hill.

Taylor, M. (1990). Clean intermittent catheterization. In C. J. Graff, M. M. Ault, D. Guess, M. Taylor, & B. Thompson (Eds.), *Health care for students with disabilities* (pp. 241–252). Baltimore: Paul H. Brookes.

Treaster, J. B. (1993, February 16) For children of cocaine: Fresh reasons for hope. *New York Times,* pp. A1, B12.

Turnbull, A. P., Turnbull, H. R., Shank, M., & Smith, D. (2004). *Exceptional lives: Special education in today's schools* (2nd ed.). Upper Saddle River, NJ: Merrill/Prentice Hall.

Turnbull, H. R., & Turnbull, A. P (2000). *Free appropriate public education: The law and children with disabilities* (6th ed.). Denver: Love.

U.S. Cancer Statistics Working Group. (2004). *United States cancer statistics: 1999–2001 incidence and mortality web-based report version.* Atlanta (GA): Department of Health and Human Services, Centers for Disease Control and Prevention, and National Cancer Institute. Available from *www.cdc.gov/cancer/npcr/uscs*

U.S. Department of Education. (2002). *Twenty-fourth annual report to Congress on the implementation of the Individuals with Disabilities Education Act.* Washington, DC: Author.

United Cerebral Palsy, (2001). *Cerebral palsy: Facts and figures.* Washington, DC: Author.

Verhaaren, P., & Connor, F. (1981). Physical disabilities. In J. M. Kauffman & D. P. Hallahan (Eds.), *Handbook of special education.* Upper Saddle River, NJ: Merrill/Prentice Hall.

Vincent, L. J., Paulsen, M. K., Cole, C. K., Woodruff, G., & Griffith, D. R. (1991). *Born substance exposed, educationally vulnerable.* Reston, VA: Council for Exceptional Children.

8

Students with Autism Spectrum Disorders

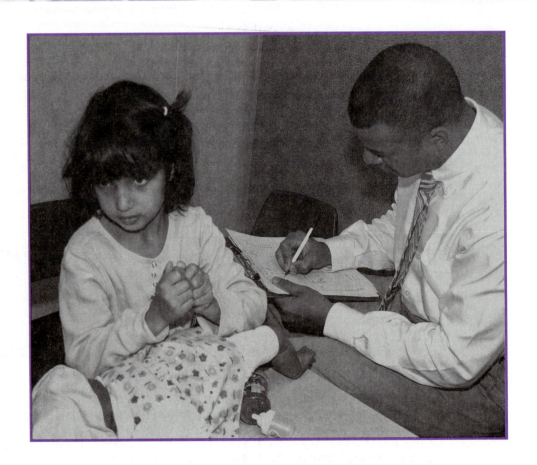

KEY TERMS

WHAT WOULD YOU DO?

Luke would play by himself most of the time. He repeated instructions before starting an activity if it was not part of a regular routine. He chose the same toys most of the time. He would imitate others. He did not like to get paint, paste, marker, or other substances on his hands. He would repeat comments other had made and he would say them with a rather flat tone.

Luke attended a preschool class for 4- to 5-year-olds for which he was age appropriate. It was a community-based preschool that encouraged full inclusion for students with special needs. Three other children with special education labels were included in Luke's class of 19 children. He was generally compliant, especially when he could see other students completing actions. He sat in circles or at tables when the class was requested to do so. He smiled to himself as he was making singsong sounds. He smiled when parents arrived. His motor control was good. He could hop, walk up ladders with alternating feet, gallop, and walk steadily. He knew the alphabet and could identify isolated letters. He could identify his own name from an array of six names of students in the preschool class. He could also identify the names of other students.

Luke had a few habits and behaviors that worried his teachers. One involved closing his eyes in class. He would close them when he was asked to do a task he did not particularly enjoy. He also closed them when other students spoke to him. Occasionally, he would place his head into a pillow or soft piece of furniture. He would face the furniture, place his head down into the seat, and stay there and hum to himself.

Another difficulty in the class was Luke's reluctance to touch "messy" substances. He would refuse to comply when he was asked to finger-paint, work with paper mache, cut out cookie dough, or play with clay. He got unreasonably upset if there was a trace of magic marker or paint on his hands, and he wanted to wash repeatedly. However, he loved to play in the sand or rice tables.

1. Does Luke appear to fit into the spectrum of autism disorders? What evidence do you have?

2. What programming modifications would appear important?

Autism spectrum disorders (ASD), including autism, Asperger syndrome, pervasive developmental disorders not otherwise specified (PDD-NOS), Rett syndrome, and childhood disintegrative disorder (CDD), are lifelong neurological disorders of unknown origin that lead to deficits in the student's ability to communicate, understand language, play, develop social skills, and relate to others (National Information Center for Children and Youth with Disabilities, 2004). Originally called infantile psychoses (Rutter, 2005), autism initially was described by Dr. Leo Kanner (1943). At about the same time, Hans Asperger (1944) noted similar types of behaviors in several of his younger patients, except that his patients used spoken language. In the middle of the 20th century, autism was identified as an emotional disorder possibly caused by parental ambivalence and rejection, but it is now generally considered as a neurobiological difficulty whose cause is as yet unknown. It is usually noted early in life by family members before it is caught by physicians or educators. There are many theories about education and treatment. Follow-up research on adults diagnosed in childhood indicates a rather poor future. A higher childhood IQ level was positively correlated with a better adult outcome, as was the existence of some communicative speech at age 6. Children with autism as diagnosed in the 1960s, 1970s, and 1980s have had poor psychosocial outcomes (Billstedt & Gillberg, 2005). Conversely, individuals with ASD may be able to analyze systems, examine relationships between components of systems, and read correlations among disparate events (Baron-Cohen, 2002; Lawson, Baron-Cohen, & Wheelwright, 2004). Many persons with ASD complete college, hold jobs, and live fulfilling lives.

DEFINITIONS

Prior to 1990, students with poor socialization, difficulty in language, and stereotypical behaviors were categorized as emotionally disturbed, mentally retarded, or as having a mental illness. PDD and ASD are overarching terms for the five syndromes listed previously. All five syndromes have been termed autism for the terms of IDEA. This category was added as a fundable category with the reauthorization of IDEA in 1990. Autism is defined legally in IDEA as:

> a developmental disability significantly affecting verbal and nonverbal communication and social interaction usually evident before age 3, that adversely affects a child's educational performance. Other characteristics often associated with autism are engagement in repetitive activities and stereotyped movement, resistance to environmental change or change in daily routines, and unusual sensory experiences. The term does not apply if the child's educational performance is adversely affected because the child has a serious emotional disturbance. (34 C.F.R., Part 300, Sec 300.7 (b)[1])

The DSM–IV definition of autism is a list of symptoms.

A. A total of six (or more) items from (1), (2), and (3), with at least two from (1), and one each from (2) and (3)
  1. qualitative impairment in social interaction, as manifested by at least two of the following:
    a) marked impairments in the use of multiple nonverbal behaviors such as eye-to-eye gaze, facial expression, body posture, and gestures to regulate social interaction
    b) failure to develop peer relationships appropriate to developmental level
    c) a lack of spontaneous seeking to share enjoyment, interests, or achievements with other people, (e.g., by a lack of showing, bringing, or pointing out objects of interest to other people)
    d) lack of social or emotional reciprocity
  2. qualitative impairments in communication as manifested by at least one of the following:
    a) delay in, or total lack of, the development of spoken language

        b) in individuals with adequate speech, marked impairment in the ability to initiate or sustain a conversation with others

        c) stereotyped and repetitive use of language or idiosyncratic language

        d) lack of varied, spontaneous make-believe play or social imitative play appropriate to developmental level

    3. restricted repetitive and stereotyped patterns of behavior, interests and activities, as manifested by at least two of the following:

        a) encompassing preoccupation with one or more stereotyped and restricted patterns of interest that is abnormal either in intensity or focus

        b) apparently inflexible adherence to specific, nonfunctional routines or rituals

        c) stereotyped and repetitive motor mannerisms (e.g., hand or finger flapping or twisting, or complex whole-body movements)

        d) persistent preoccupation with parts of objects

B. Delays or abnormal functioning in at least one of the following areas, with onset prior to age 3 years:

    1. social interaction

    2. language as used in social communication

    3. symbolic or imaginative play

C. The disturbance is not better accounted for by Rett's Disorder or Childhood Disintegrative Disorder (American Psychiatric Association, 2000).

The Autism Society of America stresses that the disorder is treatable and defines the disorder as follows:

> AUTISM is a severely incapacitating lifelong developmental disability that typically appears during the first three years of life. It occurs in approximately fifteen out of every 10,000 births and is four times more common in boys than girls. It has been found throughout the world in families of all racial, ethnic and social backgrounds. No known factors in the psychological environment of a child have been shown to cause autism. The symptoms are caused by physical disorders of the brain. They include:
>
> 1. Disturbances in the rate of appearance of physical, social and language skills.
> 2. Abnormal responses to sensations. Any one or a combination of senses or responses are affected: sight, hearing, touch, pain, balance, smell, taste, and the way a child holds his body.
> 3. Speech and language are absent or delayed while specific thinking capabilities might be present.
> 4. Abnormal ways of relating to people, objects and events.
>
> Autism occurs by itself or in association with other disorders which affect the function of the brain such as viral infections, metabolic disturbances, and epilepsy. It is important to distinguish autism from retardation or mental disorders since diagnostic confusion may result in referral to inappropriate and ineffective treatment techniques. The severe form of the syndrome may include extreme self-injurious, repetitive, highly unusual and aggressive behavior. Special educational programs using behavioral methods have proven to be the most helpful treatment (Autism Society of America, 2004b).

Defining autism and its related syndromes is difficult because, in the past, "classic" autism included developing no spoken language, engaging in repetitive behaviors, and appearing to function at a level indicating cognitive deficits. In recent decades, the concept of autism has broadened to include infants, children, youth, and adults with similar symptoms but to a less marked degree. Several other syndromes are included in the spectrum. One is **Asperger syndrome,** named after Hans Asperger, who worked with patients with autistic-like symptoms but who had spoken language. It has been termed "high-functioning autism," but many believe this is a misnomer

(Mayes, Calhoun, & Crites, 2001; Ozonoff & Griffith, 2000; Volkmar & Klin, 2001). It is defined in DSM–IV–TR as:

A. Qualitative impairment in social interaction, as manifest by at least two of the following:
   1. marked impairment in the use of multiple nonverbal behaviors such as eye-to-eye gaze, facial expression, body postures, and gestures to regulate social interaction
   2. failure to develop peer relationships appropriate to developmental level
   3. a lack of spontaneous seeking to share enjoyment, interest, or achievements with other people (e.g., by a lack of showing, bringing or pointing out object of interest)
   4. lack of social or emotional reciprocity
B. Restricted repetitive and stereotyped patterns of behavior, interests, and activities, as manifested by at least one of the following:
   1. encompassing preoccupation with one or more stereotyped and restricted patterns of interest that is abnormal either in intensity or focus
   2. apparently inflexible adherence to specific, nonfunctional routines or rituals
   3. stereotyped and repetitive motor mannerisms (e.g., hand or finger flapping or twisting, or complex whole-body movements)
   4. persistent preoccupation with parts of objects
C. The disturbance causes clinically significant impairment in social, occupational, or other important areas of functioning.
D. There is no clinically significant general delay in language (e.g., single words used by age 2 years, communicative phrases used by age 3 years).
E. There is no clinically significant delay in cognitive development or in the development of age-appropriate self-help skills, adaptive behavior (other than in social interaction), and curiosity about the environment in childhood.
F. Criteria are not met for another specific Pervasive Developmental Disorder or Schizophrenia (American Psychiatric Association, 2000).

It can be difficult to distinguish between high-functioning students with autism and students with Asperger syndrome (Howlin, 2003; Ozonoff & Griffith, 2000). Similarly, students with PDD-NOS have many of the same characteristics; the differences are in the degree. PDD-NOS includes individuals for whom autistic symptoms have a late (after age 3) onset and those person for whom the symptoms in some areas are not pronounced.

This category [PDD-NOS] should be used when there is a severe and pervasive impairment in the development of reciprocal social interaction or verbal and nonverbal communication skills, or when stereotyped behavior, interest, and activities are present, but the criteria are not met for a specific Pervasive Developmental Disorder, Schizophrenia, Schizotypal Personality Disorder, or Avoidant Personality Disorder. For example, this category includes "atypical autism"—presentations that do not meet the criteria for Autistic Disorder because of late age at onset, atypical symptomatology or subthreshold symptomatology, or all of these (American Psychiatric Association, 2000).

Rett syndrome (RTT) is a progressive neurological disorder. It is associated with the X chromosome and therefore seen only in females. Girls grow and develop normally and then deteriorate. They lose previously mastered speech and motor skills and experience stereotypical hand movements and seizures. Brain growth slows at the time of onset, resulting in abnormally small brains for developmental ages (Armstrong, 2002; Hagberg, Aicardi, Dias, & Ramos, 1983). Early death is common.

Childhood disintegrative disorder is a very rare disability. It is characterized by normal development for at least the first 2 to 4 years, followed by a significant and dramatic loss of previously acquired skills, especially vocabulary (American Psychiatric Association, 2000; Volkmar & Rutter, 2002). Primarily characterized by age of onset, many of the symptoms are similar to those of autism. Heller (1969) described the symptoms as: (a) onset between 3 and 4 years of age, (b) progressive intellectual and behavioral deterioration with loss/marked impairment of speech noted at the time of onset, (c) associated behavioral/affective symptoms (fear, overactivity) and possible hallucinations, (d) an absence of obvious signs of neurological dysfunction or apparent "organicity" (e.g., normal facial appearance; see Malhotra & Gupta, 1999).

Definitions of PDD and the syndromes in ASD share some similarities. The onset of characteristic symptoms must occur before the age of 3 (except in some cases of PDD-NOS), involve some aspect of social dysfunction, evidence difficulties in communication, and demonstrate some repetitive and stereotyped patterns of behavior. The degree to which each of these characteristics is present in one student determines the severity of the diagnosis and affects the treatment and intervention plans.

PREVALENCE

Because there are several syndromes included in the spectrum of disorders, and because there are many methods of diagnosing ASD, it is difficult to estimate how many persons have a form of autism. The Twenty-Fifth Report to Congress (U.S. Department of Education, 2005) estimates there are only 97,904 students between the ages of 6 and 21 receiving services as a result of a diagnosis in the autism spectrum. According to the Autism Society of America, the syndrome and its associated behaviors occur in approximately 15 of every 10,000 individuals. The Center for Disease Control (CDC) in Atlanta, Georgia, estimates that 2 to 6 children of every 1,000 are born with a disorder in the autism spectrum (National Center on Birth Defects and Developmental Disabilities, 2005). A study conducted by the CDC, the Metropolitan Atlanta Developmental Disabilities Surveillance Program, compared the rates of autism with other developmental disabilities. The rate of autism for children ages 3 to 10 years was 3.4 per 1,000, lower than the rate for MR (9.7 per 1,000 persons below the age of 18). Autism is identified at a higher rate than CP (2.8 per 1,000), hearing loss (1.1 per 1,000), and vision impairment (0.9 per 1,000) (Metropolitan Atlanta Developmental Disabilities Surveillance Program, 2005).

Information on the prevalence of other, less commonly occurring categories of ASD are more difficult to ascertain. Incidence of CDD may be 1 in 100,000 (Malhotra & Gupta, 1999). RTT is also rare and found at very low numbers. Misdiagnosis may be one reason for the low reported occurrence. Physicians may not be familiar with the symptoms and differential diagnoses; and the symptoms can co-occur with other categories of disabilities. It has been estimated that PDD-NOS occurs in many students with a label of MR (de Bildt, Sytema, Kraijer, & Minderaa, 2005) and probably goes unreported because it is a secondary diagnosis.

Wing (1993) postulated that the explosion of diagnoses of ASD is due to better screening and identification methods. It is also possible that it is due to increased public awareness of the characteristics of the syndrome. Because IDEA allows students so classified to receive special education programming and services, more students may be referred and subsequently found eligible. These students may have been served under different labels, or they may not have been served at all.

CHARACTERISTICS

Individuals with autism are often considered severely impaired but, in fact, autism has a range of severity. Each person is as different from others with ASD as they are alike. The student's use of language, personal behavior, and social behavior typically determine the level of severity. Symptoms generally become apparent between 18 months to 4 years of age (NICHCY, 2004). A pervasive aspect of autism is the individual's social or interpersonal detachment or nonrelatedness to others. Sensory disabilities are overresponsive or underresponsive, and students usually have impaired or delayed speech and language and display an acute sensitivity to light, noise, touch, or pain. They may exhibit either inappropriate behavior or a flat affect and engage in repetitive self-stimulatory behaviors that interfere with social interactions, adaptive behavior, and learning. Often they fail to develop typical sequences or appropriate play behaviors and may exhibit obsessive ritualistic behaviors. These behaviors are thought to provide stimulation, rendering these individuals extremely resistant to change because of the reinforcing qualities of self-stimulation (Kirk, Gallagher, Anastasiow, & Coleman, 2006). The following characteristics are found to some extent in persons with autism:

Communication problems (e.g., using and understanding language);

Difficulty in relating to people, objects, and events;

Unusual play with toys and other objects;

Difficulty with changes in routine or familiar surroundings; and

Repetitive body movements or behavior patterns (NICHCY, 2004).

In the communication area, students with ASD develop language slowly, if at all. They may reverse "you" and "I" pronouns, show evidence of **echolalia,** or the tendency to repeat phrases they hear, sometimes repeating them several times. Tone of speech may be flat or monotonous. Students with ASD may have difficulty with initiating conversations, taking turns talking, staying on subject, and responding to a question. They appear to lack imagination and are not often seen pretending during play. They may use words but not attach meaning to them, leading to an odd use of phrases. Some students with ASD experience word loss in the preschool years; that is, they use words and phrases meaningfully and then regress and do not retain the skill (Lord, Shulman, & DiLavore, 2004). Many students with ASD take language literally. An instructor of special education at Boston University, who has autism, remembers being taught about spelling rules. His teacher said to drop the e. His comment was: "I was terribly afraid for the e" (Council for Exceptional Children, 2002).

Dysfunctions in social interactions include little or no interest in making friends, preferring to be alone rather than interacting with others, lack of imitating others' actions (especially at an early age), lack of playful interaction, avoiding eye contact, evidencing little or no smiling at familiar people, and difficulty differentiating between family and strangers. The students may show little interest in making friends and, in fact, may treat others as objects, ignoring their needs. They may have what some have called an empathy disorder. Some researchers speculate students with autism do not gain empathy for others. Students with ASD may need to be taught explicitly to respond to social cues such as eye contact or smiles (Mauk, Reber, & Batshaw, 1997) because they do not accurately assess social situations (Heavey, Phillips, Baron-Cohen, & Rutter, 2000). Play is characterized by a lack of spontaneity.

Behaviorally, students with ASD tend to be physically passive and inactive, rarely responding to requests, even from familiar people. They may have picky eating habits.

They may show an extreme interest in a single item, idea, activity, or person and often show rigidity in sticking to established routines. Familiar routines seem to be an obsession for some students (Baker, 2000; Mandell, Walrath, Manteuffel, Sgro, & Pinto-Martin, 2005). Changes are difficult and require planning and advance cuing. This can cause difficulties in the classroom and in community settings. Repetitive behavior patterns appear to serve the function of providing stimulation to the student with ASD. These students may flick their fingers in front of their eyes, manipulate or spin objects, rock, or flap their hands. Sometimes the behavior increases and may be a cause for concern if the student has the potential for self-injury (Hardman, Drew, & Egan, 2005). Some students show an affinity for certain objects. This can appear to be an obsession because of the heightened interest. The interest may be manifested by using the object or part of an object to provide stimulation.

Students with ASD may throw frequent tantrums for unknown reasons. They behave aggressively toward others and material objects. They may physically attack or injure others, and they can be self-abusive. This behavior includes head banging, eye gouging, and digging into their skin. This behavior is dangerous if the student could cause injury to himself or to others.

Sensory Sensitivities

The student with ASD may overreact to the noise, movement, and number of people in a typical classroom. He or she may be hypersensitive in areas of sight, hearing, touch, smell, and taste. Unstructured times, such as lunch time, physical education classes, center times, and transitions from class to class may be overstimulating and elicit inappropriate behavior. The cafeteria food or the cleaning solution used in the hall may have smells that are confusing and overwhelming. Touch may be difficult for the student with ASD. He or she may dislike being touched by teachers or classmates. Family members have described them as "not being cuddly." Some students dislike holding objects such as pencils and books. Others show pronounced likes and dislikes for fabrics and other textured objects. Deep tissue touch or massage may be relaxing. Each person has difference preferences.

Intelligence

Students with ASD vary in intellectual functioning. The majority test in the ranges indicative of a cognitive deficit (below 70) (Kauffman, 2005; Mastropieri & Scruggs, 2000). This may be an anomaly of the testing situation, however. It is hard to obtain a useful or predictive test score for a student who repeats the examiners instructions and words, engages in repetitive behaviors, both verbal and physical, and has difficulty with communication. Pragmatics such as language use, idiomatic phrases, and multiple meanings of words may cause difficulties in language-based assessments. Students who function well and have language abilities may test well, but the results may still be depressed by their lack of understanding of social cues. Areas of skills may develop at different rates, more so than would be expected in the general population, and order of skill acquisition frequently does not follow normal developmental patterns. Some individuals with ASD show pockets of very highly perfected skills—often called splinter skills. Family members and teachers may take evidence of these skills as signs of high intelligence. The research on splinter skills, or the discrepancy between a functional impairment and a skill level in some area (Heaton & Wallace, 2004), does not explain why such an uneven cognitive profile occurs.

Physical Appearance

Students with ASD look like everyone else. There are no associated facial or body abnormalities. A diagnosis of ASD can occur in all cultures and in all social and economic levels. There is no correlation with any particular ethnic group.

Students with autism and related disorders may exhibit some physical traits or behavioral habits. **Self-stimulatory behaviors** are repetitive movements that can be grouped in four categories: (a) stereotyped motor mannerisms, (b) preoccupation with nonfunctional objects or parts of objects, (c) patterns of interest that are unusual in the narrowness or intensity of their pursuit, and (d) extreme rigidity and insistence on sameness (American Psychiatric Association, 2000). These behaviors can take the form of hand flapping, rocking, moving fingers in repeated patterns, repeated attention to zippers or collars, talking incessantly, or ritualistic play with objects. Students may spin around or walk on their toes, as if they were balancing on a tightrope. Freezing in a position is another common behavior (Vernazza et al., 2005). Repetitive behaviors may serve as stimulation or they may be a behavior a student engages in when he or she is unsure of an appropriate response. Use of social stories (Gray, 2000) is one intervention shown to be effective in reducing numbers of repetitive behaviors.

ETIOLOGY

The causes of syndromes in ASD are not known. There are several theories; some that have an evidential basis and some that do not. An **evidential basis** is a body of research that would point to the theory as being true. Current theories point to abnormalities in the brain as a function or cause of autism (Scott & Deneris, 2005). Several mechanisms are under review in ongoing research: serotonin system development, genetic mutations (Zwaigenbaum, Sonnenberg, Heshka, Eastwood, & Xu, 2005), genetic transmission from a parent, and an increased level of excitement in sensory or emotional areas (Rubenstein & Merzenich, 2003; Talebizadeh et al., 2004).

Brain studies are possible now with advances in radiologic imaging. With computerized tomography (CT), positron emission tomography (PET), single photon emission computed tomography (SPECT), and magnetic resonance imaging (MRI), we can study the structure and the functioning of the brain. Studies have shown that several major brain structures may have some association with the symptoms seen with ASD. This includes the cerebellum, cerebral cortex, limbic system, brain stem, and others (Akshoomoff, Pierce, & Courchesne, 2002; Strock, 2004). Other studies have focused on a connectivity process among areas of the brain. Wickelgren (2005) found abnormalities in number, size, and organization of neurons in some areas of the brain. Other research is focusing on the role of neurotransmitters such as serotonin, dopamine, and epinephrine.

A genetic connection has been found for RTT (Hranilovic & Bucan, 2001), lending credence to a theory of a genetic cause for ASD. It is unclear whether the genetic defects are caused by a mutation or a transformation or whether this is an inherited disorder. Peer and family studies do not give us clear information. Clearly, more research is warranted.

IDENTIFICATION PROCESS

A diagnosis in the PDD or ASD umbrella occurs only if the symptoms have occurred prior to age 3, except for PDD-NOS. In this case, the diagnosis may be made when it is not clear whether symptoms were present prior to age 3 or if sufficient symptoms are not clearly present but the symptoms indicate a disposition toward this spectrum. About three of every four students with autism may also have severe cognitive delays. Asperger syndrome is diagnosed if at least three symptoms are present from the social impairment and restricted or repetitive behavior lists discussed earlier in this chapter, but there are no significant delays in language or cognitive development.

Diagnosis of ASD is multifaceted. First, a medical exam is desirable. Along with a physical, students should be screened and perhaps have full-scale tests of sensory abilities. If there are behavioral characteristics of impaired socialization, delayed or regressive language, and restricted behavior, a more complete analysis would be warranted. Tests of intellectual ability are frequently included to determine level of functioning but not necessarily to determine eligibility. Results of tests of academic or developmental functioning combine with results from intellectual potential to provide information for comparison to a profile of typical development. Behavior rating profiles consisting of lists of behaviors, habits, and actions are completed by family members, especially parents, and other caregivers and teachers (Filipek et al., 1999). Several questionnaires are appropriate. The Childhood Asperger Syndrome Test (CAST) is a questionnaire for parents to screen for ASD (Williams et al., 2005). The Childhood Autism Rating Scale (Schopler, Reichler, & Renner, 1988) is a scale suitable for screening students as young as age 2. It is administered by a clinician or practitioner. The items, each covering a characteristic associated with ASD, are rated on a 7-point scale after direct observation and interviews with family members. The Gilliam Autism Rating Scale (GARS) (Gilliam, 1995) and the Pervasive Developmental Disorders Screening Test–II (PDDST–II) are similar but are normalized on different ages. The PDDST–II can be administered to students as young as 18 months. The Asperger Syndrome Diagnostic Scale is a 50-item, yes/no response scale that can be completed by anyone familiar with the student (Myles, Bock, & Simpson, 2001). Other screening instruments include the Checklist of Autism in Toddlers (CHAT; Baird et al., 2000), the Modified Checklist for Autism in Toddlers (M–CHAT) (Robbins, Fein, Barton, & Green, 2001), the Screening Tool for Autism in Two-Year-Olds (STAT) (Stone, Coonrod, Ousley, 2000), and the Social Communication Questionnaire) (SCQ) for children age 4 and older (Berument, Rutter, Lord, Pickles, & Bailey, 1999).

If a screening indicates a need for further diagnostic assessment, a team of persons would need to be involved (Howlin & Asgharian, 1999). Neurological and genetic assessment with comprehensive cognitive and language testing would be critical. The Autism Diagnostic Interview–Revised (Le Couteur et al., 1989; Lord, Rutter, & Le Couteur, 1994) has standardized coding criteria but flexibility in interview questions. It is designed to elicit detailed descriptions of actual behavior in situ. It consists of over 100 items covering communication, social interaction, repetitive behaviors, and age of onset (Tadevosyan-Leyfer et al., 2003). The Autism Diagnostic Observation Schedule (ADOS–G) is an observational measure with the added element of pushing the student for behaviors in the social and communicative domains (Lord et al., 2000). The Vineland Adaptive Behavior Scales have supplementary norms for assessing individuals with autism (Carter et al., 1998).

PROGRAMS

Currently, the treatment and education of students with autism varies. Of the many approaches, some are effective with certain individuals and others are not. Approaches are as diversified as the symptoms displayed by individuals and range from the use of operant techniques to punish unwanted stereotypical behaviors while reinforcing selected appropriate behaviors to auditory integration training (AIT), which relies on systematic exposure to a variety of sounds. There is a good basis for expecting that treatment of autism is a better option than not treating persons with autism (Howlin, 2003; National Research Council, 2001; Rutter, 2005), but research on treatment options is conflicting.

A diagnosis of autism or ASD does not tell the educators involved with the student what type of program is well suited to the individual or what type of placement would be optimal. Because autism can co-occur with other disabilities, and because students with autism have individual preferences, individualized programs based on the strengths and needs of each student are critical (Volkmar, Lord, Bailey, Schultz, & Klin, 2004).

BOX 8.1
WHAT EVERY TEACHER SHOULD KNOW
Principles of Applied Behavior Analysis

- Behavior is controlled by consequences.
- Antecedent events foretell consequences.
- Reinforcement increases the likelihood of the behavior.
- Immediacy of application of the reinforcer is important.
- Intermittent reinforcement strengthens the possibility of having the behavior reoccur.
- Cessation of reinforcement leads to extinction.
- Immediately following cessation of a reinforcer, the behavior escalates.
- Extinction takes time.
- Behaviors can act as their own reinforcers, or there can be unknown reinforcers acting in concert with the assigned and given reinforcer.
- Punishment of behavior will weaken the schedule of occurrence.
- Punishment is the removal of positive stimuli or the application of aversive stimuli.
- An aversive stimulus decreases the probability of a behavior's recurrence.
- Negative reinforcement is relief from aversive stimuli.
- Response cost is a procedure for the reduction of inappropriate behavior through the withdrawal of reinforcers contingent on the behavior's occurrence (a fine or penalty).
- A conditioned reinforcer is one that becomes associated with a previously established reinforcer.
- A contingency is the relationship between a behavior and its consequences.
- Differential reinforcement of other behavior is a procedure in which reinforcement is delivered when a target behavior is not emitted for a specified period of time.
- Overcorrection or exaggeration of experience of appropriate behavior can result in a decrease of inappropriate behavior.
- A reinforcer can satiate.
- A reinforcer must be reinforcing.

Education for students with ASD should emphasize developing both language and social skills. Academic skills are taught according to the student's level of cognitive or intellectual functioning. Community agencies and regional centers often provide education for parents in using behavioral approaches to further develop social and functional skills at home. These approaches lean heavily on theories of behavior modification. Box 8.1 includes 20 principles of behavior modification.

There are several approaches based on a structured, behavioral approach. One approach, developed by Ivar Lovaas (Lovaas, 1987; McEachin, Smith, & Lovaas, 1993), is based on a four-tenet behavioral theory. Lovaas espoused that (1) the laws of learning adequately account for behaviors and provide the basis for treatment; (2) there are many separate behavioral deficits (rather than a central deficit) best described as developmental delays which, if corrected, would lead to broad-based improvement; (3) there is evidence that students with ASD are able to learn when placed in special environments; and (4) failure in normal environments and success in special environments indicate that the problems are not the result of a diseased nervous system (Lovaas, 2003). Lovaas's method is time intensive and initially requires a one-to-one teacher-student relationship. At the Center for Early Intervention, the clinic-based program involves training for 35 to 40 hours per week. Programming is heavily aligned with behaviorist principles and discrete trial training (DTT). The therapist/teacher makes a request, followed by a prompt (physical, verbal, or gestural) that will ensure that the student will comply with the request. When there is compliance (regardless of the intrusiveness of the prompt), the student receives a reinforcer. As the student learns what is expected and begins to comply on his or her own, the prompts are faded. The therapist/teacher delivers one-to-one instruction for the first few months. Lovaas (1987) stated that young students with autism do not learn initially in group situations. When the student has begun to act consistently in a prescribed manner, he or she is moved to a group situation. The best situations, according to the theorists, allow students with autism to interact with students who are typically developing.

Another method used with students with autism is the Treatment and Education of Autistic and Related Communication Handicapped Children (TEACCH) program, a multidisciplinary treatment approach and an educational procedure that seek to identify the special needs of individuals and families struggling with the challenge of autism. This method also depends on individual work with students and adherence to behavioral principles but includes creating the ecological environment necessary for the student to experience success (Van-Bourgondien, Reichle, Schopler, 2003). Organizing the environment means, simply, to use schedules that vary as little as possible, a consistent method of presenting work and activities, and visual and auditory prompts for changes. Applied behavioral analytic theories support the interventions. The teacher secures the attention of the student, presents a clear **mand** (a non-yes/no request), and reinforces compliance. As in DTT, the prompts are faded as the student begins to comply. TEACCH programs, developed at the University of North Carolina at Chapel Hill, emphasize physical organization of the room. Reading activities are completed in the reading area; math activities are done in the math area. Students are given cues to the work activities and behaviors expected from the space and the organization of the space. Schedules are explicit. They are posted on desks, the wall, or other places where the students can see what is expected and what activities are planned. Task cards are provided for students to take to scheduled activities. Within areas, tasks are organized in a structure to enable the student to work as independently as possible. Articles are arranged from left to right, numbers indicate sequence, and other visual prompts provide assistance. Communication systems allow students to convey needs with and without spoken language (Lord, Bristol, & Schopler, 1993).

Learning Experiences . . . an Alternative Program (LEAP) began in 1982 as a federally funded model demonstration program serving young students with autism along with students ages 3 to 5 who were typically developing. It is based on theories of parental involvement, inclusive practices, and education across natural settings. It relies heavily on developmentally appropriate practices (Odom, Hoyson, Jamieson, & Strain, 1985; Strain & Cordisco, 1994). LEAP programs have used "reverse mainstreaming." Several students with typical development are integrated into the classroom of several students with autism. The process is "reversed" because the students with autism are not placed into a general education class. The staff of the program are trained to facilitate social interactions and language exchanges among all the students. Peer tutoring and peer facilitation of social interactions are combined with teacher facilitation of interactions to create a climate where purposeful language is encouraged.

An approach using a more relationship-driven model is the Developmental, Individual-Difference, Relationship-Based Floortime program (DIR/Floortime), in which the focus is on relating, communicating, and thinking (Greenspan & Wieder, 1998; 1999; Interdisciplinary Council on Developmental and Learning Disorders Clinical Practice Guidelines Workgroup, 2000). Floortime is an intensive program of therapies (occupation, physical, speech, or whatever is needed) at a school or agency-based site along with direct play therapy at home with parents and peers. Needed therapies follow a functional analysis of how students integrate features of their lives (motor, cognitive, language, spatial, sensory) to carry out goals, sensory preferences, motor planning, and relationships (Greenspan & Weider, 1999).

With a goal of increasing social competence, LeGoff (2004) used play with building blocks to effect improvement in the students' scores on social competence measures. He advocated use of combined methods: behaviorist methods and naturalistic strategies (peer modeling, incidental teaching, activity-based interventions) in group play for young students with ASD. O'Reilly, Sigafoos, Lancioni, Edrisinha, and Andrews (2005) conducted a functional behavior analysis and found students did not engage in self-injury when there was an absence of academic demands. By scheduling a student's day in a series of activities that progressed from no interaction, to play, to a period of demand, self-injury was reduced.

Social skills training is a critical area of instruction because social dysfunction is a determining factor in autism. By definition, these students have difficulty initiating and continuing social contacts and social interactions. There is a substantial body of research on facilitating socialization (Rogers, 2000). Recently, practitioners and researchers have moved from more adult lead interventions to those that use the ecology of the settings. Incidental teaching (McGee, Krantz, & McClannahan, 1985), peer-mediated strategies (Werts, Caldwell, & Wolery, 1996), and peer tutoring (Wolery, Werts, Snyder, & Caldwell, 1994) use natural stimuli and reinforcers. Another frequently cited technique is the use of social stories. With some stories, the student reads a narrative that contains reminders of actions to take or of viewpoints of others. In others, the card could contain a script. The student may be prompted to start a conversation and is then given a card or script starter. The partner follows the script by responding and supporting the topic. After the student masters a script, the prompts are faded so the student can initiate or continue a conversation with less and less prompting (McClannahan, & Krantz, 2005; Solomon, Goodlin-Jones, & Anders, 2004).

Other methods of teaching students with autism are evolving as research continues. Some methods work with the whole student, and others focus on symptoms and attempt to decrease inappropriate behaviors. It is difficult to determine which method is correct in the abstract. As with any disability, individual decisions must be made in relation to the severity of the condition, individual behaviors, the social validity to the family and educational providers, and the ecology of the situation. Some assistive technology may be helpful in teaching students. A list of examples is included in Box 8.2.

Because of the spectrum nature of autism and the many behavior combinations that can occur, no one approach is effective in alleviating symptoms of autism in all cases. Studies show that individuals with autism respond well to highly structured, specialized education programs tailored to their individual needs. A well-designed intervention approach may include some elements of communication therapy, social skill development, sensory integration therapy, and applied behavior analysis, delivered by trained professionals in a consistent, comprehensive, and coordinated manner. The more severe challenges of some students with autism may be best addressed by a structured education and behavior program that contains a one-on-one teacher-to-student ratio or small-group environment. Many other students with autism may be successful in a fully inclusive general education environment with appropriate support. Along with

BOX 8.2
WHAT EVERY TEACHER SHOULD KNOW
ABOUT TECHNOLOGY

- Digital cameras provide rapid access to pictures that can be used on schedules, to illustrate social stories, and in communication devices.
- Communication boards and books with pictures or representations for words have been successful ways of allowing a student with a disorder in the autism spectrum to communicate a need to others.
- Pencil grips use a material that is softer or easier to hold for students who are averse to holding the plastic or wood of a pencil.
- Thin pointed watercolor markers are good writing implements for students who do not like to use pressure when writing. The student can make a mark on the paper with a very light touch, and the teacher can reinforce differentially.
- Touch screens are sheets of plastic that contain sensors to detect pressure from either a fingertip or a pointing device. When these sensors are pressed, they perform the functions of a traditional mouse. Touch screens can be used to teach cause and effect.

appropriate educational supports in the area of academics, students with autism should have training in functional living skills at the earliest possible age.

The Autism Society of America posits several questions to be asked of any educators and parents when selecting and implementing a program of instruction:

- Will the treatment result in harm to the child?
- How will failure of the treatment affect my child and family?
- Has the treatment been validated scientifically?
- Are there assessment procedures specified?
- How will the treatment be integrated into the child's current program? Do not become so infatuated with a given treatment that functional curriculum, vocational life and social skills are ignored. (Autism Society of America, 2004b; *www.autism-society.org/site/PageServer?pagename=TreatmentOptions*).

The National Institute of Mental Health suggests a list of questions for families when planning for a person with ASD:

How successful has the program been for others?
How many students have gone on to placement in a regular school and how have they performed?
Do staff members have training and experience in working with students with autism?
How are activities planned and organized?
Are there predictable daily schedules and routines?
How much individual attention is given?
How is progress measured? Will the behavior be closely observed and recorded?
Will tasks and rewards be personally motivating?
Is the environment designed to minimize distractions?
Will the program prepare me to continue the therapy at home?
What is the cost, time commitment, and location of the program? (Strock, 2004).

Because students with ASD frequently show splinter skills in some areas but deficits in other areas, teachers and parents may have difficulty in knowing what content to teach. As with all students, content should be age appropriate and functionally appropriate. A 10-year-old should be learning information other 10-year-olds are learning. If there is an increased interest in some area, this should be encouraged, but not to the detriment of other areas of focus. For instance, prepubescent North American girls are frequently fascinated by horses and horseback riding. Several academic and social areas could be taught using this theme: calculation of costs, history of horses in the development of the North American West, balance, care of animals, and basic biology concepts. Functional skills are those that have practicality, and for some students, horseback riding may not be geographically or economically appropriate. The decision on the extent of the use of the theme should be made judiciously. Several questions need to be answered when determining appropriate instruction, including: (1) Are prerequisite skills present, (2) is the program age appropriate, (3) will it reduce behavioral problems, (4) can skills be built upon it, and (5) will the skills taught be generalized? (Volkmar et al., 2004).

ISSUES OF IMPORTANCE
Medical Issues

About one fourth of the students with ASD will develop seizures. These can start either in the preschool years or in early adolescence. They can be controlled medically using many of the same medications used with students without ASD who have seizures; however, medications have been shown to have different effects and side effects for students with ASD (Strock, 2004; Volkmar, 2000). A physician should work with the family members and the teachers to monitor behaviors closely.

Tuberous sclerosis is a genetic disorder that causes benign tumors to grow in the brain as well as in other vital organs. It is found when a gene undergoes a mutation, and it has a consistently strong association with ASD. One to 4 percent of people with ASD also have tuberous sclerosis (Smalley, 1998). Medications and surgery (dermabrasion and laser procedures) can be used to remove skin tags. Antiepileptic drugs can be used to control seizures.

Fragile X syndrome and autism appear to be linked. Fragile X is a genetic disorder named for the pinched part of the X chromosome. It is damaged in some manner and looks "fragile." Although more study is clearly needed, it appears there may be a genetic locus for autism in the same regions as for fragile X (Demark, Feldman, & Holden, 2003; Vincent et al., 2005). Many students with fragile X syndrome will also have ASD (Bailey et al., 1998; Powers, 2000).

The use of medication with students with ASD is another area in which there is much to be discovered. Although there is no medication currently thought to be a "cure" for ASD (Kwok, 2003), medications for anxiety, aggression, hyperactivity, self-injurious behavior, and severe tantrums can be effective (Ozonoff, Rogers, & Hendren, 2003). Physicians should prescribe medications and then monitor the student closely, because some medications will affect persons with autism differently from those without ASD (King et al., 2001). There also appears to be a risk for more severe side effects and for unintended effects with some medications (Aman, Lam, & VanBourgondien, 2005; Handen, Johnson, & Lubetsky, 2000).

There has been considerable debate over whether immunizations have a basis for the cause of autism. Because some forms of ASD involve an onset of symptoms that appear to be regressions, it may seem that the regressions occur just about the same time as the immunizations. Thimerosal is a preservative containing trace amounts of mercury and it was previously used in childhood vaccines. It is no longer used (Wall Street Journal, 2002). Because mercury is a neurotoxin, and ASD might be of neurological origin, there has been a suspicion of thimerosal as an agent of cause. Several studies have compared thousands of people who have had immunizations with those who have not and have found no correlations between the incidence of autism and the administration of the vaccine (Folstein & Rosen-Sheidley, 2001; Medical Research Council, 2001; Smeeth et al., 2001).

Transition from School to Work

Some students with ASD will progress through school and go to college or other secondary education. Sometimes, in a specialized environment of high interest, the student will be able to function. However, because up to 75 percent of students with ASD have a co-occurring disability of cognitive deficits, and because language and social deficits make it difficult to function independently, many will need continued support. Training in an appropriate social setting is needed to enable students to function in school settings, at home, and in the community. Adults entering the job market will need continued training. IDEA requires a transition plan for each student at age 16. The plans will be critical for these students.

Nonverbal Learning Disabilities

Nonverbal learning disability (NVLD) is a term and a syndrome under controversy. Johnson and Myklebust (1967) first described students who were adept in some areas of language but who had trouble using some language. They could read but did not understand what they were reading. They could process verbal instructions and information but had difficulty with nonverbal tasks such as visual tasks (picture instructions) and spatial tasks. This subgroup of students also had social deficits. They could not read the body language and other social cues from others. They were of average or even above average intelligence, but they did not anticipate, pretend, or respond to subtleties, gestures, or facial expressions. In more recent years, Rourke (1995) described these students as deficient in tactile perception, visual perception, complex psychomotor activities, and the ability to process novel material. Other deficits that were probably a by-product of the primary deficits included difficulties in tactile attention, visual attention, and exploratory behavior. However, these students tended to do well in school, especially in the elementary grades. As the academic tasks grew more complex, they tended to look at details rather than the overall concepts.

Several experts have compared the group of students labeled NVLD to students with autism who are high functioning and to the group labeled with Asperger syndrome. Rourke's group completed studies looking at the brain structures of students and the MRI studies while the brain was engaged in different activities. Thus far, the results have been promising but, as yet, inconclusive. The three groups may overlap. There may be only one or two types of disorders. The brain structure studies may give us clues as to the etiology and differential thinking processes. Genetic studies may give us causes and perhaps even cures for differences in our students. Until that time, teachers must continue to teach the students who are enrolled in their classrooms regardless of labels. Suggestions for classrooms are included in Box 8.3.

DIVERSITY

Except for RTT, which primarily affects females, students with ASD are mostly male. For students aged 6 to 12, 83 percent of those with ASD are male. For students aged 13 to 17, 84.8 percent are male. We are not sure of the cause of autism and therefore cannot say definitively why so many of the identified students are of one gender.

One study showed that school districts with a higher-than-average revenue were associated with higher incidences of identified cases of ASD (Palmer, Blanchard, Jean, & Mandell, 2005). Economically disadvantaged school districts do not appear to identify as many students served as ASD. The authors of the study postulated that the economically disadvantaged systems may need economic assistance to identify and serve these students. Although we do not know how effective many of the educational interventions will be, we do suspect there is no cure for autism. We also suspect there is a benefit from intense social and communicative interventions. However, these services are expensive. As the expanded definition and greater public awareness allow many more students to be identified under the label of ASD, more and more resources will be needed.

PROFESSIONALS
Medical Personnel

Medical personnel should have training and experience in dealing with persons with ASD. Family physicians may be of assistance in tracking development and growth. Nutritionists may be necessary if the student refuses food or has allergies to certain foods, causing a deficient diet. Medical personnel can also prescribe some medication to counter symptoms and behaviors that render it difficult for the student to function. Teachers may keep in touch with medical and paramedical personnel to apprise them of behavioral changes and habits of the student; however, teachers should not presume to suggest medications. In the reauthorization of IDEA in 2004, schools and educators may not require a student to be on medication.

Teachers

In consultation with parents, therapist, medical personnel, and others on the IEP team, the teacher will assist in choosing the educational program for the student with ASD. A teacher of students with ASD would need to be competent in the areas listed by CEC (see Chapter 1) and in the content areas (the core areas for elementary age and the specific subjects for secondary age students). In addition, the teacher should be skilled in collaborative skills. The intervention chosen in consultation with the IEP, IFSP (Individual Family Service Plan), or ITP team may not be one the teacher feels comfortable with personally. A professional educator recognizes that personal preference for a therapeutic intervention is not the overriding factor in effective teaching.

DISCUSSION QUESTIONS

1. Does the incidence of autism appear to be rising? Are there more autistic students now than there were two decades ago? Why is it rising?
2. What are the suspected causes of autism?

3. Discuss several types of educational treatment options for students with ASD.

4. What related service personnel should be included in the planning team for a student with autism? What would a person with each background contribute?

5. There has been discussion about immunizations being a cause of autism. How would you respond to a parent who was wondering if their children should be immunized?

6. What is a nonverbal learning disability?

PROFESSIONAL ASSOCIATIONS AND PARENT OR SELF-HELP GROUPS

Autism Hotline
Autism Services Center
P.O. Box 507
Huntington, WV 25710-0507
304-525-8014

Autism Society of America
7910 Woodmont Avenue, Suite 650
Bethesda, MD 20814
301-657-0881 or 800-328-8476

Autism National Committee
249 Hampshire Drive
Plainsboro, NJ 08536

Autism National Committee
P.O. Box 6175
North Plymouth, MA 02362-6175
www.autcom.org

Indiana Resource Center for Autism
Indiana Institute on Disability and Community
2853 East 10th Street, Indiana University
Bloomington, IN 47408-2696
812-855-6508 or 812-855-9396 (TTY)
www.iidc.Indiana.Edu/Irca

Autism Society Canada
129 Yorkville Ave, #202
Toronto, Ontario, M5R 1C4
Canada
416-922-0302
Fax: 416-922-1032

Society for Auditory Integration Training
c/o Center for the Study of Autism
Boardwalk Plaza, Suite 230
9725 SW Beaverton-Hillsdale Hwy.
Beaverton, OR 97005
503-643-4121

Tuberous Sclerosis Alliance
801 Roeder Rd
Suite 750
Silver Spring, MD 20910-4467

301-562-9890 or 800-225-6872
Fax: 301-562-9870
E-mail: info@tsalliance.org
www.tsalliance.org

Autism Network International
P.O. Box 448
Syracuse, NY 13210-0448
www.students.uiuc.edu/_bordner/ani.html

Autism Research Institute
4182 Adams Avenue
San Diego, CA 92116
619-281-7165
www.autism.com/ari/

MAAP (More Able Autistic People)
P.O. Box 524
Crown Point, IN 46307
219-662-1311

The Arc of the United States
500 East Border Street, Suite 300
Arlington, Texas 76010
817-261-6003
Fax: 817-277-3491
E-mail: thearc@metronet.com
www.thearc.org/

Asperger Syndrome Coalition of the United States (ASC-U.S.)
(formerly ASPEN of America)
P.O. Box 49267
Jacksonville Beach, FL 32240-9267
904-745-6741
E-mail: info@asc.us.org
www.asperger.org/

National Society for Children and Adults with Autism
621 Central Avenue
Albany, NY 12206

Focus on Autism and Other Developmental Disabilities
PRO-ED
8700 Shoal Creek Boulevard
Austin, TX 78757

REFERENCES

Akshoomoff, N., Pierce K., & Courchesne, E. (2002). The neuro-biological basis of autism from a developmental perspective. *Development and Psychopathology, 14,* 613–634.

Aman, M. G., Lam, K. S. L., & Van-Bourgondien, M. E. (2005). Medication patterns in patients with autism: Temporal, regional, and demographic influences. *Journal of Child and Adolescent Psychopharmacology, 15,* 116–126.

American Psychiatric Association. (2000). *Diagnostic and statistical manual of mental disorders, fourth edition, text revision* (DSM–IV–TR). Arlington, VA: Author.

Armstrong, D. D. (2002). Neuropathology of Rett syndrome. *Mental Retardation and Developmental Disabilities Research Reviews, 8,* 72–76.

Asperger, H. (1992). Autistic psychopathy in childhood. In U. Frith (Ed. & Trans.), *Autism and Asperger syndrome* (pp. 37–93). Cambridge: Cambridge University Press. (Original work published 1944)

Autism Society of America. (2004a). A brief history of the society. Retrieved August 12, 2005, from www.autism-society.org/site/PageServer?pagename=aboutasa

Autism Society of America. (2004b). Treatment options. Retrieved August 13, 2005, from www.autism-society.org/site/PageServer?pagename=TreatmentOptions

Bailey, D., Mesibov, G., Hatton, D., Clark, R., Roberts, J., & Mayhew, L. (1998). Autistic behavior in young boys with fragile X syndrome. *Journal of Autism and Developmental Disorders, 28,* 499–508.

Baird, G., Charman, T., Baron-Cohen, S., Cox, A., Swettenham, J., Wheelwright, S., et al. (2000). Screening instrument for autism at 18 months of age: A 6-year follow-up study. *Journal of the American Academy of Child and Adolescent Psychiatry, 39,* 694–702.

Baker, M. J. (2000). Incorporating the thematic ritualistic behavior of children with autism into games: Increasing social play interactions with siblings. *Journal of Positive Behavior Interactions, 2*(2), 66–84.

Baron-Cohen, S. (2002). The extreme male brain theory of autism. *Trends in Cognitive Sciences, 6,* 248–254.

Berument, S. K., Rutter, M., Lord, C., Pickles, A., & Bailey, A. (1999). Autism screening questionnaire: Diagnostic validity. *British Journal of Psychiatry, 175,* 444–451.

Billstedt, C. G., & Gillberg, C. (2005). Autism after adolescence: Population-based 13- to 22-year follow-up study of 120 individuals with autism diagnosed in childhood. *Journal of Autism and Developmental Disorders, 35,* 351–360.

Carter, A. S., Volkmar, F. R., Sparrow, S. S., Wang, J., Lord, C., Dawson, G., et al. (1998). The Vineland Adaptive Behavior Scales: Supplementary norms for individuals with autism. *Journal of Autism and Developmental Disorders, 28,* 287–302.

Council for Exceptional Children. (2002). Strategies to help students with autism. *CEC Today, 8* (8). Arlington, VA: CEC.

de Bildt, A., Sytema, S., Kraijer, D., & Minderaa, R. (2005). Prevalence of pervasive developmental disorders in children and adolescents with mental retardation. *Journal of Child Psychology and Psychiatry* (formerly *Journal of Child Psychology and Psychiatry and Allied Disciplines*), *46,* 275–286.

Demark, J. L., Feldman, M. A., Holden, J. J. A. (2003). Behavioral relationship between autism and fragile X syndrome. *American Journal on Mental Retardation, 108,* 314–326.

Epstein, M. H., Jayanthi, M., Dennis, K., Dennis, K. L., Hardy, R., Fueyo, V., et al. (1998). Educational status of children who are receiving services in an urban family preservation and reunification setting. *Journal of Emotional and Behavioral Disorders, 6,* 162–169.

Epstein, M. H., Jayanthi, M., McKelvey, J., Frankenberry, E., Hardy, R., Dennis, K. L., et al. (1998). Reliability of the wraparound observation form: An instrument to measure the wraparound process. *Journal of Child & Family Studies, 7,* 161.

Filipek, P. A., Accardo, P. J., Baranek, G. T., Cook, E. H., Dawson, G., Gordon, B., et al. (1999). The screening and diagnosis of autism spectrum disorders. *Journal of Autism and Developmental Disorders, 29,* 439–484.

Folstein, S., & Rosen-Sheidley, B. (2001). Genetics of autism: Complex aetiology for a heterogeneous disorder. *Nature Reviews: Genetics, 2,* 943–955.

Gilliam, J. E. (1995). *Gilliam autism rating scale.* Circle Pines, MN: American Guidance Service.

Gray, C. (2000). Writing social stories with Carol Gray. Arlington, TX: Future Horizons.

Greenspan, S. I., & Wieder, S. (1998). *The child with special needs: Encouraging intellectual and emotional growth.* Reading, MA: Perseus Books.

Greenspan, S. I., & Wieder, S. (1999). A functional developmental approach to autistic spectrum disorders. *Journal of Person with Severe Handicaps, 24,* 147–161.

Hagberg, B., Aicardi, J., Dias, K., & Ramos, O. (1983). A progressive syndrome of autism, dementia, ataxia, and loss of purposeful hand use in girls: Rett's syndrome: Report of 35 cases. *Annals of Neurology, 14,* 471–479.

Handen, B. L., Johnson, C. R., & Lubetsky, M. (2000). Efficacy of methylphenidate among children with autism and symptoms of attention-deficit hyperactivity disorder. *Journal of Autism and Developmental Disorders, 30,* 245–255.

Hardman, M. L., Drew, C. J., & Egan, M. W. (2005). *Human exceptionality: School, community, and family.* Upper Saddle River, NJ: Merrill.

Heaton, P., & Wallace, G. L. (2004). Annotation: The savant syndrome. *Journal of Child Psychology and Psychiatry* (formerly *Journal of Child Psychology and Psychiatry and Allied Disciplines*), *45,* 899–911.

Heavey, L., Phillips, W., Baron-Cohen, S., & Rutter, M. (2000). The awkward moments test: A naturalistic measure of social understanding in autism. *Journal of Autism and Developmental Disorders, 30,* 205–225.

Heller, T. (1969). Uber dementia infantalis. In J. G. Howells (Ed.), *Modern perspective in international child psychiatry.* Edinburgh: Oliver & Boyd. (Original work published 1930)

Howlin, P. (2003). Can early interventions alter the course of autism? In G. Bock & J. Goode (Eds.), *Autism: Neural basis and treatment possibilities* (pp. 250–265). Chichester: John Wiley & Sons.

Howlin, P., & Asgharian, A. (1999). The diagnosis of autism and Asperger syndrome: Findings from a systematic survey.

Developmental Medicine and Child Neurology, 41, 834–839.

Hranilovic, D., & Bucan, M. (2001). Social behavior as an endophenotype for psychiatric disorders: Development of mouse models. *Current Genomics, 2,* 41–54.

Interdisciplinary Council on Developmental and Learning Disorders. (2000). *Clinical practice guidelines: Redefining the standards of care for infants, children, and families with special needs.* Bethesda, MD: Author.

Johnson, D., & Myklebust, H. R. (1967). *Learning disabilities: Educational principles and practices.* New York: Grune and Stratton.

Kanner, L. (1943). Autistic disturbances of affective contact. *Nervous Child, 2,* 217–250.

Kauffman, J. (2005) *Characteristics of emotional and behavioral disorders of children and youth* (8th ed.) Upper Saddle River, NJ: Merrill.

King, B. H., Wright, D. M., Handen, B. L., Sikich, L., Zimmerman, A. W., Cantwell, E., et al. (2001). Double-blind, placebo-controlled study of amantadine hydrochloride in the treatment of children with autistic disorder. *Journal of the American Academy of Child and Adolescent Psychiatry, 40,* 658–665.

Kirk, S., Gallagher, J. J., Anastasiow, N. J., & Coleman, M. R. (2006). *Educating exceptional children* (11th ed.). Boston: Houghton Mifflin.

Kwok, H. W. M. (2003). Psychopharmacology in autism spectrum disorders. *Current Opinion in Psychiatry, 16,* 529–534.

Lawson, J., Baron-Cohen, S., & Wheelwright, S. (2004). Empathising and systemizing in adults with and without Asperger syndrome. *Journal of Autism and Developmental Disorders, 34,* 301–310.

Le Couteur, A., Rutter, M., Lord, C., Rios, P., Robertson, S., Holdgrafer, M., et al. (1989). Autism diagnostic interview: A semistructured interview for parents and caregivers of autistic persons. *Journal of Autism and Developmental Disorders, 19,* 363–387.

LeGoff, D. B. (2004). Use of LEGO© as a therapeutic medium for improving social competence. *Journal of Autism and Developmental Disorders, 34,* 557–571.

Lord, C., Bristol, M. M., & Schopler, E. (1993). Early intervention for children with autism and related developmental disorders. In E. Schopler et al. (Eds.), *Preschool issues in autism.* New York: Plenum Press.

Lord, C., Risi, S., Lambrecht, L., Cook, E. H., Leventhal, B. L., DiLavore, P. C., et al. (2000). The autism diagnostic observation schedule–generic: A standard measure of social and communication deficits associated with the spectrum of autism. *Journal of Autism and Developmental Disorders, 30,* 205–230.

Lord, C., Rutter, M., & Le Couteur, A. (1994). Autism diagnostic interview–revised. *Journal of Autism and Developmental Disorders, 24,* 659–686.

Lord, C., Shulman, C., & DiLavore, P. (2004). Regression and word loss in autistic spectrum disorders. *Journal of Child Psychology and Psychiatry* (formerly *Journal of Child Psychology and Psychiatry and Allied Disciplines*), *45,* 936–955.

Lovaas, O. I. (1987). Behavioral treatment and normal educational and intellectual functioning in young autistic children. *Journal of Consulting and Clinical Psychology, 55,* 3–9.

Lovaas, O. I. (2003). *Teaching individuals with developmental delays: Basic intervention techniques.* Austin, TX: Pro-Ed.

Malhotra, S., & Gupta, N. (1999). Childhood disintegrative disorder. *Journal of Autism and Developmental Disorders, 29,* 491–498.

Mandell, D. S., Walrath, C. M., Manteuffel, B., Sgro, G., & Pinto-Martin, J., (2005). Characteristics of children with autistic spectrum disorders served in comprehensive community-based mental health settings. *Journal of Autism and Developmental Disorders, 35,* 313–321.

Mastropieri, M. A., & Scruggs, T. E. (2000). *The inclusive classroom: Strategies for effective instruction.* Upper Saddle River, NJ: Merrill/Prentice Hall.

Mauk, J. E., Reber, M., & Batshaw, M. L. (1997). Autism and other pervasive developmental disorders (4th ed.). In M. L. Batshaw (Ed.), *Children with disabilities.* Baltimore: Paul H. Brookes.

Mayes, S. D., Calhoun, S. L., & Crites, D. L. (2001). Does DSM–IV Asperger's disorder exist? *Journal of Abnormal Child Psychology, 29,* 263–271.

McClannahan, L. E., & Krantz, P. J. (2005). *Teaching conversation to children with autism.* Bethesda, MD: Woodbine House.

McEachin, J. J., Smith, T., & Lovaas, O. I. (1993). Long-term outcome for children with autism who received early intensive behavioral treatment. *American Journal on Mental Retardation, 97,* 359–372.

McGee, G. G., Krantz, P. J. & McClannahan, L. E. (1985). The facilitative effects of incidental teaching on preposition use by autistic children. *Journal of Applied Behavior Analysis, 18,* 17–31.

Medical Research Council. (2001). *MRC review of autism research: Epidemiology and causes.* London: MRC.

Metropolitan Atlanta Developmental Disabilities Surveillance Program. Retrieved August 6, 2005, www.cdc.gov/ncbddd/dd/ddsurv.htm#prev

Myles, B., Bock, S., & Simpson, R. (2001). *Asperger syndrome diagnostic scale.* Austin, TX: Pro-Ed.

National Center on Birth Defects and Developmental Disabilities. (2005). Key findings from recent birth defects and pediatric genetics branch projects. Retrieved August 6, 2005, from www.cdc.gov/ncbddd/bd/ds.htm

National Information Center for Children and Youth with Disabilities (2004). *NICHCY connections . . . to autism resources.* Arlington, VA: Author.

National Research Council. (2001). *Educating children with autism.* Washington, DC: National Academy Press Committee on Educational Interventions for Children with Autism Division of Behavioral and Social Sciences and Education.

O'Reilly, M., Sigafoos, J., Lancioni, G., Edrisinha, C., & Andrews, A. (2005). An examination of the effects of a classroom activity schedule on levels of self-injury and engagement for a child with severe autism. *Journal of Autism and Developmental Disorders, 35,* 305–311.

Odom, S. L., Hoyson, M., Jamieson, B., & Strain, P. S. (1985). Increasing handicapped preschoolers' peer social interactions: Cross-setting and component analysis. *Journal of Applied Behavior Analysis, 18,* 3–16.

Ozonoff, S., & Griffith, E. M. (2000). Neuropsychological function and the external validity of Asperger syndrome. In A. Klin,

F. R. Volkmar, & S. Sparrow (Eds.), *Asperger syndrome* (pp. 72–96). New York: Guilford Press.

Ozonoff, S., Rogers, S. J., & Hendren, R. L. (Eds.). (2003). *Autism spectrum disorders: A research review for practitioners.* Arlington, VA: American Psychiatric Publishing.

Palmer, R. F., Blanchard, S., Jean, C. R., & Mandell, D. S. (2005). School district resources and identification of children with autistic disorder. *American Journal of Public Health, 95,* 125–130.

Powers, M. D. (2000). What is autism? In M. D. Powers (Ed.). *Children with autism: A parents' guide* (2nd ed., pp. 1–44). Bethesda, MD: Woodbine House.

Robbins, D. I., Fein, D., Barton, M. I., & Green, J. A. (2001). The modified checklist for autism in toddlers: An initial study investigating the early detection of autism and pervasive developmental disorders. *Journal of Autism and Developmental Disorders, 31,* 149–151.

Rogers, S. (2000). Interventions that facilitate socialization in children with autism. *Journal of Autism and Developmental Disorders, 30,* 399–409.

Rourke, B. P. (1995). *Syndrome of nonverbal learning disabilities.* New York: Guilford Press.

Rubenstein, J. L. R., & Merzenich, M. M. (2003). Model of autism: Increased ratio of excitation/inhibition in key neural systems. *Genes, Brain & Behavior, 2,* 225.

Rutter, M. (2005). Autism research: Lessons from the past and prospects for the future. *Journal of Autism and Developmental Disorders, 35,* 241–257.

Schopler, E., Reichler, J., & Renner, B. (1988). *The childhood autism rating scale (C.A.R.S.).* Los Angeles: Western Psychological Services.

Scott, M. M., & Deneris, E. S. (2005). Making and breaking serotonin neurons and autism. *International Journal of Developmental Neuroscience, 23,* 277–285.

Smalley, S. I. (1998). Autism and tuberous sclerosis. *Journal of Autism and Developmental Disorders, 28,* 407–414.

Smeeth, C., Cook, E., Fombonne, L., Heavey, L., Rodrigues, P., Smith, A., et al. (2001). MMR vaccination and pervasive developmental disorders: A case-control study. *The Lancet, 364,* 963–969.

Solomon, M., Goodlin-Jones, B. L., & Anders, T. F. (2004). A social adjustment enhancement intervention for high functioning autism, Asperger's syndrome, and pervasive developmental disorder. *Journal of Autism and Developmental Disorders, 34,* 649–668.

Stone, W. L., Coonrod, E. E., & Ousley, O. Y. (2000). Brief report: Screening tool for autism in two-year-olds (STAT): Development and preliminary data. *Journal of Autism and Developmental Disorders, 30,* 607–612.

Strain, P. S., & Cordisco, L. (1994). LEAP preschool. In S. Harris & J. Handleman (Eds.), *Preschool education programs for children with autism* (pp. 225–252). Austin, TX: PRO-ED.

Strock, M. (2004). *Autism spectrum disorders (pervasive developmental disorders).* NIH publication No. NIH-04-5511, National Institute of Mental Health, National Institutes of Health, Bethesda, MD: U.S. Department of Health and Human Services.

Tadevosyan-Leyfer, O., Dowd, M., Mankoski, R., Winklosky, B., Putnam, S., McGrath, L., et al. (2003). A principal components analysis of the autism diagnostic interview–revised.

Journal of the American Academy of Child and Adolescent Psychiatry, 42, 864–872.

Talebizadeh, Z., Bittel, D. C., Veatch, O. J., Butler, M. G., Takahashi, T. N., Miles, J. H., et al. (2004). Do known mutations in neuroligin genes (NLGN3 and NLGN4) cause autism? *Journal of Autism and Developmental Disorders, 34,* 735–736.

U. S. Department of Education. (2005). *Twenty-fifth annual report to Congress on the implementation of the Individuals with Disabilities Education Act.* Washington, DC: Author.

Van-Bourgondien, M. E., Reichle, N. C., & Schopler, E. (2003). Effects of a model treatment approach on adults with autism. *Journal of Autism and Developmental Disorders. 33,* 131–140.

Vernazza, M. S., Martin, N., Vernazza, A., Lepellec, M. A., Rufo, M., Massion, J., et al. (2005). Goal-directed locomotion and balance control in autistic children. *Journal of Autism and Developmental Disorders, 35,* 91–102.

Vincent, J. B., Melmer, G., Bolton, P. F., Hodgkinson, S., Holmes, D., Curtis, D., et al. (2005). Genetic linkage analysis of the X chromosome in autism, with emphasis on the fragile X region. *Psychiatric Genetics, 15*(2), 83–90.

Volkmar, F. R. (2000). Medical problems, treatments, and professionals. In M. D. Powers (Ed.), *Children with autism: A parent's guide* (2nd ed., pp. 73–74). Bethesda, MD: Woodbine House.

Volkmar, F. R., & Klin, A. (2001). Asperger's disorder and higher functioning autism: Same or different? In L. M. Glidden (Ed.), *International review of research in mental retardation: Autism* (Vol. 23, pp. 803–110). Philadelphia, PA: Elsevier Science & Technology Books.

Volkmar, F. R., Lord, C., Bailey, A. T., Schultz, R. T., & Klin, A. (2004). Autism and pervasive developmental disorders. *Journal of Child Psychology and Psychiatry, 45,* 1–35.

Volkmar, R. M., & Rutter, M. (2002). Childhood disintegrative disorder: Results of the DSM–IV autism field trial. *Journal of the American Academy of Child and Adolescent Psychiatry, 34,* 1092–1095.

Wall Street Journal. (2002). *The truth about thimerosal.* New York: *Wall Street Journal.* Retrieved Aug 2, 2005 from http://online.wsj.com/article/0,,SB1039056747469257393.djm,00.html

Werts, M. G., Caldwell, N. K., & Wolery, M. (1996). Peer modeling of response chains: Observational learning by students with disabilities. *Journal of Applied Behavior Analysis, 29,* 53–66.

Wickelgren, I. (2005). Autistic brains out of synch? *Science 308,* 1856–1858.

Williams, J., Scott, F., Stott, C., Allison, C., Bolton, P., Baron-Cohen, S., et al. (2005). The CAST (childhood Asperger syndrome test): Test accuracy. *Autism, 9,* 45–68.

Wing, L. (1993). The definition and prevalence of autism: A review. *European Child and Adolescent Psychiatry, 2,* 61–74.

Wolery, M., Werts, M. G., Snyder, E. D., & Caldwell, N. K. (1994). Efficacy of constant time delay implemented by peer tutors in general education classrooms. *Journal of Behavioral Education, 4,* 415–436.

Zwaigenbaum, L., Sonnenberg, L. K., Heshka, T., Eastwood, S., & Xu, J. (2005). A girl with pervasive developmental disorder and complex chromosome rearrangement involving 8p and 10p. *Journal of Autism and Developmental Disorders, 35,* 393–399.

9

Students with Hearing Impairments

KEY TERMS

WHAT WOULD YOU DO?

Chip's teacher and his mother had a lot to talk about. Chip was learning sign language at a rapid rate. He had been in school since right before his fourth birthday. He was the older child in his family. His sister was born when he was three. Chip was a bright-faced and engaging youngster. He was curious about all around him; he poked his nose into everything. He did not speak, though. His mother, working two jobs and taking classes on the weekend, was glad he was a happy and healthy toddler. She had arranged day care in a private home, where she thought Chip would get better care because he was not "just one of a crowd." The baby-sitter had one child of her own who was 4 years older than Chip and was in school most of the day while Chip was at her home. She played with Chip and he had full run of the playroom. She taught him to play with toys and put them away. He had a regular schedule of inside play, outside play, a little *Sesame Street*, snacks, naps, and meals. He responded well to the schedule.

When Chip's sister was about 12 months, his mother noticed she was babbling in a way Chip never did. She began to take note of other problems Chip might be having. He did not always respond to requests. Sometimes he was quick to comply and other times he seemed to ignore her completely. She had attributed this to willfulness, but then she started to wonder. He was not interested in music, but he did like to clap along and play games involving jumping and dancing. And he could sleep though anything!

A trip to the pediatrician resulted in a full workup including a hearing evaluation. Further tests indicated Chip was almost totally without hearing. On the recommendation of the intervention team, he was enrolled in a preschool for children with hearing and language deficits. He was as interested in school as he was in everything else. He loved the interactions with the other students—just as he had been engaged at the baby-sitter's house. One of the focuses of his program was to provide him with a method of communication. He was taught American sign language (ASL) and was learning rapidly. His mother could hardly keep up and repeatedly called the teachers to ask what he was saying and how to say what she wanted him to know. She would try to come a little early to pick him up so that she could watch him playing and talking and could learn his new signs. Chip, however, would make up signs and gestures for words and concepts. For instance, he was trying to tell his teacher about a cube. He held out his hand palm up, closed his fingers loosely over his palm, shook his hand side to side, and mimed throwing dice out of his hand.

Chip liked to tell his teacher about his family. He described his mother, and his teacher helped him with words: beautiful, tall, helping. He also talked about his sister. He thought she was fun. He also thought she was smarter than he was—because she could talk.

1. What would be important to do to help Chip with self-esteem?

2. What should be the main focus for Chip's educational plan?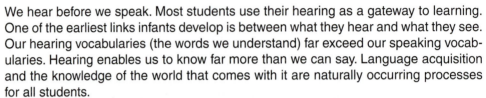

We hear before we speak. Most students use their hearing as a gateway to learning. One of the earliest links infants develop is between what they hear and what they see. Our hearing vocabularies (the words we understand) far exceed our speaking vocabularies. Hearing enables us to know far more than we can say. Language acquisition and the knowledge of the world that comes with it are naturally occurring processes for all students.

Students who are deaf or hearing impaired experience their world in a markedly different way than do their hearing peers. Spoken language may not be part of that world without early and special help. In our society, speech and language are critical avenues for effective education and socialization. Students with hearing impairments may be cut off from these processes and become isolated unless they are identified early and helped to compensate for their hearing loss by undergoing corrective medical treatment or learning to use amplification, nonoral ways of receiving and expressing language, or various types of assistive devices.

The purpose of this chapter is to define the parameters of hearing loss and present the options available for the education of students identified as hearing impaired. We will discuss the prevalence of hearing impairment, the causes of hearing loss, the characteristics of people who are hearing impaired, issues of concern to people who are hearing impaired and their families, and the professionals who can help those with hearing loss.

DEFINITIONS

Normal Hearing

Before we can understand hearing impairment and deafness, we must understand how normal hearing works. Normal hearing occurs when a listener can change sounds from the environment into signals that are sent to the brain and meaningfully interpreted. To hear and interpret a sound, we use the ear and its various structures which receives sound waves; the auditory nerve, which translates sounds into neural signals; and the brain, which decodes these neural signals and translates them into meaningful information.

Figure 9.1 illustrates the parts of the human ear. The ear is divided into the outer ear, middle ear, and inner ear. The outer ear consists of the external ear **(auricle)** and the auditory canal **(external acoustic meatus).** The outer ear collects sound and channels it through the auditory canal. These sound waves are sent to the middle ear.

The middle ear is composed of the eardrum (tympanic membrane) and three small bones called the hammer (malleus), anvil (incus), and stirrup (stapes). Together, these bones are also called the **ossicles** or **ossicular chain.** The hammer is attached to the eardrum at one end and the anvil at the other end. The anvil is attached to the stirrup,

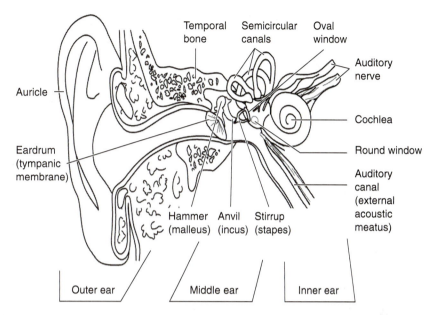

FIGURE 9.1

Parts of the human ear. The external part of the ear (auricle) and the external auditory canal make up the outer ear. The middle ear includes the eardrum (tympanic membrane), hammer, anvil, and stirrup (ossicles). The inner ear includes the round window, the oval window, the semicircular canals, vestibular mechanism, and the cochlea. Damage to any part can cause a hearing loss.

Source: Heward, *Exceptional Children: An Introduction to Special Education,* 5th ed., © 1996. Reprinted by permission of Pearson Education, Inc., Upper Saddle River, NJ.

which in turn is connected to the oval window or entrance to the inner ear. As the sound waves pass through the auditory canal, they strike the eardrum, causing it to vibrate. These mechanical vibrations are passed on to the ossicular chain. The mechanical energy is transferred in turn to the inner ear. The **eustachian tube,** which extends from the back of the throat to the middle ear, opens and closes to equalize the air pressure on both sides of the eardrum.

The inner ear is composed of the cochlea, which controls our sense of hearing; semicircular canals, which control our sense of balance; and the beginning of the auditory nerve. The **cochlea,** which looks like a snail's shell, is a fluid-filled cavity lined with small hair cells. As the movements of the ossicular chain enter the inner ear, they disturb the fluid in the cochlea, causing the hair cells to react to the motion of the fluid. The hair cell reactions are sent as signals to the auditory nerve. The impulses from the auditory nerve travel to the brain, where they are processed by the auditory cortex of the brain and become auditory information.

Hearing Loss

Hearing losses can be classified by the degree of hearing loss, the age at which the loss occurs, and the type of hearing impairment the student has acquired. These classifications will be detailed in the sections of this chapter on characteristics, etiology, and identification of hearing impairments. Normal hearing is the ability to understand speech without relying on special aids or techniques (Heward, 2006). Someone who is hearing impaired has a significant enough hearing loss that some special adaptation is required to understand speech. Being hearing impaired makes it difficult, but not impossible, to understand speech with or without amplification. People who are hearing impaired still use the auditory channel to learn, even though what they hear may be distorted. It is defined as having an impairment, either permanent or fluctuating, that negatively impacts educational performance. Hearing aids can benefit the hard of hearing. A person who is deaf cannot use hearing with or without a hearing aid to understand speech, even though that person may be able to hear some sound. Hearing impairment is a generic term that is often used to include all hearing loss. Educators may use this term when identifying any student, regardless of severity, who requires special education services due to hearing loss. Some educators prefer to use the term hard of hearing, because they feel it is less prejudicial a term than is hearing impaired.

Federal Guidelines

IDEA defines deafness as a hearing impairment that is so severe that the student is impaired in processing linguistic information through hearing with or without amplification. The hearing impairment adversely affects a student's educational performance. The same act defines hearing impairment as "an impairment in hearing, whether permanent or fluctuating, that adversely affects a student's educational performance, but which is not included under the definition of deafness" (Turnbull, Turnbull, Shank, & Smith, 2004).

PREVALENCE

Approximately 28 million people in the United States report hearing impairments (Hess, 1991), and 1 percent of the population are severely impaired (Heward, 2006). The vast majority of these people are over age 65. It is estimated that over 40 percent of the population over age 75 experience some hearing impairment (Blanchfield, Feldman, Dunbar, & Gardner, 2001). The percentage of school-age students adversely affected by hearing loss is significantly lower. It is difficult to determine exact numbers because most reports count only students with hearing impairments who receive special educational services. Other difficulties in obtaining a stable estimate result from different samples and differing definitions. Because many students with hearing loss are unidentified or not affected severely enough to be included in special education surveys, the estimates are felt to be underinclusive.

The Twenty-Fifth Annual Report to Congress on IDEA (U.S. Department of Education, 2005) reported that 1.2 percent of all students between ages 6 and 21 who received special education services were served under the hearing impairment disability category. This translates to more than 71,000 of the over 5.8 million served. Other estimates, using different, more inclusive criteria, range as high as 5 percent (Blanchfield et al., 2001). Northern and Downs (2001) reported that 1 child in 1,000 is born deaf; 2 more students in 1,000 become deaf during their early childhood years; and of the newborns that require intensive care, 1 in 50 become deaf or hard of hearing. They also reported that 10 to 15 percent of all students fail the hearing tests that are required by most public schools.

There is a higher incidence of hearing loss among students classified in other special categories than among students not identified as needing special services. This is especially true for students with Down syndrome and students with CP. In addition, deafness attributable to hereditary factors and infections such as meningitis appears to be on the rise, as are noise-induced hearing loss from repeated exposure to loud noises in the environment and hearing loss from infections such as otitis media (Heward, 2006).

CHARACTERISTICS

Degree of Hearing Loss

The degree or severity of a hearing loss will often directly correlate with the characteristic behaviors the student with the hearing impairment displays. The following five terms are frequently employed in describing the severity of a hearing loss:

1. Slight
2. Mild
3. Moderate
4. Severe
5. Profound

These descriptive labels are determined by the student's ability to hear sounds at different frequencies and at different intensities. Sound is measured by its intensity and frequency. Intensity and frequency are physical measures that are most easily understood as loudness and pitch. The loudness of a perceived sound is measured in decibels, abbreviated as dB. At 0 dB, a person with normal hearing can detect the faintest sound. Whispered speech would be about 10 dB, and conversational speech about 50 dB. A sound louder than 125 dB will cause pain and can destroy the hair cells of the cochlea.

The pitch of sound is measured in cycles per second or hertz, abbreviated as Hz. One Hz equals one cycle per second. Although humans can hear frequencies between 20 and 20,000 Hz, many of these sounds fall below or above the frequencies used for speech sounds. Most sounds in our environment fall between 125 and 8,000 Hz. The most important sounds for speech range between 300 and 3,000 Hz.

The different sounds of our language occur at different pitch levels and intensities. For example, typical sound frequencies and intensities for the sounds /f/, /s/, and /th/ occur at 20 dB at 4,000 to 6,000 Hz. The sounds /g/, /k/, /ch/, and /sh/ are conversationally spoken at 30 dB at 2,000 Hz. The sounds /m/, /b/, /d/, /n/, /ng/, /e/, /l/, and /u/ are measured at 45 dB at 3,000 Hz. Normal running conversation, which is a blend of all sounds, is typically measured at 60 dB. A rigorous dog bark will produce sound at 80 dB at 500 Hz, and the sound of a ringing telephone is typically 85 dB at 2,000 Hz. The loud sound of a lawn mower could be 100 dB at 250 Hz, and a chain saw and jet plane might be measured at 110 dB, 1,000 and 4,000 Hz, respectively.

Translating this information into the five severity categories means the following:

- A person with normal hearing will hear sounds between 0 and 20 dB with little difficulty and have no difficulty hearing in any conversational setting.

- A person with slight hearing loss will hear sounds at an intensity of 20 to 40 dB or louder and may have difficulty with faint speech. School difficulties are not usually present and can be remedied with careful seating near the teacher.

- A person with mild hearing loss cannot hear sounds produced at less than 40 to 60 dB but can usually understand face-to-face conversation. The student may miss as much as 50 percent of classroom conversations, especially in noisy environments. The student may have a limited vocabulary and oral speech problems. Special services are usually indicated.

- A person with moderate hearing loss cannot hear sounds less intense than 60 to 75 dB, which excludes all but loud conversation. Impaired speech and language are usual, and the student will most often require special class placement or a resource teacher.

- A person with severe hearing loss cannot hear sounds below 75 to 90 dB as exemplified by loud voices less than one foot from his or her ear. These students may identify environmental noises but cannot hear most consonant sounds. Speech and language is usually impaired or nonexistent if the loss occurred prior to 1 year of age. Special education placement and special classroom placement are likely.

- A person with profound hearing loss cannot hear sounds quieter than 90 dB, which means that he or she cannot hear conversational speech. This student may sense vibrations more than hear sounds and rely on vision rather than hearing for learning. This student is unlikely to develop oral speech or language and will usually rely on sign language and be placed in a special class or school for the deaf.

The characteristics described here are a general picture that will vary from student to student. Different students will react differently to the same degree of impairment.

Language Skill Characteristics

By far the most severely affected area of development for a person who is hearing impaired is the comprehension and use of oral language. Both speech and language may be affected. Speech development relies on the discrimination of the differing sounds in any language and the accurate production of these sounds. Language development is far more complex and requires the mastery of not only the sounds of a language but also its system of rules for combining sounds into words and words into sequences that express thoughts, feelings, intentions, and experiences. Phonology (combining sounds meaningfully), morphology (putting sounds into words), and syntax (combining words into sentences) compose the structure of any language. Semantic development (using language meaningfully) and pragmatic development (using language appropriately) constitute the communicative components of a language, but much language learning is the result of experiences combined with hearing the language of others.

This automatic combining of hearing and language learning may be absent to differing degrees for each student with a hearing impairment. Although all students who are neurologically intact are able to learn some form of language, oral speech and language learning are directly related to the severity of a hearing loss.

The greatest challenge to those who do not rely on hearing for information (those who are severely and profoundly hard of hearing) is learning to use the oral language of their society. Most are severely deficient in the languages used by the hearing people with whom they live. We will discuss the compensations made when we discuss the educational approaches used to educate people who are deaf and hearing impaired in the "Programs" section of this chapter. However, depending on each student's reactions to his or her hearing loss, a general characteristic that students with

hearing impairments share is minimally a difficulty in learning the speech system of their native language, and maximally a great deal of difficulty in learning the complexities of oral language in all of its parameters.

Academic Performance Characteristics

When discussing the academic performance of students with hearing impairment, it is important to remember that the majority of them possess normal intelligence. They have the same IQ-score distribution as do people who hear (Paul & Quigley, 1994; Schlesinger, 1983; Vernon, 2005). However, they are typically underachievers, lagging far behind their peers in math and reading (Bess, 1988; Moores, 2004). In the early 1980s, the average reading level of students who were deaf or hearing impaired was at the third-grade level. In the mid-1990s, the level was measured at a low fourth-grade level (Karchmer & Mitchell, 2003). One obvious problem with performance tests is that they tend to measure language competence along with academic achievement. Because nonverbal IQ tests show that people who are deaf have intelligence scores that approximate those of their hearing peers (Heward, 2006), it becomes obvious that the previously discussed difficulties with language skills are at least partially to blame for the depressed academic performance scores. Five major variables appear to correlate with academic achievement for students with hearing impairment (see Box 9.1).

Social and Psychological Characteristics

Social and personality adjustments of normally hearing students depend heavily on communication skills and interactions with family members and others in their environment. The same rules are true for people who are hearing impaired. Students who are deaf and have parents who are also deaf show higher levels of social maturity, adjustment to deafness, and control of their behavior than do students who are deaf and have hearing parents, possibly due to the earlier use of manual communication (Hallahan & Kauffman,

BOX 9.1
WHAT EVERY TEACHER SHOULD KNOW
Five Variables of Academic Achievement

1. *The severity of the hearing impairment.* The greater the hearing loss, the more likely the student will have difficulty learning language and developing academic skills.
2. *The age of onset of the hearing loss.* Hearing lost before language develops (prelingual loss) is much more debilitating than hearing loss after language has developed (postlingual loss).
3. *Intelligence test scores.* The higher a student scores on IQ tests, the better his or her chance at achieving academic success will be.
4. *Socioeconomic status of the family.* Students with hearing impairments and students who are deaf from higher socioeconomic families are generally more successful academically than their lower socioeconomic counterparts.
5. *Hearing status of parents.* A student who is deaf and has parents who are also deaf is likely to have a better chance for academic success than a student who is deaf and has parents with normal hearing. This is especially true if the parents who are deaf are highly educated. This appears to be the result of more appropriate early stimulation for the student and the earlier use of sign language in communication.

Sources: From "Educational Programs and Services for Hearing Impaired Children: Issues and Options," by D. F. Moores, 1985, in F. Powell, T. Finitzo-Hieber, S. Friel-Patti, and D. Henderson (Eds.), *Deaf Children in America* (pp. 105–123), San Diego, CA: College-Hill; and *Education and Deafness* (p. 219), by P. V. Paul and S. P. Quigley, 1994, New York: Longman.

2006; Heward, 2006). The most disruptive students who are deaf are found also to be those with the worst reading-level achievement (Kluwin, 1985), a point that emphasizes that the characteristics being discussed in this section of the chapter are not unrelated. Understandably, people who are deaf have a tendency to associate with others who are deaf when possible, to the exclusion of the hearing. Other characteristics—such as increased reliance on visual cues, which may cause the person who is hearing impaired to appear to stare at the normally hearing person's face, lips, and hands, and the excessive use of gestures and body language—may also be considered rude and further isolate the student with a hearing impairment.

ETIOLOGY

Conditions that cause hearing loss can impair the hearing mechanism to different degrees of severity, can impair the mechanism at different times in a person's life, and can cause different types of hearing loss. Severity has already been discussed. In this section, we will highlight how damage to different parts of the hearing structures will bring about different types of hearing loss to people of differing ages.

It is important to be aware that hearing loss can affect one ear only (unilateral hearing loss) or both ears (bilateral hearing loss), and that each ear may be affected differently. In most instances, the results of bilateral hearing losses are more debilitating than are those of unilateral hearing losses.

Types of Hearing Loss

As previously discussed, we hear by channeling sounds from the environment into the external ear, converting those sounds into mechanical vibrations in the middle ear, and converting the vibrations into the neural signals that go to the brain. The types of hearing loss parallel these processes. When sounds are prevented from entering the outer or middle ear, the resultant condition is a **conductive hearing loss.** When the inner ear does not function appropriately, the result is a **sensorineural hearing loss.** When the brain is unable to interpret the signals sent to it, a **central auditory processing disorder** is the result. A person with a mixture of the types described is said to have a **mixed hearing loss.** The four major types of hearing loss are:

1. Conductive hearing loss
2. Sensorineural hearing loss
3. Mixed hearing loss
4. Central auditory processing dysfunction

Conductive hearing losses can be the result when sound does not get through the outer and middle ear structures efficiently. Any blockage of the ear canal, such as a buildup of excessive ear wax (cerumen) or the failure of the canal to develop at birth, can interfere with sound transmission. Conductive hearing loss is often caused by a buildup of fluids in the middle ear due to infections (otitis media). This buildup of fluid impedes the work of the ossicular chain in transmitting sound to the inner ear. Infections and diseases may also cause the eardrum or the ossicles to work inefficiently. Otosclerosis, a disease characterized by the growth of spongy bone on the ossicles, prevents them from vibrating in a way that will send sound to the cochlea efficiently. Quite often, conductive loss can be overcome by surgery, medical treatment, or amplification of incoming sounds so they can get past the middle ear and stimulate the inner ear structures. Many conductive losses are transitory, lasting no longer than several days. Repeated untreated infections can lead to permanent damage of the hearing mechanism.

Sensorineural hearing losses occur when sound that gets to the inner ear is not transmitted to the brain or is transmitted in a distorted manner. Damage to the cochlea and the auditory nerve will bring about sensorineural hearing loss. The most common causes of this damage are viral diseases, Rh incompatibility, medications that have the side effect of harming the hearing mechanism (ototoxic medicines) while correcting other conditions in the body, normal aging, and repeated exposure to loud noise. Sensorineural hearing loss is usually permanent; it is treated with amplification but is not usually treatable medically or surgically.

A mixed hearing loss occurs when a person has a combination of both a conductive hearing loss and a sensorineural hearing loss.

Central auditory processing problems do not result from the inability of the mechanism to deliver the auditory signal to the brain, but rather from the inability of the brain to process or interpret the signals that are delivered. This symbolic processing disorder may show itself in the inability of a person to perceive sounds, discriminate among sounds, or even comprehend language that is received. People with auditory processing problems will usually have difficulty learning or using language. Central auditory processing problems are the result of lesions or growths within the nervous system or direct damage to those parts of the brain and nervous system that are dedicated to the processing of auditory signals.

Emotions may also enter into the causation of hearing disorders. For a small number of people, hearing may be impaired due to causes unrelated to any structural anomaly. For these people, the apparent loss in the ability to hear is a reaction to emotional disturbance. Quite often this conversion of emotional disturbance into the unwillingness to hear can happen without the conscious consent of the person affected. This type of hearing problem is called a functional hearing loss in recognition of the fact that the hearing mechanism is apparently functioning appropriately. The most appropriate treatment is usually counseling rather than special educational placement for hearing impairment. When a person consciously pretends not to hear to avoid some task or responsibility, such as being inducted into military service, the condition is labeled malingering.

Age of Onset

The onset of hearing loss at different times in a student's development can have markedly different implications. Onset is usually identified as being either prelingual or postlingual.

Prelingual hearing loss occurs before a student develops linguistic skills and the reliance on hearing to obtain information from the environment. Prelingual hearing loss makes the acquisition of speech and language a much more difficult process. Following are some of the most prevalent causes of prelingual hearing loss:

- *Maternal rubella (German measles)*—When contracted during pregnancy, especially the first trimester, rubella can cause deafness, visual impairment, and heart deficits. The most recent major epidemic, from 1963 to 1965, accounted for more than 50 percent of the students with hearing impairments receiving special education services during the 1970s and 1980s.

- *Heredity*—Even though 90 percent of students who are congenitally deaf are born to hearing parents, about 30 percent of school-age students who are deaf have close relatives who are deaf or hearing impaired (Keats, 2002; McKusick, 1983). Hereditary childhood deafness can be related to more than 150 distinct genetic syndromes. Estimates indicate that at least 60 percent of those with moderate to profound prelingual sensorineural hearing loss acquired it as the result of genetic factors (Marazita et al., 1993). In residential schools for the deaf, it is not uncommon to find students who are the second or third generation of their families attending the school. The high incidence of marriage between people with hearing impairments may be a contributing factor in the genetic transmission of deafness and hearing impairment (Lowenbraun & Thompson, 1990).

- *Prematurity and complications that arise during pregnancy*—These are also directly related to prelingual hearing impairments of differing levels of severity.

- *Viral infections*—Meningitis in particular can destroy the inner-ear hair cells and lead to early and permanent damage.

- *Congenital cytomegalovirus*—This herpes-related virus infects approximately 1 percent of all newborn babies. For almost 3 percent of all students under age 6 who report hearing loss (approximately 10,000), cytomegalovirus is listed as its cause, and 4,000 of those students have hearing losses ranging from mild to profound. Of the students who require special educational services, approximately 90 percent have been affected by prelingual hearing loss with damage most often to the cochlea (Strauss, 1997).

Postlingual hearing loss occurs after a student or adult has developed linguistic skills and learned to use sound for learning. Educational treatment for postlingual hearing loss usually centers on the maintenance of speech and learning skills that were developed prior to the onset of the hearing problem. Following are some of the most prevalent causes of postlingual hearing loss:

- *Infections of all types*—Meningitis, a leading cause of prelingual hearing impairment, is also a leading cause of postlingual impairment. Otitis media is a generic term for infections of the middle ear that cause fluid buildup in that chamber. If these infections are untreated, the fluids can not only disrupt sound transmission but also burst the eardrum, leading to conductive hearing problems.

- *Side effects of medication*—Some medications may be **ototoxic,** causing permanent damage to the hearing mechanism. These drugs, if identified, are usually prescribed when the disorder being treated is of such a serious nature that the risk to hearing is an acknowledged factor.

- *Noise-induced hearing loss*—Sustained levels of noise can bring about sensorineural hearing loss. Recognition of this fact has led many industrial settings (airports, construction sites, etc.) to require that their employees wear sound-absorbing ear protectors. Young males are at greater risk than young females due to male-oriented activities such as gun firing and automobile engine repair activities (Hallahan & Kauffman, 2006).

- *Unknown causes*—Almost 50 percent of all postlingual hearing losses are of undetermined origin (Smith, 2006). It is often difficult to determine the etiology of many hearing losses because they either take time to develop or are the result of repeated exposure to several circumstances or conditions, each of which could result in hearing loss.

IDENTIFICATION PROCESS

For some students the identification process begins at birth. A growing number of states now require that the hearing of newborns considered at risk be tested immediately after birth. However, most students experience their first hearing testing at preschool centers, pediatricians' offices, or routine school screenings. Most public schools and many preschools offer routine hearing testing programs. Often these programs are run in cooperation with university training programs to help university students with an interest in hearing and communication disorders gain practical experience testing students. Most students with severe hearing losses are identified by parents or others in their environment prior to school screenings. However, school and preschool screenings do discover students with mild and moderate losses who have not been previously diagnosed. Students detected by these screening examinations are usually referred for more intensive audiometric and other testing.

Early Detection

Significant hearing losses are often discovered by parents or caregivers who notice that the student is not attending to environmental sounds or speech. Perhaps the student does not startle when loud noises occur or does not respond to people he or she is not looking at. Green and Fischgrund (1993) listed many signs that can be clues to parents and others in the student's environment that hearing may be of concern.

1. Does not appear to attend
2. Has frequent earaches or any discharge from the ears
3. Makes speech sounds poorly or omits age-appropriate sounds completely
4. Often misinterprets verbal requests
5. Does not respond to direct attempts at communication
6. Appears to attend better when facing a speaker
7. Frequently requests repetition
8. Sets the volume on electronic equipment to levels that are unreasonably loud

Students suspected by parents of having hearing loss are usually referred for audiometric testing.

Audiometric Testing

Pure-Tone Audiometry

Initial hearing testing is usually performed by a procedure called pure-tone audiometry, using a machine called an audiometer. Audiometers are electronic devices capable of generating sounds at different levels of intensity (dB) and at differing frequencies (Hz). When the person being tested hears a tone being produced by the audiometer, usually through earphones, he or she signals the examiner that the sound was heard. Normally hearing students will usually respond to tones presented at most frequencies between 0 and 15 dB (Northern & Downs, 2001). A student with a hearing loss of 45 dB at 1,000 Hz will not respond to the signal from the audiometer until it exceeds 45 dB in loudness.

The results of pure-tone audiometry hearing tests are mapped out on audiograms. Audiograms are graphic representations of a person's hearing ability (acuity) at different frequencies. Figures 9.2, 9.3, and 9.4 are samples of typical audiograms representing the hearing acuity of students with moderate, severe, and profound hearing losses, respectively. The circles (O) and crosses (X) represent the responses of the left and right ears, respectively. As the hearing loss becomes more severe, the symbols appear lower on the audiogram, indicating decreasing hearing acuity.

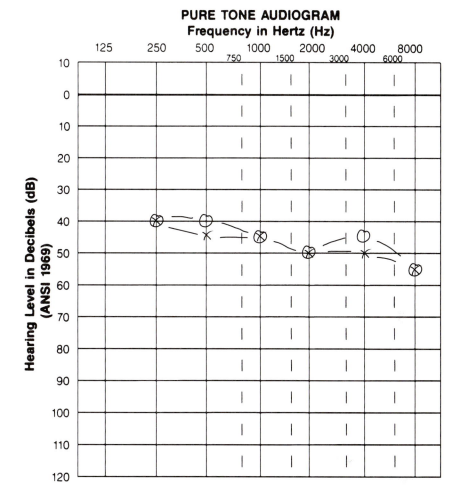

FIGURE 9.2
Moderate hearing loss.

Bone Conduction Testing

Another component of the testing procedure is bone conduction testing, which allows the examiner to bypass the outer and middle ear and present signals directly to the inner ear by vibrating the bones of the skull. This procedure helps the examiner to determine the presence of sensorineural components of hearing losses.

Other Types of Hearing Tests

Play audiometry is often used with students who are too young to respond in a conventional manner. During play audiometry, usually administered in a sound-treated booth, the student is taught to respond actively to presented tones. For example, an assistant will place a block in a pail each time a sound is presented and teach the student to perform the same activity. By carefully noting the intensity and frequency of the sounds the student responds to, the examiner can determine the student's hearing acuity.

Speech audiometry provides a measure of a listener's ability to hear and understand speech. By presenting a series of two-syllable words at different intensity levels,

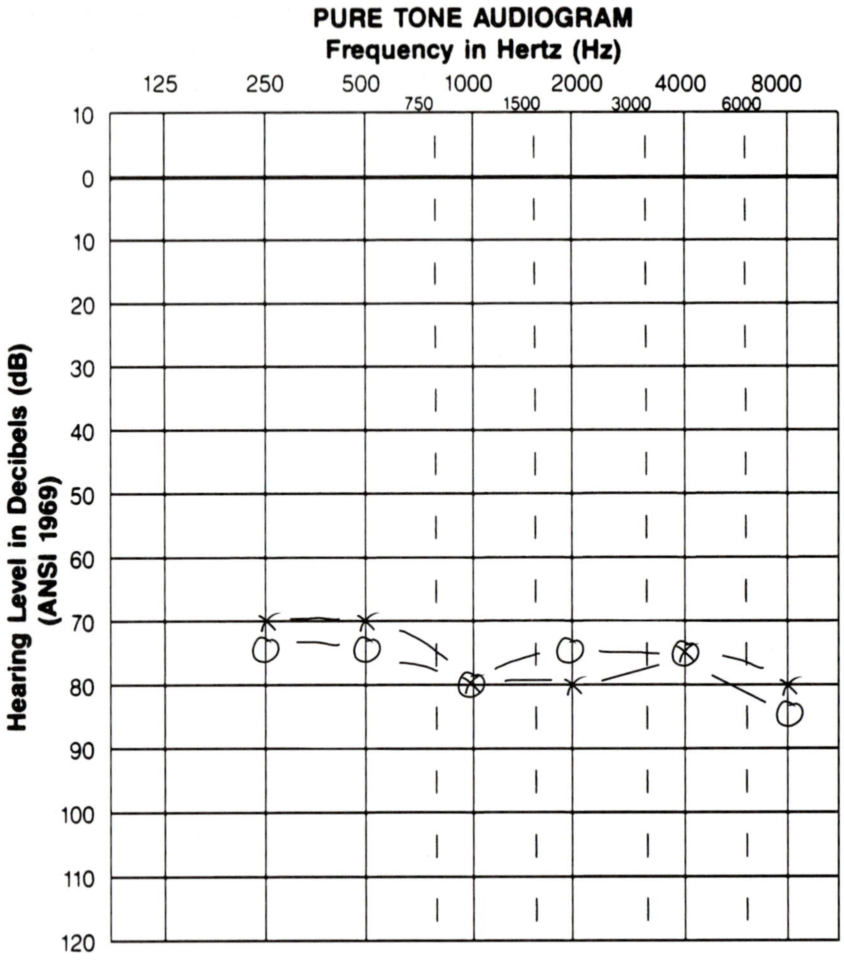

PURE TONE AUDIOGRAM
Frequency in Hertz (Hz)

FIGURE 9.3
Severe hearing loss.

the examiner can establish a student's speech recognition threshold (SRT), which is the softest level at which one can understand 50 percent of the words presented. Recognition tests present similar-sounding words and measure how well the listener can tell them apart at varying loudness levels. Speech recognition abilities can also be tested by presenting information at various loudness levels to determine the optimal conditions for maximizing the understanding of speech.

Immittance audiometry helps to determine how well the middle ear is functioning by testing how the eardrum (tympanic membrane) is working. This information is particularly helpful in diagnosing middle ear problems such as otitis media.

Evoked-response audiometry is a procedure that uses electronic sensors to determine whether the auditory nerve is sending signals to the brain. This procedure is most applicable to very young children and infants or those who cannot respond accurately or consistently.

Otoacoustic emission testing can help determine if the cochlea is intact. Using microcircuitry, a probe containing a miniature loudspeaker presents a stimulus, and a tiny microphone picks up any response. This test identifies the responding regions of

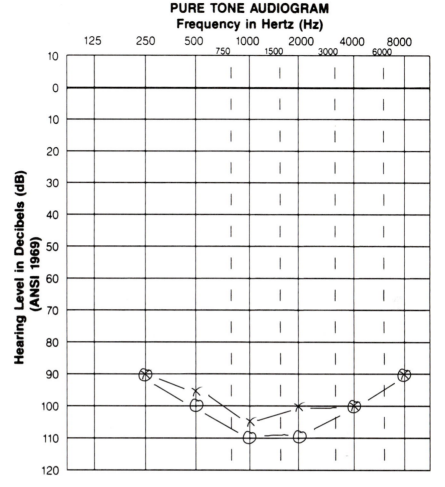

FIGURE 9.4
Profound hearing loss.

the cochlea; it can be very helpful with patients who cannot or will not cooperate on voluntary hearing tests (Martin, 2000).

Once hearing acuity is determined to be below the levels expected for a student, the next step is to determine what, if any, compensations must be made to help the student obtain a quality education.

Educational Assessment

Each student will react differently to a hearing impairment. Simply measuring a student's hearing level will not always provide all the information necessary to construct an educational program that will meet the student's needs. It is often difficult to compile a valid educational assessment for a student who is severely hearing impaired or deaf because English language competencies are often significantly delayed. Test questions written in English often confound the assessment of mastery of English as well as mastery of content. Attempts to change instructions run the risk of invalidating the tests, the result of which is that test scores cannot be used for comparisons with students who are not hearing impaired (Prezbindowski & Lederberg, 2003; Salvia & Ysseldyke, 2004). Intelligence, achievement, and communication and language assessments are vital in helping members of the educational team determine how the student is using his or her hearing and what plans might be appropriate to meet any unfilled educational needs the student may have.

Communication and Language Assessments

Assessment of the linguistic abilities of a student with hearing impairment must provide information in at least the following three areas:

1. *Expressive and receptive vocabulary skills*—How much can the student understand and how well can the student express needs? A fair assessment will test not only spoken and hearing abilities but also abilities in sign language, finger spelling, speechreading, reading, and writing.
2. *Syntactical or grammatical skills*—The planning team needs some measure of how well the student can string words together in English or grammatically correct ASL.
3. *Nonlinguistic language competence*—At what level can educators expect the student to understand and use nonlinguistic communication channels such as gestures, postures, and facial expressions that are situationally and socially appropriate?

If the student uses spoken language, some assessment must be made of articulation skills, or the ability to say the sounds of a language correctly and with phonological competence, which is the ability to use the rules for combining sounds in acceptable ways (Salvia & Ysseldyke, 2004).

Intelligence Testing

Intellectual capabilities of persons who are deaf have the same distribution as persons who are hearing. Of course, the typical IQ tests containing verbal items are not appropriate for students who are deaf or hearing impaired. However, a national survey indicated that 73 percent of school psychologists serving deaf children have administered a verbal intelligence scale to students who are deaf and 66 percent included the results in psychological reports (Maller, Konold, & Glutting, 1998). Although some students may use speechreading to access the items, the results are clearly a translated and nonstandardized adaptation (Maller, 1996, 1997). There are alternatives. One is the Universal Nonverbal Intelligence Test (UNIT), an individually administered, nonverbal intelligence test designed for use with non-English-speaking, limited English proficient, or deaf children (Maller & French, 2004). Other options include using performance test items from other normative assessment instruments.

Achievement Testing

The test used most frequently to assess achievement of students who are hearing impaired or deaf is the Stanford Achievement Test–Hearing Impaired Version (SAT–HI; 1989). It has been normed and standardized on students who are deaf and covers primary grades and high school students. The data from these tests are considered to be a reasonable estimate of students' academic performance (Moores, 2005; Traxler, 2000).

Once the educational planning team has studied the results of these and similar tests and combined them with information solicited from parents, teachers, peers, and consulting professionals, they can design, propose and, if accepted by those responsible for the student's welfare, implement educational programming plans. Periodic reviews will help them determine the effectiveness of those plans.

PROGRAMS

Answers to the following questions are often necessary before any educational program can be devised and implemented for students who are hard of hearing: When should students with hearing impairment begin formal instruction? Where should they be taught? What should they be taught? How should they be taught? (Turnbull et al., 2004). The belief systems of a society at any given time, as well as the information that any given student presents, will often interact when decisions are made. The brief historical review that follows will illustrate how the views of a society can determine the programming available, sometimes in direct opposition to the data generated by the student in need.

History of Educational Programming for Students with Hearing Impairment

A brief summary of educational practices for students living in the United States who are severely hearing impaired or deaf begins by noting that the American Asylum for the Education of the Deaf and Dumb opened in Hartford, Connecticut, in 1817. The governing philosophy at this time was that people who were deaf were best served in special schools that were isolated from normal (hearing) society. The word dumb in the title reflects the mistaken idea that people who were deaf were incapable of learning oral speech and thus were mute. Most schools were residential and were established in small communities. In the 1850s, attempts at instructing the students to use speech and lipreading became a part of the curriculum. In fact, there was such an overreaction to the use of speech instruction that there was a movement to outlaw sign language (Moores, 2004/2005). In 1864, Abraham Lincoln signed legislation creating the National Deaf Mute College, known today as Gallaudet University (Lowenbraun & Thompson, 1990). Located in Washington, DC, Gallaudet offers a wide variety of undergraduate and graduate programs for students with hearing impairments. Approximately 100 years later, the National Technical Institute for the Deaf (NTID) was established in Rochester, New York. NTID provides technical training in business and vocational fields such as computer science, hotel management, and medical technology. Both schools are supported by federal funds and each enrolls approximately 1,500 students.

After Word War II, more than 70 percent of all students with a hearing impairment attended either residential schools or day schools for students who were deaf. At the time of passage of PL 94-142 (IDEA) in 1975, the number had dropped to about 50 percent. At that time, the concept of providing the LRE in which to educate students with special needs came into focus. As with most special education placements, the least restrictive educational environment was deemed to be one wherein the student was afforded as much interaction as possible with students who can hear. This conceptualization may not always be appropriate for students who are deaf. In recognition of this fact, in 1988, the Commission on the Education of the Deaf recommended to Congress that the general education classroom not be automatically interpreted as the LRE for students who are deaf. Approximately 85 percent of students who are deaf in the United States attend local public schools; about 60 percent of these students are integrated into a general classroom for a majority of the school day (U.S. Department of Education, 2005).

A recent moment of historical significance for the deaf community occurred in 1988 when, after much unrest and political activism, Gallaudet University became the first and only university in the world to have a president who is deaf.

Early Identification and Early Intervention

Early identification and intervention is critical for students who are deaf or severely hearing impaired. Because communication skills develop from early infancy, withholding service until the school years will put these students irretrievably behind in the development of speech, oral language, and reading skills (Yoshinaga-Itano & Sedey, 2000). The connection between what a student says and the use of hearing begins long before first words are ever spoken. Even though first words usually are spoken between 12 and 18 months of age, students as young as 3 months begin to use their hearing skills to repeat the nonlinguistic sounds they are producing. This patterned babbling stage of speech development appears to be critical in the development of speech. Students who are severely hearing impaired or deaf and are unable to hear their early babbling sounds will fall silent at this stage of development. If left untreated, they will begin to fall behind their hearing peers in the development of speech and language. Students with adequate hearing have learned the basics of spoken language by age 3 and are stable enough in their linguistic skills by age 6 to use language to learn the academic concepts presented in early schooling. Students need language skills to develop the reading skills that are their main way of obtaining information about the world in which they live (Gentry, Chinn, & Moulton, 2004/2005).

Preschool early intervention programs are not only for the student; direct parent and family instruction is a vital reason for their existence. Much needs to be done for parents, especially hearing parents of students who are severely and profoundly hearing impaired or deaf. These parents will probably not know or use sign language or be aware of the reliance that their student will have on the visual rather than auditory aspects of the environment. Hearing parents of students who are deaf may have a greater tendency than parents who are deaf with students who are deaf to see their children in a negative light. As a result, they may treat them as more abnormal than the hearing impairment may warrant (Hallahan & Kauffman, 2006). Bodner-Johnson (1987) suggested that early intervention programs should focus on helping the student with hearing impairment develop within the structure of the family. To facilitate this development, parents must be aware of normal child development as well as what their child's hearing abilities will allow. They will need help in developing the skills needed to accomplish this assimilation of a family member with a hearing impairment. Most critical are skills in developing communication, knowledge of language development, and the transmission of a positive self-concept to the student (Swanwick & Watson, 2005).

Preschool programs are equally vital for students with hearing impairments. For many such students, preschool programs provide the first opportunity for them to interact with other students, both hearing and hard of hearing. They become the vehicle for the student to learn group functioning skills; the rules of group interaction such as how to play, share, and take turns; and the variety of social skills needed for later success in the classroom (Mayer, 1996). On a preacademic level, preschool programs provide a place for students and parents to practice signing; learn how to use residual hearing through auditory training and hearing aid operation; and develop readiness skills in English, reading, and arithmetic (Kirk, Gallagher, Anastasiow, & Coleman, 2006). Without these experiences, transition to any of the educational placement options will be difficult, and chances of success will be diminished.

Placement Options

Students with unilateral hearing losses (one ear affected) usually learn speech and language, even though they may have problems identifying where some sounds originate or hearing in noisy environments. Students with bilateral hearing losses (in both ears) are most in need of special services.

Five basic educational placement options are available to students with hearing impairment. Many factors go into helping parents and other members of the educational placement team decide what might constitute the LRE. The five options are:

1. Full-time placement in a general classroom
2. Part-time placement in a general classroom and part-time placement in a special education classroom
3. Special class placement in a general school
4. Separate day school placement
5. Separate residential school placement

General Classroom Placement

Depending on the severity of the hearing loss and the student's ability to compensate for the hearing loss, general classroom placement must be considered as an option. Students with mild to moderate hearing loss may be able to function in a general classroom with appropriate support. This support may consist of special seating that will help the student hear the majority of what the teachers present and hearing aids or FM amplification systems that allow teachers wearing transmitting microphones to broadcast what they are saying to students wearing special receivers. The students might require the services of speech-language pathologists to help them use speech and language to their maximal potential. In some instances, educational interpreters or note takers may accompany a student to general classrooms. The general education classroom teacher may need to periodically consult with an itinerant teacher of the deaf for information on how to present or modify lessons. The student may also require tutoring after class to help explain material they might not have understood. General classroom placement does not mean putting students with hearing impairments into a general classroom and ignoring the hearing loss, thereby placing the burden for compensation solely on the students and their families.

Part-Time General Classroom Placement and Part-Time Special Class Placement

Students who are hearing impaired may spend a part of their school day in special resource rooms, where special educators address their unique needs and the rest of the day in a general classroom that has been modified as described in the previous section. This type of placement requires coordination between the general and special education teachers to make sure that they are working in concert to maximize learning.

Special Classes in General Education Schools

Students who are hearing impaired may spend most of their school day in a special education class but may be included in one or more academic classes in a general classroom, perhaps with the help of an interpreter. They may also participate in nonacademic activities with hearing peers, such as library study or gym. Social inclusion for lunch, recess, and other school activities may be stressed. Students in special classes may be taught with special educational approaches and be exposed to separate curricula that will be discussed in the following sections of this chapter.

Separate Day Schools

A student with a severe or profound hearing loss may, depending on needs, attend a separate day school with other students with hearing impairments. Separate day schools are both public and private in nature. In these schools, usually in cities large enough to have groups of students with hearing impairments, inclusion opportunities with peers who are normally hearing may be limited to after-school hours or those special occasions when the students with hearing impairments are transported to adjacent general education facilities. Special approaches to teaching are routinely used in these settings. Specially trained teachers of the deaf are most likely employed to present specially modified curricula.

Separate Residential Schools

There are approximately 60 public residential schools for the deaf in the United States and a group of privately financed residential schools. These schools tend to be large and independent in their functioning. Students who live close enough to a given residential school may use it as a day school placement. These schools are often the centerpieces of the deaf communities that surround them. Members of the deaf community often gravitate toward areas that have special residential schools. They argue that by putting together enough students in a supportive environment, it is possible to obtain the special services needed for quality education (Higgins, 1992; Kluwin, 1992; Scheetz, 2001). Some argue that residential schools are crucial in fostering the supportive concept of a deaf community, which combats the difficulty in succeeding in hearing environments and the isolation that inclusion attempts often bring about (Ladd, 2003; Padden & Humphries, 1988). We will discuss these views in greater depth in the "Issues of Importance" section in this chapter. Residential schools employ specially trained teachers of the deaf and use any of a number of educational approaches designed exclusively to teach students who are severely hearing impaired or deaf.

There are conflicts over which placements best serve students who are hearing impaired, and there is conflicting evidence to bolster all points of view. Placements in general public schools have grown with the passage of federal legislation making it possible for students with hearing impairment to attend them, better hearing aid and other technological assistance availability, and increased demands for public school placement by parents and citizens who are deaf. Although 85 percent of students with hearing impairments are educated in local schools, few are fully included. Most of those integrated have hearing losses less than 90 dB (Schildroth & Holt, 1991). Successful experiences in general classrooms for students with hearing impairments seem to correlate with possession of good oral communication skills, strong parental support, average or above average intelligence, self-confidence, and adequate support services (Schirmer, 2000).

Academic Curriculum

The academic content presented to students who are hearing impaired parallels the content presented to students who hear normally. Box 9.2 has some general tips for teachers. However, specially modified programs and materials do exist for subject areas such as math, science, and the arts. Luetke-Stahlman and Luckner (1991) contended that educators have the following five choices in the selection and implementation of a curriculum for students who are hard of hearing:

1. Use a curriculum that has been specifically designed for students who are hearing impaired or deaf.

2. Use the general education curriculum, attempting to meet the same standards as for other students by allowing for special services and special teaching methods.

3. Use the general curriculum, but reduce the level of complexity of the material presented.

BOX 9.2
WHAT EVERY TEACHER SHOULD DO

Effective Teaching Strategies

- If using an interpreter, take time outside of class to discuss with the interpreter the general lesson, key vocabulary, and main concepts.
- Face the student when speaking; don't speak when facing the blackboard.
- Use videotapes and films with captioning.
- Allow the student to teach some sign language or other personal skills to classmates.
- Be sensitive to social cues that the student who is deaf may not hear. Explain the situations to the student.
- Have a system in place for identifying cues in schools that are conveyed only by sound, such as tardy bells, fire drills, fire alarms, and intercom announcements.
- If using sign language, wear solid-color clothing that contrasts with your skin color.
- Communicate with parents frequently when the student is learning new signs for carryover between settings.
- Instead of using a chalkboard, use a projector. The light on your face is helpful for speechreading.
- Be aware of extraneous noises in the classroom that can be distracting for students with hearing aids.
- Allow the students to move freely about the classroom so they can speechread from other students as well as the teacher.
- Make sure the classroom is well lit with the light on your face and not behind you. Stand in front of walls rather than windows.

4. Use a curriculum from a lower grade level.

5. Use curricula that have been developed for students with other exceptionalities.

Of major concern is the language curriculum. Even though students who are hearing impaired learn language the same way other students do, they may have special problems with spoken and written English. They might need to learn about language through curricular activities that stress the structure and grammar of English, because they may not learn the complexities of grammar through hearing (Quigley & Paul, 1990). In addition, the language curriculum may need to be stressed to a greater extent than it would be with normally hearing students. Some educators believe that some of the poor achievement results displayed by students with hearing impairments in academics is due in part to the fact that so much instructional time is spent on communication and language skills that the academic areas are compromised.

Luckner and Muir (2001) listed 10 factors given by interviewees when asked about what helped to make education in a general classroom setting successful.

1. Family involvement

2. Self-determination. Allow students to have choices as much as possible and appropriate.

3. Extracurricular activities. Students should determine individual interest and be encouraged to take an active part in school and community activities.

4. Friendships and social skills. Social skills may need to be taught.

5. Self-advocacy skills. Students need to learn to recognize when they need help and learn how to ask for assistance from adults and peers.

6. Collaboration and communication with general education teachers

7. Preteach/teach/postteach content and vocabulary being learned in the general education classroom

8. Collaboration with early identification and early intervention service providers

9. Reading. Students should read for enjoyment as well as reading through expository texts.

10. High expectations

Educational Approaches

A variety of approaches are available to transmit information to students who are hard of hearing. In this section, we will explain some of the different approaches used with these students. The "Issues of Importance" section will highlight how the selection of which approach to use may equally depend on the belief systems of educators and members of the deaf community and on whether an approach is educationally effective. Table 9.1 highlights effects of differents degrees of hearing loss and what a teacher might expect to do.

Oral/Aural, Manual (Nonoral), and Simultaneous Communication Approaches

Oral/aural approaches emphasize speech and sound as a part of the curriculum. Oral language is used as a vehicle to transmit information. Teachers use their voices and rely on speechreading skills and students' use of their residual hearing. Amplification in the form of hearing aids and other assistive amplification devices are employed in the teaching process. Students are encouraged to use their voices when they speak.

TABLE 9.1

Effects of different degrees of hearing loss on speech and language and probable educational needs.

Faintest Sound Heard	Effects on Understanding Language and Programs	Probable Educational Needs and Speech
27 to 40 dB (slight loss)	• May have difficulty hearing faint or distant speech • Will not usually have difficulty in school situations	• May benefit from a hearing aid as loss approaches 40 dB • Attention to vocabulary development • Needs favorable seating and lighting • May need speechreading instruction • May need speech correction
41 to 55 dB (mild loss)	• Understands conversational speech at a distance of 3 to 5 feet (face to face) • May miss as much as 50% of class discussions if voices are faint or not in line of vision • May have limited vocabulary and speech irregularities	• Should be referred for special education evaluation and educational follow-up • May benefit from individual hearing aid and training in its use • Favorable seating and possible special education supports, especially for primary-age students • Attention to vocabulary and reading • May need speechreading instruction • Speech conservation and correction, if indicated
56 to 70 dB (moderate loss)	• Can understand loud conversation only • Will have increasing difficulty with group discussions • Is likely to have impaired speech • Is likely to have difficulty in language use and comprehension • Probably will have limited vocabulary	• Likely to need resource teacher or special class • Should have special help in language skills, vocabulary development, usage, reading, writing, grammar, etc. • Can benefit from individual hearing aid through evaluation and auditory training • Speechreading instruction • Speech conservation and speech correction
71 to 90 dB (severe loss)	• May hear loud voices about 1 foot from the ear • May be able to identify environmental sounds • May be able to discriminate vowels but not all consonants • Speech and language likely to be impaired or to deteriorate • Speech and language unlikely to develop spontaneously if loss is present before 1 year of age	• Likely to need a special education program for students with emphasis on all language skills, concept development, speechreading, and speech • Needs specialized program supervision and comprehensive supporting services • Can benefit from individual hearing evaluation • Auditory training on individual and group aids • Part-time regular class placement as profitable for student
91 dB or more (profound loss)	• May hear some loud sounds but senses vibrations more than tonal pattern • Relies on vision rather than hearing as primary avenue for communication • Speech and language likely to be impaired or to deteriorate • Speech and language unlikely to develop spontaneously if loss is prelingual	• Will need a special education program for students who are deaf, with emphasis on all language skills, concept development, speechreading, and speech • Needs specialized program supervision and comprehensive support services • Continuous appraisal of needs in regard to oral or manual communication • Auditory training on individual and group aids • Part-time regular class placement may be feasible

Source: W. L. Heward, *Exceptional Children: An Introduction to Special Education*, © 1996. Reprinted by permission of Pearson Education, Inc., Upper Saddle River, NJ.

Manual approaches rely more exclusively on sign language and nonoral means to communicate information to students. The use of signs to transmit information is on the rise in all educational programs.

Simultaneous communication approaches use both speech and signing at the same time. They often use finger spelling along with signing.

Auditory-Verbal Training

Auditory training programs help students make better use of their residual hearing. Many students with hearing impairments have more auditory potential than they actually use. Auditory training, with its emphasis on amplification of sounds, can help them maximize the hearing potential they have, with the goal of developing oral skills. Auditory training can focus on basic sound detection (awareness of sounds), discrimination among sounds, and identifying sounds that are critical in comprehending messages. It focuses on listening as well as hearing (Heward, 2006). A significant amount of time is spent with the parents of younger students, familiarizing them with hearing aid use and maintenance.

An auditory-verbal approach encourages the student to use residual hearing to the greatest extent possible. The student practices directed listening activities in which visual cues are removed and speechreading is deemphasized. In an attempt to stimulate auditory development, the rehabilitation specialist might even cover his or her mouth and face to eliminate nonverbal cues (Schow & Nerbonne, 2002).

Hearing aids are the most widely used technology for the hearing impaired. Essentially, hearing aids are amplification instruments that make sounds louder. Dozens of different types of hearing aids are available. Each attempts to amplify sounds in ways that are most helpful to a given person. Some aids amplify sounds across the entire speech frequency band. Others emphasize the lower, middle, or higher ranges of frequencies, hoping to match their amplification of those sounds to the particular person's hearing loss. Some aids are worn in the ear canal and some behind the outer ear. Hearing aids increase the awareness of sounds as well as simply amplifying them. However, hearing aids do not "cure" hearing problems. They can make sounds louder but not clearer. The person using the aid must interpret the sound being amplified. The earlier a student is fitted with hearing aids, the sooner he or she can begin to use the aids for awareness of environmental sounds and learning. Advocates of amplification feel that for aids to be maximally effective, they should be worn throughout the day so that the student can learn to process all sounds, not just speech (Heward, 2006).

For some students, classroom amplification systems can overcome the problems caused by teachers moving about while they talk and room noise that cancels or masks speech signals. A typical system uses an FM broadcasting system that the student can receive either through an earpiece or a hearing aid equipped to receive FM signals. The teacher wears a lapel microphone and can be totally mobile. These systems do not usually interfere with other classroom activities and have the potential of bringing amplified sounds to students who are hearing impaired without forcing them to sacrifice mobility.

Speechreading

The term lipreading has recently been changed to **speechreading** because the skill involves more than just looking at people's lips as they talk. Rather, careful observation of the entire face helps the speechreader decipher a message. Visual cues are more helpful in discriminating some sounds than others. When speechreading is combined with residual hearing, familiarity with the listener, and some familiarity with the context of the message, students' comprehension increases. Students need to be trained in the tactic of speechreading. Because many sounds and words look similar and people use facial expressions and gestures in different ways, speechreading is a difficult skill to acquire, and the concentration it requires is often tiring. It appears to be more difficult for young students than for adults (Lyxell & Holmberg, 2000), probably because of a facility with language. It is estimated that the best speechreaders can get as much as 25 percent of a message through speechreading, whereas the average student who is deaf might get only as much as 5 percent of a message through speechreading (Vernon & Koh, 1970).

Cued Speech

Cued speech is a system that relies on learning and using a specific set of hand signals to supplement oral speech. These signals, which are different from sign language or finger spelling, are given by hand positions used near the chin while speaking. The signals do not stand alone and must be used with oral speech. Basically, eight hand shapes indicate consonant sounds and four hand positions around the mouth and chin indicate vowels. The hand shape and its location near the mouth and chin provide cues in understanding the speaker's oral message. Although this system has a degree of popularity throughout the world, it has never been particularly embraced by people who are hearing impaired or educators in the United States.

Sign Language

Sign languages use gestures to represent words, ideas, and concepts. Some signs are iconic, which means that they look like what they represent or that they act out a message. Most signs are not iconic. There are several sign languages. ASL is the language of the deaf culture of the United States and Canada. It is estimated that ASL has a vocabulary of more than 6,000 signs that represent concepts. Advocates consider it the natural language of people who are deaf. ASL is a valid linguistic form with its own rules of syntax, semantics, and pragmatics (Turnbull et al., 2004). The shape and movement of the hands in relation to the body, the intensity of the movements made, and the accompanying facial expressions all convey meaning. Space and movement are the linguistic elements. The rules of ASL do not correlate with those of spoken English. Translating ASL is similar to translating a foreign language. Most students who are deaf learn ASL from other students in residential schools and not from their parents, who are usually hearing. Grammatical problems can occur when some systems use Pidgin Sign English, which is the use of ASL signs in oral English grammatical forms. Advocates of ASL feel that this practice is detrimental to the effective use of ASL. Use of ASL has been shown to have some correlation with reading mastery in English, but the research is mixed (Lichtenstein, 1998; Luetke-Stahlman, 1998; Lyxell & Holmberg, 2000). In the past few years, enrollment in sign language courses in college have risen dramatically. Some speculate that ADA has spurred an interest in accessibility (Orlans, 2004).

Finger Spelling

Finger spelling, or the manual alphabet, consists of twenty-six special hand and finger positions that represent English letters. A person using finger spelling spells out each word letter by letter, using one hand almost like a typewriter. Sign language uses finger spelling for proper names and when it is necessary to clarify specific concepts. Figure 9.5 shows the hand positions required to finger spell each letter of the alphabet.

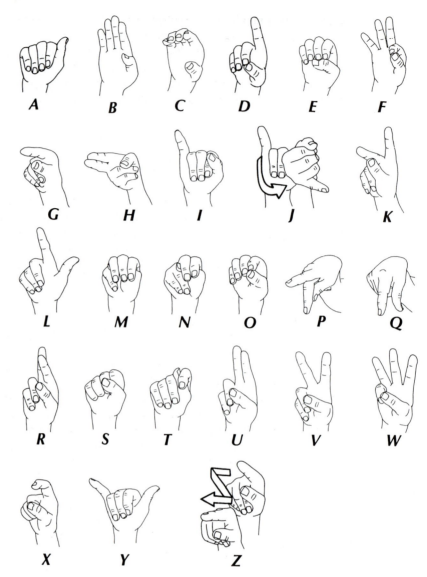

FIGURE 9.5
The American manual alphabet.

Total Communication

Total communication relies on the simultaneous presentation of signs and speech. It uses residual hearing, amplification systems, and speechreading in combination with manual systems. Total communication provides students with the most options. It is a method that is mired in controversy. Proponents argue that it provides the most language for students who are deaf. It assists them in entry into the "mainstream," and it is more normalizing. Those arguing against its use are arguing for the use of ASL as a language in its own right. The language is a cultural bond for people who are deaf, and to use English is denying their deafness.

Regardless of the approach or combination of approaches used in presenting information, several commonsense modifications in the classroom setting can help facilitate the transfer of information. Visual aids along with lectures help provide cues, as does the use of overhead projectors rather than blackboards, which often cause teachers to turn away from students. Appropriate lighting, as well as seat placement close to the teacher, will make speechreading easier. Swivel chairs help students more easily position themselves to follow classroom discussion. The assignment of alert peers to give cues when fire alarms ring or class bells chime can also be helpful (Turnbull et al., 2004).

Technology

The technologies most closely associated with people who are hearing impaired are hearing aids and amplification systems such as the FM amplification system discussed earlier. In this section, we will highlight descriptions of current medical and assistive technology—specifically, cochlear implants, computers, assistive devices, and captioning and alerting devices. A list of types of amplification is included in Box 9.3.

Cochlear Implants

Surgical implants are available to those with severe and profound sensorineural hearing loss. The procedure involves implanting a set of electrodes into the patient's cochlea. These electrodes are connected to a receiver that captures sounds and encodes them into electrical stimulation, which the electrodes then transmit through the neural pathways to the brain for processing. When this process is successful, it allows the recipient to hear environmental sounds such as telephone bells, automobile horns, and traffic noise. Cochlear implants may also make it easier for students who are severely and profoundly hearing impaired to learn speech. This is a relatively new

---

BOX 9.3

WHAT EVERY TEACHER SHOULD KNOW ABOUT TECHNOLOGY

Examples of Types of Assisted Listening Devices

- *Microphones or one-to-one communicators.* If the student is in a noisy situation (cafeteria, large classroom, gym, etc.), the teacher or other person can be given a microphone set to be picked up by the student's hearing aid or headset. Directions, safety messages, and feedback can be conveyed.
- *FM systems.* These are essentially radio stations that operate on special frequencies assigned by the FCC. The transmitter is used by the speaker and the receiver is worn by the student.
- *Infrared systems.* These work much like the FM systems but sound is transmitted using light waves. These systems work well with home televisions.
- *Amplification systems.* These are available for both land lines and for cell phones. Some modifications of ringer sounds and volume of speakers' voices can be made on regular models.

procedure and it has sparked some controversy; it is expensive, and long-term data documenting its effectiveness is only now becoming available. Some members of the deaf community are opposed to the procedure for these reasons and because they believe that it is an attack on the cultural identity of people who are deaf, undermining their self-concepts as healthy, competent members of society. Cochlear implants have been approved for children as young as 18 months.

Computers

Computers and the educational programs written for them help students who are hearing impaired in many of the same ways that they help hearing students. In addition, specific programming targeted for students with hearing impairments is useful in helping them learn reading and writing skills and become more proficient in finger spelling and sign language (Barker, 2003; Liles, 2005; Zazove, Meador, & Derry, 2004). Computer programs can also help normally hearing users learn sign language. One program, *Fingerspelling,* allows users to wear a special glove and sign letters, then the computer will text the message (Scarlatos & Nesterenko, 2004). An advantage of these programs is that they allow family members and peers to practice without having a professional available to monitor their practice sessions.

Assistive Communication Devices

Teletypewriters (TTY) and telecommunication devices for the deaf (TDD) are essentially specially designed telephone systems that allow users to type messages into the telephone system and receive typed replies. These devices are also called text telephones (TT). Special 800 numbers allow people who do not own a TTY or TDD to communicate by telephone with people who are hard of hearing. Special operators act as translators, reading messages to the hearing listener or writing them for the listener who is hearing impaired. An increasing number of businesses have their own systems

as part of their telephone service and as a result do not need to use the interpreting operator. ADA (PL 101-336) of 1990 requires that all telephone companies offer this service all day and every day.

Captioning

Captions are written transcriptions of dialogue that appear on a screen during television programs, films, and even some operas. Most television entertainment, sports, and news shows are closed captioned. This means that viewers with a decoder on their television can receive these transcriptions of dialogue as they watch. Since July 1993, all television sets 13 inches or larger sold or built in the United States have been equipped with a caption chip that allows viewers to choose whether they want to see the captions accompanying all available programs (Bowe, 1991; Hardman, Drew, & Egan, 2005). Captioning has enabled people who are hearing impaired to learn about current events and social issues without delay. Many normally hearing people use captions when they wish to watch television in circumstances that make listening to the soundtrack difficult.

Alerting Devices

Most alerting devices used by hearing people have been adapted for use by people who are hard of hearing. Doorbells have been adapted so that they flash lights as well as chime. Vibrating pillows respond to the sounds of alarm clocks. Fire detectors can be modified to give visual signals as well as auditory ones. Catalogs offering many types of ingenious and constantly improving alerting devices are available from all professionals who provide services to the hearing impaired.

ISSUES OF IMPORTANCE

Many important issues have an impact on the education of people who are hearing impaired. We have already discussed some of them. In this section, we will discuss two particularly critical issues: (1) the controversy surrounding the effectiveness of educational practices and (2) the special meaning that LRE may have for students who are hard of hearing.

Effectiveness of Academic Instruction

The most difficult problem in educating students who are deaf is teaching them spoken language. Many students who leave school are unable to read or write proficiently in English. The average student with a hearing impairment who completes a secondary education program reads at a level equal to that of a 9- to 10-year-old hearing student (Paul & Quigley, 1994). Many students who are deaf cannot communicate effectively with their hearing family members or hearing peers. Their rate of unemployment and underemployment is high. Advocates of oral/aural and simultaneous communication approaches believe that their way of teaching helps the student who is severely hearing impaired or deaf integrate better into mainstream society. However, students with severe or worse hearing losses who develop good speech are a select group. They typically score above average on IQ tests, have parents who are highly involved in their education, and have access to the resources and support services that higher socioeconomic status provides (Geers & Moog, 1989). Deaf students with deaf parents appear to make better progress in language acquisition than students with hearing parents.

Advocates of nonoral instruction fundamentally disagree about the extent to which learning spoken English is necessary. They are skeptical about the value of spending so much time teaching students who are severely impaired to express themselves through speech and attempting to perceive the communication of others through speechreading and the use of residual hearing. They argue that greater-than-ever numbers of hearing people are learning sign language and finger spelling. In fact, coursework in sign language and finger spelling is offered in many schools, colleges, and universities as a part of the curriculum for hearing students (Orlans, 2004). Public service professionals such as police, firefighters, and emergency medical technicians are becoming more proficient in sign language and finger spelling, and the mass media are using captioning and interpreters as a matter of course in many presentations. Most significantly, the data quoted earlier seem to indicate that current methods do not produce literate graduates with hearing impairments from secondary schools. There is no hard evidence that the use of sign language by students who are deaf inhibits their acquisition of speech (Burch, 2000; Lyxell & Holmberg, 2000; Yoshinaga-Itano & Sedey, 2000). However, some specialists feel that it is difficult for students to process both oral language and sign language when they are presented together. Ling (1984) suggested that students should learn oral and manual skills at different times rather than concurrently to avoid possible confusion.

There is no existing proof that either of these two approaches is better than the other. Some students become frustrated with oral/aural programs only. Others may not develop good oral skills because they were not given the opportunity to develop them. A goal appears to be to develop methods to determine which approach or approaches might provide the best educational opportunity.

Least Restrictive Environment

For most exceptional students, the LRE translates into mainstreaming and the opportunity to take part in as many general classroom and school activities as are feasible. However, this may not be the case for many students who are severely and profoundly hearing impaired. Some feel that, due to the low incidence and resulting small number of students who are hearing impaired, inclusion in general classrooms is really exclusion and results in isolation (Ohna, 2005). If students who are deaf are placed in an environment where they are unable to communicate with their peers and with most of the educational staff, this isolation might lead to loneliness and depression. Perhaps residential schools for the deaf with staff and peers able to communicate with the student are in fact less restrictive (Bowe, 1991). Any setting, including a general classroom, that prevents the student who is deaf from receiving an appropriate educational experience, including communication, may not be the LRE for that student. Special services might also be more readily accessible when more students who are deaf are in one central location. Inclusion in a general classroom does not always guarantee that all support services will be automatically supplied.

The following examples illustrate how court rulings about support services can be mixed and based on the individual needs and merits of each case. The courts ruled in *Board of Education of the Hendrik Hudson Central School District v. Rowley* (1982) that the local school district was not required to provide, at its expense, an interpreter for a student with hearing impairment performing adequately in general classes without an interpreter. However, in *Barnes v. Converse College* (1977), it was ruled that a private college had to provide, at its own expense, an interpreter for a student who was hearing impaired. It is not an easy decision to legislate, and most cases probably can only be decided individually.

DIVERSITY

Two concerns isolated from the general concerns we have been discussing in this chapter are the needs of minorities within the hard-of-hearing population and the concept of whether the deaf community forms a distinct cultural minority within the United States.

Needs of Students from Diverse Groups

Approximately 42 percent of all students aged 6 to 21 in programs for deaf and hearing impaired represent racial, linguistic, or ethnic minority groups (U.S. Department of Education, 2005). An explanation for these high incidence figures is probably tied to the limited health care and access to timely medical care experienced by a disproportionately large number of families within these groups.

Educational programming for many of these students is particularly challenging. Until relatively recently, students from non-English-speaking families were included in special programs with English-speaking peers with little or no thought to their special linguistic needs (Mayer, 1996). Although many programs seek to meet the needs of students from culturally diverse backgrounds, it is a particularly complex problem to teach English communication skills to a student who is deaf when a language other than English is spoken at home (Heward, 2006; Pagliaro, 2001).

Non-English-speaking families may be struggling on many fronts and be unable to fully use available services. Some may be struggling with feelings of isolation in their adopted communities. Others may be limited by economic constraints that curtail the amount of time they can devote to participating in the educational process available for their student. Still others may not understand the benefits of early amplification and resist it as unnecessary. Cultural insensitivity and the lack of understanding of how different cultural groups will react to a student in need of special services can further complicate an already formidable task.

Deaf Culture

Some consider people who are deaf as a distinct minority population and deafness as a defining cultural characteristic. Those that espouse the deaf culture do not consider deafness a disability, but a trait. The rationale is that deaf people, like people of other cultural groups, are united by their common physical characteristics (deafness and hearing loss), a common language (sign language), and common needs (special accommodations in communication; Lott, Easterbrooks, Heller, & O'Rourke, 2001; Scheetz, 2001). Advocates of deaf culture feel it is appropriate to capitalize the D when referring to themselves as a specific population; they use the word deaf as an adjective. Thus, deaf people have hearing losses. Others are careful to refer to themselves as people who are deaf, emphasizing their cultural bond (Turnbull et al., 2004).

The members of the deaf community see ASL as the deaf student's first language and believe that English is a second language. English is best taught, they contend, as a second language after the student has mastered ASL. Reagan (1990) noted six areas that make the deaf culture a true culture.

1. There is a linguistic difference. Deaf people speak a language that is different from English (Ladd, 2003).

2. *Attitudinal deafness* is a state of mind in which a person thinks of him- or herself as deaf regardless of the degree of severity of the impairment.

3. Behavioral norms are different in the deaf community. The culture values informality and physical contact in their interactions. The culture also calls for frank discussions that get right to the point.

4. People from the culture tend to approve of intermarriages among the deaf community. Members of this culture marry each other at rates as high as 90 percent and pass on a social awareness of the deaf and events that are of particular significance to them.

5. There is an awareness of a history of deafness. The elder persons are valued for their wisdom and knowledge.

6. The deaf community has an abundance of their own volunteer organizations, such as the National Association of the Deaf, the National Theatre of the Deaf, and the Deaf Olympics.

Others have reported that mainstreaming often isolates students who are deaf from the deaf community and puts them at risk of isolation, loneliness, and depression because they may have few people with whom they can communicate (Moores, 2001). Students who are deaf feel more secure if they are in consistent contact with other people who are deaf with whom they can communicate (Burch, 2000; Lane, Hoffmeister, & Bahan. 1996). As a result, many people who are deaf socialize to a great extent with others who are deaf. This contact has led to the transmission of sign language and the learning of the deaf culture.

In the past, this self-imposed isolation from the hearing community was seen as a social pathology. Some professionals now see this as a natural condition arising from the common bond of sign language. However, common language is but one bond. Reagan (1990) outlined other factors that may validate the deaf culture. It may be described as a bilingual group comparable to the Hispanic culture, except that the two languages are ASL and English instead of Spanish and English. There are attitudes and perceptions about deafness not shared by the hearing community, such as the view that hearing impairments are not a sickness or disability that needs to be cured (Case, 2000; Pagliaro, 2001). Members of the deaf community advocate for each other and feel that by working together they have gained many of the benefits they now enjoy, such as greater access to jobs, legislation for captioning, and the availability of assistive technology in public places. Because the transmission of deaf cultural values most easily occurs in residential schools for people who are deaf, there is even concern that Deaf culture is under attack by policies such as educational inclusion and the interpretation of LRE for education as being placement in general classrooms. Some are seeking to have classes in deaf culture and history for students who are isolated from the community and taught in nonresidential schools (Gaustad & Kluwin, 1992; Janesick & Moores, 1992).

Arguments and counterarguments about a separate cultural assignment may continue forever between professionals and deaf people. Dr. I. King Jordan, the president of Gallaudet University and the only president of a university who is deaf, writes about the conflict with the following words:

> Any labels that define one group to its satisfaction, . . . exclude another. While deaf is a pronouncement to the world of great pride in culture, deaf can also be used to exclude those who describe themselves as deaf. . . . We will constantly be defining and refining ourselves and seeking new language to reflect that expanded vision. (Jordan, 1992)

PROFESSIONALS

The needs of families with students who are hearing impaired will vary depending on the degree of hearing loss the student has and his or her accommodation to it. All or most of the professionals described in this section will probably have at least cursory contact with each student who is hearing impaired. The services of other professionals may be needed for coexisting conditions that are either related or unrelated to hearing impairments.

Educational Team Members

An educational team is responsible for producing an IEP for each student identified as having a hearing impairment severe enough to warrant special educational services. Audiologists, in cooperation with otorhinolaryngologists or otologists, must assess the hearing loss and its physical and functional dimensions. Speech-language pathologists can assist the student in reaching his or her potential in speechreading and speech production. Special teachers for students who are deaf or hearing impaired will develop the IEP and help carry it through with the general education teacher. Interpreters and teachers of students who are deaf who present curricular subjects may also be part of the team. Parents will need to be in close contact with each of these professionals and may also require counseling by genetic specialists.

Audiologists

Audiologists are specially trained professionals who are concerned with the evaluation of a student's hearing ability. They can be responsible for planning and implementing treatment that will help the student hear as efficiently as possible. They identify the degree of hearing loss, determine the student's perceptual abilities, and chart this information on audiograms. Some audiologists are aural rehabilitation specialists who provide training in the use of residual hearing and the use of hearing aids. Counseling activities include an emphasis on the social and educational impact of hearing loss. ASHA provides national certification to those who complete coursework at the master's-degree level and serve a 1-year clinical fellowship while employed.

Otorhinolaryngologists and Otologists

Otorhinolaryngologists, also known as ENT specialists, are physicians who specialize in disorders of the ears, nose, and throat. Otology is a medical subspecialty of otorhinolaryngology. Otologists specialize in the diagnosis and treatment of disorders and diseases of the ear.

Speech-Language Pathologists

Speech-language pathologists are professionals trained to work with students to develop skills in articulating the sounds of language, using their voices efficiently, and developing both receptive and expressive language skills. National certification for speech-language pathologists is acquired from ASHA after successfully completing master's-level training and serving a paid clinical fellowship year.

Deaf Educators

Deaf educators provide a variety of services. Some are classroom teachers who present curricular content to students who are deaf, similar to general education math, history, and science teachers. Others may provide service as special education coordinators, ensuring that IEPs are followed and reviewed as needed. They may serve as resource personnel for general educators or staff resource rooms. The Council for Exceptional Children (2003) proposed guidelines for the approximately 80 colleges and universities in the United States that offer training programs in the education of people who are deaf and hard of hearing. The council believes that graduates of these training programs should possess knowledge and skills in at least the following eight areas:

1. Philosophical, historical, and legal aspects of education of people who are hearing impaired or deaf. This would include knowledge of incidence, identification techniques, theories of teaching, cultural knowledge, educational placement options, and the rights and responsibilities of parents and educators.

2. Characteristics of students who are deaf or hard of hearing, including the cognitive, emotional, and social impact of deafness and hearing impairment on students and their families.

3. Assessment, diagnosis, and evaluation procedures, including the appropriate terminology used and the legal guidelines concerning referrals and placements.

4. Instructional content and practice, including sources of specialized materials; knowledge of nonverbal communication systems, including ASL; and familiarity with language development and practices to maximize residual hearing.

5. Planning and managing the teaching environment, including knowledge of model programs and cultural factors that might influence classroom management.

6. Management of student behavior and social interaction skills, and the facilitation of interactions between students who are deaf and deaf communities.

7. Communication and collaborative partnerships, including how to obtain governmental and nongovernmental resources for parents and knowledge of the responsibilities of general teachers and support personnel.

8. Professional and ethical practices, including proficiency in obtaining information on education, philosophy, and relevant consumer and professional organizations for people who are hearing impaired or deaf.

Teachers of students who are hearing impaired or deaf are certified by state departments of education. The credentials needed vary, with some states requiring at least master's-level training in deaf education before granting certification.

Educational Interpreters

These professionals, who sign the spoken content of what teachers and other speakers say, became a recognized professional group in 1964. Their umbrella organization is called the Registry of Interpreters for the Deaf (RID); (Hallahan & Kauffman, 2006). RID advocates for quality in interpretation through professional certification, professional development for interpreters, and promotion of ethical practices. RID sets standards for the competencies needed to become a certified interpreter. Freelance interpreters work primarily with adults in needed medical or legal situations. Educational interpreters, also called educational transliterators, make it possible for students who are deaf to enroll in postsecondary educational programs. Educational interpreters are being used in increasing numbers in elementary and secondary classrooms, where their duties can vary from strictly translating to tutoring, assisting general and special education teachers, keeping records, and supervising students with hearing impairments (Frasu, 2005). Tips for using an interpreter in a classroom are included in Box 9.4.

Genetics Specialists

A significant percentage of hearing losses are either inherited or occur during prenatal, perinatal, or postnatal development. The geneticist plays an important role in family counseling and prenatal screening to determine which families are at risk and informing them of the current knowledge available about hereditary transmission and its consequences.

Professional Organizations

Professional organizations and parent or self-help groups that are concerned with the needs and rights of the hard of hearing are listed at the end of this chapter. Two organizations that provide direct service are the Registry of Interpreters for the Deaf and the individual state vocational rehabilitation departments. They are highlighted here.

Registry for Interpreters of the Deaf (RID)

RID maintains a national listing of members who are skilled in the use of ASL and other sign systems. It also provides information about interpreting and the certification of interpreters.

BOX 9.4
WHAT EVERY TEACHER SHOULD KNOW

Tips for Using an Interpreter

- Speak naturally.
- Allow the interpreter to help you set up the room for maximum efficiency in communication.
- Allow for extra time in your lecture or comments, as interpreting is slightly delayed because the interpreter must hear and then sign.
- Maintain eye contact with the student—not the interpreter. The student will look at the interpreter.
- Say only what you want to be interpreted. The interpreter is ethically bound to sign everything you say. The interpreter will not leave out parts of the message nor will they add to it to make the information more clear.
- Provide occasional breaks.
- Allow students to speak one at a time. This will avoid confusion.
- All interpreted information is confidential. The interpreter will not become involved in a situation and will not offer opinions or advice.
- Summaries of upcoming information, video content, outlines, etc. can give the interpreter a background that will allow better interpretation of the material you are teaching.
- Have adequate lighting in the room.
- The student who is deaf should have an unobstructed line of sight for the interpreter, the teacher, and other media presentations.
- If you are using *PowerPoint,* videos, or other media, the student can visually attend only to the media presentation or the interpreter. All content must be presented visually if the student is to attend to the presentation. Use captioning—or do not show the video.

Vocational Rehabilitation Departments

Each state has a vocational rehabilitation office that will provide assistance in vocational evaluations, availabilities, and eligibility requirements for financial assistance, educational training, and job placements.

DISCUSSION QUESTIONS

1. Explain how a cochlear implant assists hearing.
2. What are some causes of hearing loss?
3. Identify approaches to teaching communication to a student who is deaf. Which do you believe is preferable?
4. Why is it difficult to measure the intellectual capacity of a student with a hearing loss?
5. Why is American Sign Language preferred over finger spelling?
6. Why do proponents of deaf culture prefer schools for students who are deaf and hearing impaired over inclusion into general education classes?

7. What specialists may be needed at an IEP meeting for a student with a hearing impairment? What could each contribute?
8. How can a general education teacher work collaboratively with an interpreter for the deaf?

PROFESSIONAL ASSOCIATIONS AND PARENT OR SELF-HELP GROUPS

Alexander Graham Bell Association for the Deaf
3417 Volta Place NW
Washington, DC 20007
202-337-5220 or TTY: 202-337-5221
Fax: 202-337-8314

American Athletic Association of the Deaf
1134 Davenport Drive
Burton, MI 48529

American Deafness and Rehabilitation Association
P.O. Box 55369
Little Rock, AR 72225

American Society for Deaf Children
P.O. Box 3355
Gettysburg, PA 17325
717-334-7922 (also TTY)
Fax: 717-334-8808
Parent Hotline: 800-942-ASDC
E-mail: ASDC1@aol.com

American Speech-Language-Hearing-Association (ASHA)
10801 Rockville Pike
Rockville, MD 20852
301-897-5700 or 800-498-2701 or TTY: 301-897-0157
E-mail: actioncenter@asha.org

American Tinnitus Association
P.O. Box 5
Portland, OR 97207-0005
503-248-9985 or 800-634-8978
Fax: 503-248-0024
E-mail: tinnitus@ata.org
Cheryl McGinnis
Executive Director
E-mail: cheryl@ata.org

Beginnings for Parents of Hearing Impaired Children
3900 Barrett Drive, Suite 100
Raleigh, NC 27609

Better Hearing Institute
515 King Street, Suite 420
Alexandria, VA 22314
703-684-3391

Center on Deafness
3444 W. Dundee Road
Northbrook, IL 60062

Cochlear Implant Association
5335 Wisconsin Avenue NW, Suite 440
Washington, DC 20015-2052
202-895-2781
Fax: 202-895-2782

Cochlear Implant Club
P.O. Box 464
Buffalo, NY 14223

Cued Speech Discovery
23970 Hermitage Road
Cleveland, OH 44122-4008
800-459-3529 (also TTY)

Deaf Artists of America
87 N. Clinton Avenue, Suite 408
Rochester, NY 14604

Deafness Research Foundation
1050 Seventeenth Street NW, Suite 701
Washington, DC 20036

Deafpride
1350 Potomac Avenue SE
Washington, DC 20003

Dogs for the Deaf
10175 Wheeler Road
Central Point, OR 97502
541-826-9220
Fax: 541-826-6696

Gallaudet University
800 Florida Avenue NE
Washington, DC 20002-3695

Hearing Speech & Deafness Center
Renton Office
4300 Talbot Road S.
Suite 201
Renton, WA 98055
425-226-6111 (also TTY)
Fax: 425-226-0514

Hearing, Speech & Deafness Center
Seattle Office
1620 Eighteenth Avenue
Seattle, WA 98122
206-323-5770 (also TTY)
Fax: 206-328-6871

Hear Now
9745 E. Hampden Avenue, Suite 300
Denver, CO 80231

National Association of the Deaf
814 Thayer Avenue
Silver Spring, MD 20910-4500
301-587-1788 or TTY: 301-587-1789
Fax: 301-587-1791

National Association for Hearing and Speech Action
10801 Rockville Pike
Rockville, MD 20852

National Center for Law and the Deaf
Gallaudet University
800 Florida Avenue NE
Washington, DC 20002

National Cued Speech Association
P.O. Box 31345
Raleigh, NC 27622

National Foundation for Children's Hearing Education and Research
928 McLean Avenue
Yonkers, NY 10704

National Information Center on Deafness
Gallaudet University
800 Florida Avenue NE
Washington, DC 20002

National Technical Institute for the Deaf
One Lomb Memorial Drive
Rochester, NY 14623

North Carolina Cooperative Extension Service (NNCC)
Karen DeBord, Ph.D., CFLE
Associate Professor & State Extension Specialist, Child Development
Box 7605, 101 Ricks Hall
NC State University
Raleigh, NC 27695-7605
919-515-9147
Fax: 919-515-2786
E-mail: karen_debord@NCSU.EDU

Paws with a Cause
4646 South Division
Wayland, MI 49348
616-877-7297 (also TTY) or 800-253-PAWS (7297)
Fax: 616-877-0248

Registry of Interpreters for the Deaf
51 Monroe Street, Suite 1107
Rockville, MD 20850

Self-Help for Hard of Hearing People
Brenda Battat, Director of State Development
7910 Woodmont Avenue, Suite 1200
Bethesda, MD 20814
301-657-2248 or TTY: 301-657-2249
Fax: 301-913-9413

USA Deaf Sports Federation (USADSF)
Dr. Bobbie Beth Scoggins, President
911 Tierra Linda Drive
Frankfort, KY 40601-4633
801-393-7916 (TTY)
Fax: 801-393-2263

American Annals of the Deaf
814 Thayer Avenue
Silver Spring, MD 20910

The Endeavor
American Society for Deaf Children
East 10th and Tahlequah
Sulphur, OK 73086

Journal of the American Deafness and Rehabilitation Association
P.O. Box 251554
Little Rock, AR 72225

Our Kids Magazine
Alexander Graham Bell Association for the Deaf
3417 Volta Place NW
Washington, DC 20007

Sign Language Studies
Linstok Press
9306 Mintwood Street
Silver Spring, MD 20910

Volta Review
Alexander Graham Bell Association for the Deaf
3417 Volta Place NW
Washington, DC 20007

REFERENCES

Barker, L. J. (2003). Computer-assisted vocabulary acquisition: The CSLU vocabulary tutor in oral-deaf education. *Journal of Deaf Studies and Deaf Education, 8,* 187–198.

Barnes v. Converse College, 436 F. Supp. 635 (1977).

Bess, F. H. (1988). *Hearing impairment in children*. Parkton, MD: York.

Blanchfield, B. B., Feldman, J. J., Dunbar, J. L., & Gardner, E. N. (2001). The severely to profoundly hearing impaired population in the United States: Prevalence estimates and demographics. *Journal of American Academy of Audiology, 12*(4), 183–189.

Board of Education of the Hendrik Hudson Central School District v. Rowley, 102 S. Ct. 3034 (1982).

Bodner-Johnson, B. (1987). Helping the youngest ones. Gallaudet Today, 18, 8–11.

Bowe, F. (1991). Approaching equality: Education of the deaf. Silver Spring, MD: TJ Publications.

Burch, S. (2000). In a different voice: Sign language preservation and America's deaf community. Bilingual Research Journal, 24, 443–464.

Case, B. A. (2000). Using analogy to develop an understanding of deaf culture. Multicultural Education, 7(3), 41–44.

Council for Exceptional Children. (2003). What every special educator must know: Ethics, standards, and guidelines for special educators. Reston, VA: Author.

Frasu, A. (2005). Working with an ASL-English interpreter and providing visual accessibility. DeafLink. Retrieved October 10, 2005 from www.deaflinx.com/userterp.html

Gaustad, M. G., & Kluwin, T. N. (1992). Patterns of communication among deaf and hearing adolescents. In T. N. Kluwin, D. F. Moores, & M. G. Gaustad (Eds.), Toward effective public school programs for deaf students: Context, process, & outcomes (pp. 107–128). New York: Teachers College Press.

Geers, A., & Moog, J. (1989). Factors predictive of the development of literacy in profoundly hearing-impaired adolescents. Volta Review, 91, 69–86.

Gentry, M. M., Chinn, K. M., & Moulton, R. D. (2004/2005). Effectiveness of multimedia reading materials when used with children who are deaf. American Annals of the Deaf, 148, 394–403.

Green, W. W., & Fischgrund, J. E. (1993). Students with hearing loss. In A. E. Blackhurst & W. H. Berdine (Eds.), An introduction to special education (3rd ed., pp. 271–309). New York: HarperCollins.

Hallahan, D. P., & Kauffman, J. M. (2006). Exceptional children. Upper Saddle River, NJ: Merrill/Prentice Hall.

Hardman, M. L., Drew, C. J., & Egan, M. W. (2005). Human exceptionality: Society, school, and family (8th ed.). Needham, MA: Allyn & Bacon.

Hess, D. (1991, July 23). Say what? Albuquerque Journal, pp. A1–A2.

Heward, W. L. (1996). Exceptional children (5th ed.). Upper Saddle River, NJ: Merrill/Prentice Hall.

Heward, W. L. (2006). Exceptional children: An introduction to special education. (8th ed.). Upper Saddle River, NJ: Merrill/Prentice Hall.

Higgins, P. C. (1992). Working at mainstreaming. In P. M. Ferguson, D. L. Ferguson, & S. J. Taylor (Eds.), Interpreting disability (pp. 103–123). New York: Teachers College Press.

Janesick, V. J., & Moores, D. F. (1992). Ethnic and cultural considerations. In T. N. Kluwin, D. F. Moores, & M. G. Gaustad (Eds.), Toward effective public school programs for deaf students: Context, process, & outcomes (pp. 49–65). New York: Teachers College Press.

Jordan, I. K. (1992). Language and change. Viewpoints on deafness: A Deaf American Monograph, 42, 69–71.

Karchmer, M. A. & Mitchell. R. E. (2003). Demographic and achievement characteristics of deaf and hard of hearing students. In M. Marschark & P. E. Spence (Eds.), Oxford Handbook of deaf studies, language, and education (p. 21–37). New York: Oxford University Press.

Keats, B. J. B. (2002). Genes and syndromic hearing loss. Journal of Communication Disorders, 35, 355–366.

Kirk, S. A., Gallagher, J. J., Anastasiow, N. J., & Coleman, M. R. (2006). Educating exceptional children (11th ed.). Boston: Houghton Mifflin.

Kluwin, T. N. (1985). Profiling the deaf student who is a problem in the classroom. Adolescence, 20, 863–875.

Kluwin, T. N. (1992). What does "local public school" mean? In T. N. Kluwin, D. F. Moores, & M. G. Gaustad (Eds.), Toward effective public school programs for deaf students: Context, process, & outcomes (pp. 30–48). New York: Teachers College Press.

Ladd, P. (2003). Understanding deaf culture: In search of deafhood. Cleavdon, England: MultiLingual Matters.

Lane, H. R., Hoffmeister, R., & Bahan, B. (1996). Journey into the deaf world. San Diego: DawnSignPress.

Lichtenstein, E. (1998). The relationship between reading processes and English skills of deaf college students. Journal of Deaf Studies and Deaf Education, 3(2), 80–130.

Liles, M. (2005). Interactive whiteboard system drives increased achievement at Texas school for the deaf. THE Journal, 32(10), 49–50.

Ling, D. (Ed.). (1984). Early intervention for hearing-impaired children: Total communication options. San Diego, CA: College-Hill.

Lott, V. G., Easterbrooks, S. R., Heller, K. W., & O'Rourke, C. M. (2001). Work attitudes of students who are deaf and their potential employers. Journal of the American Deafness and Rehabilitation Association, 34, 31–49.

Lowenbraun, S., & Thompson, M. (1990). Hearing impairments. In N. G. Haring, L. McCormack, & T. G. Haring (Eds.), Exceptional children and youth. Upper Saddle River, NJ: Merrill/ Prentice Hall.

Luckner, J. L., Muir, S. (2001). Successful students who are deaf in general education settings. American Annals of the Deaf, 146, 435–446.

Luetke-Stahlman, B., & Luckner, J. (1991). Effectively educating students with hearing impairments. White Plains, NY: Longman.

Luetke-Stahlman, B. (1998). Language issues in deaf education. Hillsboro, OR: Butte.

Lyxell, B., & Holmberg, I. (2000). Visual speechreading and cognitive performance in hearing-impaired and normal hearing children (11–14 years). British Journal of Educational Psychology, Volume 70, Number 4 (December 1, 2000), pp. 505–518.

Maller, S. J. (1996). WISC–III verbal item invariance across samples of deaf and hearing children of similar measured ability. Journal of Psychoeducational Assessment, 14, 152–165.

Maller, S. J. (1997). Deafness and WISC–III item difficulty: Invariance and fit. Journal of School Psychology, 35, 299–314.

Maller, S. J., & French, B. F. (2004). Universal nonverbal intelligence test: Factor invariance across deaf and standardization samples. Educational and Psychological Measurement, 64, 647–660.

Maller, S. J., Konold, T. R., & Glutting, J. J. (1998). WISC–III factor invariance across samples of children exhibiting appropriate and inappropriate test-session behaviors. Educational and Psychological Measurement, 58, 467–474.

Marazita, M. L., Ploughman, L. M., Rawlings, B., Remington, E., Arnos, K. S., & Nance, W. E. (1993). Genetic epidemiological studies of early-onset deafness in the U.S. school-age population., *American Journal Medical Genetics, 46,* 486–491.

Martin, F. (2000). *Introduction to audiology* (7th ed.). Needham Heights, MA: Allyn & Bacon.

Mayer, M. H. (1996). Children who are deaf or hard of hearing. In E. L. Meyen (Ed.), *Exceptional children in today's schools* (pp. 315–350). Denver: Love.

McKusick, V. (1983). *Mendelian inheritance in man* (6th ed.). Baltimore: Johns Hopkins Press.

Moores, D. F. (1985). Educational programs and services for hearing impaired children: Issues and options. In F. Powell, T. Finitzo-Hieber, S. Friel-Patti, & D. Henderson (Eds.), *Deaf children in America* (pp. 105–123). San Diego, CA: College-Hill.

Moores, D. F. (2001). *Educating the deaf: Psychology, principles, and practices.* (5th ed.). New York: Houghton Mifflin.

Moores, D. F. (2004). Documenting the status and academic progress of deaf and hard of hearing students: An increasingly complex task. *American Annals of the Deaf, 149,* 307–308.

Moores, D. F. (2005). Progress is not our most important product. *American Annals of the Deaf, 150,* 249–250.

Moores, D. F. (2004/2005). The search for magic solutions. *American Annals of the Deaf, 148,* 373–374.

Northern, J. L., & Downs, M. P. (2001). *Hearing in children* (5th ed.). Baltimore: Williams & Wilkins.

Ohna, S. E. (2005). Researching classroom processes of inclusion and exclusion. *European Journal of Special Needs Education, 20,* 167–178.

Orlans, H. (2004). Sign language enrollment zooms. *Change, 36,* 6–7.

Padden, C., & Humphries, T. (1988). *Deaf in America: Voices from a culture.* Cambridge, MA: Harvard University Press.

Pagliaro, C. (2001). Addressing deaf culture in the classroom. *Kappa Delta Pi Record, 37*(4), 173–176.

Paul, P. V., & Quigley, S. P. (1994). *Education and deafness.* San Diego, CA: Singular Publishing Group.

Prezbindowski, A. K., & Lederberg, A. R. (2003). Vocabulary assessment of deaf and hard of hearing children: From infancy through the preschool years. *Journal of Deaf Studies and Deaf Education, 8,* 383–400.

Quigley, S. P., & Paul, P. V. (1990). *Language and deafness.* San Diego, CA: College-Hill.

Reagan, T. (1990). Cultural considerations in the education of deaf children. In D. F. Moores & K. P. Meadow-Orleans (Eds.), *Educational and developmental aspects of deafness* (pp. 73–84). Washington, DC: Gallaudet University Press.

Salvia, J., & Ysseldyke, J. E. (2004). *Assessment in special and inclusive education* (9th ed.). Boston: Houghton Mifflin.

Scarlatos, T., & Nesterenko, D. (2004). FINGERSPELL: Let your fingers do the talking. *Journal of Educational Technology Systems, 33,* 165–172.

Scheetz, N. (2001). *Orientation to deafness.* Needham Heights, MA: Allyn & Bacon.

Schildroth, A. N., & Holt, S. A. (1991). Annual survey of hearing-impaired children and youth: 1989–90 school year. *American Annals of the Deaf, 136*(2), 155–163.

Schirmer, B. R. (2000). *Language and literacy development in children who are deaf.* Riverside, NJ: Macmillan.

Schlesinger, H. (1983) Early intervention: The prevention of multiple handicaps. In G. Mencher & S. Gerber (Eds.), *The multiply handicapped hearing-impaired child* (pp. 83–116). New York: Grune & Stratton.

Schow, R., & Nerbonne, M. (2002). *Introduction to audiologic rehabilitation.* Boston: Allyn & Bacon.

Smith, D. D. (2006). *Introduction to special education: Teaching in an age of opportunity* (5th ed.). Needham, MA: Allyn & Bacon.

Stanford Achievement Test—Hearing Impaired Version (8th ed.). (1989). Hyattsville, MD: Psychological Corporation.

Strauss, M. (1997). Hearing loss and cytomegalovirus. *Volta Review, 99*(5), 71–74.

Swanwick, R., & Watson, L. (2005). Literacy in the homes of young deaf children: Common and distinct features of spoken language and sign bilingual environments. *Journal of Early Childhood Literacy, 5,* 53–78.

Traxler, C. B. (2000). *The Stanford Achievement Test,* 9th edition: National. The Stanford Achievement Test, 9th Edition: National norming and performance standards for deaf and hard-of-hearing students. *Journal of Deaf Studies and Deaf Education 5,* 337–348.

Turnbull, A. P., Turnbull, H. R., Shank, M., & Smith, S. (2004). *Exceptional lives: Special education in today's schools* (4th ed.). Upper Saddle River, NJ: Merrill/Prentice Hall.

U.S. Department of Education. (2005). *Twenty-fifth annual report to Congress on the implementation of the Individuals with Disabilities Education Act.* Washington, DC: Author.

Vernon, M. (2005). Fifty years of research on the intelligence of deaf and hard of hearing children: A review of literature and discussion of implications. *Journal of Deaf Studies and Deaf Education, 10,* 225–231.

Vernon, M., & Koh, S. D. (1970). Effects of manual communication on deaf children's educational achievement, linguistic competence, oral skills, and psychological adjustment. *American Annals of the Deaf, 115,* 527–536.

Yoshinaga-Itano, C., & Sedey, A. L. (Eds.). (2000). *Language, speech, and socialemotional development of children who are deaf or hard of hearing: The early years.* (Monographs of The Volta Review, Vol. 100, No. 5). Washington, DC: Alexander Graham Bell Association for the Deaf.

Zazove, P., Meador, H. E., & Derry, H. A. (2004). Deaf persons and computer use. *American Annals of the Deaf, 148,* 376–384.

10 *Students with Visual Impairments*

KEY TERMS

WHAT WOULD YOU DO?

Lindy and Joanna, neighbors and best friends, entered the first-grade classroom. They sat in their chosen seats right next to each other and eagerly placed their crayons, markers, pencils, pads of writing paper, and other supplies in their desks. Cliff and John had the desks on the other side of the four-person table. The four friends chatted happily as they got out paper and pencils and got ready to copy sentences from the board. The teacher moved among all the foursomes in the room, helping with tying shoes, blowing noses, encouraging students as they worked, and talking with them about events from the previous evening. The regular activity for starting the day was to copy the sentences from the board. The words were familiar. The sentences were short and contained words used in the basal reading stories from the previous week. The students could talk quietly among themselves as they were working. Mrs. Baker had used this activity for years. She found it helped to get the students settled down before she gathered them together for opening exercises. She was pleased with the quality of work from both Lindy and Joanna. What she did not notice was that Lindy was reading the sentences and Joanna was writing them down. Joanna did not look at the board. When she did look, she had difficulty. She could distinguish the wall from the chalkboard but she could not see any writing on the board. Reading from the board was impossible because the words were indistinguishable from the background. At 6 years of age, Joanna did not know that her vision was different from that of her classmates. She thought it was good that Lindy could see the board, because she could read it to her. Joanna became adept at transcription.

1. How should the teacher modify the assignment or make accommodations for Joanna?

2. How could this situation be avoided?

Educationally, we learn from the printed and visual materials that give us a greater understanding of our world and its many wonders. Environmentally, we move from place to place based on visual signs we recognize. Socially, we read each other's faces and body language to help determine whether our behavior is appropriate, and we change it if it is not. We select friends, play sports, work, and relax with the help of the visual information we hardly pause to consider. Obviously, this is not so for students with visual impairments. Depending on the amount of residual vision each individual possesses, accommodations in learning, socialization, recreation, and career choices must be implemented in a logical and meaningful way to help compensate for the information not gained because the individual cannot see.

The incidental learning process guides so much of the acquisition of social and education competencies valued in our society. We can teach a person to fry an egg, but when individuals can see, they also learn that the egg has color, butter bubbles as it sizzles, the burner is flaming or red, and the clear part of the egg turns white but the yellow part stays close to the same color. A person without vision must be taught all these things. In the same manner, we see our peers' reactions to beauty, to our invitations, and to questions. We see pictures in books that illustrate what we read about. We see the sky darken when it is about to storm. Sighted students automatically depend on and use vision for many tasks without thought to the obstacles that are present for peers who have visual impairments.

DEFINITIONS

As a part of defining blindness and visual impairment, it is necessary to understand how normal vision works. It is also helpful to master some of the many terms that make up the vocabulary for defining visual impairment. Once the normal vision system is understood and the most appropriate terms are familiar, it will be easier to define malfunctions of the system. As with many other areas covered in this text, people use different definitions of visual impairment and blindness for different purposes. The differing legal and educational conceptualizations and their implications are fairly straightforward and understandable once you have mastered this prerequisite knowledge.

Unimpaired vision has four components:

1. The object to be viewed
2. The light that reflects from the object to the eye
3. A normally functioning eye to receive the reflections
4. The occipital lobes of the brain to interpret the signals transmitted from the eye (Hunt & Marshall, 2006)

As light reflects off an object and strikes the eye, the reflected image is converted into electrical impulses that are received by the brain and translated into what we perceive. Figure 10.1 is a schematic illustration of the parts of the eye and how they work.

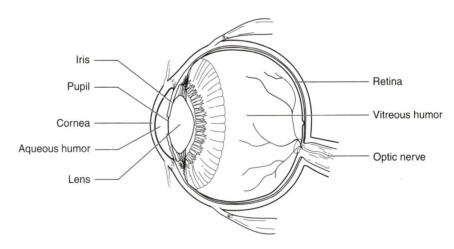

FIGURE 10.1
The human eye.

You may wish to refer to it as you read the following explanation of the visual process. The reflected light rays enter the eye through the transparent curved part of the front of the eye, which is called the cornea. They pass through the watery aqueous humor on the way to the hole in the center of the eye, which is called the pupil. The pupil is housed in the center of the iris, the colored part of the eye. The pupil changes size by expanding and contracting, which allows differing amounts of light into the eye. The lens, which is behind the iris, changes in thickness and brings the reflected light rays into focus. This process is called accommodation. These focused light rays pass through the vitreous humor, a transparent gelatinous substance, and onto the retina or inside lining of the eye. The job of the cells of the retina is to translate the reflected visual information into electrical impulse messages that are sent via the optic nerve to the occipital lobe of the brain. The occipital lobe, located in the back of the brain, is where the messages are deciphered so that the viewer can interpret the image (Hallahan & Kauffman, 2006; Menaker & Batshaw, 1997).

Six pairs of muscles that enable the eye to move from side to side and up and down control the movements of the eyes. While gazing straight ahead, a normal eye can see objects within a range of about 160 degrees. This is called the **visual field.** When the eyes are functioning normally, a person can maintain **visual attention,** which means that he or she is alert enough to be visually sensitive to the environment, is able to select the visual information the environment offers, is attentive enough to change from one visual stimulus to another, and has the processing ability to decode the information received from the visual channel (Heward, 2006; Smith, 2005).

Students with visual impairment may be described in a number of ways for differing purposes. The two major categorizations define students with visual impairments for legal purposes and for educational purposes. A person who is legally blind is eligible for a wide variety of services, materials, and benefits from government agencies. For example, they may be provided with tapes and audio recorded books from the Library of Congress. Their schools can obtain specialized materials and books from the American Printing House for the Blind. They are also eligible for free occupational training, free mail service, and special income tax exemptions (Heward, 2006). Educational definitions are concerned with the changes or accommodations that will be needed to ensure that a student will receive the most appropriate and effective educational experience.

Educational definitions are more varied because **visual acuity,** the relative ability of the eye to see detail, is not the only factor in predicting visual functioning. According to Public Law 108-446 (IDEA), a visual handicap is a "visual impairment that, even with correction, adversely affects a child's educational performance. The term includes both partially seeing and blind children" (42 Fed. Reg. 42474). Two widely used defining terms are low vision and blind. Both groups can use braille, but most students with low vision use some form of print for reading. Large-print texts or ocular devices help these students read. The American Foundation for the Blind defines those with low vision as possessing visual acuity between 20/200 and 20/70 in their better eye with the best possible correction, or those who in the opinion of an eye specialist need temporary or permanent special education services (Hallahan & Kauffman, 2006). Some have proposed slightly differing definitions in an attempt to clarify the needs of students with low vision. For example, Corn (1989) defined low vision as a level of vision that, with standard correction, hinders an individual in the planning or execution of a task but permits enhancement of functional vision through the use of optical or nonoptical devices and environmental accommodations or techniques. Individuals with low vision can generally read print, although they may depend on optical aids such as magnifying glasses. Some use both braille and print, but they can use vision to learn (Lewis, 1995).

Students who are legally blind have clinically measured visual acuity of 20/200 in the better eye with best correction or visual field of 20 degrees or less. Functional limitation refers to the consequence of different levels of visual ability for performance of common activities such as reading. Functional limitation in seeing print is measured by self-report for two levels:

1. Severe functional limitation in seeing refers to people who said they "are unable" to see words and letters in ordinary print, even with their eyeglasses on.

2. Nonsevere functional limitation in seeing refers to people who said they "have difficulty" seeing words and letters in ordinary print, even with their eyeglasses on (American Foundation for the Blind, 2000).

Teachers may be able to use the general curriculum with some **accommodations,** changes that allow students access to the instruction, for students who have some functional vision. Individuals who are totally blind do not receive meaningful information through vision, but more readily through auditory and tactile learning methods. Those who are functionally blind typically use braille for efficient reading and writing. They may use their residual sight for other tasks, such as traveling and doing daily chores. Their limited vision supplements the tactile and auditory learning to which they are exposed (Corn, DePriest, & Erin, 2000; Lewis, 1995).

Another way of defining and grouping students who are visually impaired might be helpful for educational planning. Barraga (1986) proposed the concept of moderate, severe, and profound visual impairments.

• Moderate visual disability can be almost entirely corrected with the help of visual aids or special lighting in general classrooms or resource rooms.

• Severe visual disability is helped only marginally with aids. However, the student can still use vision for learning, with additional time and energy needed to perform visual tasks. Severe visual disability is the rough equivalent of low vision.

• Profound visual disability occurs when a student cannot use vision as an educational tool. Touch and hearing are the primary channels. Although possible, the performance of most gross visual tasks may be difficult. Detailed tasks cannot be performed visually. This is the equivalent of legal blindness.

Although the definitions and categorizations differ for legal and educational reasons, the single most defining characteristic is a visual restriction of sufficient severity that it interferes with a student's normal progress in a general education setting without some accommodation (Scholl, 1986). The student must exhibit one or more of the following characteristics: visual acuity loss, visual field loss, or a changing or degenerating visual condition.

PREVALENCE

About 1 student in 10 begins school with some degree of visual impairment. However, a large majority of these students can be helped with corrective glasses or direct medical treatment. As a result, their vision problems have little or no effect on social or educational development. Approximately 1 in 1,000 has a visual problem so severe that it cannot be corrected (Kirk, Gallagher, Anastasiow, & Coleman, 2006). During the 1995–1996 school year, 25,845 students between the ages of 6 and 21 received special education services as a result of their visual impairments (U.S. Department of Education, 2005), or 0.04 percent of the students receiving special education services. There are an additional 1,615 students who are classified as deaf-blind.

Visual impairments occur in individuals under the age of 18 at a rate of 12.2 per 1,000. Severe visual impairments (legally or totally blind) occur at a rate of 0.06 per 1,000 (NICHCY, 2004). Visual impairments are fairly evenly divided between boys (55 percent) and girls (45 percent). Incidence figures may vary somewhat because of students with visual impairment who are not identified for educational services, varied state definitions, and the number of individuals with multiple disabilities who have visual impairments and other categories of disability (Smith, 2005). Many students with mild or perhaps even moderate visual disabilities are not being identified or are not eligible for educational services and are therefore not receiving services. The population around which figures fluctuate remains relatively stable due to visual impairment caused by hereditary factors. However, there does appear to be a steady increase in the number of students reported as visually impaired since the late 1970s (Kirchner, 1990). The data collected by the American Printing House for the Blind (1992b) indicated a 9 percent increase between 1987 and 1991. The data also revealed that enrollment in infant programs increased by 25 percent and the number of preschool students in programs increased by 41 percent. This rise can be credited in part to better and earlier identification of visual impairments and in particular to the ability of the medical community to save premature infants and sustain the lives of newborn infants with severe medical problems to a greater extent than ever before. Some have congenital visual impairments or sustain visual impairments as a result of the procedures used to keep them alive. This will be further discussed in the "Etiology" section of this chapter. Finally, it must be noted that visual impairments are highly correlated with increasing age. The vast majority of people who are legally blind are over age 65 (American Foundation for the Blind, 2000).

CHARACTERISTICS

Assigning characteristics to students with visual impairments must be done cautiously. Adaptations and reactions to limited sight vary from person to person. Most students with visual impairment are more like students who are normally sighted than they are different from them. They are a diverse and multicultural population. Some are gifted and talented, whereas others are average in most ways; still others have other disabilities. This section of the chapter will highlight their uniqueness, but the reader should bear in mind the similarities of students with visual impairments to students who are sighted. Still, as a group, those with visual impairment have a higher-than-average number of concomitant multiple disabilities, and all share a limited capacity for incidental environmental learning (Heward, 2006).

Motor Development

There is no indication that the motor development and innate motor skills of students with visual impairments are necessarily different from those of students with sight. However, the student with visual impairment, depending on the severity of the impairment, may not be motivated to move and explore. Celeste (2002) reported that infants and toddlers in her study demonstrated delays in all gross motor milestones, but the greatest delays were in such mobility milestones as cruises around furniture, walks independently, and walks up and down stairs. However, more than half of the participants had additional disabilities, including CP. The lack of visually driven imitative behaviors and the restrictions of an environment that is overly protective may retard the development of some motor skills.

Academic Skills

The aptitude of students who are visually impaired does not appear to be significantly different from that of their peers who use sight (Hatton, Bailey, Burchinal, & Ferrell, 1997; Hull & Mason, 1995; Warren & Hatton, 2002). However, measuring their intellectual abilities can be challenging when using measurement instruments standardized on their peers using vision. Many items on the most popular intelligence tests are unrealistic for those who are visually impaired. Obviously, tasks used to measure abilities that range from color sorting to describing pictures or other visually presented stimuli might place the student with visual impairment at a disadvantage. However, no innate intellectual impairment appears to exist in this population of students (Hallahan & Kauffman, 2006).

Language abilities of students with visual impairments do not seem to differ in regard to acquisition and development of the major components of language. Minor differences tend to revolve around restricted experiences; these students may have difficulties because of their impairment and the corresponding lack of linguistic experiences that are related to their limited interaction with the environment. Some differences are logical and predictable. For example, the language of those with visual impairment is more self-centered and refers to fewer objects and people than does the language of their sighted peers (House & Davidson, 2000). Other research has revealed that students with visual impairments may have difficulty with concept development, particularly with concepts concerning spatial relationships (Skellenger & Hill, 1997). Of course, some of the limited language development and vocabulary relates to the age of onset of the visual impairment.

Students who have a visual impairment from a very young age may have some delay in verbalizations, but in the long run there is little difference in the language abilities of students with and without vision. The initial delay may be a function of learning that words can describe abstract concepts as well as objects. They may describe the rise and fall of the ocean waves or the darkening of the sky before a storm approaching with no real understanding of what they are describing. Language development and cognitive or concept developments are intertwined for most students who are visually impaired. Some concepts may never be fully understood without vision. Height, distance, and the atmosphere of a candlelit room can be examples of visually based concepts. Often, special educational experiences can and must be devised to help compensate for the information lost through the visual channel. However, touch and hearing information tends to be perceived in sequences; for example, you feel a puppy from nose to tail in some order and hear a kitten purr when you stroke it. It requires mental imagery to integrate these experiences into a meaningful whole. Vision provides the whole and its parts simultaneously and automatically. Relationships do not have to be constructed, because they are visible. Construction of concepts from hearing and touch is not only less efficient, but it is also more prone to error and misunderstanding (Moore & McConachie, 1990; Sacks, Rosen, & Gaylord-Ross, 1990).

These learning difficulties are often reflected in academic performance. Unless multiple disability factors exist that cause other learning problems, there is no reason to believe that students with visual impairment, with appropriate accommodations in the learning environment, will not perform well academically (Hodges, 1983). However, as a group, these students do tend to lag behind their sighted peers. Basic intellectual aptitude is variable, just as it is in the general population.

Social Skills

The development and practice of social skills is the area in which students with visual impairment tend to differ most from their peers. Some believe the lack of social skills directly relates to negative attitudes transmitted by our society to people who are visually impaired. The image of a helpless and dependent person, coupled with parental overprotection, can retard social development—as can isolation and lack of contact with sighted people (Caton, 1993). Although there do not appear to be innate personality problems automatically associated with visual impairment, older people with visual impairments are often characterized as socially immature, self-conscious, isolated, passive, withdrawn, and dependent (Tuttle, 1981).

Many skills acquired automatically by others must be taught to students with visual impairment. Eye contact provides students with functional sight with information about the appropriateness of behavior. Appropriate smiling and facial expression and postural messages are all a part of socialization that is difficult for people with visual impairments (Hallahan & Kauffman, 2006). Often students with visual impairments are rejected by their classmates because they lack social skills. They may ask too many questions or engage in inappropriate acts of affection (Perez-Pereira & Conti-Ramsden, 1999). They may also be rejected because their knowledge of play experiences is limited. Because they often find it difficult to hold sighted playmates' interest, their conversations become brief and self-centered rather than focused on shared activities (MacCuspie, 1992). Rejection might even begin when parents react negatively when they are not reinforced with smiles and appropriate eye contact (Warren, 1994).

A final and critical impediment to social adjustment may be the stereotypical behaviors that some students with visual impairment display. Body rocking, eye rubbing, and inappropriate hand and finger movements are all distracting and off-putting to peers and interfere with attempts at social interaction. These behaviors are sometimes termed "blindisms" (Hallahan & Kauffman, 2006) and are also exhibited by students with autism (see Chapter 8). Aside from their social consequences, these behaviors can interfere with learning by consuming time needed for other activities. Stereotypical behaviors, once learned and ingrained into the student's behavior pattern, are often very difficult, but not impossible, to eliminate. There is debate over whether teachers should have a tolerance for repetitive and stereotypical behaviors or whether they should be extinguished (McHugh & Leiberman, 2003).

As with all the other disabilities covered in this text, the list of characteristics discussed here will not be found in all students or even in any one student. However, the composite picture presented here should help you understand some of the consequences of being visually impaired.

ETIOLOGY

We have defined the categories of visual impairment, shared the prevalence statistics, and sketched some of the most common characteristics of students who are visually impaired. Unlike some of the other disabilities covered in this text, we can accurately describe most of the conditions that lead to visual impairments. Unfortunately, we are not always aware of what causes each condition. Although this section on the causes of visual impairment covers many of the most commonly occurring conditions, it does not cover all possible causes or every condition that can lead to blindness or visual impairments.

Heredity is by far the largest causal link in visual impairments and is responsible for more than 37 percent of the most serious visual disabilities in young students. Infectious diseases during pregnancy cause another 15 percent of impairments, and approximately 10 percent more are due to injuries and the oxygen poisoning that result from attempts to sustain premature infants. Another 10 percent of visual impairments are attributable to tumors and other neoplasms affecting the optic nerve (Kirk et al., 2006). The 30 different causes and types of the eye dysfunctions discussed in this section can be grouped into major categories. The causal category deals with injuries, infections, substance abuse problems, and nutrition problems. The major types or conditions are grouped as being primarily refractive disorders, retinal and optic nerve problems, eye muscle disorders, and central vision insufficiencies. These categorizations and a listing of causes and conditions appear in Figures 10.2 and 10.3. Figure 10.2 lists potential causes of visual impairment, such as vitamin A deficiency and substance abuse. Figure 10.3 lists the most frequently seen conditions of impairment, such as myopia and retinitis pigmentosa. This attempt to present a comprehensive listing is intended as a useful checksheet for understanding the causes of visual dysfunction.

Injury, Infection, Substance Abuse, and Malnutrition

These conditions are not eye impairments themselves, but they can cause vision problems. For example, injuries to the prenatal nervous system and fetal alcohol syndrome are not vision problems, but both can lead to optic nerve hypoplasia, which is a visual problem (Koenig & Holbrook, 2000). Eye injuries of all types can lead to visual impairment or blindness. Many eye injuries are preventable and can be avoided with the proper use of safety goggles and other safety measures. Neoplasms (tumors) are a variety of growths that can affect an organ. An example is a retinoblastoma, a malignant tumor of the eye. It usually affects both eyes and occurs before age 3 (Sacks et al., 1990). Malnutrition in a severe form can lead to blindness. Vitamin A deficiency is particularly

EYE INJURIES	INFECTIONS
NEOPLASMS	Measles
Tumors	Trachoma
MALNUTRITION	Onchocerciasis
Vitamin A deficiency	AIDS
SUBSTANCE ABUSE	Chlamydia
SYSTEMIC DISEASES	Gonorrhea
Diabetes	POISONING
	Excess oxygen

FIGURE 10.2
Causes of visual impairment.

REFRACTIVE DISORDERS	RETINAL AND OPTIC NERVE
Hyperopia	PROBLEMS
Myopia	Retinal degeneration
Astigmatism	Retinal detachment
Cataracts	Macular degeneration
Aniridia (ocular albinism)	Retinitis pigmentosa
EYE MUSCLE PROBLEMS	Coloboma
Strabismus	Glaucoma
Nystagmus	Optic nerve atrophy
CENTRAL VISION LOSS	Color vision problems
Visual cortex damage	Retrolental fibroplasia
	Retinoblastoma
	Diabetic retinopathy
	Optic tumors

FIGURE 10.3
Conditions of the eye.

critical as a cause of visual impairment. Vitamin supplements, as well as increasing the student's intake of fruits, vegetables, milk, protein, and eggs when possible in a deficient diet, can prevent nutritional blindness, also known as xerophthalmia. Substance abuse during pregnancy, especially during the first trimester, can cause visual impairments in a newborn and could be partially responsible for the current increase in visual impairments (Smith, 2005). Systemic diseases such as diabetes, if untreated or treated inconsistently, can lead to visual impairment or blindness. Diabetic retinopathy is causally linked to diabetes and results when the blood supply to the retina is compromised due to the diabetic condition. A host of viral infections can cause visual problems. Measles (rubella) affects vision when contracted by pregnant women during the first trimester of pregnancy. A major outbreak of rubella in the early 1960s left many infants with varying degrees of visual impairment. Trachoma and river blindness (onchocerciasis) are both spread by infection-bearing flies and lead to scarring of the cornea and blindness if untreated. More common in underdeveloped countries, they can be controlled, when possible, by keeping eyes clear of flies and, in the case of river blindness, using the medications ivermectin and amocarzine to kill the parasites that damage vision (Smith, 2005). Sexually contracted and transmitted infections such as the AIDS virus, chlamydia, and gonorrhea can be passed from a mother to her infant. Accommodation of delivery procedures or, in cases of chlamydia or gonorrhea, application of topical ointments can prevent damage if the infection is diagnosed soon enough. Finally, poisoning can occur as a result of excessive amounts of oxygen administered to some premature infants in an attempt to keep them alive. The resulting condition, called retinopathy of prematurity (ROP), causes damage to the retina and can range from mild impairment to blindness (Heward, 2006).

Refractive Problems

Refraction is the ability of the eye to focus light rays on the retina. Several visual conditions can be classified as refractive disorders. For the purposes of this section, we have classified hyperopia, myopia, astigmatisms, cataracts, and ocular albinism as refractive disorders.

Hyperopia, most commonly known as farsightedness, results from the failure of the cornea and the lens of the eye to focus light appropriately. As a result, the individual can focus on objects at a distance but not objects that are close. **Myopia,** or nearsightedness, is similar, except that individuals with this condition can focus on objects that are close but not objects at a distance. **Astigmatisms** result in blurred vision. They are caused by an uneven curve of the cornea or lens of the eye. This produces images on the retina that are not equally in focus. Astigmatisms occur frequently and are almost always correctable with surgery or corrective glasses. If undetected or uncorrected, astigmatisms can lead to visual and educational difficulties. Cataracts occur when the lens becomes clouded and vision is masked. The opacity of the lens can cause severe visual loss. Surgical procedures are usually the major course of treatment. Ocular albinism, also called aniridia, is characterized by a lack of color in the iris of the eye. This leads to extreme sensitivity to light, reduced visual acuity, and sometimes nystagmus (defined in a following section). Color vision may also be impaired. Aside from the accommodations needed in the classroom and the use of light-reducing lenses, this condition is often not an educational problem of real consequence (Heward, 2006; Menaker & Batshaw, 1997; Sattler & Evans, 2002).

Retinal and Optic Nerve Problems

Numerous conditions of the retina and optic nerve have serious consequences on vision and, in turn, on education. The following is only a partial listing and definitions of the most commonly occurring retinal and optic nerve problems.

The most common retinal and optic nerve disorders are retinal degeneration and retinal detachment. Retinal degeneration can be the result of infection, or it may be inherited. Often, the underlying cause of the deterioration is unknown. This is a particularly difficult condition because there is no widely accepted treatment and the rate of degeneration is often uncontrollable. Students with retinal degeneration are usually enrolled in special educational programs as soon as the condition is diagnosed (Caton, 1993).

Retinal detachments occur when the retina becomes separated from the outer layers of the eye tissue. This condition causes interruption in the transmission of visual signals for the brain to interpret. This condition, when correctly diagnosed, can often be repaired surgically.

A similar but somewhat less devastating condition is macular degeneration, a condition that causes the macula, a small area near the center of the retina, to gradually deteriorate. A result is that peripheral vision is retained while central vision is lost, causing difficulties in writing and reading. Fortunately, macular degeneration is rare in elementary and secondary students (Heward, 2006).

Retinitis pigmentosa is a hereditary disorder that causes degeneration of the retina and a resulting narrowing of the field of vision. It is progressive in nature and leads to eventual blindness. One of its earliest symptoms is night blindness or extreme difficulty seeing in dimly lit environments. Coloboma is another congenital disorder wherein the retina is malformed, resulting in both visual field and visual acuity problems.

Glaucoma occurs when the flow of fluids in the eye is restricted. Increased fluid pressure in the eye can eventually sever the blood supply to the optic nerve, damaging the retina and causing blindness. The cause of glaucoma is unknown; onset may be gradual or sudden. Glaucoma can be counteracted if detected early. During its earliest stages, those affected report that lightbulbs and other illumination sources appear to have halos surrounding them (Sattler & Evans, 2002).

Cortical visual impairment results from damage or dysfunction of parts of the brain responsible for visual functioning. A variety of causes have been noted, including infections and stroke. Some infants are blind at birth and have an improvement of vision over time. Students with cortical visual impairment are sometimes subject to fluctuations in vision (Hallahan & Kauffman, 2006).

Less severe in terms of their impact on educational and social functioning are color vision problems. Problems of the retina can result in diminished abilities to differentiate colors. Usually these problems have little or no effect on visual acuity. They can cause problems at any time but can be noticeable at the primary level of education, where many curriculum activities revolve around color-matching tasks and the identification of learning-center materials by color. Color vision problems occur in varying degrees of severity.

Eye Muscle Problems

The two major eye muscle problems are strabismus and nystagmus. **Strabismus** is the result of improper muscle functioning that causes either or both eyes to be directed inward. When this occurs, two separate images may be sent to the visual cortex of the brain. The brain disregards one of the images sent by the affected eyes, which can lead to eventual blindness in one eye. Strabismus frequently can be corrected by surgery or corrective lenses. **Nystagmus** is characterized by rapid, involuntary movements of the eyes, usually laterally. These movements make it difficult to focus on objects and cause dizziness and nausea. Nystagmus is often a sign of concomitant inner ear or brain dysfunction (Hallahan & Kauffman, 2006; Menaker & Batshaw, 1997; Sattler & Evans, 2002).

Central Vision Loss

Damage to the visual cortex, the area of the brain responsible for decoding the signals sent along the optic nerve, can lead to visual insufficiency at many different levels. It can result in figure-ground discrimination problems, an inability to distinguish items in the foreground from items in the background, which in turn makes it difficult to distinguish objects from one another. In addition, cortical visual problems usually occur with other disorders, such as CP or epilepsy. A given student's coexisting attention span difficulties might lead to visual functioning fluctuations, making the measurement of the visual impairment a difficult task.

IDENTIFICATION PROCESS

The most widely used institutional strategies for identifying students with visual impairments are acuity screenings and functional visual assessments. Often, these screenings and assessments are used together to obtain the information needed prior to suggesting educational placement changes. In addition, parents, other family members, and teachers should be alert for specific signs of potential visual difficulty.

Visual Acuity Screenings

The screening test used most often for visual acuity uses the Snellen chart and is routinely administered by the school nurse or a pediatrician. The two most popular versions use the letter E presented in different sizes and placed in different positions, or alphabet letters of different sizes. The chart, or sometimes a projection of the chart, is placed 20 feet from the person being tested. The eight rows of symbols or letters correspond to normal vision at 15, 20, 30, 40, 50, 70, 100, and 200 feet (Heward, 2006; Smith, 2005). Normal visual acuity is measured by how accurately a person can see a symbol or letter at 20 feet. Thus, normal vision is 20/20. A score of 20/40 means that the person being tested can see at 20 feet what a person with normal vision can see from a distance of 40 feet. The distance of 20 feet is used because at this distance, when light rays enter the eyes, no accommodation is required of the eye to focus the rays; the eye is at rest. This is thought to give the truest measure of sharpness and clarity of vision. People with visual acuity measures between 20/70 and 20/200 in the better eye with correction are considered to have low vision. Acuity below 20/200 classifies a person as legally blind (Hallahan & Kauffman, 2006). Referrals for further testing and possible correction with lenses are usually made when students screened using the Snellen chart obtain the following results: 3-year-olds, 20/50 or less; 4-year-olds, 20/40 or less; and 5-year-olds, 20/30 or less (National Society for the Prevention of Blindness, 1990).

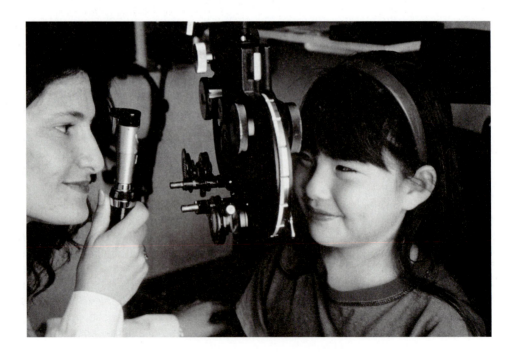

The Snellen chart procedure, despite its relative ease of administration and widespread use, has some limits in identification of visual impairment. Most obvious is that it measures visual acuity at a distance. Distance vision is not nearly as critical for school activities as is the near vision required for reading and other activities. The procedure also does not provide the schools with any measure or prediction about a student's ability to use sight to learn to read. Visual acuity and visual efficiency are not the same skill (Hallahan & Kauffman, 2006). Another measure of visual acuity is called contrast sensitivity. Size alone as measured by the Snellen chart procedure may not be an adequate measure of acuity. It may also be necessary to determine how well a person can see something in contrast to its background.

Functional Vision Assessments

Students who share similar visual impairments may use their residual vision in markedly different ways. Although visual acuity is certainly important, it does not in and of itself determine how well or poorly a student can compensate and function in the environment. Visual capacity, visual attention, and visual efficiency are other factors that are often considered when conducting a functional vision assessment. **Visual capacity** is in some ways an expansion of visual acuity. What can actually be seen includes acuity, the amount of usable visual field, and how the student responds to information presented visually. Visual attention consists of four distinct parameters:

1. Visual alertness, or how sensitive a student is to environmental visual stimuli
2. Visual selection, which is the ability to select information from different sources
3. Degree of attention, which is measured by the ability to change attention from one visual stimulus to another
4. Processing capability, or the ability to make sense of visual input

Visual efficiency depends on how well the individual can use instructional accommodations or alternate methods that depend on auditory or tactile stimuli (Smith, 2005). Changing seat placement can enhance efficiency. Other techniques include providing appropriate lighting, adapting materials, using specialized equipment, and modifying classroom teaching techniques.

Assessment of functional vision can be complicated with students who have not fully developed their language skills or who have multiple handicaps that make accurate assessment challenging (Batista & Rassi, 2001; Sattler & Evans, 2002). Examples of the types of test items that provide information for the functional vision assessments discussed here might be learning at what distance a student can imitate facial expressions, testing the ability to identify classmates, or even monitoring the ability to use sight to locate a cubby or personal possessions in a closet. Can the student visually track moving objects? Can he or she move efficiently over different surfaces? Is the student able to visually complete puzzles? Does changing the contrast between the test items and the background change the performance? Functional evaluations also try to test the ability to use visual skills in different settings and for different activities. Different visual skills are needed to function in brightly lit playgrounds and dimly lit hallways or to read labels on cans and direction signs on walls. A well-conceived assessment will enable the team working with the student and parents to make decisions about whether to use print or braille, the level of assistive services needed, types of changes in the materials, use of visual enhancement devices, and the type of educational placement required for the optimal educational experience.

Even before the vision screenings mandated by law are conducted, parents and others in a student's environment should be alert for specific signs that suggest visual impairment. The Kentucky Society for the Prevention of Blindness (1990) listed nine signs that may be significant (see Box 10.1). Other signs include recurring styes; reports of dizziness, headaches, or nausea following close eye work; and reports of blurred or double vision.

In summary, systematic identification processes should involve comprehensive screenings, referrals for complete evaluations, and follow-up activities to be certain that recommendations are followed. The usual steps in the process can be outlined as follows:

1. Concern about vision by a family member
2. Visual acuity screening test failure
3. Ophthalmologist determination of disorder
4. Optometrist and low vision expert determination of whether the impairment can be corrected
5. Functional evaluation of low vision
6. Evaluation by an orientation and mobility specialist
7. Intelligence testing by a school psychologist
8. Comprehensive determination of the potential effects of the visual impairment on academic, communication, social/emotional, sensorimotor, and orientation and mobility functioning by a teacher of students who are visually impaired, an orientation and mobility specialist, a speech-language pathologist, and a general education teacher

---

BOX 10.1
WHAT EVERY TEACHER SHOULD KNOW

Nine Warning Signs

Does the child exhibit any of the following behaviors?

1. Clumsiness and trouble walking in unfamiliar settings
2. Holding the head in an awkward position or holding material close to the eyes to see it
3. Lack of attention to written information on blackboards or other visual presentations
4. A constant need for explanation of what is happening at events
5. Extreme sensitivity to glare or loss of vision in different types of light
6. Extreme squinting
7. Excessive eye rubbing
8. Poking the eyes with fingers or knuckles
9. Physical anomalies such as swollen eyes or strabismus

Source: From *Handbook for Preschool Vision Screening* (p. 17), by the Kentucky Society for the Prevention of Blindness, 1990, Louisville, KY: Author.

9. Estimate of social and daily living skills needs by a teacher of students who are visually impaired, an orientation and mobility specialist, a daily living professional, and family members

PROGRAMS

Understanding educational programming for students with visual impairments requires more than simply looking at curriculum changes. This section will explore some introductory information about the settings and service delivery models in which educational experiences are offered to students with low vision and students who are blind and the educational assessments beyond identification needed to construct meaningful, individually designed educational programs. Programming initiated through early intervention and preschool services; primary, secondary, and postsecondary curriculum accommodations; and transition services in the form of adult living instruction will be discussed. The special listening, orientation, and mobility skills that are vital to independent functioning and socialization will be highlighted. No discussion of programming for people who are visually impaired can ignore the role of technology, from the use of canes to the latest computer technology. Box 10.2 provides some examples of low- and high-technological assistance.

The primary goal of special education for students with visual impairments is to reduce as much as possible the vision-related handicaps they experience (Topor, Rosenblum, & Hatton, 2004). Although this primary goal is simple to state, implementing it for each individual with visual impairment requires a willingness to amass diagnostic information, sensitivity to students and their families, and access to the necessary facilities and equipment needed to ensure success. The majority of students eligible for special education services have some useful vision. Students classified as having low vision account for between 75 and 80 percent of school-age students who are visually impaired (Batshaw, 2003). In addition, within the group more than 80 percent who are classified as blind use print as their primary way of learning. They use their residual vision as a primary means of learning and usually learn to read print (Ferrell & Muir, 1996; Heward, 2006).

BOX 10.2
WHAT EVERY TEACHER SHOULD KNOW ABOUT TECHNOLOGY

- Watches with digital output can announce the time in a voice when a button is pushed or can be set to announce the time hourly.
- Paper with dark, bold lines can facilitate writing. Another easily constructed aid is a card stock template with a cutout section in the place where the student is to sign a paper, a check, etc.
- Magnifiers are available in many sizes and strengths. Some are designed to be used with small areas and some are as large as a page. Magnification of computer screens is available in most operating systems and word processing programs.
- Scanners can provide enlarged print on computer screens. Documents or pictures can be scanned into a computer program and then adjusted to the intensity, contrast, or size needed by the student.
- Screens can be adjusted so that color and contrast are optimized for the individual.

Educational Settings for Students Who Are Visually Impaired

Most of the students attending residential schools for students who are blind or visually impaired have multiple conditions of special needs or have visual problems that are difficult to handle in the student's home. Some lack the necessary services in their home communities. Some are enrolled because their parents prefer the concentration of special services that residential schools can provide (Heward, 2006). It was not always this way. In 1940, only 10 percent of students with visual impairments were in the public schools. By 1992, 80 percent were enrolled in the public schools and 9 percent were in residential schools (American Printing House for the Blind, 1992a). The increase in students with visual impairments during the 1960s due to a rubella epidemic strained the capacity of the residential schools. At the same time, parents began to lobby for "mainstream" education or access to the general curriculum. They believed that there were many social and life skill advantages in functioning in general classrooms, living at home, and being a more integral part of normal family life (Pillips, 2003). As a result, students with visual impairments are now enrolled in general classrooms at their neighborhood public schools. They and their teachers receive itinerant or consultative special education services to support their general classroom placements (Smith, 2005). Only about 17 percent of the students are placed in separate classrooms within public schools (Heward, 2006).

This change of placement for students has changed the role of the residential schools drastically. They now serve as statewide resource centers, providing materials and specialists to consult with general education teachers. They are able to offer short courses and special intensive summer programs for teachers and students. Often they are responsible for maintaining all types of outreach programs designed to meet family needs. The remaining full-time educational programs for residential students characteristically maintain a "separate but equal" approach to education from kindergarten through grade 12. Their students are usually isolated from sighted students except for any classes in which the residential students may be enrolled at the local public schools. The programming at residential schools allows for a concentration of specialized services, such as orientation, mobility, and independent living skills training managed by on-site specialists (Corn & Koenig, 2002). A current issue of importance is whether these special services outweigh the benefits of inclusion in general schools. This issue is more fully discussed in the "Issues of Importance" section of this chapter.

Local schools operate under some combination of the following five plans to provide an educational setting for students with visual impairments. The first plan is the special class plan, sometimes called the self-contained classroom. In this setting, students are housed in a special classroom and receive most instruction there. There may be some nonacademic integration, but it is not usually the practice to provide academic integration with students who are sighted. This setting is most appropriate for students with multiple disabilities who are not able to benefit from general education classes. The second plan is known as the cooperative class plan. In this rarely used plan, the students are grouped into a special education class and divide their time between the special class and the general classroom for academic subjects. Most nonacademic experiences are with general educators. The third plan is the resource room setting. Students with visual impairments are placed in general education settings and leave them to go to a resource room for special help in academic areas in which they are having difficulty. Thus, they spend most of their time in the general classroom, leaving only when it is necessary. The fourth plan is the itinerant teacher plan. Students are housed in a general classroom, and a specially trained teacher who serves several schools provides special instructions and materials. The fifth plan, the teacher-consultant plan, is similar to the itinerant plan except that with the teacher-consultant plan, the specially trained itinerant teacher works with general teachers and other school personnel rather than directly with students.

In practice, schools employ combinations of the plans described, varying the setting depending on the needs of the student and the resources available to the school district. Placement decisions are always made by IEP committees, who use the data from eye examinations and medical, developmental, social history, and behavioral reports provided by parents, teachers, and other appropriate specialists. These plans and settings change as the student changes and becomes more independent.

Early intervention services are usually home based, with itinerant specialists providing information and programs for family members and for the student (Topor et al., 2004). Preschoolers and toddlers are also educated in self-contained classrooms or in other locations where students with visual impairments can be integrated into play and other activities with sighted peers.

Educational Assessments

Once a setting is determined, a plan must be developed to guide professionals and parents. After determining that the student has visual impairments and possibly assessing how the student uses his or her residual sight to learn, the task is to determine what, if any, special educational experiences are desired. Educational assessments help determine what special services are needed. They can be based on a given student's specific needs in academic skills, communication skills, social/emotional skills, sensory/motor skills, orientation and mobility skills, daily living skills, or career and vocational skills.

As an IEP team of professionals and parents evaluates each of these areas, a plan will evolve to meet the individual needs of each student. The school evaluation team should minimally consist of a school psychologist, a speech-language pathologist, an orientation and mobility specialist, and a teacher of students with visual impairments. Specific characteristics displayed by any given student might also call for the inclusion of an occupational therapist, a behavior specialist, an audiologist, a low vision specialist, or a physical therapist, among others on the evaluation and planning team. Parents, caretakers, and other family members form a vital part of the team.

Each professional will use assessment tools specific to his or her specialty area. In general, the assessment tools will be either specially designed for the student who is visually impaired, adapted for the student's needs, or used in their original form with no accommodation for the visual impairment (Caton, 1993). Assessment tools designed specifically for young students with visual impairments include tests such as the Cognitive Test for the Blind (CTB) (Nelson, Dial, & Joyce, 2002); the Oregon Project for Visually Impaired and Blind Preschool Children (OR Project) (Brown, Simmons, & Methvin, 1986); the Mangold Developmental Program of Tactile Perception and Braille Letter Recognition (Mangold, 1977); the Intelligence Test for Visually Impaired Children (ITVIC) (Dekker, 1993); and the Revised Peabody Mobility Scale (Harley, Wood, & Merbler, 1981).

Other factors considered during the educational assessment include the etiology of the impairment, because some conditions require a special setting or accommodations such as bright lighting or highly contrasted print; whether the condition is degenerative and will eventually lead to blindness and a reliance on braille; and the age of onset of the condition so that teachers will know how much sight memory the student may have (Bishop, 1996; Erin & Koening, 1997; Lussenhop & Corn, 2002).

Curricular Accommodations and Special Programming

Once the educational assessment is completed, teachers and other specialists can begin to help students and their families by implementing the plan they have cooperated in conceiving. Although each student may have different needs, no one student is so different that his or her needs cannot be anticipated and provided for with either curricular accommodations or special programming. In addition, the degree of impairment will dictate the level and intensity of programming. Regardless of their classification, all students with visual impairments share some of the same goals. They need to learn to read, write, and move about in their environment. The degree of visual impairment does not change this need; it only structures how students, their families, and their teachers go about accomplishing these goals.

The most dramatic change has been in how students with low vision are being educated. Most educators credit Barraga (1964, 1970, 1980, 1983) with changing the basic philosophy and implementation of intervention strategies for students with low vision. Prior to her work, "sight conservation classes" were the norm for students with visual impairment. These classes were designed to help the students preserve their sight, as if it were a limited commodity that could be exhausted if not used sparingly. Barraga demonstrated that students with low vision should be helped to use their vision in a proactive way. For most of the students, this meant getting the maximum use of their residual vision rather than attempting to ration it. The students needed to be taught how to get information directly from visual experiences. They also needed to learn to appreciate visual input and use their vision when planning and carrying out tasks (Corn, 1989; Heward, 2006).

Early Intervention

Special services begin with early intervention. There are valid reasons to offer early assistance to families that goes beyond kindness. Failure to provide experiences and information early in the life of a student with visual impairment can complicate all the attempts to achieve normal functioning that follow. Primary behaviors such as crawling and early socialization may be delayed due to a lack of the motivation that is inherent in infants and toddlers who use sight. Infants and toddlers with visual impairment explore close to their bodies and need to be stimulated to reach beyond themselves (Topor et al., 2004). It is also critical to prevent secondary disabilities from developing. These problems are not automatically part of visual impairment but can be the result of failure to compensate for visual deficits. Examples might be the failure to infants to bond with parents, delays in ear-and-hand coordination, or the development of inappropriate self-stimulating behaviors (Warren & Hatton, 2002).

Parents and other family members are critical in early intervention programs. They often need support in physically managing and in understanding the extra effort that will be required to provide needed experiences, from early socialization to providing games that help in all types of exploration (Chen, 1996). The line between overprotection, which disables a student's development, and poor judgment, which places a student in danger, must be constantly redrawn. The fears that all parents feel for their students are magnified when visual impairment may be seen as preventing the most primary of self-protective behaviors from developing.

Preschool Programs

Preschool programs in both homes and centers continue the work begun with early intervention. In the best of circumstances, preschool programs are staffed by a teacher of students who are visually impaired, an orientation and mobility specialist, a speech-language pathologist, an occupational therapist, and a physical therapist. All these professionals should be available to parents and encourage their involvement in the preschool activities (Koenig & Holbrook, 2000). A goal of preschool programs is to help students develop the skills needed to transfer successfully from the home to the school setting. Often, preschool activities are practice for the behavior that will be necessary at school. They can be as specific as drill in language and listening skills, preacademics, initial literacy skills, and fine and gross motor play. They might deal with the use of residual vision for mobility or for planning and executing tasks. At times, socialization, confidence-building, and independence-fostering activities are appropriate. Preschool programs might also introduce unfamiliar assistive technology that will later aid in learning. As with early intervention programs, preschool programs focus on continuing to support families in their efforts to rear students in the most positive environment possible. Through these programs and the experiences, support, and counseling they offer, students will develop and gain a strong sense of themselves and their capabilities (Smith, 2005).

Reading and Writing

Once school formally begins, the program emphasis shifts to the reading, writing, and listening skills necessary to learn. The social emphasis is on the development of peer relationships and friendships. Skills allowing the students to get around in the school and other environments with independence, orientation and mobility skills are now needed as much as ever to help navigate the school setting as well as the after-school environment (Hallahan & Kauffman, 2006). Reading and writing skills have traditionally been presented with some combination of modified type size and braille.

Braille uses a coded system of raised dots to represent letters, words, numbers, special contractions, and codes for different types of reading. This system was developed in 1829 by Louis Braille, who was blind. Braille is a fairly complicated system to learn and takes a good deal of practice to master. Training in braille with a teacher of students who are visually impaired usually begins during kindergarten (Sacks et al., 1990). Writing in braille requires the use of a slate and stylus. The slate is a metal frame that holds paper in the appropriate position while the stylus, a penlike device, punches the code onto the paper. A brailler or braillewriter can also be used to write in braille. The braillewriter is a six-key machine that embosses braille dots onto paper in the coded form or cells necessary to spell in braille. Writing in braille requires the manual dexterity that is usually developed by the fifth grade (Sacks et al., 1990). Computers have also been developed that can print and translate regular print into braille. Using braille is a comparatively slow process. The good braille reader can read about 100 words per minute. Once the primary system of literacy for the blind (Heward, 2006), braille is now less popular than in the past. In 1963, more than 50 percent of students who were severely visually impaired used braille to read and write. In 1978, the figure had dropped to 20 percent; by 1992, only 10 percent of students who were blind relied on braille (American Printing House for the Blind, 1992b).

Modified type size is the other major alternative for developing literacy skills. Figure 10.4 provides some examples of different sizes of type. The goal with large type is to use the smallest magnification that will be useful and then try to transfer to normal-size type as the student matures (Heward, 2006).

All accommodation systems have advantages and disadvantages: Large type is easy to use, funds are available to get books and materials, and the materials themselves are not particularly delicate and are sometimes easy to carry. The problems include the following: Magnification often distorts printed material; when photocopies

This is 12 point type.
AN UPPERCASE SAMPLE.
A lowercase sample.

This is 14 point type.
AN UPPERCASE SAMPLE.
A lowercase sample.

This is 18 point type.
AN UPPERCASE SAMPLE.
A lowercase sample.

This is 24 point type.
AN UPPERCASE SAMPLE.
A lowercase sample.

This is 36 point type.
AN UPPERCASE SAMPLE.
A lowercase sample.

FIGURE 10.4
Examples of different sizes of type fonts.

are used to magnify print, the material is usually limited to only black-and-white reproductions; and despite their portability, large-type books often become unwieldy and difficult to manage. The most serious drawback is the limited availability of large-type works after the school years. People who rely only on large type run the risk of becoming nonfunctional readers (Heward, 2006). Some authorities suggest that students who are able to use large print should also be taught braille (Koenig & Holbrook, 2000). Audiocassette versions of material and personal readers are also available, but limited, options. For some, minor accommodations such as book placement or special lighting enable the use of normal print for learning.

Regardless of the method, many students have difficulty learning to read. It can be a fatiguing process, and students often require more practice, more drill, and more repetition than their sighted peers (Hallahan & Kauffman, 2006; Lewis & Tolla, 2003).

It is a challenge for teachers to provide these experiences without overusing any one type of drill. Students with visual impairments must rely on auditory (listening) skills as well as tactile skills to compensate for the information they might miss visually (Craig, Hough, & Churchwell, 2002). Listening skills do not develop automatically and are becoming more and more critical as the availability of recorded material is increasing. Smith (1972) divided listening skills into five categories: attentive, analytic, appreciative, marginal, and selective. Attentive listening takes place when the listener focuses on one form or source of communication. Telephone use requires attentive listening, as does following directions. Analytic listening requires that the listener not only listen but also prepare to analyze or interpret the information received. Asking a student to explain what the author meant by a "slippery character" in a story means the student must not only attend to the story but also interpret the author's intent. Appreciative listening occurs when listening purely for the sake of enjoyment. Marginal listening takes place when the auditory signal is part of the background and not a primary part of activity. Background music in a restaurant during a conversation requires marginal listening. Selective listening, on the other hand, requires focusing on one signal and disregarding others. Selective listening for a person with visual impairment takes place when he or she ignores the background music on an elevator and listens for the chimes that announce the number of each floor. Listening skills need to be a part of the curriculum for students who are visually impaired. An understanding of the type of listening required for the various situations the student will encounter can guide the teacher in structuring learning experiences that will hone the needed auditory skills.

Developing peer relationships for many students who are visually impaired does not occur without some family or teacher help (D'Allura, 2002; Golub, 2004; Kef, 2002; Lewis, 2002). Informal interactions are particularly difficult to initiate. These interactions, which usually occur during lunch, physical education, or recess periods, are often visually and auditorily confusing for the student who is visually impaired. Quite often, such interactions emphasize the student's weaknesses, such as shooting a basketball or playing tag. Teacher-initiated activities that call for pairing allow for social as well as task-related conversations. One-to-one interactions are always easier than group interactions. Many adolescents with vision problems struggle with social acceptance even though they may have a best friend; they must work harder at establishing and maintaining friendships (Dimigen, Roy, & Horn, 2001). It is important for teachers and parents to attempt to keep the skills needed to complete a task balanced so that the sighted student is not always the leader. Peer interactions with other students who are visually impaired are often helpful because they can provide a forum for sharing experiences.

Orientation and Mobility Training

Orientation and mobility skills allow students with visual impairments to move about in their environment and interact within it for many types of learning and for socialization, concept development, and independence (Lahav & Mioduser, 2004). The special instruction necessary is intensified during the primary school years. In addition to using residual sight, students with visual impairment have a choice of four mobility aids: long canes, guide dogs, human guides, and electronic devices.

The long cane or Hoover cane was developed by Richard Hoover in 1944. Users sweep the long white cane in front of them, touching the ground lightly as they walk. They receive cues by echo and tactile feedback about uneven surfaces, holes, stairways, and other barriers. The cane is reliable, with no batteries or moving parts to fail. However, using it efficiently requires training. The traditional approach of waiting until school age to train users is being reconsidered. A more current view suggests that students begin to use them as soon as they can walk independently (Hill, 1997; Hill & Black, 2003). Some youngsters will require shorter canes or other accommodations.

Guide dogs are not recommended very often for students. The size of the dogs, their relatively fast walking pace, and their need for care are drawbacks for young people. However, they do provide faster reactions to potential danger than do walking canes.

Human guides provide the greatest freedom of movement. However, dependence on human guides is not practical in most cases. In addition, some feel that the use of human guides can disrupt or retard the development of orientation and mobility skills (Hallahan & Kauffman, 2006).

Electronic devices may be the wave of the future for enhancing orientation and mobility. Many that are currently available are both expensive and experimental in nature. Typically they use some form of laser beam or sonic wave to provide feedback. Orientation and mobility training is a well-developed specialty taught by orientation and mobility specialists, described in the "Professionals" section of this chapter.

Daily Living Skills

Daily living skills such as eating, bathing, dressing, and toileting are not usually taught in the school setting but rather at home. Many of these skills are acquired by observation and incidental learning. However, they require special effort during home teaching

(Lewis & Iselin, 2002; Lindo & Nordholm, 1999). Teachers monitor students' acquisition of skills and report to the parents and the educational team if intervention is necessary. When students who are visually impaired fail to acquire daily living skills at home, the responsibility falls to the schools. Obviously, daily living skills are needed in the classroom as well as at home.

Middle and Secondary Schools

Middle and secondary school experiences follow the guidelines established during the primary years. However, there may need to be greater emphasis on experiences that will reinforce self-confidence and self-esteem. The learning process should parallel that of sighted students, using whatever accommodations are needed to master the information presented. Special curricular packages such as MAVIS (Materials Adaptation for Students with Visual Impairments in the Social Studies) and SAVI (Science Activities for the Visually Impaired) are available to assist teachers and can be obtained from agencies, residential school libraries, or itinerant teachers.

Because the majority of students who are visually impaired are placed in general classroom settings, many suggestions are available to help the general classroom teacher be as effective as possible in reaching these students with as little disruption in teaching style as possible. For example, all students learn better when given previews of information that will be presented. All are helped by advanced organizers such as highlighting critical vocabulary, giving appropriate background information, and presenting outlines of information to be presented (Carter, Wehby, & Hughes, 2005; Deshler et al., 2001; Garb, 2000; Smith, 2005). Students with low vision benefit from teacher attempts to use descriptive oral language, rather than speech that refers to visually based material. For example, a teacher who says, "Look at the number next to the letter I have written on the board," would be more effective if she said, "Look at the number 4 next to the letter A that I have written on the board." The habitual reading aloud of information on blackboards and overheads will not disrupt class teaching, but it will help a student with visual impairment. Large-type overheads and handouts, when possible, will also help while not disrupting general classroom activity. Sometimes special actions such as giving written copies of orally presented material and audiotaping lectures may be necessary. See Box 10.3 for more suggestions.

Students who are blind often can be taught in general classrooms with minor accommodations (Abner & Lahm, 2002; Corn et al., 2003). Suggestions from experts (Barraga & Morris, 1980; Lewis & Allman, 2000; Lussenhop & Corn, 2002) range from making certain that the student is seated close to the teacher's desk, blackboard, and door to explaining the social rules of the classroom to the student as often as necessary. Providing adequate lighting and space necessary for special equipment and making the classroom as obstacle free as possible will also enhance the learning environment. Simple rules such as opening and closing all doors fully, placing materials in consistent places, and keeping distracting noises to a minimum will also reduce the amount of time needed to care for the needs of the student who is blind. Routinely checking with students to find out whether their classroom needs are being met will often short-circuit problems before they can develop. Specialists and consultants are almost always available to share the concerns of students and their teachers and assist in solving problems.

Transition to Independent Living

The transition from the educational system to independent living is also a critical time in the life of a person with visual impairment. Some educators are concerned that schools place too much emphasis on teaching academic skills and too little on teaching

BOX 10.3
WHAT EVERY TEACHER SHOULD DO

Effective Teaching Strategies

- Eliminate clutter in the classroom so that the student can move without surprises. Make tactile maps of the classroom, school, and other places so the student will know how to move easily through the areas.
- Place braille labels on items in the classroom. The student with a visual impairment will learn braille vocabulary and so will some of the other students in the class.
- Allow the student with a visual impairment to use a computer to produce work. Use a speech synthesizer with the computer so the student will know what has been written. A braille printer is useful for proofreading (although braille printers are noisy). A laser or inkjet printer will facilitate grading the work.
- Learn some braille. A student who is a braille reader does not spell words in a letter-by-letter correspondence to Standard English. The student will need to learn contracted braille. Allow the student as much mobility as possible.
- Have another student read assignments from books not available in braille or on tape. Students may also make tapes of the chapters. In this manner, both students will benefit from the readings. Other students may listen as the student with a visual impairment is listening to the science or social studies chapter.
- Recognize that some vocabulary words mean nothing to a person who has never seen the item. Allow other students to explain or make models or line drawings with string or puffy paint to convey concepts such as "Conestoga wagon" and other unknown words.
- If the student has some vision, use large print with lots of contrast, such as black letters on yellow paper. Do not assume that the enlarger on the copier is as good as large-print type.
- If the student has some vision, use a marker and allow the student to use a marker to write. The lines will be wider and easier to see.

living skills such as cooking, shopping, financial management, decision making, personal hygiene, social behavior, and recreational activities (Hallahan & Kauffman, 2006; Jorgensen-Smith & Lewis, 2004; Nagle, 2001).

The process of obtaining needed services itself is complicated. Despite the low incidence of visual handicaps, more than 1,000 agencies provide services and programs in the United States alone (Heward, 2006). Accessing these programs and obtaining eligibility to use their services can be an educational experience in itself. Some suggest that people who are blind should take courses in how to access the services of the variety of programs available to them.

Career assistance is needed to help people with visual handicaps become a productive part of the workforce. Only 29.4 percent of young adults with visual impairments were competitively employed 3 to 5 years after they left school, compared with 56.8 percent of all youths with disabilities and 69 percent of youths in general (Blackorby & Wagner, 1996). Many others are underemployed, working at jobs below their skill levels. Some guidance is clearly needed to help people with visual impairments make the transition from the sheltered school environment to independent adult living.

Technology

Including technology as a subheading of programming is merely a convenient way to provide the information. Technology does not exist in a vacuum; rather it is part of the continuum of attempts to provide better ways to accomplish the goals previously listed. Identifying aids to mobility, daily living, information accessing, and recreation will be the focus of this section.

Probably the simplest and most effective aid to mobility is the previously discussed Hoover cane. High-tech offshoots of the basic cane are devices such as the Miniguide (Hill & Black, 2003), which sends out ultrasonic beams that bounce off objects. Sensors pick up the reflected beams and provide electronic feedback to the user about their distance from objects and other spatial information. Daily living can be made easier by devices such as the Note Teller ("Talking Wallet," 1992), which identifies the denomination of paper money, or the Personal Companion, which accesses and dials phone numbers, keeps an appointment schedule, and even turns appliances on and off (Feinsilber, 1989). The ID Mate is a portable bar code reader for cans of vegetables or the flavor of a container of yogurt (Ingber, 2005).

Technology has made its most important contributions in the area of information transmission for educational and recreational purposes (Corn, 2000). Tactile, auditory, and visual enhancing aids, as either independent devices or parts of computers, provide access to the printed information vital to functioning in our society. The Optacon (optical-to-tactile converter) consists of a handheld scanner that, when passed over printed material, converts the print into tactile letters. It was one of the first "high-tech" portable units available. Many other devices have been marketed since (Hallahan & Kauffman, 2006).

The Kurzweil reader, first produced in 1975 and updated and improved since then, converts print into synthesized speech. The Kurzweil Omni 3000, the latest improvement for converting almost any typeface, also produces voice when a scanner moves over a line of type. The rate of speech and the gender of the voice are programmable (Kurzweil, 1996). An obvious advantage for students using this device is that they can use the same materials as their classmates without waiting for special versions. The downside is that exclusive use of this or similar devices can have a negative impact on reading skills or the desire to improve them.

For braille readers, a refreshable braille device such as the VersaBraille saves time and space by converting braille onto tape cassettes, then replaying those tapes onto the machine's reading board. These devices consist of a portable laptop on which students can take notes, complete tests, or prepare papers. It can print in braille or conventional type. This enables more rapid communication with teachers not proficient in braille. Many can also be connected to talking word processors to obtain printed information (Heward, 2006). The Mountbatten Brailler is a braille embosser, a printer that creates the raised dots on the heavy paper. It also has a small screen that converts the braille created by the student into English text for a teacher, family member, or peer to read. It includes a speech option to announce letters or words and they are written. Teachers and others can input text using a computer keyboard and the device will braille it for a student, reducing the amount of time needed for access to the braille format (D'Andrea, 2005). Portable braille notetakers such as the BrailleLite, BrailleNote, and Braille-N-Speak can be used in class. Although very useful, many braille readers and professionals who work with them find that full function desktop and laptop computers can offer more features than a braille notetaker (Chong, 2004).

Electronic book readers such as Book Port, from American Printing House for the Blind, and BookCourier, from Springer Design Incorporated, allow students to access text files and to listen to MP3 players. They are portable, easy to use, and relatively inexpensive (Leventhal, 2004). Closed circuit television (CCTV) is being used to enlarge print size and broadcast it onto a television screen for almost instant access to printed materials (Holbrook & Healy, 2002). Less sophisticated but most highly used are talking books. Available since 1934, these recordings are readings of a large catalog of many kinds of books. In their latest form they allow for speech compression, which in turn allows greater amounts of information to be transmitted in shorter periods of time.

A service that parallels captioning for people who are deaf, called audiodescription, is now available for making television, plays, and movies more understandable for people who are visually impaired (Cronin & King, 1990). Descriptive Video Services of Boston, developed by WGBH, the National Public Radio station in Boston, provides a narration about television shows, plays, and movies that fills in the information missing when listening to the soundtracks alone. It provides descriptions of costumes, scenes, actors' body language, and other critical visual information. The narration is provided during silences in the action.

The future of technology is constrained only by the cost of the devices and the ability of those who need them to select the appropriate equipment. Currently, these are formidable drawbacks. Financial resources are limited for many people with visual impairments, and it is not clear whether social service agencies are responsible for providing and upgrading the latest in technology at the expense of the public. Providing services and programs is not a cut-and-dried science. Many controversies exist, and attempts are always being made to improve services.

ISSUES OF IMPORTANCE

The four issues discussed in this section are not the only issues of importance. However, they represent major concerns of educators, parents, and people who are visually impaired. Doubts have arisen about whether or not full inclusion in the public schools is truly the LRE. Some feel that a return to the residential school concept might be more effective. The decline in literacy that has accompanied the rejection of braille has led to a backlash and the proposal of the so-called braille bills, which call for increased availability of braille for people who are visually impaired. The sexual information deficits and vulnerability that seem to accompany visual impairments are the third issue to be highlighted. Finally, technological advances are both exciting and expensive; the issue is who is responsible for paying for them.

Inclusion

The movement of students with visual impairments from residential to public schools was discussed in the previous section. It was a time of optimism. Educators hoped that the isolation imposed by the segregation of students who were visually impaired would evaporate as they became a more integrated part of the general education system and a more functional part of their own families. However, despite the obvious advantages of family and educational integration, many educators are voicing concerns that the graduates of general school systems do not attain the skills needed for independent living. They are concerned that students who are visually impaired need direct, intensive special instruction in social skills, use of assistive technology, career education, leisure education, braille, and orientation and mobility, which are not a part of the general curriculum (Corn et al., 2000; D'Allura, 2002; Koenig & Holbrook, 2000; Lewis, 2002; Lewis & Allman, 2000). Sacks (1992) reported that even though students with visual impairments have spent their entire academic careers with sighted peers, they are still socially isolated and academically limited. Physical proximity does not automatically ensure that social and living skills will be met. Centers or residential schools might be the best placement for students with moderate and severe visual problems. Other educators take a more conciliatory view (Turnbull, Turnbull, Shank, & Smith, 2004), refusing to select one placement over another and voicing the opinion that a student's needs should dictate placement. Representatives from eight North American associations concerned about this issue formed a Joint Organizational Committee (1993) and issued the position paper reprinted in Figure 10.5.

Although the viewpoints presented in Figure 10.5 are well conceived, there is little data available to support any of the recommendations about which settings are most successful (Kirk et al., 2006). Harrell and Curry (1987) reported that there is no compelling evidence that integrated programs are of more benefit than the segregated residential programs that offer only limited and carefully planned opportunities to interact with nondisabled peers. Until more persuasive data-based arguments can be presented, this issue will remain unresolved.

Back to Braille

One of the side effects of the historical work of Barraga (1964) that placed more of an emphasis on the use of residual vision was a decrease in tactile learning. Students whose level of impairment falls between low vision and blindness are in danger of becoming functionally illiterate, unable to read print, and untutored in braille (Caton, 1993). The use of braille declined, and other methods to access information (electronic books, closed circuit television, audio aids) were taught. Along with the decline in the use of braille, a parallel decline in the literacy capabilities of students with visual impairments occurred (Hallahan & Kauffman, 2006). In the early 1990s, about half of people with visual impairments polled were nonreaders (American Printing House for the Blind, 1992a). A reaction to this disturbing trend was a return to teaching braille reading. Advocates feel that braille readers have advantages over those who rely on current technology in that they can skim read, take notes, and financially afford the

STATEMENT BY THE JOINT
ORGANIZATIONAL EFFORT

"Full inclusion," a philosophical concept currently advanced by a number of educators, is not a federal requirement of special education law. Proponents of "full inclusion" nevertheless take the position that all students with disabilities must receive their total instruction in the regular public school classroom regardless of individual needs. Unfortunately, "full inclusion" would eliminate all special placements, including "pull-out" services, resource rooms, and specialized schools. Such an arrangement would be seriously detrimental to the educational development of many students with disabilities.

   We, the national organizations of and for the blind, listed below, are firmly committed to appropriate educational opportunities designed to provide students with the competencies necessary to ensure full participation in society. It is significant to recognize that our field was the first to develop a broad range of special education options beginning with specialized schools as early as 1829, and extending to public school programs since 1900. These options have provided critically important educational preparation for several generations of highly successful and independent blind people. Based on this long and impressive record of success in making optimal use of both special and public school programs to meet the diverse needs of blind students, we strongly agree upon the following:

- If provided with timely and adequate specialized services by appropriately certified teachers, students who are blind or visually impaired can develop skills that will enable them to achieve success and independence as responsible citizens in a fully integrated society. If these students do not receive appropriate instruction designed to develop competencies that meet the sensory deficits of blindness and low vision, critical learning opportunities will be lost, thus diminishing the potential for future accomplishments. In this context, ample opportunities for instruction in such areas as braille, abacus, orientation and mobility, and use of prescribed optical devices must be made available to students, as needed.
- Educational decisions must be made on a case-by-case basis consistent with the Individuals with Disabilities Education Act (IDEA), which guarantees a Free, Appropriate Public Education in the "Least Restrictive Environment" (LRE) from among a "Full Continuum of Alternative Placements," based on the Individual Education Plan for each student. Educational decisions should not be made simply on the basis of philosophy, limited school budgets, administrative convenience, or concerns about socialization.
- Full inclusion in regular education classrooms for all students with disabilities irrespective of individual needs is in sharp conflict with procedural guarantees of IDEA.
- Least Restrictive Environment and Full Continuum of Alternative Placements are critically important IDEA

FIGURE 10.5
Making a difference.

system. Thirty-two states have passed Braille Bills (National Federation for the Blind, 2003). These legislative initiatives do not mandate the use of braille. Rather, they stress that students not be denied the opportunity to learn braille or to have braille learning made part of their IEPs. The two major components of most bills are that braille is to be available for students if any members of the IEP team, including parents, feel that it is indicated, and that teachers of students with visual impairments be proficient in braille (Hallahan & Kauffman, 2006).

Sexuality

Sex education and vulnerability to sexual assault are critical issues for people with visual impairments and those interested in their welfare. Students with visual impairments often mature with serious misconceptions and knowledge gaps about sex in general and reproduction in particular. Parents and teachers are uncomfortable giving information, and modesty makes getting information by touch impractical. In some European countries, live human models are used to familiarize students who are blind with anatomy. This is not a common practice in the United States. Persons who are visually impaired

provisions. LRE is not one sole physical location. It is, rather, a principle, which if properly applied, matches the need of the student with an appropriate school setting which provides meaningful challenges, realistic expectations, and maximum opportunities for achievement and development of healthy self-esteem.

- The regular education classroom may be considered the LRE if the student possesses sufficient readiness and survival skills and can be provided adequate supports, specialized services (from personnel trained in education of the visually impaired), and opportunities to develop skills commensurate with his or her potential. Extreme caution must be exercised so that full inclusion does not result in "full submersion," social isolation, "lowered" self-esteem, poor performance, or a setting in which services are unavailable.

- In cases where the needs of the student cannot be met in the regular classroom, an alternative education must be provided and be recognized as the LRE for that particular student. Such alternative placements should not be negatively viewed as discriminatory or as "segregated" settings when legitimately warranted to develop the needed skills for future integration in school and society.

- Since it has been clearly demonstrated that blind children benefit from interacting with disabled and non-disabled children, both interaction opportunities should be fully encouraged in whatever setting that is considered appropriate. We believe that the mandate in IDEA which states that "to the maximum extent appropriate, children with disabilities [should be] educated with children who are nondisabled," does not intend that blind children avoid interaction with each other.

We strongly urge that decision makers carefully consider and be sensitive to the impact of reform initiatives on the education of students with visual disabilities. Caution must be exercised to ensure that educational philosophy and trends such as full inclusion do not seriously endanger appropriate and specialized services for students who are blind or visually impaired. If properly implemented, IDEA can provide legal safeguards to ensure that all individual children can realize their full potential for independence and success.

American Council of the Blind
American Foundation for the Blind
Association for Education and Rehabilitation
    of the Blind and Visually Impaired
Blinded Veterans Association
Canadian Council of the Blind
Canadian National Institute for the Blind
National Federation of the Blind
National Library Service for the Blind and
    Physically Handicapped

need information not only about the social and emotional aspects of sexuality but also about the genetic transmission of visual impairments. Sexual safety is also a concern in what appears to be an increasingly hostile sexual environment in which AIDS and other sexually transmitted diseases are occurring in what some consider to be epidemic proportions. The vulnerability to sexual assault, especially for women who are visually impaired, should also be of concern. Pava (1994) reported survey results that indicate that one of three respondents had been the target of either attempted or actual sexual assault. Pava, Bateman, Appleton, and Glascock (1991) developed a rape prevention and self-defense curriculum for women with visual impairments.

Privacy, morality, religious beliefs, community standards, and a host of other societal concerns and taboos make it difficult to implement any standardized policies or guidelines regarding sexuality and people who are visually impaired. The difficulty in coping with this topic does not lessen its priority or necessity for attention.

Responsibility for Providing Needed Technology

The marvels of technology that are becoming available for people with visual impairments come with a curse for many who need them. The costs of these devices and aids are often beyond the means of the families that need them most. Although some agencies and community charitable organizations will help in providing needed equipment, most costs still fall on the individual or the family. Some equipment can be loaned only during the school year and must be returned during school breaks or permanently at graduation. Finding out about new equipment and choosing wisely among options is a task that requires technological sophistication that is not readily available to most families. Equipment that is obtained needs to be repaired or upgraded often, as it rapidly becomes obsolete. The question is a simple one: Who should pay for equipment that will enhance the lives of people who are visually impaired when they cannot afford to buy their own equipment? The answer is a jumble of reasons why specific agencies and institutions cannot be responsible. State educational institutions simply do not have the funds. IDEA does not automatically provide the money. Some feel it should; others feel it should not. Even when charitable organizations can purchase equipment initially, they cannot afford to maintain it or routinely replace it. The more militant feel that people with visual impairments should not be dependent on the kindness of charity for devices that will ensure that they are productive citizens. The more conservative may believe that there are many ways to make everyone's life, disabled or not, more productive, but that the costs of these life-improving sources are not and should not be the burden of taxpayers, beyond providing equal educational opportunities. Arguments and counterarguments can be made from all perspectives. Perhaps all have some degree of merit. However, regardless of philosophy, the problem remains that a good deal of the latest technology is beyond the means of those for whom it was designed.

DIVERSITY

A greater percentage of students from culturally and linguistically diverse backgrounds have severe visual impairment than do their peers from the mainstream culture (Kirchner & Peterson, 1988). The reasons for the higher incidence are not clear. However, speculation points toward higher rates of inadequate prenatal care, higher instances of prematurity for minority women, and less adequate health care in general for this population. Perhaps, linguistically and culturally diverse families would benefit from improved preventive health care procedures more than others.

Educational concerns for minority students with visual impairments are in reality no different from the concerns for sighted minority students. Culturally biased assessments and instructional techniques should be avoided. Sensitivity to familial structures needs to be developed, and unique cultural attitudes need to be respected. This is especially true because a large part of the programming during early intervention and the preschool years takes place in the home setting. Respect for individuals and their culture is a teacher characteristic highly correlated to student success. Because the numbers of minority professionals who work with students with visual impairments from culturally diverse backgrounds are not proportionately equal to those of their students, these professionals must make attempts to understand how insensitivity to diversity can have a negative impact on service provision. Scorn for a family that turns to a traditional healer before accepting programming, or failure to understand the resistance to encourage independence in a Hispanic student, can only lead to mistrust and delay in providing the best possible plan for a minority student with visual impairment.

PROFESSIONALS

Although many professionals can be a part of the life of a student with visual impairments, the primary ones we will discuss are medical (ophthalmologists, optometrists, opticians), educational (teachers of students who are visually impaired), orientation and mobility, and transitional specialists. Any given student may also need the care of physical therapists, occupational therapists, speech-language pathologists, dietitians, social workers, family counselors, and many other related professional workers who can provide care directly to the student who is visually impaired and his or her family.

Medical Professionals

The physical care of the vision falls to ophthalmologists, who are medical doctors who specialize in eye disorders. They are trained to perform surgery, conduct physical examinations, and prescribe medications and corrective lenses. Optometrists are able to measure vision and prescribe corrective lenses. Opticians fill prescriptions for glasses and corrective lenses.

Educators

The Council for Exceptional Children (2003) published suggested standards for the initial preparation and certification of teachers of students with visual impairments. The council mandates that university training programs prepare teachers who, upon completion of their program of studies, have knowledge and skills in the following eight areas as they relate to students who are visually impaired:

1. Philosophy, history, and legal foundations
2. Characteristics of learners who are visually impaired
3. Assessment, diagnosis, and evaluation of students with visual impairment
4. Instructional content and practices geared toward students who are visually impaired
5. Planning and managing the teaching and learning environment
6. Managing student behavior and social skills
7. Communication and collaborative partnerships
8. Professionalism and ethical practices

Among other skills, teachers of students who are visually impaired should be skillful in explaining the current trends in education, interpreting reports and diagnostic information from all professional sources, using and adapting assessment instruments, maintaining reports and records, developing individualized strategies, and choosing and using appropriate technologies to accomplish objectives. They need to be skillful in implementing generalization and maintenance plans and preparing and obtaining specially modified materials. It is their responsibility to lead in structuring an optimal learning environment for their students. They should be proficient in all aspects of braille and handwriting for students with low vision. They should have up-to-date knowledge of technological advances and devices and the ability to determine the devices' usefulness to individual students. Teachers of students who are visually impaired must be current in methods used to teach sexuality, recreational skills, social skills, and daily living skills. They are often critical in helping with transition services, counseling families, and consulting with appropriate professionals.

Certification of teachers of students who are visually impaired occurs at the state level. Information about the specific guidelines and requirements for any given state can be obtained by contacting the state director of special education at the address listed in Appendix A.

Orientation and Mobility Professionals

We have already discussed the tasks of the orientation and mobility specialist in the section on programming. The Association for Education and Rehabilitation of the Blind and Visually Impaired (AER) certifies orientation and mobility specialists. It also recognizes the orientation and mobility assistant, who provides selected services to students who are visually impaired under the direction and supervision of the orientation and mobility specialist. Specific requirements for certification can be obtained from the AER, which is listed in the "Professional Associations" section of this chapter. Generally speaking, certification usually requires at least 2 years of study at either the undergraduate or graduate level.

Transitional Specialists

Transitional specialists are a relatively new arrival on the care provision team. They are usually housed in school districts or within a state department of rehabilitation (Sacks & Pruett, 1992). Many have specialized training in helping those with visual impairments. The transition specialist monitors the implementation of an ITP with respect to the establishment of the student's relationships with adult agencies and employers. They are available for follow-up services and career counseling, referrals for continuing education, and similar necessary services (Sacks & Reardon, 1992; Siegel, Greener, Prieuer, Robert, & Gaylord-Ross, 1989). Transition specialists may be responsible for teaching skills such as advocating for individuals' rights with landlords, accessing public buildings with service dogs, and employing and supervising sighted assistants for driving, accounting, and reading mail (Turnbull et al., 2004). Given the high levels of unemployment and underemployment of people with visual impairment and the increasing complexity in selecting technological equipment and even locating agencies to help, the role of transition specialists is clearly becoming increasingly critical for full service provision.

DISCUSSION QUESTIONS

1. Should persons who are visually impaired but who have some usable vision be taught to read and write braille?
2. How have technological advances changed the curriculum for persons with visual impairments?
3. What is the prevalence of visual impairment?
4. Do students with visual impairment do better academically in a residential school, center-based day school, or neighborhood public school?
5. What causes visual impairments?
6. What delays can be expected for students with visual impairments?

7. How can early intervention assist with development for learners who are visually impaired?

8. What educational decisions should be addressed by the IEP team?

PROFESSIONAL ASSOCIATIONS AND PARENT OR SELF-HELP GROUPS

American Council of the Blind
1155 15th St. N.W., Suite 1004
Washington, DC 20005
202-467-5081 or 800-424-8666
E-mail: info@acb.org
www.acb.org

American Foundation for the Blind
11 Penn Plaza, Suite 300
New York, NY 10001
800-232-5463 (Hotline)
For publications, call: 800-232-3044
E-mail: afbinfo@afb.net
www.afb.org

Blind Children's Center
4120 Marathon Street
Los Angeles, CA 90029-0159
323-664-2153 or 800-222-3566
E-mail: info@blindchildrenscenter.org
www.blindchildrenscenter.org

National Association for Parents of the Visually Impaired, Inc.
P.O. Box 317
Watertown, MA 02472-0317
617-972-7441 or 800-562-6265
E-mail: napvi@perkins.org
www.napvi.org

National Association for Visually Handicapped
22 West 21st Street, 6th Floor
New York, NY 10010
212-889-3141
E-mail: staff@navh.org
www.navh.org

National Braille Association, Inc. (NBA)
3 Townline Circle
Rochester, NY 14623-2513
585-427-8260
E-mail: nbaoffice@nationalbraille.org
www.nationalbraille.org

National Braille Press
88 St. Stephen Street
Boston, MA 02115
617-266-6160 or 800-548-7323
E-mail: orders@nbp.org
www.nbp.org

National Eye Institute
31 Center Drive, MSC 2510
Bethesda, MD 20892-2510
301-496-5248
E-mail: 2020@nei.nih.gov
www.nei.nih.gov

National Federation of the Blind, Parents Division
1800 Johnson Street
Baltimore, MD 21230
410-659-9314, ext. 360
E-mail: nfb@nfb.org
www.nfb.org/nopbc.htm

National Library Service for the Blind and Physically Handicapped
Library of Congress
1291 Taylor Street, N.W.
Washington, DC 20011
202-707-5100 or 202-707-0744 (TTY) or 800-424-8567
E-mail: nls@loc.gov
www.loc.gov/nls

Prevent Blindness America
500 E. Remington Road
Schaumburg, IL 60173
847-843-2020 or 800-221-3004
E-mail: info@preventblindness.org
www.preventblindness.org

The Foundation Fighting Blindness (formerly the National Retinitis Pigmentosa Foundation)
11435 Cronhill Drive
Owings Mills, MD 21117-2220
888-394-3937 or 800-683-5551 (TTY)
410-568-0150 or 410-363-7139 (TTY)
E-mail: info@blindness.org
www.blindness.org

American Printing House for the Blind
P.O. Box 6085
1839 Frankfort Avenue
Louisville, KY 40206

Division for the Visually Handicapped
Council for Exceptional Children
1110 North Glebe Road, Suite 300
Arlington, VA 22201-5704

Journal of Visual Impairment and Blindness
15 West 16th Street
New York, NY 10011

RE:view (formerly *Education of the Visually Handicapped*)

Association for Education and Rehabilitation of the Blind and Visually Impaired (AER)
206 N. Washington Street
Alexandria, VA 22314

REFERENCES

Abner, G. H., & Lahm, E. A. (2002). Implementation of assistive technology with students who are visually impaired: Teachers' readiness. *Journal of Visual Impairment & Blindness, 96,* 98–105.

American Foundation for the Blind. (2000). *A teacher education for those who serve blind children and youth.* New York: Author.

American Printing House for the Blind. (1992a). *Annual report.* Louisville, KY: Author.

American Printing House for the Blind. (1992b). *Distribution of federal quota based on the January 1992 registration of eligible students.* Research report. Louisville, KY: Author.

Barraga, N. (1986). Sensory perceptual development. In G. T. Scholl (Ed.), *Foundations of education for blind and visually handicapped children and youth: Theory and practice.* New York: American Foundation for the Blind.

Barraga, N. C. (1964). *Increased visual behavior in low vision children.* New York: American Foundation for the Blind.

Barraga, N. C. (1970). *Teacher's guide for development of visual learning abilities and utilization of low vision.* Louisville, KY: American Printing House for the Blind.

Barraga, N. C. (1980). *Source book on low vision.* Louisville, KY: American Printing House for the Blind.

Barraga, N. C. (1983). *Visual handicaps and learning* (Rev. ed.). Austin, TX: Exceptional Resources.

Barraga, N. C., & Morris, J. E. (1980). *Program to develop efficiency in visual function: Sourcebook on low vision.* Louisville, KY: American Printing House for the Blind.

Batista, C. G., & Rassi, M. O. M. (2001). Assessment of visual acuity in toddlers and children with developmental delays: The joint contribution of ophthalmology, orthoptics, and psychology. *Visual Impairment Research, 3,* 17–30.

Batshaw, M. L. (2003). *Children with disabilities* (5th ed.). Baltimore: Paul H. Brookes.

Bishop, V. E. (1996). *Teaching visually impaired children* (2nd ed.). Springfield, IL: Charles C. Thomas.

Blackorby, J., & Wagner, M. (1996). Longitudinal postschool outcomes of youth with disabilities: Findings from the National Longitudinal Transition Study. *Exceptional Children, 62,* 399–413.

Brown, D., Simmons, V., & Methvin, J. (1986). *The Oregon project for visually impaired & blind preschool children—Skills inventory.* Medford, OR: Jackson Education Service District.

Carter, E. W., Wehby, J., & Hughes, C. (2005). Preparing adolescents with high-incidence disabilities for high-stakes testing with strategy instruction. *Preventing School Failure, 49,* 55–62.

Caton, H. R. (1993). Students with visual impairments. In A. E. Blackhurst & W. H. Berdine (Eds.), *An introduction to special education* (3rd ed.). New York: HarperCollins.

Celeste, M. (2002). A survey of motor development for infants and young children with visual impairments. *Journal of Visual Impairment and Blindness, 96,* 169–174.

Chen, D. (1996). Parent-infant communication: Early intervention for very young children with visual impairment or hearing loss. *Infants and Young Children, 9*(2), 1–2.

Chong, C. (2004). Appropriate use of the electronic notetaker in school. *Braille Monitor, 47,* 29–31.

Corn, A. L. (1989). Instruction in the use of vision for children and adults with low vision: A proposed program model. *RE:view, 21,* 26–38.

Corn, A. L. (2000). Technology and assistive devices. In B. Silverstone, M. A. Lang, B. P. Rosenthal, & E. E. Faye (Eds.), *Visual impairment and visual rehabilitation: Volume 2* (pp. 901–1004). New York: Oxford University Press.

Corn, A. L., & Koenig, A. J. (2002). Literacy instruction for students with low vision: A framework for delivery of instruction. *Journal of Visual Impairment and Blindness, 96,* 305–321.

Corn, A. L., Bell, J. K., Andersen, E., Bachofer, C., Jose, R. T., & Perez, A. M. (2003). Providing access to the visual environment: A model of low vision services for children. *Journal of Visual Impairment & Blindness, 97,* 261–272.

Corn, A. L., DePriest, L., & Erin, J. N. (2000). Visual efficiency. In A. J. Koenig & C. Holbrook (Eds.), *Foundations of education for children and youths with visual impairments* (pp. 464–499). New York: AFB Press.

Council for Exceptional Children. (2003). *What every special educator must know: Ethics, standards, and guidelines for special educators.* Reston, VA: Author.

Craig, C. J., Hough, D. L., & Churchwell, C. (2002). A statewide study on the literacy of students with visual impairments. *Journal of Visual Impairment and Blindness, 96*(6), 452–455.

Cronin, B. J., & King, S. R. (1990). The development of the descriptive video service. *Journal of Visual Impairment and Blindness, 86*(2), 101–104.

D'Andrea, F. M. (2005). The Mountbatten pro: More than just an electronic brailler. *Journal of Visual Impairment and Blindness, 99,* 115–118.

D'Allura, T. (2002). Enhancing the social interaction skills of preschoolers with visual impairments. *Journal of Visual Impairment & Blindness, 96,* 576–584.

Dekker, R. (1993). Visually impaired children and haptic intelligence test scores: Intelligence test for visually impaired children (ITVIC). *Developmental Medicine & Child Neurology, 35,* 478–489.

Deshler, D. D., Schumaker, J. B., Lenz, B. K., Bulgren, J. A., Hock, M. F., Knight, J., et al. (2001). Ensuring content-area learning by secondary students with learning disabilities. *Learning Disabilities Research & Practice, 16,* 96–108.

Dimigen, G., Roy, A. W. N., & Horn, J. (2001). Integration of visually impaired students into mainstream education: Two case studies. *Journal of Visual Impairment and Blindness, 95,* 161–164.

Erin, J. N., & Koening, A. J. (1997). The student with a visual disability and a learning disability. *Journal of Learning Disabilities, 30,* 309–320.

Feinsilber, M. (1989, June 28). New machine can be big help for visually impaired. *Albuquerque Journal,* p. B3.

Ferrell, K. A., & Muir, D. W. (1996). A call to end vision stimulation training. *Journal of Visual Impairment and Blindness, 90,* 364–366.

Garb, E. (2000). Maximizing the potential of young adults with visual impairments: The metacognitive element. *Journal of Visual Impairment and Blindness, 94,* 574–583.

Golub, D. (2004). Exploration of factors that contribute to a successful work experience for adults who are visually impaired. *Journal of Visual Impairment and Blindness, 97*(12), 774–778.

Hallahan, D. P., & Kauffman, J. M. (2006). *Exceptional learners: Introduction to special education* (10th ed.). Upper Saddle River, NJ: Merrill/Prentice Hall.

Harley, R., Wood, T., & Merbler, J. (1981). *Peabody mobility scale.* Chicago: Stoelting.

Harrell, L., & Curry, S. A. (1987). Services to blind and visually impaired children and adults: Who is responsible? *Journal of Visual Impairment and Blindness, 81*(8), 368–376.

Hatton, D., Bailey, D., Burchinal, M., & Ferrell, K. (1997). Developmental growth curves of preschool children with vision impairments. *Child Development, 68,* 788–806.

Heward, W. L. (2006). *Exceptional children* (8th ed.). Upper Saddle River, NJ: Merrill/Prentice Hall.

Hill, A. (1997, April). Teaching can travel blind? *Braille Monitor,* 222–225.

Hill, J., & Black, J. (2003). The Miniguide: A new electronic travel device. *Journal of Visual Impairment and Blindness, 97,* 655–656.

Hodges, H. L. (1983). Evaluating the effectiveness of programs for the visually impaired: One state's approach. *Journal of Visual Impairment and Blindness, 77*(1), 97–99.

Holbrook, C., & Healy, M. S. (2002). Children who are blind or have low vision. In N. Hunt & K. Marshall (Eds.), *Exceptional children and youth: An introduction to special education* (pp. 443–501). Boston: Houghton Mifflin.

House, S. S., & Davidson, R. C. (2000). Increasing language development through orientation and mobility instruction. *RE:view, 31*(4), 149–153.

Hull, T., & Mason, H. (1995). Performance of blind children on digit-span tests. *Journal of Visual Impairment & Blindness, 892,* 166–169.

Hunt, N., & Marshall, K. (2006). *Exceptional children and youth: An introduction to special education* (4th ed.). Boston: Houghton Mifflin.

Ingber, J. (2005). Product evaluation: Breaking the code: A review of two portable bar code scanners. *AccessWorld, 6*(5), 1–5.

Joint Organizational Committee. (1993). *Full inclusion of students who are blind or visually impaired: A position statement.* Author.

Jorgensen-Smith, T., & Lewis, S. (2004). Meeting the challenge: Innovation in one state rehabilitation system's approach to transition. *Journal of Visual Impairment and Blindness, 98,* 212–227.

Kef, S. (2002). Psychosocial adjustment and the meaning of social support for visually impaired adolescents. *Journal of Visual Impairment and Blindness, 96,* 22–37.

Kentucky Society for the Prevention of Blindness. (1990). *Handbook for preschool vision screening.* Louisville, KY: Author.

Kirchner, C. (1990). Trends in the prevalence rates and numbers of blind and visually impaired schoolchildren. *Journal of Visual Impairment and Blindness, 84,* 478–479.

Kirchner, C., & Peterson, R. (1988). Estimates of race: Ethnic groups in the U.S. visually impaired and blind population. In C. Kirchner (Ed.), *Data on blindness and visual impairment in the U.S.: A resource manual on social demographic characteristics, education, employment and income, and service delivery* (2nd ed.). New York: American Foundation for the Blind.

Kirk, S. A., Gallagher, J. J., Anastasiow, N. J., & Coleman, M. R. (2006). *Educating exceptional children* (11th ed.). Boston: Houghton Mifflin.

Koenig, A. J., & Holbrook, C. (Eds.). (2000). *Foundations of education for children and youths with visual impairments.* New York: AFB Press.

Kurzweil, R. (1996, November). Why I am building reading machines again. *Braille Monitor,* 568–581.

Lahav, O., & Mioduser, D. (2004). Exploration of unknown spaces by people who are blind using a multi-sensory virtual environment. *Journal of Special Education Technology, 19*(3), 15–23.

Leventhal, J. (2004). A review of e-book readers: The Book Port and the BookCourier. *Journal of Visual Impairment and Blindness, 98,* 373–377.

Lewis, S. (1995). Blindness and low vision. In A. P. Turnbull, H. R. Turnbull, M. Shank, & D. Leal, *Exceptional lives: Special education in today's schools* (pp. 662–710). Upper Saddle River, NJ: Merrill/Prentice Hall.

Lewis, S. (2002). Some thoughts on inclusion, alienation, and meeting the needs of children with visual impairments. *RE:view, 34,* 99–101.

Lewis, S., & Allman, C. B. (2000). Educational programming. In M. C. Holbrook & A. J. Koenig (Eds.), *Foundations of education: History and theory of teaching children and youth with visual impairments* (2nd ed., pp. 218–259). New York: American Foundation for the Blind Press.

Lewis, S., & Iselin, S. (2002). A comparison of the independent living skills of primary students with visual impairments and their sighted peers: A pilot study. *Journal of Visual Impairment and Blindness, 96,* 335–344.

Lewis, S., & Tolla, J. (2003). Creating and using tactile experience books for young children with visual impairments. *Teaching Exceptional Children, 35*(3), 22–28.

Lindo, G., & Nordholm, L. (1999). Adaptation strategies, well-being, and activities of daily living among people with low vision. *Journal of Visual Impairment, 93,* 434–466.

Lussenhop, K., & Corn, A. L. (2002). Comparative studies pertaining to the reading performance of students with low vision using large print, standard print, and standard print with optical devices. *RE: view, 34,* 57–69.

MacCuspie, A. P. (1992). The social acceptance and interaction of visually impaired children in integrated setting. In S. Z. Sacks, L. S. Kekelis, & R. J. Gaylord-Ross (Eds.), *The development of social skills by blind and visually impaired students: Exploratory studies and strategies.* New York: American Foundation for the Blind.

Mangold, S. (1977). *Mangold developmental program of tactile perception and braille letter recognition.* Castro Valley, CA: Exceptional Teaching Aids.

McHugh, E., & Leiberman, L. (2003). The impact of developmental factors on stereotypical rocking of children with visual impairments. *Journal of Visual Impairment and Blindness, 97,* 453–473.

Menaker, S. J., & Batshaw, M. L. (1997). Vision: Our window to the world. In M. L. Batshaw (Ed.), *Children with disabilities* (4th ed., pp. 211–240). Baltimore: Paul H. Brookes.

Moore, V., & McConachie, H. (1990). *Early language development in blind and severely visually impaired children: Interim report on pilot study* (Report No. ED331204). London: Institute of Child Health, The Wolfson Centre. (ERIC Document Reproduction Service No. ED 331 204, Clearinghouse No. EC 300 185.)

Nagle, K. M. (2001). Transition to employment and community life for youths with visual impairments: Current status and future directions. *Journal of Visual Impairment and Blindness, 95,* 725–738.

National Federation for the Blind (2003). *Blind literacy legislation adopted by states.* www.nfb.org/brailstates.htm

National Society for the Prevention of Blindness. (1990). *Vision screening in schools.* New York: Author.

Nelson, P. A., Dial, J. G., & Joyce, A. (2002). Validation of the Cognitive Test for the Blind as an assessment of intellectual functioning. *Rehabilitation Psychology, 47,* 184–193.

NICHCY. (2004). *Visual impairments: Fact sheet 13.* Arlington, VA: Author.

Pava, W. S. (1994). Visually impaired persons' vulnerability to sexual and physical assault. *Journal of Visual Impairment and Blindness, 88,* 103–112.

Pava, W. S., Bateman, P., Appleton, M. K., & Glascock, J. (1991). Self-defense training for visually impaired women. *Journal of Visual Impairment and Blindness, 85,* 397–401.

Perez-Pereira, M., & Conti-Ramsden, G. (1999). *Language interaction and social interaction in blind children.* East Sussex, England: Psychology Press, Ltd.

Pillips, J. E. (2003). An initial study of students' perceptions of their educational placement at a special school for the blind, *RE:view, 35,* 89–95.

Sacks, S. Z. (1992). The social development of visually impaired children: A theoretical perspective. In S. Z. Sacks, L. S. Kekelis, & R. J. Gaylord-Ross (Eds.), *The development of social skills by blind and visually impaired students: Exploratory studies and strategies* (pp. 54–71). New York: American Foundation for the Blind.

Sacks, S. Z., & Pruett, K. M. (1992). Summer transition training project for professionals who work with adolescents and young adults. *Journal of Visual Impairment and Blindness, 86,* 211–214.

Sacks, S. Z., & Reardon, M. P. (1992). Maximizing social integration for visually impaired students: Applications and practice. In S. Z. Sacks, L. S. Kekelis, & R. J. Gaylord-Ross (Eds.), *The development of social skills by blind and visually impaired students: Exploratory studies and strategies.* New York: American Foundation for the Blind.

Sacks, S. Z., Rosen, S., & Gaylord-Ross, R. J. (1990). Visual impairment. In N. G. Haring & L. McCormick (Eds.), *Exceptional children and youth* (5th ed., pp. 332–364). Upper Saddle River, NJ: Merrill/Prentice Hall.

Sattler, J. M., & Evans, C. A. (2002). Visual impairments. In J. M. Sattler (Ed.), *Assessment of children: Behavioral and clinical applications* (4th ed., pp. 367–376). San Diego: Jerome M. Sattler.

Scholl, G. T. (1986). Growth and development. In G. T. Scholl (Ed.), *Foundations of education for blind and visually handicapped children and youth: Theory and practice.* New York: American Foundation for the Blind.

Siegel, S., Greener, K., Prieuer, J., Robert, M., & Gaylord-Ross, R. (1989). The community vocational training program. *Career Development for Exceptional Individuals, 12,* 48–64.

Skellenger, A. C., & Hill, E. W. (1997). The preschool learner. In B. B. Blasch, W. R. Wiener, & R. L. Welsh, (Eds.), *Foundations of orientation and mobility* (2nd ed., pp. 407–438). New York: American Foundation for the Blind.

Smith, D. D. (2005). *Introduction to special education: Teaching in an age of opportunity* (5th ed.). Needham, MA: Allyn & Bacon.

Smith, J. A. (1972). *Adventures in communication.* Needham, MA: Allyn & Bacon.

Talking Wallet. (1992). *Journal of Visual Impairment and Blindness, 86,* 411.

Topor, I., Rosenblum, L. P., & Hatton, D. D. (2004). *Visual conditions and functional vision in young children with visual impairments: Early intervention issues.* Chapel Hill: University of North Carolina, FPG Child Development Institute.

Turnbull, A. P., Turnbull, H. R., Shank, M., & Smith, S. (2004). *Exceptional lives: Special education in today's schools.* Upper Saddle River, NJ: Merrill/Prentice Hall.

Tuttle, D. W. (1981). Academics are not enough: Techniques of daily living for visually impaired children. In *Handbook for teachers of the visually handicapped.* New York: American Printing House for the Blind.

U.S. Department of Education. (2005). *Twenty-fifth annual report to Congress on the implementation of the Individuals with Disabilities Education Act.* Washington, DC: Author.

Warren, D. H. (1994). *Blindness and children: An individual differences approach.* New York: Cambridge University Press.

Warren, D. H., & Hatton, D. D. (2002). Cognitive development in visually impaired children. In I. Rapin & S. Segalowitz (Eds.), *Elsevier's handbook of neuropsychology* (2nd ed.). New York: Elsevier.

11

Students with Severe or Multiple Disabilities

KEY TERMS

WHAT WOULD YOU DO?

Luis dashed into the room with his eyes sparkling. He limped to one side because one leg and one arm were affected by CP from birth. He had been helped off the van by the driver and the assistant and he moved quickly into the classroom for breakfast. His teacher met him with a smile and a greeting, and Luis, who was not yet using words, smiled back and repeated his oft used phrase, "Ah-dah." He was hungry and he and his teacher, Dolores, worked at using his adapted spoon to eat oatmeal. The handle of the spoon was built up so that he could hold it more easily, and his task was to scoop the oatmeal out of the bowl and move it to his mouth. Dolores used a hand-over-hand technique with graduated guidance—she helped him scoop and move the spoon when he needed it, but if he was making the correct movements, her hand remained in place but did not impede or assist. His objective was to move the spoon from the bowl to his mouth without spilling. Dolores sighed as another blob of oatmeal slid from the spoon to the table and he spread the cereal around by waving his other arm. Another difficulty with the task was Luis' interest span. He cared less for the food than the activity around him. His mother put him on the bus without breakfast, but he liked to look at the other students and the teachers. He liked to listen to the conversations. He had a jerking movement of his head. He was not always able to control it, and when he looked at others by moving his head, he frequently jerked his head sideways. Dolores recalled the meeting when the team decided it was not in Luis' best interest to eat breakfast in a separate room because he needed the stimulation. He generally did calm down over the course of the day, but having so many students and teachers in the room at first seemed like he was on "sensory overload." Dolores knew Luis needed to hear conversations, to learn what was expected at meal times, and to increase his receptive language. So, she just wiped up the oatmeal, took his hand, and said, "Luis, eat another mouthful."

1. Would you change Luis' objective of eating breakfast with a spoon?

2. What disability labels might be appropriate for Luis? How might having multiple disability conditions change choices for interventions?

Students with severe or multiple disabilities may have an extensive range of physical problems, and they may or may not have coexisting intellectual challenges. These students may need intensive assistance or support their entire lives. Some are also mentally retarded to some degree. Some have learning disabilities. Some have difficulties maintaining appropriate focusing on tasks. Some have sensory deficits. Some are typically developing. Some students with severe or multiple disabilities may be cognitively gifted and talented. Some students are ambulatory; others need wheelchairs or other prostheses such as crutches or braces. They may experience mild physical or neurological difficulties, severe impairments of language, other communication disorders, or impairments of body movements (Batshaw & Perret, 1992; Bowe, 2000; Kennedy & Horn, 2004; Kirk, Gallagher, Anastasiow, & Coleman, 2006; Orelove, Sobsey, & Silberman, 2004). It is difficult to provide an all-inclusive definition of students with severe or multiple disabilities because no single definition would include all the prevailing conditions. Under the law (IDEA), a student with multiple disabilities must have two or more concomitant disability conditions, and the conditions must have an impact that causes difficulties in educational settings to the extent that one disability cannot be adequately addressed because of the concurrent problems.

DEFINITIONS

The reauthorization of IDEA (IDEA, 2004) has no new definition for students with multiple disabilities and so relies on the previous laws for this population. The section of IDEA that specifies 13 different categories of exceptionality defines multiple disabilities as follows:

> Multiple disabilities means concomitant impairments (such as mental retardation–blindness, mental retardation–orthopedic impairment, etc.), the combination of which causes such severe educational problems such that they cannot be accommodated in special education programs solely for one of the impairments. The term does not include deaf-blindness. (IDEA, 34 C.F.R., pt. 300, § 300.7).

IDEA does describe students with severe disabilities in regard to their instructional needs:

> "Children with severe disabilities" refers to children with disabilities who, because of the intensity of their physical, mental, or emotional problems, need highly specialized education, social, psychological, and medical services in order to maximize their full potential for useful and meaningful participation in society for self-fulfillment. (IDEA, 34 C.F.R. 300 [315.4[d]] 1977)."

Different agencies and researchers have defined severe disabilities. Generally, severe disabilities are defined as a degree of impairment that reduces one's ability to complete activities necessary for an independent lifestyle in general settings (Westling & Fox, 2004). Any disability can occur in severe forms and would probably require different programming and more services. AAMR characterizes severe mental handicaps as a human manifestation in which different levels of support are required to adequately meet the needs of persons with reduced intellectual functioning and adaptive behaviors (Taylor, Brady, & Richards, 2005; Westling & Fox, 2004). Two major themes are as follows: (1) The extent of disability is beyond mild or moderate levels, and (2) there are typically, but not always, two or more disabilities occurring simultaneously.

The Association for Persons with Severe Disabilities, formerly known as The Association for Persons with Severe Handicaps (TASH), has offered a useful definition of severe disabilities. As defined by this organization, persons with severe disabilities may or may not have multiple diagnoses. Their definition is as follows:

> Persons with severe handicaps include individuals of all ages who require extensive ongoing support in more than one life activity in order to participate in integrated

community settings and to enjoy a quality of life that is available to citizens with fewer or no disabilities. Support may be required for life activities such as mobility, communication, self-care, and learning as necessary for independent living, employment, and self-sufficiency. (Kirk, Gallagher, & Anastasiow, 1997, p. 470)

Several special and major categories are associated with people with severe or multiple disabilities. These problems are unique and challenging, and they often require special services notably different from and more sophisticated than those routinely provided to people with exceptionalities.

Students with Deaf-Blind Impairment

Students who are deaf and blind were included as a separate category with a funding base in 1969, when maternal rubella was causing a significant increase in the number of babies born with sensory deficits and multiple sensory deficits (Smith, 2001). Since that time, medical advances have reduced the occurrence of maternal rubella, although the condition still exists as a low-incidence category. IDEA 97 defines the condition as follows:

Deaf-blindness means concomitant hearing and visual impairments, the combination of which causes such severe communication and other developmental and learning needs that the persons cannot be appropriately educated in special education programs solely for children and youth with hearing impairments, or severe disabilities, without supplementary assistance to address their educational needs due to these dual concurrent disabilities. (U.S. Department of Education, 1999, p. 12422)

The Helen Keller National Center defines a person who is deaf-blind more specifically as someone (1) with central vision acuity of 20/200 or worse in the better eye with corrective lenses and/or a visual field of 20 degrees or less in the better eye or with a progressive visual loss; (2) who has a chronic hearing impairment so severe that most speech cannot be understood; and (3) for whom the combination of impairments . . . causes extreme difficulty in daily life activities (Everson, 1995).

People who are deaf-blind may need help at its most basic level. For the infant who is deaf-blind, the outside world extends only as far as they can reach; this is augmented by any residual hearing or vision through the use of auxiliary supports such as hearing aids, glasses, or sonic directional devices, which give the infant feedback about the location of objects through vibration (Bower, 1989). It is important to realize that only a small percentage of the students are totally deaf or totally blind. There is, for the majority of students, a modicum of residual sensory ability. However, there are challenges due to the impairment of the senses. Janssen, Riksen-Walraven, & Van Dijk (2003) stressed the importance of responsiveness in forming attachments. Caregivers must be responsive to an infant's signals, must interpret them correctly, and must respond so the infant begins to understand and be understood. The reciprocity of the interactions is a basis for communication. If the infant is deaf and blind, the caregiver must be sensitive to any signal given by the infant and then allow the infant to receive the reciprocal interactions—through touch. The infant must learn that (1) they exist, (2) others exist, (3) they have needs, (4) these needs can be met, (5) they can meet some of their needs, and (6) some, if not most, of their needs will be met by others (Murphy & Byrne, 1983). Many infants who are deaf-blind can go beyond point 6 and, as they develop, begin to meet many of their own needs. The need for reciprocal interactions and communication continues through life. Students who do not bond with others are at risk of having problems with insecurity and incompetence as well as problems with emotional regulation, self-injurious behavior, aggression, withdrawal, or depression (Luiselli, 1992; Marks, 1998; Sisson, Hersen, & Van Hasselt, 1993).

A program of interaction for infants and others who are deaf-blind is described through eight core objectives:

1. *Initiatives*—Starting an interaction or raising something new as part of a reaction.
2. *Confirmation*—Clear acknowledgment that an initiative has been noticed and recognized.
3. *Answers*—Positive (approving) or negative (disapproving) reaction to an utterance of the partner.
4. *Turns*—Turn taking, or becoming the actor, and turn giving, or allowing the other to become the actor.
5. *Attention*—Focus on the interaction partner, the content of the interaction, and the people and/or objects within the interaction context.
6. *Regulation of intensity of the interaction*—For the educator: waiting while the deaf-blind student regulates the intensity of the interaction. For the student: appropriate regulation of intensity by, for example, withdrawing (turning his or her head away) or some other individual signal (such as laying his or her hand on the partner's hand) and apparent processing of information, and inappropriate regulation of intensity by, for example, self-abusive or aggressive behaviors.
7. *Affective involvement*—Mutual sharing of emotions.
8. *Independent acting*—For the educator: acting with no focus on the student. For the student: executing actions independently (e.g., putting a garment or part of a garment on alone) (Janssen et al., 2003).

Persons with deaf-blindness often develop self-stimulatory behaviors (much like persons with autism). These behaviors probably persist as a substitute for the lost or diminished use of sight and hearing. They may serve as social or sensory reinforcements (Tang, Patterson, & Kennedy, 2003). Changes occur with maturity; a student who is unable to see or hear does not get the normal sensory stimulation that facilitates normal growth. Other stimulation must be provided.

One aspect of learning important to persons without sensory deficits is incidental learning in which students learn about the environment, subtle cultural rules, manners and mores, directions, and other information helpful in everyday life. Persons with impaired vision and hearing do not have opportunities to learn incidentally and frequently need to be taught directly. However, some students with deaf-blindness can be included in general education classrooms (Mar & Sall, 1995). Mar described a case report of a fifth-grade student who was successful with a variety of variables such as direct administrative involvement, effective teaming, teachers' and peers' problem-solving skills, adaptation of materials and activities, consideration of the physical environment, and a positive attitude about inclusion (Sall & Mar, 1999).

Students with Mental Retardation and Cerebral Palsy

There are many causes of multiple disabilities. Some have been virtually eradicated, but others may be on the rise. One that may be increasing because of shorter hospital stays for newborns is **kernicterus.** It is a type of brain damage that causes athetoid CP, hearing loss, and MR. Some newborns who have a severe case of jaundice and do not get treatment can be at risk. Jaundice is caused by an excess of bilirubin in the system. This frequently occurs in newborns because their systems may not be able to slough off excess red blood cells or there may be an imbalance. If the infants leave the hospital and the jaundice occurs, it may not be noticed by the new parents. Checkups within a day or two after leaving the hospital could be beneficial in detecting this condition. The treatment is simple for most. The infant needs to be placed under a certain type of light, but if the phototherapy is not sufficient, then an exchange transfusion might be necessary (O'Keefe, 2001). If not treated, the high levels of bilirubin can result in brain damage (The National Center on Birth Defects and Developmental Disabilities [NCBDDD], 2004).

Although students with physical and other disabilities can also have low cognitive functioning (MR), the danger of diagnosing a dual disability with traditional testing methods exists. Alternative methods, including some normed tests, observations, examples of work, and assigned tasks, can provide a reasonable guess as to the intelligence or potential of a person unable to complete a traditional IQ test. In general, IQ tests have serious limitations when evaluating students with multiple disabilities. The samples of persons on whom the tests were normalized generally do not include persons with severe and multiple disabilities and therefore do not account for differences in receptive and expressive modalities.

Often the poor speech and uncontrolled movements of students with CP give the impression that these individuals are mentally retarded. Actually, little relationship exists between the degree of physical impairment and intelligence in students with CP. A student who is severely physically impaired may be intellectually gifted; another with mild physical involvement may be mildly or severely retarded (Kirk et al., 2006).

PREVALENCE

Students with multiple disabilities account for slightly over 2 percent of the total special education population. However, it is difficult to achieve an accurate count because many are counted only in the category of their primary disorder. Students who are deaf-blind comprise approximately one quarter of 1 percent. According to the report to Congress, of the approximately 5 million students with disabilities between ages 6 and 21 served during the 2000–2001 school year, 128,552 students were identified as experiencing multiple disabilities and 1,615 were diagnosed with deaf-blindness (U.S. Department of Education, 2005).

CHARACTERISTICS

Individuals with severe or multiple disabilities exhibit wide behavioral differences, abilities, and characteristics due to sensory and motor impairments, physical and orthopedic anomalies, communication deficits, and cognitive abilities. They may have MR, seizure disorders, CP or other motor disabilities. Other individuals included in this category may have multiple difficulties. Many students with severe disabilities may exhibit adjustment problems or be self-injurious or self-abusive (Giangreco, Edelman, Macfarland, & Luiselli, 1997; Hardman, Drew, & Egan, 2005; Kirk et al., 2006; Westling & Fox, 2004). Others can learn to perform many skills (Friend, 2005; Wolery, Anthony, Snyder, Werts, & Katzenmeyer, 1997). The difficulty in defining severe or multiple disabilities carries over into attempts to describe all characteristics of all individuals with severe and multiple disabilities. We can categorize characteristics such as intellectual functioning, adaptive behavior, physical and sensory development, health care needs, and communication needs. Throughout this section, keep in mind that some individuals with severe or multiple disabilities may have normal intelligence, be ambulatory, and become fully integrated into society.

Intellectual Functioning

Some, but not all, individuals with severe or multiple disabilities have severe impairments in intellectual functioning as determined by intelligence test scores and by performance of adaptive skills. Others have normal or high intelligence and test well on standardized tests. Still other students, who have average to above average potential to learn, need modifications in test items, directions, or the mode of responding during testing. Several assessment instruments have been adapted to special populations. It is inappropriate to administer a standardized test that has not been normalized and validated on the population from which an individual comes. The validity of information from such an administration is often in doubt. There may be some indication of what a student is able to do, but the standard scores are useless. The scores do not indicate what a teacher is to teach nor do they indicate how to teach it.

Academic Skills

Most individuals with severe or multiple disabilities cannot perform traditional academic tasks if the mix of disabilities includes lowered cognitive functioning. However, others can benefit from traditional standard curricula and should, by law, be given access to it. In addition, many of these students will need IEP goals that focus on self-help skills and functional curricular areas, such as manipulation of money for vending machines, mobility training, and safety issues. **Functional skills** are those needed to be successful in the environment in which the student participates. Students with severe or multiple physical disabilities who have sufficient cognitive abilities can succeed in general education classes (Giangreco et al., 1997; Turnbull, Turnbull, Shank, & Smith, 2004).

Self-Care Skills

Many individuals with severe or multiple disabilities, with appropriate support, can learn to care for their own needs, such as dressing, personal hygiene, toileting, and feeding, and may successfully master some household chores (Friend, 2005; Kirk et al., 2006). Others can learn to live independently with the help of case managers, trained dog guides, assistive devices, low- and high-tech assistance, and an appropriately modified environment.

Social Skills

The majority of individuals with severe or multiple disabilities do not have typical social skills because they may lack opportunities for the social interactions that would enable them to develop and practice social skills. However, reports indicate that these individuals can engage in reciprocal interpersonal relationships with teachers, peers, and family members. The facilitating key appears to be providing enriching opportunities for participation in the community, with appropriate employment and living situations if

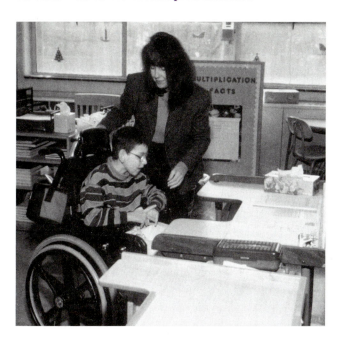

possible (Hardman et al., 2005). Research has shown that high school students with severe disabilities who are likable have friends and achieve social success; those that are not tend to be shunned by their peers. In other words, social relationships mirror those of their peers without disabilities (Cushing & Kennedy, 2002).

Delayed Motor Development

Individuals with severe or multiple disabilities may exhibit a delay in motor development, including sensorimotor impairments and abnormal orthopedic muscle tone. However, many of these individuals can learn to walk with or without assistance, play sports, participate in competitions such as Special Olympics, and enjoy playing with their peers (Nisbet, 1992; Turnbull et al., 2004). Adaptations in games and sports have made it possible for persons to participate in wheelchair races and basketball. Adapted equipment such as balls with lights or sound functions allows persons with sensory impairments to be included with peers who do not have disabilities. Sometimes delayed motor development can be a problem when involving the student in physical activities, but with some creativity, the student should be able to participate at some level.

Sensory Impairment

Unlike other senses, hearing and vision are distance senses (Smith, 2001), providing us with information that is outside our bodies. People deprived of these two senses require modifications for independence. Because only a small number of individuals are classified as deaf-blind, few teachers will encounter these students. The occurrence of one of these sensory impairments is common among individuals with other disabilities. Teaching a student with multiple disabilities is more difficult than teaching a student who is blind or physically impaired. The combinations are numerous. Specialists are available in most areas to help with sensory impairments.

Health Care Needs

Students with health care needs who also experience severe or multiple disabilities may need school and other staff members to assist with intermittent catheterization; gastronomy tube feeding; respiratory ventilation; and the administration of medications for controlling seizures, hyperactivity, and muscle relaxation. Clean intermittent catheterization involves inserting a catheter (tube) into the urethra to the bladder to drain off urine. Gastronomy tube feeding is used with individuals who cannot ingest adequate amounts of nutrition normally. Cleaning stomas and collection bags for urine or feces are necessary for students who do not have full use of their colons or bladders and instead must eliminate waste through **stomas,** which are openings in the abdominal area. Respiratory ventilation involves suctioning mucus from the respiratory tract by machine through a small tube (Kirk et al., 2006; Turnbull et al., 2004). Although some students learn to perform these tasks for themselves, at least to some degree, it is important for teachers to learn to perform these life-sustaining duties.

Communication Skills

The majority of individuals with severe or multiple disabilities display communication problems or fail to acquire speech and language. However, in spite of speech and language problems, they can and do communicate with others. Nonverbal communication and communication using assistive devices can be critical for these students. Some of these devices may be as simple as pictures on a board or sign language, and some involve sophisticated **assistive technology,** or tools and processes to help with tasks, and computerized communication devices (Beukelman & Mirenda, 1998; Friend, 2005).

Summary

Educators need to be aware of the multiple factors that may affect the learning and functioning of students with severe or multiple disabilities. Often learning is not only possible but also probable because there are more similarities between these students and their typically developing peers than differences. The many characteristics exhibited by individuals with severe or multiple disabilities that we have described may appear in a variety of combinations for any given student. These life needs must be met with substantial assistance if the student is to attain any measure of integration into society (Hardman et al., 2005).

ETIOLOGY

There are multiple causes for the conditions that result in severe or multiple disabilities. Teratogens are agents that cause defects in a developing fetus (Graham & Morgan, 1997). Prior to conception, there are genetic determinants. **Autosomal disorders** are those disorders resulting from a defect or disorder in the 22 pairs of chromosomes that are not related to gender. **Sex-linked disorders** are those resulting from a defect or disorder in the X and Y chromosomes. Prior to birth, several other factors, such as maternal substance abuse, blood incompatibility, or viral diseases,

BOX 11.1
WHAT EVERY TEACHER SHOULD KNOW
Causes of Multiple Handicaps

Time of Injury	Affecting Agent	Agent Activity	Typical Results
Conception	Genetic disorder; inherited; inborn errors of metabolism	Serious change in embryo and fetus; inability to carry out normal metabolic processes	Down syndrome; Tay Sachs; many other disorders that if untreated will lead to severe mental retardation
Prenatal	Mother has German measles or other viral infection; uses toxic substances (crack, heroin); or has RH blood incompatibility	Interferes with development of central nervous system	Visual, hearing, and motor impairments; mental retardation
Natal	Anoxia	Destroys brain cells	Cerebral palsy, mental retardation, and other defects
	Low birth weight (less than 5.5 lb); prematurity	Immature organism not ready for environmental stimulation	From normal to severe mental retardation and disabilities
	Very low birth weight (less than 3 lb)	Damage to brain organization	From normal to severe and profound disabilities
Postnatal	Encephalitis, meningitis, physical abuse	Damage to brain cells	Epilepsy, mental retardation, motor disabilities

Source: S. A. Kirk, J. J. Gallagher, & N. J. Anastasiow. From *Educating Exceptional Children* (8th ed.), Copyright © 1997 by Houghton Mifflin Company. Used with permission.

may be causes of severe disabilities. During the birth process, oxygen deprivation or extremely low birth weight associated with prematurity can contribute to severe and multiple disabilities. After birth, accidents, infections, poisoning, malnutrition, or physical and emotional child abuse may cause severe or multiple disabilities (Hardman et al., 2005; Kirk et al., 2006; Taylor et al., 2005). Many known causes of severe or multiple disabilities relate to prenatal biomedical factors such as chromosomal abnormalities, genetic metabolic disorders, disorders of the central nervous system, and prenatal noxious environmental influences. Advances in medicine have allowed us to identify and to remedy several syndromes; however, for other children born with severe or multiple disabilities, there is no identifiable cause (Taylor et al., 2005; Turnbull et al., 2004). Box 11.1 lists some of the more identifiable causes of severe or multiple disabilities, indicating the time of injury, affecting agent, agent activity, and typical results.

Some causes, but not all, are preventable. Generally, causes are related to randomly occurring genetic or medical conditions rather than cultural factors. It is often difficult to determine or document causality; these conditions affect all social, economic, racial, and linguistic groups equally.

IDENTIFICATION PROCESS
Medical Evaluation

Infants with severe or multiple disabilities are usually identified at birth during routine screening processes required by physicians, such as checking for observable disabilities, genetic and metabolic disorders, and potential developmental problems (Turnbull et al., 2004). One screening process for newborns is the Apgar test. A physician ranks the infant on five physical traits (heart rate, respiratory effort, muscle tone, gag reflex, and skin color) 1 minute and 5 minutes after birth. A rating indicates his or her level of risk for being disabled. The neonate may have disabilities common to a given syndrome or show symptoms that are easily recognized. Later parents may report that the infant is having unusual difficulties sleeping, eating, or attaining developmental milestones. These reports will lead to genetic investigations and physical evaluations that might include vision and hearing tests, blood tests, metabolic workups, or a variety of other screening procedures that reveal the presence of disabling conditions (Turnbull et al., 2004).

Prenatal genetic testing gives information about identifiable syndromes. **Amniocentesis,** an analysis of a sample of amniotic fluid, and testing using a sample of placental tissue give information about chromosomal structure. Blood tests provide information about proteins and hormones that are associated with difficulties such as spina bifida.

Educational Evaluation

Concurrent with medical identification and assessment procedures, the child is referred to educational and therapeutic specialists who are experts in remediation and treatment. For example, as a result of screening procedures, a child, at birth, may be suspected of having respiratory problems with possible neurological impairments along with low Apgar scores. The child is referred for evaluation; if the presenting problems indicate a physical impairment such as CP, these results will lead to vision, hearing, and other evaluations. The possible combination of problems and their potential severity will prompt a variety of specialists to become part of the service provision team that evaluates and plans treatment. In addition to medical personnel, speech-language pathologists, physical therapists, special educators, family counselors, and other appropriate professionals will prepare for future educational and therapeutic needs. Early intervention programs will be notified; they will provide supportive services from infancy through the preschool years.

Educational placement procedures that parallel those described in previous chapters are then set in motion. Assessment activities for students with severe or multiple handicaps or disabilities should analyze student performance under natural, normal situations and settings where they learn, live, work, and recreate. Individualized intelligence tests should be administered following guidelines that ensure the most accurate scores possible. Many students with severe or multiple disabilities have IQ scores that indicate severe cognitive impairments (Turnbull et al., 2004). However, examiners must be cautious about applying results and interpretations derived from tests designed for students with intact neurological and sensory systems. Commercial assessment instruments may need to be interpreted not only according to each student's age and disability but also with consideration of the environment and people in the homes and communities. Students with multiple disabilities will be at a disadvantage if the assessment instruments are scored in a standard manner.

Adaptive behavior scales should also be a part of the assessment battery. Adaptive behavior tests focus on behaviors important to an individual's adjustment to cultural, social, and age standards of performance.

Many assessment tools are available for determining developmental problems, educational diagnoses, and programming.

Following are some diagnostic instruments:

- AAMD Adaptive Behavior Scale: School (Lambert, Nihira, & Leland, 1993)
- The TARC Assessment Inventory for Severely Handicapped Children (Sailor & Mix, 1976)
- The Behavior Rating Instrument for Autistic and Other Atypical Children (BRIAAC) (Ruttenberg, Wolf-Schein, & Wenar, 1991)

These instruments are useful in evaluating students with severe or multiple disabilities because they rely to some extent on the developmental approach and the ecological assessment model in which the teacher considers particular skills the student needs to perform a particular behavior and the settings within which the student is expected to function. Severe or multiple disabilities are often diagnosed when a student scores significantly below average in two or more areas of adaptive behavior. These results usually indicate problems in areas such as communication, daily living skills, socialization, and coordination abilities. The educational team must consider the intensity of the support the student will require. A **person-centered approach** is necessary. This approach focuses on the unique needs of the person (Gardner & Carran, 2005; Wehmeyer, 2000). Major areas to be considered are communication, self-care, social skills, home living, community involvement, health, and safety (Turnbull et al., 2004). From results of these assessment instruments, observations, and consultations with family members and the multidisciplinary team, an IEP evolves that will serve as the guideline for the student's educational experience.

PROGRAMS

Historically, students with severe or multiple disabilities were often isolated from their community and society in large institutions, or they were kept at home and services focused primarily on protection and care. Currently, educational practices emphasize including students with disabilities in their community and local school to the extent that inclusion is possible and reasonable. Hardman et al. (2005) identified several aspects of instructional emphasis that characterize quality school programs for students with severe or multiple disabilities: Student preferences and needs are considered in developing educational objectives; the school values and supports involvement of family members; and instruction focuses on frequently used functional skills that are meaningful in daily life or activities that will be meaningful in their next setting. Quality programs offer opportunities for interaction between students with severe or multiple disabilities and their nondisabled peers. Box 11.2 provides general suggestions for teachers.

Curriculum

Current curriculum emphasis for students with severe or multiple disabilities focuses on the critical environments in which the student is expected to function now and in the future and identifies the skills and activities he or she needs to participate successfully in these environments (Browder, Flowers, & Ahlgrim-Delzell, 2004; Clark,

BOX 11.2
WHAT EVERY TEACHER SHOULD DO

Effective Teaching Strategies

- Be familiar with the medical history of the student and have clear and written instructions for what to do and whom to call in case of an emergency.
- Be familiar with any special medical procedures such as ventilation, catheterization, and positioning.
- Know how to operate assistive devices such as switches, speech synthesizers, and electric wheelchairs.
- Work cooperatively with other professionals and family members who implement educational and social programming in the school, home, and community.
- Use research-validated teaching practices that are also efficient for the particular student.
- Systematically collect data on objectives. Use graphs and clear data decision rules so you will know when skills have been mastered.
- Read the IEP and implement activities that will assist the student with meeting the objectives. It is helpful to keep a chart of objectives in an inconspicuous place to remind yourself of IEP objectives and goals.
- Use differential teaching. For example, when teaching fractions, you can also teach number recognition to individual students.
- Task analyze each learning task. Evaluate the student on each step of the task analysis and in the fluency of moving from one step to another.
- Use time wisely. Time changing diapers can be used for speech development. Time waiting for buses or for doctors' appointments can be used for sensory stimulation.

Cushing, & Kennedy, 2004; Snell, 1992). Students should first be taught to function in their present environment and then in other environments. Emphasis on functional curriculum content is concerned not only with what is taught but also with how and where teaching occurs. Educators are taking responsibility for teaching domestic skills that span the entire range of self-care needs, so that students will be better able to function within a home environment. School skills now include not only traditional academic areas but also activities related to successful functioning within schools, such as interacting with peers; working in groups; and participating, communicating, and complying with schedules and adult requests. Community skills needed for moving about the community (i.e., obtaining transportation), shopping, participating in recreation and leisure activities, spending time in socially acceptable and enjoyable ways, and vocational training, including getting and keeping a job, are also the responsibility of the educational team that outlines a plan for the student (Browder, Spooner, Ahlgrim-Delzell, 2003; Ryndak & Alper, 2003). These skills are termed **community-based instruction,** or skills needed in a community taught in the community.

Instructional Priorities

Special education for persons with severe or multiple disabilities consists of individually devised programs that may include instructional processes dealing with cognitive and social skills, interpersonal skills, tasks of daily living, as well as discovering accommodations that increase individual freedom. Special education for these students, and for all students with disabilities, is "made special by the nature of the skills that are taught and the methods used to teach them" (Westling & Fox, 2004). High-quality special education programs should include the following features:

1. Each student should be treated with dignity.
2. Students should be able to self-determine as much as possible.
3. There should be an attitude that all students will learn meaningful skills that will lead them toward independence.
4. Students will be involved in the normal routines of school as much as possible.
5. Instruction should occur not only in the least restrictive placement but also in the most natural environments to maximize **generalization,** application of known information in new settings, and **maintenance,** ability to apply and use taught information for a length of time.
6. Meaningful learning activities should comprise the majority of instruction.
7. Materials used and instructional activities should not be contrived but should be a natural part of the student's environment.
8. Instructional procedures should be as precise as necessary, but no more than necessary.
9. Data should be collected on student performance, and regular meetings to analyze the data and make decisions about programmatic changes should take place.
10. Specific efforts should be made to improve the attitudes of all people in school environments toward students with disabilities.
11. Family members should be acknowledged as the primary and long-term teachers of students, and they should be included in each programming decision (Westling & Fox, 2004).

Instructional Methods

Task analysis is the process of isolating, describing, and sequencing all subtasks that must be mastered for the student to acquire a skill. The skill being taught, the student's prior knowledge or practice of the skill, and sometimes the severity of the student's condition determine the number of steps necessary. Often a student with more significant disabilities requires additional steps or extra time to acquire a step. There are several ways to teach a sequence of skills. One frequently used method has the teacher begin with the simplest or first step and proceed sequentially to the more difficult steps until the entire task has been accomplished **(forward chaining).** An alternative method is to start with the final step, giving the student a sense of accomplishment for a completed task, and then adding steps back to the beginning **(backward chaining).** Both methods, forward and backward chaining, consist of breaking skills that need to be learned into simpler, easier, or smaller steps. Teaching skills in related clusters promotes the student's understanding of the interdependence of some naturally occurring behaviors (Alberto & Troutman, 2006; Wolery, Ault, & Doyle, 1992).

This systematic instruction requires that teachers follow a series of specific procedures and collect performance results to document the effectiveness of their instruction. Teachers help students learn the correct steps in a skill sequence through the abundant use of positive reinforcement, prompts, cues, and demonstrations. Immediate reinforcers are necessary in the beginning sequences of skill mastery. External reinforcers are paired with natural cues in the environment so the cues will eventually

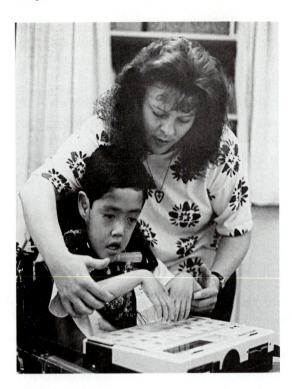

trigger the performance of the behaviors being learned (Alberto & Troutman, 2006; Turnbull et al., 2004).

Another instructional method shown to be effective with students with significant disabilities, as well as with students with mild disabilities and those typically developing, is direct instruction with response prompting. This strategy is straightforward, effective, and efficient. It is especially useful with students with more severe disabilities when used to embed curricular aspects that are not appropriate for the majority of students in the class. Each trial takes approximately 4 seconds, and it has been shown to be effective for students and easily taught to teachers (Werts, 2005; Wolery et al., 1997). The teacher uses a one- or two-trial sequence during transitions (moving from student to student providing help) and at other times during the day. Positive learning effects have been shown with as few as four trials per day (Werts, Caldwell, & Wolery, 1996; Werts, Wolery, Venn, Demblowski, & Doren, 1996).

To further increase the efficiency of learning for students with substantial disabilities, a technique called instructive feedback can add extra information into regular curricular activities. This technique has been used effectively with many direct instructional strategies to increase the efficiency of teaching. It involves adding extra information in the consequent event to a trial (i.e., adding information after the praise or reinforcement) (Werts, Wolery, Gast, & Holcombe, 1996; Werts, Wolery, Holcombe, & Gast, 1995). Instructive feedback provides students with additional information that is not central to the primary lesson; it is especially effective in teaching IEP goals that are not needed by the majority of the class. The information is merely presented to the student at the conclusion of a direct trial, following or concurrently with the praise statement or positive consequence. To illustrate: The teacher holds a card with a word printed on it, asks the student to look, and then delivers the direction, "What word?" If the student reads the word correctly, the teacher praises the student and adds, "This word means _____." Students are not expected to respond to this second stimulus and are not reinforced if they do.

Teachers have been able to implement instructive feedback reliably in a variety of instructional groupings (one-to-one, small-group, whole-class, and computer-assisted instruction). Instructive feedback has been presented verbally, visually, and in combination. The use of instructive feedback does not appear to interfere with the rapidity with which target behaviors are acquired, nor does it substantially increase the length of instructional sessions. Students have acquired information when (1) one stimulus is presented for each target behavior, (2) two stimuli are presented for each target behavior either simultaneously or on alternating trials, and (3) the stimuli are related and unrelated to the target stimulus. In small-group instruction, students sometimes acquire some of their peers' target and instructive feedback stimuli (Anthony, Wolery, Werts, Caldwell, & Snyder, 1996; Caldwell, Wolery, Werts, & Caldwell, 1996; Werts, Caldwell, et al., 1996; Werts, Wolery, Gast, et al., 1996).

One additional consideration for students with severe or multiple disabilities is that they not be denied access to daily routine activities simply because they are unable to function independently. Appropriate modifications can often enable these students to participate and learn with their peers. One of the tenets of IDEA is that students should have, as appropriate, access to the general educational curricula and environments. Family members and teachers are currently taking the position that participation (as much as is reasonable) in the whole range of school and other experiences is required for an appropriate educational experience.

Technology

There is widespread national support for the development and use of computer and other technologies for people with disabilities in education, assessment, vocational training, and transition from school to employment. Numerous programs have been designed for students with learning, hearing, vision, motor, and cognitive disabilities. Assistive technology is composed of services and aids: mechanical, electronic, computer based, nonmechanical, and nonelectronic. These devices are designed to assist individuals to function in their environments. Individuals with disabilities and their teachers can use these devices to (a) assist them in learning, (b) make the environment more accessible, (c) enable them to compete in the workplace, (d) enhance their independence, or (e) otherwise improve their quality of life. These may include commercially available or "homemade" devices that are specially designed to meet the idiosyncratic needs of a particular individual (Blackhurst, 2005; Blackhurst & Lahm, in press).

Adaptive devices such as head pointers allow some students to type, and other students with limited dexterity are able to use voice-activated software for help with reading and responding to curriculum materials. Communication boards, keyboards, and other electronic devices can be adapted electronically or mechanically through the use of specifically designed switches that enable people with disabilities to enhance whatever motor skills are available to them. Computer programs can translate print into braille and braille into print or electronic voice. Toys can be adapted to make noise or light up to aid in location. Switches can be activated by blowing on a straw, through the use of head sticks, or by small body movements. Box 11.3 lists several questions that may be important to ask when considering use of a device.

Video games and videotaping can be used to teach social skills and communication and to simulate community-based instruction and behavioral management. Teachers can use current technology for administrative tasks and to obtain data for making instructional decisions, as well as other decisions about their students (Braddock, Rizzolo, & Thompson, 2004; Edyburn, 2005; Wehman, 1997).

BOX 11.3
WHAT EVERY TEACHER SHOULD KNOW
ABOUT TECHNOLOGY

Many factors must be considered when deciding to adopt or purchase a piece of equipment as an assistive device.

- Is the equipment going to do what you need? Many times the device is a great help for some problems but it may not be a help with the specific task for the student. Developmental and physical functioning levels must be considered.
- How easy is it to learn and to operate? A piece of equipment that is harder to operate than the task it is to replace is not functional. Is the manual readable?
- How sturdy or reliable is it? Is it going to hold up under normal wear? It is frustrating and expensive to have a device in for repairs.
- How much help is available? Are there people in the community or the student's family who can help with the device especially when it is being learned? Are there toll-free numbers to call if the device breaks or will not operate?
- Have others had good experiences with the device? Are there other students who have used this piece of equipment or adaptation to a piece of equipment? Do these students have any advice or recommendations?

Placement

Determining the most appropriate, reasonable, and natural settings for the education of students with severe or multiple disabilities has engendered serious debates in special education and educational circles. Students with severe or multiple disabilities are guaranteed by legislation and court decisions educational services in the LRE for their individual needs. This may include their home or local schools, community programs, partial or full participation in chronologically age-appropriate environments, and extracurricular activities that are educationally and socially responsive to their special needs. Because the most appropriate setting for maximal learning must be determined individually, there are no definitive answers as to what constitutes the LRE for all students. Considerable evidence supports the educational and socialization benefits of integrating students with severe disabilities into the regular classroom (Kavale & Forness, 1997; Leyser & Kirk, 2004; Salisbury, Evans, & Palombaro, 1997). Inclusion is occurring more and more frequently (Sailor, Gee, & Karasoff, 2000; U.S. Department of Education, 2005), and there are levels of participation in inclusive practices ranging from unadapted participation to receiving a functional curriculum in the general education classroom (Wolfe & Hall, 2003). Kirk et al. (2006) reviewed numerous studies that indicated that inclusion positively influences the attitudes of nondisabled individuals toward their peers with severe or multiple disabilities at various age levels. Inclusion may improve the social and communication skills of students with severe or multiple disabilities and positively improve interactions among all students. An appropriate inclusive placement may facilitate adjustment to community settings as adults. Students with severe or multiple disabilities become more responsive to others, increase reciprocal interactions, and increase displays of affection toward others.

In practice, students with severe or multiple disabilities may have full-time placement in regular classes, part-time placements in regular classes and resource rooms, or placements in special self-contained programs. An IEP based on professional judgments that account for family wishes; the student's age and abilities; the services needed; the content of instructional approaches; and the student's need for a more-or-less structured educational, community, and work environment will determine the best placement (Giangreco et al., 1997; Jackson, Ryndak, & Billingsley, 2000; Wolfe & Hall, 2003).

The question of where to teach students with severe or multiple disabilities is centered on selecting a setting that maximizes skill development and use. It is important to realize that special education is a service and education is a process; neither is equated with a setting. A range of service options is necessary to select the most appropriate placement for each student. Therefore, depending on the severity, number, and kinds of disabilities, these students could be provided services (education and treatment) in institutions, residential settings, or their community or home schools.

Students with severe or multiple disabilities are increasingly being educated in general education classes. These students' schedules are designed so they receive supportive services such as speech-language and physical therapy, orientation and mobility services, and other services unique to their disabilities while attending their home schools. The help of specialists to assist these students is critical. However, the traditional use of specialists who work in isolation in separate classes or schools may not work well in the context of the regular classroom. Many special service providers must learn to integrate their services within regular classroom instruction (French & Chopra, 1999; Werts, Zigmond, & Leeper, 2001).

The low incidence of this population and the limited availability of specially trained teachers and specialists will sometimes dictate the placement for students with severe or multiple disabilities. Other factors, such as conflicting educational goals and different agendas between specialists and regular classroom teachers, specialists disrupting the regular classes, and incompatible school schedules and routines, can also interfere with full inclusion. However, there is a great deal of support and advocacy for full access to homes, neighborhoods, local schools, regular classrooms, and job sites. These support and advocacy activities maximize the importance of specialized services in inclusive settings (Giangreco et al., 1997; Kennedy & Horn, 2004; Meyen, 1996).

ISSUES OF IMPORTANCE
Confusing the Effects of Disabilities

Persons with more than one disability present problems to schools in terms of choice of significant areas for intervention. An individual with a hearing loss may also be mentally retarded. A student with CP may be blind. A student with autism may be LD. However, a careful and appropriate assessment of a student with a hearing loss may reveal that poor academic performance is primarily the result of one aspect of the student's functioning levels. If low test scores are a function of poor hearing, then intervention should focus on remediation and accommodation of the hearing loss. If more than one condition exists, however, then the intervention should accommodate both.

Often, one disability area must be accommodated before another can be addressed. These decisions are almost always made on an individual basis, and there are no rules to follow. For example, a nonverbal student who has difficulty using traditional communication devices must be evaluated with the types of switches and devices that he or she is able to use before any academic areas can be addressed.

Another issue is the confusion of MR with mental illness. One of the major concerns of TASH is the faulty assumption that people with MR are mentally ill, an assumption often based on these individuals' challenging behaviors. Individuals with MR are prone to magical thinking and confusing reality because of their cognitive deficits, but this is not mental illness (Rojahn, Matson, & Naglieri, 2004; Singh et al., 2004). People with MR may have some rigid rule-oriented or ritualistic behaviors, and they may exhibit self-stimulating behaviors, but these behaviors do not signify emotional or behavioral disorders. MR does not necessarily include mental illness. On the other hand, persons with MR can have mental illnesses. If there is a multiple diagnosis, both issues and the combination of issues probably will need intervention.

Collaboration

Any combination of disabilities can cause confusion between family members and professionals. This confusion underlies the importance of collaboration among persons involved in the education and care of students with multiple and severe disabilities.

Students with severe and multiple disabilities and their families need a complicated and extensive array of support and services from educators, physical and occupational therapists, vocational counselors, speech-language pathologists, and medical personnel. These involved professionals and paraprofessionals need to cooperate in special health-related services ranging from the administration of medication to assistance with respiratory ventilation to engaging the student in activities deemed important by the IEP team. Turnbull et al. (2004) reported that if students with severe or multiple disabilities are to be successful in integrated schools and communities, collaboration between families and all involved professionals is essential. In the past decade, a greater number of families have kept persons at home, out of institutions, and this has produced different family and student needs. Educational, medical, and related service professionals must provide enabling support either directly to families or through community schools and agencies. The era of the independent professional treating his or her "part" of the student in isolation from the entire rehabilitation program seems to have no place in modern service provision to students with severe or multiple disabilities. This method of service provision is not as helpful to families because they may receive conflicting information. A more collaborative provision of service is needed.

Collaboration may also mean enlisting the support and friendship of the peer group of the student with disabilities. Adults can encourage social interpersonal relationships with other students in the school by fostering peer tutor programs, cooperative small-group learning, and buddy systems (Turnbull et al., 2004; Meyer, 2001). The importance of cooperation and collaboration on behalf of students with severe or multiple disabilities cannot be overemphasized; nor can the profound benefits of engendering peer relationships for these students.

Generalization, Maintenance, and the Use of Aversive Procedures

A persistent concern in the education and treatment of students with severe or multiple disabilities is that students often fail to generalize the behaviors targeted in their programs. They seem unable to maintain learned behaviors after reinforcement and other procedures have been discontinued. Generalization and maintenance programs, when applied, are often haphazardly constructed and poorly monitored. Attainment of behaviors in the controlled safety of the classroom is a far cry from the active use of an acquired behavior in everyday life outside the classroom.

Several issues are apparent in this problem. First, the curriculum written in the IEP for the student should be functional. Behaviors that are functional have a greater possibility of being used in other settings outside the teaching venue. Second, the behaviors must be age appropriate. Again, only age-appropriate behaviors are likely to be needed in independent or partially independent settings. Sorting colored blocks is not age appropriate for older students, but sorting knives, forks, and spoons or sorting laundry items by color are useful behaviors. Third, the behaviors must be developmentally appropriate. Activities that a person is not expected to perform are not acceptable as IEP benchmarks because they will not be used by the student. For behaviors to be generalized and maintained, they must be meaningful and under the control of the student. Fourth, teaching expected and important behaviors must take place in the setting in which they will occur. Students who are expected to communicate with peers should receive communication training in the presence of peers. Students who are expected to order lunch should do so in a restaurant, and students who are expected to use public transportation should be given practice in the community. Family members, teachers, and peers are an underused resource in assisting a student in generalizing and maintaining newly learned skills.

An older and less frequently used method of teaching students with severe behaviors is to discourage troubling and inappropriate behaviors through the use of aversive or punishing procedures, including electric shock, ammonia spray, pinching, and forced body movements. The effectiveness of these procedures is short lived, and the process is ethically suspect (Meyen & Skrtic, 1988). Teaching and rewarding alternatives that are incompatible with unwanted behaviors, rather than punishing inappropriate behaviors, is more desirable and effective. Positive intervention is constructive and teaches the student what to do rather than what not to do. For each inappropriate behavior that serves a purpose for the student (stimulation, attention getting, communication, etc.), an appropriate behavior must be substituted. This is termed the "fair pair rule" (Wolery, Bailey, & Sugai, 1988). Nonaversive procedures, such as rewarding sought-after behavior, facilitate the generalization and maintenance of behaviors that are incompatible with those formerly punished (Alberto & Troutman, 2006).

Family Issues

Families of students with severe or multiple disabilities face many pressures and heartrending issues that most families never need to confront. These families require more financial planning and professional support and services than other families just to help them keep family members at home. They need information about how to deal with everyone's needs and how to become more cogent advocates when dealing with schools, community agencies, and professionals who may not share their philosophies (Dunst, 2002; Lambie, 2000). Families of persons with severe or multiple disabilities may also need direct physical assistance to help with caregiving tasks. They may also need qualified persons to provide some respite and release time from the constant demands of caregiving (Turnbull et al., 2004). Many times, families need counseling and caring professionals to help them understand that their personal needs are as important as those of the student. When making demands of families including persons with severe or multiple disabilities, professionals must be sensitive to the effect their mandates might have on the already-strained family.

PROFESSIONALS

Every professional that we have described in each of the preceding chapters might conceivably be on the service provision team for any given student with severe or multiple disabilities. However, no one team will require all of the services available to all exceptional students. Coordination of the array of personnel requires a team that can work supportively. The student should be on the team. Typically, the team includes the family members, a general education teacher, a special education teacher, a speech-language pathologist, and a physical therapist. Physicians, occupational therapists, vision specialists, audiologists, vocational rehabilitation counselors, movement specialists, and medical and nonmedical paraprofessionals of all types may also be on the team. The composition of the team is obviously driven by the combination and severity of the multiple disabilities and by the needs of the student. How any given team functions is critical to efficient service provision to the family and the student. Sometimes a family member is able and willing to coordinate the services, but frequently a case manager is needed.

The quality of service personnel and the number of services needed, combined with the ability of each cooperating party to work together, determines the efficacy of any team. A **transdisciplinary team,** one that is a coordinated effort of more than one discipline, involves persons from each discipline working cooperatively from the outset of program design and implementation. Team members exchange information, share skills, and train each other to implement specialized programs. Specific team members, especially family members, teachers, and paraprofessionals, have continuous contact with the student and deliver the educational and therapeutic services with support and training from the specialist team members. Programs are implemented in the school, the home, and the community, as well as in specialized settings.

Many students with severe disabilities (one or several coexisting types) require the services of a paraprofessional in the classroom and other school settings. These persons generally stay with the student during the day and assist with tasks of daily living such as hygiene skills, redressing when appropriate, feeding, and mobility. NCLB requires that

paraeducators employed in Title I schools or programs must have 2 years of college coursework (or demonstrate basic literacy skills in math and reading); however, many paraeducators will be required to complete daily tasks for which they are untrained. These tasks may include suctioning, catheterization, cleaning ostomies, and maintaining equipment (e.g., wheelchairs, standing boards, communication devices). In addition, they are frequently asked to provide monitoring for other students in the class, help with computers, provide noninstructional assistance (helping with snacks, grading papers, providing classroom displays, etc.), and perform some instructional tasks.

In IDEA 97, language was added allowing paraprofessionals to be involved in instruction under the direct supervision of a licensed professional. Recent research indicates that such supervision does not occur during instructional times and sometimes not at all (Werts, Roark, et al., 2001). Paraprofessionals indicate that a major barrier to doing a better job is their lack of training to do their job.

Another barrier to ideal performance is the lack of planning time with teachers and other professionals (Tillery, Werts, Roark, & Harris, 2003). Parents report that students talk about their paraprofessional, as well as their teacher, when discussing school activities; they perceive both persons as "teachers."

DISCUSSION QUESTIONS

1. Multiple disabilities means concomitant impairments such as MR–blindness or MR–orthopedic impairment. Why does it not include deaf-blindness?

2. What function might self-stimulatory behaviors serve?

3. What are the difficulties in assessing the intellectual capabilities of a student with severe or multiple disabilities?

4. What are functional skills?

5. Is it appropriate for a student with a need for daily medical-type procedures (e.g., catheterization, feeding tubes, medication) to be educated in a general education setting?

6. Why are generalization and maintenance important for a student?

7. What is task analysis?

8. Write a task analysis for (a) tying your shoe laces; (b) making toast; and (c) computing a problem in long division. Have a colleague follow your instructions.

9. What can a teacher do in the classroom with a student with multiple disabilities that will be helpful to the family of the student?

PROFESSIONAL ASSOCIATIONS AND PARENT OR SELF-HELP GROUPS

American Association of the Deaf-Blind
814 Thayer Avenue
Silver Spring, MD 20910
812-855-6508

Association of Birth Defect Children
3526 Emerywood Lane
Orlando, FL 32812

Association for Persons with Severe Handicaps
11201 Greenwood Avenue N
Seattle, WA 98133

Helen Keller National Center for Deaf-Blind
Youths and Adults
111 Middle Neck Road
Sands Point, NY 11050

The Advance
Association for Persons in Supported Employment
5001 W. Broad Street, Suite 34
Richmond, VA 23230

Supported Employment InfoLines
Training Resource Network
316 St. George Street
St. Augustine, FL 32084

United Cerebral Palsy Association
66 East 34th Street
New York, NY 10016

REFERENCES

Alberto, P. A., & Troutman, A. C. (2006). *Applied behavior analysis for teachers* (7th ed.). Upper Saddle River, NJ: Merrill/Prentice Hall.

Anthony, L., Wolery, M., Werts, M. G., Caldwell, N. K., & Snyder, E. D. (1996). Effects of daily probing on acquisition of instructive feedback responses. *Journal of Behavioral Education, 6,* 111–133.

Batshaw, M. L., & Perret, Y. M. (Eds.). (1992). *Children with handicaps: A medical primer* (3rd ed.). Baltimore: Paul H. Brookes.

Beukelman, D. R., & Mirenda, P. (1998). *Augmentative and alternative communication: Management of severe communication disorders in children and adults.* Baltimore: Paul H. Brookes.

Blackhurst, A. E. (2005). Perspectives on applications of technology in the field of learning disabilities. *Learning Disability Quarterly, 28,* 175–178.

Blackhurst, A. E., & Lahm, E. A. (in press). Foundations of technology and exceptionality. In J. Lindsey (Ed.), *Technology and exceptional individuals* (4th ed.). Austin, TX: Pro-Ed.

Bowe, F. G. (2000). *Physical, sensory, and health disabilities: An introduction.* Upper Saddle River, NJ: Merrill/Prentice Hall.

Bower, T. G. R. (1989). *The rational infant.* New York: Freeman.

Braddock, D., Rizzolo, M. C., & Thompson, M. (2004). Emerging technologies and cognitive disability. *Journal of Special Education Technology, 19*(4), 49–56.

Browder, D., Flowers, C., & Ahlgrim-Delzell, L. (2004). The alignment of alternate assessment content with academic and functional curricula. *The Journal of Special Education, 37,* 211–223.

Browder, D., Spooner, F., & Ahlgrim-Delzell, L. (2003). A content analysis of the curricular philosophies reflected in states' alternate assessment performance indicators. *Research and Practice for Persons with Severe Disabilities, 28,* 165–181.

Caldwell, N. K., Wolery, M., Werts, M. G., & Caldwell, Y. (1996). Embedding instructive feedback into student–teacher interactions during independent seatwork. *Journal of Behavioral Education, 6,* 459–480.

Clark, N. M., Cushing, L. S., & Kennedy, C. H. (2004). An intensive onsite technical assistance model to promote inclusive educational practices for students with disabilities in middle school and high school. *Research and Practice for Persons with Severe Disabilities, 29,* 253–262.

Cushing, L. S., & Kennedy, C. H. (2002). Adolescents: Putting research into practice. In H. Goldstein & L. K. Kaczmarek (Eds.), *Promoting social communication: Children with developmental disabilities from birth to adolescence. Communication and language intervention series* (Vol. 10, pp. 331–344). Baltimore: Paul H. Brookes.

Dunst, C. J. (2002). Family-centered practices: Birth through high school. *The Journal of Special Education, 36,* 139–147.

Edyburn, D. L. (2005). Assistive technology for students with mild disabilities: From consideration to outcome measurement. In D. Edyburn, K. Higgins, & R. Boone (Eds.), *Handbook of special education technology research and practice* (pp. 239–269). Whitefish Bay, WI: Knowledge by Design, Inc.

Everson, J. (Ed.). (1995). *Supporting young adults who are deaf-blind in their communities.* Baltimore: Paul H. Brookes.

French, N. K., & Chopra, R. V. (1999). Parent perspectives on the roles of paraprofessionals. *The Association for Persons with Severe Handicaps, 24*(4), 259–272.

Friend, M. (2005). *Special education: Contemporary perspectives for school professionals.* Boston: Allyn & Bacon.

Gardner, J. F., & Carran, D. T. (2005). Attainment of personal outcomes by people with developmental disabilities. *Mental Retardation, 43,* 157–174.

Giangreco, M. F., Edelman, S. W., Macfarland, S., & Luiselli, T. E. (1997). Attitudes about educational and related services for students with deaf-blindness and multiple disabilities. *Exceptional Children, 63,* 329–342.

Graham, E. M., & Morgan, M. A. (1997). Growth before birth. In M. L. Batshaw (Ed.), *Children with disabilities* (4th ed., pp. 53–69). Baltimore: Brookes.

Hardman, M. L., Drew, C. J., & Egan, M. W. (2005). *Human exceptionality: Society, school, and family* (7th ed.). Needham, MA: Allyn & Bacon.

Individuals with Disabilities Education Improvement Act (IDEA). (2004). 20 U.S.C.: 1400 et seq.

Jackson, L., Ryndak, D. L., & Billingsley, F. (2000). Useful practices in inclusive education: A preliminary view of what experts in moderate to severe disabilities are saying. *Journal of The Association for Persons with Severe Handicaps, 25*(3), 129–141.

Janssen, M. J., Riksen-Walraven, J. M., & Van Dijk, J. P. M. (2003). Toward a diagnostic intervention model for fostering harmonious interactions between deaf-blind children and their educators. *Journal of Visual Impairment & Blindness, 97,* 197–214.

Kavale, K. A., & Forness, S. R. (1997). Defining learning disabilities: Consonance & dissonance. In J. W. Lloyd, E. J. Kameenui, & D. Chord (Eds.), *Issues in educating students with disabilities.* Mahwah, NJ: Erlbaum.

Kennedy, C. H., & Horn, E. (2004). *Including students with severe disabilities*. Boston: Allyn & Bacon.

Kirk, S. A., Gallagher, J. J., Anastasiow, N. J., & Coleman, M. R. (2006). *Educating exceptional children* (11th ed.). Boston: Houghton Mifflin.

Kirk, S. A., Gallagher, J. J., & Anastasiow, N. J. (1997). *Educating exceptional children* (8th ed.). Boston: Houghton Mifflin.

Lambert, N., Nihira, K., & Leland, H. (1993). *AAMR adaptive behavior scale–school* (2nd ed.). Austin, TX: Pro-Ed.

Lambie, R. (2000). *Family systems within educational contexts: Understanding at-risk and special needs students*. Denver: Love.

Leyser, Y., & Kirk, R. (2004). Evaluating inclusion: An examination of parent views and factors influencing their perspectives. *International Journal of Disability, Development and Education, 51*(3), 271–285.

Luiselli, J. K. (1992). Assessment and treatment of self-injury in a deaf-blind child. *Journal of Developmental and Physical Disabilities, 4,* 219–226.

Mar, H. H., & Sall, N. (1995). Enhancing social opportunities and relationships of children who are deaf-blind. *Journal of Visual Impairment and Blindness, 89,* 280–286.

Marks, S. B. (1998). Understanding and preventing learned helplessness in children who are congenitally deaf-blind. *Journal of Visual Impairment & Blindness, 93,* 200–212.

Meyen, E. L. (1996). *Exceptional children in today's schools* (3rd ed.). Denver: Love.

Meyen, E. L., & Skrtic, T. M. (1988). *Exceptional children and youth: An introduction* (3rd ed.). Denver: Love.

Meyer, L. H. (2001). The impact of inclusion on children's lives: Multiple outcomes and friendship in particular. *International Journal of Disability, Development, and Education, 48*(1), 9–31.

Murphy, K., & Byrne, D. (1983). Selection of optimal modalities as avenues of learning in deaf, blind, multiply disabled children. In G. Mencher & S. Gerber (Eds.), *Multiply handicapped hearing-impaired child*. New York: Grune & Stratton.

National Center on Birth Defects and Developmental Disabilities (NCBDDD). (2004). *Kernicterus*. Atlanta, GA: Author.

Nisbet, J. (1992). *Natural supports at home, school and in the community for people with severe disabilities*. Baltimore: Paul H. Brookes.

O'Keefe, L. (2001). Increased vigilance needed to prevent kernicterus in newborns. *AAP News, 18,* 231.

Orelove, F. P., Sobsey, R., & Silberman, R. K. (2004). *Educating children with multiple disabilities: A collaborative approach*. Baltimore: Paul H. Brookes.

Rojahn, J., Matson, J. L., & Naglieri, J. A. (2004). Relationships between psychiatric conditions and behavior problems among adults with mental retardation. *American Journal on Mental Retardation, 109*(1), 21–33.

Ruttenberg, B. A., Wolf-Schein, E. G., & Wenar, C. (1991). *BRIAAC: Behavior Rating Instrument for Autistic and Other Atypical Children* (2nd ed.). Wood Dale, IL: Stoelting.

Ryndak, D. L., & Alper, S. K. (2003). *Curriculum and instruction for students with significant disabilities in inclusive settings*. Boston: Allyn & Bacon.

Sailor, W., & Mix, B. J. (1976). *TARC assessment system*. Lawrence, KS: H & H Enterprises.

Sailor, W., Gee, K., & Karasoff, P. (2000). Inclusion and school restructuring. In M. E. Snell & F. Brown (Eds.), *Instruction of students with severe disabilities* (5th ed., pp. 31–66). Upper Saddle River, NJ: Merrill/Prentice Hall.

Salisbury, C. L., Evans, I. M., & Palombaro, M. M. (1997). Collaborative problem-solving to promote the inclusion of young children with significant disabilities in primary grades. *Exceptional Children, 63,* 195–209.

Sall, N., & Mar, H. H. (1999). In the community of a classroom: Inclusive education of a student with deaf-blindness. *Journal of Visual Impairment and Blindness, 93,* 197–210.

Singh, N. N., Lancioni, G. E., Winton, A. L. S., Molina, E. J., Sage, M., Brown, S., et al. (2004). Effects of Snoezelen room, activities of daily living skills training, and vocational skills training on aggression and self-injury by adults with mental retardation and mental illness. *Research in Developmental Disabilities, 25*(3), 285–293.

Sisson, L. A., Hersen, M., & Van Hasselt, V. B. (1993). Improving the performance of youth with dual sensory impairment: Analyses and social validation of procedures to reduce mal-adaptive responding in vocational and leisure settings. *Behavior Therapy, 24,* 553–571.

Smith, D. D. (2001). *Introduction to special education: Teaching in an age of challenge* (4th ed.). Needham, MA: Allyn & Bacon.

Snell, M. A. (1992). *Systematic instruction of persons with severe handicaps* (4th ed.). Upper Saddle River, NJ: Merrill/Prentice Hall.

Tang, J., Patterson, T. G., & Kennedy, C. H. (2003). Identifying specific sensory modalities maintaining the stereotypy of students with multiple profound disabilities. *Research in Developmental Disabilities, 24,* 433–451.

Taylor, R. L., Brady, M., & Richards, S. B. (2005). *Mental retardation: Historical perspectives, current practices, and future directions*. Boston: Allyn & Bacon.

Tillery, C. Y., Werts, M. G., Roark, R. R., & Harris, S. H. (2003). Perceptions of paraeducators on job retention. *Teacher Education and Special Education, 3,* 154–168.

Turnbull, A. P., Turnbull, H. R., Shank, M., & Smith, S. (2004). *Exceptional lives: Special education in today's schools* (4th ed.). Upper Saddle River, NJ: Merrill/Prentice Hall.

U.S. Department of Education. (1999). Assistance to states for education of children with disabilities and the early intervention program for infants and toddlers with disabilities: Final regulations. *Federal Register, 64*(48), CFR parts 300 and 303.

U.S. Department of Education. (2005). *Twenty-fifth annual report to Congress on the implementation of the Individuals with Disabilities Education Act*. Washington, DC: Author.

Wehman, P. (1997). *Exceptional individuals in school, community, and work*. Austin, TX: Pro-Ed.

Wehmeyer, M. L. (2000). *Teaching students with mental retardation: Providing access to the general curriculum*. Baltimore: Paul H. Brookes.

Werts, M. G. (2005). *Instructive feedback as a tool for differentiating instruction*. Proceedings: International Association of Special Education, Halifax, Nova Scotia.

Werts, M. G., Caldwell, N. K., & Wolery, M. (1996). Peer modeling of response chains: Observational learning by students with disabilities. *Journal of Applied Behavior Analysis, 29,* 53–66.

Werts, M. G., Roark, R. R., Harris, S. H., & Tillery, C. Y. (April, 2001). Tasks and activities of paraeducators in the classrooms, National Conference on Training and Employment of Paraeducators, Minneapolis, MN.

Werts, M. G., Wolery, M., Gast, D. L., & Holcombe, A. (1996). Sneak in some extra learning by using instructive feedback. *Teaching Exceptional Children, 28*(3), 70–71.

Werts, M. G., Wolery, M., Holcombe, A., & Gast, D. L. (1995). Instructive feedback: Review of parameters and effects. *Journal of Behavioral Education, 5,* 55–75.

Werts, M. G., Wolery, M., Venn, M. L., Demblowski, D., & Doren, H. (1996). Effects of transition-based teaching with instructive feedback on the acquisition of skills by children with and without disabilities. *Journal of Educational Research, 90,* 75–86.

Werts, M. G., Zigmond, N., & Leeper, D. C. (2001). Paraprofessional proximity and academic engagement: Primary-aged students with disabilities in general education classrooms. *Education and Training in Mental Retardation and Developmental Disabilities, 36,* 424–440.

Westling, D. L., & Fox, L. (2004). *Teaching students with severe disabilities* (4th ed.). Upper Saddle River, NJ: Merrill/ Prentice Hall.

Wolery, M., Anthony, L., Snyder, E. D., Werts, M. G., & Katzenmeyer, J. (1997). Training elementary teachers to embed instruction during classroom activities. *Education and Treatment of Children, 20,* 40–58.

Wolery, M., Ault, M. J., & Doyle, P. M. (1992). *Teaching students with moderate to severe disabilities.* New York: Longman.

Wolery, M., Bailey, D. B., & Sugai, G. M. (1988). *Effective teaching: Principles and procedures of applied behavior analysis with exceptional students.* Boston: Allyn & Bacon.

Wolfe, P. S., & Hall, T. E. (2003). Making inclusion a reality for students with severe disabilities. *Teaching Exceptional Children, 35*(4), 56–61.

12

Students Who Are Gifted and Talented

KEY TERMS

WHAT WOULD YOU DO?

Austin was a well-formed male aged 9 years. He was born at term with no complications. He started kindergarten at the age of 5 years 0 months. He had been reading since the age of 3 and playing counting and preliteracy games with his younger brother and his mother. The parents were both in the home. The father was a scientist with a Ph.D. in radiation oncology, and the mother was a special education teacher with a master's degree and earning hours toward her Ph.D. She taught special education in the local district for the first 3 years of Austin's life and then stayed at home when the younger sibling was born. Reading was one of Austin's favorite activities. He had a measured total IQ of 132 on a Stanford-Binet, administered at the end of first grade. His current Stanford Achievement scores ranged from 99th percentile in reading comprehension to 69th percentile in math calculations. He was taught a general education curriculum for all subjects.

He had been in a public school in a small Midwestern town with good grades and good reports from his teachers. The kindergarten through third-grade years had been remarkable for small classes and project-based learning. Prior to fourth grade, Austin's family moved to a large urban area and he was enrolled in a public school in a suburban area. The class was larger and he was expected to follow a Joplin-type plan of changing classes for some subjects, attending lecture-type classes, and taking notes and tests from textbooks, with an emphasis on facts. This was contrary to the model to which he was accustomed. He was also asked to write in a different handwriting system (Peterson rather than D'Nealian) and was graded on his handwritten responses for correctness as well as for correct handwriting.

His grades, following the first quarter, were at C and D levels. After several parent conferences and student, parent, and teacher conferences, a plan was put in place requiring the mother to assist Austin with homework. No improvement was noted. A subsequent assignment allowed Austin (and any other student who wished to do so) to choose a project to illustrate a book report in place of a written report. Austin did very well on this assignment, but the teacher reverted to his general mode of requiring written reports and tests. Subsequent plans called for most work to be completed at school, and the mother was to give assistance only when Austin asked for it. No improvements were noted by the teacher.

At first Austin accepted the help given to him but then began to rebel against it. He "forgot" to bring his books home. He would complete his homework but forget to take it to school. He would not turn it in if he had it. He was compliant in class and responded to teachers' questions and prompts. He was correct more often than he was incorrect. He would analyze the material being taught and extrapolate further meaning from it. Often this activity caused him to miss the next phase of the class discussion. Tutors were engaged to work with Austin after school. Still, improvements were noted by the teacher.

Outside of school, Austin played soccer on a town team. He played goalie and halfback and was named to the all-star team in his first year. He took piano lessons, had played the piano since the age of 5, and was playing complex pieces and sight reading. He also played baseball in the backyard with neighborhood friends and his father and brother.

1. Does Austin meet the definition for the label "gifted and talented?"

2. Is there any evidence of causality for giftedness in Austin? What may be conflicting factors resulting in misidentification?

The special gifts and talents that some students possess may, with nurturing and care, blossom into contributions a society values, or they may be ignored and wither on the vine. It is difficult to define giftedness and talent, identify those students with these traits, and provide relevant and meaningful programs that will enhance their development. There are unresolved conflicts about which students should be identified; what training, experiences, and skills are necessary; and even whether the school systems should assume any responsibility for providing special educational opportunities for these students. All of these questions are debated, concerns are discussed, and ultimately decisions are made while generations of gifted and talented students mature and remain underserved. Some are never identified. Others' chances to excel evaporate in poverty. Many are too culturally distinct for their teachers to appreciate or even acknowledge them. A number have other disabilities that may make it difficult to concentrate on their talents, and others, for a variety of reasons, are unable to achieve their potential. Others blossom and reach artistic, academic, and creative heights without special programming.

DEFINITIONS

The definition of who is gifted and talented is evolving and becoming less restrictive. The earliest definitions were based exclusively on intellectual potential as measured by intelligence tests, primarily those in the Wechsler Intelligence tests series or the Stanford-Binet. More recently proposed definitions are wider in scope and recognize many facets of exceptional talent. They stress multiple evaluation measures and encourage family member and community collaboration with school personnel. Regardless of the definition, all seem to agree that students who are gifted and talented need services not ordinarily provided by schools.

Definitions are of practical importance. Hardman, Drew, and Egan (2006) suggested that how we define giftedness and talent will ultimately have an impact on the following:

- The number of students labeled to receive services
- The choice of tests used to evaluate potential gifted students
- The cutoff scores needed to qualify
- Which students are offered enriched curricula
- The type of education provided

- The amount of funding allocated by school systems for programs for gifted and talented students
- The qualifications needed by teachers who wish to instruct students and youth who are gifted and talented

Although factors such as intelligence, creativity, and talent are the keys to many definitions (Davis, 2003; Davis & Rimm, 2004; Howell, Heward, & Swassing, 1996; Stephens & Karnes, 2000), they are not universal to all definitions, nor do all available definitions use these three terms exclusively. In this section, we will share some of the many terms that make up the vocabulary used for defining students who are gifted and talented. Then we will illustrate some of the many federal government and state educational agency definitions. Finally, we will offer a sampling of how some of the most influential scholars define students with gifts and talents.

Federal and State Definitions of Giftedness

In 1972, Sidney Marland, U.S. Commissioner of Education, proposed a definition of giftedness and talent, signaling that educators should be aware of more than just superior intellectual ability when determining which students in their school systems were to be considered for special programming. Marland (1972) proposed the following:

> Gifted and talented children are those identified by professionally qualified persons who, by virtue of outstanding abilities, are capable of high performance. These are children who require differentiated educational programs and/or services beyond those normally provided by the regular school program in order to realize their contribution to self and society.
>
> Children capable of high performance include those with demonstrated achievement and/or potential ability in any of the following areas, singly or in combination:
>
> 1. general intellectual ability
> 2. specific academic aptitude
> 3. creative or productive thinking
> 4. leadership ability
> 5. visual and performing arts
> 6. psychomotor ability.
>
> It can be assumed that utilization of these criteria for identification of the gifted and talented will encompass a minimum of 3 to 5 percent of the school population. (p. 2)

Many students who are gifted and talented benefit from different educational experiences than their age peers to allow maximum growth from school experiences. If these students are already proficient in areas of the curriculum, they have little to gain from the general education pathway. With the passage of PL 95-561 in 1978 and PL 100-297, the Jacob K. Javits Gifted and Talented Children's Education Act of 1988, and NCLB in 2002, Congress incorporated Marland's conceptualizations into law. According to PL 95-561 and its similarly worded mate, PL 100-297:

> Gifted and talented means children, and whenever possible, youth who are identified at the preschool, elementary, or secondary level as possessing demonstrated or potential abilities that give evidence of high performance capability in areas such as intellectual, creative, specific academic or leadership ability, or in the performing or visual arts, and who by reason thereof require services or activities not ordinarily provided by the school.

In 1994, the U.S. Department of Education proposed the following definition for this special group in its publication, *National Excellence: A Case for Developing American Talent* (U.S. Department of Education, 1994):

> Children and youth with outstanding talent perform or show the potential for performing at remarkably high levels of accomplishment when compared with others of their age, experience or environment. These children and youth exhibit high performance capability in intellectual, creative and/or artistic areas, possess an unusual leadership capacity or excel in specific academic fields. They require the services or activities not ordinarily provided in the schools. Outstanding talents are present in children and youth from all cultural groups, across all economic strata and in all areas of human endeavor. (p. 26)

The term *gifted* is noticeably absent from this definition. **Gifted** implies that the student has a mature or developed intellect or talent rather than a developing ability. In stressing the developing aspect of abilities, the U.S. Department of Education underscored the case for services to nurture these abilities and emphasized that teachers need to look beyond scores on tests of intelligence and traditional academic areas for students with talents. This definition explicitly mandates sensitivity to multicultural and diverse populations, who may not automatically meet the expectations of the prevailing cultural standards, and who are currently underrepresented in gifted and talented programs.

Federal legislation has provided a definition for identifying a population of students as gifted and talented, but has left to the states the right to use or modify that definition. Specific definitions appear either in statutes or in state department of education regulations, many of which require special education for those identified as gifted and talented (Davis & Rimm, 2004). Most states have incorporated aspects of the federal definition into their definitions. However, states are by no means uniform in their selection of criteria for inclusion in their individual programs. The most common elements among state definitions are that gifted and talented students must show (1) general intellectual ability, (2) specific academic aptitudes, (3) creative thinking skills, (4) advanced abilities in the fine or performing arts, or (5) leadership abilities (Council of State Directors of Programs for the Gifted, 2001). In a survey reported in 2000, Stephens and Karnes reported that in the decade prior to the study, 29 states had changed their definition of gifted and talented in some manner. Some states added elements, and others deleted some. Five states (Minnesota, Massachusetts, New Hampshire, New Jersey, and South Dakota) reported no longer having a state definition for this population. The most efficient way to obtain and study the definition of any given state is to contact the state department of special education and request a copy of the definition and guidelines for inclusion in gifted and talented programs. A list of addresses and phone numbers for each state appears in Appendix A.

Scholarly Definitions

In this section, we will summarize the conceptualizations of some of the most influential scholars devoted to better understanding students who are gifted and talented. It is from their work, both historical and current, that our understanding of the nature of these students arises.

Terman (1925, 1947, 1959) most influenced the early definitions of giftedness as based on performance on individual IQ test scores. He postulated that precocious students would fare better as adults. He initiated a longitudinal study of students identified as gifted (referred to as "Termites") followed to adulthood. The study is slated for completion in the year 2020. He identified as gifted those persons whose IQ scores were in the 98th or 99th percentile. Terman's standard—that is, students whose IQ scores were at least 130 or who were more than two standard deviations from the mean on a test of intelligence—is still used as a numerical way to describe the intellectual capabilities of students who are gifted. Stephens and Karnes (2000) reported that most states still focus on intellectual ability, at least in part, in defining giftedness. As scholars became more informed about the way students who are gifted and talented function, components other than intellectual functioning were added to the definition. In fact, even our conceptualization of intelligence has expanded. Witty (1951) expanded the definition to include special skills and talents when he described students who are gifted and talented as those who show performance that is remarkable, not only in intellectual functioning, but also in any area valuable to society. Guilford (1959) added that creativity should be considered; he found creativity to be the driving force behind the contributions of scientists and inventors who were gifted. **Creativity** is the ability to sense relationships that are not readily apparent, ask critical questions, and generate novel or unexpected responses to situations.

The belief among researchers studying individuals who are gifted and talented is that intelligence and giftedness are more complex than tests alone can measure. IQ test scores may not accurately reflect thinking ability or insightfulness (Gallagher, 2000; Reis, 1989; Sternberg & Davidson, 1983; Vaughn, Bos & Schumm, 2000). A single number cannot capture giftedness (Haensly, 1999; Hallahan & Kauffman, 2006; Renzulli & Reis, 2002); it is a multifaceted combination of different types of abilities. The person who is gifted will show **analytical understanding,** which allows for dividing problems into their critical components; **synthetic insights,** shown by the intuitive ability to cope with novel situations; or **practical application skills,** which makes it possible to use the analytical and synthetic skills to solve problems.

Renzulli (2000) expanded the definition to include students who might not achieve high IQ scores, but who demonstrate above-average ability in an area, combined with task commitment and creativity. This combination of talents should make these students eligible for special programming he termed "schoolwide enrichment."

Gardner (1983, 1993) postulated a theory of intelligences encompassing the ideas that people have a blend of intelligences. The challenge is to take advantage of the uniqueness of world view of each person (Smith, 2002). He initially listed seven modes of intelligence that rarely operate separately. This widely accepted acknowledgment of the multiple components of intelligence recognizes logical-mathematical intelligence, evidenced by high-level inductive and deductive reasoning and computational skills; linguistic intelligence, seen in written and oral language performance; musical intelligence, the ability to understand and manipulate components of music, either in performance or composition; spatial intelligence, the ability to perceive and manipulate visual-spatial configurations; bodily kinesthetic intelligence, evidenced by the ability to control body movements or handle objects with great skill; interpersonal intelligence, shown by abilities to understand an act insightfully in response to other people's actions or feelings; and intrapersonal intelligence, the ability to use one's own feelings and perceptions as guides to understanding. Gardner and Hatch (1989) expanded the concepts to use in the schools, providing a set of questions and rules for teachers to use in their practice and planning. There is little empirical research indicating such planning results in more effective or efficient teaching.

Sternberg (1996) redefined intelligence to include results of practical experience. He stated it is important to conceptualize success as a measure of how one succeeds in life, not as how one does in school. Experiential and contextual factors also influence the intelligence of a person and should be measured. Sternberg's **Triarchic Model,** intelligence, experience, and context, has been a base for broadening the definitions of mental functioning.

Being gifted and talented means a student has talent at the high end of a continuum. It also indicates a propensity for creative thinking. It does not mean the student has good conceptualization of ideas already articulated but, rather, those ideas and ways of being intelligent that we do not know about yet. It includes high abilities (including high intelligence), high creativity (as seen in the generation of novel ideas and the application of those ideas to solve problems), and high task commitment (shown in the ability to see projects through to their conclusion; Brown, Renzulli, & Gubbins, 2005). In this chapter, we will see how many of the concepts and definitions have an impact on the lives of students who are gifted and talented and the family members and teachers responsible for their well-being.

PREVALENCE

Considering the differences in state and local educational agency definitions used, an accurate count of students who are gifted and talented would seem impossible. However, methods of estimating the number of students who may be served do exist. The talent pool approach used by Renzulli and Reis (1991) and Renzulli (1994) suggests that approximately 15 to 20 percent of the school population could qualify in any variety of areas. Gagne (2000) proposed a metric-based system in which each of five levels of giftedness (in each field of talent) reflects a prevalence that is one tenth that of the previous level. This system suggests that 30 to 40 percent of the population is mildly gifted in at least one area. The U.S. Department of Education accumulates records of students receiving services and has found that approximately 6 percent of the school population receives special education services. Davis and Rimm (2004) reported that traditional methods of identifying students would result in a figure of 3 to 5 percent of school populations. Because the variance of these estimates is so wide, there seems to be little usefulness in identifying a global number. Each educational agency responsible for the provision of services must determine its own estimate for staffing and funding based on the definition used.

CHARACTERISTICS

Common stereotypes of students who are gifted and talented as little adults with thick glasses, pocket protectors, and arcane mathematics textbooks in each hand do not mirror reality. Being considered gifted and talented may cover a wide variety of possibilities, abilities, and skills, each occurring individually or in combination with others. As a result, a correspondingly wide variety of characteristics are applicable to students who are gifted and talented. However, common characteristics do exist. These traits are generalizations based for the most part on observations, standardized tests, and each individual observer's familiarity with students who are gifted and talented. Like all generalizations, they fail to describe each individual student, but rather provide large inclusive categories that help family members, teachers, and other interested community members recognize the behavioral characteristics these special students are likely to exhibit.

Beginning in 1920, Terman (1925, 1947, 1959) studied 1,528 students with average IQ scores of 151. His discoveries over more than 40 years helped to contradict the most widely held stereotypes of students who are gifted and talented. He discovered that these students tended to be superior to their age mates in almost every measure applied. They were not intellectually gifted at the cost of physical weakness, social timidness, or emotional immaturity. In fact, as a group, they were taller, heavier, stronger, more energetic, and healthier than their age mates. They were more emotionally stable and even showed, as measured by Terman, superior moral character (Terman, 1926). It must be noted that Terman's students were selected as the result of their performance on group intelligence scores and teacher recommendations. Overall they were a white middle-class group of students who were high achievers (Shurkin, 1992). Culturally diverse and economically disadvantaged students did not make up a significant portion of the sample. It must be emphasized that these are general characteristics. Students who are gifted show as much individual variation as any other group of students. As we recognize more types of giftedness, the relationships Terman described may be less observable. However, others, including Gallagher (1985), also reported that the students they observed were socially and emotionally equal to or ahead of their age peers' developmental levels and above average in their concerns about moral and ethical issues and behaviors. They tended to be well liked by peers, social leaders, self-sufficient, and demonstrated a wide variety of interests; although not immune to problems, they were less prone to neurotic or psychotic episodes than their contemporaries (Piechowski, 1997; Reis & Renzulli, 2004; VanTassel-Baska, 1992).

Creativity, in many different forms, appears repeatedly as a characteristic of students who are gifted and talented. The characteristics of creativity are varied. We often see gifted and talented students who produce large numbers of novel, divergent ideas and solutions to problems (Clark, 1997). These sometimes unusual or unexpected ideas can be produced rapidly in great detail and can be paired with unlikely alternative solutions to problems (Guilford, 1987). Creativity is difficult to measure. Several testing instruments have been developed to tap into creativity. In a Remote Association Task (Mednick & Mednick, 1967), students are given three words and are asked to come up with the word that associates the other three together. For example, cottage, blue, and mouse are all associated with cheese. The Khatena-Torrance Creative Perception Inventory (KTCPI) (Khatena & Torrance, 1976) has two subtests: Something About Myself (SAM) and What Kind of Person Are You? (WKOPAY). The Screening Assessment for Gifted Elementary and Middle School Students, Second Edition (SAGES–2) (Johnsen & Corn, 2001) is an assessment for identifying students who are gifted in academics and reasoning. These and other assessment instruments attempt to elicit original responses to questions and problems. Rather than looking for "correct" answers, they look for unusual and creative answers to questions that indicate that the student is imaginative and understands the problems presented. Generally, the tests are adequate but not reliable (Cooper, 1991; Gallucci, Middleton, & Kline, 2000; Morse, 1994).

Students who are gifted and talented can show exceptional academic skills, and in general, they are able to grasp concepts, generalize, analyze, and synthesize new ideas or problems with greater facility than their age peers (Clark, 1997; Hallahan & Kauffman, 2006). Sometimes they have unusual aptitude in only a given area or areas. They sometimes learn to read easily before entering school, either teaching themselves or learning from minimal input from family members. Reading is often a preferred leisure activity (Hardman et al., 2006). They learn a great deal of information quickly, retain and use what they learn, have an excellent command of language, enjoy acquiring and manipulating abstract material, and are stimulated and excited by the learning process in general. Students who are gifted and talented characteristically do more than just absorb knowledge. They have the ability to see the "big picture," as evidenced by their ability to deal with a variety of concepts at any time and organize them into large, comprehensive, and meaningful patterns. They may have a developed sense of moral justice, which leads them to see and to act in ways to benefit the greater good (Hallahan & Kauffman, 2006). They have an intellectual curiosity that fires a need for mental stimulation and an intuitive sense of appropriateness reflected in good judgment (Clark, 1997; Gallagher & Gallagher, 1994; Piirto, 1994; Silverman, 1995).

Students who are gifted are often confident students, exhibiting an advanced appreciation of humor along with an intellectual playfulness that brings a sense of relaxation to their creative pursuits. They do not fear being different and will uninhibitedly express opinions and, if sufficiently challenged, express their opinions in a spirited and tenacious manner (Berger, 1994; Neihart, Reis, Robinson, & Moon, 2002; Winebrenner, 1992).

We can more easily catalog the characteristics of students who are academically gifted than we can those who are extremely talented or creative. Talents usually refer to outstanding skills or potentials, primarily those in the visual or performing arts. Students who are talented might show highly developed nonverbal skills, exceptional physical coordination, and spatial talents. They might display skills in music, dance, storytelling, drawing, or painting (Turnbull, Turnbull, Shank, & Smith, 2004). Many persons who evidence creativity have predicative signs in early childhood (Piirto, 1999). Students who are visually talented seem to show more control over artistic media of all types than do their age mates. This is often most noticeable in early drawing skills (Clark & Zimmerman, 1984).

Students who are gifted and talented often show the potential for leadership. Although there are many different types of leaders and many skills appropriate to leadership, some characteristics have emerged. Highly developed communication skills seem to head the list, along with coexisting social skills, empathy, superior decision-making skills, the ability to motivate others, and the ability to keep groups united and on task; these all appear to be a part of the leadership component of giftedness (Turnbull et al., 2004). Even though these students may show leadership skills, they are often very independent. They can plan and execute projects with little need

for or interest in supervision. Some authors believe these students should be guided in their development of leadership traits (Bisland, Karnes, & Cobb, 2004) Many of these students rely on their own judgment and self-evaluation more than on the evaluations of their peers or teachers.

One might conclude that being gifted and talented excuses students from the negatives in their lives. This is not the case at all. Students who are gifted are, in many ways, like all other students. They suffer emotional traumas, have physical problems, and evidence all the types of behavior that all their peers demonstrate. In addition, their talents often bring some special problems. These students are often impatient with the routines of regular classroom life. Although they may do very well in analysis, argument, and debate, tasks and rote exercises are often met with resistance and noncompliance (Smith, 2001; Vaughn et al., 2000). Conforming to routines in general may be difficult for some of these students. Their self-evaluations may lead them toward perfectionism and to applying unreasonably high standards not only to their own efforts but also to the efforts of others in their environment. Driven, domineering, and aloof describe some students who are gifted and talented (Howell et al., 1996). Clark (1997) synthesized the work of many investigators and developed a comprehensive list of the characteristics of students who are gifted and talented and the problems that might arise as a consequence of outstanding ability. She summarized their characteristics and potential problems within five domains: cognitive (thinking), affective (feeling), physical (sensation), intuitive, and societal.

ETIOLOGY

At this time, we can make only informed guesses and point out what seem to be important factors for those already diagnosed as gifted and talented. We are unable to predict or perfectly explain why giftedness occurs. Many factors such as heredity and early childhood environment appear to be important. The interaction between heredity and environment seems to be the key to helping giftedness develop (Reis, 1989).

Heredity

The statistical probability of a student being gifted increases when his or her parents have higher-than-average intelligence and are able to provide a nurturing environment (Delisle, 2003a). Studies of higher incidence of giftedness in both twins and the close relationship between the talents of adopted children and their natural, rather than custodial, parents indicate some inherited properties in giftedness (Gottfredson, 2003; Plomin, 1989; Rothenberg & Wyshak, 2004). Clark (1997) presented a genetically based cause for giftedness, but stated that psychosocial factors are important as well.

Environment

Heredity may predispose talent, but talent is also nurtured and developed by environment (Hallahan & Kauffman, 2006; Kirk, Gallagher, & Anastasiow, 2000). The proportional mix of heredity and environment necessary to produce and develop a student who is gifted remains unknown. The nurturing environment includes not only intellectual and artistic stimulation but also more basic components such as appropriate nutrition and escaping the effects of neurological trauma. Although basic nutrition and care are necessary for growth and realization of potential, it is not sufficient. It is impossible to simplistically conclude that because malnutrition can bring about mental deficiency in students who might otherwise have been normal or even above average, a superior diet and health care system will produce students who are gifted. Parents, families, peer group interactions, and even community experiences can have a strong influence on the development of a student's talents. Bloom (1982) and Bloom and Sosniak (1981) traced what they believed to be critical experiences in the developing years of persons eventually identified as gifted. As adults, they were able to recall some or many of the following experiences:

- A specific person in their family who took a personal interest in their development and provided support for that development
- Family members who were role models in a skill or talent area
- Family members who encouraged an exploration of interests and curiosities
- Family members who communicated their belief that the student would do well in a given talent area
- Expectations of high performance standards with enforced schedules of accomplishment
- A variety of learning experiences, often informal
- Provision of private tutors and mentors to guide in the attainment of performance standards
- Direct parental observation of practice sessions, with rewards for accomplishment
- Parental encouragement to participate in public events to showcase talents

Several characteristics may be unexpected in students with high to extremely high IQ scores. These characteristics, some of which may not be those that teachers generally find desirable in classroom settings, include exhibiting high sensitivity or an excessive amount of energy, resisting authority unless it is democratically presented, needing the presence of stable and secure adults, an inability to sit still unless the task or conversation is extremely interesting, and giving up on tasks after early failure. These reports seem to undermine any argument for leaving students who might potentially be gifted and talented to their own devices with the expectation that they will somehow blossom as highly productive, talented adults (Davis & Rimm, 2004).

IDENTIFICATION PROCESS

The most common strategies for identifying students who are gifted and talented usually include some combination of the several methods. A survey recently conducted revealed that teachers, principals, and parents favored a multipronged approach, looking at individual expression criteria, ongoing assessment, multiple criteria for identification, and consideration of contextual factors. Respondents were opposed to using IQ scores as a sole criterion. Generally, the following are used to identify students who may benefit from programming:

- Standardized tests of aptitude and achievement are administered to identify potential candidates.
- Nominations are solicited from creditable sources such as teachers and family members.
- Products illustrating the student's outstanding potential are collected.

Testing

Three types of tests are used most frequently. Achievement tests are designed to indicate whether a student demonstrates abilities or learned skills in particular subject areas. Aptitude or intelligence tests, both group and individual, may signal a teacher to look for abilities whether or not academic achievement has been outstanding. Tests of creativity measure divergent and novel thinking processes by seeking creative rather than "correct" responses.

Tests have both benefits and liabilities. The traditional method of identifying students who are gifted and talented has been to use intelligence tests administered in a group setting and then limit the pool of eligible students to those with IQ scores in the 98th or 99th percentile (Howell et al., 1996; Pendarvis, 1993). Because group aptitude tests can be administered without the services of a psychologist, they are less costly for initial screening. However, group tests are not as reliable as individually administered tests. Most of the tests used have been designed for average students and may not be sufficiently discriminative for students who are gifted. Achievement tests will isolate only those students doing well academically, and neither type of test will routinely measure creative thinking in areas other than academic subjects. Some students, regardless of how gifted they are, simply do not do well on timed tests. Many researchers also believe that culturally diverse students do not perform well on these tests (Kirk et al., 2000).

Individual aptitude assessment instruments are more reliable and have been accepted as valid for predicting students who will do well in school. The interpretation of the results of individual tests can be critical in the evaluation of potential. Tests of creativity might deal with some of these concerns. For example, the Torrance Tests of Creative Thinking (TTCT) (Torrance, 1966) test giftedness by measuring fluency (the ability to give many answers to questions), flexibility (different types of answers or the ability to shift from one type of answer to another), originality (responding in unique yet appropriate ways), and elaboration (developing answers in detail). However, data on the correlation of these measures with creative performance are lacking (Sattler, 2002). Other tests designed to be more culturally sensitive include the Subcultural Indices of Academic Potential (Renzulli, 1973) and the Kranz Talent Identification Instrument (Kranz, 1982).

All types of tests, when used with some degree of sensitivity by a professional trained and experienced in working with students from diverse groups, help to provide some information but cannot be the sole criterion for identification. A multifaceted approach using tests, nominations, observations, analysis of work and work habits, informal tests of divergent thinking (Sattler, 2002), and student-generated products provides a more complete assessment of potential. **Divergent thinking** is the ability to start from a given idea or concept and branch into different directions from the starting point.

Nominations

Students who might be gifted and talented may be nominated by classroom teachers, family members, other students, or in some instances the students themselves. A checklist or questionnaire is usually provided to help with the nomination. The checklists rely on observations of performance or on reports from memory. Classroom teachers may mention grades, academic awards earned, outstanding test scores, and other achievements. Items such as the student's ability to learn rapidly, work unsupervised, use vocabulary skills beyond classmates, be imaginative, show curiosity, complete and exceed assignment requirements, and use advanced and original oral or written language are often included in the checklists (Sattler, 2002).

Nominations by teachers are not a consistently reliable source for identification. Teachers refer attractive students more than students they find unattractive. Females are nominated less often than males, although this is slowly changing. Parents may be more familiar with their children and as a result may be a more creditable referral source in the early grades. Both parents and teachers show biases in opinions about students who may benefit from special programming. Research on the validity of peer and self-nominations is limited. Behavioral checklists, parent interviews, and direct observations of a student's performance may be less formal than standardized tests but are especially important for culturally different or disabled students who might be both gifted and have a concomitant disability (Wolf, 1990). Nominations should not stand alone as a gateway to enrichment programs for gifted students. Too many aspects of the process can be skewed by personal biases.

Products

Stories, poems, paintings, and videotapes of outstanding performances often compose a portfolio of products, which is becoming a more common and useful method employed in discovering gifts and talents. This is proving to be most critical in the evaluation of outstanding performances in nonacademic areas (Gardner, 1999; Reis & Renzulli, 1991; Renzulli, 2004). Specialists outside of the normal decision-making process can be more easily asked for their input on a portfolio than on the other strategies outlined earlier.

Early Intervention

A final concern in the identification process is the relative delay of most identification systems for all but the students who are most exceptionally gifted and talented. Students with the potential to develop talents are often not identified until the third or fourth grade. Early identification may prove to be important, both to help schools prepare for the eventual enrollment of students who are gifted and talented (Eby & Smutny, 1990) and to help the individual student begin as early as possible to develop his or her potential. However, there is little empirical data to support this view. Clearly, more research is needed in this area.

PROGRAMS

Historical Background

Interest in students who might be gifted and talented has always been with us, but the effort to identify these students began in France in the early 1900s when Binet and Simon, at the request of the French government, created the first developmental assessment test to identify students with intellectual disabilities. They began to look at students' ability to attend, remember, use judgment, reason, and understand. As a result, they were able to differentiate among students who differed in these measures of intelligence (Binet & Simon, 1905a, 1905b). Soon, American psychologists were using this test to measure mental abilities (Davis & Rimm, 2004). At Stanford University, Terman modified and Americanized the Binet-Simon test; in 1916, he published the Stanford-Binet Intelligence Scale and developed the term IQ. Terman identified some

1,500 students with outstanding IQ scores. This group became the first group to be identified as gifted and was and still is the most studied group of gifted individuals. In the years that followed, others have added to the criteria used to identify those who might be considered gifted. Memory, divergent thinking, and vocabulary use were considered, as was the idea that intelligence is the result of multiple factors. Creativity measures were developed, and skills in visual and performance arts were recognized as components of giftedness.

In 1957, Russia launched the Sputnik satellite. Many scholars and politicians in the United States felt this accomplishment was a technological defeat for the United States. Commissions, reports, and books indicated that the U.S. educational system was providing meager intellectual stimulation for students who were gifted. As a result, there was an initial but short-lived "talent mobilization" (Tannenbaum, 1979), which emphasized teaching gifted and talented students in math and science, primarily at the high school and college levels.

NCLB reauthorized ESEA and replaced the Jacob Javits Act. Although the funding was retained for grants and for synthesis of results from research projects, there is no provision for what a program for students consists of or for what they should be taught. Currently, no federal mandate requires specific services or protections for gifted students in public schools. Further, no nationally adopted curriculum or standardized set of instructional procedures exists for the gifted and talented. Programs are often intuitively designed and based on the opinions of leading educators, with little data to support their validity. However, the National Association for Gifted Children has published guidelines to assist persons in developing programs (Landrum, Callahan, & Shaklee, 2001). Only 21 states provide funding for gifted programs. In 29 states, gifted education is mandated through one of the following: a state law specific to gifted education ($n=14$), a law specific to disabilities and gifted education ($n=7$) or administrative rule ($n=6$), or state-level policy ($n=3$) (Council of State Directors of Programs for the Gifted, 2001; Ehlers, 2003).

Programs for students who are identified as gifted and talented are usually composed of curriculum enrichment, special classes, special schools, and special educational experiences (Shaunessy, 2003).

Curriculum Enrichment

Enrichment may have several meanings and may be used to describe any of a variety of attempts to extend or broaden a student's knowledge (Schiever & Maker, 1991; Smith, 2001). It most often refers to attempts planned and made within the classroom setting by the classroom teacher to add depth, detail, and challenges to the curriculum in place for students at a given grade level. Acting independently or with the aid of specially trained consultant teachers, the classroom teacher might provide students who are gifted and talented with special activities such as independent study with advanced texts, independent small-group projects, or access to computer programs or other activities that can replace drills. To be successful, enrichment activities need a purpose and specified outcomes (Riley, 2003). They should be systematic in extending student learning, stress higher order thinking skills, and be interdisciplinary to allow students to view a subject from different perspectives (Banks, 1994a, 1994b). In-class enrichment allows the student who is gifted to study in depth and detail and still maintain social contact with age peers. However, enrichment in the classroom and clustering small groups of students for advanced study within a classroom is difficult because many teachers, administrators, and parents believe that the general classroom teacher

is already too burdened with general classroom responsibilities to provide the necessary meaningful enrichment activities (Kirk et al., 2000).

Compacting the curriculum occurs when a teacher deletes many of the repetitions, drills, and practices unnecessary for students who can grasp concepts quickly. Compacting allows the student who is gifted the opportunity to spend the time saved in more challenging activities (Troxclair, 2000; Winebrenner, 2003). Compacting requires an intimate knowledge of the curriculum and sensitivity to exactly what is critical to concept mastery and when a student has mastered a concept. Renzulli and Reis (1998) described **compacting curriculum** as a three-step process: (1) Define the objectives or outcomes from the planned instruction; (2) identify the students who have already mastered the objectives and who may benefit from enrichment activities; and (3) decide on the activities to be put in place for students who opt out of the general curriculum. Reis (1995) found that the 436 teachers in her study were able to eliminate 40 to 50 percent of content without any detrimental effects on the 738 students they taught who were identified as gifted and talented. In fact, the students achieved higher scores in math and science concepts after the critical areas were compacted. Box 12.1 provides general suggestions for teachers.

Special Classes Within the Regular School Setting

The two most frequently used types of special classes for students who are gifted are resource rooms and self-contained classrooms. In the self-contained classroom, students who are gifted and talented are grouped together and receive specialized instruction from a specially trained teacher or teachers. Self-contained classrooms are rare, because they depend on a school system identifying enough students to fill a full-time classroom and providing the funding for an additional teacher. In addition, many students who are gifted may not be above average in all subjects or in all affective domains and thus may be ineligible for full class participation. Some educators report that being isolated in a self-contained classroom may contribute to an increase in social problems for the students and may even have a negative impact on overall school morale in high schools due to its exclusionary and elitist nature (Delisle, 1994).

BOX 12.1
WHAT EVERY TEACHER SHOULD DO

Effective Teaching Strategies

- Have resource materials (reference books, computers) accessible in the classroom.
- Allow students to express their interests in subjects you are teaching. Let them go on tangents while you teach the main points.
- Let students who have done extra research on subjects display it for others to learn from. Let them do bulletin boards, poster presentations, PowerPoint slide shows, packets, or centers of interactive activities.
- Allow divergent thinkers to speak up and add to the class discussion. Then guide them into finding information on their own so that the rest of the class does not lose the train of thought and the sequence of the lesson.
- Have guest speakers on subjects that interest one or two of the students. Others may find an interest in the subject as well.
- Praise and encourage novel ideas and ways of completing assignments.
- Encourage a depth of understanding in an area by letting the student go to other teachers' classrooms while they are teaching a subject that interests the student. Let them go to advanced classes if their interest continues.
- Alert librarians to have materials on a higher level for the student's area of interest.
- Find outlets for the products of the students—publications for creative writing, places in town (such as the public library) for projects.
- Ensure that the gifted and talented student has a firm grasp of the core material as well as the enrichment curricula.

The resource room is a popular method of providing special instruction because it provides a special education experience and still allows the individual student to remain with age mates within the general classroom environment. Students identified as gifted and talented leave their home classroom on a regular basis to go to a resource room where they receive instruction from a specially trained teacher. This pull-out method of instruction is usually assigned on a once- or twice-a-week basis, often for only 1 or 2 hours at a time. The teacher of the gifted and talented is usually an itinerant teacher assigned to several schools in a district. Although this model may not offer much continuity or in-depth instruction, it is a method often used at the elementary school level. At the high school level, it may be a special class (Clarkson, 2003). The potential social isolation problems still exist because the student is pulled out of class to go to the resource room, sometimes, depending on scheduling, missing out on desirable activities or important assignments. An even more critical concern is that classroom teachers may feel that the resource room and special teacher have the sole responsibility to care for the needs of students who are gifted and give up responsibility as a team member in the student's overall program.

Special Schools

Two kinds of special schools are available to some students who are gifted and talented: magnet schools and state-sponsored schools. Magnet schools offer both regular programming and accelerated classes in specific subjects within the same school. Students enrolled in magnet schools are not expected to be outstanding in all areas and are assigned to a variety of classes during the school day. Magnet schools are often found in large urban areas because they require a large pool of students and reasonable, efficient transportation.

State-sponsored or governor's schools are often residential schools with a special emphasis on science or arts. They feature special programming and specially trained teachers and are usually located close to universities with access to special experiences for their students. Even though these schools offer intense special instruction, they are often not popular with family members because their residential format separates students from their communities and families. Large urban areas may also have commuter high schools such as the High School of Performing Arts, the Bronx High School of Science, or Brooklyn Technical High School, available to residents of New York City.

Special Experiences

Students who are gifted and talented are often eligible for special educational experiences. The most controversial special experience for a student who is gifted is acceleration, in which the student is allowed to move through academic levels or grades at his or her own pace. This entails skipping grades, cross-grade placement, being allowed to attend advanced classes, or early entrance into kindergarten, high school, or college (Clarkson, 2003). The concerns about students accelerating beyond the experiences of their age mates are obvious. There is fear of social isolation, negative social and emotional experiences, and a loss of perspective. However, acceleration is the most efficient way to provide content without special classes or schools. Educators researching the effects of acceleration are stressing that when acceleration is implemented wisely, students show increased interest in school and higher levels of academic achievement (Smutny, 2003a). They also receive more recognition of their accomplishments and complete higher levels of education in less time (Robinson & Noble, 1991; Southern & Jones, 1991). Having authentic mastery experiences can lead to a heightened sense of self (Bandura, 1997) and can translate into gains in achievement (Multon, Brown, & Lent, 1991; Pajares & Valiante, 1997). Acceleration with dual enrollment in high school and college seems to be most effective for students who excel in math (Brody & Stanley, 1991; Stanley, 1989). Fears about premature burnout and undue pressure seem to have no basis in fact. Students who willingly participate in accelerated programs do not seem to suffer socially, academically, or emotionally (Feldhusen, 1992a; Swiatek, 1993; see Smutny, 2003b). For some students, not only academic achievement but also extracurricular activities and social and emotional adjustments are positive experiences (see Prager & Alderman, 2003). Some educators suggest that accelerated placement spares these students the negative experiences of always being first to answer or being most correct and may lead to a more reasonable self-concept and toleration for the weaknesses of others (Southern & Jones, 1991). Benefits or problems cannot be generalized. Acceleration requires sensitivity to the individual student's needs. Counseling and support services are critical (Brody & Stanley, 1991; Matthews & Menna, 2003; Noble & Drummond, 1992; Peterson, 2003). Students who are gifted and talented are still students, and they require the concern and protection of adults. Acceleration combined with enrichment allows both appropriate social experiences and academic programs equal to students' abilities.

As might be expected, the counseling and interest of those most concerned about any given student often prove critical in structuring that student's experiences.

Traditional programs such as advanced placement (AP), in which high schools offer college-level instruction on the high school campus, are fairly widespread. Often the student can receive college credit for these courses by "testing out" of the college course of similar content. In some instances, high school students are allowed to enroll in classes taught at local colleges or universities. Larger schools are often able to sponsor special interest clubs either as part of the school day or as extracurricular activities. Periodically, in-depth seminars can be offered on topics not in the regular curriculum. These seminars can be presented along with independent study, in which a teacher assists the student in locating resources and defining topics and goals for independent projects. Tutorials are more formal, individually designed relationships between a selected student and an expert who meet to share interests in a given topic. The experts can be adult volunteers or older students knowledgeable in a content area and willing to share expertise with a younger student. A more hands-on experience can be provided through mentorships and internships, in which students who are gifted and talented are placed in settings or with willing community experts at the site where the experience is to be offered. Both internships and mentorships provide the opportunity to learn in depth from practitioners, often while the service is being performed or the product created.

For younger students, the extracurricular Odyssey of the Mind program provides a nationally sponsored competitive program in which students are guided by volunteer coaches to present solutions to complex problems, perform self-generated skits, and construct projects illustrating scientific or artistic concepts. The Junior Great Books Program employs teachers specifically trained to help students produce sophisticated analysis and discussion of classical, philosophical, fictional, and poetic works of literature. Addresses to contact for more information about these programs can be found in the listings of parent and self-help groups at the end of this chapter.

The addition of a personal computer to the world of the student who is gifted and talented has opened up new pathways to knowledge. Appropriately used and supervised, computers can help dissolve distances and rural or urban disadvantages to learning and facilitate global communication. The evaluation of the possibilities for learning and perils of enhanced computerized educational experiences for students who are gifted and talented are only beginning to be studied. Programs such as the Fifth Dimension (Blanton, Moorman, Hayes, & Warner, 1997; Cole, 1995; Nicopolou & Cole, 1993) are enabling primary school students to experience affiliation, play, education, and peer interaction while being introduced to computers and computer networking. Other uses of technology are suggested in Box 12.2.

Programs such as the Schoolwide Enrichment Model (Renzulli & Reis, 1986), the Integrated Curriculum Model (Maker, 1993), the Responsive Learning Environment (Clark, 1986), and the Autonomous Learner Model (Betts, 1985) were designed by scholars attempting to establish more fully integrated systems of education for students who are gifted. Others have argued that providing such programs has enabled administrators to cut funds and emphasis on programs for the gifted. The "dumbing down" of programs has given them a more widespread access but perhaps deprived the higher testing students of more intense programs (Delisle, 2003b).

Several goals of programming seem to be shared by educators. Students who are gifted need a facilitator to help them master the appropriate analytical, expressive, and conceptual prerequisite skills to extend their educational experiences. They need to develop strategies and skills that foster independence and creativity. Students who are gifted and talented should be allowed to develop a joy for and excitement about learning that will carry them through the drill and routine that is also a part of the learning

BOX 12.2
WHAT EVERY TEACHER SHOULD KNOW
ABOUT TECHNOLOGY

- Palm-sized computers can assist in notetaking.
- Digital audio and video players can be used to download newscasts and lectures. "Podcasting" can give students access to information in a timely manner.
- Encourage creativity by encouraging students to create Web spaces or Web pages. Blogs (Web logs) can become a way of expressing oneself. Student can load writings, art work, photographs of travels or three dimensional art, or other creative work into a format accessible by families and classmates.
- International communication is easy with e-mail. Students conversant or wanting to become more conversant in second languages can use e-mail or Internet telephone. With Web sites such as Skype, students can talk over the Internet through headsets, speakers, or USB phones to other students worldwide also connected to the Internet site.
- *Princeton Review* has launched an SAT-preparation product that is accessible on cell phones. Other applications for cell phones are portable, mobile, and accessible.

process (Kirk et al., 2000). The concept of the differentiated curriculum or a pyramid of learning goals is currently gaining favor as a way of accomplishing these goals. The differentiated curriculum uses a variety of curricular targets and a combination of instructional techniques, models, and practices individually designed to meet the needs of the student who is gifted and talented (Clark, 1997; Van Tassel-Baska, 1992; Yong & McIntyre, 1992). The combination seems to be the key. Success seems to be dependent on cooperation among the regular classroom teachers, the teacher of gifted and talented students, administrators, family members, and community agencies.

ISSUES OF IMPORTANCE

The issues to be discussed here are not an all-inclusive list of all the conflicts and unresolved problems facing those responsible for educating students who are gifted and talented. They represent only some of the concerns, and those are presented only briefly.

Responsibility for Providing Services

To support the development of talent in the United States, the U.S. Congress passed the Jacob K. Javits Gifted and Talented Students Education Act in 1988 (Willard-Holt, 1997). This legislation authorizes the U.S. Department of Education to fund grants, provide leadership, and sponsor a national research center on the education of gifted and talented students. The department's Office of Educational Research and Improvement administers the program. Even with government support for national activities, this legislation does not provide money for direct services. So the question remains: Should the public educational system further tax its limited resources by providing special educational services for students who are gifted and talented? Those who believe that special programming is not necessary stress that these students will succeed without it and that the programs are elitist and unfairly exclusionary because many students are not identified (Detterman & Ruthsatz, 1999; Pendarvis & Howley, 1996). An even more troubling concern is that students are often not identified fairly due to cultural and economic prejudice. Those who are identified are often separated from their age mates and community, risking potential social and emotional problems. Also, research results do not seem to indicate that special educational programs contribute to the development or maintenance of giftedness (Herr, 1999).

Proponents argue that some students who are gifted will perform at high levels without special help, but most will not come close to achieving their potential unless they are challenged by programs that will foster the development of their advanced abilities (Kauffman, 1997; Sternberg, 1996). Most students who are gifted and talented do not succeed on their own. Some become dropouts, delinquents, counseling problems, and underachievers (Vaughn et al., 2000; Willard-Holt, 1997). The idea that students who are gifted and talented will learn automatically or spontaneously is persistent. Ideas and the strategies needed to learn efficiently must be explicitly taught. They are not likely to be spontaneously discovered by an individual who is gifted and talented. Occasionally, a student who is gifted will intuitively perform in an innovative manner, but unless the potential is recognized, reinforced, and honed, the student will not likely develop the strategies needed for consistent performance.

Characteristics of students who are gifted and talented often include a high degree of morality, concern for others, and heightened emotional sensitivity in general (Winebrenner, 1992). A more basic argument is that students who are gifted and talented are entitled to a public education that meets their special needs. Denying them such an education denies them the right to equal opportunity to fulfill their potential. Society is best served when these students achieve their potential and become productive adults (Hallahan & Kauffman, 2006).

As Sternberg (1996) reported, attitudes toward the gifted and talented are on a perpetual roller coaster. He noted that they are alternately applauded and attacked, mined as a resource and then ignored. This issue remains unresolved. As a society we have not determined whether we have the same moral obligation to the gifted and talented that we have to other students.

Terminology

The use of the word *gifted* in identifying or placing students is a cause for concern. The most recently proposed definition (U.S. Department of Education, 1994) does not include the term because it implies that the skills or abilities isolated are already developed and might not need special services to develop further. Some are concerned that this belief may result in schools ignoring the needs of this special population, leading to further underachievement (Howell et al., 1996). Feldhusen (1992b) argued that "there is no physiological, genetic or neurological justification for a diagnostic category called 'gifted.' The very term implies hereditary transmission, for how else could a 'gift' be placed in a child?" (p. 3). Perhaps, as Ring and Shaughnessy (1993) and Sternberg (1996) suggested, the trend toward deleting the term gifted comes in response to the public perception of elitism that the term implies. Heward (2006) suggested that deleting references to giftedness may be the start of a movement away from giftedness as a unidimensional perception of high intellectual functioning and toward recognition of many types of special talents and aptitudes.

Underachievement

Because the potential for students who are gifted and talented is so great, their apparent underachievement is particularly troubling. The discussions of underachievement fall into several categories. There is a concern that the students identified as gifted and talented are disproportionately underachievers (Rimm, 1996). More specifically, females do not appear to achieve their potential as often as their male peers. In addition, minority students may be at more of a risk to underachieve than their dominant-culture counterparts. A more basic concern with minority students is the failure to identify them at all.

Some students who are gifted and talented become underachievers, regardless of their talents, for the same reasons that cause all students to fail. They are not immune to emotional conflicts; debilitating family situations; hostile home, school, or community environments; and specific physical or social impairments. Some students who are gifted may have specific learning disabilities that contribute to underachievement (Coben & Vaughn, 1994; Hua, 2002; Vaughn et al., 2000). Like all students, those who are gifted may develop poor study habits and lack the self-confidence needed to achieve their potential. Students who are gifted and talented are more likely to underachieve because the instruction they receive is too easy or slow paced (Vaughn et al., 2000). An unchallenging or monotonous curriculum might foster poor attitudes toward the learning process for students who grasp concepts quickly. Minority students and students from diverse cultural environments may lack exposure to the mainstream culture to thrive in its educational system (Thorne, 1995). The special challenges faced by students with exceptional talents need to be recognized and dealt with by family members and professionals with an understanding and sensitivity to the needs for both the support and challenge these students require.

Females who are gifted face some unique challenges to achieving their potential. As more and more women have left traditional roles, the issue of gender bias is recognized (Gavin & Reis, 2003; Inzlicht & Ben-Zeev, 2003; Noble, Subotnik, & Arnold, 1999). Although there is little evidence of biological differences, boys' and girls' achievements are different. At the primary level of education, girls achieve better grades than boys (Wentzel, 1988). However, by the end of high school, boys outperform girls on achievement tests (Hallinan & Sorensen, 1987; Lupart & Pyryt, 1996). More adult males than females are identified as gifted and creative. Perhaps social and cultural experiences shape females differently than males, causing them to increasingly yield to boys and men in achievement and competitiveness. This may explain their occasional failure to pursue advanced studies or careers commensurate with their abilities (Luscombe & Riley, 2001; Pendarvis, Howley, & Howley, 1990). Sex role stereotyping, as evidenced by lack of equal opportunity or lack of motivation to enter traditionally male fields, may establish barriers to the development of female giftedness. Cultural barriers and expectation also seem to play a role in limiting female achievements (Eccles, 1985; Reis, 1995). Conflicts between careers and marriage and family responsibilities can also act as barriers (Kerr, 1985). The "fear of success" analogy (Butler-Por, 1987; Dai, 2000; Strop & Goldman, 2002; Thorne, 1995) illustrates how the negative consequences of outstanding achievement, such as the animosity of classmates and pressure from others to succeed, produced girls who were more fearful of success than boys.

Solutions to these problems may be to motivate girls who are gifted and talented by making them aware of role models who challenge sex stereotypes and by providing, early in the educational programming, information about careers in nonstereotypical fields and disciplines (Freeman, 2003; Gavin & Reis, 2003). Single-sex classrooms for math and science may cancel the incentives to underachieve for females who are gifted. Parental education may be necessary to alter attitudes toward girls who are gifted and their potential to choose nontraditional fields of endeavor. Teachers may need to be sensitized about potentially damaging sex-based instructional practices (Fox, Brody, & Tobin, 1980). In the operating room, not all brain surgeons are male, nor all nurses female. Math professors may be male or female. It appears that progress is being made. Kerr (1991) reported that young women who are gifted are choosing professional careers in almost equal proportions to men. In the same report, the author stated that business has replaced education as the most popular career choice of bright young women.

Early Identification

The evidence available overwhelmingly supports the notion that students who are gifted and talented need special encouragement and nurturing to achieve their potential. Early intervention with other areas of exceptionality may lead to a more successful result. However, no comprehensive plan is in place for the early identification of students who are gifted. There is no equivalent of Project Child Find or similar programs for early identification. Although programs such as early admissions to kindergarten and primary levels might offer advantages, relatively few preschoolers who are gifted can overcome the age restrictions needed for admission. This is especially true because their social and motor development might be age appropriate, making placement burdensome to the teachers of these classes. Worse still, preschool students who are gifted and talented may find themselves in situations in which expectations of their social and emotional skills are equal to expectations for their advanced cognitive and language skills. Little thought has been given to perhaps teaching social skills to precocious students to make them eligible for accelerated placements (Baum, 1986; Roedell, 1985). It appears logical that students who are gifted and talented will not only profit from but may also require early intervention (Bayley, 2002; Lewis, 2002; Piirto, 1999; Rotigel, 2003; Sankar-DeLeeuw, 2002). It also appears logical that the arguments that special experiences are necessary to help achieve potential during the school years can be extrapolated to the preschool years. Little empirical data is available to document the loss of potential due to the lack of early intervention.

DIVERSITY

The most overriding issue for minority groups is that they are underrepresented in gifted and talented programs (Brown, 1997; Howell et al., 1996; Perrone & Male, 1981) and overrepresented in other categories of disabilities. "Gifts and talents exist in students of every race, culture, and socioeconomic group. However, gifted program planners have often been criticized for not looking hard enough to find talents in students who may not represent the majority culture or its values" (Delisle, 1994, p. 592). The underidentification seems to be a result of an interaction among tests, teachers, and opportunities.

Rose (2001) examined patterns of academic progress and outcomes in different inner-city school settings (identified as gifted or general education) for African American and European American lower, middle, and upper socioeconomic strata students. The author followed 287 students' progress from kindergarten through high school graduation; 185 were considered gifted and enrolled in a self-contained gifted program for all subjects in elementary school and core academic subjects in secondary school. Students' grades for math, reading, and science were recorded over time. Overall academic outcomes (grades and standardized test scores) were higher for gifted students enrolled in the program sometime during their school career than for general education students. Graduation rates were higher for gifted students who remained in the gifted program than for gifted students who left for general education or for general education students. European American students remained in the gifted program at a higher rate than they did in the general education program. Income was a factor in gifted students' graduation outcomes and grades, and standardized test scores varied by grade, program placement, race, and gender.

Tests

The cultural bias inherent in many of the tests used to identify students who might be gifted and talented often makes it difficult to obtain a fair estimate of students' (including minority students') abilities. Although totally culturally fair tests may not be possible, special procedures might be appropriate in the identification of minority students who are potentially gifted and talented. Suggestions range from using separate norms for large minority groups or those who are economically disadvantaged to including the top scoring 2 to 5 percent of minority students, regardless of their test scores (Maker, Morris, & James, 1981; Pendarvis et al., 1990). Special tests, such as the previously discussed Subcultural Indices of Academic Potential (Renzulli, 1973), the Kranz Talent Identification Instrument (Kranz, 1982), and the DISCOVER problem-solving system (Maker, 1993), have been suggested as alternative instruments to measure the potential of minority students. Other language free tests, such as the series of Raven's Progressive Matrices (Raven, 1998), can be used (Mills & Tissot, 1995). Most schools use traditional methods and tests to identify potentially gifted and talented students (Scott, Prior, Urbano, Hogan, & Gold, 1992).

Teachers

Negative teacher attitudes may be a significant factor in the underidentification of gifted minority students. Due to a lack of cultural sensitivity, minority students may be passed over because they do not always display giftedness in the same manner as their dominant-class cohorts (Lohman, 2005; Plummer, 1995; Rhodes, 1992;

Van Tassel-Baska, Patton, & Prillaman, 1991). Their teachers may not recognize the signs of their giftedness. Haring, McCormick, and Haring (1990) suggested that dominant-culture teachers educating minority students may need specific training that will enable them to identify culturally different students who have the potential to be gifted.

Culturally different students may be raised in environments that conflict with the conventional ideas of giftedness. For example, in some Hispanic families, highly verbal students may not be as prized for their verbal skills as are their dominant-culture peers.

Opportunities

Students reared in poverty, regardless of race, may not have the opportunity to interact with toys or reading materials. They might not have positive travel and other enriching experiences. They may be malnourished and receive inadequate medical care. They may be denied many or all of the opportunities and experiences that facilitate the development of talents (Ford, 1996; Kauffman, 1997). Their basic skills may suffer from this impoverishment and mask their superior abilities. When Standard English is not the student's primary language, this lack of facility might in and of itself be enough to deny the student access to programs for the gifted (Maker, 1977). Despite the increasing use of computers and their ability to bring information into the classroom, students who are gifted and live in isolated or rural areas may not have access to the resources necessary to develop their potential.

All of these factors contribute to the underidentification of minority students. Underidentification, in turn, prohibits these students from participating in critical experiences that might help in the full development of their potential. This lack of inclusion appears to make other minority issues secondary in nature.

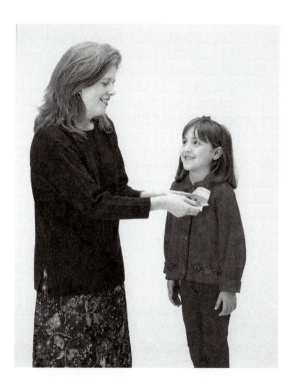

PROFESSIONALS

The certification of teachers of students who are gifted and talented is individually administered by each state. Karnes and Whorton (1991) were able to report specific certification requirements for only 21 states. As of 1991, their inquiries revealed that 25 states had no specific requirements for obtaining a teaching certificate for teaching this population. Information about the specific guidelines and requirements for any given state can be obtained by contacting the state director of special education at the address listed in Appendix A.

Should teachers of students who are gifted be gifted themselves? Most educators feel that a teacher of students who are gifted need not be gifted in the same way the students are but must have enough intellectual capability to understand the student's thinking processes. A shopping list of proposed characteristics includes intellectual curiosity, a developed literary and cultural interest, a high tolerance for ambiguity, high-quality verbal skills, a variety of interests, appreciation for achievement, a high energy level, a good sense of humor, enthusiasm, and a love of learning (Mills, 2003; Piirto, 1994; Story, 1985).

Others believe that effective teachers of students who are gifted and talented must also show some combination of the following skills and practices in their classroom instruction: They must demonstrate a high quality and quantity of verbal interactions with their students, be flexible and open to new ideas and unusual responses, and be process oriented rather than content driven, yet still maintain appropriately high standards and respect high-quality work. However, they also need to be well prepared in content, have mastered teaching techniques, and be flexible in time scheduling. They should want to teach students who are gifted and talented and be comfortable with the idea that for any given topic, students may be more knowledgeable than the teacher. Silverman (1983) suggested that Renzulli's (1978) characteristics for giftedness (above-average intelligence, creativity, and task commitment) are appropriate criteria for the selection of teachers of students who are gifted. She also stressed that teachers of students who are gifted and talented are often more like facilitators than directors and need to be comfortable in that role.

These lists form quite an impressive profile. Effective teacher training programs must attempt to meet these expectations when training college students who wish to teach the gifted. The CEC has recently published suggested standards for the initial preparation and certification of teachers of students with gifts or talents (Council for Exceptional Children, 2003). The council mandates that university training programs prepare teachers who have knowledge and skills in the following eight areas as they relate to students who are gifted and talented: philosophy, history, and legal foundations; characteristics of students who are gifted and talented; assessment, diagnosis, and evaluation of potentially gifted students; instructional content and practices geared toward students who are gifted; planning and managing the teaching and learning environment; managing student behavior and social skills; communication and collaborative partnerships; and professionalism and ethical practices.

DISCUSSION QUESTIONS

1. Should more fiscal resources be allocated for research on effective teaching of students who are gifted and talented?

2. Should students be given specially designed instruction because they are gifted and talented?

3. Should the category be broad enough to reflect the needs of all students with talents or narrowed to reflect those who are extremely gifted?

4. Should money be allocated for public school programs for students who are markedly gifted? Why or why not?

5. What legal protections and rights for education are available for students who are gifted and talented?

6. What steps should be taken, if any, to address the gender and racial overrepresentation in students identified as gifted and talented?

PROFESSIONAL ASSOCIATIONS AND PARENT OR SELF-HELP GROUPS

American Association for Gifted Children
New York City Partnership
200 Madison Avenue
New York, NY 10016

American Association for Gifted Children
c/o Talent Identification Program
Duke University
1121 W. Main Street, Suite 100
Durham, NC 27701

American Creativity Association
P. O. Box 26068
St. Paul, MN 55126

Future Problem Solving International
315 W. Huron, Suite 140B
Ann Arbor, MI 48103-4203

Gifted Children's Information Office
12657 Fee Fee Road
St. Louis, MO 63146

Gifted Child Society
190 Rock Road, Suite 6
Glen Rock, NJ 07425

Junior Great Books Foundation
40 E. Huron
Chicago, IL 60611

Mensa
Gifted Children Program
2626 East 14th Street
Brooklyn, NY 11235

National Association for Creative Children and Adults
8080 Spring Valley Drive
Cincinnati, OH 45236

National Association for Gifted Children
1707 L Street, N.W., Suite 550
Washington, DC 20036
202-785-4268
Fax: 202-785-4248
E-mail: nagc@nagc.org
www.nagc.org

National Association for Gifted Children
4175 Lovell Road, Suite 140
Circle Pines, MN 55014

National Research Center on the Gifted and Talented (NCR/GT)
University of Connecticut
Stoors, CT 06269

National/State Leadership Training Institute on the Gifted and Talented
One Wilshire Building, Suite 1007
624 S. Grand Avenue
Los Angeles, CA 90017

Odyssey of the Mind
OM Association
P. O. Box 547
Glassboro, NJ 08028

Supporting Emotional Needs of the Gifted
A 501 (c) (3) nonprofit organization
P. O. Box 6074
Scottsdale, AZ 85261
773-857-6250
E-mail: office@sengifted.org

Project Zero
Harvard Graduate School of Education
124 Mount Auburn Street, Fifth Floor
Cambridge, MA 02138
617-496-7097
Fax: 617-495-9709
E-mail: Info@Pz.Harvard.Edu

The Association for the Gifted (TAG)
c/o Council for Exceptional Children
1110 North Glebe Road, Suite 300
Arlington, VA 22201-5704

The Association for the Gifted (TAG)
2216 Main Street
Cedar Falls, IA 50613

World Council for Gifted and Talented Children
Lamar University
P. O. Box 10034
Beaumont, TX 77710

World Council for Gifted and Talented Children
HMS, Room 414
University of South Florida
Tampa, FL 33620

World Council for Gifted and Talented Children, Inc.
370 S. Carmelo Ave.
Pasadena, CA 91107
626-584-9751
Fax: 626-584-9751
Secondary Fax: 818-700-0028 (Use if primary fax does not work)
E-mail: worldgt@earthlink.net

Gifted Child Newsletter
Gifted and Talented Publications
213 Hollydell Drive
Sewell, NJ 08080

Gifted Child Quarterly
National Association for Gifted Children
4175 Lovell Road, Suite 140
Circle Pines, MN 55014

Gifted Child Today
P. O. Box 637
Holmes, PA 19043

Gifted Education International
A. B. Academic Publishers
P. O. Box 42
Bicester, Oxon OX6 7NW, England

Gifted International
Trillium Press
P. O. Box 209
Monroe, NY 10950

Journal of Creative Behavior
Creative Educational Foundation
1050 Union Road
Buffalo, NY 14222

Journal for the Education of the Gifted
Association for the Gifted
University of North Carolina Press
P. O. Box 2288
Chapel Hill, NC 27515

Prufrock Journal: The Journal of Secondary Gifted Education
1617 N. Valley Mills Drive, Suite 237
Waco, TX 76710

Roeper Review
Roeper City and County Schools
2190 N. Woodward
Bloomfield Hills, MI 48013

REFERENCES

Bandura, A. (1997). *Self-efficacy: The exercise of control.* New York: Freeman.

Banks, J. A. (1994a). *An introduction to multicultural education.* Boston: Allyn & Bacon.

Banks, J. A. (1994b). *Multiethnic education: Theory and practice.* Nova Scotia: Canada Journal.

Baum, S. (1986). The gifted preschooler: An awesome delight. *Gifted Child Today, 9*(4), 42–45.

Bayley, R. (2002). Thinking skills in the early years. *Gifted Education International, 16,* 248–260.

Berger, S. L. (1994). *College planning for gifted students.* Reston, VA: Council for Exceptional Children.

Betts, G. (1985). *The autonomous learner model.* Greeley, CO: Autonomous Learning Publications Specialists.

Binet, A., & Simon, T. (1905a). Méthodes nouvelles pour le diagnostic du niveau intellectual des anormaux. *L'Année Psychologique, 11,* 191–244.

Binet, A., & Simon, T. (1905b). Sur la nécessité d' établir un diagnostic scientifique des états inférieurs de l'intelligence. *L'Année Psychologique, 11,* 191–244.

Bisland, A., Karnes, F. A., & Cobb, Y. B. (2004). Leadership education: Resources and web sites for teachers of gifted students. *Gifted Child Today, 27,* 50–56.

Blanton, W., Moorman, G., Hayes, B., & Warner, M. (1997). Effects of participation in the Fifth Dimension on far transfer. *Journal of Educational Computing Research, 16*(4), 371–396.

Bloom, B. S. (1982). The role of gifts and markers in the development of talent. *Exceptional Children, 48,* 510–522.

Bloom, B. S., & Sosniak, L. A. (1981). Talent development vs. schooling. *Educational Leadership, 39,* 86–94.

Brody, L. E., & Stanley, J. C. (1991). Young college students: Assessing factors that contribute to success. In W. T. Southern & E. D. Jones (Eds.), *Academic acceleration of gifted children.* New York: Teachers College Press.

Brown, C. N. (1997). Gifted identification as a constitutional issue. *Roeper Review, 19*(3), 157.

Brown, S. W., Renzulli, J. S., & Gubbins, E. J. (2005). Assumptions underlying the identification of gifted and talented students. *Gifted Child Quarterly, 49,* 68–79.

Butler-Por, N. (1987). *Underachievers in school: Issues and intervention.* New York: Wiley.

Clark, B. (1986). The integrative education model. In J. S. Renzulli (Ed.), *Systems and models for developing programs for the gifted and talented.* Mansfield Center, CT: Creative Learning.

Clark, B. (1997). *Growing up gifted: Developing the potential of children at home and at school* (5th ed.). Upper Saddle River, NJ: Merrill/Prentice Hall.

Clark, G., & Zimmerman, E. (1984). Identifying artistically talented students. *School Arts, 83*(3), 26–31.

Clarkson, W. P. (2003). Beautiful minds. *American School Board Journal, 190*(8), 24–29.

Coben, S. S., & Vaughn, S. (1994). Gifted students with learning disabilities: What does the research say? *Learning Disabilities: A Multidisciplinary Journal, 5*(2), 87–94.

Cole, M. (1995). Socio-cultural-historical psychology: Some general remarks and a proposal for a new kind of cultural genetic methodology. In J. Wertsch, P. del Rio, & A. Alveron (Eds.), *Sociocultural studies of mind.* Cambridge, MA: Cambridge University Press.

Cooper, E. (1991). A critique of six measures for assessing creativity. *Journal of Creative Behavior 25,* 194–204.

Council for Exceptional Children. (2003). *What every special educator must know: Ethics, standards, and guidelines for special educators.* Reston, VA: Author.

Council of State Directors of Programs for the Gifted. (2001). *The 2000 state of the states gifted and talented education report.* Washington, DC: Author.

Dai, D. Y. (2000). To be or not to be (challenged), that is the question: Task and ego orientations among high-ability, high-achieving adolescents. *The Journal of Experimental Education, 68,* 311–330.

Davis, G. A. (2003). Identifying creative students, teaching for creative growth. In N. Colangelo & G. A. Davis (Eds.), *Handbook of gifted education* (pp. 311–324). Boston: Allyn & Bacon.

Davis, G. A., & Rimm, S. B (2004). *Education of the gifted and talented* (5th ed.). Boston: Allyn & Bacon.

Delisle, J. (1994). Children who are gifted and talented. In N. Hunt & K. Marshall (Eds.), *Exceptional children and youth: An introduction to special education.* Boston: Houghton Mifflin.

Delisle, J. R (2003a). To be or to do: Is a gifted child born or developed? *Roeper Review, 26*(1) 12–13.

Delisle, J. R. (2003b). The false security of inclusivity. *Understanding Our Gifted, 15*(2), 3–7.

Detterman, D. K., & Ruthsatz, J. (1999). Toward a more comprehensive theory of exceptional abilities. *Journal for the Education of the Gifted, 22,* 148–158.

Eby, J. W., & Smutny, J. F. (1990). *A thoughtful overview of gifted education.* New York: Longman.

Eccles, J. S. (1985). Why doesn't Jane run? Sex differences in educational and occupational patterns. In F. D. Horowitz & M. O'Brien (Eds.), *Gifted and talented: Developmental perspectives.* Washington, DC: American Psychological Association.

Ehlers, K. (2003). *GT programs.* Arlington, VA: Council for Exceptional Children.

Feldhusen, J. F. (1992a). Early admission and grade advancement. *Gifted Child Today, 15,* 45–49.

Feldhusen, J. F. (1992b). *Talent identification and development in education (TIDE).* Sarasota, FL: Center for Creative Learning.

Ford, D. Y. (1996). *Reversing underachievement among gifted Black students: Promising practices and programs.* New York: Teachers College Press.

Fox, L., Brody, L., & Tobin, D. (Eds.). (1980). *Women and the mathematical mystique.* Baltimore: Johns Hopkins University Press.

Freeman, J. (2003). Gender differences in gifted achievement in Britain and the U.S. *Gifted Child Quarterly, 47,* 202–211.

Gagne, F. (2000). How many persons are gifted or talented? *Understanding Our Gifted, 12*(2), 10–13.

Gallagher, J. J. (1985). *Teaching the gifted child* (3rd ed.). Needham, MA: Allyn & Bacon.

Gallagher, J. J. (2000). Changing paradigms for gifted education in the United States. In K. A. Heller, F. J. Monks, R. J. Sternberg, & R. F. Subotnik, (Eds.). *International handbook of giftedness and talent* (2nd ed., pp. 681–693). New York: Pergamon.

Gallagher, J. J., & Gallagher, S. (1994). *Teaching the gifted child* (4th ed.). Needham, MA: Allyn & Bacon.

Gallucci, N. T., Middleton, G., & Kline, A. (2000). Perfectionism and creative strivings. *Journal of Creative Behavior, 34*(2), 135–141.

Gardner, H. (1983). *Frames of mind: The theory of multiple intelligence.* New York: Simon & Schuster.

Gardner, H. (1993). *Multiple intelligences: The theory in practice.* New York: Simon & Schuster.

Gardner, H. (1999). *The disciplined mind: What all students should understand.* New York: Simon & Schuster.

Gardner, H., & Hatch, T. (1989). Multiple intelligences go to school: Educational implications of the theory of multiple intelligences. *Educational Researcher, 18*(8), 4–9.

Gavin, M. K., & Reis, S. M. (2003). Helping teachers to encourage talented girls in mathematics. *Gifted Child Today, 26*(1), 32–44, 64.

Gottfredson, L. S. (2003). The science and politics of intelligence in gifted education. In N. Colangelo and G. Davis (Eds.). *The handbook of gifted education* (3rd ed. pp. 24–40). Boston: Allyn & Bacon.

Guilford, J. P. (1959). Traits of creativity. In H. H. Anderson (Ed.), *Creativity and its cultivation.* New York: Harper & Brothers.

Guilford, J. P. (1987). Creativity research: Past, present and future. In S. Isaksen (Ed.), *Frontiers of creativity research.* Buffalo, NY: Bearly.

Haensly, P. A. (1999). My view of the "top 10" events that have influenced the field of gifted education during the past century. *Gifted Child Today Magazine, 22*(6), 33–37.

Hallahan, D. P., & Kauffman, J. M. (2006). *Exceptional children: Introduction to special education.* Needham, MA: Allyn & Bacon.

Hallinan, M. T., & Sorensen, A. B. (1987). Ability grouping and sex difference in mathematics achievement. *Sociology of Education, 60,* 64–72.

Hardman, M. L., Drew, C. J., & Egan, M. W. (2006). *Human exceptionality: School, community, and family, IDEA 2004 update edition* (8th ed.). Needham, MA: Allyn & Bacon.

Haring, N. G., McCormick, L., & Haring, T. G. (1990). *Exceptional children and youth* (6th ed.). Upper Saddle River, NJ: Merrill/Prentice Hall.

Herr, K. (1999). Private power and privileged education: De/constructing institutionalized racism. *International Journal of Inclusive Education, 3,* 111–129.

Heward, W. L. (2006). *Exceptional children: An introduction to special education* (8th ed.). Upper Saddle River: Merrill/Prentice Hall.

Howell, R., Heward, L., & Swassing, R. (1996). Gifted and talented students. In W. L. Heward, *Exceptional children: An introduction to special education* (pp. 532–574). Upper Saddle River, NJ: Merrill/Prentice Hall.

Hua, C. B. (2002). Career self-efficacy of the student who is gifted/learning disabled: A case study. *Journal for the Education of the Gifted, 25,* 375–404.

Inzlicht, M., & Ben-Zeev, T. (2003). Do high-achieving female students underperform in private? The implications of threatening environments on intellectual processing. *Journal of Educational Psychology, 95,* 796–805.

Johnsen, S. K., & Corn, A. L. (2001). *Screening assessment for gifted elementary and middle school students, second edition (SAGES–2).* Austin, TX: Pro-Ed.

Karnes, F. A., & Whorton, J. E. (1991). Teacher certification and endorsement in gifted education: Past, present and future. *Gifted Child Quarterly, 35,* 148–150.

Kauffman, J. (1997). *Exceptional children* (7th ed.). Needham, MA: Allyn & Bacon.

Kerr, B. (1985). Smart girls, gifted women: Special guidance concerns. *Roeper Review, 8*(1), 30–33.

Kerr, B. (1991). Educating gifted girls. In N. Colangelo & G. A. Davis (Eds.), *Handbook of gifted education* (pp. 209–221). Needham, MA: Allyn & Bacon.

Khatena, J., & Torrance, E. P. (1976). *Khatena-Torrance creative perception inventory.* Chicago, II: Stoelting Company.

Kirk, S. A., Gallagher, J. J., & Anastasiow, N. J. (2000). *Educating exceptional children* (9th ed.). Boston: Houghton Mifflin.

Kranz, B. (1982). *Kranz talent identification instrument.* Moorehead, MN: University of Minnesota Press.

Landrum, M. S., Callahan, C. M., & Shaklee, B. D. (Eds.). (2001). *Aiming for excellence: Gifted program standards.* Waco, TX: Prufrock Press.

Lewis, G. (2002). Alternatives to acceleration for the highly gifted child. *Roeper Review, 24*(3), 130–133.

Lohman, D. F. (2005). Review of Naglieri and Ford (2003): Does the Naglieri Nonverbal Ability Test identify equal proportions of high-scoring White, Black, and Hispanic students? *Gifted Child Quarterly, 49,* 19–26.

Lupart, J. L., & Pyryt, M. C. (1996). "Hidden gifted" students: Underachiever prevalence and profile. *Journal for the Education of the Gifted, 20,* 36–53.

Luscombe, A., & Riley, T. L. (2001). An examination of self-concept in academically gifted adolescents: Do gender differences occur? *Roeper Review, 24*(1), 20–22.

Maker, C. J. (1977). *Providing programs for the gifted handicapped.* Reston, VA: Council for Exceptional Children.

Maker, C. J. (1993). Creativity, intelligence, and problem solving: A definition and design for cross-cultural research and measurement related to giftedness. *Gifted Education International, 9*(2), 68–77.

Maker, C. J., Morris, E., & James, J. (1981). The Eugene field project: A program for potentially gifted young children. In *National/state leadership training on the gifted: Balancing the scale for the disadvantaged gifted.* Ventura, CA: Office of the Ventura County Superintendent of Schools.

Matthews, D., & Menna, R. (2003). Solving problems together: Parent/school/community collaboration at a time of educational and social change. *Education Canada, 43,* 20–23.

Marland, S. (1972). *Education of the gifted and talented.* Report to Congress by the U.S. Commissioner of Education. Washington, DC: U.S. Government Printing Office.

Mednick, S. A., & Mednick, M. T. (1967). *Examiner's manual: Remote Associates Test.* Boston, MA: Houghton Mifflin.

Mills, C. J. (2003). Characteristics of effective teachers of gifted students: Teacher background and personality styles of students. *Gifted Child Quarterly, 47,* 272–281.

Mills, C. J., & Tissot, S. L. (1995). Identifying academic potential in students from under-represented populations: Is using the Ravens Progressive Matrices a good idea? *Gifted Child Quarterly, 39,* 209–217.

Morse, D. T. (1994). Reliability estimates for total, factor, and group mean scores on the Khatena-Torrance Creative Perception Inventory. *Perceptual and Motor Skills, 79,* 155–162.

Multon, K., Brown, S., & Lent, R. (1991). Relation of self-efficacy beliefs to academic outcomes: A meta-analytic investigation. *Journal of Counseling Psychology, 38,* 30–38.

Neihart, M., Reis, S. M., Robinson, N. M., & Moon, S. M. (Eds.). (2002). *The social and emotional development of gifted children: What do we know?* Waco, TX: Prufrock Press.

Nicopolou, A., & Cole, M. (1993). The Fifth Dimension, its playworld, and its institutional contexts: The generation and transmission of shared knowledge in the culture of collaborative learning. In E. A. Foreman, N. Minnick, & C. A. Stone (Eds.), *Contexts for learning: Sociocultural dynamics in children's development.* New York: Oxford University Press.

Noble, K. D., & Drummond, J. E. (1992). But what about the prom? Students' perceptions of early college entrance. *Gifted Child Quarterly, 36,* 106–111.

Noble, K. D., Subotnik, R. F., & Arnold, K. D. (1999). To thine own self be true: A new model of female talent development. *Gifted Child Quarterly, 43,* 140–149.

Pajares, E., & Valiante, G. (1997). Influence of writing self-efficacy beliefs on the writing performance of upper elementary students. *Journal of Educational Research, 90,* 353–360.

Pendarvis, E. (1993). Students with unique gifts and talents. In A. Blackhurst & W. Berdine, *An introduction to special education* (3rd ed.). New York: HarperCollins.

Pendarvis, E., & Howley, A. (1996). Playing fair: The possibilities of gifted education. *Journal for the Education of the Gifted, 19,* 215–233.

Pendarvis, E., Howley, A., & Howley, C. (1990). *The abilities of gifted children.* Upper Saddle River, NJ: Merrill/Prentice Hall.

Perrone, P. A., & Male, R. A. (1981). *The developmental education and guidance of talented learners.* Rockville, MD: Aspen.

Peterson, J. S. (2003). An argument for proactive attention to affective concerns of gifted adolescents. *Journal of Secondary Gifted Education, 14*(2), 62–71.

Piechowski, M. M. (1997). Emotional giftedness: The measure of intrapersonal intelligence. In M. Colangelo & G. A. Davis (Eds.), *Handbook of gifted education* (2nd ed., pp. 336–381). Boston: Allyn & Bacon.

Piirto, J. (1994). *Talented children and adults: Their development and education.* Upper Saddle River, NJ: Merrill/Prentice Hall.

Piirto, J. (1999). Precocity as a hallmark of giftedness. In W. L. Heward (Ed.), *Exceptional children: An introduction to special education* (p. 580). Upper Saddle River, NJ: Merrill/Prentice Hall.

Plomin, R. (1989). Environment and genes: Determinants of behavior. *American Psychologist, 44,* 105–111.

Plummer, D. (1995). Serving the needs of gifted children from a multicultural perspective. In J. L. Genshaft, M. Bireley, & C. L. Hollinger (Eds.), *Serving gifted and talented students: A resource for school personnel.* Austin, TX: Pro-Ed.

Prager, D., & Alderman, C. (2003). Stand by to roll. . . . *Gifted Child Today, 26*(2), 18–25, 65.

Raven, J. C. (1998). *Raven's progressive matrices: Comprehensive technical manual.* San Antonio, TX: Psychological Corporation.

Reis, S. (1995). What gifted education can offer the reform movement. In J. L. Genshaft, M. Bireley, & C. L. Hollinger (Eds.), *Serving gifted and talented students: A resource for school personnel* (pp. 371–387). Austin, TX: Pro-Ed.

Reis, S. M. (1989). Reflections on policy affecting the education of gifted and talented students: Past and future perspectives. *American Psychologist, 44,* 399–408.

Reis, S. M., & Renzulli, J. S. (1991). The assessment of creative products in programs for gifted and talented students. *Gifted Child Quarterly, 35,* 128–134.

Reis, S. M., & Renzulli, J. S. (2004). Current research on the social and emotional development of gifted and talented students: Good news and future possibilities. *Psychology in the Schools, 41,* 119–130.

Renzulli, J. S. (1973). Talent potential in minority group students. *Exceptional Children, 39,* 128–134.

Renzulli, J. S. (1978). What makes giftedness? Reexamining a definition. *Phi Delta Kappan, 84,* 180–185.

Renzulli, J. S. (1994). *Schools for talent development: A practical plan for total school improvement.* Mansfield Center, CT: Creative Learning Press.

Renzulli, J. S. (2000). The identification and development of giftedness as a paradigm for school reform. *Journal of Science Education and Technology, 9*(2), 95–114.

Renzulli, J. S. (2004). Expanding the umbrella: An interview with Joseph Renzulli. *Roeper Review, 26*(2), 65–67.

Renzulli, J., & Reis, S. (1986). The enrichment triad/revolving door model: A schoolwide plan for the development of creative productivity. In J. Renzulli (Ed.), *Systems and models for developing programs for the gifted and talented* (pp. 303–326). Mansfield Center, CT: Creative Learning.

Renzulli, J. S., & Reis, S. M. (1991). The schoolwide enrichment model: A comprehensive plan for the development of creative productivity. In N. Colangelo & G. A. Davis (Eds.), *Handbook of gifted education* (pp. 184–203). Needham, MA: Allyn & Bacon.

Renzulli, J. S., & Reis, S. M. (1998). Talent development through curriculum differentiation. *NASSP Bulletin, 82*(595), 61–64.

Renzulli, J. S., & Reis, S. M. (2002). What is schoolwide enrichment and how do gifted programs relate to total school improvement? *Gifted Child Today, 25*(4), 18–25.

Rhodes, L. (1992). Focusing attention on the individual in identification of gifted black students. *Roeper Review, 14,* 108–110.

Riley, T. (2003). International perspectives: Practicing what we preach: The reality factors in talent development. *Gifted Child Today, 26,* 45–49.

Rimm, S. B. (1996). *Why bright kids get poor grades and what you can do about it.* New York: Three Rivers Press.

Ring, B., & Shaughnessy, M. F. (1993). The gifted label, gifted children, and the aftermath. *Gifted Education International, 9*(1), 33–35.

Robinson, N. M., & Noble, K. D. (1991). Social-emotional development and adjustment of gifted children. In M. C. Wang, M. C. Reynolds, & H. J. Walberg (Eds.), *Handbook of special education: Research and practice. Volume 4: Emerging programs* (pp. 57–76). New York: Pergamon.

Roedell, W. C. (1985). Developing social competence in gifted preschool children. *Remedial and Special Education, 6*(4), 6–11.

Rose, E. A. (2001). *A longitudinal study of the course of academic achievement of urban and minority gifted and general education students.* Paper presented at the annual meeting of the American Educational Research Association, Seattle, WA.

Rothenberg, A., & Wyshak, G. (2004). Family background and genius. *Canadian Journal of Psychiatry, 49*(3), 185–191.

Rotigel, J. V. (2003). Understanding the young gifted child: Guidelines for parents, families, and educators. *Early Childhood Education Journal, 30,* 209–214.

Sankar-DeLeeuw, N. (2002). Gifted preschoolers: Parent and teacher views on identification, early admission, and programming. *Roeper Review, 24,* 172–177.

Sattler, J. M. (2002). *Assessment of children: Behavioral and clinical applications* (4th ed.). La Mesa, CA: Jerome M. Sattler.

Schiever, S. W., & Maker, C. J. (1991). Enrichment and acceleration: An overview and new directions. In N. Colangelo & G. A. Davis (Eds.), *Handbook of gifted education* (pp. 99–110). Needham, MA: Allyn & Bacon.

Scott, M. S., Prior, R., Urbano, R., Hogan, A., & Gold, S. (1992). The identification of giftedness: A comparison of white, Hispanic and black families. *Gifted Child Quarterly, 36,* 131–139.

Shaunessy, E. (2003). State policies regarding gifted education. *Gifted Child Today Magazine, 26,* 1076–2175.

Shurkin, J. N. (1992). *Terman's kids: The groundbreaking study of how the gifted grow up.* Boston: Little, Brown.

Silverman, L. K. (1983). Personality development: The pursuit of excellence. *Journal for the Education of the Gifted, 6*(1), 5–19.

Silverman, L. K. (1995). Highly gifted children. In J. L. Genshaft, M. Bireley, & C. L. Hollinger (Eds.), *Serving gifted and talented students: A resource for school personnel* (pp. 217–240). Austin, TX: Pro-Ed.

Smith, D. D. (2001). *Introduction to special education: Teaching in an age of opportunity* (4th ed.). Needham, MA: Allyn & Bacon.

Smith, M. K. (2002). Howard Gardner and multiple intelligences. *The encyclopedia of informal education.* www.infed.org/thinkers/gardner.htm 3/24/2006

Smutny, J. F. (Ed.). (2003a). *Designing and developing programs for gifted students.* St. Paul, MN: National Association for Gifted Children.

Smutny, J. F. (Ed.). (2003b). Underserved gifted populations: Responding to their needs and abilities. *Perspectives on Creativity Research.* St. Paul, MN: National Association for Gifted Children.

Southern, W. T., & Jones, E. D. (Eds.). (1991). *The academic acceleration of gifted children.* New York: Teachers College Press.

Stanley, J. C. (1989). A look back at educational non-acceleration: An international tragedy. *Gifted/Creative/Talented, 12*(4), 60–61.

Stephens, K. R., & Karnes, F. A. (2000). Classroom to community: Student products as the link. *Gifted Child Today Magazine, 23*(6), 14–19.

Sternberg, R. J. (1996). The sound of silence: A nation responds to its gifted. *Roeper Review, 18,* 168–172.

Sternberg, R. J., & Davidson, J. E. (1983). Insight on the gifted. *Educational Psychologist, 18,* 51–57.

Story, C. (1985). Facilitator of learning: A microethnographic study of the teacher of the gifted. *Gifted Child Quarterly, 29*(4), 155–159.

Strop, J., & Goldman, D. (2002). The affective side: Emotional issues of twice exceptional students. *Understanding Our Gifted, 14*(2), 228–229.

Swiatek, M. A. (1993). A decade of longitudinal research on academic acceleration through the study of mathematically precocious youth. *Roeper Review, 15*(3), 120–123.

Tannenbaum, A. J. (1979). Pre-Sputnik to post-Watergate concern about the gifted. In A. H. Passow (Ed.), The gifted and the talented: Their education and development. *Seventy-eighth yearbook of the National Society for the Study of Education, Part 1.* Chicago: University of Chicago Press.

Terman, L. M. (Ed.). (1925, 1947, 1959). *Genetic studies of genius:* Vols. 1, 4, 5. Stanford, CA: Stanford University Press.

Terman, L. M. (1926). *Genetic studies of genius: Vol. 1. Mental and physical traits of a thousand gifted children* (2nd ed.). Palo Alto, CA: Stanford University Press.

Thorne, Y. M. (1995). Achievement motivation in high achieving latina women. *Roeper Review, 18*(1), 44–49.

Torrance, E. P. (1966). *Tests of creative thinking.* Princeton, NJ: Personnel.

Troxclair, D. A. (2000). Differentiating instruction for gifted students in regular education social studies classes. *Roeper Review, 22*(3), 195–198.

Turnbull, A. P., Turnbull, H. R., Shank, M., & Smith, D. (2004). *Exceptional lives: Special education in today's schools* (4th ed.). Upper Saddle River, NJ: Merrill/Prentice Hall.

U.S. Department of Education. (1994). *National excellence: A case for developing American talent.* Washington, DC: Author.

Van Tassel-Baska, J. (1992). *Planning effective curriculum for gifted learners.* Denver: Love.

Van Tassel-Baska, J., Patton, J. M., & Prillaman, D. (1991). *Gifted youth at risk: A report of a national study.* Reston, VA: Council for Exceptional Children.

Vaughn, S., Bos, C. S., & Schumm, J. S. (2000). *Teaching mainstreamed, diverse, and at-risk students in the general education classroom* (2nd ed.). Boston: Allyn & Bacon.

Wentzel, K. R. (1988). Gender differences in math and English achievement: A longitudinal study. *Sex Roles, 18*(11/12), 691–699.

Willard-Holt, C. (1997). *Gifted education and the law: PAGE bulletin.* Norristown, PA: Pennsylvania Association for Gifted Education.

Winebrenner, S. (1992). *Teaching gifted kids in the regular classroom.* Minneapolis: Free Spirit Publishing.

Winebrenner, S. (2003). Teaching strategies for twice-exceptional students. *Intervention in School and Clinic, 38*(3), 131–133.

Witty, P. A. (Ed.). (1951). *The gifted child.* Boston: D. C. Heath.

Wolf, J. (1990). The gifted and talented. In N. G. Haring, L. McCormack, & T. G. Haring, *Exceptional children and youth.* Upper Saddle River, NJ: Merrill/Prentice Hall. 445–501.

Yong, F. L., & McIntyre, J. D. (1992). A comparative study of the learning style preferences of students with learning disabilities and students who are gifted. *Journal of Learning Disabilities, 25,* 124–132.

APPENDIX A

Addresses of State Offices of Teacher Licensure and Certification

The addresses and phone numbers of the state offices that can supply you with information about the requirements for licensing and certification are listed in this appendix.

Alabama

Certification—Division of Professional Services
Department of Education
Gordon Persons Building
50 N. Ripley Street
Montgomery, AL 36130-3901
334-242-9977

Alaska

Teacher Education and Certification
Department of Education
Alaska State Office Building
Pouch F
Juneau, AK 99811-1894
907-465-2831

Arizona

Teacher Certification Unit
Department of Education
1535 W. Jefferson Street
P.O. Box 25609
Phoenix, AZ 85007
602-542-4368

Arkansas

Office of Teacher Education and Licensure
Department of Education
#4 Capitol Mall, Room 106B/107B
Little Rock, AR 72201
501-682-4342

California

Commission of Teacher Credentialing
1812 9th Street
Sacramento, CA 95814
916-445-7254

Colorado

Teacher Certification
Department of Education
201 E. Colfax Avenue
Denver, CO 80203-1799
303-866-6628

Connecticut

Bureau of Certification and Accreditation
Department of Education
P.O. Box 2219
Hartford, CT 06145
860-713-7017

Delaware

Office of Certification
Department of Public Instruction
Townsend Building
P.O. Box 1402
Dover, DE 19903
302-739-4688

District of Columbia

Division of Teacher Services
District of Columbia Public Schools
415 12th Street NW
Room 1013
Washington, DC 20004-1994
202-724-4250

Florida

Division of Human Resource Development
Teacher Certification Offices
Department of Education, FEC, Room 201
325 W. Gaines Street
Tallahassee, FL 32399-0400
800-445-6739

Georgia

Professional Standards Commission
Department of Education
1454 Twin Towers East
Atlanta, GA 30334
404-656-2604

Hawaii

Office of Personnel Services
Department of Education
P.O. Box 2360
Honolulu, HI 96804
808-586-3420

Idaho

Teacher Education and Certification
Department of Education
Len B. Jordan Office Building
650 W. State Street
Boise, ID 83720
208-334-3475

Illinois

Certification and Placement
State Board of Education
100 N. First Street
Springfield, IL 62777-0001
217-782-2805

Indiana

Professional Standards Board
Department of Education
State House, Room 229
Indianapolis, IN 46204-2790
317-232-9010

Iowa

Board of Education Examiners
State of Iowa
Grimes State Office Building
Des Moines, IA 50319-0146
515-281-3245

Kansas

Certification, Teacher Education & Accreditation
Department of Education
120 S.E. Tenth Avenue
Topeka, KS 66612
785-291-3678

Kentucky

Teacher Education and Certification
Department of Education
500 Mero Street, Room 1820
Frankfort, KY 40601
502-564-4606

Louisiana

Teacher Certification
Department of Education
P.O. Box 94064
626 N. 4th Street
Baton Rouge, LA 70804-9064
504-342-3490

Maine

Department of Education
Certification and Placement
State House Station 23
Augusta, ME 04333
207-289-5800

Maryland

Division of Certification & Accreditation
Department of Education
200 W. Baltimore Street
Baltimore, MD 21201
410-333-2142

Massachusetts

Bureau of Teacher Certification
Department of Education
350 Main Street
Maiden, MA 02148
617-338-3300

Michigan

Teacher/Administrator Preparation and Certification
Department of Education
P.O. Box 30008
608 W. Allegan Street
Lansing, MI 48909
517-373-3310

Minnesota

Personnel and Licensing
Department of Education
1500 Highway 36 West
Roseville, MN 55113
651-582-8807

Mississippi

Office of Teacher Certification
Department of Education
P.O. Box 771
Jackson, MS 39205
601-359-3483

Missouri

Teacher Education
Missouri Teacher Certification Office
Department of Elementary and Secondary Education
P.O. Box 480
Jefferson City, MO 65102-0480
573-751-0051
573-751-3847

Montana

Certification Services
Office of Public Instruction
State Capitol
Helena, MT 59620
406-444-3150

Nebraska

Teacher Certification/Education
301 Centennial Mall, South
Box 94987
Lincoln, NE 68509
402-471-2496

Nevada

Teacher Licensure
Department of Education
1850 E. Sahara, Suite 200
State Mail Room
Las Vegas, NV 89158
702-486-6457

New Hampshire

Bureau of Teacher Education and Professional Standards
Department of Education
State Office Park South
101 Pleasant Street
Concord, NH 03301-3860
603-271-2407

New Jersey

Teacher Certification and Academic Credentials
Department of Education
3535 Quakerbridge Road, CN 503
Trenton, NJ 08625-0503
609-292-2070

New Mexico

Educator Preparation and Licensure
Department of Education
Education Building
Santa Fe, NM 87501-2786
505-827-6587

New York

Office of Teacher Certification
Department of Education
Cultural Education Center, Room 5A11
Albany, NY 12230
518-474-3901

North Carolina

Division of Certification
Department of Public Instruction
114 W. Edenton Street
Raleigh, NC 27603-1712
919-733-4125
919-733-0377

North Dakota

Teacher Certification Division
Department of Public Instruction
600 E. Boulevard Avenue
Bismarck, ND 58505-0440
701-224-2264

Ohio

Teacher Certification
Department of Education
65 S. Front Street, Room 1012
Columbus, OH 43266-0308
614-466-3593

Oklahoma

Department of Education
2500 N. Lincoln Blvd., Room 211
Oliver Hodge Education Building
Oklahoma City, OK 73105-4599
405-521-3337

Oregon

Teacher Standards and Practices Commission
580 State Street, Room 203
Salem, OR 97310
503-378-3586

Pennsylvania

Bureau of Teacher Preparation and Certification
Department of Education
333 Market Street, 3rd Floor
Harrisburg, PA 17126-0333
717-787-2967

Rhode Island

School and Teacher Accreditation, Certification and Placement
22 Hayes Street
Roger Williams Building, 2nd Floor
Providence, RI 02908
401-277-2675

South Carolina

Teacher Education and Certification
Department of Education
1015 Rutledge
1429 Senate Street
Columbia, SC 29201
803-734-8466

South Dakota

Office of Certification
Division of Education and Cultural Affairs
Kneip Office Building
700 Governor's Drive
Pierre, SD 57501
605-773-3553

Tennessee

Office of Teacher Licensing
Department of Education
6th Floor, North Wing
Cordell Hull Building
Nashville, TN 37243-0377
615-741-1644

Texas

Division of Personnel Records
William B. Travis Office Building
1701 N. Congress Avenue
Austin, TX 78701
512-463-8976

Utah

Certification and Personnel Development
State Office of Education
250 East 500 South
Salt Lake City, UT 84111
801-538-7740

Vermont

Licensing Division
Department of Education
Montpelier, VT 05620
802-828-2445

Virginia

Office of Professional Licensure
Department of Education
P.O. Box 2120
Richmond, VA 23216-2120
804-225-2022

Washington

Director of Professional Preparation
Office of the Superintendent of Public Instruction
Old Capitol Building
Box 47200
Olympia, WA 98504-7200
360-725-6400

West Virginia

Office of Professional Preparation
Department of Education
Capitol Complex, Room B-337, Building 6
Charleston, WV 25305
304-558-2703
800-982-2378

Wisconsin

Bureau of Teacher Education, Licensing and Placement
Department of Public Instruction
125 S. Webster Street
P.O. Box 7841
Madison, WI 53707-7841
608-266-1027

Wyoming

Certification and Licensing Unit
Department of Education
2300 Capitol Avenue
Hathaway Building
Cheyenne, WY 82002-0050
307-777-6261

U.S. Department of Defense Overseas

Dependent Section
Teacher Recruitment
2461 Eisenhower Avenue
Alexandria, VA 22331-1100
703-325-0690

APPENDIX B

National Toll-Free Numbers and Web Sites

The following is a selected list of toll-free numbers and Web sites for national organizations concerned with disability and students' issues. Inclusion on this list does not imply endorsement by NICHCY or the Office of Special Education Programs. There are also many national disability organizations providing services and information that do not have toll-free numbers. If you would like additional help in locating assistance, contact NICHCY at 800-695-0285 (Voice/TTY) or visit our Web site (*www.nichcy.org*). This information is copyright free. Readers are encouraged to copy and share it, but please credit the National Dissemination Center for Children with Disabilities (NICHCY).[1]

Adoption / Foster Care

AdoptUSKids
888-200-4005
www.adoptuskids.org

Adoptive Families *(national adoption magazine; information for families before, during, and after adoption)*
800-372-3300 (to subscribe)
www.adoptivefamilies.com

Fostering Families Today *(a bimonthly magazine with foster care and adoption resources)*
888-924-6736
www.fosteringfamiliestoday.com

National Adoption Center
800-TO ADOPT (862-3678)
www.adopt.org

---

[1]NICHCY
P.O. Box 1492
Washington, DC 20013
800-695-0285 (V/TTY)
202-884-8441 (fax)
E-mail: nichcy@aed.org
www.nichcy.org

National Adoption Information Clearinghouse
888-251-0075
http://naic.acf.hhs.gov

AIDS

AIDSinfo *(for information on HIV/AIDS, treatment, prevention, and research)*
800-448-0440 (V, English/Spanish)
888-480-3739 (TTY)
www.aidsinfo.nih.gov

CDC-INFO *(formerly the CDC National AIDS Hotline)*
800-232-4636 (V, English/Spanish)
888-232-6348 (TTY)
www.cdc.gov/hiv/dhap.htm

CDC National Prevention Information Network
800-458-5231 (V, English/Spanish)
800-243-7012 (TTY)
www.cdcnpin.org

Alcohol and Drug Abuse

American Council for Drug Education (ACDE)
800-488-3784
www.acde.org

Families Anonymous
800-736-9805
www.familiesanonymous.org

National Clearinghouse for Alcohol and Drug Information
800-729-6686 (V)
877-767-8432 (Spanish)
800-487-4889 (TTY)
www.health.org

National Council on Alcoholism & Drug Dependence
800-622-2255
www.ncadd.org

Americans with Disabilities Act (ADA)

ADA InfoLine–U.S. Department of Justice
800-514-0301 (V, English/Spanish)
800-514-0383 (TTY)
www.usdoj.gov/crt/ada/adahom1.htm

Center for Universal Design
800-647-6777
www.design.ncsu.edu/cud

Equal Employment Opportunity Commission

800-669-4000 (V, English/Spanish)

800-669-6820 (TTY)

www.eeoc.gov

Job Accommodation Network

800-526-7234 (V/TTY)

800-232-9675 (V/TTY; ADA information)

http://janweb.icdi.wvu.edu

U.S. Access Board

800-872-2253 (V)

800-993-2822 (TTY)

www.access-board.gov

U.S. Department of Housing and Urban Development–HUD User

800-245-2691 (V)

800-927-7589 (TTY)

www.huduser.org

Assistive Technology / Devices

ABLEDATA

800-227-0216

www.abledata.com

AbleNet

800-322-0956

www.ablenetinc.com

Alliance for Technology Access

800-914-3017

www.ataccess.org

Apple Store for Education

800-MY APPLE (692-7753)

www.apple.com/education/accessibility

Georgia Tech Center for Assistive Technology and Environmental Access (CATEA)

800-726-9119 (V/TTY)

www.assistivetech.net

IBM Accessibility Center

800-426-4832 (V)

800-426-4833 (TTY)

www.ibm.com/able

National Lekotek Center's Toy Resource Helpline

800-366-7529 (V)

800-573-4446 (TTY)

www.lekotek.org

Blindness / Visual Impairments

American Council of the Blind
800-424-8666 (English/Spanish)
www.acb.org

American Foundation for the Blind
800-232-5463
www.afb.org

American Printing House for the Blind
800-223-1839
www.aph.org

Blind Childrens Center
800-222-3566
www.blindcntr.org

The Foundation Fighting Blindness
888-394-3937 (V)
800-683-5555 (TTY)
www.blindness.org

Library Reproduction Service
800-255-5002
www.lrs-largeprint.com

Lighthouse International
800-829-0500 (V)
212-821-9713 (TTY)
www.lighthouse.org

National Association for Parents of Children with Visual Impairments
800-562-6265
www.spedex.com/napvi

National Library Service for the Blind and Physically Handicapped
800-424-8567
www.loc.gov/nls

Prevent Blindness America
800-331-2020
www.preventblindness.org

Recording for the Blind and Dyslexic
800-221-4792
www.rfbd.org

Burns

Burn Survivors Throughout the World
800-503-8058
www.burnsurvivorsttw.org

Phoenix Society for Burn Survivors

800-888-2876

www.phoenix-society.org

Shriners Hospitals for Children

800-237-5055

www.shrinershq.org

Cancer

American Cancer Society

800-227-2345 (English/Spanish)

www.cancer.org

American Cancer Research Center

Cancer Information and Counseling Line

800-525-3777

www.amc.org

Candlelighters Childhood Cancer Foundation

800-366-2223

www.candlelighters.org

National Brain Tumor Foundation

800-934-2873 (English/Spanish)

www.braintumor.org

National Cancer Institute Information Service

800-422-6237 (V, English/Spanish)

800-332-8615 (TTY)

http://cis.nci.nih.gov

Support for People with Oral and Head and Neck Cancer

800-377-0928

www.spohnc.org

Child Abuse

National Center for Missing and Exploited Children

800-843-5678 (V, English/Spanish)

800-826-7653 (TTY)

www.missingkids.com

National Child Abuse Hotline

800-422-4453

www.childhelpusa.org

National Clearinghouse on Child Abuse and Neglect Information

800-394-3366 (English/Spanish)

http://nccanch.acf.hhs.gov

Prevent Child Abuse America

800-244-5373 (English/Spanish)

www.preventchildabuse.org

Child Care

Child Care Aware

800-424-2246 (English/Spanish)

www.childcareaware.org

National Child Care Information Center

800-616-2242 (V, English/Spanish)

800-516-2242 (TTY)

http://nccic.org

National Resource Center for Health and Safety in Child Care

800-598-5437

http://nrc.uchsc.edu

Communication Disorders

American Speech-Language-Hearing Association

800-638-8255

www.asha.org

National Institute on Deafness and Other Communication Disorders Clearinghouse

800-241-1044 (V, English/Spanish)

800-241-1055 (TTY)

www.nidcd.nih.gov

National Stuttering Association

800-937-8888

www.nsastutter.org

Stuttering Foundation of America

800-992-9392

www.stuttersfa.org

Craniofacial Syndromes

Aboutface USA

888-486-1209

www.aboutfaceusa.org

Children's Craniofacial Association

800-535-3643

www.ccakids.org

Craniofacial Foundation of America

800-418-3223

www.craniofacialcenter.com

FACES–National Craniofacial Association
800-332-2373
www.faces-cranio.org

Foundation for Nager and Miller Syndromes
800-507-3667
www.nagerormillersynd.com

Crisis Intervention

Air Care Alliance
888-260-9707
www.aircareall.org

Angel Flight America
877-858-7788
www.angelflightamerica.org

National Hopeline Network
800-SUICIDE (784-2433)
www.hopeline.com

National Suicide Prevention Lifeline
800-273-TALK (8255)
800-799-4TTY (4889) (TTY)
www.suicidepreventionlifeline.org

Nineline Crisis Hotline
800-999-9999
www.nineline.org

Deafness / Hearing Impairments

Alexander Graham Bell Association for the Deaf and Hard of Hearing
866-337-5220
www.agbell.org

American Academy of Audiology
800-222-2336
www.audiology.org

American Society for Deaf Children
800-942-2732 (V/TTY)
www.deafchildren.org

American Speech-Language-Hearing Association
800-638-8255
www.asha.org

Better Hearing Institute
800-327-9355 (V/TTY)
www.betterhearing.org

Hear Now

800-648-4327 (V/TTY)

www.sotheworldmayhear.org

Hearing Aid Helpline

800-521-5247 (V/TTY)

http://ihsinfo.org

John Tracy Clinic

800-522-4582 (V/TTY, English/Spanish)

213-748-5481 (V in 213 area)

213-747-2924 (TTY in 213 area)

www.johntracyclinic.org

National Cued Speech Association

800-459-3529

www.cuedspeech.org

National Information Clearinghouse on Children Who are Deaf-Blind (DB–LINK)

800-438-9376 (V)

800-854-7013 (TTY)

www.tr.wou.edu/dblink

National Institute on Deafness and Other Communication Disorders Clearinghouse

800-241-1044 (V, English/Spanish)

800-241-1055 (TTY)

www.nidcd.nih.gov

Postsecondary Education Programs Network Resource Center (PEPNet)

888-684-4695 (V/TTY)

http://prc.csun.edu

Disability Awareness / Community Inclusion

Best Buddies

800 89-BUDDY (892-8339)

www.bestbuddies.org

Kids on the Block

800-368-5437

www.kotb.com

Friends Who Care (from Easter Seals)

800-221-6827

www.easterseals.com

VSA Arts

800-933-8721

www.vsarts.org

Yes I Can! Foundation for Exceptional Children
800-224-6830, Ext. 450
http://yesican.sped.org

Education

American Association for Vocational Instructional Materials
800-228-4689
www.aavim.com

Association for Career & Technical Education
800-826-9972 (V/TTY)
www.acteonline.org

Association for Childhood Education International
800-423-3563
www.acei.org

The Center for Comprehensive School Reform and Improvement
877-277-2744
www.csrclearinghouse.org

Early Childhood and Parenting Collaborative
877-275-3227 (V/TTY)
http://ecap.crc.uiuc.edu

ERIC System (Educational Resources Information Center)
800-538-3742
www.eric.ed.gov

Federal Student Aid Information Center
800-433-3243 (V, English/Spanish)
800-730-8913 (TTY)
http://studentaid.ed.gov

HEATH Resource Center *(for information on postsecondary education for individuals with disabilities)*
800-544-3284 (V/TTY)
www.heath.gwu.edu

National Alliance of Black School Educators
800-221-2654
www.nabse.org

National Association for the Education of Young Children (NAEYC)
800-424-2460
www.naeyc.org

National Clearinghouse for English Language Acquisition & Language Instruction Educational Programs (NCELA)
800-321-6223
www.ncela.gwu.edu

National Information Center for Educational Media

800-926-8328 (V/TTY)

www.nicem.com/

National Institute for Literacy–Literacy Hotline

800-228-8813 (V, English/Spanish)

877-576-7734 (TTY)

www.nifl.gov

National Library of Education (NLE)

800-424-1616 (English/Spanish)

www.ed.gov/NLE

National Middle School Association

800-528-6672

www.nmsa.org

U.S. Department of Education Information Resource Center

800-872-5327 (V, English/Spanish)

800-437-0833 (TTY)

www.ed.gov/about/offices/list/oiia/irc.html

Employment / Independent Living

Disabled and Alone, Inc.

800-995-0066

www.disabledandalone.org

Education, Career, and Community Program *(a program of the Northwest Regional Educational Laboratory)*

800-547-6339

www.nwrel.org

Employer Assistance Referral Network

866-327-6669 (V/TTY)

www.earnworks.com

Equal Employment Opportunity Commission

800-669-4000 (V, English/Spanish)

800-669-6820 (TTY)

www.eeoc.gov

Job Accommodation Network

800-526-7234 (V/TTY)

800-232-9675 (V/TTY; ADA information)

http://janweb.icdi.wvu.edu

National Center on Workforce and Disability/Adult

888-886-9898 (V/TTY)

www.onestops.info

National Collaborative on Workforce and Disability/Youth

877-871-0744

www.ncwd-youth.info

National Council on Independent Living

877-525-3400

www.ncil.org

National Resource Center on Supported Living and Choice: Center on Human Policy

800-894-0826

http://thechp.syr.edu/nrc.html

Proyecto Visión Hotline

866-EMPLEO-1 (866-367-5361)

www.proyectovision.net

Financial Counseling

National Foundation for Consumer Credit

800-388-2227

800-682-9832 (Spanish)

www.nfcc.org

Hospice

Caring Connections

800-658-8898

www.caringinfo.org

Children's Hospice International

800-242-4453 (V/TTY)

www.chionline.org

Hospice Education Institute

800-331-1620

www.hospiceworld.org

Information Centers

ABLEDATA *(for information on assistive technology)*

800-227-0216 (V/TTY)

www.abledata.com

HRSA Information Center (U.S. Dept. of Health & Human Services)

888-275-4772 (V, English/Spanish)

877-489-4772 (TTY)

www.ask.hrsa.gov

March of Dimes

888-663-4637 (English/Spanish)

www.marchofdimes.com

National Center on Birth Defects and Developmental Disabilities
800-CDC-INFO (232-4636)
www.cdc.gov/ncbddd

National Center on Low-Incidence Disabilities (NCLID)
800-395-2693 (V/TTY)
http://nclid.unco.edu/newnclid

National Dissemination Center for Children with Disabilities (NICHCY)
800-695-0285 (V/TTY, English/Spanish)
www.nichcy.org

National Health Information Center
800-336-4797
www.health.gov/nhic

National Library of Medicine
888-346-3656
www.nlm.nih.gov

Office of Minority Health Resource Center
800-444-6472 (English/Spanish)
www.omhrc.gov

Zero to Three/National Center for Infants, Toddlers, and Families
800-899-4301
www.zerotothree.org

Literacy

National Institute for Literacy–Literacy Hotline
800-228-8813 (V, English/Spanish)
877-576-7734 (TTY)
www.nifl.gov

ProLiteracy Worldwide
888-528-2224 (English/Spanish)
www.proliteracy.org

Reading is Fundamental
877-743-7323
www.rif.org

Medical / Health Disorders

American Academy of Allergy, Asthma, and Immunology
800-822-2762
www.aaaai.org

American Association of Kidney Patients
800-749-2257
www.aakp.org

American Behcet's Disease Association
800-7-BEHCETS (723-4238)
www.behcets.com

American Brain Tumor Association
800-886-2282
http://hope.abta.org

American Cancer Society
800-227-2345 (English/Spanish)
www.cancer.org

American Diabetes Association
800-342-2383 (English/Spanish)
www.diabetes.org

American Heart Association
800-242-8721 (English/Spanish)
www.americanheart.org

American Kidney Fund
800-638-8299
www.kidneyfund.org

American Liver Foundation
800-GO-LIVER (465-4837)
888-4HEP-USA (443-7872)
www.liverfoundation.org

American Lung Association
800-586-4872 (English/Spanish)
www.lungusa.org

American Stroke Association
888-478-7653
www.strokeassociation.org

American Syringomyelia Alliance Project
800-272-7282
www.asap.org

Angioma Alliance
866-432-5226
www.angiomaalliance.org

Aplastic Anemia & MDS International Foundation
800-747-2820 (English/Spanish)
www.aamds.org

Arthritis Foundation
800-568-4045
www.arthritis.org

Asthma and Allergy Foundation of America
800-727-8462
www.aafa.org

Celiac Sprue Association
877-CSA-4CSA (272-4272)
www.csaceliacs.org

Children's Tumor Foundation *(formerly the National Neurofibromatosis Foundation)*
800-323-7938 (English/Spanish)
www.ctf.org

Chronic Fatigue and Immune Dysfunction Syndrome Association (CFIDS)
800-442-3437
www.cfids.org

Cleft Palate Foundation
800-24-CLEFT (242-5338)
www.cleftline.org

Cooley's Anemia Foundation
800-522-7222
www.thalassemia.org

Crohn's and Colitis Foundation of America
800-932-2423
www.ccfa.org

Cystic Fibrosis Foundation
800-344-4823
www.cff.org

Cystinosis Foundation
800-392-8458
www.cystinosisfoundation.org

Dystrophic Epidermolysis Bullosa Research Association of America (DebRA)
866-332-7276 (nurse line)
www.debra.org

Epilepsy Foundation
800-332-1000 (English/Spanish)
www.epilepsyfoundation.org

Family Voices: A National Coalition Speaking for Children with Special Health Care Needs
888-835-5669
www.familyvoices.org

First Candle/SIDS Alliance
800-221-7437
www.sidsalliance.org

Foundation for Ichthyosis and Related Skin Types

800-545-3286

www.scalyskin.org

Huntington's Disease Society of America

800-345-4372

www.hdsa.org

Immune Deficiency Foundation

800-296-4433

www.primaryimmune.org

International Foundation for Functional Gastrointestinal Disorders

888-964-2001

www.iffgd.org

Juvenile Diabetes Research Foundation International

800-533-CURE (2873)

www.jdrf.org

Kennedy Krieger Institute

888-554-2080

www.kennedykrieger.org

Leukemia and Lymphoma Society

800-955-4572

www.leukemia-lymphoma.org

Lupus Foundation of America

800-558-0121

800-558-0231 (Spanish)

www.lupus.org

Lyme Disease Foundation Hotline

800-886-LYME (5963)

www.lyme.org/index.html

MAGIC Foundation (Major Aspects of Growth Disorders In Children)

800-3-MAGIC-3 (362-4423)

www.magicfoundation.org

Malignant Hyperthermia Association

800-644-9737

www.mhaus.org

March of Dimes

888-663-4637 (English/Spanish)

www.marchofdimes.com

National Association of Hospital Hospitality Houses (NAHHH)

800-542-9730

www.nahhh.org/

National Brain Tumor Foundation

800-934-2873 (English/Spanish)

www.braintumor.org

National Diabetes Information Clearinghouse

800-860-8747

http://diabetes.niddk.nih.gov

National Digestive Diseases Information Center

800-891-5389

www.niddk.nih.gov

National Eating Disorders Association

800-931-2237

www.nationaleatingdisorders.org

National Foundation for Transplants

800-489-3863

www.transplants.org

National Health Information Center

800-336-4797

www.health.gov/nhic

National Heart, Lung, and Blood Institute Information Center

800-575-9355 (English/Spanish)

www.nhlbi.nih.gov

National Hemophilia Foundation

800-424-2634

www.hemophilia.org

National Institute of Arthritis and Musculoskeletal and Skin Diseases Clearinghouse

877-226-4267 (English/Spanish)

www.niams.nih.gov

National Institute of Child Health and Human Development

800-370-2943

www.nichd.nih.gov

National Jewish Medical and Research Center

800-222-5864

www.njc.org

National Kidney Foundation

800-622-9010

www.kidney.org

National Lymphedema Network

800-541-3259

www.lymphnet.org

National Marfan Foundation

800-8-MARFAN (862-7326)

www.marfan.org

National Multiple Sclerosis Society

800-344-4867

866-KIDS-W-MS (543-7967) (English/Spanish)

www.nmss.org

National Organization for Albinism and Hypopigmentation

800-473-2310

www.albinism.org

National Patient Travel Helpline

800-296-1217

www.patienttravel.org

National Scoliosis Foundation

800-673-6922

www.scoliosis.org

National Tay-Sachs & Allied Diseases Association

800-906-8723

www.ntsad.org

Neurofibromatosis, Inc.

800-942-6825

www.nfinc.org

Osteogenesis Imperfecta Foundation

800-981-2663

www.oif.org

Oxalosis & Hyperoxaluria Foundation

800-OHF-8699 (643-8699)

www.ohf.org

Scleroderma Foundation

800-722-4673

www.scleroderma.org

Shriners Hospital for Children

800-237-5055

www.shrinershq.org

Sickle Cell Disease Association of America

800-421-8453

www.sicklecelldisease.org

United Leukodystrophy Foundation

800-728-5483

www.ulf.org

United Ostomy Association
800-826-0826
www.uoa.org

Vestibular Disorders Association
800-837-8428
www.vestibular.org

Weight-Control Information Network (WIN)
877-946-4627
http://win.niddk.nih.gov/index.htm

Williams Syndrome Association
800-806-1871
www.williams-syndrome.org

Wilson's Disease Association
800-399-0266
www.wilsonsdisease.org

Mental Health

American Psychiatric Association
888-35-PSYCH (357-7924)
www.psych.org

American Psychological Association's Consumer Help Center
800-964-2000
www.apahelpcenter.org

Depression and Bipolar Support Alliance
800-826-3632
www.dbsalliance.org

Families Anonymous
800-736-9805
www.familiesanonymous.org

National Alliance for the Mentally Ill
800-950-6264 (English/Spanish)
www.nami.org

National Association for the Dually Diagnosed
800-331-5362
www.thenadd.org

National Hopeline Network
800-SUICIDE (784-2433) (English/Spanish)
www.hopeline.com

National Institute of Mental Health (NIMH) Information Center
866-615-6464 (English/Spanish)
www.nimh.nih.gov

National Mental Health Association

800-969-6642 (V, English/Spanish)

800-433-5959 (TTY)

www.nmha.org

National Mental Health Consumer Self-Help Clearinghouse

800-553-4539 (English/Spanish)

www.mhselfhelp.org

National Mental Health Information Center

800-789-2647 (English/Spanish)

www.mentalhealth.org

National Suicide Prevention Lifeline

800-273-TALK (8255)

800-799-4TTY (4889) (TTY)

www.suicidepreventionlifeline.org

Minority Issues

Gates Millennium Scholars

877-690-4677

www.gmsp.org

Hispanic Scholarship Fund

877-473-4636

www.hsf.net

National Alliance of Black School Educators

800-221-2654

www.nabse.org

National Clearinghouse for English Language Acquisition (NCELA)

800-321-6223

www.ncela.gwu.edu

National Native American Families Together Parent Center

877-205-7501

www.nativefamilynetwork.com

Office of Minority Health Resource Center

800-444-6472 (English/Spanish)

www.omhrc.gov

Proyecto Visión Hotline

866-Empleo-1 (367-5361)

www.proyectovision.net

Parent Support

Compassionate Friends *(grief support after the death of a child)*

877-969-0010

www.compassionatefriends.org

MUMS: National Parent to Parent Network

877-336-5333

www.netnet.net/mums

National Organization of Mothers of Twins Clubs

877-540-2200

www.nomotc.org

Parent Advocacy Coalition for Educational Rights (PACER Center)

888-248-0822

www.pacer.org

Special Needs Advocate for Parents (SNAP)

888-310-9889

www.snapinfo.org

Specialized Training of Military Parents (STOMP)

800-5-PARENT (572-7368)

www.stompproject.org

Through the Looking Glass

800-644-2666

www.lookingglass.org

Physical Disabilities

Canine Companions for Independence

800-572-BARK (2275)

www.caninecompanions.org

Christopher and Dana Reeve Paralysis Resource Center

800-539-7309

www.paralysis.org

Courage Center

888-846-8253

www.courage.org

Craniofacial Foundation of America

800-418-3223

www.craniofacialcenter.com

Easter Seals-National Office

800-221-6827 (V)

312-726-4258 (TTY)

www.easterseals.com

Families of Spinal Muscular Atrophy

800-886-1762

www.fsma.org

Human Growth Foundation

800-451-6434

www.hgfound.org

Muscular Dystrophy Association

800-572-1717

www.mdausa.org

National Institute of Arthritis and Musculoskeletal and Skin Diseases Information Clearinghouse

877-226-4267

www.niams.nih.gov

National Library Service for the Blind and Physically Handicapped

800-424-8567

www.loc.gov/nls

National Limb Loss Information Center

888-267-5669 (English/Spanish)

www.amputee-coalition.org

National Scoliosis Foundation

800-673-6922

www.scoliosis.org

National Spasmodic Torticollis Association

800-487-8385

www.torticollis.org

National Spinal Cord Injury Hotline

800-962-9629

www.spinalcord.org

Pathways Awareness Foundation

800-955-2445

www.pathwaysawareness.org

Spina Bifida Association of America

800-621-3141 (English/Spanish)

www.sbaa.org

United Cerebral Palsy Associations

800-872-5827

www.ucp.org

Winners on Wheels (WOW)

800-WOW-Talk (969-8255)

www.wowusa.com

Rare Syndromes

Genetic Alliance

800-336-4363

http://geneticalliance.org

Genetic & Rare Diseases Information Center

888-205-2311 (V, English/Spanish)

888-205-3223 (TTY)

http://rarediseases.info.nih.gov

National Organization for Rare Disorders (NORD)
800-999-6673 (V/TTY)
www.rarediseases.org

Recreation

Adventures in Movement for the Handicapped
800-332-8210
www.aimforthehandicapped.org

Best Buddies
800-89-BUDDY (892-8339)
www.bestbuddies.org

Girl Scouts of the USA
800-478-7248
www.girlscouts.org

National Center on Physical Activity and Disability
800-900-8086 (V/TTY)
www.ncpad.org

National Lekotek Center's Toy Resource Helpline
800-366-7529 (V)
800-573-4446 (TTY)
www.lekotek.org

North American Riding for the Handicapped, Inc.
800-369-7433
www.narha.org

Rehabilitation

ABLEDATA
800-227-0216 (V/TTY)
www.abledata.com

ADED: Association for Driver Rehabilitation Specialists
800-290-2344
www.driver-ed.org

National Rehabilitation Information Center
800-346-2742
www.naric.com

Respiratory Disorders

American Lung Association
800-586-4872
www.lungusa.org

National Heart, Lung, and Blood Institute Information Center

800-575-9355 (English/Spanish)

www.nhlbi.nih.gov

National Jewish Medical & Research Center

800-222-5864

www.njc.org

Respite Care

National Family Caregivers Association

800-896-3650

www.thefamilycaregiver.org

Rural

Rural Institute on Disabilities

800-732-0323

http://ruralinstitute.umt.edu

Specific Disabilities

American Association on Mental Retardation

800-424-3688 (outside Metro DC area)

202-387-1968 (in DC)

www.aamr.org

Angelman Syndrome Foundation

800-432-6435

www.angelman.org/angel

The Arc of the United States

800-433-5255

www.thearc.org

Autism Society of America

800-3-AUTISM (328-8476)

www.autism-society.org

Beckwith Wiedemann Support Network

800-837-2976

http://beckwith-wiedemann.org

Brain Injury Association Family Helpline

800-444-6443 (English/Spanish)

www.biausa.org

Center for the Study and Treatment of Usher Syndrome at Boys Town National Research Hospital

800-835-1468 (V/TTY)

www.boystownhospital.org

Charge Syndrome Foundation

800-442-7604

www.chargesyndrome.org

Children and Adults with Attention-Deficit/ Hyperactivity Disorder (CHADD)

800-233-4050

301-306-7070 (in Washington, DC metro area)

www.chadd.org

Cornelia de Lange Syndrome Foundation

800-223-8355

860-676-8166 (in CT)

www.cdlsusa.org

Family Empowerment Network: Support for Families Affected by FAS/E

800-462-5254 (for families)

www.fammed.wisc.edu/fen

Fetal Alcohol Spectrum Disorders Center

866-786-7327

www.fascenter.samhsa.gov/index.cfm

International Dyslexia Association

800-222-3123

www.interdys.org

International Rett Syndrome Association

800-818-7388

www.rettsyndrome.org

Learning Disabilities Association of America

888-300-6710

www.ldaamerica.org

Little People of America

888-572-2001

www.lpaonline.org

National Center for Learning Disabilities

888-575-7373

www.ncld.org

National Down Syndrome Congress

800-232-6372

www.ndsccenter.org

National Down Syndrome Society

800-221-4602 (English/Spanish)

www.ndss.org

National Fragile X Foundation

800-688-8765

www.fragilex.org

National Gaucher Foundation

800-428-2437

www.gaucherdisease.org

National Niemann-Pick Disease Foundation

877-287-3672

www.nnpdf.org

National Organization on Fetal Alcohol Syndrome

800-666-6327

www.nofas.org

National Reye's Syndrome Foundation

800-233-7393

www.reyessyndrome.org

National Stuttering Association

800-937-8888

www.nsastutter.org

Prader-Willi Syndrome Association

800-926-4797

www.pwsausa.org

Spina Bifida Association of America

800-621-3141 (English/Spanish)

www.sbaa.org

Sturge-Weber Foundation

800-627-5482

www.sturge-weber.com

Stuttering Foundation of America

800-992-9392

www.stuttersfa.org

Support Organization for Trisomy 18, 13, and Related Chromosomal Disorders

800-716-7638

www.trisomy.org

Tuberous Sclerosis Alliance

800-225-6872

www.tsalliance.org

United Cerebral Palsy Association

800-872-5827

www.ucp.org

Williams Syndrome Association

800-806-1871

www.williams-syndrome.org

Suicide Prevention

American Foundation for Suicide Prevention

888-333-2377

www.afsp.org

National Hopeline Network

800-SUICIDE (784-2433)

www.hopeline.com

National Suicide Prevention Lifeline

800-273-TALK (8255)

www.suicidepreventionlifeline.org

Nineline Crisis Hotline

800-999-9999

www.nineline.org

Supplemental Security Income (SSI)

Social Security Administration

800-772-1213 (V, English/Spanish)

800-325-0778 (TTY)

www.ssa.gov

Trauma

American Trauma Society

800-556-7890

www.amtrauma.org

Brain Injury Association Family Helpline

800-444-6443

www.biausa.org

National Spinal Cord Injury Association

800-962-9629

www.spinalcord.org

Wishes for Children

Believe in Tomorrow National Children's Foundation

800-933-5470

www.believeintomorrow.org

Name Index

SUBJECT INDEX